1 9 9 9

Compiled and Edited by Reg Cade and Barry Gallafent

Published by
Marwain Publishing Limited,
Marwain House, Clarke Road, Mount Farm, Milton Keynes MK1 1LG

Design
Richard Cade

Administration
Vicky Jones

Colour Reproduction by
HiLo Colour Printers, Telford Way, Colchester, Essex, C04 4QP

Printed by
Acorn Web Offset, Normanton, West Yorkshire

Distributed by (Booktrade)
Bravo Limited
7 Spectrum House, 32-34 Gordon House Road, London, NW5 1LP

(Camping and Caravan Trade)
Marwain Publishing Limited

ISBN 0 - 905377 - 79 - 6

Each edition is conscientiously revised and updated with prevailing periodic amendments accommodated. For instance the current Local Authority reorganisation has created many new unitary authorities, together with the creation of some new counties and the reinstatement of some traditional county names.

With the exception of the new or reinstated counties the new unitary authorities remain for ceremonial purposes in the counties from which they were formed. Where counties have been abolished, i.e. Cleveland, the towns of Hartlepool and Stockton (North of the River Tees) deemed part of County Durham, Langbaurgh, Middlesbrough and Stockton (South of the River Tees) deemed part of North Yorkshire.

To make life easier for you the reader, we have used the traditional county names for England.

For Scotland and Wales the review has totally changed the map and we have had to use the new authority names, (a new boundary map is included in the Scottish and Welsh sections for your assistance).

Every entry detailed in this guide will provide you with the most essential information on each caravan and camping park enabling you to make the most of your touring holiday. Key symbols make direct comparisons of sites a simple process, the guide will also leave you in no doubt as to whether your interest and requirement is catered for. For instance it will inform you as to how many pitches are available, whether the ground is sloping or level, if the park has electric hook-ups as well as the range of leisure activities available not only on the park, but in the nearby area.

We pride ourselves as always on the accuracy of the detailed information in our guide. We must however, point out that we are not agents of the sites and publish only such information as is supplied to us by the owner or operator in good faith and cannot therefore be responsible for any conditions or facilities that differ from those published. We strongly advise that you check directly with the site before booking that the particular facilities you require will be available at the time of your visit.

The full address and telephone numbers of each site are published to help with your inquiries. Do remember that advance bookings are advised, especially in the peak season.

I would like to take this opportunity to thank you for supporting CADE'S and wish you very happy and successful touring in 1999.

REG CADE
(MANAGING DIRECTOR, MARWAIN PUBLISHING LIMITED)

Haven
Touring

SYMBOLS

- Tents
- Motor Caravans
- Touring Caravans
- Nearest Station
- Facilities for Disabled
- No Motorcycles
- Electricity Hook-ups
- Fully Serviced Pitches
- Hard Standings
- Flush Toilets
- Water
- Showers
- Shaver Points
- Washing Facilities
- Ironing Facilities
- Launderette
- Chem. Toilet Disposal
- Site Shop
- Mobile Shop
- Local Shop
- Gas
- Public Telephone
- Café Restaurant
- Licensed Club
- T.V.
- Games Room
- Childs Play Area
- Swimming Pool
- Sports Area
- Pets Welcome
- Parking by Unit
- Credit Cards Accepted
- Money-Off Vouchers Accepted

Nearby Facilities

- Golf
- Fishing
- Sailing
- Boating
- Riding
- Water Ski-ing
- Tennis
- Climbing

SYMBOLES FRANÇAIS

- Tentes
- Auto-Caravanes
- Caravanes
- Gare Locale
- Handicapés
- Branchments Electrique Pour Caravanes
- Emplacement Service Complet
- Emplacement Surface Dure
- Motorcyclettes Non-Admises
- Toilettes
- Eau
- Douches
- Prises Electrique pour Rasoirs
- Bains
- Repassage
- Laverie Automatique
- Décharge pour W.C. Chemique
- Magasin du Terrain
- Magasin Mobile
- Magasin du Quartier
- Gaz
- Cabines Téléphoniques
- Café
- Club/Bar Patenté
- Salle de Télévision
- Salle de Jeux
- Terrain de Jeux Enfants
- Piscine du Terrain
- Terrain de Sports et de Jeux
- Stationment à côté de la caravane permis
- Carte Credit Accepter
- Bon Remise 'Cades' Accepter

Nearby Facilities

- Golf
- Pêche
- Voile
- Canotage
- Equitation
- Ski Nautique
- Tennis
- Ascension

ENGLAND

BEDFORDSHIRE

RIDGMONT

Rose & Crown, 89 High St., Ridgmont, Bedfordshire.
Std: 01525 **Tel:** 280245
Nearest Town/Resort Woburn/Ampthill
Directions Midway between Ampthill and Woburn on A507 2 miles south of junc 13 M1.
Acreage 3 **Open** All Year
Access Good **Site** Level
Sites Available **Total** 20
Facilities
Nearby Facilities
Ridgmont
Adjacent to Woburn Safari Park and 4 miles from Woburn Abbey.

BERKSHIRE

DORNEY REACH

Amerden Caravan Site, Off Old Marsh Lane, Dorney Reach, Nr. Maidenhead, Berkshire.
Std: 01628 **Tel:** 627461
Nearest Town/Resort Maidenhead.
Directions Leave M4 junc 7, Slough West, then A4 towards Maidenhead. Third turn left signposted Dorney Reach and caravan site, then first turn right.
Acreage 3 **Open** April **to** October
Access Good **Site** Level
Sites Available
Facilities
Nearby Facilities
Taplow.
Near River Thames.

HURLEY

Hurley Farm Caravan & Camping Park, Shepherds Lane, Hurley, Nr. Maidenhead, Berkshire, SL6 5NE.
Std: 01628 **Tel:** 823501/824493
Std: 01628 **Fax:** 825533
Nearest Town/Resort Maidenhead/ Henley-on-Thames.
Directions Maidenhead, A4130 west towards Henley. After 3¼ miles turn right, ¾ mile past East Arms PH into Shepherds Lane. Entrance 200 yards on left.
Acreage 15 **Open** March **to** October
Access Good **Site** Level
Sites Available **Total** 200
Facilities
Nearby Facilities
Maidenhead
✓✓✓✓Graded Park. On picturesque River Thames. Ideal touring centre for Henley, Windsor, Oxford and London. Launching ramp. Walks along riverside and into nearby forest. Site shop in peak season only. Disabled toilet facilities. David Bellamy Silver Award.

NEWBURY

Oakley Farm Caravan Park, Oakley Farm House, Penwood Road, Wash Water, Newbury, Berkshire, RG20 0LP.
Std: 01635 **Tel:** 36581
Nearest Town/Resort Newbury.
Directions 2¼ miles south of Newbury on the A343, approx 300mtrs after the Hants, Berks boundary. Turn left at car sales garage into Penwood Road and follow signs to site.
Acreage 3 **Open** March **to** October
Access Good **Site** Gentle Slope
Sites Available **Total** 30
Facilities
Nearby Facilities
Newbury

READING

Loddon Court Farm, Beech Hill Road, Spencers Wood, Reading, Berkshire, RG7 1HT.
Std: 0118 **Tel:** 988 3153
Nearest Town/Resort Reading.
Directions From Reading and M4 junction 11, go south on the old A33 to Spencers Wood, signposted. From Basingstoke take the old A33 north to Spencers Wood, signposted from Riseley roundabout.
Acreage 4 **Open** All Year
Access Good **Site** Level
Sites Available **Total** 30
Facilities
Nearby Facilities
Reading.
Quiet farm site.

RISELEY

Wellington Country Park, Riseley, Nr Reading, Berkshire, RG7 1SP.
Std: 01189 **Tel:** 326444
Std: 01189 **Fax:** 326445
Nearest Town/Resort Reading
Directions Between Reading and Basingstoke. Signposted from the A33, approx. 4 miles south of the M4 junction 11 and 5 miles north of the M3 junction 5.
Acreage 350 **Open** March **to** October
Access Good **Site** Level
Sites Available **Total** 60
Facilities
Nearby Facilities
Reading
✓✓✓✓Graded Park. In part of the Duke of Wellingtons estate. Childrens animal farm, adventure playground, nature trails, crazy golf, boating and a gift shop.

WOKINGHAM

California Chalet & Touring Park, Nine Mile Ride, Finchampstead, Wokingham, Berks, RG40 4HU.
Std: 0118 **Tel:** 973 3928
Std: 0118 **Fax:** 932 8720
Nearest Town/Resort Wokingham.
Directions A321 towards Sandhurst, in 1¼ miles turn right onto B3016. In 1 mile turn right at California crossroads onto the B3430, park is ¼ mile on the right.
Acreage 5¼ **Open** March **to** October
Access Good **Site** Level
Sites Available **Total** 35
Facilities
Nearby Facilities
Wokingham
✓✓✓✓Graded Park. Lakeside, wooded park, ideal for visiting Windsor, Oxford, Thames Valley and London.

BUCKINGHAMSHIRE

OLNEY

Emberton Country Park, Emberton, Nr. Olney, Bucks, MK46 5DB.
Std: 01234 **Tel:** 711575
Std: 01234 **Fax:** 711575
Nearest Town/Resort Olney
Directions On the A509 between Newport Pagnell/Olney, M1 junction 14.
Acreage 175 **Open** April **to** October
Access Good **Site** Level
Sites Available **Total** 200
Facilities
Nearby Facilities
Milton Keynes Central
✓✓✓Graded Park. In the Ouse Valley by the River Ouse with five beautiful lakes for fishing, boating and sailing. Golf and climbing on site.

CAMBRIDGESHIRE

BURWELL

Stanford Park, Weirs Road, Burwell, Cambridgeshire, CB5 0BP.
Std: 01638 **Tel:** 741547
Nearest Town/Resort Cambridge/ Newmarket.
Directions From Cambridge take B1102 to Burwell from Newmarket take B1103 to Burwell.
Acreage 20 **Open** All year
Access Good **Site** Level
Sites Available **Total** 150
Facilities
Nearby Facilities
Newmarket.
✓✓✓✓Graded Park. Near to rivers, on the Fens for birdwatching etc., Newmarket Horse Racing. RAC appointed and AA 4 Pennants. You can also call us on 0802 439997.

CAMBRIDGE

Highfield Farm Camping Park, Highfield Farm, Long Road, Comberton, Cambridge, CB3 7DG.
Std: 01223 **Tel:** 262308
Std: 01223 **Fax:** 262308
Nearest Town/Resort Cambridge.
Directions From Cambridge. Leave A1303/ A428 (Bedford) after 3 miles, follow camping signs to Comberton. From M11. Leave junction 12, take A603 (Sandy) for ½ mile then B1046 to Comberton (2 miles).
Acreage 8 **Open** April **to** October
Access Good **Site** Level
Sites Available **Total** 120
Facilities
Nearby Facilities
Cambridge.
✓✓✓✓✓Graded Park. Well maintained, long established family run Touring Park. Close to the historic University City of Cambridge, and the Imperial War Museum, Duxford. Awarded AA camp site of the year 1991/92 Midlands winner.

CAMBRIDGE

Roseberry Tourist Park, Earith Road, Willingham, Cambs.
Std: 01954 **Tel:** 260346
Nearest Town/Resort Cambridge
Directions Leave M11 at junction 16 (Bar Hill) onto the B1050. Site is on the left in 6 miles.
Acreage 9 **Open** March **to** October
Access Good **Site** Level
Sites Available **Total** 80
Facilities
Nearby Facilities
Cambridge
Sheltered orchard site. Ideal for touring Cambridge, Ely and Huntindon area. AA 3 Pennants and RAC listed.

CAMBRIDGE

Toad Acre Caravan Park, Mills Lane, Longstanton, Cambridgeshire, CB4 5DF.
Std: 01954 **Tel:** 780939
Nearest Town/Resort Cambridge
Directions A14 from Cambridge towards Huntingdon. Exit at the B1050 flyover (Barhill) following Army Barrick signs. Go over the flyover and travel about 1½ miles. Take a right hand fork in the road, turn right at the church then the first left (Mills Lane).
Acreage 1 **Open** All Year
Access Good **Site** Level
Sites Available **Total** 12
Facilities
Nearby Facilities
Cambridge
Quiet site in a small village, yet only 5½ miles from Cambridge centre.

ELY

Riverside Caravan & Camping Park, 21 New River Bank, Little Port, Ely, Cambridgeshire, CB7 4TA.
Std: 01353 **Tel:** 860255
Nearest Town/Resort Little Port
Directions ½ mile from the village, signposted. Near the Black Horse Public House.
Acreage 3¾ **Open** 1 March **to** 30 October
Access Good **Site** Level
Sites Available **Total** 40
Facilities
Nearby Facilities
Little Port
Quiet site. Fishing in the Great River Ouse only 10 yards away.

GRAFHAM

Old Manor Caravan Park, Church Road, Grafham, Huntingdon, Cambridgeshire, PE18 0BB.
Std: 01480 **Tel:** 810264
Nearest Town/Resort Huntingdon
Directions From the A1 at Buckden roundabout follow caravan park signs. From the A14 leave at Ellington and follow caravan park signs from the village.
Acreage 6½ **Open** February **to** November
Access Good **Site** Level
Sites Available **Total** 80
Facilities
Nearby Facilities
Huntingdon
✓✓✓✓Graded Park. Near to Grafham Water.

GREAT SHELFORD

Camping & Caravanning Club Site, 19 Cabbage Moor, Great Shelford, Cambs, CB2 5NB.
Std: 01223 **Tel:** 841185
Directions Leave the M11 at junction 11 onto the B1309 signposted Cambridge. At the first set of traffic lights turn right, after ½ mile you will see the site sign on the left hand side pointing down the lane.
Open 22 March **to** 1 Nov
Site Level
Sites Available **Total** 120
Facilities
Nearby Facilities
Great Shelford
✓✓✓✓Graded Park. On the outskirts of the city of Cambridge. 6 miles from Duxford Imperial War Museum. AA 4 Pennants.

HUNTINGDON

Burliegh Hill Camping Site, Burliegh Hill Farm, Somersham Road, St. Ives, Huntingdon, Cambs, PE17 4LY.
Std: 01480 **Tel:** 462173/461490
Std: 01480 **Fax:** 462173
Nearest Town/Resort St. Ives
Directions From St. Ives take the B1040 to Somersham, approx ½ mile from St. Ives. Look for signs on the left for Burliegh Hill Farm. Take this private, tarmac driveway for a third of a mile, campsite is on the left.
Acreage 6 **Open** All Year
Access Good **Site** Level
Sites Available **Total** 10
Facilities
Nearby Facilities
Huntingdon
Quiet, country park atmosphere, but close to the M11, A14 and main towns including Cambridge. St. Ives is a historic market town and the birthplace of Oliver Cromwell.

HUNTINGDON

Park Lane (Touring), Park Lane, Godmanchester, Huntingdon, Cambs, PE18 8AF.
Std: 01480 **Tel:** 453740
Std: 01480 **Fax:** 453740
Nearest Town/Resort Huntingdon
Directions From A14 northbound, turn left for Godmanchester/Huntingdon. Follow signs in Godmanchester on lamp posts, turn right at Black Pub Public House to Park Lane.
Acreage 2¼ **Open** March **to** October
Access Good **Site** Level
Sites Available **Total** 50
Facilities
Nearby Facilities
Huntingdon.
✓✓✓✓Graded Park. A great deal of History and buildings in the towns of Huntingdon and Godmanchester. Wash-up and vegetable preperation facilities. Restaurant and public house 50 metres.

HUNTINGDON

Quiet Waters Caravan Park, Hemingford Abbots, Huntingdon, Cambridgeshire, PE18 9AJ.
Std: 01480 **Tel:** 463405
Nearest Town/Resort St Ives/Huntingdon
Directions West of Cambridge on the A14, after 12 miles look for Hemingford Abbots, we are 1 mile into the village. 3 miles east of Huntingdon on the A14.
Acreage ½ **Open** April **to** October
Access Good **Site** Level
Sites Available **Total** 20
Facilities
Nearby Facilities
Huntingdon
✓✓✓✓Graded Park. In the centre of a riverside village, good for fishing and boating.

HUNTINGDON

The Willows Caravan Park, Bromholme Lane, Brampton, Huntingdon, Cambs, PE18 8NE.
Std: 01480 **Tel:** 454961
Std: 01480 **Fax:** 432828
Nearest Town/Resort Huntingdon.
Directions Brampton is situated on the A1 and the A14 (formerly A604). Follow the B1514 through Brampton towards Huntingdon, taking right hand signposted turning into Bromholme Lane.
Acreage 4 **Open** March **to** October
Access Good **Site** Level
Sites Available **Total** 40
Facilities
Nearby Facilities
Huntingdon.
Situated on Ouse Valley Way, attractive walks. Launching area for boats and canoes. Country park, Grafham Water and sports facilities nearby.

MARCH

Floods Ferry Touring Park, Staffurths Bridge, March, Cambridgeshire, PE15 0YP.
Std: 01354 **Tel:** 677302
Nearest Town/Resort March

Directions 4 miles from March. Take the A141 from March towards Chatteris, look for Floods Ferry and golf course sign and take this turn, continue for 3 miles and look for park sign on the right, single lane road to the park.
Acreage 7 **Open** All Year
Access Good **Site** Level
Sites Available **Total** 100
Facilities
Nearby Facilities
March
Relaxed, remote location adjacent to the Old Nene River. Slipway for boating and a ramp for disabled access. Ideal for walking, fishing and bird watching. Cycle route. Disabled fishing access. Views across Fenland.

ST. IVES

Crystal Lakes Touring & Fishing Site, Crystal Lakes, The Low Road, Fenstanton, St. Ives, Cambridgeshire, PE18 9HU.
Std: 01480 **Tel:** 497728
Nearest Town/Resort St. Ives
Directions Turn off the A14 at Fenstanton and follow signs.
Acreage 10 **Open** March **to** October
Access Good **Site** Level
Sites Available **Total** 76
Facilities
Nearby Facilities
Huntingdon
✓✓✓Graded Park. Horse riding, fishing lakes and car boot sales.

ST. NEOTS

Camping & Caravanning Club Site, Rush Meadow, St Neots, Cambridgeshire, PE19 2UD.
Std: 01480 **Tel:** 474404
Nearest Town/Resort St Neots
Directions From the A1 take the A428, at the second roundabout turn left to Tesco's, go past the sports centre and follow the international signs to the site.
Acreage 10 **Open** 22 March **to** 1 Nov
Access Good **Site** Level
Sites Available **Total** 180
Facilities
Nearby Facilities
St Neots
✓✓✓✓Graded Park. On the banks of the River Ouse for fishing and a small boating lake on site. Ideal for walking. Pitch 'n' Putt. Close to the Ouse Valley Way. Next door to a sports centre.

WILLINGHAM

Alwyn Tourist Park, Over Road, Willingham, Cambridgeshire, CB4 5EU.
Std: 01954 **Tel:** 260977
Std: 01954 **Fax:** 261797
Nearest Town/Resort Cambridge.
Directions Take the A14 to Huntingdon and turn off at Bar Hill, follow signs for Willingham. 8 miles from Cambridge.
Acreage 7 **Open** March **to** October
Access Good **Site** Level
Sites Available **Total** 90
Facilities
Nearby Facilities
Cambridge.
14 miles from Duxford Air Museum.

WISBECH

Orchard View Caravan & Camp Park, 100 Broadgate, Sutton St Edmund, Near Spalding, Lincs.
Std: 01945 **Tel:** 700482
Nearest Town/Resort Wisbech
Directions A47 Peterborough to Wisbech road, at Guyhirn turn at signpost for Guyhirn/Wisbech St Mary, turn left at T-Junction signposted Parson Drove, over Clough Bridge into Lincolnshire. Take the second right signposted Sutton St Edmund.
Acreage 2½ **Open** 31 March **to** October
Access Good **Site** Level
Sites Available **Total** 37
Facilities
Nearby Facilities
Peterborough
✓✓✓Graded Park. Rural site, peace and quiet. Waterways and cycling. Fenland touring centre. 6 berth statics available for hire.

WISBECH

Virginia Lake & Caravan Park, Virginia House, St John's Fen End, Wisbech, Cambridgeshire, PE14 8JF.
Std: 01945 **Tel:** 430332
Std: 01945 **Fax:** 430128
Nearest Town/Resort Wisbech/Kings Lynn
Directions On the A47 7 miles from Wisbech and 7 miles from Kings Lynn. Follow tourist board signs from the A47.
Acreage 5 **Open** All Year
Access Good **Site** Level
Sites Available **Total** 40
Facilities
Nearby Facilities
Kings Lynn
✓✓✓Graded Park. 2 acre course fishing lake on site. 30 minutes from Sandringham and 45 minutes from the coast.

CHANNEL ISLANDS

GUERNSEY

Fauxquets Valley Farm Camping Site, Fauxquets de Bas, Catel, Guernsey, Channel Islands.
Std: 01481 **Tel:** 55460
Std: 01481 **Fax:** 51797
Nearest Town/Resort St. Peter Port.
Directions Follow sign for Catel, turn left onto Queens Road. Turn right at the sign for the German Underground Hospital
Acreage 3 **Open** Easter **to** 20 September
Site Level
Sites Available **Total** 90
Facilities
Nearby Facilities
1½ miles from sea, beautiful countryside, quiet site. Fully equipped tents available for hire.

GUERNSEY

La Bailloterie Camp Site, Vale Guernsey, Channel Islands.
Std: 01481 **Tel:** 43636
Std: 01481 **Fax:** 43225
Nearest Town/Resort St. Sampsons
Directions Turn right at roundabout proceed along front until you come to Halfway Plantation. Turn left and proceed to second traffic lights turn right and first left.
Acreage 7½ **Open** May **to** 15th Sept
Access Good **Site** Level
Sites Available **Total** 120
Facilities
Nearby Facilities
Near beach 12 minutes. Fully equipped, 2/4/6 berth tents for hire.

JERSEY

Rozel Camping Park, Summerville, St Martin, Jersey, Channel Islands, JE3 6AX.
Std: 01534 **Tel:** 856797
Std: 01534 **Fax:** 856127
Nearest Town/Resort St. Helier
Directions 5 miles from St. Helier. A6 to Martin's Church then B38 to Rozel.
Acreage 3 **Open** May **to** Mid Sept
Site Level
Sites Available **Total** 80
Facilities
Nearby Facilities
Hire tents available, own tents welcome. Nearby a picturesque beach and harbour aswell as Gerald Durrell's Zoo.

CHESHIRE

CHESTER

Birch Bank Farm, Stamford Lane, Christleton, Chester, Cheshire, CH3 7QD.
Std: 01244 **Tel:** 335233
Nearest Town/Resort Chester
Directions Take the A51 (Nantwich), first turn right after the Little Chef signposted Christleton/Waverton.
Acreage 1 **Open** April **to** October
Access Good **Site** Level
Sites Available **Total** 10
Facilities
Nearby Facilities
Chester
A small site on a working farm, free from traffic noise.

CHESTER

Chester Southerly Caravan Park, Balderton Lane, Marlston-cum-Lache, Chester, Cheshire, CH4 9LF.
Std: 0976 **Tel:** 743888
Nearest Town/Resort Chester.
Directions 3 miles south side of Chester. Turn off the A55 towards Wrexham, at the A483 junction the road sign will immediately direct you to the site.
Acreage 8 **Open** March **to** November
Access Good **Site** Level
Sites Available **Total** 90.
Facilities
Nearby Facilities
Chester
Chester is noted for its walls, gates, towers and rows (arcaded streets with balconies).

CHESTER

Netherwood Touring Site, Netherwood House, Whitchurch Road, Nr. Chester, Cheshire, CH3 6AF.
Std: 01244 **Tel:** 335583
Std: 01244 **Fax:** 335583
Nearest Town/Resort Chester.
Directions On A41, approx. 1 mile from Chester bypass.
Acreage 1½ **Open** March **to** October
Access Good **Site** Level
Sites Available **Total** 15
Facilities
Nearby Facilities
Chester.
On Shropshire Union Canal. 5 miles from Zoo.

CHESTER

Northwood Hall Country Touring Park, Dog Lane, Kelsall, Chester, Cheshire, CW6 0RP.
Std: 01829 **Tel:** 752569
Std: 01829 **Fax:** 751157
Nearest Town/Resort Chester
Directions 7 miles east of Chester off the A54, adjacent to Delamere Forest.
Acreage 5 **Open** All Year
Access Good **Site** Level
Sites Available **Total** 30
Facilities
Nearby Facilities
Chester
Delamere Forest and the walled city of Chester.

MACCLESFIELD

Capesthorne Hall Caravan Park, Capesthorne, Macclesfield, Cheshire, SK11 9JY.
Std: 01625 **Tel:** 861779
Std: 01625 **Fax:** 861619
Nearest Town/Resort Alderley Edge
Directions On the A34 approx 3 miles south of Alderley Edge. Accessible from junctions 17, 18 and 19 off the M6 and junction 6 off the M56.
Acreage 5½ **Open** Easter **to** End Sept
Access Good **Site** Level/Slope
Sites Available **Total** 30
Facilities
Nearby Facilities
Alderley Edge
Situated in the grounds of a stately home. Ideal base for attractions in the area including other stately homes, Jodrell Bank and Granada Studio Tours. Ideal touring.

WARRINGTON

Holly Bank Caravan Park, Warburton Bridge Road, Rixton, Warrington, Cheshire, WA3 6HU.
Std: 0161 **Tel:** 775 2842
Nearest Town/Resort Warrington.
Directions 2 miles from M6 junction 21 on A57 (Irlam) turn right at lights into Warburton Bridge Road entry on left, warrington 5 miles.
Open All Year
Access Good **Site** Level
Sites Available **Total** 85.
Facilities
Nearby Facilities
Irlam.
✓✓✓✓Graded Park. Dunham Park, Tatton Park, and ideal touring North Cheshire.

WINSFORD

Lamb Cottage Camping & Caravan Park, Dalesford Lane, Whitegate, Nr. Northwich, Cheshire, CW8 2BN.
Std: 01606 **Tel:** 888491/882302
Std: 01606 **Fax:** 882302
Nearest Town/Resort Northwich/ Winsford
Directions Leave M6 at Junction 19 onto A556 to Chester, turn at lights by Sandiway Post Office into Dalesford Lane, site is located 1 mile on right, past garage on the left.
Acreage 4 **Open** March **to** October
Access Good **Site** Level
Sites Available **Total** 70
Facilities
Nearby Facilities
Cuddington
Ideal touring, walks in Delamere Forest, 45 mins to Chester, Manchester Airport etc.. Discounts for rallies and club outings.

CORNWALL

BODMIN

Camping & Caravanning Club Site, Old Callywith Road, Bodmin, Cornwall, PL31 2DZ.
Std: 01208 **Tel:** 73834
Directions From the north stay on the A30 until signpost 'Bodmin', turn right crossing over the dual carriageway in front of industrial estate, then turn immediately left at international sign. Site is on the left down Old Callywith Road.
Acreage 11 **Open** 22 March **to** 1 Nov
Site Lev/Slope
Sites Available **Total** 175
Facilities
Nearby Facilities
Bodmin Parkway
✓✓✓✓Graded Park. On the edge of Bodmin Moor. Within easy reach of the coast.

BODMIN

Glenmorris Park, Longstone Road, St. Mabyn, Bodmin, Cornwall, PL30 3BY.
Std: 01208 **Tel:** 841677
Std: 01208 **Fax:** 841677
Nearest Town/Resort Bodmin/ Wadebridge.
Directions ½ mile south west of Camelford on the A39, turn left onto B3266 for 6 miles. Turn right signposted St. Mabyn, ¼ mile to site. 5½ miles north of Bodmin.
Acreage 10 **Open** Easter **to** October
Access Good **Site** Level
Sites Available **Total** 80
Facilities
Nearby Facilities
Bodmin Parkway.
✓✓✓✓Graded Park. Quiet and secluded, between the moors and the shores. Centrally located for touring and beaches. E-mail : gmpark@dircon.co.uk

BODMIN

Lanarth Hotel & Caravan Park, St. Kew Highway, Bodmin, Cornwall, PL30 3EE.
Std: 01208 **Tel:** 841215
Nearest Town/Resort Wadebridge.
Directions On the A39 at St. Kew Highway, approx 4 miles east of Wadebridge and 8 miles west of Camelford.
Acreage 10 **Open** April **to** October
Access Good **Site** Lev/Slope
Sites Available **Total** 86
Facilities
Nearby Facilities
Bodmin
Beautiful rural setting, conveniently situated for beaches and moor. Ideal for touring Cornwall and Devon.

BODMIN

Ruthern Valley Holiday Park, Ruthernbridge, Nr. Bodmin, Cornwall, PL30 5LU
Std: 01208 **Tel:** 831395
Nearest Town/Resort Bodmin
Directions Through Bodmin on A389 towards St. Austell, on outskirts of Bodmin Ruthernbridge signposted right. Follow signs for Ruthern or Ruthernbridge.
Acreage 2 **Open** April **to** October
Access Good **Site** Level
Sites Available **Total** 30
Facilities
Nearby Facilities
Bodmin Parkway
✓✓✓✓Graded Park. Quiet peaceful wooded location centrally based for touring.

BOSCASTLE

Lower Pennycrocker Farm, St. Juliot, Boscastle, Cornwall.
Std: 01840 **Tel:** 250257
Nearest Town/Resort Boscastle
Directions 2½ miles north of Boscastle on B3263, turn left signposted Pennycrocker.
Acreage 4 **Open** Easter **to** September
Access Good **Site** Level
Sites Available **Total** 40
Facilities
Nearby Facilities
Bodmin
Scenic views, ideal touring.

BOSCASTLE

West End Camping Site, West End Farm, Tresparrett, Camelford, Cornwall.
Std: 01840 **Tel:** 261612
Nearest Town/Resort Boscastle
Directions On coastal road between Bude and Boscastle. A39 onto the B3263.
Acreage 1 **Open** Easter **to** September
Access Good **Site** Level
Sites Available **Total** 25
Facilities
Nearby Facilities
Bodmin

A COLOUR MAP SECTION FEATURES AT THE BACK OF THIS GUIDE

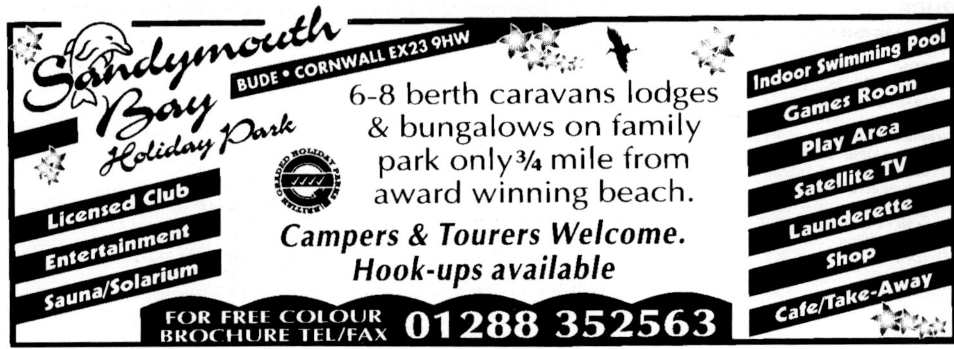

BUDE

Bude Holiday Park, Maer Lane, Bude, Cornwall, EX23 9EE.
Std: 01288 **Tel:** 355955
Std: 01288 **Fax:** 355980
Nearest Town/Resort Bude
Directions Take the A39 to Bude town centre, signposted.
Acreage 21 **Open** April **to** October
Access Good **Site** Lev/Slope
Sites Available **Total** 250
Facilities
Nearby Facilities
Exeter
✓✓✓✓Graded Park. Close to three beaches and the town centre.

BUDE

Budemeadows Touring Holiday Park, Poundstock, Bude, Cornwall, EX23 0NA.
Std: 01288 **Tel:** 361646
Std: 01288 **Fax:** 361646
Nearest Town/Resort Bude
Directions From Bude take A39 south for 3 miles.
Acreage 9 **Open** All Year
Access Good **Site** Level
Sites Available **Total** 140
Facilities
Nearby Facilities
Exeter
✓✓✓✓✓Graded Park. 1 mile from sandy beaches, cliff walks and rolling surf of Widmouth Bay. Spectactular coastal scenery.

BUDE

Camping & Caravanning Club Site, Gillards Moor, St Gennys, Bude, Cornwall, EX23 0BG.
Std: 01840 **Tel:** 230650
Directions Going south on the A39 the site is on the right in lay-by 9 miles from Bude. Going north on the A39 the site is on the left in lay-by 9 miles from Camelford, approx. 3 miles from the B3262 junction. Brown camping signs ½ mile either side of the site, also on both ends of the lay-by.
Acreage 6 **Open** 22 March **to** 27 Sept
Site Lev/Slope
Sites Available **Total** 105
Facilities
Nearby Facilities
Exeter
✓✓✓✓✓Graded Park. Near the coastal paths in the heart of King Arthur's Country.

BUDE

Cornish Coasts Caravan Park, Middle Penlean, Poundstock, Bude, Cornwall, EX23 0EE.
Std: 01288 **Tel:** 361380
Nearest Town/Resort Bude/Widemouth Bay
Directions On seaward side of A39 Bude to Camelford road, 5 miles south of Bude.
Acreage 3 **Open** Easter **to** October
Access Good **Site** Lev/Slope
Sites Available **Total** 67
Facilities
Nearby Facilities
Exeter
Peaceful, friendly site. Superb views over countryside and coast line. Ideal touring location with many beaches nearby. Good base for spectacular coastal path, walking groups transport arranged. Holiday caravans to let.

BUDE

Red Post Inn Holiday Park, Launcells, Bude, Cornwall, EX23 9NW.
Std: 01288 **Tel:** 381305
Nearest Town/Resort Bude
Directions 4 miles from Bude on the A3072 road to Holsworthy.
Acreage 4 **Open** March **to** October
Access Good **Site** Sloping
Sites Available **Total** 50
Facilities
Nearby Facilities
Barnstaple
Ideal for touring, easy access. Adventure playground and a public house on site. AA 3 Pennants.

BUDE

Sandymouth Bay Holiday Park, Sandymouth Bay, Bude, Cornwall, EX23 9HW.
Std: 01288 **Tel:** 352563
Std: 01288 **Fax:** 352563
Nearest Town/Resort Bude
Directions A39 from Kilkhampton to Bude. Turn right immediately after Penstowe, through Stibb. 3 miles from Bude.
Acreage 14 **Open** April **to** October
Access Good **Site** Level
Sites Available **Total** 55
Facilities
Nearby Facilities
Barnstaple
✓✓✓✓Graded Park. Overlooking miles of sea and countryside. Level terraced grassland. ½ mile from an award winning beach. Sauna and solarium.

BUDE

Upper Lynstone Camping & Caravan Park, Upper Lynstone Farm, Bude, Cornwall.
Std: 01288 **Tel:** 352017
Nearest Town/Resort Bude
Directions ½ mile south of Bude on Widemouth Bay road.
Acreage 5 **Open** Easter **to** October
Access Good **Site** Lev/Slope
Sites Available **Total** 90
Facilities
Nearby Facilities
≠ Exeter
✓✓✓✓Graded Park. Within easy reach of good surfing beaches. Access to cliff walks. Families and couples only, no groups.

BUDE

Widemouth Bay Caravan Park, John Fowler Holidays, Widemouth Bay, Nr. Bude, Cornwall, EX23 0DF.
Std: 01288 **Tel:** 361208
Nearest Town/Resort Widemouth/Bude
Directions 2 miles south of Bude, just off the A39.
Acreage 50 **Open** March **to** October
Access Good **Site** Level
Sites Available **Total** 300
Facilities
Nearby Facilities
✓✓✓✓Graded Park. Adjacent to an excellent surfing beach.

BUDE

Willow Valley Holiday Park, Bush, Bude, Cornwall, EX23 9LB.
Std: 01288 **Tel:** 353104
Nearest Town/Resort Bude
Directions 2 miles north of Bude on the A39 towards Kilkhampton.
Acreage 4 **Open** March **to** December
Access Good **Site** Level
Sites Available **Total** 41
Facilities
Nearby Facilities
≠ Exeter
River runs through the site. 2 miles from the nearest beach and town. Many tourist attractions nearby. AA 3 Pennants.

BUDE

Wooda Caravan Park, Poughill, Bude, Cornwall.
Std: 01288 **Tel:** 352069
Std: 01288 **Fax:** 355258
Nearest Town/Resort Bude
Directions Take road to Poughill 1¼ miles, go through village. At crossroads turn left. Site 200yds along road on right hand side.
Acreage 12 **Open** April **to** October
Access Good **Site** Lev/Slope
Sites Available **Total** 160
Facilities
Nearby Facilities
≠ Exeter
✓✓✓✓✓Graded Park. Overlooks sea and coastline, woodland walks, coarse fishing, large childrens play area, dog exercise field, short golf course. Contact Mrs Q. Colwill. Sandy beaches 1½ miles. Licensed farm restaurant.

CAMELFORD

Juliots Well Holiday Park, Camelford, Cornwall.
Std: 01840 **Tel:** 213302
Nearest Town/Resort Tintagel
Directions Leave Camelford on A39 Wadebridge Road. 1 mile out turn right at Valley Truckle, then first left towards Lanteglos, site 400 yards on right.
Acreage 8¼ **Open** March **to** October
Access Good
Sites Available **Total** 80
Facilities
Nearby Facilities
≠ Bodmin
✓✓✓✓✓Graded Park. AA 4 Pennants.

CAMELFORD

Lakefield Caravan Park, Lower Pendavey Farm, Camelford, Cornwall, PL32 9TX.
Std: 01840 **Tel:** 213279
Std: 01840 **Fax:** 213279
Nearest Town/Resort Camelford/Tintagel.
Directions 1¼ miles north of Camelford on the B3266 - Boscastle road.
Acreage 5 **Open** Easter **to** October
Access Good **Site** Level
Sites Available **Total** 30
Facilities
Nearby Facilities
≠ Bodmin.
Scenic views, own lake. Ideal for touring Cornwall. Full equestrian facilities providing lessons, site rides and hacks for all the family. British Horse Society Qualified Instruction.

CARLYON BAY

Carlyon Bay Camping Park, Cypress Avenue, Carlyon Bay, St. Austell, Cornwall, PL25 3RE.
Std: 01726 **Tel:** 812735
Std: 01726 **Fax:** 815496
Nearest Town/Resort St. Austell
Directions From St Austell head east on the A390 to the Britannia Inn and the roundabout, turn onto the A3082 and follow the Carlyon Bay signs.

CORNWALL

Acreage 32 **Open** April **to** September
Access Good **Site** Lev/Slope
Sites Available **Total** 180
Facilities
Nearby Facilities
Par
✓✓✓✓Graded Park. Within walking distance of the beach and an 18 hole golf course.

COVERACK

Little Trevothan Caravan Park, Coverack, Helston, Cornwall, TR12 6SD.
Std: 01326 **Tel:** 280260
Std: 01326 **Fax:** 280260
Nearest Town/Resort Helston
Directions A39 to Helston, follow B3083 to Culdrose, turn left B3293 signposted to Coverack. Go past BT Goonhilly, turn right before Zoar Garage, third turning on left, 300yds on the right.
Open April **to** October
Access Good **Site** Level
Sites Available **Total** 60
Facilities
Nearby Facilities
Redruth
Beach nearby, flat meadows, off road.

COVERACK

Penmarth Farm Camp Site, Coverack, Helston, Cornwall.
Std: 01326 **Tel:** 280389
Nearest Town/Resort Helston
Directions 10 miles from Helston.
Acreage 2 **Open** March **to** October
Access Good **Site** Level
Sites Available **Total** 28
Facilities
Nearby Facilities
Cambourne
¼ mile to beach and walks. Milk, cream and eggs at farm.

CRACKINGTON HAVEN

Hentervene Caravan & Camping Park, Crackington Haven, Nr. Bude, Cornwall, EX23 0LF.
Std: 01840 **Tel:** 230365
Std: 01840 **Fax:** 230514
Nearest Town/Resort Bude
Directions 10 miles southwest of Bude, turn off A39 opposite Otterham Garage, signed Crackington Haven. After 2½ miles turn left onto Crackington Road at Hentervene sign, park is ½ mile on right - 2 miles from beach.
Acreage 8¼ **Open** All Year
Access Good **Site** Level
Sites Available **Total** 35
Facilities
Nearby Facilities
Bodmin
Sands, swimming and surfing. Ideal touring centre - 2 miles to the beach. All year parking, tourers caravans sales. Take-away meals available in season.

DELABOLE

Planet Park, Delabole, Cornwall, PL33 9DT.
Std: 01840 **Tel:** 213361
Std: 01840 **Fax:** 212195
Nearest Town/Resort Tintagel
Directions On the main B3314 coast road at the western end of village, on the left hand side.
Acreage 3½ **Open** All Year
Access Good **Site** Level
Sites Available **Total** 40
Facilities
Nearby Facilities
Bodmin Parkway
Ideal touring centre with fantastic views. No noisy clubhouse or bar.

FALMOUTH

Maen Valley Holiday Park, Falmouth, Cornwall, TR11 5BJ.
Std: 01326 **Tel:** 312190
Std: 01326 **Fax:** 211120
Nearest Town/Resort Falmouth
Directions Take the A39 to Falmouth, turn right at Hillhead roundabout, go straight on for 1½ miles, turn right at Maen Valley sign to the site.
Open March **to** October
Access Good **Site** Level
Sites Available
Facilities
Nearby Facilities
Falmouth
✓✓✓✓Graded Park. Close to safe, sandy beaches. David Bellamy Silver Conservation Award.

FALMOUTH

Pennance Mill Farm Chalets & Camping, Pennance Mill Farm, Maenporth, Falmouth, Cornwall, TR11 5HJ.
Std: 01326 **Tel:** 317431/312616
Std: 01326 **Fax:** 317431
Nearest Town/Resort Falmouth
Directions Take the A39 from Truro to Falmouth, follow the brown international camping signs to Hillhead roundabout and turn right. Straight across at the next crossroads, site is on the left in 2 miles at the bottom of the hill.
Acreage 5 **Open** Easter **to** October
Access Good **Site** Level

Sites Available **Total** 55
Facilities
Nearby Facilities
Falmouth
✓✓Graded Park. Set in a sheltered valley on a working dairy farm. See the cows being milked. ½ mile to Maenporth beach. National Trust gardens and Helford River within 2½ miles.

FOWEY

Penhale Caravan & Camping Park, Fowey, Cornwall, PL23 1JU.
Std: 01726 **Tel:** 833425
Std: 01726 **Fax:** 833425
Nearest Town/Resort Fowey
Directions 1 mile west of Lostwithiel on the A390, turn left onto the B3269. After 3 miles turn right at the roundabout onto the A3082. Penhale is 500yds on the left.
Acreage 5 **Open** April **to** October
Access Good **Site** Lev/Slope
Sites Available **Total** 56
Facilities
Nearby Facilities
Par
✓✓✓Graded Park. Splendid views, close to sandy beaches with many lovely walks nearby. Central for touring.

FOWEY

Polruan Holiday Centre, Polruan-by-Fowey, Cornwall, PL23 1QH.
Std: 01726 **Tel:** 870263
Std: 01726 **Fax:** 870263
Nearest Town/Resort Fowey.
Directions From Plymouth A38 to Dobwalls, left onto A390 to East Taphouse, then left onto B3359. After 4¼ miles turn right signposted Polruan.
Acreage 2 **Open** April **to** September
Access Good **Site** Lev/Slope
Sites Available **Total** 32
Facilities
Nearby Facilities
Par
Coastal park surrounded by sea, river and National Trust farmland.

FOWEY

Yeate Farm Camp and Caravan Site, Bodinnick-by-Fowey, Cornwall.
Std: 01726 **Tel:** 870256
Nearest Town/Resort Fowey
Directions A38 Liskeard by-pass, fork left A390. Left at East Taphouse B3359 follow signs to Bodinnick. Site on right of Bodinnick ferry road.
Acreage 1 **Open** April **to** October
Access Good **Site** Level
Sites Available **Total** 30
Facilities
Nearby Facilities
Par/Lostwithiel
Private quay, slip and storage for small boats. Good walks over mainly National Trust Land. Only individual motorcycles accepted not groups.

GORRAN HAVEN

Trelispen Caravan and Camping Park, Gorran, St. Austell, Cornwall.
Std: 01726. **Tel:** 843501
Std: 01726 **Fax:** 843501
Nearest Town/Resort Gorran Haven.
Directions From A390 at St. Austell take B3293 for Mevagissey, nearing Mevagissey take road for Gorran Haven, nearing Gorran Haven look for Trelispen Camping Park signs.
Acreage 1½ **Open** April **to** October
Access Good **Site** Level
Sites Available **Total** 40.
Facilities
Nearby Facilities
St. Austell.
✓✓Graded Park. Small site in pleasant rural surroundings near impressive cliff scenery and several safe sandy beaches.

HAYLE

Atlantic Coast Park, 53 Upton Towans, Gwithian, Hayle, Cornwall, TR27 5BL.
Std: 01736 **Tel:** 752071
Nearest Town/Resort Hayle
Directions When entering Hayle from Camborne by-pass (A30), turn right at the double roundabout onto the B3301, Atlantic Coast Park is approx. 1 mile on the left.
Acreage 4½ **Open** April **to** October
Access Good **Site** Level
Sites Available **Total** 32
Facilities
Nearby Facilities
Hayle
Situated in sand dunes close to a bathing and surfing beach, excellent walks.

HAYLE

Beachside Holiday Park, Hayle, Cornwall, TR27 5AW.
Std: 01736 **Tel:** 753080
Std: 01736 **Fax:** 757252
Nearest Town/Resort Hayle
Directions Leave the A30 at Hayle and follow brown tourist signs to 'Beachside'.
Acreage 20 **Open** Easter **to** 30 Sept
Access Good **Site** Lev/Slope
Sites Available **Total** 90
Facilities
Nearby Facilities
Hayle
Right beside a golden sandy beach.

HAYLE

Higher Trevaskis Caravan & Camping Park, Gwinear Road, Connor Downs, Hayle, Cornwall, TR27 5JQ.
Std: 01209 **Tel:** 831736
Nearest Town/Resort Hayle/St Ives.
Directions At Hayle roundabout (Little Chef) on A30 take the first exit (signposted Connor Downs). After 1 mile turn right to Carnhell Green. Park is on the right in ¾ of mile.
Acreage 5¼ **Open** April **to** October
Access Good **Site** Level
Sites Available **Total** 75
Facilities
Nearby Facilities
Hayle
✓✓✓✓Graded Park. Pleasant, secluded, family run, countryside park with good clean facilities. Sheltered fields. Some facilities for the disabled.

HAYLE

Parbola Holiday Park, Wall, Gwinear, Cornwall, TR27 5LE.
Std: 01209 **Tel:** 831503
Std: 01209 **Fax:** 831503
Nearest Town/Resort Hayle
Directions Travel on A30 to Hayle, at roundabout leave first exit to Connor Downs. At end of village turn right to Carnhell Green, right at T-Junction, Parbola is 1 mile on the left.
Acreage 17 **Open** April **to** September
Access Good **Site** Level
Sites Available **Total** 115
Facilities
Nearby Facilities
No dogs allowed July/August.

HAYLE

Sunny Meadow Holiday Park, Lelant Down, Hayle, Cornwall.
Std: 01736 **Tel:** 752243
Nearest Town/Resort Hayle/St Ives.
Directions Take the Hayle by-pass, turn off for St Ives to the mini roundabout. Take the first left onto the B3311. We are ¼ mile up on the left.

Acreage 1 **Open** March **to** November
Access Good **Site** Level
Sites Available **Total** 10
Facilities
Nearby Facilities
St Erth
A few miles from both north and south coasts offering ideal opportunity to tour the Peninsula.

HELSTON

Boscrege Caravan Park, Ashton, Helston, Cornwall.
Std: 01736 **Tel:** 762231
Std: 01736 **Fax:** 762231
Nearest Town/Resort Praa Sands.
Directions From Helston follow Penzance road (A394) to Ashton, turn right by post office along road signposted to Godolphin and continue about 1½ miles to Boscrege Park.
Acreage 7 **Open** Easter/1 April **to** Oct
Access Good **Site** Level
Sites Available **Total** 50
Facilities
Nearby Facilities
Penzance.
✓✓✓✓✓Graded Park. Quiet family park in garden setting. No club. Near sandy beaches. Ideal for exploring West Cornwall. Microwave for campers.

HELSTON

Gunwalloe Caravan Park, Gunwalloe, Helston, Cornwall, TR12 7QP.
Std: 01326 **Tel:** 572668
Nearest Town/Resort Helston
Directions Take the A3083 from Helston towards Lizard for 2 miles, turn right to Gunwalloe for 1 mile, on the right signposted.
Acreage 2½ **Open** Easter **to** October
Access Good **Site** Level
Sites Available **Total** 40
Facilities
Nearby Facilities
Redruth
Central for the Lizard Peninsula. 1 mile from coastal walks.

HELSTON

Lower Polladras Touring Park, Carleen, Nr. Helston, Cornwall, TR13 9NX.
Std: 01736 **Tel:** 762220
Std: 01736 **Fax:** 762220
Nearest Town/Resort Helston.
Directions From Helston take the A394 to Penzance and turn right at the Hilltop Garage along the B3302. After ½ mile turn left to Carleen village. From the A30 turn left in Camborne along the B3303, then take the first right turning after junction of 3303 and 3302.
Acreage 4 **Open** April **to** October
Access Good **Site** Level
Sites Available **Total** 60
Facilities
Nearby Facilities
Camborne.
Pleasant views of surrounding hills. Ideal touring situation.

HELSTON

Poldown Caravan & Camping Site, Carleen, Breage, Helston, Cornwall.
Std: 01326 **Tel:** 574560
Nearest Town/Resort Helston.
Directions Take A394 (signed Penzance) from Helston. At top of the hill on outskirts of Helston take the B3303 signed Hayle/St Ives. Take the second left on this road and we are ¼ mile along.
Acreage 1¼ **Open** April **to** October
Access Good **Site** Level
Sites Available **Total** 10
Facilities
Nearby Facilities
Penzance
✓✓✓✓Graded Park. Ideal for touring West Cornwall. Small, secluded, pretty site.

ISLES OF SCILLY

Garrison Campsite, Tower Cottage, The Garrison, St. Marys, Isles of Scilly, Cornwall, TR21 0LS.
Std: 01720 **Tel:** 422670
Std: 01720 **Fax:** 422670
Nearest Town/Resort St Marys
Directions From the quay in Hugh Town, follow the road past Star Castle and we are 300 yards on. Camp shop and reception is the white building facing you.
Acreage 9 **Open** March **to** November
Site Level
Sites Available **Total** 120
Facilities
Nearby Facilities
Penzance
Quiet, family run site with superb views. Near the town.

ISLES OF SCILLY

Jenford, Bryher, Isles of Scilly, Cornwall.
Std: 01720 **Tel:** 422886
Std: 01720 **Fax:** 423092
Nearest Town/Resort Penzance.
Acreage 1 **Open** April **to** October
Site Level
Sites Available **Total** 37.
Facilities
Nearby Facilities

ISLES OF SCILLY

St. Martins Campsite, St. Martins, Isles of Scilly, Cornwall, TR25 0QN.
Std: 01720 **Tel:** 422888
Std: 01720 **Fax:** 422888
Directions Take a ferry, plane or helicopter from Penzance, St. Marys to St. Martins.
Acreage 2 **Open** March **to** October
Site Level
Sites Available **Total** 50
Facilities
Nearby Facilities
Penzance
✓✓✓✓Graded Park. Adjacent to a south facing beach on a picturesque, peaceful island.

ISLES OF SCILLY

Troytown Campsite, Troytown Farm, St. Agnes, Isles of Scilly, Cornwall, TR22 OPL.
Std: 01720 **Tel:** 422360
Nearest Town/Resort St Marys
Directions Ship or helicopter from Penzance, cars stay at Penzance. Take the boat from St Marys to St Agnes (15 minutes). Tractor for luggage from quay to the site.
Acreage 1¾ **Open** March **to** October
Site Lev/Slope
Sites Available **Total** 38
Facilities
Nearby Facilities
Penzance
✓✓✓Graded Park. TENT ONLY site on an island, beside the sea. Wonderful views to the sea and other islands.

JACOBSTOW

Edmore Tourist Park, Edgar Road, Wainhouse Corner, Jacobstow, Bude, Cornwall, EX23 0BJ.
Std: 01840 **Tel:** 230467
Nearest Town/Resort Bude
Directions 8 miles south of Bude on the A39.
Acreage 2 **Open** Easter **to** October
Access Good **Site** Level
Sites Available **Total** 28
Facilities
Nearby Facilities
Bodmin
3 miles from the beach. Ideal touring.

LANDS END

Cardinney Caravan & Caravan Park, Main A30, Lands End Road, Crows-An-Wra, Lands End, Cornwall, TR19 6HJ.
Std: 01736 **Tel:** 810880
Nearest Town/Resort Sennen Cove

Directions From Penzance follow Main A30 to Lands End, approx 5¼ miles. Entrance on right hand side on Main A30, large name board at entrance.
Acreage 5 **Open** 1 Feb **to** End Nov
Access Good **Site** Level
Sites Available **Total** 105
Facilities
Nearby Facilities
Penzance
✓✓✓✓Graded Park. Sennen Cove Blue Flag, scenic coastal walks, ancient monuments, scenic flights, Minack Ampitheatre, trips to the Isles of Scilly. Ideal for touring Lands End Peninsula. AA 3 Pennants and West Country Tourist Board Graded 4 Ticks.

LANDS END

Lower Treave Caravan Park, Crows-an-Wra, St. Buryan, Penzance, Cornwall, TR19 6HZ.
Std: 01736 **Tel:** 810559
Std: 01736 **Fax:** 810559
Nearest Town/Resort Penzance
Directions On A30 Penzance/Lands End road, ½ mile west of Crows-an-Wra.
Acreage 4½ **Open** April **to** October
Access Good **Site** Level
Sites Available **Total** 80.
Facilities
Nearby Facilities
Penzance.
Quiet family site in the heart of Lands End peninsular with panoramic rural views to the sea. Sheltered, level grass terraces. Blue Flag beach 2½ miles. AA 3 Pennants, Camping & Caravan Club Listed and Caravan Club Listed.

LAUNCESTON

Chapmanswell Caravan Site, St. Giles on the Heath, Launceston, Cornwall, PL15 9SG.
Std: 01409 **Tel:** 211382
Nearest Town/Resort Launceston.
Directions Chapmanswell Caravan Park is situated 6 miles from Launceston along the A388 on your left hand side going towards Holsworthy, just past the pub and garage in Chapmanswell.
Acreage 12 **Open** 15 March **to** 5 Nov
Access Good **Site** Level
Sites Available **Total** 81.
Facilities
Nearby Facilities
Exeter
Very central for Cornwall and Devon, easy reach of North Devon beaches, Dartmoor and Cornish resorts. Village pub meals 200 yards. Caravan storage available.

LISKEARD

Colliford Tavern, Colliford Lake, St Neot, Liskeard, Cornwall, PL14 6PZ.
Std: 01208 **Tel:** 821335
Std: 01208 **Fax:** 821335
Nearest Town/Resort Bodmin
Directions Signed from the A30 between Bodmin and Launceston.
Acreage 3¼ **Open** Easter **to** End Sept
Access Good **Site** Level
Sites Available **Total** 40
Facilities
Nearby Facilities
Bodmin Parkway
✓✓✓✓✓Graded Park. Quiet site, not suitable for boisterous families. Ideal base for exploring Cornwall. Booking is recommended fpr peak times. AA 4 Pennants.

LISKEARD

Pine Green Caravan Park, Double Bois, Liskeard, East Cornwall.
Std: 01579 **Tel:** 320183
Nearest Town/Resort Liskeard.
Directions 3 miles from Liskeard towards Bodmin. Just off the main A38 at Double Bois.
Acreage 3 **Open** January **to** November
Access Good **Site** Level
Sites Available **Total** 50
Facilities
Nearby Facilities
Liskeard
✓✓✓✓✓Graded Park. Overlooking beautiful wooded valley and open countryside.

LISKEARD

Trenant Chapel House, Trenant Caravan Park, St Neot, Liskeard, Cornwall.
Std: 01579 **Tel:** 320896
Nearest Town/Resort Liskeard
Directions Take St Cleer road off A38 at Dobwalls, 1 mile left SP St. Neot, 1 mile right SP Trennant, ½ mile right SP Trennant.
Acreage 1 **Open** April **to** October
Site Level
Sites Available **Total** 8
Facilities
Nearby Facilities
Liskeard
Siblyback and Colliford Reservoirs close, fishing, boardsailing and bird watching. Site in sheltered corner upper Fowey valley bounded by tributary of Fowey river, close Bodmin moor, ideal walking, touring.

LIZARD

Chy-Carne Holiday Park, Kuggar, Kennack Sands, Ruan Minor, Helston, Cornwall, TR12 7LX.
Std: 01326 **Tel:** 290200
Nearest Town/Resort Helston
Directions From Helston follow the A3083 for approx. 2 miles, at mini roundabout turn left onto the B3293 signposted St Keverne. Approx. 1 mile past Goonhilly Earth Satellite Station turn right, onto T-Junction turn left, site is on the left.
Open Easter **to** October
Access Good **Site** Level
Sites Available **Total** 94
Facilities
Nearby Facilities
Penzance
¼ mile from the beach, ideal for touring.

LIZARD

Gwendreath Farm Caravan Park, Kennack Sands, Helston, Cornwall, TR12 7LZ.
Std: 01326 **Tel:** 290666
Nearest Town/Resort The Lizard
Directions A3083 from Helston, left on B3293 after R.N.A.S. Culdrose. After Goonhilly Earth Station, take the first right then first left. At end of lane go through Seaview Caravan Site to second shop.
Acreage 3 **Open** Easter **to** October
Access Good **Site** Level
Sites Available **Total** 30
Facilities
Nearby Facilities
Redruth
Attractive, peaceful family site overlooking the sea in an area of outstanding natural beauty. Short woodland walk to safe sandy beaches.

LIZARD

Henry's Campsite, Caerthillian Farm, The Lizard, Helston, Cornwall, TR12 7NX.
Std: 01326 **Tel:** 290596
Nearest Town/Resort Helston
Directions Take the main A3083 Helston to Lizard road, enter the village and take the first turn right across the village green, then turn second right.
Acreage 1½ **Open** All Year
Access Good **Site** Lev/Slope
Sites Available **Total** 30
Facilities
Nearby Facilities
Redruth
Farm park with outstanding views. Close to secluded or popular beaches and near coastal footpaths.

LIZARD

Sea Acres Holiday Park, Kennack Sands, Ruan Minor, Helston, Cornwall, TR12 7LT.
Std: 01326 **Tel:** 290064
Std: 01326 **Fax:** 290063
Nearest Town/Resort Helston.
Directions Take the B3293 from Helston towards St Keverne, after the Goonhilly Earth Station turn right to Kennack Sands. In Kuggar turn left at the T-Junction and head towards the beach.
Acreage 20 **Open** 27 March **to** 30 October
Access Good **Site** Gentle Slope
Sites Available **Total** 30
Facilities
Nearby Facilities
Redruth.
✓✓✓Graded Park. Overlooking the beach, creche and golf on site.

LIZARD

Silver Sands Holiday Park, Kennack Sands, Gwendreath, Ruan Minor, Helston, Cornwall, TR12 7LZ.
Std: 01326 **Tel:** 290631
Std: 01326 **Fax:** 290631
Nearest Town/Resort Helston.
Directions On entering Helston take the A3083 Lizard road, pass R.N.A.S. Culdrose then turn left at roundabout onto the B3293 signposted St Keverne. In 4 miles, immediately past Goonhilly Satellite Station, turn right to Kennack. After 1 mile turn left.
Acreage 9 **Open** May **to** September
Access Good **Site** Lev/Slope
Sites Available **Total** 34
Facilities
Nearby Facilities
Redruth
✓✓✓Graded Park. 800mts to safe sandy beach, ideal touring and walking. Quiet, family site in area of outstanding natural beauty.

LONGDOWNS

Calamankey Campsite, Calamankey Farm Campsite, Longdowns, Penryn, Cornwall, TR10 9DL.
Std: 01209 **Tel:** 860314
Nearest Town/Resort Falmouth
Directions A394 from Penryn, 2½ miles.
Acreage 2½ **Open** Easter **to** October
Access Good **Site** Sloping
Sites Available **Total** 60
Facilities
Nearby Facilities
Penryn
Farming area. Beach 4½ miles. Ideal touring.

LOOE

Camping Caradon, Trelawne, Looe, Cornwall, PL13 2NA.
Std: 01503 **Tel:** 272388
Nearest Town/Resort Polperro/Looe
Directions From Looe on the A387, take right turn onto B3359. First turning on the right, approx 200yds on the left.
Acreage 2¼ **Open** April **to** October
Access Good **Site** Level
Sites Available **Total** 85.
Facilities
Nearby Facilities
Looe.
✓✓✓ Graded Park. Friendly, family run park with rural surroundings.

LOOE

Carbeil Holiday Park, Treliddon Lane, Downderry, Near Torpoint, Cornwall, PL11 3LS.
Std: 01503 **Tel:** 250636
Nearest Town/Resort Looe
Directions Travel along the A38 following signs for Liskeard. At Trerule Foot roundabout follow signs for Seaton then Downderry.
Acreage 1¼ **Open** Easter **to** October
Access Average **Site** Sloping
Sites Available **Total** 30
Facilities
Nearby Facilities
Looe/Liskeard
5 minutes from the beach, and attractions within 20 minutes.

LOOE

Looe Valley Touring Park, (Formerly Treble B), Polperro Road, Looe, Cornwall, PL13 2JS.
Std: 01503 **Tel:** 262425
Std: 01503 **Fax:** 265411
Nearest Town/Resort Looe
Directions 2 miles west Looe on A387 midway between Looe/Polperro.
Acreage 20 **Open** May **to** September
Access Good **Site** Lev/Slope
Sites Available **Total** 450
Facilities
Nearby Facilities
Looe
✓✓✓✓ Graded Park. Formerly Trable B Holiday Centre. Family site, ideal base for touring all Cornwall. R.A.C. appointed. Free coloured brochure. Enquiries to Dept. 06. Free showers.

LOOE

Polborder House Caravan & Camping Park, Bucklawren Road, St. Martin, Looe, Cornwall, PL13 1QR.
Std: 01503 **Tel:** 240265
Std: 01503 **Fax:** 240700
Nearest Town/Resort Looe.
Directions 2¼ miles east of Looe off B3253, follow signs for Polborder and Monkey Sanctuary.
Acreage 3 **Open** April **to** October
Access Good **Site** Level
Sites Available **Total** 36
Facilities
Nearby Facilities
Looe.
✓✓✓✓✓ Graded Park. Small, select, award winning park set in beautiful countryside, 1¼ miles from the sea.

LOOE

Talland Barton Caravan Park, Talland Bay, Looe, Cornwall, PL13 2JA.
Std: 01503 **Tel:** 272715
Nearest Town/Resort Looe.
Directions Take A387 from Looe towards Polperro. After 1 mile turn left. Follow this road for 1½ miles. The site is on the left hand side by Talland Church.
Acreage 1¼ **Open** Easter **to** October
Access Poor **Site** Lev/Slope
Sites Available **Total** 30
Facilities
Nearby Facilities
Looe.
Between Looe and Polperro, near a beach. Peaceful countryside, ideal touring.

LOOE

Tencreek Caravan & Camping Park, Looe, Cornwall, PL13 2JR.
Std: 01503 **Tel:** 262447
Std: 01503 **Fax:** 262447
Nearest Town/Resort Looe
Directions 1½ miles west of Looe on the A387 Looe to Polperro road.
Acreage 14 **Open** All Year
Access Good **Site** Level
Sites Available **Total** 250
Facilities
Nearby Facilities
Looe.
✓✓✓✓ Graded Park. Extensive coastal and countryside views. The nearest park to Looe. 45m water flume. Free use of all facilities. Practical Caravan Top 100, E.T.B. 4 Tick Grading and Rose Award.

LOOE

Tregoad Farm Touring Caravan & Camping Park, St. Martins, Looe, Cornwall, PL13 1PB.
Std: 01503 **Tel:** 262718
Std: 01503 **Fax:** 262718
Nearest Town/Resort Looe.
Directions Situated approx. 1½ miles from Looe and 200yds off the Plymouth to Looe road (B3253).
Acreage 10 **Open** April **to** October
Access Good **Site** Level
Sites Available **Total** 150
Facilities
Nearby Facilities
Looe/Liskeard
✓✓✓ Graded Park. Ideally situated on southerly slopes with magnificent views to Looe Bay and the rolling Cornish Hinterland.

LOOE

Trelawne Manor Holiday Village, Looe, Cornwall, PL13 2NA.
Std: 01503 **Tel:** 272151
Nearest Town/Resort Looe.
Directions A38 from Liskeard through Dobwalls, turn left onto the A390 for St. Austell. Go through Taphouse, then turn left onto the B3359. Trelawne is on the left after 8¼ miles.
Open Easter **to** October
Access Good **Site** Level
Sites Available
Facilities
Nearby Facilities
Liskeard
✓✓✓✓ Graded Park. Centred around a stately manor house (former home of Lady Jane Grey). Just 1¼ miles from the sea. Tennis on site.

LOOE

Trelay Farmpark, Pelynt, Looe, Cornwall, PL13 2JX.
Std: 01503 **Tel:** 220900
Std: 01503 **Fax:** 220900
Nearest Town/Resort Looe/Polperro.
Directions From Looe take the A387 towards Polperro. After 2 miles turn right onto the B3359. Trelay Farmpark is clearly signed ¾ mile on the right.
Acreage 3 **Open** Easter **to** October
Access Good **Site** Level
Sites Available **Total** 55
Facilities
Nearby Facilities
Looe.
✓✓✓ Graded Park. A quiet, uncommercialised park surrounded by farmland. Wide views over open countryside. Large pitches on a gentle south facing slope.

LOSTWITHIEL

Downend Camp, Lostwithiel, Cornwall.
Std: 01208 **Tel:** 872363
Nearest Town/Resort Lostwithiel.
Directions On the A390.
Acreage 5 **Open** April **to** October
Access Good **Site** Level
Sites Available **Total** 30
Facilities
Nearby Facilities
Lostwithiel.
Ideal touring. ½ mile to woods.

LOSTWITHIEL

Powderham Castle Tourist Park, Lanlivery, Nr. Fowey, Cornwall.
Std: 01208. **Tel:** 872277
Nearest Town/Resort Fowey/St. Austell.
Directions 1½ miles southwest Lostwithiel on A390, turn right at signpost, up road 400 yards.
Acreage 10 **Open** April **to** October
Access Good **Site** Level
Sites Available **Total** 75

Looe Valley
Touring Park

Looe Valley, formerly Treble B, is set in glorious countryside and is ideally situated for touring beautiful South East Cornwall. Close to beautiful, safe, sandy beaches, secluded coves and picturesque villages.

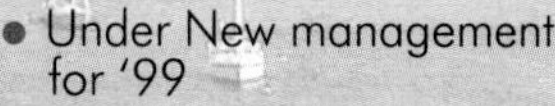

- Under New management for '99
- **NEW** & refurbished toilet & shower blocks
- **NEW** Eurotents for '99
- 4 large utility blocks with Free hot water
- Level well drained pitches with electric hook-ups
- **FREE** heated swimming pool
- Licensed club
- **FREE** entertainment & children's club
- TV & Games rooms
- Shop, Restaurant, Takeaway & Launderette
- 4 large toilet blocks
- Holiday homes & apartments available
- Rallies welcome
- Semi seasonal pitches & winter storage available

Looe Valley Touring Park, Polperro Road, Looe PL13 2JS

AA ▸▸▸ **01503 262425** QUOTE CODE: CP

Facilities
Nearby Facilities
Lostwithiel.
Quiet spacious site, uncommercialised. Central touring position. Battery charging, freezer pack service. Dish washing and vegetable preparation facilities. Indoor Badmington and soft tennis court, putting green, childrens pool and multiactivity games area. Seasonal pitches/storage. Winner AA Award for Sanitation and Environmental Facilities.

MARAZION

Kenneggy Cove Holiday Park, Higher Kenneggy, Rosudgeon, Penzance, Cornwall, TR20 9AU.
Std: 01736 **Tel:** 763453
Std: 01736 **Fax:** 763453
Nearest Town/Resort Penzance
Directions Midway between Penzance and Helston on the A394, turn south onto signed lane, go down ½ mile.
Acreage 4 **Open** Easter **to** End October
Access Good **Site** Level
Sites Available **Total** 70
Facilities
Nearby Facilities
Penzance
Sea views. Near the South West Coastal Path and a safe secluded beach. Centrally situated for West Cornwall attractions.

MARAZION

Lower Pentreath, Lower Pentreath Farm, Praa Sands, Penzance, Cornwall, TR20 9TL.
Std: 01736 **Tel:** 763221
Nearest Town/Resort Penzance
Directions From Penzance take the A394 towards Helston. Go through Rosudgeon, take Pentreath Lane immediately before the garage on the right hand side, we are at the bottom of the hill.
Acreage 1 **Open** April **to** October
Access Good **Site** Lev/Slope
Sites Available **Total** 15
Facilities
Nearby Facilities
Penzance
Small friendly site, 400 yards from the beach.

MARAZION

Trevair Touring Site, South Treveneague Farm, St. Hilary, Penzance, Cornwall, TR20 9BY.
Std: 01736 **Tel:** 740647
Nearest Town/Resort Marazion
Directions 3 miles from Marazion, B3280 through Goldsithney signposted South Treveneague.
Acreage 3½ **Open** End March **to** October
Access Good **Site** Level
Sites Available **Total** 35
Facilities
Nearby Facilities
Set in the peace and quiet of a secluded sunny valley, clean and friendly. Goats, donkey and tame birds.

MARAZION

Wheal Rodney, Marazion, Cornwall.
Std: 01736 **Tel:** 710605
Std: 01736 **Fax:** 710605
Nearest Town/Resort Marazion.
Directions ½ mile north Marazion.
Acreage 4¼ **Open** 1 April or Easter **to** Oct
Access Good **Site** Level
Sites Available **Total** 45
Facilities
Nearby Facilities
Penzance.
½ mile from safe beach. Sauna, solarium, spa bath on site.

MAWGAN PORTH

Magic Cove Touring Park, Mawgan Porth, Newquay, Cornwall, TR8 4BZ.
Std: 01637 **Tel:** 860263
Nearest Town/Resort Newquay
Directions A30 Bodmin by-pass, turn right 4¼ miles from the end. At the roundabout take the second left (Newquay) then right 400yds past Shell Garage. Pass the airport, T-Junction right to Mawgan Porth. Right after garage and Magic Co
Acreage 1 **Open** Easter **to** October
Access Good **Site** Level
Sites Available **Total** 26
Facilities
Nearby Facilities
Newquay
300yds from beach, ideal for touring Cornwall. Water and drainage on each pitch, hook-ups include T.V. point.

MAWGAN PORTH

Sun Haven Valley Holiday Park, Mawgan Porth, Newquay, Cornwall, TR8 4BQ.
Std: 01637 **Tel:** 860373
Std: 01637 **Fax:** 860373
Nearest Town/Resort Newquay/Padstow
Directions From the A30 follow signs for Newquay Airport, pass the airport and turn right into Mawgan Porth petrol station, turn right and the site is ¾ mile on the left.
Acreage 7 **Open** May **to** September
Access Good **Site** Level
Sites Available **Total** 118
Facilities
Nearby Facilities
Newquay
✓✓✓✓Graded Park. Sheltered site in beautiful countryside. Close to a sandy beach and coast walks.

MEVAGISSEY

Pengrugla Caravan Park, Mevagissey, Cornwall, PL26 6EL.
Std: 01726 **Tel:** 842714
Nearest Town/Resort Mevagissey.
Acreage 20 **Open** All Year
Access Good **Site** Lev/Slope
Sites Available **Total** 120
Facilities
Nearby Facilities
St Austell
✓✓✓✓Graded Park. Site is next door to Heligan Gardens. Rose Award Caravans and Top 100 Parks in the UK.

MEVAGISSEY

Seaview International, Boswinger, Gorran, St. Austell, Cornwall, PL26 6LL.
Std: 01726 **Tel:** 843425
Std: 01726 **Fax:** 843358
Nearest Town/Resort Mevagissey.
Directions From St. Austell take B3273 to Mevagissey, prior to village turn right. Then follow signs to Gorran.
Acreage 16 **Open** April **to** September
Access Good **Site** Level
Sites Available **Total** 165
Facilities
Nearby Facilities
St Austell.
✓✓✓✓Graded Park. Beautiful level park overlooking the sea, surrounded by sandy beaches graded among cleanest in Britain, nearest ½ mile. Free sports and pastimes on site. Holiday caravans also for hire. AA Best Campsite of the Year 1995/6 and AA 5 Pennant Premier Park.

MEVAGISSEY

Tregarton Park, Gorran, St. Austell, Cornwall, PL26 6NF.
Std: 01726. **Tel:** 843666
Std: 01726 **Fax:** 844481
Nearest Town/Resort Mevagissey.
Directions From St Austell take the B3273 signposted Mevagissey. At the top of Pentewan Hill turn right signposted Gorran. Park is 3 miles on the right (signposted).
Acreage 12 **Open** April **to** September
Access Good **Site** Lev/Slope
Sites Available **Total** 150
Facilities
Nearby Facilities
St. Austell.
✓✓✓✓Graded Park. Beautiful sheltered park with views of the sea through the valley. Nearest beach is 1½ miles. Lost Garden of Heligan 2 miles.

MULLION

Criggan Mill, Mullion Cove, Cornwall, TR12 7EU.
Std: 01326 **Tel:** 240496
Nearest Town/Resort Helston
Directions Take the A3083 towards Lizard. After approx. 7 miles turn right onto the B3296 to Mullion. Follow signs through the village to the cove and Criggan Mill is on the left approx. 200 yards before the road ends at the harbour.
Open May **to** October
Access Good **Site** Level
Sites Available **Total** 5
Facilities
Nearby Facilities
Penzance/Truro
✓✓✓✓Graded Park. In a secluded valley, 200 yards from the sea.

MULLION

Mullion Holiday Park, Mullion, Nr. Helston, Cornwall, TR12 7LJ.
Std: 01326 **Tel:** 240000
Std: 01392 **Fax:** 445202
Nearest Town/Resort Mullion
Directions Follow the A3083 from Helston to the Lizard for approx. 5 miles, we are on the left.
Acreage 10 **Open** May **to** September
Access Good **Site** Level
Sites Available **Total** 150
Facilities
Nearby Facilities
Redruth
✓✓✓✓Graded Park. In an area of outstanding natural beauty on the Lizard Peninsula, within easy reach of the beautiful Helford River, Kynance Cove, other sandy beaches and top attractions.

MULLION

Teneriffe Farm Caravan Site, A.B. Thomas, Teneriffe Farm, Mullion, Helston, Cornwall TR12 7EZ.
Std: 01326 **Tel:** 240293
Std: 01326 **Fax:** 240293
Nearest Town/Resort Helston.
Directions 10 miles Helston to The Lizard, turn right for Mullion. Take Mullion Cove road, turn left Predannack.
Acreage 3 **Open** Easter **to** October
Access Good **Site** Lev/Slope
Sites Available **Total** 20
Facilities
Nearby Facilities
Redruth.
Views of sea. S.A.E. required. Tumble drying facility.

NEWQUAY

Camping & Caravanning Club Site, Tregurrian, Near Newquay, Cornwall, TR8 4AE.
Std: 01637 **Tel:** 860448
Nearest Town/Resort Newquay
Directions On the A39 turn right onto the A3059 towards Newquay. In 1½ miles turn right at Airport sign, take the next left then right and follow Watergate Bay Campsite signs.
Acreage 4¼ **Open** 22 March **to** 27 Sept
Access Good **Site** Level
Sites Available **Total** 90
Facilities
Nearby Facilities
Newquay
✓✓✓Graded Park. ¾ mile from Watergate Bay. Adjacent to a coastal path for walks. Close to the popular resort of Newquay.

NEWQUAY

Cottage Farm Touring Park, Treworgans, Cubert, Newquay, Cornwall, TR8 5HH.
Std: 01637 **Tel:** 831083
Nearest Town/Resort Newquay.
Directions Newqauy to Redruth road A3075, turn right onto High Lanes. Follow signs to Cubert, before Cubert Village turn right signposted Crantock-Wesley road. Down the lane for ¼ mile then turn left signposted Tresean and Treworgans.
Acreage 2 **Open** April **to** October
Access Good **Site** Level
Sites Available **Total** 45
Facilities
Nearby Facilities
Newquay.
Within easy reach of three National Trust beaches. Small, family site, peaceful and in a rural location.

NEWQUAY

Crantock Plains Touring Park, Crantock, Newquay, Cornwall, TR8 5PH.
Std: 01637 **Tel:** 831273/830955
Nearest Town/Resort Newquay.
Directions From the A30 at Indian Queens take the A392 to Newquay. At Quintrell Downs roundabout go straight across to the next roundabout, then take the A3075 to Redruth and take second signposted road to Crantock.
Acreage 6 **Open** April **to** September
Access Good **Site** Level
Sites Available **Total** 40
Facilities
Nearby Facilities
Newquay.
Spacious site with peace and quiet. 2½ miles from Newquay with its beaches and 1½ miles from the picturesque village of Crantock.

NEWQUAY
CORNWALL

Excellent Camping & Touring Facilities - Luxury Static Caravans

Free Entertainment • Cabaret • Children's Pirate Den Licensed Bars • Marios Bar • Fish and Chip Shop Sauna • Supermarket • Food Bar • Amusements Games Fields • Train Rides • Pitch n Putt • Heated Swimming Pools and Waterslide • Adventure Playparks

To ensure everyones enjoyment, Hendra Holiday Park caters exclusively for families and couples only!

AA ROSE AWARD

Hendra
HOLIDAY PARK

Brochure Hotline 0500 242523

Hendra Holiday Park, Newquay, Cornwall TR8 4NY
Tel: 01637 875778

e.mail: hendra.cornwall@dial.pipex.com
http://www.hendra-holidays.com

HOLIDAY PARK

Between Watergate Bay & Mawgan Porth, Newquay

Personally supervised by the proprietors Dave & Tish Phillips.
Write or phone for free colour brochure:
Trevarrian Holiday Park, Mawgan Porth, Newquay, Cornwall

(01637) 860381
(01637) 860495 Oct 1st - May 1st only

"Quiet and Caring family site, exceptionally good value"

- Super Facilities
- Heated pool
- Individual pitches
- Electric hook-ups
- No overcrowding
- Self service shops
- Laundrette
- Park lighting
- TV/Video & Games Room
- Children's Play area
- Tennis Court and Pitch & Putt
- Free evening entertainment during peak season
- Licenced Bar
- Bar Snacks
- Modern Toilets & Hot Showers

June and September - Children FREE, discounted rates for the over 50's

EXCELLENT!

Trevella & Newperran

CARAVAN AND CAMPING PARK — TOURIST PARK

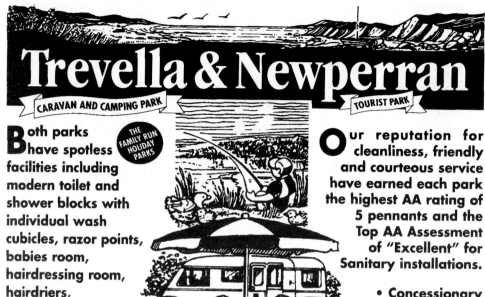

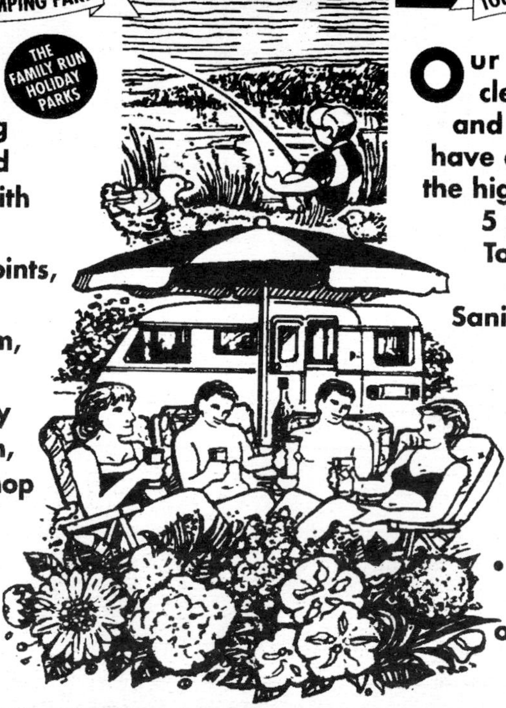

THE FAMILY RUN HOLIDAY PARKS

Both parks have spotless facilities including modern toilet and shower blocks with individual wash cubicles, razor points, babies room, hairdressing room, hairdriers, launderette, crazy golf, games room, TV room, cafe, shop and off licence, free heated swimming pools and adventure play areas.

Our reputation for cleanliness, friendly and courteous service have earned each park the highest AA rating of 5 pennants and the Top AA Assessment of "Excellent" for Sanitary installations.

- **Concessionary green fees at Perranporth's excellent links golf course.**
- **The well stocked lake at Trevella offers Free Fishing (no closed season).**

VOTED TWO OF THE TOP 10 TOURING PARKS IN CORNWALL

TREVELLA PARK

20 CRANTOCK, NEWQUAY, CORNWALL
TR8 5EW. TEL: 01637 830308

Trevella just outside Newquay and its seven golden beaches. A breathtakingly beautiful secluded family park. As well as touring pitches there are holiday caravans for hire with toilet, shower and colour Satellite TV.

NEWPERRAN TOURIST PARK

20 REJERRAH, NEWQUAY, CORNWALL
TR8 5QJ. TEL: 01872 572407

Newperran has been developed from a small Cornish farm in a picturesque, beautifully cared for setting. It is a level park with perimeter pitching ideal for caravans, tents, motor homes and the perfect family holiday.

TELEPHONE FOR COLOUR BROCHURES
01637 830308 (24 HOURS)
OR WRITE FOR BROCHURE TO THE SITE OF YOUR CHOICE.

Newquay
HOLIDAY PARKS
Choose from 2 parks, each offering great value for money!
HOLYWELL
NEWQUAY
Fantastic, picturesque locations.
If you want a high quality Holiday Park in a beautiful country setting, or one close to a glorious sandy beach then Newquay Holiday Park or Holywell Bay Holiday Park are just what you're looking for...
FOR FREE
PHONE NOW!
01637 871111
ext 6
BROCHURE
Great family value and so much to enjoy!
★ FREE Heated swimming pools with Giant water slides
★ FREE Children's playgrounds
★ FREE Nightly entertainment for all the family
★ FREE Children's clubs
★ Crazy Golf
★ Pool/Snooker rooms
★ Amusement arcades
BRITISH GRADED HOLIDAY PARKS
EXCELLENT
ROSE AWARD
CARAVAN HOLIDAY PARK
AA
Excellent facilities
★ Electric Hook-ups
★ Free showers
★ Launderette
★ Self-service shop
★ Take-away food
NEWQUAY HOLIDAY PARKS 6, NEWQUAY, CORNWALL TR8 4HS
http://www.newquay-holiday-parks.co.uk

LUXURY HOLIDAY CARAVANS

QUALITY EURO TENTS

SUPERB TOURING & CAMPING

MONKEY TREE HOLIDAY PARK

REJERRAH NEWQUAY CORNWALL TR8 5QL

FAMILY PARK IN RURAL SURROUNDS - CLOSE TO BEACHES

Plenty of Excellent Amenities to include...

- *Heated Swimming Pool & Sauna* ● *Lounge Bar Restaurant/Take-Away*
- *Regular Entertainment* ● *Ample Toilet & Washing Facilities* ● *On-Site Shop*
- *Games Room & Outdoor Play Area* ● *Electric Hook-Ups & Winter Storage*

NEWQUAY - PERRANPORTH

Tel: 01872 572032 Fax: 01872 571298

E-mail: walker.group@virgin.net Web site: www.chycor.co.uk/monkey-tree

RAC

A holiday to remember in **NEWQUAY** at

TRELOY HOLIDAY PARK

A friendly family site for touring vans, tents and motorcaravans. Convenient for beaches and beauty spots. We cater for families and couples only.

Facilties include:

• Heated swimming pool • Licenced club with family room • • Free entertainment • Children's Club • • Sports and swimming galas • Cafeteria / takeaway food • • Electric hook-ups • Shop • • Laundry • Private washing cubicles • Showers • • Baby baths • Games room • •TV room • Indoor dishwashing sinks • • Adventure playground • COARSE FISHING NEARBY •

400 yards from the Park TRELOY GOLF COURSE

Our own superb 9 HOLE PAR 32 GOLF COURSE built to an exceptionally high standard with sculptured American style greens * Golf shop * Clubs for hire * Concessionary green fees for golfers staying at the park * Special golfing weeks April, May, June and September * Golfing societies welcome * Coffee shop * Licenced Clubhouse

Write or telephone please for free colour brochure

TRELOY TOURIST PARK, NEWQUAY
CORNWALL TR8 4JN TEL: (01637) 872063 / 876279

NEWQUAY

Hendra Holiday Park, Newquay, Cornwall, TR8 4NY.
Std: 01637 **Tel:** 875778
Std: 01637 **Fax:** 879017
Nearest Town/Resort Newquay.
Directions A30 to Cornwall to Indian Queens, take the Newquay road to Quintrell Downs. Hendra is 1¼ miles before Newquay Town Centre.
Acreage 36 **Open** April **to** October
Access Good **Site** Lev/Slope
Sites Available **Total** 600
Facilities
Nearby Facilities
Newquay.
✓✓✓✓✓Graded Park. Scenic country views. Waterslide and train rides. Brochure Line - FREEPHONE 0500 242523.

NEWQUAY

Holywell Bay Holiday Park, Holywell Bay, Near Newquay, Cornwall, TR8 5PR.
Std: 01637 **Tel:** 871111
Std: 01637 **Fax:** 850818
Nearest Town/Resort Newquay
Directions From Newquay take the A3075 towards Goonhavern until you reach a sign for Cubert/Holywell, turn right.
Acreage 10 **Open** Easter **to** October
Access Good **Site** Level
Sites Available **Total** 75
Facilities
Nearby Facilities
Newquay
✓✓✓✓✓Graded Park. A short walk to the beach. FREE entertainment. Web address: http://www.newquay-holiday-parks.co.uk

NEWQUAY

Monkey Tree Holiday Park, Scotland Road, Rejerrah, Near Newquay, Cornwall, TR8 5QL.
Std: 01872 **Tel:** 572032/571298
Std: 01872 **Fax:** 571298
Nearest Town/Resort Newquay/Perranporth
Directions From the A30 take the turning onto the B3285 to Perranporth. Take the second turning on the right signposted Monkey Tree Holiday Park. The park can be found 1 mile on the left hand side.
Acreage 19 **Open** All Year
Access Good **Site** Level
Sites Available **Total** 295
Facilities
Nearby Facilities
Within 3 miles of sandy beaches, 4 miles from Newquay and 8 miles from Truro. Easily accessible to all parts of Cornwall with its location adjacent to the A30.

NEWQUAY

Newperran Tourist Park, Rejerrah, Newquay, Cornwall, TR8 5QJ.
Std: 01872 **Tel:** 572407
Nearest Town/Resort Newquay.
Directions Take A30 turn right 2½ miles past the village of Mitchell. On reaching A3075 at Goonhaven turn right and after ¼ mile, sign on righthand side turning on left.
Acreage 25 **Open** Mid May **to** Mid Sept
Access Good **Site** Level
Sites Available **Total** 270
Facilities
Nearby Facilities
✓✓✓✓✓Graded Park. Concessionary green fees, own fishing lake nearby, scenic views and central to nine golden beaches. AA 5 Pennants.

NEWQUAY

Newquay Holiday Park, Newquay, Cornwall, TR8 4HS.
Std: 01637 **Tel:** 871111
Std: 01637 **Fax:** 850818
Nearest Town/Resort Newquay
Directions East of Newquay on the A3059 towards St Columb.
Open Mid May **to** September
Access Good **Site** Sloping
Sites Available **Total** 350
Facilities
Nearby Facilities
✓✓✓✓✓Graded Park. South facing park, 2 miles outside of Newquay. FREE entertainment. Web address: http://www.newquay-holiday-parks.co.uk

NEWQUAY

Perran-Quay Tourist Park, Rejerrah, Newquay, Cornwall, TR8 5QP.
Std: 01872 **Tel:** 572561
Nearest Town/Resort Newquay.
Directions On the A3075 midway between Perranporth and Newquay.
Acreage 7 **Open** Easter **to** 21 October
Access Good **Site** Level
Sites Available **Total** 135
Facilities
Nearby Facilities
Newquay.
Country location with walks. 4 miles from seven beaches.

NEWQUAY

Porth Beach Tourist Park, Porth, Newquay, Cornwall, TR7 3NH.
Std: 01637 **Tel:** 876531
Std: 01637 **Fax:** 871227

Nearest Town/Resort Newquay.
Directions Take the A30 and turn right at Indian Queens onto the A392, then take the A3058, turn right onto the B3276.
Open March **to** October
Access Good **Site** Level
Sites Available
Facilities
Nearby Facilities
Riverside touring pitches, beside Porth Beach. Satellite TV Hook-ups.

NEWQUAY

Resparva House Camping & Caravanning, Summercourt, Newquay, Cornwall, TR8 5AH.
Std: 01872 **Tel:** 510332
Nearest Town/Resort Newquay.
Directions From east on A30, ¼ mile west of Summercourt turn left signposted Chapel Town/ Summercourt. Site entrance is on the right.
Acreage 1 **Open** Easter **to** October
Access Good **Site** Level
Sites Available **Total** 15
Facilities
Nearby Facilities
Truro
✓✓✓Graded Park. Secluded touring site with views over farm meadows. Pitches are separated by hedges. In the centre of Cornwall, near the A30.

NEWQUAY

Rosecliston Park, Trevemper, Newquay, Cornwall.
Std: 01637 **Tel:** 830326
Nearest Town/Resort Newquay
Directions Take A3075 from Newquay, Rosecliston is 1 mile on left.
Acreage 8 **Open** Whitsun **to** September
Access Good **Site** Lev/Slope
Sites Available **Total** 130
Facilities
Nearby Facilities
Entertainment in July and August. All ages welcome.

NEWQUAY

Summer Lodge Holiday Park, Whitecross, Newquay, Cornwall, TR8 4LW.
Std: 01726 **Tel:** 860415
Std: 01726 **Fax:** 861490
Nearest Town/Resort Newquay
Directions A30 turn right at Indian Queens onto A392. Approx 2 miles along the A392 you come to Whitecross, holiday park signposted left.
Acreage 10 **Open** Easter **to** September
Access Good **Site** Level
Sites Available **Total** 50
Facilities
Nearby Facilities
✓✓✓✓Graded Park. Set in beautiful countryside and ideally situated for touring. Short distance from beach and main town of Newquay.

NEWQUAY

Sunnyside Holiday Park, Quintrell Downs, Newquay, Cornwall.
Std: 01637 **Tel:** 873338
Std: 01637 **Fax:** 851403
Nearest Town/Resort Newquay
Directions From Newquay take the A392. Site is situated at Quintrell Downs, 2¼ miles from the town centre.
Acreage 11 **Open** April **to** 30 October
Sites Available **Total** 100
Facilities
Nearby Facilities
Quintrell Downs
Cornwalls leading site for 18-35 age group. On site night club plus a minibus service to town.

NEWQUAY

Trebarber Farm, St. Columb Minor, Newquay, Cornwall, TR8 4JT.
Std: 01637 **Tel:** 873007
Std: 01637 **Fax:** 873007
Nearest Town/Resort Newquay.
Directions 3 miles from Newquay on A3059, Newquay to St. Columb Major road.
Acreage 5 **Open** June **to** September
Access Good **Site** Level
Sites Available
Facilities
Nearby Facilities
Newquay.
Quiet Ideal family centre for touring, beaches. Walking distance to Porth reservoir (coarse fishing) and to Golf course.

NEWQUAY

Trekenning Tourist Park, Newquay, Cornwall, TR8 4JF.
Std: 01637 **Tel:** 880462
Std: 01637 **Fax:** 880500
Nearest Town/Resort Newquay.
Directions Just off the A39 on the A3059. 6½ miles from Newquay town centre and ¼ mile from St Columb Major.
Acreage 6½ **Open** April **to** September
Sites Available **Total** 75
Facilities
Nearby Facilities
Friendly, family run park set in beautiful Cornish countryside. Within a 10 minute drive to the beach.

NEWQUAY

Treloy Tourist Park, Newquay, Cornwall, TR8 4JN.
Std: 01637 **Tel:** 872063
Std: 01637 **Fax:** 872063
Nearest Town/Resort Newquay.
Directions 5 minutes from Newquay on the A3059 Newquay to St Columb Major Road
Acreage 11¼ **Open** April **to** September
Access Good **Site** Level
Sites Available **Total** 141
Facilities
Nearby Facilities
Newquay.
✓✓✓✓Graded Park. Ideal site for touring the whole of Cornwall. Coarse fishing nearby. Own golf course ½ mile, concessionary Green Fees. Free entertainment.

NEWQUAY

Trenance Caravan & Chalet Park, Edgcumbe Avenue, Newquay, Cornwall, TR7 2JY.
Std: 01637 **Tel:** 873447
Std: 01637 **Fax:** 852677
Nearest Town/Resort Newquay
Directions On the main A3075 Newquay to Truro road, approx. 1 mile from Newquay town centre.
Acreage 12 **Open** April **to** 11 October
Access Good **Site** Sloping
Sites Available **Total** 50
Facilities
Nearby Facilities
Newquay
✓✓✓✓Graded Park.

NEWQUAY

Trencreek Holiday Park, Trencreek, Newquay, Cornwall, TR8 4NS.
Std: 01637 **Tel:** 874210
Nearest Town/Resort Newquay.
Directions A392 to Quintrell Downs, turn right Newquay East/Porth, at Porth crossroads, ¾ mile outside Newquay, turn left to Trencreek.
Acreage 10 **Open** April **to** September
Access Good **Site** Level
Sites Available **Total** 150
Facilities
Nearby Facilities
Newquay.
Coarse fishing on site, 15 minutes footpath walk to Newquay, 1 mile by road.

NEWQUAY

Trethiggey Touring Park, Quintrell Downs, Newquay, Cornwall. TR8 4LG
Std: 01637 **Tel:** 877672
Nearest Town/Resort Newquay
Directions Follow main route signposted to Newquay and turn left onto the A3058 at Quintrell Downs, the site is in ¼ mile.
Acreage 15 **Open** 1st March **to** 1st January
Access Good **Site** Level
Sites Available **Total** 157
Facilities
Nearby Facilities
Quintrell Downs
✓✓✓✓Graded Park. Peaceful location with scenic views, close to several sandy beaches. NO overcrowding. Caravan storage. Touring caravans to let. Take-away food available.

NEWQUAY

Trevarrian Holiday Park, Mawgan Porth, Newquay, Cornwall, TR8 4AQ.
Std: 01637 **Tel:** 860381
Nearest Town/Resort Newquay
Directions Follow the A30 dual carriageway to the end at Bodmin, continue for 5 miles. After going under a railway bridge turn right signposted St Mawgan. Follow to the roundabout and take the second exit to Newquay. When you pass the garage take the next turn right and we are ¾ mile along on the left.
Acreage 12
Access Good **Site** Level
Sites Available **Total** 185
Facilities
Nearby Facilities

≠ Newquay
✓✓✓✓✓Graded Park. Family run park with 25 years experience. ¾ mile to beautiful beaches and 4½ miles from the popular resort of Newquay. Families and couples only. Special reductions in June and September. You can also call us on 01637 860495 from 1st October to 1st May only.

NEWQUAY

Trevella Park, Crantock, Newquay, Cornwall, TR8 5EW.
Std: 01637 **Tel:** 830308
Nearest Town/Resort Newquay.
Directions 2 miles south of Newquay on the A3075, turn right signposted Crantock.
Acreage 15 **Open** Easter **to** October
Access Good **Site** Level
Sites Available **Total** 270
Facilities
Nearby Facilities
≠ Newquay.
✓✓✓✓✓Graded Park. ½ mile from the beach, concessionary green fees, own fishing lake. AA 5 Pennants.

NEWQUAY

Trevornick Holiday Park, Holywell Bay, Newquay, Cornwall, TR8 5PW.
Std: 01637 **Tel:** 830531
Std: 01637 **Fax:** 831000
Nearest Town/Resort Newquay.
Directions Take Newquay to Perrenporth A3075 road. Take turning for Cubert/Holywell.
Acreage 30 **Open** Easter **to** September
Access Good **Site** Level
Sites Available **Total** 500
Facilities
Nearby Facilities
✓✓✓✓✓Graded Park. Next to the beach, stunning sea views. Tourers and static tents. Golf, fishing and tennis on site.

NEWQUAY

Watergate Bay Holiday Park, Watergate Bay, Newquay, Cornwall.
Std: 01637 **Tel:** 860387
Std: 01637 **Fax:** 860387
Nearest Town/Resort Newquay
Directions 4 miles north of Newquay on the B3276 Coast Road to Padstow. Follow directions shown from Watergate Bay.
Acreage 30 **Open** March **to** November
Access Good **Site** Level
Sites Available **Total** 171
Facilities
Nearby Facilities
≠ Newquay
½ mile from Watergate Bay in a rural location in an area of outstanding natural beauty.

Welcome to Carnevas

BH & HPA,
English Tourist Board

ROSE AWARD
CARAVAN HOLIDAY PARK
1998

Situated in the unspoilt country of the North Cornish coast, our park is ideal for touring Cornwall, Newquay - 10 miles and Padstow - 4 miles.

We are pleased to offer:

- MODERN 6+8 CARAVANS
- HOLIDAY BUNGALOWS
- SITES FOR TOURING CARAVANS
- ELECTRIC HOOK-UPS
- TOILET BLOCKS AND SHOWERS
- LAUNDRY FACILITIES
- MODERN SHOP
- TREYARNON BAY - NATURAL SWIMMING POOL
- PORTHCOTHAN BAY - SWIMMING AND SURFING
- TREVOSE GOLF COURSE NEARBY

For our colour brochure please write:
CARNEVAS HOLIDAY PARK, ST. MERRYN,
Nr. PADSTOW, CORNWALL Telephone: (01841) 520230

Harlyn Sands Holiday Park

Family owned, family run, for families!
Camp overlooking this glorious golden sandy bay & there are 7 bays for 7 days to enjoy a family bucket & spade holiday.
Enjoy the wonderful coastal walks & SAFE bathing at Harlyn.

SPECIAL RATES FOR TRAILER TENTS IN AUGUST.
STRICTLY FAMILIES ONLY!

Shop, Launderette, Shavers, Club House, Amusements, Restaurant, Take-Away, Entertainment Every Night, Children's Activities Daily.

We are 4 miles from Padstow
12 miles from Newquay.

HOLIDAY HOMES FOR HIRE

Prices & Brochure. (01841) 520720, (01752) 847949

TRERETHERN

TOURING PARK
PADSTOW
Tel/Fax: 01841 532061

Padstow's top rated caravan site. Easy access to quite rural setting of 13.5 acres for 100 units. Panoramic views over Camel Estuary and countryside. Footpath to Padstow. Assessed excellent, clean showerblocks, some individual cubicals. En-suite pitches with private WC and hand basin. Picnic tables, many sandy beaches from 1.5 m. Food and gas accessory shop. Doggy area.

Friendly welcome resident proprietor

PADSTOW

Carnevas Farm Holiday Park, Carnevas Farm, St. Merryn, Padstow, Cornwall, PL28 8PN.
Std: 01841. **Tel:** 520230
Std: 01841 **Fax:** 520230
Nearest Town/Resort Padstow.
Directions Take Newquay coast road from Padstow, turn right at Tredrea Inn just before getting to Porthcothan Bay. Site ¼ mile up road on right.
Acreage 8 **Open** April **to** October
Access Good **Site** Lev/Slope
Sites Available **Total** 198
Facilities
Nearby Facilities
Newquay
✓✓✓✓Graded Park. Near numerous sandy beaches in lovely rural position, ideal touring, well run family park. AA 3 Pennants and Rose Award Park 1998.

PADSTOW

Dennis Cove Camping, Dennis Cove, Padstow, Cornwall, PL28 8DR.
Std: 01841 **Tel:** 532349
Nearest Town/Resort Padstow
Directions Signposted off A389 on outskirts of Padstow Town.
Acreage 5 **Open** Easter **to** September
Access Fair **Site** Lev/Slope
Sites Available **Total** 62
Facilities
Nearby Facilities
Bodmin Parkway
Site adjoins Camel Estuary and town of Padstow. Scenic views and ideal base for variety of watersports. 5 Touring caravan pitches only. No large groups without prior reservation.

PADSTOW

Harlyn Sands Holiday Park, Lighthouse Road, Trevose Head, Nr. Padstow, Cornwall.
Std: 01841 **Tel:** 520720
Std: 01841 **Fax:** 521251
Nearest Town/Resort Padstow
Directions From Padstow take the B3276 Newquay coast road. After 1 mile follow signs for Harlyn Sands.
Open April **to** October
Access Good **Site** Level
Sites Available **Total** 100
Facilities
Nearby Facilities
Bodmin Parkway
✓✓✓Graded Park. 300 yards from the beach.

PADSTOW

Higher Harlyn Park, St Merryn, Padstow, Cornwall, PL28 8SG.
Std: 01841 **Tel:** 520022
Std: 01841 **Fax:** 520942
Nearest Town/Resort Padstow
Directions Take the B3296 from Padstow to St Merryn, at the crossroads in the village take Harlyn Bay road, we are the first caravan site on the left (¼ mile).
Open Easter **to** Mid October
Access Good **Site** Level
Sites Available **Total** 350
Facilities
Nearby Facilities
Newquay
Very flat site near the beach and Harlyn Bay.

PADSTOW

Mother Iveys Bay Caravan Park, Trevose Head, Padstow, Cornwall, PL28 8SL.
Std: 01841 **Tel:** 520990
Std: 01841 **Fax:** 520550
Nearest Town/Resort Padstow
Directions Padstow to Newquay coast road B3276 4 miles west of Padstow pick up Mother Iveys signs.
Acreage 1½ **Open** Easter **to** October
Access Busy **Site** Lev/Slope
Sites Available **Total** 100
Facilities
Nearby Facilities
Bodmin Parkway
✓✓✓✓Graded Park. Own private sandy beach.

PADSTOW

Music Water Touring Park, Rumford, Wadebridge, Cornwall, PL27 7SJ.
Std: 01841 **Tel:** 540257
Std: 01841 **Fax:** 540257
Nearest Town/Resort Padstow.
Directions Wadebridge A39 to roundabout take B3274 signposted Padstow. Turn left, 2 miles 500yds Park on right.
Acreage 7 **Open** April **to** October
Access Good **Site** Level
Sites Available **Total** 145
Facilities
Nearby Facilities
Bodmin.
Scenic views, ideal walking, clean friendly family site, splash pool.

PADSTOW

Seagull Tourist Park, St Merryn, Padstow, Cornwall, PL28 8PT.
Std: 01841 **Tel:** 520117
Nearest Town/Resort Padstow.
Acreage 8 **Open** Easter/1 April **to** End Oct
Access Good **Site** Level
Sites Available **Total** 100
Facilities
Nearby Facilities
Bodmin Parkway
Seven golden sandy beaches within 10 minutes drive. Small family park, quiet farmland. Coastal walks, golf, fishing, boating, surf and cycle hire.

PADSTOW

Trerethern Touring Park, Padstow, Cornwall, PL28 8LE.
Std: 01841 **Tel:** 532061
Std: 01841 **Fax:** 532061
Nearest Town/Resort Padstow
Directions On A389 1 mile south south west of Padstow
Acreage 13¼ **Open** April **to** October
Access Good **Site** Level
Sites Available **Total** 100
Facilities
Nearby Facilities
✓✓✓✓Graded Park. Panoramic views, several sandy beaches within 3 miles. Extra large pitches, footpath to padstow. En-suite pitches. No statics. Separate dog exercise area. Free brochure.

THIS GUIDE IS NOW AVAILABLE ON CD-ROM CALL OR WRITE TO US FOR MORE INFORMATION SEE PAGE 1 FOR OUR ADDRESS & TELEPHONE NUMBER

PAR

Par Sands Holiday Park, Par Beach, St. Austell Bay, Cornwall, PL24 2AS.
Std: 01726. **Tel:** 812868
Std: 01726 **Fax:** 817899
Nearest Town/Resort St. Austell/Fowey.
Directions 4 miles east of St Austell on road to Fowey A3082.
Acreage 12 **Open** April **to** October
Access Good **Site** Level
Sites Available **Total** 200
Facilities
Nearby Facilities
Par.
✓✓✓✓Graded Park. Alongside safe sandy beach and freshwater wildlife lake. Indoor heated swimming pool with aquaslide. Rose Award.

PENTEWAN

Pentewan Sands Holiday Park, Pentewan, St. Austel, Cornwall, PL26 6BT.
Std: 01726 **Tel:** 843485
Std: 01726 **Fax:** 844142
Nearest Town/Resort Mevagissey.
Directions From A390 at St. Austell take B3273 south towards Mevagissey. Entrance is 4 miles on left.
Acreage 27 **Open** April **to** October
Access Good **Site** Level
Sites Available **Total** 480
Facilities
Nearby Facilities
St. Austell.
✓✓✓✓Graded Park. Large individual marked pitches (many with electric hook-ups) on well equipped site with own safe sandy beach.

PENZANCE

Arden-Sawah Farm, Arden-Sawah, St. Levan, Penzance, Cornwall, TR19 6JL.
Std: 01736 **Tel:** 871238
Std: 01736 **Fax:** 352002
Nearest Town/Resort Penzance
Directions Take the A30 from Penzance to Sennen, then take the B3315 to Porthcurno. The site is 100 yards on the right towards Porthcurno Village.
Acreage 10 **Open** 31st July **to** 28th August
Access Good **Site** Level
Sites Available **Total** 240
Facilities
Nearby Facilities
Penzance
This TEMPORARY campsite is being opened for the month of the Total Eclipse (11th August 1999) and is very near to the "dead centre". Expected duration at this point is 2 minutes and 2 seconds. Breathtaking coastline. 3 miles from Lands End, 5 minute walk to Porthcurno beach and 1 mile from the Minack Open Air Theatre.

PENZANCE

Boleigh Farm Site, Boleigh Farm, Lamorna, Penzance, Cornwall.
Std: 01736 **Tel:** 810305
Nearest Town/Resort Penzance.
Directions Site is 4½ miles southwest of Penzance on the B3315, first on the right after turn to Lamorna Cove.
Acreage 1½ **Open** March **to** October
Access Good **Site** Level
Sites Available **Total** 30
Facilities
Nearby Facilities
Penzance.
Local Prehistoric Stones, Pipers and Merry Maidens, etc. Sea 1 mile. Coastal walks. Spin dryer. 7 miles to Lands End, 5 miles Minac (open air) theatre.

PENZANCE

Bone Valley Caravan Park, Heamoor, Penzance, Cornwall, TR20 8UJ.
Std: 01736 **Tel:** 360313
Nearest Town/Resort Penzance
Directions 1 mile north of Penzance. Follow the A30 (Penzance Bypass) to roundabout and turn right signposted Heamoor. Follow road through the village past Sportsman Pub to signpost on the right. Go downhill to signpost on the left, site is 200 yards on the left.
Acreage 1 **Open** March **to** 15 December
Access Good **Site** Level
Sites Available **Total** 18
Facilities
Nearby Facilities
Penzance
Clean, tidy and quiet site, supervised. Very sheltered, flat pitches. Very good location for touring the Penwith area.

PENZANCE

Camping & Caravanning Club Site, Higher Tregiffian Farm, St Buryan, Penzance, Cornwall, TR19 6JB.
Std: 01736 **Tel:** 871588
Directions Follow the A30 towards Lands End, turn right onto the A3306 St. Just to Pendeen road, site is 50 yards on the left.
Acreage 4 **Open** 22 March **to** 27 Sept
Site Level
Sites Available **Total** 75
Facilities
Nearby Facilities
Penzance

✓✓✓✓ Graded Park. 2½ miles from Sennen Cove. Within walking distance of Lands End.

PENZANCE

Garris Farm, Gulval, Penzance, Cornwall, TR20 8XD.
Std: 01736 **Tel:** 365806
Std: 01736 **Fax:** 365806
Nearest Town/Resort Penzance
Directions Leave A30 turning right at Growlas on road to Luogvan B3309 to Castlegate. Follow road to Chysauster ancient village.
Acreage 8 **Open** May **to** October
Access Good **Site** Sloping
Sites Available
Facilities
Nearby Facilities
Penzance.

PENZANCE

River Valley Caravan Park, Relubbus, Marazion, Penzance, Cornwall, TR20 9ER.
Std: 01736 **Tel:** 763398
Std: 01736 **Fax:** 763398
Nearest Town/Resort Marazion.
Directions From the A30 Penzance/St Michaels Mount roundabout, turn left Helston A394, left at next roundabout, signposted Relubbus.
Acreage 18 **Open** March **to** 5th Jan
Access Good **Site** Level
Sites Available **Total** 150
Facilities
Nearby Facilities
Penzance.
✓✓✓✓✓ Graded Park. Quiet park, no clubhouse, in sheltered valley. Top grade toilets. Now under NEW ownership.

PENZANCE

Wayfarers Caravan & Camping Park, St. Hilary, Penzance, Cornwall, TR20 9EF.
Std: 01736 **Tel:** Penzance 763326
Nearest Town/Resort Marazion.
Directions 2 miles east of Marazion on B3280.
Acreage 4 **Open** March **to** November
Access Good **Site** Level
Sites Available **Total** 60
Facilities
Nearby Facilities
Penzance.
Quiet, family park. Easy reach of Mounts Bay and beaches. Modern holiday caravans for hire. Short breaks and couple discounts. AA 3 Pennant. Members of the Cornish Tourist Board.

PERRANPORTH

Penrose Farm Touring Park, Goonhavern, Truro, Cornwall, TR4 9QF.
Std: 01872 **Tel:** 573185
Nearest Town/Resort Perranporth.
Directions Leave A30 onto the B3285 signed Perranporth, site 1½ miles on the left.
Acreage 9 **Open** April **to** September
Access Good **Site** Level
Sites Available **Total** 100
Facilities
Nearby Facilities
Newquay/Truro
✓✓✓✓ Graded Park. Quiet, clean and sheltered park with animal centre and adventure play area. Good spacing. Close to Perranporth beach. Private Superloos.

PERRANPORTH

Perran Sands Holiday Centre, Perranporth, Cornwall, TR6 0AQ.
Std: 01872 **Tel:** 573551
Std: 01872 **Fax:** 571158
Nearest Town/Resort Perranporth.
Directions Take the A30 through Cornwall. 3 miles after Mitchell turn right onto the B3285 towards Perranporth. Perran Sands is on the right just before Perranporth.
Acreage 25 **Open** 6 May **to** 7 October
Access Good **Site** Level

CORNWALL

Sites Available **Total** 450
Facilities
Nearby Facilities
Truro.
✓✓✓✓Graded Park. On a cliff top amid dunes and grassl
and. A short walk from the beach.

PERRANPORTH

Perran Springs Touring Park, Goonhavern, Truro, Cornwall, TR4 9QG.
Std: 01872 **Tel:** 540568
Nearest Town/Resort Perranporth.
Directions Leave the A30 and turn onto the B3285 signposted Perranporth. Follow the brown tourism signs marked "Perran Springs" for 1½ miles. Entrance will then be clearly seen.
Acreage 8 **Open** April **to** October
Access Good **Site** Level
Sites Available **Total** 120
Facilities
Nearby Facilities
Truro
Quiet family park with panoramic countryside views. Award winning amenities. Takeaway food available. Within a few minutes drive of the sand and surf of Perranporth Beach and Newquay.

PERRANPORTH

Rosehill Farm Tourist Park, Goonhavern, Cornwall, TR4 9LA.
Std: 01872 **Tel:** 572448
Nearest Town/Resort Perranporth
Directions 200 yds from The New Inn in Goonhavern on the B3285 Perranporth road.
Acreage 6 **Open** Easter **to** October
Access Good **Site** Lev/Slope
Sites Available **Total** 65
Facilities
Nearby Facilities
Truro & Newquay
Quiet family site, 1¼ miles from Perranporth beach, ideal touring base. Free hot showers, separate dog walking field. Cleanliness insured by resident owners. Booking is essential July and August, discount for advance bookings.

POLPERRO

Killigarth Manor Caravan Park, Polperro, Looe, Cornwall.
Std: 01503. **Tel:** 272216
Std: 01503 **Fax:** 272065
Nearest Town/Resort Polperro.
Directions From Looe take the A387, after approx 4 miles turn left, signposted Killigarth. Park is about 400yds on the left.
Acreage 7 **Open** Easter **to** October
Access Good **Site** Level
Sites Available **Total** 202
Facilities
Nearby Facilities
Looe.
✓✓✓✓✓Graded Park. Set in an area of outstanding natural beauty. AA 5 Pennants.

POLZEATH

South Winds Camping & Caravan Park, Old Polzeath Road, Polzeath, Near Wadebridge, Cornwall, PL27 6QU.
Std: 01208 **Tel:** 863267
Std: 01208 **Fax:** 862080
Nearest Town/Resort Wadebridge.
Acreage 7 **Open** Easter **to** October
Access Good **Site** Level
Sites Available **Total** 100
Facilities
Nearby Facilities
Bodmin Road.
Outstanding views of countryside and sea.

POLZEATH

Tristram Caravan & Camping Park, Polzeath, Nr Wadebridge, Cornwall, PL27 6SR.
Std: 01208 **Tel:** 863267/862215
Std: 01208 **Fax:** 862080
Nearest Town/Resort Wadebridge
Acreage 5 **Open** Easter **to** October
Access Good **Site** Level
Sites Available **Total** 130
Facilities
Nearby Facilities
Bodmin Parkway
Cliff top site. Direct access onto Polzeath beach.

PORTHTOWAN

Porthtowan Tourist Park, Mile Hill, Porthtowan, Truro, Cornwall, TR4 8TY.
Std: 01209 **Tel:** 890256
Std: 01209 **Fax:** 890011
Nearest Town/Resort Porthtowan/ Redruth
Directions Take signpost off A30 Redruth/ Porthtowan. Cross the A30, through north country to T-Junction, right up the hill, past Woodlands Restaurant, park is on the left.
Acreage 5½ **Open** Easter **to** October
Access Good **Site** Level
Sites Available **Total** 50
Facilities
Nearby Facilities

⇌ Redruth
A completely level site in an area of outstanding natural beauty. ½ mile from the beach. Ideal touring base.

PORTHTOWAN

Rose Hill Touring Park, Porthtowan, Truro, Cornwall, TR4 8AR.
Std: 01209 **Tel:** 890802
Nearest Town/Resort Redruth
Directions A30 then the B3277 St Agnes road. Turn left at 7 Milestone Shell Garage signposted Porthtowan, 2 miles to the park.
Acreage 3 **Open** April **to** October
Access Good **Site** Level
Sites Available **Total** 40
Facilities
Nearby Facilities
⇌ Redruth
Sheltered site, only a 4 minute walk from the beach. Coastal walks. Ideal touring site. AA 3 Pennants.

PORTREATH

Cambrose Touring Park, Portreath Road, Redruth, Cornwall.
Std: 01209 **Tel:** 890747
Std: 01209 **Fax:** 890747
Nearest Town/Resort Redruth/Portreath.
Directions From Redruth, B3300 (Portreath road) north.
Acreage 6 **Open** Easter **to** October
Access Good **Site** Level
Sites Available **Total** 60
Facilities
Nearby Facilities
⇌ Redruth.
✓✓✓✓Graded Park. 1½ miles sandy beaches, centrally situated as a base from which to tour. Adventure playground. Under the personal supervision of the resident proprietors - R.G. & J. Fitton.

PORTREATH

Tehidy Holiday Park, Harris Mill, Redruth, Cornwall, TR16 4JQ.
Std: 01209 **Tel:** 216489
Std: 01209 **Fax:** 216489
Nearest Town/Resort Portreath.
Directions Take Redruth Porthtowan exit from A30. Take Porthtowan North Country exit from double roundabout, turn left at first crossroads. Cross next two crossroads Tehidy Holiday Park 200 yards on left pass Cornish Arms Public House.
Acreage 1 **Open** Easter **to** October
Access Good **Site** Level
Sites Available **Total** 18
Facilities
Nearby Facilities
⇌ Redruth.
✓✓✓✓Graded Park. Near beach, scenic views, ideal touring.

REDRUTH

Tresaddern Holiday Park, St. Day, Redruth, Cornwall, TR16 5JR.
Std: 01209 **Tel:** 820459
Nearest Town/Resort Redruth
Directions From A30 2 miles east of Redruth take A3047 Scorrier, in 400yds B3298 Falmouth, site 1½ miles on right.
Acreage ½ **Open** Easter **to** October
Access Good **Site** Lev/Slope
Sites Available **Total** 25
Facilities
Nearby Facilities
⇌ Redruth
Quiet rural site, central for touring south Cornwall.

RUAN MINOR

The Friendly Camp, Tregullas Farm, Penhale, Ruan Minor, Helston, Cornwall, TR12 7LJ.
Std: 01326 **Tel:** 240387
Nearest Town/Resort Mullion
Directions 7 miles south of Helston on left hand side of A3083, just before junction of B3296 to Mullion which is 1 mile.
Acreage 1¼ **Open** April **to** November
Access Good **Site** Level
Sites Available **Total** 18
Facilities
Nearby Facilities
⇌ Redruth
Nice views, ideal touring, nice moorland walks.

SALTASH

Dolbeare Caravan & Camping Park, Landrake, Saltash, Cornwall, PL12 5AF.
Std: 01752 **Tel:** 851332
Nearest Town/Resort Saltash.
Directions 4 miles west of Saltash, turn off A38 at Landrake immediately after footbridge into Pound Hill, signposted.
Acreage 9 **Open** All Year
Access Good **Site** Lev/Slope
Sites Available **Total** 60.
Facilities
Nearby Facilities
⇌ Saltash.
✓✓✓✓✓Graded Park. Quality touring park in magnificent countryside. Free, plentiful hot water. Level hard standings and large grass areas. Please telephone for a brochure.

SALTASH

Notter Bridge Caravan & Camping Park, Notter Bridge, Saltash, Cornwall, PL12 4RW.
Std: 01752 **Tel:** 842318
Nearest Town/Resort Plymouth
Directions A38, 3½ miles west of Tamar Bridge, Plymouth, signposted Notter Bridge.
Acreage 6¼ **Open** April/Easter **to** October
Access Good **Site** Level
Sites Available **Total** 33
Facilities
Nearby Facilities
⇌ Plymouth
Sheltered, level site in a picturesque wooded valley with river frontage. Fishing, pool, pub food opposite. Ideal centre for Plymouth, Cornwall and Devon. AA 3 Pennants.

SALTASH

Stoketon Touring Park, Trematon, Saltash, Cornwall, PL12 4RZ.
Std: 01752 **Tel:** 848177
Std: 01752 **Fax:** 843203
Nearest Town/Resort Plymouth
Directions Off the main A38 1½ miles from the Tamar Bridge.
Acreage 10 **Open** April **to** October
Access Good **Site** Level

CORNWALL

Sites Available **Total** 80
Facilities
Nearby Facilities
Saltash.
Ideal touring.

ST. AGNES

Beacon Cottage Farm Camping Park, Beacon Drive, St. Agnes, Cornwall.
Std: 01872 **Tel:** 552347
Nearest Town/Resort St. Agnes.
Directions From A30, take B3277 to St. Agnes, take road to the Beacon. Follow signs to site.
Acreage 2 **Open** April **to** September
Access Good **Site** Level
Sites Available **Total** 50
Facilities
Nearby Facilities
Truro.
✓✓✓✓✓Graded Park. On working farm, surrounded by National Trust Land. Sandy beach 1 mile, beautiful sea views.

ST. AGNES

Chiverton Park, Blackwater, Truro, Cornwall, TR4 8HS.
Std: 01872 **Tel:** 560667
Std: 01872 **Fax:** 560667
Nearest Town/Resort St Agnes
Directions Travel along the A30 to Chiverton Cross roundabout 4 miles east of Redruth. Take the St. Agnes road, after 500 yards turn left and the park is 200 yards down on the left.
Open Easter **to** End October
Access Good **Site** Level
Sites Available **Total** 30
Facilities
Nearby Facilities
Truro
Quiet park, close to beaches. Easy access to the north and south coast.

ST. AGNES

Presingoll Farm Caravan & Camping Park, St. Agnes, Cornwall, TR5 0PB.
Std: 01872 **Tel:** 552333
Nearest Town/Resort St. Agnes
Directions Leave the A30 at Chiverton Cross roundabout and take the B3277 for St. Agnes. Site is 3 miles on the right.
Acreage 3½ **Open** Easter **to** End October
Access Good **Site** Level
Sites Available **Total** 90
Facilities
Nearby Facilities
Truro
Working farm overlooking the North Cornwall coastline. Near the Cornish Coastal Path and surf beaches within 2 miles. Ideal for walking.

ST. AUSTELL

Croft Farm Touring Park, Luxulyan, Bodmin, Cornwall, PL30 5EQ.
Std: 01726 **Tel:** 850228
Std: 01726 **Fax:** 850498
Nearest Town/Resort St. Austell
Directions From A390 (Liskeard to St Austell) turn right past the level crossing in St Blazey (signposted Luxulyan). In ¼ mile turn right at T-Junction, continue to next T-Juntion and turn right. The park is on the left within ½ mile. N.B. DO NOT take any other routes signposted Luxulyan/Lux Valley.
Acreage 4 **Open** End March **to** End Oct
Access Good **Site** Level
Sites Available **Total** 53
Facilities
Nearby Facilities
Luxulyan
✓✓✓✓Graded Park. David Bellamy Silver Conservation Award winners.

ST. AUSTELL

Penhaven Touring Park, Pentewan Road, St. Austell, Cornwall, PL26 6DL.
Std: 01726 **Tel:** 843687
Nearest Town/Resort Mevagissey
Directions 3 miles south of St Austell on the B3273 Mevagissey road, 1 mile after the village of London Apprentice.
Acreage 13 **Open** Easter/1 April **to** 31 October
Access Good **Site** Level
Sites Available **Total** 105
Facilities
Nearby Facilities
St Austell
✓✓✓✓✓Graded Park. Situated in a sheltered valley of outstanding natural beauty. 1 mile from a river and a woodland walk to the beach. Central for touring Cornwall.

ST. AUSTELL

River Valley Holiday Park, London Apprentice, St Austell, Cornwall, PL26 7AP.
Std: 01726 **Tel:** 73533
Std: 01726 **Fax:** 73533
Nearest Town/Resort St Austell
Directions Take the B3273 from St Austell to Mevagissey, 1 mile to London Apprentice, site is on the left hand side.
Acreage 4 **Open** April **to** September
Access Good **Site** Level

Sites Available **Total** 40
Facilities
Nearby Facilities
St Austell
✓✓✓✓ Graded Park. Alongside a river with woodland walk and a cycle trail.

ST. AUSTELL

Sun Valley Holiday Park, Pentewan Road, St. Austell, Cornwall.
Std: 01726 **Tel:** 843266
Nearest Town/Resort Mevagissey.
Directions Take B3273 from St. Austell, site 1 mile past 'London Apprentice', on right.
Acreage 20 **Open** April **to** October
Access Good **Site** Level
Sites Available **Total** 22
Facilities
Nearby Facilities
St. Austell.
✓✓✓✓✓ Graded Park. Site situated in woodland and pasture surrounding. 1 mile from sea. Ideal touring centre. Tennis on site.

ST. AUSTELL

Trencreek Farm Holiday Park, Hewaswater, St. Austell, Cornwall, PL26 7JG.
Std: 01726 **Tel:** 882540
Std: 01726 **Fax:** 882540
Nearest Town/Resort St. Austell.
Acreage 56 **Open** Easter **to** End October
Access Good **Site** Level
Sites Available **Total** 198
Facilities
Nearby Facilities
St. Austell.
Kids Club in main season and 4 fishing lakes on site.

ST. AUSTELL

Treveor Farm Caravan & Camping Park, Gorran, St Austell, Cornwall.
Std: 01726 **Tel:** 842387
Std: 01726 **Fax:** 842387
Nearest Town/Resort Gorran Haven.
Directions Take the B2373 from St Austell. After Pentewan beach at top of hill turn right to Gorran. Approx 4 miles on turn right at signboard.
Acreage 4 **Open** April **to** October
Access Good **Site** Level
Sites Available **Total** 50
Facilities
Nearby Facilities
St Austell
Near to beach, coastal path and the Lost Gardens of Heligan.

ST. AUSTELL

Trewhiddle Holiday Estate, Trewhiddle, St. Austell, Cornwall, PL26 7AD.
Std: 01726 **Tel:** 67011
Std: 01726 **Fax:** 67010
Nearest Town/Resort St. Austell.
Directions From St Austell roundabout on the By-Pass, take the B3273 road towards Mevagissey, the site entrance is ½ mile from the roundabout on the right.
Acreage 16 **Open** March **to** January
Access Good **Site** Lev/Slope
Sites Available **Total** 105
Facilities
Nearby Facilities
St. Austell.
✓✓✓✓ Graded Park. Set in 16 acres of beautiful grounds. Excellent facilities for family holidays. Heated pool with water flume. Ideal touring centre.

ST. BURYAN

Tower Park Caravans & Camping, St. Buryan, Penzance, Cornwall, TR19 6BZ.
Std: 01736 **Tel:** 810286
Nearest Town/Resort Penzance.
Directions From the A30 Lands End road turn left onto the B3283 towards St. Buryan. In the village turn right then right again and the park is 300 yards on the right.
Acreage 12 **Open** March **to** January
Access Good **Site** Level
Sites Available **Total** 102
Facilities
Nearby Facilities
Penzance.
✓✓✓✓ Graded Park. Quiet, rural park located midway between Penzance and Lands End. Ideal touring and walking in West Cornwall.

ST. IVES

Ayr Holiday Park, Ayr, St. Ives, Cornwall, TR26 1EJ.
Std: 01736 **Tel:** 795855
Std: 01736 **Fax:** 798797
Nearest Town/Resort St. Ives.
Open April **to** October
Access Good **Site** Sloping
Sites Available
Facilities
Nearby Facilities
St. Ives.
✓✓✓✓✓ Graded Park.

ST. IVES

Carbis Bay Holiday Village, Laity Lane, Carbis Bay, St. Ives, Cornwall, TR26 3HW.
Std: 01736 **Tel:** 797580
Std: 01736 **Fax:** 797580
Nearest Town/Resort St. Ives
Directions Follow the A30 Hayle bypass, at the roundabout turn north west onto the A3074 signposted St. Ives. After 3 miles at Carbis Bay site is signposted left opposite the junction to the beach, turn and follow for 150 yards to the crossroads, go straight across and the site is directly on your right.
Acreage 36 **Open** 31 March **to** 31 October
Access Good **Site** Lev/Slope
Sites Available **Total** 486
Facilities
Nearby Facilities
Carbis Bay
Spacious site with superb facilities. Relaxed atmosphere and plenty of room for everyone. Within walking distance of the beach. Ideal base to explore the countryside of West Cornwall.

ST. IVES

Higher Chellew Touring Caravan & Camping Park, Higher Chellew, Nancledra, Penzance, Cornwall, TR20 8BD.
Std: 01736 **Tel:** 364532
Nearest Town/Resort St Ives
Directions Take the A30 to the village of Crowlas, turn right onto the B3309 signposted Ludgvan and Nancledra. After 2 miles at the T-Junction turn right onto the B3311, turn right after ¾ mile into a private lane signed Higher Chellew.
Acreage 1¼ **Open** All Year
Access Good **Site** Level
Sites Available **Total** 30
Facilities
Nearby Facilities
Penzance/St Ives
Quiet, rural site with spectacular panoramic, countryside views. Immaculate facilities. Easy access to all that makes West Cornwall special.

ST. IVES

Penderleath Caravan & Camping Park, Towednack, St. Ives, Cornwall, TR26 3AF.
Std: 01736 **Tel:** 798403
Nearest Town/Resort St. Ives
Directions B3311 from St. Ives, after Halsetown first right to Towednack.
Acreage 8 **Open** Easter **to** October
Access Good **Site** Lev/Slope
Sites Available **Total** 75
Facilities
Nearby Facilities
St. Ives
Set in classified area of outstanding natural beauty with unrivalled views. Peaceful family run site.

ST. IVES

Polmanter Tourist Park, Halsetown, St. Ives, Cornwall, TR26 3LX.
Std: 01736 **Tel:** 795640
Std: 01736 **Fax:** 795640
Nearest Town/Resort St. Ives.
Directions Take the A3074 to St. Ives from the A30. First left at the mini-roundabout taking Holiday Route to St. Ives (Halsetown). Turn right at the Halsetown Inn, then first left.
Acreage 13 **Open** Easter **to** October
Access Good **Site** Level
Sites Available **Total** 240
Facilities
Nearby Facilities
St. Ives.
✓✓✓✓✓ Graded Park. Just 1½ miles from St. Ives and beaches. Central for touring the whole of West Cornwall. Tennis on site. TV to individual pitches.

ST. IVES

St. Ives Bay Holiday Park, Upton Towans, Hayle, Cornwall, TR27 5BH.
Std: 01736 **Tel:** Hayle 752274
Std: 01736 **Fax:** 754523
Nearest Town/Resort Hayle.
Directions A30 from Camborne to Hayle, at roundabout take Hayle turn-off and then turn right onto B3301, 600yds on left enter park.
Acreage 12 **Open** May **to** September
Access Good **Site** Lev/Slope
Sites Available **Total** 200
Facilities
Nearby Facilities
Hayle.
✓✓✓✓ Graded Park. Park adjoining own sandy beach, onto St. Ives Bay. Children very welcome. Sea views. Dial-a-Brochure 24 hours, Mr R. White. (See full page colour advertisment).

ST. IVES

Trevalgan Family Camping Park, St. Ives, Cornwall, TR26 3BJ.
Std: 01736 **Tel:** 796433
Nearest Town/Resort St. Ives
Directions Follow the holiday route round St. Ives. From the B3306 follow brown camping park signs.
Acreage 5 **Open** May **to** September
Access Good **Site** Level
Sites Available **Total** 120
Facilities
Nearby Facilities
St. Ives
✓✓✓✓ Graded Park. Rural park with own stretch of Cornish coast. Superb views and walking. Some facilities for the disabled.

ST. JUST

Bosavern Garden Caravan Site, Bosavern House, St. Just, Penzance, Cornwall.
Std: 01736 **Tel:** 788301
Std: 01736 **Fax:** 788301
Nearest Town/Resort St. Just/Penzance.
Directions Take the A3071 from Penzance towards St. Just. Approximately 550yds before St. Just turn left onto the B3306 signposted Lands End and airport. Bosavern Garden Caravan Park is 500yds from the turn off, behind Bosavern House.
Acreage 2¼ **Open** March **to** October
Access Good **Site** Level
Sites Available **Total** 12
Facilities
Nearby Facilities
Penzance

Sea and moorland views, walled garden site surrounded by trees and flowers. Excellent walking country, good beaches nearby. Local authorities licensed site.

ST. JUST

Kelynack Caravan & Camping Park, Kelynack, St. Just, Nr. Penzance, Cornwall.
Std: 01736 **Tel:** 787633
Nearest Town/Resort St. Just in Penwith.
Directions From Penzance take A3071 St. Just road, then after 6 miles turn left onto the B3306 Lands End coast road, ½ mile to site sign.
Acreage 2 **Open** April **to** October
Access Good **Site** Level
Sites Available **Total** 20
Facilities
Nearby Facilities
Penzance.
✓✓✓✓Graded Park. ¾ mile beach, alongside stream in valley setting. Ideal for touring. On coast road. Sheltered site. Rose Award Park.

ST. JUST

Levant House, Levant House, Levant Road, Pendeen, Penzance, Cornwall, TR19 7SX.
Std: 01736 **Tel:** 788795
Nearest Town/Resort St. Just-in-Penwith.
Directions From St. Just-in-Penwith take the B3306 towards St. Ives. At Trewellard turn left. Site is in two fields 200yds on the left.
Acreage 2½ **Open** April **to** October
Access Good **Site** Lev/Slope
Sites Available **Total** 43
Facilities
Nearby Facilities
Penzance.
Approx. 8 minutes wlak to the Coastal Path. Rock climbing at Bosegran.

ST. JUST

Trevaylor Caravan and Camping Park, Botallack, St Just, Cornwall.
Std: 01736 **Tel:** 787016
Nearest Town/Resort Penzance
Directions Situated on the B3306 Lands End to St Ives road, approx 1 mile to the north of St Just.
Acreage 5 **Open** Mid March **to** October
Access Good **Site** Level
Sites Available **Total** 85
Facilities
Nearby Facilities
Penzance
Easy access to the golden sands, white surf from the Atlantic Ocean, rugged cliffs and coastal paths. Off License and take-away on site.

ST. MAWES

Trethem Mill Touring Park, St. Just-in-Roseland, Truro, Cornwall.
Std: 01872 **Tel:** 580504
Std: 01872 **Fax:** 580968
Nearest Town/Resort St. Mawes.
Directions From Tregony follow the A3078 to St. Mawes. Approx. 2 miles after passing through Trewithian look out for caravan and camping sign.
Acreage 4 **Open** April **to** October
Access Good **Site** Lev/Slope
Sites Available **Total** 84
Facilities
Nearby Facilities
Truro.
✓✓✓✓Graded Park. St. Mawes.

ST. MERRYN

Tregavone Farm Touring Park, St. Merryn, Padstow, Cornwall, PL28 8JZ.
Std: 01841 **Tel:** 520148
Nearest Town/Resort Padstow
Directions Turn right off A39 (Wadebridge-St. Columb) onto A389 (Padstow) come to T junction turn right in 1 mile turn left, entrance on left after 1 mile.
Acreage 4 **Open** March **to** October
Access Good **Site** Level
Sites Available **Total** 40
Facilities
Nearby Facilities
Newquay
Quiet family run site situated near sandy surfing beaches, country views, well maintained and grassy. AA 2 Pennants.

ST. MERRYN

Trethias Farm Caravan Park, St. Merryn, Padstow, Cornwall.
Std: 01841 **Tel:** 520323
Nearest Town/Resort Padstow.
Directions From Wadebridge follow signs to St. Merryn, go past Farmers Arms, third turning right (our signs from here).
Acreage 5 **Open** April **to** September
Access Good **Site** Level
Sites Available **Total** 62
Facilities
Nearby Facilities
Bodmin Parkway
✓✓✓Graded Park. Near beach, scenic views. Couples and family groups only.

ST. MERRYN

Trevean Farm Caravan & Camping Park, St. Merryn, Padstow, Cornwall, PL28 8PR.
Std: 01841 **Tel:** 520772
Nearest Town/Resort Padstow
Directions From St. Merryn village take the B3276 Newquay road for 1 mile. Turn left for Rumford, site ¼ mile on the right.
Acreage 2 **Open** April **to** October
Access Good **Site** Level
Sites Available **Total** 36
Facilities
Nearby Facilities
Newquay
✓✓✓✓Graded Park. Situated near several sandy, surfing beaches.

ST. MERRYN

Treyarnon Bay Caravan Park, Treyarnon Bay, Padstow, Cornwall, PL28 8JR.
Std: 01841 **Tel:** 520681
Nearest Town/Resort Padstow.
Directions Follow road for Treyarnon from B3276 Newquay to Padstow road. Follow lane and into car park at the bottom of the village. (Holiday park adjoins car park).
Acreage 4 **Open** April **to** September
Site Level
Sites Available **Total** 60
Facilities
Nearby Facilities
Newquay
Overlooking bay. Ideal for touring, surfing, golf, swimming or just lazing by the sea.

ST. MINVER

Dinham Farm Caravan & Camping Park, St. Minver, Wadebridge, Cornwall, PL27 6RH.
Std: 01208 **Tel:** 812878
Nearest Town/Resort Rock
Directions 3 miles west of Wadebridge on the B3314.
Acreage 2½ **Open** April **to** October
Access Good **Site** Lev/Slope
Sites Available **Total** 40
Facilities
Nearby Facilities
Bodmin Parkway.
Lovely secluded park, overlooking the River Camel and surrounded by trees and shrubs. Own heated swimming pool. Near golden sandy beaches.

ST. MINVER

St. Minver Holiday Village, St. Minver, Nr. Wadebridge, Cornwall, PL27 6RR.
Std: 01208 **Tel:** 862305
Nearest Town/Resort Wadebridge
Directions Take the A39 from Camelford to Wadebridge, then take the B3314. Turn right at the mini-roundabout heading for Port Isaac. After 3¼ miles turn left at the road signposted to Rock. The park is 250yds along on the right hand side.
Acreage 6 **Open** 8 April **to** 7 October
Access Good **Site** Sloping
Sites Available **Total** 120
Facilities
Nearby Facilities
Bodmin Parkway
✓✓✓✓Graded Park. Set amidst 40 acres of wooded countryside, in the grounds of a lovely old Cornish Manor House.

TINTAGEL

Bossiney Farm Caravan Site, Tintagel, Cornwall, PL34 OAY.
Std: 01840 **Tel:** 770481
Nearest Town/Resort Tintagel
Directions ¾ miles from centre of Tintagel on main Boscastle road.
Acreage 2 **Open** April **to** October
Access Good **Site** Lev/Slope

Sites Available **Total** 20
Facilities
Nearby Facilities
Bodmin Parkway
✓✓✓✓Graded Park. Ideal touring centre, near beach, inland views.

TINTAGEL

The Headland Caravan & Camping Park, Atlantic Road, Tintagel, Cornwall, PL34 0DE.
Std: 0184. **Tel:** 770239
Std: 01840 **Fax:** 770925
Nearest Town/Resort Tintagel.
Directions Follow camping/caravan signs from B3263 through village to Headland.
Acreage 4 **Open** Easter **to** October
Access Good **Site** Lev/Slope
Sites Available **Total** 60
Facilities
Nearby Facilities
Bodmin Parkway
Three beaches walking distance. Scenic views. Ideal touring centre.

TORPOINT

Whitsand Bay Holiday Park, Millbrook, Torpoint, Cornwall, PL10 1JZ.
Std: 01752 **Tel:** 822597
Std: 01752 **Fax:** 823444
Nearest Town/Resort Torpoint.
Directions From Plymouth take the Torpoint Ferry (10 minutes). From Torpoint take the main road out, 3 miles to Anthony bear left, 2 miles turn left at T-Junction, 1 mile past Tregantle Fort turn right onto coast road. After 2½ miles turn left into the park.
Acreage 27 **Open** March **to** December
Access Good **Site** Lev/Slope
Sites Available **Total** 60
Facilities
Nearby Facilities
Plymouth.
✓✓✓✓Graded Park. Situated in an historic fort with spectacular views from every pitch. 10 minutes from the beach. 6 miles from Plymouth.

TRURO

Camping & Caravanning Club Site, Tretheake Manor, Veryan, Truro, Cornwall, TR2 5PP.
Std: 01872 **Tel:** 501658
Directions Take the A390 from St. Austell, leave at the A3078 sign on the left, turn left at the filling station and follow international signs.
Acreage 9 **Open** 22 March **to** 1 Nov
Site Lev/Slope
Sites Available **Total** 150
Facilities
Nearby Facilities
✓✓✓✓✓Graded Park. Ideal for exploring the beaches and coves of the Cornish Coast. Fishing on site.

TRURO

Carnon Downs Caravan & Camping Park, Carnon Downs, Truro, Cornwall, TR3 6JJ.
Std: 01872 **Tel:** 862283
Std: 01872 **Fax:** 862800
Nearest Town/Resort Truro.
Directions On the A39 Falmouth road, 3 miles West of Truro.
Acreage 9 **Open** April **to** October
Access Good **Site** Level
Sites Available **Total** 150
Facilities
Nearby Facilities
Truro
✓✓✓✓✓Graded Park. Ideally central for touring. Excellent location for sailing and water sports.

TRURO

Chacewater Camping & Caravan Park, Coxhill, Chacewater, Truro, Cornwall.
Std: 01209 **Tel:** 820762
Std: 01209 **Fax:** 820544
Nearest Town/Resort Truro.
Directions From A30 take the A3047 to Scorrier. Turn left at Crossroads Hotel onto the B3298. 1½ miles left to Chacewater ½ mile sign directs you to the park.
Acreage 6 **Open** May **to** End September
Access Good **Site** Level
Sites Available **Total** 80
Facilities
Nearby Facilities
Truro.
✓✓✓✓Graded Park. ADULTS ONLY. Quiet, rural meadow, well off main road. Family run. Ideal for couples and families.

TRURO

Cosawes, Perranarworthal, Truro, Cornwall, TR3 7QS.
Std: 01872 **Tel:** 863724
Std: 01872 **Fax:** 870268
Nearest Town/Resort Falmouth
Directions Midway between Truro and Falmouth on the A39.
Acreage 100 **Open** All Year

Access Good **Site** Level
Sites Available **Total** 50
Facilities
Nearby Facilities
Perranwell
Situated in a 100 acre wooded valley, an area of outstanding natural beauty.

TRURO

Leverton Place, Greenbottom, Nr. Truro, Cornwall, TR4 8QW.
Std: 01872 **Tel:** 560462
Std: 01872 **Fax:** 560668
Nearest Town/Resort Truro.
Directions 3 miles west of Truro. Take the A390 to Truro, right at the first roundabout signposted Chacewater. Right at the mini roundabout and Leverton Place is 100yds on the right.
Acreage 10 **Open** All Year
Access Good **Site** Level
Sites Available **Total** 110
Facilities
Nearby Facilities
Truro.
✓✓✓✓✓Graded Park. Ideal touring and exploring centre for Cornwall. Excellent swimming pool, lounge bar and bistro.

TRURO

Liskey Touring Park, Greenbottom, Truro, Cornwall, TR4 8QN.
Std: 01872 **Tel:** 560274
Std: 01872 **Fax:** 560274
Nearest Town/Resort Truro.
Directions 3½ miles west of Truro, off A390 between Threemilestone and Chacewater.
Acreage 8 **Open** April **to** September
Access Good **Site** Lev/slope
Sites Available **Total** 68
Facilities
Nearby Facilities
Truro.
✓✓✓✓✓Graded Park. Small family site, central for exploring Cornwall. Adventure play barn, games field, family bathroom and dishwashing sinks. 10 minutes to the sea.

TRURO

Ringwell Valley Holiday Park, Bissoe Road, Carnon Downs, Truro, Cornwall, TR3 6LQ.
Std: 01872 **Tel:** 862194
Std: 01872 **Fax:** 862194
Nearest Town/Resort Truro
Directions From Truro take the A39 towards Falmouth. Turn right at Carnon Downs roundabout into the village, take the third right following Ringwell signs.
Acreage 12 **Open** Easter **to** Mid October
Access Good **Site** Lev/Slope
Sites Available **Total** 33
Facilities
Nearby Facilities
Truro/Perranwell
✓✓✓✓✓Graded Park. Set in a valley, picturesque and relaxing. Family entertainment in season. Central for touring. All the facilities without the crowds.

TRURO

Summer Valley Touring Park, Shortlanesend, Truro, Cornwall.
Std: 01872. **Tel:** 277878
Nearest Town/Resort Truro.
Directions 2 miles out of Truro on Perranporth road (B3284). Sign on left just past Shortlanesend.
Acreage ½ **Open** April **to** October
Access Good **Site** Level
Sites Available **Total** 60
Facilities
Nearby Facilities
Truro.
✓✓✓✓✓Graded Park. Ideal centre for touring Cornwall.

WADEBRIDGE

Gunvenna Caravan & Camping Park, St. Minver, Wadebridge, Cornwall, PL27 6QN.
Std: 01208 **Tel:** 862405
Std: 01208 **Fax:** 862405
Nearest Town/Resort Wadebridge
Directions Take the A30 to Bodmin then the A389 to Wadebridge. Take the A39 to Polzeath then the B3314, remain on this road and Gunvenna Caravan Park is on the right hand side.
Acreage 10 **Open** Easter **to** October
Access Good **Site** Lev/Slope
Sites Available **Total** 75
Facilities
Nearby Facilities
Bodmin
Polzeath and rock beaches. Good sandy beaches.

WADEBRIDGE

Little Bodieve Holiday Park, Bodieve Road, Wadebridge, Cornwall, PL27 6EG.
Std: 01208 **Tel:** 812323
Nearest Town/Resort Wadebridge
Directions 1 mile north of Wadebridge Town centre off the A39 trunk road. 1/3rd mile on the B3314 road to Rock and Port Isaac.
Acreage 22 **Open** Late March **to** October
Access Good **Site** Level
Sites Available **Total** 195
Facilities

Nearby Facilities
Bodmin Parkway
✓✓✓✓Graded Park. Nearest park to the Camel Trail, close to superb beaches. Ideal touring centre. 6 golf courses within a 20 minute drive. Club Rallies welcome.

WADEBRIDGE

Lundynant Caravan Site, Polzeath, Nr. Wadebridge, Cornwall, PL27 6QX.
Std: 01208 **Tel:** 862268
Nearest Town/Resort Polzeath
Directions From Wadebridge take the B3314 to Polzeath, 7 miles.
Acreage 3 **Open** April **to** October
Access Fair **Site** Lev/Slope
Sites Available **Total** 49
Facilities
Nearby Facilities
Bodmin Parkway
Alongside a public footpath to the beach and village (with several shops) a 5-10 minute walk. Ideally situated for coastal walking.

WADEBRIDGE

The Laurels, Whitecross, Wadebridge, Cornwall, PL27 7JQ.
Std: 01208 **Tel:** 813341
Nearest Town/Resort Wadebridge/ Padstow
Directions On the junction of the A39 Newquay to Wadebridge road and the A389 to Padstow.
Acreage 3 **Open** Easter **to** End October
Access Good **Site** Level
Sites Available **Total** 30
Facilities
Nearby Facilities
Bodmin Parkway
✓✓✓✓Graded Park. Ideal touring.

CUMBRIA

ALLONBY

Manor House Caravan Park, Edderside Road, Allonby, Nr Maryport, Cumbria, CA15 6RA.
Std: 01900. **Tel:** 881236
Std: 01900 **Fax:** 881160
Nearest Town/Resort Allonby.
Directions B5300 from Maryport, through Allonby, 1 mile turn right, park 1 mile on right. Signposted on main road.
Acreage 2 **Open** March **to** 15th Nov
Access Good **Site** Level
Sites Available **Total** 30
Facilities
Nearby Facilities
Maryport.
✓✓✓Graded Park. 1 mile from beach, quiet park. Ideal for touring North Lakes.

ALSTON

Horse & Waggon Caravan Park, Nentsberry, Alston, Cumbria, CA9 3LH.
Std: 01434 **Tel:** 382805
Nearest Town/Resort Alston
Directions 3 miles east of Alston on the A689.
Acreage ½ **Open** Mid March **to** October
Access Good **Site** Level
Sites Available **Total** 10
Facilities
Nearby Facilities
Penrith
Area of outstanding natural beauty.

ALSTON

Hudgill Caravan Park, South Hudgill, Alston, Cumbria, CA9 3LG.
Std: 01434 **Tel:** 381731
Nearest Town/Resort Alston
Directions 2 miles from Alston on the A689.
Acreage 12 **Open** March **to** 14 November
Access Good **Site** Level
Sites Available **Total** 15
Facilities
Nearby Facilities
Penrith
Highest market town of Alston, golf club, Kilhope Mines & Museum, high force waterfall, near the Lake District and Nenthead Mines.

AMBLESIDE

Low Wray Campsite, The National Trust Campsite, Low Wray, Near Ambleside, Cumbria, LA22 0JA.
Std: 015394 **Tel:** 32810
Std: 015394 **Fax:** 32810
Nearest Town/Resort Ambleside
Directions Signposted off the B5286 road to Hawkshead, approx 3 miles from Ambleside.
Acreage 10 **Open** Easter **to** End October
Site Sloping
Sites Available **Total** 200
Facilities
Nearby Facilities
Windermere
Family site, near a lake.

AMBLESIDE

Skelwith Fold Caravan Park, Ambleside, Cumbria, LA22 0HX.
Std: 01539 **Tel:** 432277
Std: 01539 **Fax:** 434344
Nearest Town/Resort Ambleside
Directions Leave Ambleside on the A593, at Clappersgate take the B5286 signposted Hawkshead, park is 1 mile on the right hand side.
Acreage 125 **Open** 1 March **to** 15 Nov
Access Good **Site** Level
Sites Available **Total** 150
Facilities
Nearby Facilities
Windermere
✓✓✓✓✓Graded Park. Magnificent scenery and excellent walking. Abundance of wildlife, plants and trees. Ideal touring.

AMBLESIDE

Waterson Ground Camping Site, Waterson Ground, Outgate, Ambleside, Cumbria, LA22 0NJ.
Std: 015394 **Tel:** 36225
Nearest Town/Resort Hawkshead
Directions 600 yards south of Outgate on the B5286 Ambleside to Hawkshead road.
Acreage 6 **Open** All Year
Access Fair **Site** Lev/Slope
Sites Available **Total** 45
Facilities
Nearby Facilities
Windermere
6 acres of camping overlooking the Esthwaite Valley and Esthwaite Lake. Ideal base for walking, fishing and mountain biking.

APPLEBY

Silverband Park, Silverband, Knock, Nr Appleby, Cumbria, CA16 6DL.
Std: 017683 **Tel:** 61218

Nearest Town/Resort Appleby
Directions Turn right off the A66 Brough to Penrith at Kirkby Thore. After 2 miles turn left at the T-Junction, then turn right after 100yards, site is on the right in 1 mile.
Acreage ½ **Open** All Year
Access Good **Site** Sloping
Sites Available **Total** 12
Facilities
Nearby Facilities
Appleby
Ideal for touring the lakes and Penines. Penine Way 4 miles. Off license on site. Fell walking.

APPLEBY

Wild Rose Park, Ormside, Appleby, Cumbria, CA16 6EJ.
Std: 017683 **Tel:** 51077
Std: 017683 **Fax:** 52551
Nearest Town/Resort Appleby.
Directions Centre Appleby take B6260 Kendal for 1½ miles. Left Ormside and Soulby 1½ miles left, ½ mile turn right.
Acreage 40 **Open** All year
Access Good **Site** Lev/Slope
Sites Available **Total** 184
Facilities
Nearby Facilities
Appleby.
✓✓✓✓✓Graded Park. Quiet park in unspoilt Eden Valley, superb views. Midway between Lakes and Yorkshire Dales.

ARNSIDE

Fell End Caravan Park, Slackhead Road, Hale, Near Milnthorpe, Cumbria, LA7 7BS.
Std: 015395 **Tel:** 62122
Nearest Town/Resort Arnside/Silverdale
Directions Leave the M6 at junction 35, take the A6 north and turn left at Wildlife Oasis after driving past Esso Fuel Station and follow caravan tourism signs.
Acreage 12 **Open** March **to** January
Access Good **Site** Level
Sites Available **Total** 68
Facilities
Nearby Facilities
Arnside
✓✓✓✓✓Graded Park. In an area of outstanding natural beauty, Fell End is a meticulously kept site with mature gardens and a country inn. Close to Lakes and Dales.

ASKAM IN FURNESS

Marsh Farm, Askam-in-Furness, Cumbria, LA16 7AW.
Std: 01229 **Tel:** 462321
Nearest Town/Resort Barrow-in-Furness.
Directions Leave A590 at Dalton, take A595 from Dalton to Askam, turn left at railway crossing.
Acreage 3 **Open** April **to** September
Access Good **Site** Level
Sites Available **Total** 40
Facilities
Nearby Facilities
Near beach, adjacent golf course. Scenic views.

BASSENTHWAITE

Herdwick Croft Caravan Park, Ouse Bridge, Bassenthwaite, Keswick, Cumbria, CA12 4RD.
Std: 017687 **Tel:** 76605
Nearest Town/Resort Keswick
Directions Take the A66 from Keswick to Cockermouth, turn right onto the B5291. 1 mile from the A66.
Acreage 2 **Open** Easter **to** October
Access Good **Site** Level
Sites Available **Total** 10
Facilities
Nearby Facilities
Carlisle

BASSENTHWAITE

Robin Hood Caravan Park, Bassenthwaite, Keswick, Cumbria, CA12 4RJ.
Std: 017687 **Tel:** 76334
Std: 017687 **Fax:** 76334
Nearest Town/Resort Keswick
Directions Take A591 from Keswick towards Carlisle. After 7 miles turn right at the Castle Inn (signposted Ireby/Caldbeck), after 1 mile turn right to Robin Hood. The site is ½ mile on the right.
Acreage 2 **Open** Easter/1st April **to** 15 Nov
Access Good **Site** Level
Sites Available **Total** 16
Facilities
Nearby Facilities
Carlisle
Elevated, quiet, country site overlooking Bassenthwaite Lake and the surrounding mountains.

BASSENTHWAITE

Trafford Caravans, Lowood, Bassenthwaite, Keswick, Cumbria, CA12 4QX.
Std: 017687 **Tel:** 76298
Nearest Town/Resort Keswick
Directions From Keswick take the A66 then the A591.
Acreage 5½ **Open** 31 March **to** 31 October
Access Good **Site** Level
Sites Available **Total** 50
Facilities
Nearby Facilities
Penrith
Quiet site in the Lake District with superb mountain views. Ideal base for touring.

BOTHEL

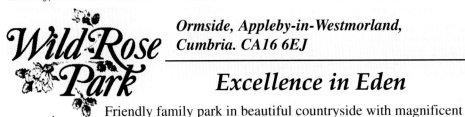

Skiddaw View Holiday Park, Bothel, Carlisle, Cumbria, CA5 2JG.
Std: 016973 **Tel:** 20919
Nearest Town/Resort Keswick

Directions Signposted off the A591 near the junction with the A595.
Acreage 3 **Open** March **to** 5th November
Access Good **Site** Sloping
Sites Available **Total** 20
Facilities
Nearby Facilities
Carlisle
Panoramic views of the Northern Fells.

BRAMPTON

Irthing Vale Caravan Park, Old Church Lane, Brampton, Cumbria, CA8 2AA.
Std: 016977 **Tel:** 3600
Nearest Town/Resort Brampton.
Directions From the M6 junction 43 take the A69 to Brampton, then the A6071 signposted Longtown for ½ mile. Turn into Old Church Lane, site is on the left in 400yds (signposted).
Acreage 4 **Open** March **to** October
Access Good **Site** Level
Sites Available **Total** 40
Facilities
Nearby Facilities
Brampton Junction.
Ideal location for Hadrians (Roman) Wall, days out and visiting Carlisle and the romantic Border country. Near Gretna Green and South West Scotland.

BROUGHTON IN FURNESS

Birchbank Farm, Birchbank, Blawith, Ulverston, Cumbria.
Std: 01229 **Tel:** 885277
Nearest Town/Resort Coniston Water
Directions A5092 ¼ mile west of Gawthwaite turn for Woodland. Site is 2 miles on the right along an unfenced road.
Acreage ¼ **Open** Mid May **to** October
Access Good **Site** Level
Sites Available **Total** 8
Facilities
Nearby Facilities
Kirkby in Furness
Small farm site, ideal for walking or touring the southern lakes.

CARLISLE

Dalston Hall Caravan Park, Dalston Road, Carlisle, Cumbria.
Std: 01228. **Tel:** 710165
Nearest Town/Resort Carlisle.
Directions Leave M6 at junction 42, take road to Dalston. At Dalston turn onto the B5299, site on right after ¾ mile.
Acreage 4 **Open** March **to** October
Access Good **Site** Level
Sites Available **Total** 60
Facilities
Nearby Facilities
Carlisle.
✓✓✓✓Graded Park. Fishing, ideal for touring Lake District, Hadrian's Wall etc. Nine hole golf course.

CARLISLE

Dandy Dinmont Caravan & Camping Site, Blackford, Carlisle, Cumbria, CA6 4EA.
Std: 01228 **Tel:** 674611
Nearest Town/Resort Carlisle
Directions On A7 at Blackford, 4¼ miles north of Carlisle. Leave M6 at intersection 44, take the A7 Galashiels road (site approx 1½ miles on the right). After Blackford sign, follow road directional signs to site.
Acreage 4 **Open** March **to** October
Access Good **Site** Level
Sites Available **Total** 47
Facilities
Nearby Facilities
Carlisle
✓✓✓✓Graded Park. Historic Carlisle-Castle, Cathedral, Roman Wall, Border Country only 45 minutes to Lake District.

CARLISLE

Green Acres Caravan Park, High Knells, Houghton, Carlisle, Cumbria, CA6 4JW.
Std: 01228 **Tel:** 577403/75418
Std: 01228 **Fax:** 577403
Nearest Town/Resort Carlisle
Directions Leave the M6 at junction 44 onto the A74 (North Carlisle). Take the A689 for 1 mile, turn left signposted Scaleby. Site is 1 mile on the left.
Acreage 1 **Open** Easter **to** October
Access Good **Site** Level
Sites Available **Total** 30
Facilities
Nearby Facilities
Carlisle
✓✓✓✓Graded Park. Ideal touring base for Hadrians Wall, Carlisle City, Lake District and Scottish Borders.

CARLISLE

Orton Grange Caravan Park, Wigton Road, Carlisle, Cumbria, CA5 6LA.
Std: 01228 **Tel:** 710252
Nearest Town/Resort Carlisle.
Directions 4 miles west of Carlisle on A595.
Acreage 6 **Open** All year
Access Good **Site** Level
Sites Available **Total** 50
Facilities
Nearby Facilities
Dalston
✓✓✓✓Graded Park. Ideal for touring, north lakes, the Roman Wall plus Border country. Camping shop/Tent sales.

COCKERMOUTH

Violet Bank Holiday Home Park, Simonscales Lane, off Lorton Road, Cockermouth, Cumbria, CA13 9TG
Std: 01900 **Tel:** 822169
Nearest Town/Resort Cockermouth
Directions From Cockermouth town centre take the Lorton road (A5292), signed Lorton, Buttermere for about ¼ mile then turn right up Vicarage Lane leading to site.
Acreage 6 **Open** March **to** 15 Nov
Access Good **Site** Level
Sites Available **Total** 30
Facilities
Nearby Facilities
Workington
✓✓✓Graded Park. Quiet park with superb view. Centre for touring Lakes and fell walking. S.A.E. for brochure and terms.

COCKERMOUTH

Wheatsheaf Inn Caravan Park, Low Lorton, Cockermouth, Cumbria, CA13 9UW.
Std: 01900 **Tel:** 85268
Std: 01900 **Fax:** 85199
Nearest Town/Resort Cockermouth.
Directions 4 miles from Cockermouth on the B5292 towards Buttermere and Loweswater.
Open 1 March **to** 1 November
Access Good **Site** Level
Sites Available **Total** 15
Facilities
Nearby Facilities
Penrith.
Very quiet site alongside a river, nestling in a valley surrounded by mountains and fells.

COCKERMOUTH

Whinfell Camping, Lorton, Nr Cockermouth, Cumbria, CA13 0RQ.
Std: 01900 **Tel:** 85260/85057
Nearest Town/Resort Cockermouth.
Directions Take the A66 then the B5292 at Braithwaite into Low Lorton, follow caravan and camping signs. Or take the 5289 from Cockermouth.
Acreage 5 **Open** 15 March **to** 15 Nov
Access Good **Site** Level
Sites Available **Total** 40
Facilities
Nearby Facilities
Workington.
Ideal touring and walking. Near to many attractions including Whinlatter Visitor Centre, Sellafield Visitor Centre, Ravenglass Miniature Steam Railway, Muncaster Castle & Gardens and an Owl centre.

COCKERMOUTH

Wyndham Holiday Park, Old Keswick Road, Cockermouth, Cumbria, CA13 9SF.
Std: 01900 **Tel:** 822571/825238
Nearest Town/Resort Cockermouth
Directions ¼ of an hours drive from Keswick on the A66 or 3 minutes from Cockermouth town centre.
Acreage 12 **Open** March **to** November
Access Good **Site** Lev/Slope
Sites Available **Total** 40
Facilities
Nearby Facilities
Workington
Cockermouth is the birthplace of Wordsworth also Fletcher Christian of Mutiny on the Bounty. Next door to an indoor swimming pool.

CONISTON

Coniston Hall Camping Site, Coniston, Cumbria.
Std: 015394 **Tel:** 41223
Nearest Town/Resort Coniston.
Directions 1 mile south of Coniston.
Acreage 200 **Open** March **to** October
Site Level
Sites Available
Facilities
Nearby Facilities
Windermere.
Lake access. Dogs to be kept on leads.

CONISTON

Hoathwaite Farm Caravan & Camping Site, Torver, Coniston, Cumbria, LA21 8AX.
Std: 015394 **Tel:** 41349
Nearest Town/Resort Coniston.
Directions A593 to Torver, after 3 miles turn left at green railings. After 100yds turn left over first farm cattlegrid, follow road to farm.
Acreage 30 **Open** All Year
Access Good **Site** Lev/Slope
Sites Available
Facilities
Nearby Facilities
Ulverston.
Scenic, ideal for touring and walking. Lake access from the site for boating etc..

CROOK

Ratherheath Lane Camping & Caravan park, Chain House, Bonningate, Kendal, Cumbria, LA8 8JU.
Std: 01539 **Tel:** 821154
Nearest Town/Resort Bowness on Windermere
Directions From Kendal A591 take B5284

to Crook, turn right at sign to Burneside.
Acreage 1 **Open** March **to** 15 Nov
Access Good **Site** Level
Sites Available **Total** 20
Facilities
Nearby Facilities
Burneside
✓✓✓✓Graded Park. Lake District National Park. Pool table on site.

CUMWHITTON

Cairndale Caravan Park, Cumwhitton, Headsnook, Carlisle, Cumbria CA4 9BZ.
Std: 01768 **Tel:** 896280
Nearest Town/Resort Carlisle.
Directions Follow A69 to Warwick Bridge and then follow unclassified road through Great Corby to Cumwhitton, approx. 9 miles.
Acreage 2 **Open** March **to** October
Access Good **Site** Level
Sites Available **Total** 5
Facilities
Nearby Facilities
Carlisle.
✓✓✓Graded Park. Scenic views, ideal touring, quiet site, water and electricity to individual touring sites. Windsurfing nearby.

DENT

Conder Farm, Deepdale Road, Dent, Sedbergh, Cumbria, LA10 5QJ.
Std: 015396 **Tel:** 25277
Nearest Town/Resort Kendal
Directions 17 miles east of the M6 junction 37.
Open All Year
Access Good **Site** Sloping
Sites Available **Total** 47
Facilities
Nearby Facilities
Dent
Scenic views, ideal touring.

DENT

Ewegales Farm, Dent, Sedbergh, Cumbria, LA10 5RH.
Std: 01539 **Tel:** 625440
Nearest Town/Resort Dent
Directions 3½ miles from Dent.
Acreage 11½ **Open** All Year
Access Good **Site** Level
Sites Available **Total** 60
Facilities
Nearby Facilities
Dent
Alongside a river.

DENT

Millbeck Farm, Dent, Sedbergh, Cumbria, LA10 5TB.
Std: 015396 **Tel:** 25272/25424/25275
Nearest Town/Resort Sedbergh
Directions From M6 junc. 37 onto A684 to sedbergh on to Dent, site ½ mile west of Dent.
Acreage 1 **Open** Easter **to** October
Access Good **Site** Lev/Slope
Sites Available
Facilities
Nearby Facilities
Oxenholme
Near river, scenic views, ideal for walking. Caravan to let on site.

EGREMONT

Home Farm Caravan Park, Rothersyke, Egremont, Thornhill, Cumbria, CA22 2UD.
Std: 01946 **Tel:** 824023
Nearest Town/Resort Egremont/St. Bees
Directions From the south on the A595 to Calderbridge, take the first right after Blackbeck roundabout and follow St Bees signs on the B5435. From the north on the A595 to Egremont Bypass, follow the new bypass and turn right after the third bypass B5345.
Acreage 2 **Open** March **to** October
Access Good **Site** Lev/Slope
Sites Available **Total** 18
Facilities
Nearby Facilities
✓✓✓Graded Park. Near beaches, lakes and mountains.

ESKDALE

Fisherground Farm, Eskdale, Cumbria,CA19 1TF.
Std: 019467 **Tel:** 23319
Nearest Town/Resort Broughton in Furness
Directions ¾ mile past Broughton on A595 turn RT. up Duddon Valley (signed Ulpha). 4 miles to Ulpha, then turn LT., (signed Eskdale). 6 miles over Birker Moor, descend to Eskdale turn RT. at King George IV Inn. Fisherground is first farm on LT.
Acreage 3 **Open** March **to** November
Access Good **Site** Level
Sites Available **Total** 100
Facilities
Nearby Facilities
Ravenglass
✓✓✓Graded Park. Quiet family site in the heart of the Lake District. 7 mile miniature railway 100yds (private station). Adventure playground, pond and laundry. Camp fires allowed. Voted Northern Campsite of the Year 1997 by Camping Magazine and AA Award for Excellence. Brochure on request.

GOSFORTH

Seven Acres Caravan Park, Holmrook, Cumbria, CA19 1YD.
Std: 019467 **Tel:** 25480
Nearest Town/Resort Whitehaven
Directions Half way between Gosforth and Holmrook on the A595 (Broughton-in-Furness to Workington road) west coast road.
Acreage 3 **Open** March **to** Mid November
Access Good **Site** Level
Sites Available **Total** 103
Facilities
Nearby Facilities
Seascale
Family owned and run site at the foot of Wasdale Valley, 3 miles of coast. Ideal for touring the Western Lake District, walking, golf, fishing, riding and relaxing.

GRANGE-OVER-SANDS

Greaves Farm Caravan Park, c/o Prospect House, Barber Green, Grange-over-Sands, Cumbria, LA11 6HU.
Std: 015395 **Tel:** 36329/36587
Nearest Town/Resort Grange-over-Sands
Directions Come off the A590 approx 1 mile south of Newby Bridge at the sign "Cartmel 4 miles". Proceed 1½ miles to sign for caravan park.
Acreage 3 **Open** March **to** October
Access Good **Site** Level
Sites Available **Total** 10
Facilities
Nearby Facilities
Grange-over-Sands
✓✓✓✓Graded Park. Quiet, select, family run park. Ideal base for exploring the Lake District.

GRANGE-OVER-SANDS

Lakeland Leisure Park, Moor Lane, Nr Grange-over-Sands, Cumbria, LA11 7LT.
Std: 015395 **Tel:** 58556
Std: 015395 **Fax:** 58559
Nearest Town/Resort Grange-over-Sands.
Directions Take exit 36 off M6 onto the A590, turn left onto A6/A590 for Barrow-in-Furness. Then take the B5277 through Grange-over-Sands and into Flookburgh, turn left at the village square and drive 1 mile down this road.
Open March **to** October
Access Good **Site** Level
Sites Available **Total** 125
Facilities
Nearby Facilities
Cark
✓✓✓✓✓Graded Park. Gateway to the

lakes, ideal base for touring. Horse riding on site. Kids Club and a full family entertainment programme. Rose Award.

GRANGE-OVER-SANDS

Oak Head Caravan Park, Ayside, Grange-over-Sands, Cumbria.
Std: 015395 **Tel:** Newby Bridge 31475
Nearest Town/Resort Grange-over-Sands.
Directions M6 junction 36 follow signs for Newby Bridge, site is signposted on left hand side of A590, 2 miles from Newby Bridge, 13 miles from M6.
Acreage 2½ **Open** March **to** October
Access Good **Site** Lev/slope
Sites Available **Total** 90
Facilities
Nearby Facilities
Grange-over-Sands.
Scenic views, ideal touring. Within easy reach of all lakes.

GRANGE-OVER-SANDS

Old Park Wood Caravan Park, Holker, Cark-in-Cartmel, Grange-over-Sands, Cumbria, LA11 7PP.
Std: 015395 **Tel:** 58266
Std: 015395 **Fax:** 58101
Nearest Town/Resort Grange-over-Sands
Directions Take the A590 to Grange-over-Sands then onto the B5278. Head for Holker Hall, ½ mile past the main gates turn left and follow the road for 1 mile, signposted.
Open March **to** October
Access Good **Site** Level
Sites Available
Facilities
Nearby Facilities
Cark-in-Cartmel
✓✓✓✓Graded Park. Alongside an estuary with views of the mountains.

GREYSTOKE

Whitbarrow Hall Caravan Park, Berrier, Penrith, Cumbria, CA11 0XB.
Std: 017684 **Tel:** 83456
Nearest Town/Resort Keswick.
Directions Leave M6 at junction 40, A66 towards Keswick after 8 miles turn right at signpost Hutton Roof site ½ mile from A66.
Acreage 8 **Open** March **to** October
Access Good **Site** Level
Sites Available **Total** 80
Facilities
Nearby Facilities
Penrith.
Views. 5 miles Ullswater. Lake District. AA 3 Pennants.

HAWKSHEAD

Camping & Caravanning Club Site, Grizedale Hall, Hawkshead, Ambleside, Cumbria, LA22 0GL.
Std: 01229 **Tel:** 860257
Directions From the M6 take the A591, A590 turn right onto the A5092 to Broonodd, ½ mile to Pony Bridge, look for minor road on the right signposted Colton, Oxon Park. Stay on this road DO NOT deviate to Grizedale, look for Caravan & Camping sign, the next entrance on the right (approx. 6 miles from Greenodd).
Acreage 5 **Open** 22 March **to** 27 Sept
Site Lev/Slope
Sites Available **Total** 60
Facilities
Nearby Facilities
Windermere
✓✓✓✓Graded Park. Located in the Grizedale Forest. There is a theatre in the forest with a variety of entertainment.

HAWKSHEAD

Hawkshead Hall Farm, Near Ambleside, Cumbria, LA22 0NN.
Std: 015394 **Tel:** 36221
Nearest Town/Resort Hawkshead
Directions 5 miles south of Ambleside on the B5286.
Acreage 5 **Open** March **to** 15 November
Access Good **Site** Lev/Slope
Sites Available **Total** 60
Facilities
Nearby Facilities
Windermere

HAWKSHEAD

The Croft Caravan & Camp Site, North Lonsdale Road, Hawkshead, Nr. Ambleside, Cumbria, LA22 0NX.
Std: 015394 **Tel:** 36374
Std: 015394 **Fax:** 36544
Nearest Town/Resort Hawkshead.
Directions From Ambleside 5 miles on the B5286 at village of Hawkshead.
Acreage 5 **Open** March **to** November
Access Good **Site** Level
Sites Available **Total** 100
Facilities
Nearby Facilities
Windermere.
✓✓✓Graded Park.

KENDAL

Camping & Caravanning Club Site, Millcrest, Shap Road, Kendal, Cumbria, LA9 6NY.
Std: 01539 **Tel:** 741363
Directions On the A6, 1½ miles north of Kendal, site entrance is 100 yards north of the nameplate 'Skelsmergh'.
Acreage 3 **Open** 22 March **to** 1 Nov
Site Lev/Slope
Sites Available **Total** 53
Facilities
Nearby Facilities
Kendal
✓✓✓✓Graded Park. Right in the middle of the Lake District.

KENDAL

Lambhowe Caravan Park, Crosthwaite, Kendal, Cumbria.
Std: 015395 **Tel:** 68483
Nearest Town/Resort Bowness on Windermere.
Directions A590, join the A5074 towards Bowness on Windermere. Just opposite Damson Dene Hotel.
Acreage 4 **Open** March **to** October
Access Good **Site** Level
Sites Available **Total** 14
Facilities
Nearby Facilities
Windermere.
Situated in the beautiful Lyth Valley, 15 minutes drive Lake Windermere.

KENDAL

Pound Farm Caravan Park, Crook, Kendal, Cumbria, LA8 8JZ.
Std: 01539 **Tel:** 821220
Nearest Town/Resort Bowness-on-Windermere
Directions Leave the M6 junction 36, turn onto the A591. After 10 miles at large roundabout take the B5284 to Crook, and Pound Farm is 2 miles on the left.
Acreage 4 **Open** 1 March **to** 14 Nov
Access Good **Site** Sloping
Sites Available **Total** 20
Facilities
Nearby Facilities
Kendal
✓✓✓✓Graded Park. Ideal for touring the Lake District.

KESWICK

Ashness Camp Site, Ashness Farm, Keswick, Cumbria, CA12 5UN.
Std: 017687 **Tel:** 77361
Nearest Town/Resort Keswick.
Directions Take the B5289 from Keswick for 2 miles, turn left signposted Ashness Bridge and Watendath, 1 mile Ashness farm on left.
Acreage 5 **Open** March **to** November
Access Good **Site** Lev/Slope
Sites Available **Total** 60
Facilities
Nearby Facilities
Penrith.
Centre of lakes, Derwentwater 1 mile, wonderful views from site, fully working farm.

KESWICK

Burns Farm Caravan Site, St. Johns-in-the-Vale, Keswick, Cumbria, CA12 4RR.
Std: 017687 **Tel:** 79225
Nearest Town/Resort Keswick
Directions Turn left off the A66 (Penrith to Keswick road) ½ mile past B5322 junction signposted Castlerigg Stone Circle. Site is on the right, farm is on the left. 2¼ miles from Keswick.
Acreage 1¼ **Open** Easter **to** October
Access Good **Site** Level
Sites Available **Total** 40
Facilities
Nearby Facilities
Penrith
Ideal touring, walking and climbing. Beautiful views, quiet family site.

KESWICK

Burnside Caravan Park, Underskiddaw, Keswick, Cumbria, CA12 4PF.
Std: 017687 **Tel:** 72950
Nearest Town/Resort Keswick
Directions At the junction of the A66 and the A591, 1 mile from the centre of Keswick.
Acreage 2 **Open** March **to** November
Access Good **Site** Level
Sites Available **Total** 25
Facilities
Nearby Facilities
Penrith
✓✓Graded Park. A stream runs through the site.

KESWICK

Camping & Caravanning Club Site, Derwentwater, Keswick, Cumbria, CA12 5EP.
Std: 01768 **Tel:** 772392
Nearest Town/Resort Keswick
Directions From the A66 roundabout at Keswick take the Carlisle road and turn sharp right, then right again onto the site, signposted.
Acreage 14 **Open** 1 Feb **to** 29 Nov
Access Good **Site** Level
Sites Available **Total** 253
Facilities
Nearby Facilities
Penrith

✓✓✓✓✓Graded Park. Situated on the banks of Derwentwater, ideal for fishing and water sports. Good hillwalking area. Close to the centre of Keswick.

KESWICK

Castlerigg Hall Caravan & Camping Park, Castlerigg Hall, Keswick, Cumbria, CA12 4TE.
Std: 017687 **Tel:** 72437
Nearest Town/Resort Keswick.
Directions 1¼ miles south east of Keswick off the A591.
Acreage 4 **Open** Easter **to** Mid November
Access Good **Site** Lev/Slope
Sites Available **Total** 140
Facilities
Nearby Facilities
Penrith.
✓✓✓✓Graded Park. Scenic views, good walking. Breakfasts available.

KESWICK

Dalebottom Holiday Park, Dalebottom, Naddle, Keswick, Cumbria, CA12 4TF.
Std: 017687 **Tel:** 72176
Nearest Town/Resort Keswick
Directions 2 miles south of Keswick on the A591 towards Windermere. .
Acreage 7 **Open** March **to** October
Access Good **Site** Sloping
Sites Available
Facilities
Nearby Facilities
Penrith
Ideal for touring.

KESWICK

Scotgate Holiday Park, Braithwaite, Keswick, Cumbria, CA12 5TF.
Std: 017687 **Tel:** 78343
Std: 017687 **Fax:** 78099
Nearest Town/Resort Keswick
Directions 2 miles west of Keswick, just off the A66 on the B5292.
Acreage 9½ **Open** March **to** November
Access Good **Site** Level
Sites Available **Total** 150
Facilities
Nearby Facilities
Penrith
✓✓✓✓Graded Park. Ideal for walking.

KIRKBY LONSDALE

Woodclose Caravan Park, Casterton, Carnforth, Lancs, LA6 2SE.
Std: 015242 **Tel:** 71597
Nearest Town/Resort Kirkby Lonsdale.
Directions ½ mile south east of Kirkby Lonsdale on the A65.
Acreage 9¼ **Open** March **to** October
Access Good **Site** Level
Sites Available **Total** 70
Facilities
Nearby Facilities
Oxenholme
Near River Lune, within easy driving distance of Lake District, Dales or seaside.

KIRKBY STEPHEN

Bowberhead Caravan Site, Bowberhead Farm, Ravenstonedale, Kirkby Stephen, Cumbria, CA17 4NL.
Std: 015396 **Tel:** 23254
Nearest Town/Resort Kirkby Stephen.
Directions 4½ miles south of Kirkby Stephen off the A683 road to Sedgbergh.
Acreage 1¼ **Open** All Year
Access Good **Site** Lev/Slope
Sites Available **Total** 7
Facilities
Nearby Facilities
Kirkby Stephen
Settle to Carlisle Line, beautiful views, best fell walking. TV hook-ups.

KIRKBY THORE

Low Moor, Kirkby Thore, Penrith, Cumbria, CA10 1XG.
Std: 017683 **Tel:** 61231
Nearest Town/Resort Appleby
Directions On the A66 7 miles south east of Penrith, between Temple Sowerby and Kirkby Thore villages.
Acreage 1½ **Open** April **to** October
Access Good **Site** Level
Sites Available **Total** 12
Facilities
Nearby Facilities
Penrith
Open country.

LAMPLUGH

Inglenook Caravan Park, Lamplugh, Workington, Cumbria.
Std: 01946 **Tel:** 861240
Std: 01946 **Fax:** 861240
Nearest Town/Resort Cockermouth.
Directions Leave A66 road at Cockermouth and take A5086 road (Egremont). 6 miles on turn left at caravan sign.
Acreage 3½ **Open** All Year
Access Good **Site** Level
Sites Available **Total** 30
Facilities
Nearby Facilities
Workington.
✓✓✓✓Graded Park. Scenic surroundings. Golf 4C. 9 miles beach. Ideal touring and walking area. Luxury holiday homes for hire. A.A. recommended 3 Pennant site and A.A. Award for Excellence. Attractive environment.

LEVENS

Sampool Caravan Park, Levens, Nr. Kendal, Cumbria, LA8 8EQ.
Std: 015395 **Tel:** 52265
Nearest Town/Resort Kendal.
Directions Kendal - south A6 for 3 miles to slip road onto A591. Follow signs for Milnthorpe to Levens Bridge A6. Turn right onto A590, 250yds on left.
Open 15 March **to** October
Site Level
Sites Available **Total** 15
Facilities
Nearby Facilities
Oxenholme.
Alongside river, country side, quiet. Handy for lakes.

LONGTOWN

Camelot Caravan Park, Sandysike, Longtown, Carlisle, Cumbria.
Std: 01228 **Tel:** 791248
Nearest Town/Resort Longtown
Directions On left 1¼ miles south of Longtown on A7, northbound leave M6 at exit 44, take A7 (Longtown) site on right in 4 miles.
Acreage 1¼ **Open** March **to** October
Access Good **Site** Level
Sites Available **Total** 20
Facilities
Nearby Facilities
Carlisle.
Ideal for Solway coast, Carlisle Settle railway, romantic Gretna Green, base for Hadrians Wall and border towns, Carlisle Castle. AA 3 Pennants.

MARYPORT

Spring Lea Caravan Park, Allonby, Maryport, Cumbria, CA15 6QF.
Std: 01900 **Tel:** 881331
Std: 01900 **Fax:** 881209
Nearest Town/Resort Maryport
Directions 5 miles north of Maryport on the B5300 coast road.
Acreage 5 **Open** March **to** October
Access Good **Site** Level
Sites Available **Total** 35
Facilities
Nearby Facilities
Maryport
✓✓✓✓Graded Park. 300 yards from the beach with views of Lakeland and Scottish hills. Leisure centre for sauna etc.. Bar/restaurant on site.

MEALSGATE

The Larches Caravan Park, Mealsgate, Carlisle, Cumbria, CA5 1LQ.
Std: 016973 **Tel:** 71379/71803
Std: 016973 **Fax:** 71782
Nearest Town/Resort Wigton.
Directions From the north take the A57/A74/A7/A69 to Carlisle, follow the A595 to Mealsgate. From the south leave the M6 at junction 41, take the B5305 Wigton road as far as the A595. Turn left and follow the A595 to Mealsgate.
Acreage 17 **Open** March **to** October
Access Good **Site** Lev/slope
Sites Available **Total** 73
Facilities
Nearby Facilities
Wigton.
Ideal for couples, peace and quiet in the countryside with beautiful views. Excellent toilets. ADAC Yellow Award.

MELMERBY

Melmerby Caravan Park, Melmerby, Penrith, Cumbria, CA10 1HE.
Std: 01768 **Tel:** 881311
Std: 01768 **Fax:** 881311
Nearest Town/Resort Penrith
Directions Situated in Melmerby Village on the A686, 10 miles north east of Penrith.
Open Mid-March **to** October
Access Good **Site** Level
Sites Available **Total** 5
Facilities
Nearby Facilities
✓✓✓✓✓Graded Park. Excellent walking country, ideal base for touring North Pennines, Eden Valley and Lake District.

MILNTHORPE

Hall More Caravan Park, Field House, Hall More, Hale, Nr. Milnthorpe, Cumbria, LA7 7BP.
Std: 015395 **Tel:** 64163
Std: 015395 **Fax:** 63025
Nearest Town/Resort Arnside/Milnthorpe.
Directions Leave the M6 at junction 35, take the A6 north and turn left at Wildlife Oasis (after passing Esso fuel station). Follow signs to Fell End Caravan Park and Hall More is signposted from there.
Acreage 5 **Open** March **to** October
Access Good **Site** Level
Sites Available **Total** 50

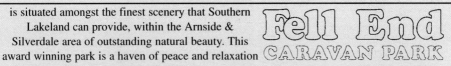

Facilities
Nearby Facilities
Arnside
Rural location, excellent for walking, rambling, etc.. Next to a Trout Fishery and Riding Centre. Easy access to the Lake District.

MILNTHORPE

Millness Hill Park, Crooklands, Milnthorpe, Cumbria.
Std: 015395 **Tel:** 67306
Std: 015395 **Fax:** 67306
Nearest Town/Resort Kendal
Directions Leave the M6 at junction 36, follow signs for Kirkby Lonsdale, at roundabout take the A65 to Crooklands, site is 100yds on the left.
Acreage 1 **Open** March **to** 14 November
Access Good **Site** Lev/Slope
Sites Available **Total** 15
Facilities
Nearby Facilities
Kendal
✓✓✓✓Graded Park. Adjoining Lancaster Canal.

MILNTHORPE

Waters Edge Caravan Park, Crooklands, Near Kendal, Cumbria, LA7 7NN.
Std: 015395 **Tel:** 67708
Std: 015395 **Fax:** 67610
Nearest Town/Resort Kendal
Directions A65 Crooklands, ¾ mile from M6 motorway junction 36.
Acreage 3 **Open** March **to** November
Access Good **Site** Level
Sites Available **Total** 40
Facilities
Nearby Facilities
Oxenholme
✓✓✓✓✓Graded Park. Set in quiet and pleasant countryside. Lakes, Yorkshire Dales and Morecambe Bay within easy reach.

NEWBY BRIDGE

Hill of Oaks & Blakeholme Caravan Estate, Newby Bridge, Near Ulverston, Cumbria, LA12 8NR.
Std: 015395 **Tel:** 31578
Nearest Town/Resort Windermere.
Directions Leave the M6 at junction 36 and follow the A590 to Newby Bridge. Take the A592 for approx. 2 miles and the Estate is on the east shore of Lake Windermere.
Acreage 83 **Open** March **to** October
Access Good **Site** Sloping
Sites Available **Total** 43
Facilities
Nearby Facilities
Windermere.
✓✓✓✓✓Graded Park. Approximately 1 mile of lake frontage, piers and slipways. Easy access to the mountains and local shopping.

PENRITH

Beckes Caravan Site, Penruddock, Penrith, Cumbria, CA11 0RX.
Std: 017684 **Tel:** 83224
Nearest Town/Resort Penrith.
Directions 7 miles from Penrith, 11 miles from Keswick. Turn right off the A66 onto the B5288, 400 yards on the right.
Acreage 3½ **Open** Easter **to** October
Access Good **Site** Lev/Slope
Sites Available **Total** 23
Facilities
Nearby Facilities
Penrith.
Ideal touring for Lakes. Discounted rates for O.A.P.s.

PENRITH

Gillside Caravan & Camping Site, Glenridding, Penrith, Cumbria, CA11 0QQ.
Std: 017684 **Tel:** 82346
Nearest Town/Resort Penrith.
Directions A592 signposted Ullswater, 14 miles from Penrith. In Glenridding turn right, follow sign for Gillside.
Acreage 8 **Open** March **to** Mid Nov
Access Good **Site** Level
Sites Available **Total** 65
Facilities
Nearby Facilities
Penrith
Foot of Helvellyn, 5 minutes walk from Lake Ullswater.

PENRITH

Hillcroft Park, Roehead Lane, Pooley Bridge, Penrith, Cumbria, CA10 2LT.
Std: 017684 **Tel:** 86363
Std: 017684 **Fax:** 86010
Nearest Town/Resort Pooley Bridge
Directions Junction 40 off M6, A592 to Ullswater. Turn left into Pooley Bridge, bear right at the church, straight across the crossroads, entrance is on the left.
Acreage 7 **Open** 6 March **to** 14 Nov
Access Good **Site** Level

Sites Available **Total** 125
Facilities
Nearby Facilities
Penrith
Scenic views, ideal touring for Lake District. Near to Lake Ullswater.

PENRITH

Lowther Caravan Park, Eamont Bridge, Penrith, Cumbria, CA10 2JB.
Std: 01768 **Tel:** 863631
Std: 01768 **Fax:** 868126
Nearest Town/Resort Penrith.
Directions 1 mile south of Penrith on the A6.
Acreage 50 **Open** March **to** November
Access Good **Site** Lev/Slope
Sites Available **Total** 225
Facilities
Nearby Facilities
Penrith.
√√√√ Graded Park. A haven of peace and tranquility in natural parkland on the banks of the River Lowther, home of the rare and fascinating red squirrel. AA Campsite of the Year for Northern England 1998/99.

PENRITH

Park Foot Caravan & Camping Site, Howtown Road, Pooley Bridge, Penrith, Cumbria, CA10 2NA.
Std: 017684 **Tel:** Pooley Bridge 86309
Std: 017684 **Fax:** 86041
Nearest Town/Resort Pooley Bridge.
Directions 5 miles southwest of Penrith. Leave M6 at junction 40, then take A66 for Ullswater, next roundabout take A592 then road for Pooley Bridge and 1 mile on Howtown Road to site.
Acreage 15 **Open** March **to** October
Access Good **Site** Lev/Slope
Sites Available **Total** 323
Facilities
Nearby Facilities
Penrith.
Family run park beside Lake Ullswater with boat and car launching access. Licensed bar, restaurant and takeaway. Pony trekking, mountain bike hire, tennis and table tennis on site.

PENRITH

Stonefold, Newbiggin, Stainton, Penrith, Cumbria, CA11 0HP.
Std: 01768 **Tel:** 866383
Nearest Town/Resort Penrith
Directions Leave the M6 at junction 40 and take the A66 Keswick road. Turn right at the sign for Newbiggin and Stonefold is one minutes drive on the left.
Acreage 2 **Open** March **to** November
Access Good **Site** Level
Sites Available **Total** 15
Facilities
Nearby Facilities
Penrith
Panoramic position overlooking Eden Valley. An ideal base for exploring and enjoying the lakes. 5 miles from Ullswater.

PENRITH

Thacka Lea Caravan Site, Thacka Lea, Penrith, Cumbria, CA11 9HX.
Std: 01768. **Tel:** 863319
Nearest Town/Resort Penrith.
Directions From south, left off A6, past Shell Station north end of town. From north, turn right Grey Bull.
Acreage 1 **Open** March **to** October
Access Good **Site** Lev/Slope
Sites Available **Total** 25
Facilities
Nearby Facilities
Penrith.
Ten minutes town centre walking. Good touring.

PENRITH

Thanet Well Caravan Park, Greystoke, Penrith, Cumbria, CA11 0XX.
Std: 017684 **Tel:** 84262
Nearest Town/Resort Penrith
Directions M6 junction 41 onto B5305 for Wigton, approx 6 miles turn left for Lamonby, follow caravan signs for approx 2 miles to park.
Acreage 3 **Open** March **to** October
Access Good **Site** Lev/Slope
Sites Available **Total** 20
Facilities
Nearby Facilities
Penrith
Scenic views, Fell walking, touring and cycling. AA 3 Pennants.

PENRITH

The Cross Fell Camping & Caravan Park, The Fox Inn, Ousby, Penrith, Cumbria, CA10 1QA.
Std: 01768 **Tel:** 881374
Std: 01768 **Fax:** 881374
Nearest Town/Resort Penrith
Directions From Penrith take the A686 towards Alston, after 6 miles turn right at the crossroads signposted Ousby. The Fox Inn is in the centre of the village.
Acreage 3 **Open** 1 March **to** 13 Nov
Access Good **Site** Level
Sites Available **Total** 9
Facilities
Nearby Facilities
Langwathby
Peaceful park in quiet countryside.

PENRITH

Waterside Farm Campsite, Waterside Farm, Howtown Road, Pooley Bridge, Penrith, Cumbria, CA10 2NA.
Std: 017684 **Tel:** 86332
Std: 017684 **Fax:** 86332
Nearest Town/Resort Pooley Bridge
Directions Leave the M6 at junction 40 and take the A66 for 1 mile, turn left onto the A592 for Ullswater and after 4 miles turn left to Pooley Bridge. Go through the village and turn right at the church then right again, we are 1 mile on the right past the other sites.
Open March **to** October
Site Lev/Slope
Sites Available
Facilities
Nearby Facilities
Penrith
√√√√ Graded Park. Genuine lakeside location with beautiful views of a lake and fells. Boat, canoe and mountain bike hire available.

PORT CARLISLE

Cottage Caravan Park, Port Carlisle, Cumbria, CA5 5DJ.
Std: 016973 **Tel:** Kirkbride 51317
Nearest Town/Resort Carlisle.
Directions 11 miles west of Carlisle on B class coastal road to Bowness-on-Solway.
Acreage 4 **Open** March **to** October
Sites Available **Total** 20
Facilities
Nearby Facilities
Carlisle.
Good walking near beach on Roman Wall route.

PORT CARLISLE

Glendale Caravan Park, Port Carlisle, Nr. Carlisle, Cumbria, CA5 5DJ.
Std: 0169 73 **Tel:** Kirkbride 51317
Nearest Town/Resort Carlisle.
Directions Take west coast road in Carlisle then fork right at McVities Biscuits Works, then right fork to Burgh-by-Sands and Bowness-on-Solway.
Acreage 12 **Open** March **to** October
Access Good **Site** Level
Sites Available **Total** 20
Facilities

Nearby Facilities
Carlisle.
Near beach, scenic, ideal touring for lakes and north.

PORT HAVERIGG
Butterflowers Holiday Homes, Port Haverigg, Cumbria, LA18 4HB.
Std: 01229 **Tel:** 772880
Std: 01229 **Fax:** 774445
Nearest Town/Resort Millom
Directions 1 mile from Millom, follow signs for beach.
Acreage 4½ **Open** All Year
Access Good **Site** Level
Sites Available **Total** 100
Facilities
Nearby Facilities
Millom.
Near the beach.

RAVENGLASS
Walls Caravan Camping Park, Ravenglass, West Cumbria, CA18 1SR.
Std: 01229 **Tel:** 717250
Nearest Town/Resort Ravenglass/ Whitehaven.
Directions A595 into Ravenglass. Site at entrance to village.
Acreage 5 **Open** 28 Feb **to** 15 Nov
Access Good **Site** Sloping
Sites Available **Total** 60
Facilities
Nearby Facilities
Ravenglass.
✓✓✓✓Graded Park. Muncaster castle, Ravenglass and Eskdale miniature railway, Ravenglass Gullery and Nature Reserve, Muncaster Watermill, Roman sites in area.

SEASCALE
Church Stile Camp Site, Church Stile Farm, Wasdale, Seascale, Cumbria, CA20 1ET.
Std: 019467 **Tel:** 26388
Nearest Town/Resort Seascale.
Directions 4 miles east of Gosforth off the A595, head for Netherwasdale village.
Acreage 4 **Open** March **to** November
Site Level
Sites Available **Total** 80
Facilities
Nearby Facilities
Seascale.
6 miles from beach, 1½ miles Wastwater Lake and fells. Scenic views, ideal for walking and touring. Muncaster Castle and railway.

SEDBERGH
Cross Hall Caravan Park, Cautley, Sedbergh, Cumbria, LA10 5LY.
Std: 015396 **Tel:** 20668
Nearest Town/Resort Sedbergh.
Directions Straight through Sedbergh on main A683 road to Kirkby Stephen. 2¼ miles from Sedbergh on right hand side.
Acreage 1½ **Open** April **to** October
Access Good **Site** Level
Sites Available **Total** 10
Facilities
Nearby Facilities
✓✓✓Graded Park. Ideal walking country, Howgill Fells. Cautley Spout 1¼ miles.

SEDBERGH
Pinfold Caravan Park, Garsdale Road, Sedbergh, Cumbria, LA10 5JL.
Std: 01539 **Tel:** 620576
Std: 01539 **Fax:** 620576
Nearest Town/Resort Sedbergh.
Directions Take A684 through Sedbergh, caravan park 450 yds from village, over Dales Bridge, on left hand side of road.
Acreage 3 **Open** March **to** October
Access Good **Site** Level
Sites Available **Total** 38
Facilities
Nearby Facilities
Oxenholme
Alongside river Rawthey below the Howgill Fells, ideal fell walking and touring. Fishing on the site. Motorcycles are permitted but no groups please.

SILLOTH
Hylton Park Holiday Centre, Eden Street, Silloth, Cumbria.
Std: 016973 **Tel:** 31707
Std: 016973 **Fax:** 32555
Nearest Town/Resort Silloth.
Directions ½ mile south of Silloth on B5300.
Open Easter **to** October
Access Good **Site** Level
Sites Available **Total** 45
Facilities
Nearby Facilities
Carlisle.
Full use of Stanwix Park facilities available - ¼ mile. See Stanwix Park advertisement.

SILLOTH
Moordale Caravan Park, Blitterlees, Silloth, Cumbria.
Std: 016973 **Tel:** 31375
Nearest Town/Resort Silloth.
Directions From Silloth take the B5300 Silloth to Maryport road. Moordale is about 2 miles on the right hand side.
Acreage 7 **Open** March **to** October
Access Good **Site** Level
Sites Available **Total** 12
Facilities
Nearby Facilities
Wigton.
Adjacent to Silloth Golf Course and beach. Ideal for touring Northern lakes and Southern Scotland.

SILLOTH
Rowanbank Caravan Park, Beckfoot, Silloth, Cumbria, CA5 4LA.
Std: 016973 **Tel:** 31653
Nearest Town/Resort Silloth.
Directions 2 miles south of Silloth on B5300.
Acreage 3¼ **Open** March **to** November
Access Good **Site** Level
Sites Available **Total** 30
Facilities
Nearby Facilities
Maryport
Across road from beach on Solway coast, overlooking Scottish Hills. Brochure sent with pleasure.

SILLOTH
Solway Holiday Village, Skinburness Drive, Silloth, Nr Carlisle, Cumbria, CA5 4QQ.
Std: 016973 **Tel:** 31236
Std: 016973 **Fax:** 32553
Nearest Town/Resort Silloth.
Directions From Carlisle take the B5302 to Silloth. At Silloth turn right before sea front, park is ¼ mile up Skinburness Road, set back on the right.
Open March **to** October
Access Good **Site** Level
Sites Available **Total** 100
Facilities
Nearby Facilities
Carlisle.
✓✓✓Graded Park. Near the beach and Lake District. Level, grassed and concrete based pitches. 10% discount on production of our advertisement or by quoting reference CCSOL.

SILLOTH

Stanwix Park Holiday Centre, Silloth (West), Cumbria.
Std: 016973 **Tel:** 32666
Std: 016973 **Fax:** 32555
Nearest Town/Resort Silloth.
Directions Enter Silloth on B5302, turn left at sea front, 1 mile to West Siloth on B5300. Site on right.
Acreage 4 **Open** Easter **to** October
Access Good **Site** Level
Sites Available **Total** 121
Facilities
Nearby Facilities
Carlisle.
✓✓✓✓✓Graded Park. Large holiday centre with full range of facilities for all the family, indoor and outdoor, including pony trekking. Sunbeds, water shoot. New indoor leisure complex. See our display advertisment. Internet site HTTP://WWW.MARTEX.CO.UK/NCC/STANWIX E-Mail ERIC.STANWIX@BTINTERNET.COM

SILLOTH

Tanglewood Caravan Park, Causewayhead, Silloth, Cumbria, CA5 4PE.
Std: 016973 **Tel:** 31253
Nearest Town/Resort Silloth.
Directions Take B5302, 1 mile inland from town on Wigton road.
Acreage 2 **Open** Easter **to** October
Access Good **Site** Level
Sites Available **Total** 31
Facilities
Nearby Facilities
Wigton.
✓✓✓✓Graded Park. Tree sheltered site, ideal for touring lakes and borders. Pets free of charge.

ST. BEES

Seacote Park, St. Bees, Cumbria, CA27 0ES.
Std: 01946 **Tel:** 822777
Std: 01946 **Fax:** 822777
Nearest Town/Resort Whitehaven
Directions From Whitehaven take the B5345 to St. Bees, approx. 4 miles then follow road to the beach.
Acreage 3 **Open** All Year
Access Good **Site** Lev/Slope
Sites Available **Total** 50
Facilities
Nearby Facilities
St. Bees
✓✓✓Graded Park. Close to the beach, hotel and shop. Ideal touring and walking area.

TEBAY

Westmorland Caravan Site Tebay, Tebay Westmorland Services M6 Northbound, Cumbria, CA10 3SB.
Std: 015396 **Tel:** 24511
Std: 015396 **Fax:** 24511
Nearest Town/Resort Penrith/Kendal
Directions M6 Motorway 1 mile north of junction 38, take the Westmorland Tebay Services exit and follow signs for Tebay Caravan Site. Access also from Tebay East Services M6 south, follow signs.
Acreage 3½ **Open** Mid-March **to** October
Access Good **Site** Level
Sites Available **Total** 70
Facilities
Nearby Facilities
Penrith/Oxenholme
✓✓✓✓✓Graded Park. Ideal base for the Lake District and the Yorkshire Dales.

TROUTBECK

Gill Head Farm, Troutbeck, Penrith, Cumbria, CA11 0ST.
Std: 017687 **Tel:** 79652
Nearest Town/Resort Keswick
Directions Just off A66 on A5091 9 miles Keswick, 5 miles Ullswater.
Acreage 10 **Open** April **to** October
Access Good **Site** Level
Sites Available **Total** 54
Facilities
Nearby Facilities
Penrith.
Ideal touring, scenic views.

TROUTBECK

Moor End Farm Caravan & Camping Site, Moor End Farm, Troutbeck, Penrith, Cumbria, CA11 0SX.
Std: 01768 **Tel:** 779615
Nearest Town/Resort Keswick
Directions On A66 9 miles west of junc 40 M6. Turn left for Wallthwaite.
Acreage 2½ **Open** Easter or 1st April **to** Nov
Access Good **Site** Sloping
Sites Available **Total** 50
Facilities
Nearby Facilities
Penrith
Walking

ULLSWATER

The Quiet Caravan & Camping Site, Ullswater, Nr. Penrith, Cumbria, CA11 0LS.
Std: 0176 84 **Tel:** 86337
Std: 0176 84 **Fax:** 86610
Nearest Town/Resort Pooley Bridge.
Directions Take A592 from Penrith, turn right at lake and right again at Brackenrigg Hotel follow road for 1½ miles, site on right hand side of road.
Acreage 6 **Open** March **to** November
Access Good **Site** Lev/Slope
Sites Available **Total** 83
Facilities
Nearby Facilities
Penrith.
✓✓✓✓✓Graded Park. Idyllic setting amongst the fells, voted Best Campsite in Britain by Camping Magazine, AA Northern Campsite of the Year. Large adventure playground and probably the best campsite bar in Britain! Top 100 Park.

ULLSWATER

Ullswater Caravan Camping & Marine Park, Watermillock, Penrith, Cumbria, CA11 0LR.
Std: 0176 84 **Tel:** 86666
Std: 0176 84 **Fax:** 86095
Nearest Town/Resort Penrith.
Directions A592 from Penrith, turn right at lake and right again at telephone kiosk, signposted Watermillock Church.
Acreage 7 **Open** March **to** 14 November
Access Good **Site** Lev/Slope
Sites Available **Total** 155
Facilities
Nearby Facilities
Penrith.
✓✓✓✓Graded Park. Lake District National Park. Scenic views. Boat launching and moorings 1 mile.

WALNEY ISLAND

South End Caravan Park, Walney, Barrow in Furness, Cumbria.
Std: 01229 **Tel:** 472823
Nearest Town/Resort Barrow in Furness
Directions A590 to Barrow, then follow Walney signs. Turn left after crossing bridge to Walney, 4 miles south from there.
Acreage 7 **Open** March **to** October
Site Sloping
Sites Available **Total** 60
Facilities
Nearby Facilities
Barrow
Close to beach, good views.

WATERMILLOCK

Cove Camping Park, Lake Ullswater, Watermillock, Penrith, Cumbria, CA11 0LS.
Std: 0176 84. **Tel:** 86549
Nearest Town/Resort Penrith
Directions Leave M6 at junction 40, turn west follow signs for Ullswater (A592). Turn right at Lake junction, then right at Brackenrigg Inn. Park is 1½ miles on left. Look for Cove Camping Park sign.
Acreage 2½ **Open** March **to** November
Access Good **Site** Lev/Slope
Sites Available **Total** 50
Facilities
Nearby Facilities
Penrith
✓✓✓✓✓Graded Park. Peaceful family park, sheltered by nearby Fells. Overlooking Lake Ullswater. Ideal for touring the Lakes. Freezer for ice packs, hairdryers, hot and cold drinks machine. Battery charging.

WATERMILLOCK

Knotts Hill Caravan Chalet Site, Watermillock, Penrith Cumbria, CA11 0JR.
Std: 017684 **Tel:** 86328
Nearest Town/Resort Penrith
Directions A592 from Penrith turn off at Gowbarrow Lodge Grill approx 8 miles from Penrith, entrance ½ mile on right.
Access Good **Site** Lev/Slope
Sites Available
Facilities
Nearby Facilities
Penrith

WIGTON

Clea Hall Holiday Park, Westward, Wigton, Cumbria, CA7 8NQ.
Std: 016973 **Tel:** 42880
Std: 016973 **Fax:** 42880
Nearest Town/Resort Wigton.
Directions M6 North junction 41, B5305 signposted Wigton. B5299 (turn left at Steadmans sign) Caldbeck, second crossroads signposted Westward and Wigton.
Acreage 10 **Open** March **to** November
Access Good **Site** Level
Sites Available **Total** 16
Facilities
Nearby Facilities
Wigton
✓✓✓✓✓Graded Park. Scenic views and ideal touring. Price Band C includes electric hook-up charge. AA 4 Pennants.

WINDERMERE

Ashes Lane Caravan & Camping Park, Ashes Lane, Staveley, Kendal, Cumbria, LA8 9JS.
Std: 01539 **Tel:** 821119
Std: 01539 **Fax:** 821282
Nearest Town/Resort Kendal
Directions M6 junction 36, take the A591 towards Windermere, 1½ miles from Kendal roundabout.
Acreage 22 **Open** 14 March **to** 14 Jan
Access Good **Site** Level
Sites Available **Total** 300
Facilities
Nearby Facilities
Staveley
✓✓✓✓Graded Park. Lake District National Park.

WINDERMERE

Fallbarrow Park, Rayrigg Road, Windermere, Cumbria, LA23 3DL.
Std: 015394 **Tel:** 44428
Std: 015394 **Fax:** 88736
Nearest Town/Resort Windermere.
Directions Just north of Bowness village on A592.
Acreage 32 **Open** 15 March **to** October
Access Good **Site** Level
Sites Available **Total** 81
Facilities
Nearby Facilities
Windermere.
✓✓✓✓✓Graded Park. On shore of Lake Windermere. Boating facilities. An AA 5 Pennant Premier Park and AA Campsite of the Year 1996/97. Tourers have direct connections to water, waste, TV and electric. Please refer to our colour advertisement.

WINDERMERE

Limefitt Park, Windermere, Cumbria, LA23 1PA.
Std: 015394 **Tel:** 32300
Nearest Town/Resort Windermere.
Directions In Lakeland valley 4 miles north of Windermere on A592 to Ullswater.
Acreage 25 **Open** 1 week before Easter **to** October
Access Good **Site** Lev/Slope
Sites Available **Total** 165
Facilities
Nearby Facilities
Windermere.
✓✓✓✓✓Graded Park. Spectacular Lakeland valley location. Ten minutes drive to Lake Windermere. Tourers and family campers welcome. Friendly Lakeland pub with bar meals. 'Do-it-Yourself' Camper's kitchen, shop, plus a full range of award winning facilities. AA 5 Pennant Premier Park. Luxurious holiday caravans for hire. No dogs. Please see our colour advertisement.

WINDERMERE

Park Cliffe Camping & Caravan Estate, Birks Road, Tower Wood, Windermere, Cumbria, LA23 3PG.
Std: 015395 **Tel:** 31344
Std: 015395 **Fax:** 31971
Nearest Town/Resort Windermere
Directions M6 junction 36, A590 to Newby Bridge. Turn right onto A592, in 4 miles turn right into Birks Road. Park is roughly ½ mile on the right.
Acreage 25 **Open** March **to** October
Access Good **Site** Lev/Slope
Sites Available **Total** 250
Facilities
Nearby Facilities
Windermere
✓✓✓✓✓Graded Park. Near to Lake Windermere with outstanding views of lakes and mountains, ideal touring. AA 3 pennants and RAC.

WINDERMERE

White Cross Bay Leisure Park & Marina, Ambleside Road, Windermere, Cumbria, LA23 1LF.
Std: 015394 **Tel:** 43937
Std: 015394 **Fax:** 88704
Nearest Town/Resort Windermere/ Ambleside
Directions Approx 15 miles from the M6 junction 36. Follow the direction signs to Windermere on the A591 until reaching the town, stay on the A591 following signs for Ambleside. Park is on the left hand side 2 miles after Windermere.
Acreage 65 **Open** 1 March **to** 14 November
Access Good **Site** Level
Sites Available
Facilities
Nearby Facilities
Windermere
✓✓✓✓Graded Park. Ideally placed between Windermere and Ambleside in the heart of walking country. The park borders Lake Windermere.

DERBYSHIRE

AMBERGATE

The Firs Farm Caravan & Camping Park, Crich Lane, Nether Heage, Ambergate, Belper, Derbys, DE56 2JH.
Std: 01773 **Tel:** 852913
Nearest Town/Resort Ambergate.
Directions 1½ miles south of Ambergate turn left off the A6 onto Broad Holme Lane. At top of lane turn left, park is 500yds on the left.
Acreage 3 **Open** All Year
Access Good **Site** Level
Sites Available **Total** 60
Facilities
Nearby Facilities
Ambergate
✓✓✓✓✓Graded Park. Magnificent views, well maintained, quiet, landscaped site. Friendly, family run park with a sauna. Host of local attractions. Gas, launderette, pub, restaurant and telephone nearby.

ASHBOURNE

Bank Top Farm, Fenny Bentley, Ashbourne, Derbyshire.
Std: 01335. **Tel:** 350250
Nearest Town/Resort Ashbourne.
Directions Take A515 from town 2 miles. Take B5056, site 200 yards opposite Bentley Brook Inn.
Acreage 2½ **Open** Easter **to** End September
Access Good
Sites Available
Facilities
Nearby Facilities
Derby.
Scenic views from site. Area ideal for touring Dovedale and other Dales, also pretty little villages. Viewing gallery to watch the milking of the cows. Washing machine and spin dryer available. Prices available on request. AA 3 Pennants.

ASHBOURNE

Callow Top Holiday Park, Buxton Road, Ashbourne, Derbyshire.
Std: 01335 **Tel:** 344020
Std: 01335 **Fax:** 343726
Nearest Town/Resort Ashbourne.
Directions The access to Callow Top is only ¼ mile from Ashbourne on the A515 Buxton road. The entrance is directly opposite Sandybrook Garage, follow the private road for ½ mile to the end.
Acreage 15 **Open** All Year
Access Good **Site** Level
Sites Available **Total** 150
Facilities

Nearby Facilities
Derby
✓✓✓Graded Park. Alton Towers only 20 minutes away, Tissington Trail cycle path is adjacent, Carsington Reservoir 5 miles. Many footpaths.

ASHBOURNE

Gateway Caravan Park, Osmaston, Near Ashbourne, Derbyshire, DE6 1NA.
Std: 01335 **Tel:** 344643
Nearest Town/Resort Ashbourne
Directions 1 mile south of Ashbourne turn right off the A52, park is 400 metres on the right hand side.
Acreage 15 **Open** All Year
Access Good **Site** Level
Sites Available **Total** 200
Facilities
Nearby Facilities
Derby
Entertainment on Saturday nights during school holidays and Bank Holiday weekends. The Peak District and only 15 minutes to Alton Towers.

ASHBOURNE

Newton Grange Caravan Site, Newton Grange, Ashbourne, Derbyshire, DE6 1NJ.
Std: 01335 **Tel:** 310214
Nearest Town/Resort Ashbourne
Directions On the A515 4½ miles north of Ashbourne.
Acreage 1 **Open** Mid March **to** End October
Access Good **Site** Level
Sites Available **Total** 15
Facilities
Nearby Facilities
Derby
Close to Buxton, Matlock and Alton Towers. Tissington Trail adjacent for cycling and walking. Ideal touring.

ASHBOURNE

Rivendale Caravan & Leisure Park, Buxton Road, Alsop-en-le-Dale, Ashbourne, Derbyshire, DE6 1QU.
Std: 01332 **Tel:** 843000
Std: 01332 **Fax:** 842311
Nearest Town/Resort Hartington
Directions 6½ miles north of Ashbourne, directly accessed from the A515 (Buxton road).
Acreage 35 **Open** March **to** January
Access Good **Site** Level
Sites Available **Total** 80
Facilities
Nearby Facilities
Buxton
Surrounded by scenic countryside, ideal for walking, cycling and outdoor hobbies. Convenient for Chatsworth, Alton Towers and many other attractions.

ASHBOURNE

Sandybrook Hall Holiday Park, Sandybrook Hall, Ashbourne, Derbyshire, DE6 2AQ.
Std: 01335 **Tel:** 342679
Nearest Town/Resort Ashbourne
Directions 1 mile north of Ashbourne on A515. MOT signed.
Acreage 5 **Open** March **to** November
Access Good
Sites Available **Total** 70
Facilities
Nearby Facilities
Peak District National Park. Near to Alton Towers.

ASHBOURNE

The Alamo Caravan Site, Wood Lane, Kniveton, Ashbourne, Derbyshire, DE6 1JF.
Std: 01335 **Tel:** 347329
Std: 01335 **Fax:** 343160
Nearest Town/Resort Ashbourne
Directions From Ashbourne follow signs for the B5035 Ashbourne to Wirksworth road. Follow for 2 miles, once past the Greyhound Pub ½ mile on the left hand junction, Kniveton Wood turn down, go past a bungalow, green gates and through the next gates into the site.
Acreage 1½ **Open** All Year
Access Good **Site** Level
Sites Available
Facilities
Nearby Facilities
Matlock/Derby
Only 20 minutes from Alton Towers. Also near to Carsington Water, Matlock, Matlock Bath, Tissington Trail, Bakewell and only 5 minutes from Ashbourne Town centre.

BAKEWELL

Camping & Caravanning Club Site, c/o Hopping Farm, Youlgreave, Bakewell, Derbyshire, DE45 1NA.
Std: 01629 **Tel:** 636555
Directions Take the A6 Bakewell to Matlock road, turn onto the B5056 Ashbourne road. After ½ mile take the right hand branch to Youlgreave, turn sharp left after the church into Bradford Lane opposite The George Hotel. Continue ½ mile to club sign then turn right into Farmers Lane for ¼ mile.
Acreage 14 **Open** 22 March **to** 27 Sept
Site Sloping
Sites Available **Total** 100
Facilities
Nearby Facilities
Matlock
✓✓✓✓Graded Park. Ideally situated for the Peak District.

BAKEWELL

Peakland Caravans, High Street, Stoney Middleton, Hope Valley, S32 4TL.
Std: 01433 **Tel:** 631414
Nearest Town/Resort Bakewell
Directions Stoney Middleton is on the A623, 3 miles west of Baslow. Approaching from Baslow turn left by the Moon Inn and Village Cross. Continue up the hill for a third of a mile, park is on the right.
Open Easter **to** End October
Site Level
Sites Available **Total** 12
Facilities
Nearby Facilities
Grindleford
✓✓✓✓Graded Park. Ideal for touring, walking and climbing. STATICS ALSO FOR HIRE.

BAKEWELL

Stocking Farm Caravan & Camp Site, Stocking Farm, Calver Bridge, Calver, Hope Valley, S32 3XA.
Tel: Hope Valley 630516
Nearest Town/Resort Bakewell
Directions Out of Bakewell on the A619 fork left onto the B6001 to traffic lights. Turn right then first left, after Derbyshire Craft Centre first left again.
Acreage 1½ **Open** April **to** October
Access Good **Site** Level
Sites Available **Total** 10
Facilities
Nearby Facilities
Grindleford
Scenic views, idea touring. Married couples and families only.

BUXTON

Cold Springs Farm, Buxton, Derbyshire, SK17 6SS.
Std: 01298. **Tel:** 22762
Std: 01298 **Fax:** 72005
Nearest Town/Resort Buxton.
Directions A5004 from Buxton 1 mile.
Acreage 4 **Open** March **to** November
Access Sloping **Site** Sloping
Sites Available **Total** 25
Facilities
Nearby Facilities
Buxton.
Scenic views. Ideal touring.

BUXTON

Cottage Farm Caravan Park, Blackwell in the Peak, Derbyshire, SK17 9TQ.
Std: 01298 **Tel:** 85330
Nearest Town/Resort Buxton.
Directions From Buxton, 6 miles east on the A6. Take an unclassified road north, signposted.
Acreage 3 **Open** March **to** October
Access Good **Site** Level
Sites Available **Total** 30
Facilities
Nearby Facilities
Buxton
✓✓✓Graded Park. Centre of a National Park, ideal for walking and touring by car.

BUXTON

Lime Tree Park, Dukes Drive, Buxton, Derbyshire, SK17 9RP.
Std: 01298 **Tel:** 22988
Nearest Town/Resort Buxton.
Directions From Buxton proceed south on the A515 for ½ mile, sharp left after Buxton Hospital, ½ mile along on the right.
Open March **to** October inc.
Access Good **Site** Lev/Slope
Sites Available **Total** 100

Facilities
Nearby Facilities
Buxton.
✓✓✓✓Graded Park. Ideal location for touring the Peak District. TV room.

BUXTON

Newhaven Caravan & Camping Park, Newhaven, Nr. Buxton, Derbyshire.
Std: 01298 **Tel:** 84300
Nearest Town/Resort Buxton.
Directions Midway between Ashbourne and Buxton on A515. At the junction with A5012.
Acreage 27 **Open** March **to** October
Access Good **Site** Level
Sites Available **Total** 125
Facilities
Nearby Facilities
Buxton.
✓✓✓Graded Park. Ideal centre for touring Peak District, National Park and Derbyshire Dales.

BUXTON

Pomeroy Caravan & Camping Park, Street House Farm, Pomeroy, Nr. Flagg, Buxton, Derbyshire, SK17 9QG.
Std: 01298 **Tel:** 83259
Nearest Town/Resort Buxton
Directions From Buxton take the A515 towards Ashbourne, site is 5 miles on the right, go over the cattle grid, 200 yard tarmac drive to the site.
Acreage 2 **Open** Easter/1 April **to** 31 October
Access Good **Site** Level
Sites Available **Total** 40
Facilities
Nearby Facilities
Buxton
✓✓✓Graded Park. Site adjoins the northern end of Cromford High Peak Trail. Cycle hire centre 3 miles. Ideal walking and cycling.

BUXTON

Shallow Grange, Chelmorton, Near Buxton, Derbyshire, SK17 9SG.
Std: 01298 **Tel:** 23578
Std: 01298 **Fax:** 78242
Nearest Town/Resort Buxton
Directions From Buxton take the A515 Ashbourne road and travel for 2 to 3 miles. Turn left onto the A5270 and Shallow Grange is ½ mile on the left.
Acreage ¾ **Open** April **to** October
Access Good **Site** Sloping
Sites Available **Total** 20
Facilities
Nearby Facilities
Buxton
Walking in the SSSI Dale. Chatsworth House, Haddon Hall and Bakewell nearby.

DERBY

Shardlow Marina Caravan Park, London Road, Shardlow, Derby, Derbyshire, DE72 2GL.
Std: 01332 **Tel:** 792832
Nearest Town/Resort Derby
Directions Leave the M1 at junction 24, follow the A6 towards Derby. Follow signs to Shardlow and Cavendish Bridge. In Shardlow Village, marina is on the right, entrance beside the Navigation Inn.
Open April **to** October
Access Good **Site** Level
Sites Available **Total** 70
Facilities
Nearby Facilities
Derby
Adjacent to a marina. Convenient for Derbyshire Dales, Nottinghamshire and The American Adventure. AA 3 Pennants.

DOVERIDGE

Cavendish Cottage Camping & Caravan Site, Doveridge, Ashbourne, Derbys, DE6 5JR.
Std: 01889 **Tel:** 562092
Nearest Town/Resort Uttoxeter.
Directions On the main road in Doveridge take the sign posts for (Doveridge).
Acreage 2 **Open** All Year
Access Good **Site** Level
Sites Available **Total** 15
Facilities
Nearby Facilities
Uttoxeter
Alton Towers, Dovedale, Sudbury Hall and many pleasant walks. Owner Mr G Wood.

EDALE

Cooper's Camp & Caravan Site, New Fold Farm, Edale, Sheffield, Derbyshire, S30 2ZD.
Std: 01433 **Tel:** 670372
Nearest Town/Resort Edale
Directions We are in the centre of Edale Village, opposite the school.
Acreage 7 **Open** All Year
Access Good **Site** Sloping
Sites Available **Total** 150
Facilities
Nearby Facilities
Edale
Walking on the Pennine Way.

EDALE

Highfield Farm, Highfield Farm, Near Upper Booth, Edale, Hope Valley, S33 7ZJ.
Std: 01433 **Tel:** 670245
Nearest Town/Resort Buxton
Directions Leave the A625 at Hope Church, take minor road to Edale. Follow road, pass turning for Edale, at bottom of hill turn right, pass picnic area, access to farm.
Acreage 50 **Open** Easter **to** October
Access Good **Site** Lev/Slope
Sites Available
Facilities
Nearby Facilities
Edale.
Good walking country, near Pennine Way. Good views, quiet.

EDALE

Upper Booth Farm, Mrs. E. Hodgson, Edale, Hope Valley, S33 7ZJ.
Std: 01433 **Tel:** 670250
Nearest Town/Resort Buxton.
Acreage 3 **Open** All Year
Site Level
Sites Available **Total** 30
Facilities
Nearby Facilities
Edale.
Ideal centre for walking, climbing, caving etc. 2 miles from start of,and on Pennine Way. Tent numbers limited. Booking advisable. Stream nearby. Camping barn available (for 12).

EDALE

Waterside Camp & Caravan Site, Waterside, Barber Booth Road, Edale, Hope Valley, S33 7ZL.
Std: 01433 **Tel:** 670215
Nearest Town/Resort Sheffield.
Open April **to** September
Access Good **Site** Level
Sites Available **Total** 10
Facilities
Nearby Facilities
Edale.
Ideal for hill walking, near to the start of the Pennine Way.

HARTINGTON

Barracks Farm Caravan & Camping Site, Beresford Dale, Hartington, Buxton, Derbyshire, SK17 0HQ.
Std: 01298 **Tel:** 84261
Nearest Town/Resort Buxton
Directions Buxton A515 approx 10 miles. After leaving Buxton go on for 7 miles, turn right for Hartington B5054. Go through village for 1½ miles, turn left for Beresford

Dale, continue for ¼ mile then turn left again signposted Beresford Dale. The site is second on the left.
Acreage 5 **Open** Easter **to** End Oct
Access Good **Site** Level
Sites Available **Total** 40
Facilities
Nearby Facilities
Buxton.
Alongside river, scenic views and ideal touring.

HARTINGTON

Waterloo Inn, Main Street, Biggin, By Hartington, Derbyshire, SK17 0DH.
Std: 01298 **Tel:** 84284
Nearest Town/Resort Buxton
Directions From Buxton take the main A515 to Ashbourne, first turning right at Newhaven, Biggin well signposted. 10 miles from Buxton, 10 miles from Ashbourne.
Acreage 2 **Open** All Year
Access Good **Site** Sloping
Sites Available **Total** 20
Facilities
Nearby Facilities
Buxton
Ideal for touring, walking and cycling, pony trekking.

HATHERSAGE

Swallow Holme Caravan Park, Station Road, Bamford, Hope Valley, S33 0BN.
Std: 01433 **Tel:** 650981
Directions A6013 12 miles west of Sheffield.
Acreage 2¼ **Open** April **to** October
Access Good **Site** Level
Sites Available **Total** 60
Facilities
Nearby Facilities
Bamford
Scenic views and ideal touring.

HAYFIELD

Camping & Caravanning Club Site, Kinder Road, Hayfield, High Peak, Derbyshire, SK22 2LE.
Std: 01663 **Tel:** 745394
Directions On the A624 Glossop to Chapel-en-le-Frith road, the Hayfield by-pass. Well signed to the village, follow wooden carved signs to the site.
Acreage 7 **Open** 22 March **to** 1 Nov
Site Level
Sites Available **Total** 90
Facilities
Nearby Facilities
New Mills
✓✓✓✓Graded Park. On the banks of the River Sett. Ideal for fell and moorland walkers. 6 miles from a Victorian style swimming pool.

HOPE

Hardhurst Farm Camping & Caravan Site, Hardhurst Farm, Brough Lane Ends, Hope, Hope Valley, S33 6RB.
Std: 01433 **Tel:** 620001
Nearest Town/Resort Sheffield/Buxton/Castleton
Directions Take the A625 west from Sheffield, travel for 12 miles.
Acreage 3 **Open** All Year
Access Good **Site** Level
Sites Available **Total** 37
Facilities
Nearby Facilities
Hope
Ideal area for walking, touring and climbing.

MATLOCK

Birchwood Farm Caravan Park, Wirksworth Road, Whatstandwell, Matlock, Derbyshire, DE4 5HS.
Std: 01629 **Tel:** 822280
Std: 01629 **Fax:** 822280
Nearest Town/Resort Matlock Bath
Directions Leave to A6 at Whatstandwell, take the B5035 towards Wirksworth, about 1 mile.
Acreage 4 **Open** April **to** October
Access Good **Site** Lev/Slope
Sites Available **Total** 70
Facilities
Nearby Facilities
Whatstandwell
✓✓Graded Park. Near High Peak Trail, ideal touring area. Carsington Water 20 minutes. Table Tennis on site.

MATLOCK

Darwin Forest Country Park, Darley Moor, Two Dales, Matlock, Derbyshire, DE4 5LN.
Std: 01629 **Tel:** 732428/735015
Std: 01629 **Fax:** 735015
Nearest Town/Resort Matlock.
Directions From Chesterfield take the A632 for Matlock, turn onto the B5057 for Darley Dale. Park is on the right hand side.
Open March **to** December
Access Good **Site** Level
Sites Available **Total** 50
Facilities
Nearby Facilities
Matlock
✓✓✓✓✓Graded Park. Set in superb woodland, excellent touring area with many attractions. Tennis on site.

MATLOCK

Merebrook Caravan Park, Derby Road, Whatstandwell, Derbyshire, DE4 5HH.
Std: 01773 **Tel:** 852154
Nearest Town/Resort Matlock/Belper.
Directions A6, 5¼ miles either way.
Acreage 1 **Open** All Year
Access Good **Site** Level
Sites Available **Total** 75
Facilities
Nearby Facilities
Whatstandwell.
✓✓✓✓Graded Park. Alongside river, scenic views. Ideal for local attractions. Open for tents March to October, Tourers all year. Fishing on site.

MATLOCK

Packhorse Farm, Packhorse Farm Bungalow, Tansley, Matlock, Derbyshire, DE4 5LF.
Std: 01629 **Tel:** 582781
Nearest Town/Resort Matlock
Directions Take the A615 from the M1, 4 miles from Matlock.
Acreage 2 **Open** All Year
Access Good **Site** Level
Sites Available **Total** 30
Facilities

Nearby Facilities
Matlock
✓✓✓✓Graded Park. Ideal for fishing and touring the Peak District.

MATLOCK

Pinegroves Caravan Park, High Lane, Tansley, Matlock, Derbys.
Std: 01629 **Tel:** 534815
Nearest Town/Resort Matlock.
Directions From the M1 junction 28, take the A38 then the A615 towards Matlock. 2 miles past Wessington, turn left at crossroads into High Lane. Site is 600yds on the left.
Acreage 7 **Open** April **to** 30 October
Access Good **Site** Level
Sites Available **Total** 60
Facilities
Nearby Facilities
Matlock
Quiet site in woodland and open countryside. Static caravans for sale.

MATLOCK

Sycamore Caravan Park, Lant Lane, Nr. Tansley, Matlock, Derbyshire, DE4 5LF.
Std: 01629 **Tel:** 55760
Fax: On Request
Nearest Town/Resort Matlock
Directions From the A615 in Tansley, turn onto Church Street and follow for 1½ miles, turn left after a row of bungalows on the left.
Acreage 3 **Open** 15 March **to** 31 October
Access Good **Site** Level
Sites Available **Total** 35
Facilities
Nearby Facilities
Matlock
✓✓✓✓Graded Park. Quiet, country site, set amongst the rolling Derbyshire Dales. Well equipped site, perfect for families.

WHALEY BRIDGE

Ringstones Caravan Park, Yeardsley Lane, Furness Vale, Whaley Bridge, Derbyshire.
Std: 01663 **Tel:** 732152
Nearest Town/Resort Whaley Bridge.
Directions From Whaley Bridge take A6 towards Stockport, in Furness Vale turn left at Pelican crossing (Cantonese resturant on corner).
Acreage 3 **Open** March **to** October
Access Good **Site** Lev/Slope
Sites Available
Facilities
Nearby Facilities
Furness Vale.

DEVON

ASHBURTON

Ashburton Caravan Park, Waterleat, Ashburton, Devon, TQ13 7HU.
Std: 01364 **Tel:** 652552
Std: 01364 **Fax:** 652552
Nearest Town/Resort Ashburton/Newton Abbot.
Directions Off A38, Ashburton Centre North Street bear right before bridge signposted Waterleat 1½ miles.
Acreage 2 **Open** Easter **to** September
Access Reasonable **Site** Level
Sites Available **Total** 35
Facilities
Nearby Facilities
Newton Abbot.
✓✓✓✓✓Graded Park. In beautiful wooded valley, River Ashburn flowing through. Within Dartmoor National Park.

ASHBURTON

Landscove Camping Site, Landscove, Ashburton, Newton Abbot, Devon.
Std: 01803 **Tel:** 762225
Nearest Town/Resort Ashburton
Directions From A38 at Ashburton take Slipway (Peartree). Follow signs to Landscove for 2¼ miles to Woolston Green.
Acreage ¼ **Open** Easter **to** End of Sept
Site Level
Sites Available **Total** 6
Facilities
Nearby Facilities
Quiet country site by village green. Near Dartmoor and within easy reach of the sea.

ASHBURTON

Parkers Farm Holiday Park, Higher Mead Farm, Ashburton, Devon, TQ13 7LJ.
Std: 01364 **Tel:** 652598
Std: 01364 **Fax:** 654004
Nearest Town/Resort Ashburton
Directions Take the A38 to Plymouth, when you see the sign 26 miles Plymouth take second left at Alston Cross marked Woodland - Denbury. The site is behind the bungalow.
Acreage 10 **Open** April **to** October
Access Good **Site** Level Terrace
Sites Available **Total** 60
Facilities
Nearby Facilities
Newton Abbot
✓✓✓✓Graded Park. A real working farm enviroment with goats, sheep, pigs, cows, ducks and rabbits set amidst beautiful countryside.

ASHBURTON

The River Dart Country Park, Holne Park, Ashburton, Devon, TQ13 7NP.
Std: 01364 **Tel:** 652511
Std: 01364 **Fax:** 652020
Nearest Town/Resort Ashburton
Directions A38 Devon expressway at Exeter/Plymouth. Follow brown signs from Ashburton.
Acreage 90 **Open** Easter/1 April **to** Sept
Access Good **Site** Level
Sites Available **Total** 120
Facilities
Nearby Facilities
Newton Abbot
✓✓✓✓✓Graded Park. Magnificent site alongside the River Dart. Ideal touring site for Dartmoor and the South Devon coast.

AXMINSTER

Andrewshayes Caravan Park, Dalwood, Axminster, Devon.
Std: 01404 **Tel:** 831225
Std: 01404 **Fax:** 831893
Nearest Town/Resort Seaton.
Directions A35 Axminster 3 miles. Honiton 6 miles. Take 2nd. turning signpost Dalwood and Stockland. Site entrance 100yds. off A35.
Acreage 10 **Open** March **to** 31 January
Access Good **Site** Sloping
Sites Available **Total** 90
Facilities
Nearby Facilities
Axminster.
✓✓✓✓Graded Park. Peaceful, clean park in beautiful countryside. Ideal for family holiday. Easy reach of resorts. New toilet building with family rooms and disabled room.

BARNSTAPLE

Midland Holiday Park, Braunton Road, Ashford, Barnstaple, North Devon, EX31 4AU.
Std: 01271 **Tel:** 343691
Std: 01271 **Fax:** 326355
Nearest Town/Resort Barnstaple
Directions Take the A361 from Barnstaple signposted Braunton and Ilfracombe. The park is on the right 3 miles out of Barnstaple.
Acreage 8 **Open** Easter **to** Mid-Nov
Access Good **Site** Level
Sites Available **Total** 95
Facilities
Nearby Facilities
Barnstaple
On the River Taw Estuary. Ideally situated for all beaches, shops, attractions and all sports. Exmoor and The Tarka Trail.

BERRYNARBOR

Watermouth Cove Holiday Park, Berrynarbor, Nr. Ilfracombe, North Devon, EX34 9SJ.
Std: 01271 **Tel:** 862504
Nearest Town/Resort Ilfracombe/Combe Martin.
Directions Leave the M5 at junction 27 and join the North Devon link road. Leave the link road at Aller Cross roundabout and follow signs for Combe Martin. Go through Combe Martin and Watermouth is 2 miles on.
Acreage 27 **Open** Easter **to** End October
Access Good **Site** Level
Sites Available **Total** 90
Facilities
Nearby Facilities
Barnstaple.
√√√Graded Park. Picturesque views and private sandy beach. Headland walks. Adjacent to small craft harbour.

BIDEFORD

Steart Farm Touring Park, Horns Cross, Bideford, Devon, EX39 5DW.
Std: 01237 **Tel:** 431836
Nearest Town/Resort Bideford
Directions From Bideford follow the A39 west (signed Bude). Pass through Fairy Cross and Horns Cross, 2 miles after Horns Cross site will be on the right. 8 miles from Bideford.
Acreage 10¼ **Open** Easter **to** October
Access Good **Site** Lev/Slope
Sites Available **Total** 60
Facilities
Nearby Facilities
Barnstaple
√√√Graded Park. Set in 17 acres overlooking Bideford Bay, 1 mile from the sea. 2¼ acre dog exercise area and daytime dog kenelling. 2 acre childrens play area.

BRATTON FLEMING

Greenacres Farm Touring Caravan Park, Bratton Fleming, Barnstaple, North Devon, EX31 4SG.
Std: 01598 **Tel:** 763334
Nearest Town/Resort Barnstaple.
Directions From North Devon link road (A361), turn right at Northaller roundabout (by Little Chef). Take the A399 to Blackmoor Gate, approx 10 miles. Park signed (300yds from the A399).
Acreage 4 **Open** April **to** October
Access Good **Site** Level
Sites Available **Total** 30
Facilities
Nearby Facilities
Barnstaple
√√√√Graded Park. Moors and coast 5 miles, towns 10 miles. Peaceful, secluded park with scenic views. Ideal for touring, walking and cycling.

BRAUNTON

Chivenor Caravan Park, Chivenor Cross, Braunton, Barnstaple, North Devon, EX31 4BN.
Std: 01271 **Tel:** 812217
Nearest Town/Resort Braunton
Directions On the A361 Barnstaple to Braunton road, on the only roundabout between the two.
Acreage 3 **Open** March **to** November
Access Good **Site** Level
Sites Available **Total** 40
Facilities
Nearby Facilities
Barnstaple
100 yards from the Tarka Trail. Saunton Sands 3 miles. Central for touring North Devon.

BRAUNTON

Lobb Fields Caravan & Camping Park, Saunton Road, Braunton, Devon, EX33 1EB.
Std: 01271 **Tel:** 812090
Std: 01271 **Fax:** 812090
Nearest Town/Resort Braunton
Directions A361 to Braunton, turn left onto B3231. The park is 1 mile on the right.
Acreage 14 **Open** 28 March **to** 31 Oct
Access Good **Site** Level
Sites Available **Total** 180
Facilities
Nearby Facilities
Barnstaple
√√√√Graded Park. Facing south with panoramic views. Quiet site with Saunton beach and golf course 1¼ miles away. Dogs on leads.

BRIXHAM

Centry Touring Caravans & Tents, Mudberry House, Centry Road, Brixham, Devon, TQ5 9EY.
Std: 01803 **Tel:** 853215
Nearest Town/Resort Brixham
Directions Approach on the A3022 and go into Brixham town centre, at the traffic lights turn right into Bolton Street, at the next traffic lights turn left up Rea Barn Hill, bear right past the rugby club and we are ½ mile on the left.
Acreage 1½ **Open** Easter **to** October
Access Good **Site** Level
Sites Available **Total** 30
Facilities
Nearby Facilities
Paignton
√√Graded Park. Adjacent to Berry Head Country Park and coastal path. Only a 10 minute walk from the town and harbour. Ideal for all leisure activities.

BRIXHAM

Galmpton Touring Park, Greenway Road, Galmpton, Brixham, Devon, TQ5 0EP.
Std: 01803 **Tel:** 842066
Std: 01803 **Fax:** 844405
Nearest Town/Resort Brixham
Directions Signposted right off the A379 Brixham road ¼ mile past the end of the A380 Torbay ring road.
Acreage 10 **Open** Easter **to** September
Access Good **Site** Lev/Slope
Sites Available **Total** 120
Facilities
Nearby Facilities
Paignton
√√√√Graded Park. Terraced site with stunning River Dart views, in a central Torbay location.

BRIXHAM

Hillhead Camp, Brixham, Devon, TQ5 0HH.
Std: 01803 **Tel:** Off842336 Site853204
Nearest Town/Resort Brixham.
Directions Follow A380 towards Brixham. Turn on to A379 (Dartmouth) at Gliddon Ford Garage (avoiding Brixham town centre.) After B.P. garage Take left fork (Kingswear Lower Ferry) camp 300 yds
Acreage 12½ **Open** Easter **to** October
Site Lev/Slope
Sites Available **Total** 330
Facilities
Nearby Facilities
Paignton.
Near beaches and river overlooking sea. Panoramic views of sea and country.

BUCKFAST

Churchill Farm, Buckfastleigh, Devon, TQ11 0EZ.
Std: 01364 **Tel:** 642844
Nearest Town/Resort Buckfastleigh/Buckfast.
Directions Exit A38 at Dartbridge, follow signs for Buckfast Abbey, proceed up hill to crossroads. Turn left into no-through road towards church. Farm entrance is opposite the church 1½ miles from the A38.
Acreage 2 **Open** Easter **to** October

Access Good **Site** Lev/Slope
Sites Available **Total** 25
Facilities
Nearby Facilities
Totnes.
Stunning views of Dartmoor and Buckfast Abbey, the latter being within easy walking distance as are the Steam Railway, Butterfly Farm, Otter Sanctuary and local inns. Seaside resort 10 miles.

BUCKFASTLEIGH

Beara Farm Camping Site, Colston Road, Buckfastleigh, Devon.
Std: 01364. **Tel:** 642234
Nearest Town/Resort Buckfastleigh.
Directions Coming from Exeter take first left after passing South Devon Steam Railway and Butterfly Centre at Buckfastleigh, signpost marked Beara, fork right at next turning then 1 mile to site, signposted on roadside and junctions.
Acreage 3¼ **Open** All Year
Access Good **Site** Level
Sites Available **Total** 30
Facilities
Nearby Facilities
Totnes.
Quiet, select, sheltered site adjoining River Dart. Within easy reach of sea and moors and 1½ miles southeast of Buckfastleigh.

CHAGFORD

Woodland Springs Touring Park, Venton, Near Chagford, Devon, EX6 6PG.
Std: 01647 **Tel:** 231695
Nearest Town/Resort Okehampton
Directions From Exeter take the A30, after 17 miles turn left at Merrymeet roundabout onto the A382 towards Moretonhampstead, after 1½ miles the park is on the left, signpost Venton.
Acreage 4 **Open** 14 March **to** 14 Nov
Access Good **Site** Level
Sites Available **Total** 85
Facilities
Nearby Facilities
Exeter
Secluded site within the Dartmoor National Park, ideal for walking on the moor. Central for touring Devon and Cornwall.

CHUDLEIGH

Finlake Holiday Park, Chudleigh, Nr. Newton Abbot, Devon, TQ13 0EJ.
Std: 01626 **Tel:** 853833
Std: 01626 **Fax:** 854031
Nearest Town/Resort Newton Abbot/ Teignmouth
Directions Take the A38 towards Plymouth, exit at Chudleigh Knighton slip road. Turn right and Finlake is ½ mile on the right.
Acreage 130 **Open** All Year
Access Good **Site** Level
Sites Available **Total** 420
Facilities
Nearby Facilities
Newton Abbot
Situated in a wooded valley, some pitches overlooking a lake.

CHUDLEIGH

Holmans Wood Tourist Park, Harcombe, Cross, Chudleigh, Devon, TQ13 0DZ.
Std: 01626 **Tel:** 853785
Nearest Town/Resort Chudleigh.
Directions From Exeter take the A38 Towards Plymouth. Go past the racecourse and after 1 mile take the B3344 for Chudleigh. We are on the left at the end of the sliproad.
Acreage 11 **Open** March **to** End October
Access Good **Site** Level
Sites Available **Total** 144
Facilities
Nearby Facilities
Newton Abbot.
✓✓✓✓Graded Park. Ideal touring for Dartmoor, Haldon Forest, Exeter and Torbay.

CLOVELLY

Dyke Green Farm, Clovelly, Bideford, Devon, EX39 5RU.
Std: 01237 **Tel:** 431279
Nearest Town/Resort Clovelly.
Directions On roundabout at Clovelly Cross.
Acreage 3½ **Open** March **to** October
Access Good **Site** Level
Sites Available
Facilities
Nearby Facilities
Barnstaple.
Clovelly village and beach. Sheltered bays, ideal walks etc.

COMBE MARTIN

Newberry Farm, Combe Martin, North Devon, EX34 0AT.
Std: 01271 **Tel:** 882334
Nearest Town/Resort Combe Martin/ Ilfracombe.
Directions Leave the M5 at junction 27 and take the A361 to Aller Cross Roundabout. A399 to Combe Martin.
Acreage 6 **Open** Easter **to** October
Access Good **Site** Level
Sites Available **Total** 100
Facilities

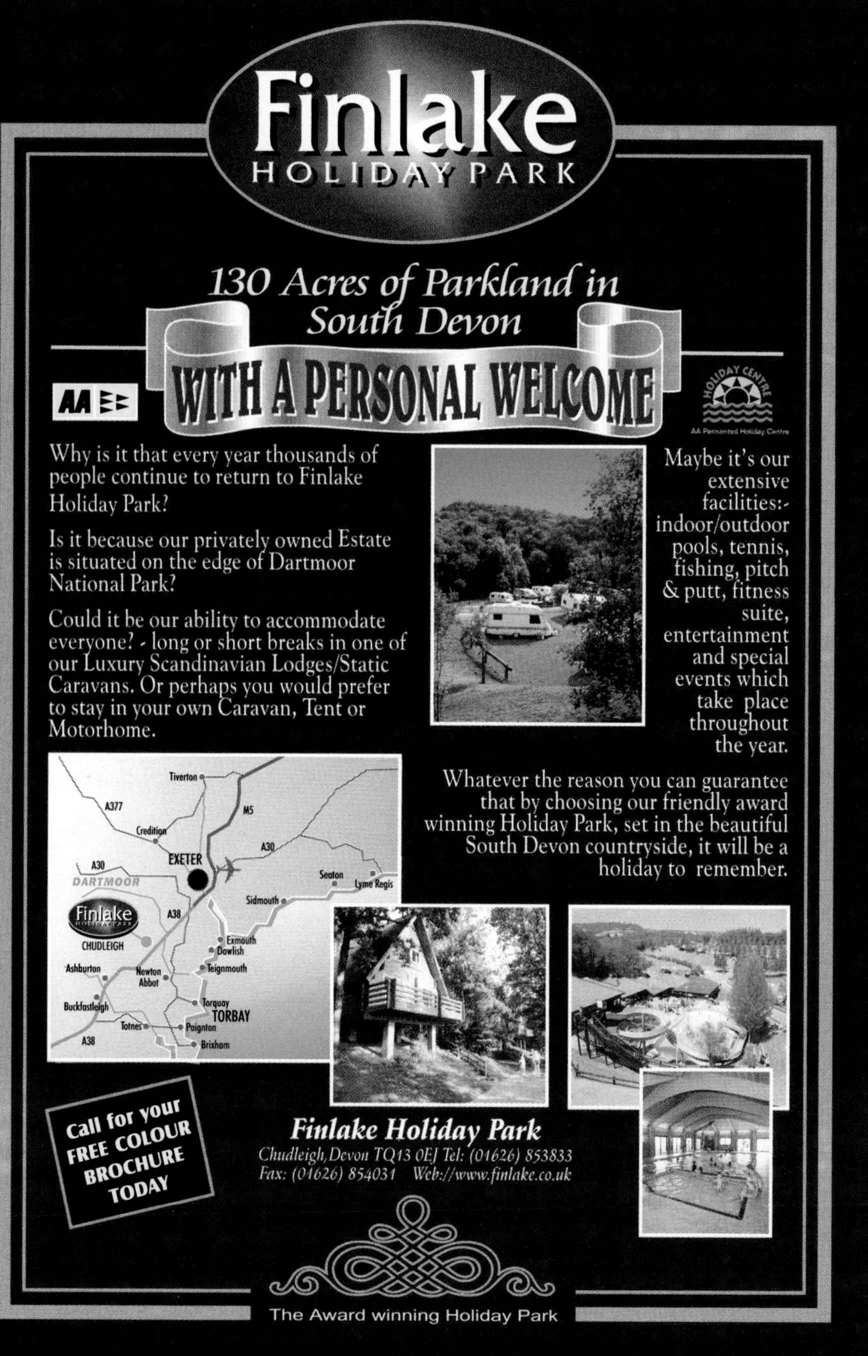
Finlake
HOLIDAY PARK
130 Acres of Parkland in South Devon
WITH A PERSONAL WELCOME
AA
HOLIDAY CENTRE
AA Pennanted Holiday Centre
Why is it that every year thousands of people continue to return to Finlake Holiday Park?
Is it because our privately owned Estate is situated on the edge of Dartmoor National Park?
Could it be our ability to accommodate everyone? - long or short breaks in one of our Luxury Scandinavian Lodges/Static Caravans. Or perhaps you would prefer to stay in your own Caravan, Tent or Motorhome.
Maybe it's our extensive facilities:- indoor/outdoor pools, tennis, fishing, pitch & putt, fitness suite, entertainment and special events which take place throughout the year.
Whatever the reason you can guarantee that by choosing our friendly award winning Holiday Park, set in the beautiful South Devon countryside, it will be a holiday to remember.
Tiverton
A377
M5
Crediton
A30
EXETER
A30
DARTMOOR
Seaton
Lyme Regis
Sidmouth
Finlake
A38
CHUDLEIGH
Exmouth
Dawlish
Teignmouth
Ashburton
Newton Abbot
Buckfastleigh
Torquay
TORBAY
Totnes
Paignton
A38
Brixham
Call for your FREE COLOUR BROCHURE TODAY
Finlake Holiday Park
Chudleigh, Devon TQ13 0EJ Tel: (01626) 853833
Fax: (01626) 854031 Web://www.finlake.co.uk
The Award winning Holiday Park

YEATHERIDGE FARM

(Touring) Caravan & Camping Park

E. WORLINGTON, CREDITON, DEVON. EX17 4TN

OFF THE A377 AND B3137 (OLD A373)

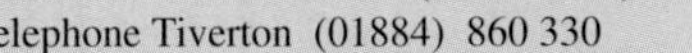

Telephone Tiverton (01884) 860 330

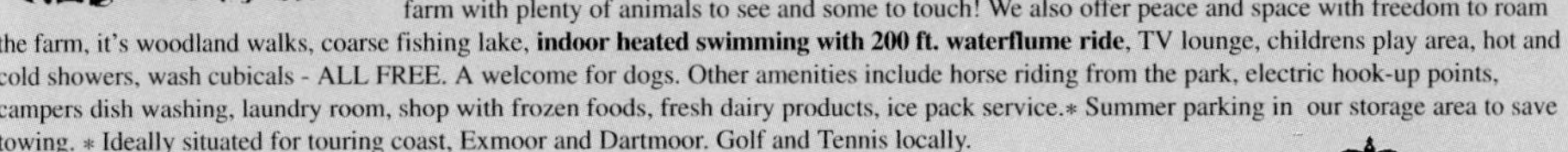

WHY ARE WE DIFFERENT? We are a small Central Park with panoramic views on a genuine working farm with plenty of animals to see and some to touch! We also offer peace and space with freedom to roam the farm, it's woodland walks, coarse fishing lake, **indoor heated swimming with 200 ft. waterflume ride**, TV lounge, childrens play area, hot and cold showers, wash cubicals - ALL FREE. A welcome for dogs. Other amenities include horse riding from the park, electric hook-up points, campers dish washing, laundry room, shop with frozen foods, fresh dairy products, ice pack service.* Summer parking in our storage area to save towing. * Ideally situated for touring coast, Exmoor and Dartmoor. Golf and Tennis locally.

ALSO: 2 CARAVANS TO LET - PROPRIETORS/OWNERS-GEOFFREY & ELIZABETH HOSEGOOD
W.C.T.B. Member WRITE, PHONE OR FAX FOR FREE COLOUR BROCHURE.

RAC

International Caravan & Camping Park

The Best of British CARAVAN & CAMPING PARKS

ROSE AWARD CARAVAN HOLIDAY PARK

A small country estate surrounded by forest in which deer roam.

LARGE, FLAT, SHELTERED CAMPING/TOURING PITCHES
MODERN FACILITIES BUILDING, LUXURY 2/6 BERTH FULL SERVICE HOLIDAY HOMES, ALSO SELF CONTAINED FLAT FOR 2 PERSONS.
FOREST GLADE HOLIDAY PARK, CULLOMPTON, DEVON EX15 2DT

COUNTRY HOLIDAY PARK

Shop, Take Away Food, Tennis Court, Adventure Play Area, Games Room, Electric Hook-up Points. Riding, Forest & Hill Walks, Gliding, Fishing & Golf are all nearby.
Freedom for the children, peace for the adults. Central for touring S.W. Easy access coast and moors.
Motor caravans welcome – Facilities for the Disabled. Dogs welcome. Tourers please book in advance.
FREE COLOUR BROCHURE
Tel: (01404) 841381 (Evgs to 8pm)
Fax: (01404) 841593

Little Cotton Caravan Park
Dartmouth

AA · BRITISH GRADED HOLIDAY PARKS

★ FOR TOURING CARAVANS ★

Close to Dartmouth, a beautiful Town Port and Historic Centre.

Park + Ride facility adjoining

★ Shop ★ Calor Gas ★ Electric Hook-ups ★ Beach 3 miles ★ Laundry Room ★ Dishwashing facilities ★ Luxurious Toilet and Shower Block ★ **Torbay and Dartmoor within easy reach** ★ Friendly family service ★ Disabled facilities ★ Payphone

National Winner "**Loo Of The Year**" Award 96/97.

Tel: (01803) 832558 Fax: (01803) 834887

Paul and Dorothy White.

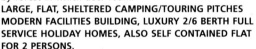

Nearby Facilities
Barnstaple.
On the edge of Exmoor National Park. 5 minute walk to Combe Martin beach and shops. NO dogs allowed.

COMBE MARTIN

Stowford Farm Meadows, Combe Martin, Devon, EX34 OPW.
Std: 01271 **Tel:** 882476
Std: 01271 **Fax:** 883053
Nearest Town/Resort Combe Martin.
Directions Situated on the A3123 Combe Martin/Woollacombe Road at Berry Down.
Acreage 140 **Open** Easter **to** October
Access Good **Site** Lev/Slope
Sites Available **Total** 570
Facilities
Nearby Facilities
Barnstaple.
✓✓✓✓Graded Park. Set in 450 acres of beautiful countryside. Ideal touring site at the heart of North Devon. Renowned for our extensive range of facilities at excellent value.

CREDITON

Yeatheridge Farm Caravan Park, East Worlington, Crediton, Devon, EX17 4TN.
Std: 01884 **Tel:** 860330
Std: 01884 **Fax:** 860330
Nearest Town/Resort Witheridge.
Directions Leave M5 at junction 27 take A361 to 1st roundabout A396 to mini-roundabout and follow A396 for approx 400yds turn right 200 yds turn left onto B3137 (Old A373) to Witheridge approx 10 miles. Turn left onto B3042 site 3¾ miles on left. Do not enter East Worlington, unsuitable for caravans. From Exeter take A377 to Barnstaple, turn right at Eggesford Station onto B3042, through Chawliegh Village the park is about 4 miles on right.
Acreage 9 **Open** Easter **to** October
Access Good **Site** Lev/Slope
Sites Available **Total** 85
Facilities
Nearby Facilities
Eggesford.
✓✓✓✓Graded Park. Heated swimming pools, coarse fishing lakes all free on site and horse riding. Scenic view from landscape park, working farm with animals.

CROYDE BAY

Bay View Farm Holidays, Bay View Farm, Croyde, Devon, EX33 1PN.
Std: 01271 **Tel:** 890501
Nearest Town/Resort Croyde
Directions At Braunton on A361 turn west on main road B3231 towards Croyde Village
Acreage 10 **Open** Easter **to** September
Site Level
Sites Available
Facilities
Nearby Facilities
Barnstaple
Near beach, 5 mins walking, Scenic views, ideal touring, booking advisable peak season. S.A.E. for information.

CROYDE BAY

Mitchums Meadow Camping/Myrtle Meadow Camping, Moor Lane, Croyde, Near Braunton, North Devon.
Std: 01271 **Tel:** 890233
Nearest Town/Resort Croyde
Directions Leave the M5 at junction 27 and take the A361 to Braunton, then take the B3231 to Croyde. Head for the centre of Croyde and follow signs for National Trust until you get to Moor Lane.
Acreage 1¼ **Open** July **to** Sept & Whitsun
Site Lev/Slope
Sites Available **Total** 30
Facilities
Nearby Facilities
Barnstaple
Small, friendly sites with outstanding views across the beach which is a 1 minute walk. Close to the village and pubs. Numerous attractions in the surrounding area. Barbecue every Saturday.

CULLOMPTON

Forest Glade Holiday Park, Cullomptom, Devon, EX15 2DT.
Std: 01404 **Tel:** 841381
Std: 01404 **Fax:** 841593
Nearest Town/Resort Cullompton.
Directions A373 Cullompton/Honiton, turn for Sheldon at Keepers Cottage Inn, 2½ miles east of Cullompton. Touring caravans via Dunkeswell Road only.
Acreage 10 **Open** Mid March **to** End Oct
Access See Directions **Site** Level
Sites Available **Total** 80
Facilities
Nearby Facilities
Honiton/Tiverton Parkway
✓✓✓✓✓Graded Park. Central for south-west twixt coast and moors. Large flat sheltered camping pitches. Caravans for hire. Free heated swimming pool and Paddling pool, riding, gliding and tennis on site.

DARTMOUTH

Deer Park Holiday Village, Dartmouth Road, Stoke Fleming, Near Dartmouth, Devon, TQ6 0RF.
Std: 01803 **Tel:** 770253
Std: 01803 **Fax:** 770320
Nearest Town/Resort Dartmouth
Directions On the A379 approx. 2 miles from Dartmouth town centre.
Acreage 8 **Open** March **to** October
Access Good **Site** Level
Sites Available **Total** 160
Facilities
Nearby Facilities
Totnes
1½ miles from the beautiful beach Blackpool Sands, lovely coastal walks. Close to historical Dartmouth.

DARTMOUTH

Leonards Cove, Stoke Fleming, Dartmouth, Devon, TQ6 0NR.
Std: 01803 **Tel:** 770206
Std: 01803 **Fax:** 770206
Nearest Town/Resort Dartmouth
Directions On A379 2 miles Dartmouth Within village of Stoke Fleming.
Acreage 1 **Open** March **to** October
Access Good **Site** Lev/Slope
Sites Available **Total** 50
Facilities
Nearby Facilities
Totnes
On clifftop spectacular views, ½ mile famous Blackpool Sands.

DARTMOUTH

Little Cotton Caravan Park, Darmouth, South Devon.
Std: 01803 **Tel:** 832558
Std: 01803 **Fax:** 834887
Nearest Town/Resort Dartmouth
Directions Leave the A38 ta Buckfastleigh, A384 to Totnes, from Totnes to Halwell on the A381. At Halwell take the A3122 Dartmouth road, park is on the right at entrance to town.
Acreage 7½ **Open** 15 March **to** October
Access Good **Site** Lev/Slope
Sites Available **Total** 95
Facilities
Nearby Facilities
Totnes
✓✓✓✓Graded Park. Scenic views, ideal touring. Park and ride service in the next field. Luxurious new toilet and shower facilities.

DARTMOUTH

Start Bay Caravan Park, Strete, Nr. Dartmouth, South Devon, TQ6 0RU.
Std: 01803 **Tel:** 770535
Std: 01803 **Fax:** 770535
Nearest Town/Resort Dartmouth
Directions 4 miles from Dartmouth on the coast road to Kingsbridge, turn right at Strete Post Office for Halwell.
Acreage 1¼ **Open** April (Easter) **to** End Sept
Access Good **Site** Level
Sites Available **Total** 25
Facilities
Nearby Facilities
Totnes
✓✓✓Graded Park. In the countryside, near the sea. Black Pool Sands and Slapton Ley.

DARTMOUTH

Woodland Leisure Park, Blackawton, Totnes, Devon, TQ9 7DQ.
Std: 01803 **Tel:** 712598
Std: 01803 **Fax:** 712680
Nearest Town/Resort Dartmouth
Directions 4 miles from Dartmouth on main road A3122 (formally B3207).
Acreage 16 **Open** 15th March **to** 15th Nov
Access Good **Site** Level
Sites Available **Total** 210
Facilities
Nearby Facilities
Totnes
✓✓✓✓✓Graded Park. Stay for TWO nights to gain FREE entrance to extensive leisure park attached, 75 acres of entertainment. 5 Water Coasters, toboggan run, 46,000 sq ft of indoor attractions, 17 playzones, animals, falconry centre and paddling pool.

DEVON'S AWARD WINNING TOURING PARK

PRACTICAL CARAVAN TOP FAMILY PARK

DARTMOUTH

VOTED THE TOP FAMILY HOLIDAY

FIRST CLASS FACILITIES

Quiet pitching lawns edged with trees and flowers surround the excellent and luxurious facilities

60 ACRES OF ENJOYMENT

Hidden in beautiful woodland are spectacular adventure zones, indoor play centres, animals and undercover Falconry

FAMOUS LEISURE PARK FREE *

3 Watercoasters,
500m Toboggan Run,
30 Slides, Bumper Boats,
Toddlers Play Villages

DISCOVER THE WONDER OF WOODLANDS

SEND FOR OUR COLOUR BROCHURE. Chris Bendall. Woodland Leisure Park, Blackawton, TOTNES TQ9 7DQ Telephone: (01803) 712598 Fax (01803) 712680

* subject to conditions

DAWLISH

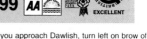

Cofton Country Holiday Park, Devon Swan Holidays, Starcross, Nr Dawlish, Devon, EX6 8RP.
Std: 01626 **Tel:** 890111
Nearest Town/Resort Dawlish Warren.
Directions On A379 Exeter - Dawlish road ½ mile after fishing village at Cockwood.
Acreage 16 **Open** Easter **to** October
Access Good **Site** Level
Sites Available **Total** 450
Facilities
Nearby Facilities
Dawlish.
✓✓✓✓✓Graded Park. In beautiful rural countryside close to sandy Dawlish Warren beach Clean and tidy family run park. Superb complex and swimming pool, Swan pub with family lounge and snack bar. Ideal centre to discover Devon. ETB Rose Award Holiday Park. See our advert on back cover.

DAWLISH

Golden Sands Holiday Park, Week Lane, Dawlish, South Devon, EX7 0LZ.
Std: 01626 **Tel:** 863099
Nearest Town/Resort Dawlish.
Directions From M5 junction 30 take the A379 Dawlish, through Starcross. After 2 miles Week Lane is the second left past filling station.
Acreage 2¼ **Open** Easter **to** October
Access Good **Site** Level
Sites Available **Total** 60
Facilities
Nearby Facilities
Dawlish
✓✓✓✓✓Graded Park. Family run for family fun! Small touring park, 2/3rds of a mile from Dawlish Warren beach with free nightly, family entertainment in the licensed club. Unique indoor/outdoor swimming pool.

DAWLISH

Lady's Mile Touring Caravan & Camping Park, Dawlish, Devon, EX7 0LX.
Std: 01626 **Tel:** 863411
Std: 01626 **Fax:** 888689
Nearest Town/Resort Dawlish.
Directions On A379 road 1 mile Exeter side of Dawlish.
Acreage 16 **Open** March **to** October
Access Good **Site** Level
Sites Available **Total** 486
Facilities
Nearby Facilities
Dawlish.
Family run popular park in green Devon countryside. Ideal touring centre. Short walk to Dawlish Warren beach. Indoor pool has a 100 foot waterslide and the outdoor pool has a 200 foot waterslide. See our colour advertisement. New 9 hole golf course, bar, disco and indoor swimming pool on site.

DAWLISH

Leadstone Camping, Warren Road, Dawlish, Devon, EX7 0NG.
Std: 01626 **Tel:** 872239/864411
Std: 01626 **Fax:** 873833
Nearest Town/Resort Dawlish.
Directions Leave the M5 at junction 30 and take signposted road A379 to Dawlish. As you approach Dawlish, turn left on brow of hill, signposted Dawlish Warren. Our site is ½ mile on right.
Acreage 7 **Open** 18 June **to** 4 September
Access Good **Site** Lev/Slope
Sites Available **Total** 160
Facilities
Nearby Facilities
Dawlish Warren.
✓✓✓✓Graded Park. Rolling grassland in a natural secluded bowl within ½ mile of sandy 2 mile Dawlish Warren Beach and nature reserve. Ideally situated for discovering Devon.

DAWLISH WARREN

Peppermint Park, Warren Road, Dawlish Warren, Devon, EX7 0PQ.
Std: 01626 **Tel:** 863436
Nearest Town/Resort Dawlish
Directions Leave M5 at Exeter and follow A379 signposted to Dawlish, turn left at Cockwood towards Dawlish Warren.
Acreage 16 **Open** Easter **to** September
Access Good **Site** Lev/Slope
Sites Available **Total** 300
Facilities
Nearby Facilities
Dawlish Warren.
✓✓✓✓✓Graded Park. Closest touring park to Dawlish Warren beach (600 metres). The only "Excellent" Graded touring park at Dawlish Warren. Grassland park sheltered by mature trees. Coarse fishing. Free nightly entertainment. AA 4 Pennants.

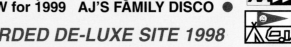

THE NEAREST TOURING PARK TO DAWLISH WARREN BEACH

Just a 680 metre level walk from Dawlish Warren's famous stretch of golden sands, you'll find Peppermint Park Touring and Camping Park. Nestled away from the road in pleasant sheltered grassland. Individually marked pitches on level terraces for touring caravans and tents – offering the best of greenery, scenery and seaside holiday fun.

Telephone now for our FREE brochure.

01626 863436 Ask for extension 1

Peppermint Park
Warren Road Dawlish Warren · South Devon EX7 0PQ

- Stylish club and bar
- Heated swimming pool and water chute
- Children's play area
- Well-stocked shop
- Coarse Fishing
- Laundrette
- Free hot water and showers.
- Electric hook-ups
- Modern toilet facilities
- Holiday homes at Peppermint Paddocks

DOLTON

Dolton Caravan Park, The Square, Dolton, Winkleigh, Devon, EX19 8QF.
Std: 01805 **Tel:** 804536
Nearest Town/Resort Great Torrington
Directions From the B3220 turn at the Beacon Garage signposted Dolton. Go into the village and turn right at the Union Inn, the site is at the rear of Royal Oak Inn.
Acreage 2¼ **Open** Mid March **to** October
Access Good **Site** Level
Sites Available **Total** 25
Facilities
Nearby Facilities
Scenic views. Ideal for touring Exmoor and Dartmoor. Walking on the Tarka Trail.

EXETER

Haldon Lodge Farm Caravan & Camping Park, Kennford, Nr. Exeter, Devon, EX6 7YG.
Std: 01392 **Tel:** 832312
Nearest Town/Resort Exeter
Directions 4¼ miles South of Exeter, ½ mile from the end of M5 turn off A38 at Kennford Services. Follow signs for Haldon Lodge turning left through Kennford Village past the Post Office. Proceed to Motorway bridge turning left to Dunchideock, 1 mile to site.
Open All Year
Access Good **Site** Lev/Slope
Sites Available
Facilities
Nearby Facilities
Exeter
Peaceful family site with beautiful forest scenery, nature walks, fishing lakes, riding holidays and barbeques. Excellent touring centre. Sea and Exeter 15 minutes.

EXETER

Heazille Barton, Rewe, Exeter, Devon, EX5 4HB.
Std: 01392 **Tel:** 860253
Std: 01392 **Fax:** 861100
Nearest Town/Resort Exeter
Directions Take the A396 from Exeter towards Tiverton. Go through Rewe and turn right ¼ mile onto unclassified road, ¼ mile on the right.
Acreage ½ **Open** May **to** October
Access Good **Site** Level
Sites Available **Total** 5
Facilities
Nearby Facilities
Exeter
Very quiet site, easily accessible to the moors and National Trust.

EXETER

Kennford International Caravan Park, Exeter, Devon, EX6 7YN.
Std: 01392 **Tel:** 833046
Nearest Town/Resort Exeter.
Directions ½ mile from end of M5 on A38. 4 miles south of Exeter.
Acreage 8 **Open** All Year
Access Good **Site** Level
Sites Available **Total** 120
Facilities
Nearby Facilities
Exeter.
✓✓✓✓Graded Park. Excellent touring centre in beautiful rural setting with easy access to main roads. Individually hedged sites. Children's adventure playground. Family lounge and bar with takeaway and the very popular log fire cabin. Holiday bungalows and caravans to rent.

EXMOUTH

Castle Brake, Castle Lane, Woodbury, Near Exeter, Devon, EX5 1HA.
Std: 01395 **Tel:** 232431
Nearest Town/Resort Exmouth
Directions M5 junction 30 take the A3052 to Halfway Inn. Turn right onto the B3180, after 2 miles turn right to Woodbury. The park is 500yds on the right.
Acreage 10 **Open** March **to** October
Access Good **Site** Level
Sites Available **Total** 42
Facilities
Nearby Facilities
Exmouth
Beautiful views of the River Exe. Exmouth beach 4 miles. Good touring centre for East Devon and beyond.

EXMOUTH

Devon Cliffs Holiday Centre, Sandy Bay, Exmouth, Devon, EX8 5BT.
Std: 01395 **Tel:** 226226
Std: 01395 **Fax:** 223111
Nearest Town/Resort Exmouth
Directions Turn off the M5 at exit 30 and take the A376 for Exmouth. At Exmouth follow the signs to Sandy Bay.
Acreage 10 **Open** Easter **to** November
Access Good **Site** Lev/Slope
Sites Available **Total** 195
Facilities
Nearby Facilities
Exmouth
✓✓✓✓Graded Park. Overlooking the beautiful Sandy Bay, with access to a private beach.

EXMOUTH

Webbers Farm Caravan Park, Castle Lane, Woodbury, Exeter, Devon, EX5 1EA.
Std: 01395 **Tel:** 232276
Std: 01395 **Fax:** 233389
Nearest Town/Resort Exmouth
Directions Leave the M5 junction 30 (Exeter Services) and follow the A376 Exmouth road. At the second roundabout take the B3179 (Budleigh Salterton/Woodbury). From the village centre follow the International signs.
Acreage 8 **Open** Easter **to** September
Access Good **Site** Lev/Slope
Sites Available **Total** 100
Facilities
Nearby Facilities
Exmouth
✓✓✓✓Graded Park. Outstanding view over the River Exe towards Dartmoor. 4 miles from the sea, quiet popular site. Van storage available.

HAWKCHURCH

Hunters Moon Touring Park, Hawkchurch, Axminster, Devon, EX13 5UL.
Std: 01297 **Tel:** 678402
Std: 01297 **Fax:** 678402
Nearest Town/Resort Lyme Regis
Directions From Axminster take A35 towards Dorchester for 3 miles. At main crossroads take left B3165 towards Crewkerne. Follow for 2¼ miles turn left to Hunters Moon.
Acreage 8 **Open** All Year
Access Good **Site** Level
Sites Available **Total** 179
Facilities
Nearby Facilities
Axminster.
✓✓✓✓Graded Park. Super views over Axe Valley. All weather bowling greens, boules pitch and pitch & putt.

HOLSWORTHY

Hedley Wood Caravan & Camping Park, Bridgerule, Near Bude, Holsworthy, Devon, EX22 7ED.
Std: 01288 **Tel:** 381404
Std: 01288 **Fax:** 381404
Nearest Town/Resort Bude
Directions Travel west on A3072 from Holsworthy for 5¼ miles, turn left on B3254 for 2¼ miles turn right, site entrance 500 yards on right (signposted).
Acreage 8 **Open** All Year
Access Good **Site** Lev/Slope
Sites Available **Total** 120
Facilities
Nearby Facilities
A friendly, family run, 16 acre woodland site with a laid back atmosphere. Daily kennelling facility and dog walk. Static and touring vans for hire and caravan storage available. Clay pigeon shooting. Nature trail. E-mail : hedleywood.demon.co.uk

HOLSWORTHY

Noteworthy, Bude Main Road, Holsworthy, Devon.
Std: 01409 **Tel:** Holsworthy 253731
Std: 01409 **Fax:** 253731
Nearest Town/Resort Holsworthy/Bude.
Directions 2½ miles west of Holsworthy on A3072.
Acreage 5 **Open** June **to** August
Access Good **Site** Level
Sites Available
Facilities
Nearby Facilities
Exeter.
Views, 6 miles Cornish coast. Rural site.

HONITON

Camping & Caravanning Club Site, Otter Valley Park, Honiton, Devon, EX14 8ST.
Std: 01404 **Tel:** 44546
Directions From the A30 leave at the first exit for Honiton, keep left off the slip road and keep going left. (Road skirts the perimeter of the site).
Acreage 5 **Open** 22 March **to** 1 Nov
Site Level
Sites Available **Total** 89
Facilities
Nearby Facilities
Honiton
✓✓✓Graded Park. In the valley of the River Otter, a great start for a visit to the South West. AA 3 Pennants.

HONITON

Fishponds House, Dunkeswell, Near Honiton, Devon, EX14 0SH.
Std: 01404 **Tel:** 891358
Std: 01404 **Fax:** 891109
Nearest Town/Resort Honiton
Directions From Honiton take the A303 and follow signs to Luppitt and Smeatharpe. At Luppitt Common crossroads, RAC sign points the direction to Fishponds House. 6 miles from Honiton.
Acreage 5 **Open** All Year
Access Good **Site** Level
Sites Available **Total** 15
Facilities
Nearby Facilities
Honiton
Lakeside pitches in an area of outstanding natural beauty. Wildlife Sanctuary.

ILFRACOMBE

Big Meadow Touring Caravan & Camping Park, Watermouth, Ilfracombe, Devon. EX34 9SJ
Std: 01271 **Tel:** 862282
Nearest Town/Resort Ilfracombe
Directions Situated on the A399 coastal road approximately 2 miles from Ilfracombe, opposite Watermouth Castle Tourist Attraction.
Acreage 9 **Open** Easter **to** 31 October
Access Good **Site** Level
Sites Available **Total** 125
Facilities
Nearby Facilities
Barnstaple
Near Watermouth Harbour, sheltered family site with stream running through.

MULLACOTT CARAVANS

Touring Caravan & Camping Pitches

Situated between the Golden Sands of Woolacombe and the picturesque seaside harbour town of Ilfracombe. All in Glorious North Devon.

Mullacott Cross Caravan Park
Ilfracombe, EX34 8NB
Or Phone - (01271) 862212

Facilities Include:

- Licensed Bar & Restaurant
- Off License & Food Shop
- Children's Play Area
- Launderette
- Telephone Kiosks
- Electric & Water Hook-ups
- On Main Bus Route
- Comprehensive Caravan & Camping Shop

FREE

- Showers
- Children Under 5
- Awnings
- Dogs (under strict control)

Napps Caravan Site

Friendly and popular, well kept family site in probably the most beautiful coastal setting you will see, offering terrific value for money and superb modern facilities.

Bar, Swimming Pool, Tennis Court etc.

THE FIVE STAR SITE BY THE SEA.

"Impressive not only for its setting but also for its state of cleanliness"
- Buccaneer Owners Club.

"One of North Devon's top six sites"
- Practical Caravan Mag.

"Simply the best"
- Owners, Staff and Regulars.

For colour brochure and full site details please write or phone:
OLD COAST ROAD, BERRYNARBOR, ILFRACOMBE, NORTH DEVON. EX34 9SW
Tel/Fax: (01271) 882557

ILFRACOMBE

Hele Valley Holiday Park, Dept C, Hele Bay, Ilfracombe, North Devon, EX34 9RD.
Std: 01271 **Tel:** 862460
Std: 01271 **Fax:** 867926
Nearest Town/Resort Ilfracombe.
Directions Take A399 to Ilfracombe turn at signpost Hele village, to bottom of lane, take righthand turning into Holiday Park.
Acreage 4 **Open** Easter **to** End October
Access Good **Site** Level
Sites Available **Total** 50
Facilities
Nearby Facilities
Barnstaple.
Only camping park in Ilfracombe. Beach only a few minutes walk. Tranquil, secluded valley. Alongside stream, scenic views.

ILFRACOMBE

Little Meadow Camp Site, Watermouth, Ilfracombe, Devon, EX34 9SJ.
Std: 01271 **Tel:** 862222
Nearest Town/Resort Ilfracombe
Directions On A399 between Ifracombe and Combe Martin.
Acreage 5 **Open** Whitsun **to** September
Access Good **Site** Terraced
Sites Available **Total** 50
Facilities
Nearby Facilities
Barnstaple
Quiet and peaceful and the best view in Devon.

ILFRACOMBE

Mill Park Touring Site, Berrynarbor, Nr. Ilfracombe. Devon, EX34 9SH.
Std: 01271 **Tel:** 882647
Nearest Town/Resort Ilfracombe.
Directions Situated on the A399 coast road between Combe Martin and Ilfracombe near Watermouth Castle. Take the turning opposite the Sawmills Inn signposted to Berrynarbor.
Acreage 30 **Open** 15th March **to** 15th Nov
Access Good **Site** Level
Sites Available **Total** 165
Facilities
Nearby Facilities
Barnstaple.
Well sheltered site with woodland walks. Coarse fishing lake. Well stocked shop, take away food, off licence, laundry, etc..

ILFRACOMBE

Mullacott Cross Caravan Park, Mullacott Cross, Ilfracombe, Devon, EX34 8NB.
Std: 01271 **Tel:** 862212
Std: 01271 **Fax:** 862979
Nearest Town/Resort Ilfracombe
Directions On A361 1½ miles south of Ilfracombe.
Acreage 5 **Open** Easter **to** Mid Oct
Access Good **Site** Lev/Slope
Sites Available **Total** 110
Facilities
Nearby Facilities
Barnstaple
✓✓✓✓Graded Park. Excellent centre for touring North Devon.

ILFRACOMBE

Napps Caravan Site, Napps, Old Coast Road, Berrynarbor, Ilfracombe, North Devon.
Std: 01271 **Tel:** 882557
Std: 01271 **Fax:** 882557
Nearest Town/Resort Ilfracombe.
Directions On A399, 1¼ miles west of Combe Martin, turn right onto Old Coast Road (signposted). Site 400yds along Old Coast Road.
Acreage 11 **Open** March **to** November
Access Good **Site** Level
Sites Available **Total** 250
Facilities
Nearby Facilities
Barnstaple.
Probably the most beautiful coastal setting you will see. Beach 200yds. Popular family site with woodland and coastal walks, tennis on site. Summer parking and Winter storage available.

ILFRACOMBE

Sandaway Beach Holiday Park, John Fowler Holidays, Combe Martin, Ilfracombe, Devon.
Std: 01271 **Tel:** 883155
Std: 01271 **Fax:** 866791
Nearest Town/Resort Ilfracombe
Directions ½ mile from Combe Martin towards Ilfracombe.
Open March **to** October
Access Good **Site** Level
Sites Available **Total** 25
Facilities
Nearby Facilities
Barnstaple
✓✓✓✓Graded Park. Breathtaking sea views and our own private beach.

IVYBRIDGE

Cheston Caravan & Camping Park, Folly Cross, Wrangaton Road, South Brent, Devon, TQ10 9HF.
Std: 01364 **Tel:** 72586
Nearest Town/Resort Ivybridge.
Directions From Exeter, after by-passing South Brent, turn left at Wrangaton Cross slip road then right A38. From Plymouth take South Brent (Woodpecker) turn, at end of slip road turn right, go under A38 and rejoin A38 and follow directions from Exeter.
Acreage 1¼ **Open** 15th March **to** 15th Jan
Access Good **Site** Level
Sites Available **Total** 23
Facilities
Nearby Facilities
Set in beautiful Dartmoor. Perfect for touring, walking and bird watching. Nearest beach 9 miles. Pets welcome. Easy access from A38.

IVYBRIDGE

Whiteoaks Caravan & Camp Site, Davids Lane, Filham, Ivybridge, Devon, PL21 0DW.
Std: 01752 **Tel:** 892340
Nearest Town/Resort Ivybridge
Directions Turn off the A38 (Exeter to Plymouth road) at signpost for Ermington and Modbury onto the B3213 (Ivybridge). In about 2 miles turn left at Daveys X. Site is on the right in 100yds.
Acreage 1 **Open** 15 March **to** 15 Nov
Access Good **Site** Level
Sites Available **Total** 24
Facilities
Nearby Facilities
Ivybridge
On the edge of Dartmoor, at the start/finish of "Two Moors Way". Ideal for walkers.

KINGSBRIDGE

Camping & Caravanning Club Site, Middle Grounds, Slapton, Kingsbridge, Devon, TQ7 1QW.
Std: 01548 **Tel:** 580538
Directions From Kingsbridge take the S379, site entrance is ¼ mile from the A379, beyond the brow of the hill approaching Slapton Village.
Acreage 5½ **Open** 22 March **to** 1 Nov
Site Level
Sites Available **Total** 115
Facilities
Nearby Facilities
✓✓✓✓✓Graded Park. Overlooking Start Bay, just a few minutes from the beach. CLUB MEMBER CARAVANS ONLY.

KINGSBRIDGE

Island Lodge, Stumpy Post Cross, Kingsbridge, Devon, TQ7 4BL.
Std: 01548 **Tel:** Kingsbridge 852956
Nearest Town/Resort Kingsbridge.
Directions Travelling from Totnes to Kingsbridge on A381 turn right onto A381 at Stumpy Post Cross then turn first left into lane leading to site entrance. Approx 200yds from Stumpy Post Cross.
Acreage 3 **Open** Easter **to** November
Access Good **Site** Level
Sites Available **Total** 35
Facilities
Nearby Facilities
Totnes.
Small, friendly site with new purpose built facilities. Sea glimpses, very central for all beaches and villages in the South Hams area. Easy reach of Dartmoor and the cities of Plymouth and Exeter. Suitable for families with young children. Proprietor - Mrs Kay Parker.

KINGSBRIDGE

Karrageen Caravan & Camping Site, Bolberry, Malborough, Kingsbridge, Devon, TQ7 3EN.
Std: 01548 **Tel:** 561230
Std: 01548 **Fax:** 560192
Nearest Town/Resort Salcombe
Directions Take the A381 Kingsbridge to Salcombe road, turn sharp right into Malborough Village. In 0.6 miles turn right (signposted Bolberry), after 0.9 miles the site is on the right and reception is at the house on the left.
Acreage 7½ **Open** 15 March **to** 15 Nov
Access Good **Site** Lev/slope
Sites Available **Total** 75
Facilities
Nearby Facilities
Totnes/Plymouth
✓✓✓✓Graded Park. Nearest and best park to Hope Cove, beaches 1 mile away. Situated in beautiful, scenic countryside and surrounded by superb National Trust coastline. Parents and baby room and family shower room. Hot take-away food. Superb cliff top walking. A site with a view. See our advertisement under Salcombe.

KINGSBRIDGE

Mounts Farm Touring Park, The Mounts, Nr. East Allington, Kingsbridge, South Devon, TQ9 7QJ.
Std: 01548 **Tel:** 521591
Nearest Town/Resort Kingsbridge.
Directions On the A381 Totnes/ Kingsbridge. 3 miles north of Kingsbridge. Entrance from A381 - DO NOT go to East Allington Village.
Acreage 6 **Open** April **to** October
Access Good **Site** Level
Sites Available **Total** 50
Facilities
Nearby Facilities
Totnes.
In an area of outstanding natural beauty. Ideal for touring all South Devon.

LYDFORD

Camping & Caravanning Club Site, Lydford, Near Okehampton, Devon, EX20 4BE.
Std: 01822 **Tel:** 820275
Nearest Town/Resort Lydford
Directions A30 take the A386 signposted Tavistock and Lydford Gorge. Pass the Fox Hounds Public House on the left, turn right signposted Lydford. At the war memorial turn right, right fork, site is on the left.
Open 22 March **to** 1 Nov
Access Good **Site** Lev/Slope
Sites Available **Total** 70
Facilities
Nearby Facilities
Lydford
✓✓✓✓Graded Park. Situated in a quiet rural setting, overlooking a river. On the edge of Dartmoor, close to the moors, Lydford Gorge and castle.

LYNTON

Camping & Caravanning Club Site, Caffyn's Cross, Lynton, Devon, EX35 6JS.
Std: 01598 **Tel:** 752379
Nearest Town/Resort Lynton
Directions For Caravans the site MUST BE approached via Blackmoor Gate not Lynton/ Lynmouth. From Blackmoor Gate follow signs for Lynton/Lynmouth for 5 miles to Caffyn's Cross. Bus shelter on the left at juntion, turn left then first right to the site.
Acreage 5½ **Open** 22 March **to** 1 Nov
Access Good **Site** Lev/Slope
Sites Available **Total** 105
Facilities
Nearby Facilities
Barnstaple
✓✓✓✓Graded Park. Quiet park with lovely views. Close to Exmoor National Park and Valley of the Rocks, ideal for walkers.

LYNTON

Channel View Caravan Park, Manor Farm, Barbrook, Lynton, North Devon, EX35 6LD.
Std: 01598 **Tel:** 753349
Nearest Town/Resort Lynton/Lynmouth
Directions 2 miles south east of Lynton on the A39.
Acreage 6 **Open** Easter **to** October
Access Good **Site** Level
Sites Available **Total** 110
Facilities
Nearby Facilities
Barnstaple
✓✓✓✓Graded Park. Panoramic views, on the edge of Exmoor overlooking Lynton/ Lynmouth. Disabled toilets being built - should be ready for the 1998 season.

MODBURY

Camping & Caravanning Club Site, California Cross, Modbury, Devon, PL21 0SG.
Std: 01548 **Tel:** 821297
Nearest Town/Resort Ivybridge
Directions On the A38 travelling south west take the A3121 to the crossroads, straight across to the B3196 to California Cross Hamlet. Turn left after California Cross Hamlet sign but before the petrol station, site is on the right.
Acreage 4 **Open** 22 March **to** 1 Nov
Access Good **Site** Lev/Slope
Sites Available **Total** 80
Facilities
Nearby Facilities
Ivybridge
✓✓✓✓✓Graded Park. Rural setting centrally situated in the South Hams. Close to the beaches of Salcombe and Torbay. Takeaway food available two nights a week.

MODBURY

Moor View Touring Park, California Cross, Near Modbury, South Devon, PL21 0SG.
Std: 01548 **Tel:** 821485
Nearest Town/Resort Modbury
Directions 3 miles east of Modbury on the B3207. From the A38 westbound leave at Wrangaton Cross signed Ermington A3121, turn left at the top of sliproad, Loddiswell Road at crossroads, follow Moor View camping signs.
Acreage 6 **Open** Easter **to** End October
Access Good **Site** Level
Sites Available **Total** 68
Facilities
Nearby Facilities
Ivybridge
✓✓✓✓✓Graded Park. 6 miles to Bigbury Bay, 12 miles to Plymouth, 5 miles to Dartmoor and 15 miles to Dartmouth.

MODBURY

Pennymoor Caravan Park, Modbury, Devon.
Std: 01548 **Tel:** 830269/830542
Nearest Town/Resort Kingsbridge/ Salcombe.
Directions Approx 30 miles West of Exeter, leave A38 at Wrangaton Cross. Turn left, then straight across at next crossroads and continue for approx 4 miles. Pass petrol garage on left, then take second left, site is 1 mile on the right.
Acreage 6 **Open** 15 March **to** 15 Nov
Access Good **Site** Level
Sites Available **Total** 155
Facilities
Nearby Facilities
Plymouth.
✓✓✓✓Graded Park. Peaceful rural site. Ideal touring base. Central to towns, moors, beaches. Bigbury-on-Sea only 5 miles. Holiday caravans to let. New superb toilet/ shower block. Free colour brochure.

MORETONHAMPSTEAD

Clifford Bridge Park, Nr. Drewsteignton, Exeter, Devon, EX6 6QE.
Std: 01647 **Tel:** 24226
Nearest Town/Resort Moretonhampstead.
Directions Leave A30 Dual carriage way to Cheriton Bishop, left at Old Thatch 2 miles to crossroads turn right, 1 mile to Clifford.
Acreage 8 **Open** Easter **to** September.
Access Good **Site** Level
Sites Available **Total** 65
Facilities
Nearby Facilities
Exeter.
✓✓✓Graded Park. The upper Teign valley and Gorge is noted for it's outstanding natural beauty, superb viewpoints and magnificent woodland tracks, it's location in Dartmoor National Park makes it a unique touring centre for walking fishing, riding and golf.

MORTEHOE

Warcombe Farm Camping Park, Mortehoe, Near Woolacombe, North Devon, EX34 7EJ.
Std: 01271. **Tel:** 870690
Std: 01271 **Fax:** 871070
Nearest Town/Resort Barnstaple.
Directions Turn left off the A361, Barnstaple to Ilfracombe road at Mullacott Cross roundabout signposted Woolacombe. After 2 miles turn right towards Mortehoe. Site is first on the right in less than a mile.
Acreage 19 **Open** 15 March **to** 31 Oct
Access Good **Site** Level
Sites Available **Total** 145
Facilities
Nearby Facilities
Barnstaple
✓✓✓Graded Park. 1¼ miles to Woolacombe beach. Panoramic sea views. Well drained level land, family run. Fishing on site.

NEWTON ABBOT

Dornafield, Two Mile Oak, Newton Abbott, Devon, TQ12 6DD.
Std: 01803 **Tel:** 812732
Std: 01803 **Fax:** 812032
Nearest Town/Resort Newton Abbot.
Directions Take the A381 (Newton Abbott to Totnes), in 2 miles at Two Mile Oak Inn turn right. In ½ mile turn first left, site is 200 yards on the right.
Acreage 30 **Open** 20th March **to** October
Access Good **Site** Level
Sites Available **Total** 135
Facilities
Nearby Facilities
Newton Abbot.
✓✓✓✓✓Graded Park. Beautiful 14th Century farmhouse location with superb facilities to suit discerning caravanners and campers.

NEWTON ABBOT

Lemonford Caravan Park, Bickington, Newton Abbot, Devon, TQ12 6JR.
Std: 01626 **Tel:** 821242
Nearest Town/Resort Ashburton
Directions From Exeter along A38 take A382 turnoff, on roundabout take 3rd exit and follow site signs to Bickington. From Plymouth take A383 turnoff, follow road for ¼ mile and turn left into site.
Acreage 7 **Open** Easter **to** October
Access Good **Site** Level
Sites Available **Total** 90
Facilities
Nearby Facilities
Newton Abbot
✓✓✓✓✓Graded Park. In a beautiful setting and scrupulously clean. Close to Torbay and the Dartmoor National Park.

NEWTON ABBOT

Ross Park, Park Hill Farm, Ipplepen, Newton Abbot, Devon, TQ12 5TT.
Std: 01803 **Tel:** 812983
Std: 01803 **Fax:** 812983
Nearest Town/Resort Newton Abbot
Directions 3 miles from Newton Abbot and 6 miles from Totnes on the A381. At Park Hill crossroads and Jet Filling Station follow the brown tourist sign.
Acreage 26 **Open** All Year
Access Good **Site** Level
Sites Available **Total** 110
Facilities
Nearby Facilities
Newton Abbot
✓✓✓✓Graded Park. Tranquil park with individually landscaped pitches, magnificent floral displays and rural views. Excllent touring centre. Centrally heated showers. Dog walks are situated in a conservation area which forms part of the park.

NEWTON ABBOT

The Dartmoor Halfway, Bickington, Newton Abbot, Devon, TQ12 6JW.
Std: 01626 **Tel:** 821270
Std: 01626 **Fax:** 821820
Nearest Town/Resort Newton Abbot
Directions From Newton Abbot take the A383 towards Ashburton and Plymouth, site is 3 miles on the right hand side.
Acreage 1½ **Open** All Year
Access Good **Site** Level
Sites Available **Total** 22
Facilities
Nearby Facilities
Newton Abbot
✓✓✓✓Graded Park. A family run site nestling on the edge of Dartmoor. Beside the River Lemon in Bickington, "Halfway" between Newton Abbot and Ashburton. Colour TV Hook-ups.

NEWTON ABBOT

Woodville Park, Totnes Road, Ipplepen, Newton Abbot, Devon, TQ12 5TN.
Std: 01803 **Tel:** 812240
Nearest Town/Resort Newton Abbot.
Directions From Newton Abbot take the A381 towards Totnes for approx. 2½ miles. At the Two Mile Oak Inn (crossroads) Woodville Park is a further ½ mile on the right hand side.
Acreage 3½ **Open** 1st March **to** 18th October
Access Good **Site** Level
Sites Available **Total** 25
Facilities
Nearby Facilities
Newton Abbot.
✓✓✓✓Graded Park. Quiet and beautiful, simply the best ADULT ONLY site. Ideal touring location for Torbay and Dartmoor. Luxury facilities.

NEWTON FERRERS

Briar Hill Caravan & Camping Park, Briar Hill Farm, Newton Ferrers, Plymouth, Devon, PL8 1AR.
Std: 01752 **Tel:** 872252
Std: 01752 **Fax:** 872252
Nearest Town/Resort Newton Ferrers
Open March **to** November
Access Good **Site** Lev/Slope
Sites Available **Total** 50
Facilities
Nearby Facilities
Plymouth
Near the beach and coastal walk. Only 8 miles from the city of Plymouth. Boat hire locally.

OKEHAMPTON

Bridestowe Caravan Park, Bridestowe, Nr. Okehampton, Devon.
Std: 01837 **Tel:** 861261
Nearest Town/Resort Bude
Directions Leave M5 for A30 to Okehampton 3 miles west of Okehampton turn off A30 to Bridestowe village, follow camping signs to site.
Open March **to** December
Access Good **Site** Level
Sites Available **Total** 53
Facilities
Nearby Facilities
✓✓✓Graded Park. Dartmoor National Park 2 miles, ideal for walking, horse riding and fishing and touring Devon and Cornwall. Within easy reach of coastal resorts.

OKEHAMPTON

Bundu Camping & Caravan Park, Sourton Down, Okehampton, Devon, EX20 4HT.
Std: 01837 **Tel:** 861611
Nearest Town/Resort Okehampton.
Directions Slip road off the A30 dual carriageway to the A386 Tavistock/Sourton. Turn left then left again after 100yds, site is at the top of the road on the right.
Acreage 4 **Open** March **to** November
Access Good **Site** Level
Sites Available **Total** 38
Facilities
Nearby Facilities
Exeter
Situated on Dartmoor, ideal for walking. Centrally based for touring Devon and Cornwall.

OKEHAMPTON

Culverhayes Camping Park, Sampford Courtenay, Nr Okehampton, Devon, EX20 2TG.
Std: 01837 **Tel:** 82431
Nearest Town/Resort Okehampton.
Directions From M5 junction 31 take the A30, at first roundabout turn left and follow yellow holiday route signs. Sampford Courtenay on A3072, in Sampford Courtenay go over mini roundabout, campsite is 300yds on the right, steep hill.
Acreage 3¼ **Open** Mid March **to** End Oct
Access Good **Site** Lev/Slope
Sites Available **Total** 50
Facilities
Nearby Facilities
Exeter
Ideal site to explore Devon and North Cornwall. Views of Dartmoor. Cycle routes and walks. FREE coarse fishing on site. E-Mail STEVEN.ALLEN1@VIRGIN.NET

OKEHAMPTON

Dartmoor View Caravan Park, Whiddon Down, Okehampton, Devon, EX20 2QL.
Std: 01647 **Tel:** 231545
Std: 01647 **Fax:** 231654
Nearest Town/Resort Okehampton.
Directions Take the A30 from Exeter (17 miles), turn left at Whiddon Down roundabout, park is ½ mile on the right.
Acreage 5 **Open** March **to** 9th November
Access Good **Site** Level
Sites Available **Total** 75
Facilities
Nearby Facilities
Exeter.
✓✓✓✓Graded Park. Excellent facilities, close to Dartmoor National Park. Letterboxing centre. Ideal for touring.

OKEHAMPTON

Olditch Farm Caravan & Camping Site, Sticklepath, Okehampton, Devon, EX20 2NT.
Std: 01837 **Tel:** 840734
Std: 01837 **Fax:** 840877
Nearest Town/Resort Okehampton
Directions We are 18 miles west of Exeter off the A30 at first roundabout and 3 miles east of Okehampton.
Acreage 3½ **Open** 15 March **to** 15 Nov
Access Good **Site** Sloping
Sites Available **Total** 35
Facilities
Nearby Facilities
Exeter
✓✓✓Graded Park. Dartmoor National Park. Ideal for touring the West Country, numerous historical sites within the vicinity.

OKEHAMPTON

Yertiz Caravan & Camping Park, Exeter Road, Okehampton, Devon, EX20 1QF.
Std: 01837 **Tel:** 52281
Nearest Town/Resort Okehampton
Directions From Okehampton town centre take the Exeter road, Yertiz is ¾ mile on the right hand side.
Acreage 3½ **Open** All Year
Access Good **Site** Lev/Slope
Sites Available **Total** 30
Facilities
Nearby Facilities
Exeter
✓✓✓Graded Park. Small, friendly site with lovely views of Dartmoor. Good for local walking and touring the West Country.

AA Listed as one of Britain's Best Parks set in 23 acres of beautiful Devon countryside but close to safe sandy beaches.

Tranquility, Fun, Peace, Entertainment, Good Food, Good Company - which ever makes your holiday

ANWB EUROPEAN CAMPSITE OF THE YEAR 1994

COME TO BYSLADES

BYSLADES CAMPING & TOURING PARK

FOR MORE INFORMATION
AND FREE COLOUR BROCHURE
PHONE 01803 - 555072
BYSLADES CAMPING & TOURING PARK,
TOTNES ROAD, PAIGNTON, DEVON TQ4 7PY

BRITISH GRADED HOLIDAY PARKS EXCELLENT · AA · RAC APPOINTED · BRITISH HOLIDAY & HOME PARKS ASSOCIATION MEMBER

Premier Riviera Holidays

TORBAY'S FUN-PACKED, SEA-VIEW HOLIDAY

Touring Park and Luxury Caravan Homes for 2-6 people – all fully equipped to the highest standard. Beautiful Parkland with wonderful views of Torbay. Fun and activities for all; indoor and outdoor heated swimming pools with Leisure Club. Entertainments, Dancing, Cabaret, Sports facilities and children's activities.

Beverley Holidays

For FREE colour brochure write to
Beverley Holidays, Dept 10, Goodrington Road,
Paignton, Devon TQ4 7JE.
Or phone: **01803 843887** (24hrs)

AA ▶▶▶▶▶ · ROSE AWARD CARAVAN HOLIDAY PARKS · BRITISH GRADED HOLIDAY PARKS GRADED EXCELLENT · DAVID BELLAMY CONSERVATION AWARD SILVER

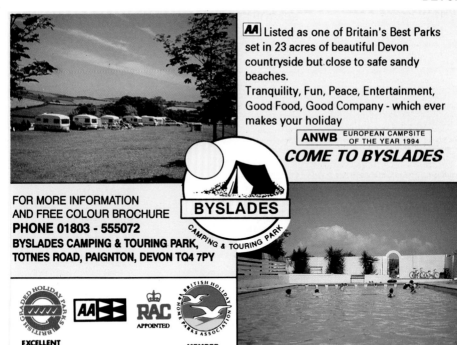

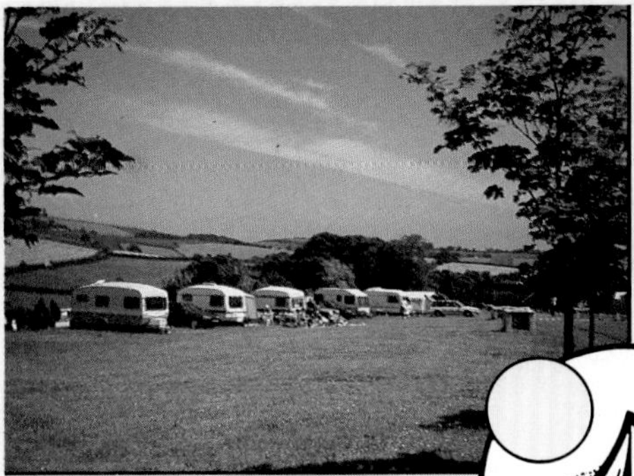

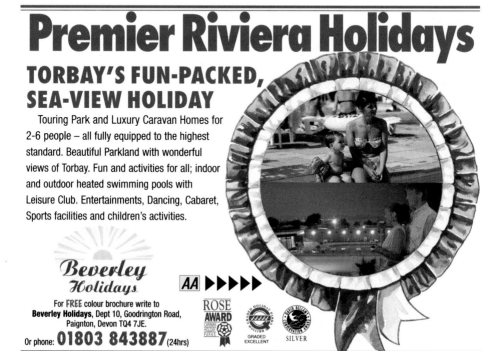

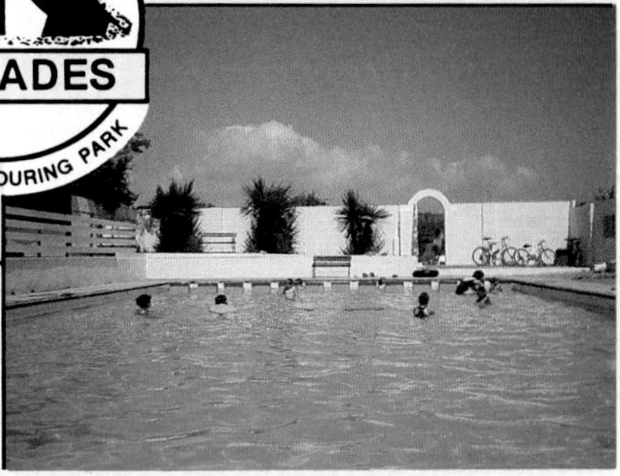

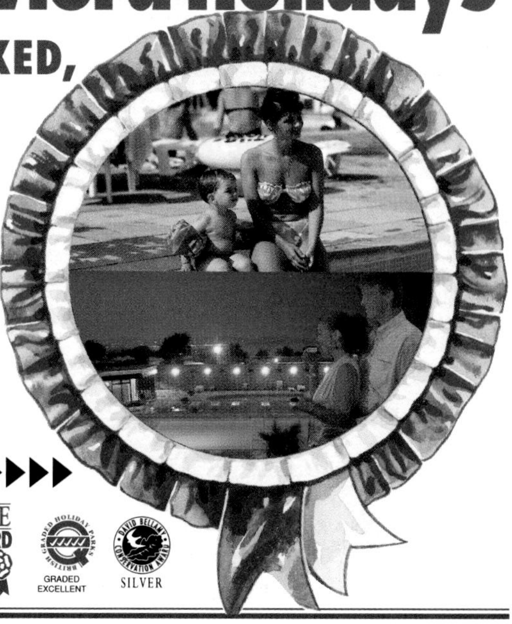

PAIGNTON

Barton Pines, Blagdon Road, Paignton, Devon, TQ3 3YG.
Std: 01803 **Tel:** 553350
Std: 01803 **Fax:** 553350
Nearest Town/Resort Paignton
Directions From Newton Abbot follow the A380 Torbay ring road. At Preston Down roundabout follow a signed right turn, after 100 yards go straight across a five lane roundabout, continue for 2 miles and turn left at the crossroads.
Acreage 4 **Open** March **to** October
Access Good **Site** Level
Sites Available **Total** 33
Facilities
Nearby Facilities
Totnes
✓✓✓✓Graded Park. Centrally located yet set in peaceful countryside. Approx. 5 miles from all of Torbay and Dartmoor attractions.

PAIGNTON

Beverley Park Holiday Centre, Goodrington Road, Paignton, Devon.
Std: 01803 **Tel:** Churston 843887
Std: 01803 **Fax:** 845427
Nearest Town/Resort Paignton.
Directions 2 miles south of Paignton (ring road) A3022. Turn left into Goodrington Road.
Acreage 9½ **Open** Easter **to** October
Access Good **Site** Level
Sites Available **Total** 194
Facilities
Nearby Facilities
Paignton.
✓✓✓✓✓Graded Park. Views across Torbay. Indoor heated swimming pool, tennis court. Sauna.

PAIGNTON

Byslades International Camping & Touring Park, Totnes Road, Paignton, Devon, TQ4 7PY.
Std: 01803 **Tel:** 555072
Std: 01803 **Fax:** 555072
Nearest Town/Resort Paignton.
Directions 2¼ miles west of Paignton on the A385
Acreage 23 **Open** April **to** October
Access Good **Site** Level
Sites Available **Total** 190
Facilities
Nearby Facilities
Paignton
✓✓✓✓Graded Park. The site is overlooking a beautiful valley and is centrally situated to visit all parts of Devon. Tennis on site.

PAIGNTON

Grange Court Holiday Centre, Grange Road, Goodrington, Paignton, Devon, TQ4 7JP.
Std: 01803 **Tel:** 558010
Std: 01803 **Fax:** 663336
Nearest Town/Resort Paignton
Directions From junc 31 of M5, travel south for approx 20 miles on A380 to junction with A385. Continue south on A380 (Paignton Ring Road) for 1 mile, turn left into Goodrington Road by Esso Filling Station. After ¾ mile turn left into Grange Road and follow signs to park.
Acreage 20 **Open** Mid-Feb **to** Mid-Jan
Access Good **Site** Sloping
Sites Available **Total** 157
Facilities
Nearby Facilities
Paignton
✓✓✓✓Graded Park. Panoramic views over Torbay, close to Goodrington beach.

PAIGNTON

Higher Well Farm Holiday Park, Stoke Gabriel, Totnes, Devon, TQ9 6RN.
Std: 01803 **Tel:** 782289
Nearest Town/Resort Paignton.
Directions From Paignton take A385 towards Totnes, turn off left at Parkers Arms Pub. Go 1½ miles then turn left again, site is 200 yards down road.
Acreage 8 **Open** Easter **to** October
Access Good **Site** Lev/Slope
Sites Available
Facilities
Nearby Facilities
Paignton.
✓✓✓Graded Park. Within 4 miles Torbay beaches, 1 mile village Stoke Gabriel and River Dart.

PAIGNTON

Holly Gruit Camp, Brixham Road, Paignton, Devon, TQ4 7BA.
Std: 01803 **Tel:** 550763
Nearest Town/Resort Paignton
Directions 1½ miles from Paignton Town on the A3022 Brixham Ring-Road.
Acreage 2½ **Open** End May **to** Mid Sept
Site Level
Sites Available **Total** 70
Facilities
Nearby Facilities
Paignton
Near Paignton Zoo.

WHITEHILL FARM
HOLIDAY PARK

Beautifully situated in rolling Devonshire countryside, yet within easy reach of the sea, Torquay and the Dartmoor National Park.

STOKE ROAD, PAIGNTON
SOUTH DEVON TQ4 7PF

(01803) 782338
Fax: (01803) 782722

Heated Swimming Pool

★

Licensed bar & adjoining family room with soft drinks bar & all ages disco.
Arcade & video machines.
Games room with pool and table tennis

★

Free hot showers.
For ladies, individual washing cubicles & heated luxury bathroom.
Dishwashing facilities.
Fully equipped launderette with free ironing

★

Shop, Café and Takeaway

★

10 acres of woodland
Children's park & play areas

★

Pitches with or without electric hook-up for tents, caravans & motorhomes

★

FAMILIES AND COUPLES ONLY. NO PETS

How to find us: Turn off the Paignton-Totnes road (A385), at the "Parkers Arms", 1/2 a mile from Paignton Zoo. Follow the signposts to Stoke Gabriel. Park 1 mile.

PAIGNTON

Lower Yalberton Holiday Park, Long Road, Paignton, Devon, TQ4 7PQ.
Std: 01803 **Tel:** 558127
Std: 01803 **Fax:** 558127
Nearest Town/Resort Paignton
Directions On the south side of Paignton on the A3022 Torquay to Brixham ring road. Turn right at Nortel into Long Road and we are ½ mile on the right.
Acreage 25 **Open** May **to** September
Access Good **Site** Lev/Slope
Sites Available **Total** 543
Facilities
Nearby Facilities
Paignton
Ideal touring centre.

PAIGNTON

Marine Park Holiday Centre, Grange Road, Paignton, Devon.
Std: 01803 **Tel:** 843887
Std: 01803 **Fax:** 845427
Nearest Town/Resort Paignton.
Directions 2 miles south of Paignton off A379.
Acreage 4 **Open** May **to** September
Access Good **Site** Lev/Slope
Sites Available **Total** 30
Facilities
Nearby Facilities
Paignton.
✓✓✓✓✓Graded Park.

PAIGNTON

Paignton Holiday Park, Totnes Road, Paignton, Devon, TQ4 7PW.
Std: 01803 **Tel:** 550504
Std: 01803 **Fax:** 529909
Nearest Town/Resort Paignton
Directions 1½ miles west of Paignton on the A385.
Acreage 20 **Open** March **to** October
Access Good **Site** Lev/Slope
Sites Available **Total** 250
Facilities
Nearby Facilities
Paignton
✓✓✓✓Graded Park. Ideal touring site near beaches yet convenient for Dartmoor National Park.

PAIGNTON

Ramslade Touring Park, Stoke Road, Stoke Gabriel, Paignton, Devon.
Std: 01803 **Tel:** 782575
Std: 01803 **Fax:** 782828
Nearest Town/Resort Paignton.
Directions From Paignton take A385, turn left at Parkers Arms, site 1½ miles on right.
Acreage 9 **Open** 15 March **to** October
Access Good **Site** Lev/Slope
Sites Available **Total** 135
Facilities
Nearby Facilities
Paignton.
✓✓✓✓✓Graded Park. Quiet site. No dogs in high season. Babies bathroom, logland play areas and paddling pool with waterfall.

PAIGNTON

Whitehill Farm Holiday Park, Stoke Road, Paignton, South Devon, TQ4 7PF.
Std: 01803 **Tel:** 782338
Std: 01803 **Fax:** 782722
Nearest Town/Resort Paignton
Directions Turn off the A385 at Parkers Arms Public House, ½ mile from Paignton Zoo, signposted Stoke Gabriel. Park is 1 mile along this road.
Acreage 30 **Open** 10th May **to** End September
Access Good **Site** Lev/Slope
Sites Available **Total** 400
Facilities
Nearby Facilities

PAIGNTON HOLIDAY PARK

A beautifully landscaped Touring and Camping Park and a wide range of luxury Caravan Holiday Homes.

For free brochure:
Tel: 01803 550504
(24hr answer 01803 521684)

or write to Paignton Holiday Park, Dept. CC, Totnes Rd, Paignton, S.Devon TQ4 7PW

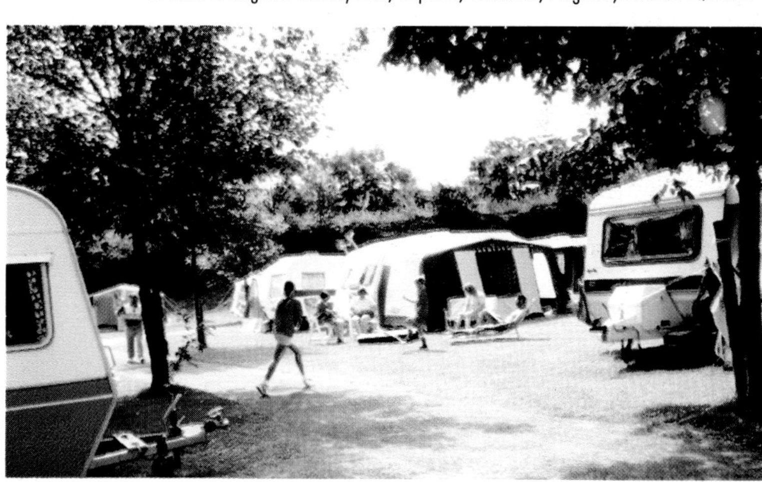

Set in an area of outstanding natural beauty and close to the beaches & attractions of the English Riviera. There is a full range of facilities for you to enjoy including a licensed club with entertainment & dancing, pool & snooker club.
Large heated swimming pool, shop, cafe,
children's activity & play area,
laundry & shower facilities.

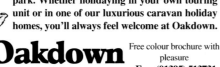

Paignton
Beautifully situated in rolling Devon countryside yet within easy reach of the sea, Torquay and the Dartmoor National Park.

PAIGNTON

Widend Touring Park, Berry Pomeroy Road, Marldon, Paignton, Devon, TQ3 1RT.
Std: 01803 **Tel:** 550116
Std: 01803 **Fax:** 550116
Nearest Town/Resort Paignton/Torquay.
Directions Turn into Five Lanes Road towards Berry Pomeroy off the main Torquay ring road (A380) new duel carriageway at Marldon. Singmore Hotel is on the corner.
Acreage 20 **Open** Easter **to** October
Access Good **Site** Level
Sites Available **Total** 185
Facilities
Nearby Facilities
Torquay
✓✓✓✓Graded Park. Quiet, family run park for families and mixed couples only. A most central site for most of the sea and country amenities in South Devon. Dogs not allowed from Mid-July to the end of August.

PLYMOUTH

Riverside Caravan Park, Longbridge Road, Marsh Mills, Plymouth, Devon, PL6 8LD.
Std: 01752 **Tel:** 344122
Std: 01752 **Fax:** 344122
Nearest Town/Resort Plymouth.
Directions 3 miles from Plymouth city centre, follow the A374.
Acreage 10½ **Open** All Year
Access Good **Site** Level
Sites Available **Total** 290
Facilities
Nearby Facilities
Plymouth.
Woodland site alongside a river.

PRINCETOWN

The Plume of Feathers Inn, The Square, Princetown, Tavistock, Devon, PL20 6QG.
Std: 01822 **Tel:** 890240
Std: 01822 **Fax:** 890780
Nearest Town/Resort Tavistock
Directions In the Square of Princetown, which is situated in Dartmoor.
Acreage 3 **Open** All Year
Site Sloping
Sites Available **Total** 75
Facilities
Nearby Facilities
Plymouth
In the heart of Dartmoor.

PUTSBOROUGH

Putsborough Sands Caravan Park, Orchard House, Putsborough, Georgeham, North Devon, EX33 1LB.
Std: 01271 **Tel:** 890230
Std: 01271 **Fax:** 890980
Nearest Town/Resort Ilfracombe/Barnstaple
Directions Directions given upon booking.
Open April **to** October
Access Poor **Site** Sloping
Sites Available **Total** 21
Facilities
Nearby Facilities
Barnstaple
Adjacent to Multi Award Winning beach, top beach in North Devon. Unique position. Booking is essential, please contact Park Management.

SALCOMBE

Alston Farm Camping & Caravan Site, Nr. Salcombe, Kingsbridge, Devon TQ7 3BJ.
Std: 01548 **Tel:** 561260
Std: 01548 **Fax:** 561260
Nearest Town/Resort Salcombe.
Directions Signposted on left of A381 between Kingsbridge and Salcombe towards Salcombe.
Acreage 15 **Open** Easter **to** October
Access Good **Site** Level
Sites Available **Total** 200
Facilities
Nearby Facilities
Totnes.
Secluded, sheltered site. Dish washing facilities.

SALCOMBE

Bolberry House Farm Camping & Caravanning Park, Bolberry, Malborough, Nr Kingsbridge, Devon, TQ7 3DY.
Std: 01548 **Tel:** 561251/560926
Nearest Town/Resort Salcombe
Directions Take the A381 from Kingsbridge to Malborough. Turn right through the village, follow signs to Bolberry ¾ mile.
Acreage 6 **Open** March **to** October
Access Good **Site** Level
Sites Available **Total** 70
Facilities
Nearby Facilities
Totnes
✓✓✓Graded Park. A friendly and peaceful, family run park on a coastal farm. Mostly level. Wonderful sea views and stunning cliff top walks. Safe sandy beaches 1 mile at the quaint old fishing village of Hope Cove.

Salcombe's scenic and pretty estuary, a boating paradise - 2½ miles. AA 3 Pennants.

SALCOMBE

Higher Rew Caravan & Camping Park, Malborough, Kingsbridge, Devon, TQ7 3DW.
Std: 01548 **Tel:** 842681/843681
Std: 01548 **Fax:** 844181
Nearest Town/Resort Salcombe
Directions When approaching from Kingsbridge on the A381 to Salcombe, turn right at Malborough and follow signs to Soar for approx. 1 mile then turn left at Rew Cross. Higher Rew is then the first turning on the right.
Acreage 5 **Open** 4 March **to** October
Access Good **Site** Terraced
Sites Available **Total** 80
Facilities
Nearby Facilities
Totnes
✓✓✓✓Graded Park. In an area of outstanding natural beauty. 1 mile from the beach. Cliff walks.

SALCOMBE

Parkland, Sorley Green Cross, Salcombe, Devon, TQ7 4AF.
Std: 01548. **Tel:** 852723
Nearest Town/Resort Kingsbridge.
Directions From Totnes follow the A381, main Kingsbridge road, to Sorley Green Cross. Go straight ahead and the site is 100 yards on the left.
Acreage 3 **Open** All Year
Access Good **Site** Level
Sites Available
Facilities

Nearby Facilities
Central for beaches and touring (river 1 mile). Well sheltered site with views over Salcombe. One pitch with hard standing, hook-up water point and T.V. point (Super Pitch). Out of season package prices available.

SALCOMBE

Sun Park, Soar, Malborough, Nr. Kingsbridge, Devon, TQ7 3DS.
Std: 01548 **Tel:** 561378
Nearest Town/Resort Salcombe.
Directions A381 fron Kingsbridge to Malborough, turn right through village, follow sign Soar Mill Cove for 1¼ miles, site on right.
Acreage 3¼ **Open** Easter **to** End October
Site Level
Sites Available **Total** 70
Facilities
Nearby Facilities
Totnes.
Within walking distance of Soar Mill Cove, in an area of outstanding natural beauty, Ideal centre for touring.

SEATON

Leacroft Touring Park, Colyton Hill, Colyton, Devon.
Std: 01297 **Tel:** 552823
Std: 01297 **Fax:** 552823
Nearest Town/Resort Seaton/Beer.
Directions A3052 Sidmouth to Lyme Regis road, 2 miles west of Seaton. Turn left at Stafford Cross international caravan sign, site is 1 mile on the right.
Acreage 10 **Open** End March **to** October
Access Good **Site** Lev/Slope
Sites Available **Total** 138
Facilities
Nearby Facilities
Axminster
✓✓✓✓✓Graded Park. Quiet, peaceful site in open countryside. Picturesque villages to explore and woodland walks nearby.

SEATON

Manor Farm Caravan Site, Seaton Down Hill, Seaton, Devon.
Std: 01297 **Tel:** 21524
Nearest Town/Resort Seaton
Directions From Lyme Regis A3052, left at Tower Cross, ½ mile entrance on left.
Acreage 22 **Open** April **to** 15th Nov
Access Good **Site** Lev/Slope
Sites Available **Total** 274
Facilities
Nearby Facilities
Axminster
Glorious scenic views of valley and Lyme Bay. Farm animals, rare breeds. A quiet site only 1 mile from beach. Ideal touring centre for glorious East Devon. Gas available nearby.

SIDMOUTH

Oakdown Touring & Holiday Home Park, Weston, Sidmouth, Devon, EX10 0PH.
Std: 01297 **Tel:** 680387
Std: 01395 **Fax:** 513731
Nearest Town/Resort Sidmouth.
Directions 1½ miles east of Sidford on A3052, take the second Weston turning at the Oakdown sign. Site 50 yards on left. Also signposted with international Caravan/ Camping signs.

Acreage 13 **Open** April **to** October
Access Good **Site** Level
Sites Available **Total** 120
Facilities
Nearby Facilities
Honiton.

✓✓✓✓✓Graded Park. Sidmouths Award Winning park set in glorious East Devon Heritage coast, near beautiful Weston Valley owned by National Trust, lovely cliff walks. Caravan storage. Field trail to nearby world famous Donkey Sanctuary. Caravan holiday homes to let. Awards for 1997-98 England for Excellence Silver Award, David Bellamy Gold Conservation Award and Loo of the Year Award.

SIDMOUTH

Popplefords, Exeter Road, Newton Poppleford, Sidmouth, Devon, EX10 0DE.
Std: 01395 **Tel:** 568672
Std: 01395 **Fax:** 568672
Nearest Town/Resort Sidmouth
Directions Leave the M5 at junction 30 and follow the A3052 for Sidmouth. The site is approx. 7 miles along this road on the left hand side just before Newton Poppleford.
Acreage 7 **Open** March **to** October
Access Good **Site** Lev/Slope
Sites Available **Total** 6+
Facilities
Nearby Facilities
Exeter

Rural setting adjacent to Woodbury Common and an RSPB Sanctuary. Only 5 miles from Sidmouth and 8 miles from Exeter.

SIDMOUTH

Salcombe Regis Camping & Caravan Park, Salcombe Regis, Sidmouth, Devon, EX10 0JH.
Std: 01395 **Tel:** 514303
Std: 01395 **Fax:** 514303
Nearest Town/Resort Sidmouth
Directions 1½ miles east of Sidmouth, signposted off the A3052 Exeter to Lyme Regis coast road. ½ mile down the lane on the left hand side.
Acreage 16 **Open** Easter **to** October
Access Good **Site** Level
Sites Available **Total** 100
Facilities
Nearby Facilities
Exeter

✓✓✓✓✓Graded Park. Situated in an area of outstanding natural beauty, within walking distance of the sea and famous Donkey Sanctuary. Own water supply available for motor caravans and tourers. Heated amenity block. Quiet, "Excellent" graded park with David Bellamy Gold Environmental Award.

SLAPTON

Newlands Farm Camping & Caravan Site, Newlands Farm, Slapton, Nr. Dartmouth, Devon.
Std: 01548 **Tel:** 580366
Nearest Town/Resort Dartmouth
Directions From Totnes take the A381 towards Kingsbridge, after Halwell Village take the fourth left signposted Slapton. Go 4 miles to Buckland Cross, proceed for ¼ mile, site is on the left hand side.
Acreage 10 **Open** 23 May **to** September
Access Good **Site** Level
Sites Available **Total** 45
Facilities
Nearby Facilities

We have a friendly, uncommercialised, quiet site overlooking beautiful countryside and sea. Within 1 mile of glorious beaches, cliff walks and a nature reserve. Woodlands Leisure Centre is close by with fun for all the family. Web Address: WWW.NEWLANDSFARM.DEMON.CO.UK

SOUTH BRENT

Webland Farm Holiday Park, Avonwick, Nr. South Brent, Devon. TQ10 9EX
Std: 01364 **Tel:** 73273
Nearest Town/Resort Totnes.
Directions Leave the A38 at Marley Head A385 exit. Follow Webland signs from the roundabout and along lane for about 1¼ miles.
Acreage 5 **Open** 15th March **to** 15th November
Access Good **Site** Lev/Gentle Slope
Sites Available **Total** 35
Facilities
Nearby Facilities
Totnes.

✓✓✓Graded Park. Overlooked by Dartmoor Hills, very quiet country park, well placed for touring the coast and Dartmoor and the many tourist attractions in the area.

SOUTH MOLTON

Molland Camping & Caravan Park, Blackcock Inn, Molland, South Molton, North Devon.
Std: 01769 **Tel:** 550297
Nearest Town/Resort Barnstaple.
Directions Proceed along the A361 from either Tiverton or South Molton, Molland and Black Cock Inn are signposted. Camping signs lead directly to the site.
Acreage 9¼ **Open** All Year
Access Good **Site** Level
Sites Available **Total** 65
Facilities
Nearby Facilities
Barnstaple/Tiverton.
Edge of Exmoor National Park. Ideal for touring, hiking, riding, etc..

SOUTH MOLTON

Romansleigh Holiday Park, Odam Hill, South Molton, North Devon, EX36 4NB.
Std: 01769 **Tel:** 550259
Nearest Town/Resort Barnstaple.
Directions Take the B3137 South Molton to Witheridge road. Site is signposted right approximately 4 miles from South Molton and 2 miles past Alswear.
Acreage 2 **Open** 15 March **to** 31 October
Access Good **Site** Level
Sites Available **Total** 20
Facilities
Nearby Facilities
Umberleigh
Secluded, wooded valley with magnificent all-round views. In the grounds of 14 acres. Ideal touring location.

STOKENHAM

Old Cotmore Farm, Old Cotmore Farm, Stokenham, South Devon, TQ7 2LR.
Std: 01548 **Tel:** 580240
Std: 01548 **Fax:** 580875
Nearest Town/Resort Kingsbridge/Salcombe
Directions Take the A379 Kingsbridge to Dartmouth road, at the Carehouse Cross in Stokenham turn right signposted Beesands. Farm is 1 mile on the right and is signposted.
Acreage 10 **Open** March **to** November
Access Good **Site** Lev/Slope
Sites Available **Total** 30
Facilities
Nearby Facilities
Totnes
2 miles from Start Point with stunning walks. The perfect spot for the Eclipse. Sandy and shingle beaches within easy reach, diving and fishing. Newly refurbished shower block. Excellent pubs.

TAVISTOCK

Harford Bridge Holiday Park, Peter Tavy, Tavistock, Devon.
Std: 01822 **Tel:** 810349
Std: 01822 **Fax:** 810349
Nearest Town/Resort Tavistock
Directions A386 Okehampton road 2 miles north of Tavistock.
Acreage 16½ **Open** March **to** November
Access Good **Site** Level
Sites Available **Total** 120
Facilities
Nearby Facilities
Plymouth
✓✓✓✓✓Graded Park. Scenic views, riverside pitches, fishing and tennis, ideal touring Dartmoor National Park. Rose Award.

TAVISTOCK

Higher Longford Farm, Moorshop, Tavistock, Devon.
Std: 01822 **Tel:** 613360
Nearest Town/Resort Tavistock.
Directions Tavistock/Princetown road, 2 miles from Tavistock on the B3357.
Acreage 4 **Open** All Year
Access Good **Site** Level
Sites Available **Total** 52
Facilities
Nearby Facilities
Plymouth.
Situated in the Dartmoor National Park, central for touring Devon and Cornwall. David Bellamy Silver Award.

TAVISTOCK

Langstone Manor Caravan & Camping Park, Langstone Manor, Moortown, Tavistock, Devon, PL19 9JZ.
Std: 01822 **Tel:** 613371
Std: 01822 **Fax:** 613371
Nearest Town/Resort Tavistock
Directions Take the B3357 from Tavistock towards Princetown, after approx. 2 miles turn right at crossroads, pass over the cattle grid then turn left following signs for Langstone Manor. We are ½ mile on the right.
Acreage 5½ **Open** 15 March **to** 15 Nov
Access Good **Site** Level
Sites Available **Total** 40
Facilities
Nearby Facilities
Plymouth
Only 6 miles from Cornwall. Near to Dartmoor. Beaches within 12 miles. AA 4 Pennant Luxury Site.

TAVISTOCK

Woodovis Holiday Park, Tavistock, Devon, PL19 8NY.
Std: 01822 **Tel:** 832968
Std: 01822 **Fax:** 832948
Nearest Town/Resort Tavistock.
Directions Take A390 Liskeard road from Tavistock. Site signposted right in 3 miles.
Acreage 14 **Open** March **to** December
Access Good **Site** Lev/Slope
Sites Available **Total** 72
Facilities
Nearby Facilities
Plymouth
✓✓✓✓Graded Park. Scenic views, close to Tamar river. Ideal place for exploring Devon and Cornwall. R.A.C. Three Stars, A.A. Three Stars, A.N.W.B. Approved and A.A. Award for Environmental Excellance. Heated indoor swimming pool.

TEDBURN ST MARY

Springfield Holiday Park, Tedburn Road, Tedburn St. Mary, Exeter, Devon, EX6 6EW.
Std: 01647 **Tel:** 24242
Std: 01647 **Fax:** 24131
Nearest Town/Resort Exeter
Directions Leave the M5 at junction 31 (Okehampton) and take the A30. Leave at the second exit for Tedburn St. Mary, go through the village and we are 1¾ miles on the right.
Acreage 9 **Open** 15 March **to** 15 Nov
Access Good **Site** Level
Sites Available **Total** 88
Facilities
Nearby Facilities
Exeter
✓✓✓✓Graded Park. On the fringe of Dartmoor National Park. Central for beaches and ideal for touring.

TEIGNMOUTH

Coast View Holiday Park, Torquay Road, Teignmouth, Shaldon, South Devon, TQ14 0BG.
Std: 01626 **Tel:** 872392
Nearest Town/Resort Teignmouth.
Directions Follow A38 from Exeter, take left fork A380 to Torquay. Proceed along the A380 for about 6 miles taking the A381 towards Shaldon. Turn right at traffic lights, cross Shaldon bridge and follow main road. Camp is on the right hand side.
Acreage 17
Access Good **Site** Level
Sites Available **Total** 100
Facilities

Nearby Facilities
Teignmouth
✓✓✓✓Graded Park. Scenic views across the sea to the South Devon coastline, Devon coast. Ideal for touring.

TEIGNMOUTH

Wear Farm Caravan Site, E. S. Coaker & Co., Newton Road, Bishopsteignton, Nr. Teignmouth, Devon, TQ14 9PT.
Std: 01626 **Tel:** 775249/779265
Std: 01626 **Fax:** 775249
Nearest Town/Resort Teignmouth.
Directions Off the A380 take the A381 towards Teignmouth, Wear Farm can be found ¼ a mile on the right from the dual carriageway.
Acreage 15 **Open** Easter **to** End October
Access Good **Site** Level
Sites Available **Total** 147
Facilities
Nearby Facilities
Newton Abbot
Alongside a river, scenic views and ideal touring.

TIVERTON

West Middlewick Farm, Nomansland, Nr. Tiverton, Devon, EX16 8NP.
Std: 01884 **Tel:** 860286
Nearest Town/Resort Tiverton.
Directions Take the old A373 (now the B3137) W.N.W.from Tiverton, farm is beside road one mile beyond Nomansland, on right (9 miles from Tiverton).
Acreage 3 **Open** All Year
Access Good **Site** Level
Sites Available **Total** 15
Facilities
Nearby Facilities
Tiverton Parkway
Panoramic view towards Exmoor, quiet surroundings, children welcome. Genuine farm with the same family management since 1933.

TIVERTON

Zeacombe House Caravan Park, Zeacombe House, East Anstey, Tiverton, Devon, EX16 9JU.
Std: 01398 **Tel:** 341279
Std: 01398 **Fax:** 341463
Nearest Town/Resort Tiverton/South Molton
Directions Junction 27 of the M5 take the A361 Barnstaple to South Molton road. Travel for 16 miles in a straight direction. Turn right signed Knowstone and travel road for 2¼ miles. Gates are on the left.
Acreage 4¼ **Open** 11 March **to** October
Access Good **Site** Level
Sites Available **Total** 70
Facilities
Nearby Facilities
Tiverton
✓✓✓✓Graded Park. Scenic views across Exmoor, ideal for touring. Flat, landscaped park with flowers, trees and shrubs.

TORQUAY

Manor Farm Camp Site, Manor Farm, Daccombe, Nr Torquay, Devon.
Std: 01803 **Tel:** 328294
Nearest Town/Resort Torquay.
Directions From Newton Abbot take the A380 for Torquay. Go through roundabout at Kerswell Gardens to next set of traffic lights, turn left into Kingskerswell Road, follow camp signs.
Acreage 4 **Open** 20 May **to** 20 Sept
Site Lev/Slope
Sites Available **Total** 75
Facilities
Nearby Facilities
Torquay
Near the beach, scenic views, ideal touring.

TORQUAY

Widdicombe Farm Touring Park, Compton, Nr. Torquay, Paignton, Devon, TQ3 1ST.
Std: 01803 **Tel:** 558325
Std: 01803 **Fax:** 559526
Nearest Town/Resort Torquay
Directions From Exeter go towards Newton Abbot and follow signs for Torquay, at the roundabout turn right into Harlyn Way. Go straight on at the next roundabout, look to the right to see our park, proceed to next roundabout and turn back following signs to Torquay.
Acreage 10 **Open** 15 March **to** 15 November
Access Good **Site** Level
Sites Available **Total** 150
Facilities
Nearby Facilities
Torquay
✓✓✓✓✓Graded Park. Quiet, well run, family site with a separate area for couples without children. Luxury facilities. Spotlessly clean. Easy access, no narrow country lanes. Bargain breaks in low season from £35.00 per week.

TORRINGTON

Greenways Valley, Torrington, Devon, EX38 7EW.
Std: 01805 **Tel:** 622153
Std: 01805 **Fax:** 622320
Nearest Town/Resort Torrington/ Westward Ho!
Directions Site is just one mile from Torrington town centre. Take B3227 (to South Molton) turn right into Borough Road then 3rd left to site entrance.
Acreage 8 **Open** Mid March **to** October
Access Good **Site** Level
Sites Available **Total** 10
Facilities
Nearby Facilities
Barnstaple
✓✓✓✓Graded Park. Peaceful well tended site with a southerly aspect overlooking a beautiful wooded valley. Tennis and heated pool on park.

TORRINGTON

Smytham Manor Holidays, Smytham Manor, Little Torrington, Devon, EX38 8PU.
Std: 01805 **Tel:** 622110
Nearest Town/Resort Westward Ho!
Directions 2 miles south Torrington on A386 to Okehampton.
Acreage 25 **Open** Mid March **to** October
Access Good **Site** Level
Sites Available **Total** 30
Facilities
Nearby Facilities
Barnstaple
✓✓✓✓Graded Park. Attractive landscaped grounds, close to moors and beach with direct access to the Tarka Trail. Good base for exploring Devon.

TOTNES

Edeswell Farm Country Caravan Park, Edeswell Farm, Rattery, South Brent, Devon, TQ10 9LN.
Std: 01364 **Tel:** 72177
Std: 01364 **Fax:** 72177
Nearest Town/Resort Totnes
Directions Fron Exeter follow the A38 approx 22 miles ignore Rattery signs leave at Marley Head Junction signposted Paignton, Totnes A358. Site ½ mile on right.
Acreage 6 **Open** March **to** October
Access Good **Site** Terraced
Sites Available **Total** 46
Facilities
Nearby Facilities
Totnes
✓✓✓✓Graded Park. Dartmoor, country site for quiet family holidays but with all facilities. Indoor heated swimming pool.

UFFCULME

Waterloo Caravan Park, Waterloo Cross, Uffculme, Devon, EX15 3ES.
Std: 01884 **Tel:** 841342
Directions 6 miles from Collumpton.
Access Good **Site** Level
Sites Available **Total** 50
Facilities
Nearby Facilities
Parkway

UMBERLEIGH

Umberleigh Camping & Caravanning Club Site, Over Weir, Umberleigh, North Devon, EX37 9DU.
Std: 01769 **Tel:** 560009
Std: 01769 **Fax:** 560387
Nearest Town/Resort Barnstaple
Directions ½ mile from Umberleigh Village on the B3227 in the direction of Atherington Village. 8 miles south of Molton and 8 miles from Torrington.
Acreage 3 **Open** 22 March **to** 27 Sept
Access Good **Site** Level
Sites Available **Total** 60
Facilities

Nearby Facilities
✓✓✓✓Graded Park. Tennis, fishing, games and a TV room on site. Pub ½ mile. Ideal for touring Exmoor and the North Devon beaches.

WOOLACOMBE

Europa Holiday Village, Station Road, Woolacombe, Devon.
Std: 01271 **Tel:** 870159
Nearest Town/Resort Woolacombe
Directions Less than a mile from and above Woolacombe on the right hand side of the main road leading into the resort.
Acreage 11 **Open** Easter **to** October
Access Good **Site** Lev/slope
Sites Available **Total** 100
Facilities
Nearby Facilities
Barnstaple
Panoramic views of surrounding countryside and Woolacombe Bay. Quietly situated informal site where well behaved animals (and children!) are welcome.

WOOLACOMBE

Little Roadway Farm Camping Park, Woolacombe, Devon, EX34 7HL.
Std: 01271 **Tel:** 870313
Nearest Town/Resort Woolacombe
Directions Barnstaple to Mullacott Cross on the A361, then the B3343 towards Woolacombe. Then take the B3231 towards Georgeham and Croyde. About 4 miles on the left.
Acreage 22 **Open** March **to** November
Site Level
Sites Available **Total** 200
Facilities
Nearby Facilities
Barnstaple

WOOLACOMBE

Twitchen Park, Mortehoe, Woolacombe, North Devon, EX34 7ES.
Std: 01271 **Tel:** 870476
Std: 01271 **Fax:** 870498
Nearest Town/Resort Woolacombe.
Directions From Barnstaple/Ilfracombe road (A361) to junction with B3343 at Mullacott Cross, first left signposted Woolacombe for 1¾ miles, then right signposted Mortehoe. Park is 1¼ miles on left.
Acreage 20 **Open** April **to** October
Access Good **Site** Sloping
Sites Available **Total** 131
Facilities
Nearby Facilities
Barnstaple.
✓✓✓✓Graded Park. Rural, scenic setting, close to Woolacombe's glorious sandy beach and spectacular coastal walks. New indoor pool opened in July 1997.

WOOLACOMBE

Woolacombe Sands Holiday Park, Beach Road, Woolacombe, North Devon, EX34 7AF.
Std: 01271 **Tel:** 870569
Std: 01271 **Fax:** 870606
Nearest Town/Resort Woolacombe
Directions Take the A361 from Barnstaple to Mullacott Cross, then the B3343 to Woolacombe. Park is on the left on the last bend before the village of Woolacombe.
Acreage 20 **Open** Easter **to** October
Access Good **Site** Lev/Slope
Sites Available **Total** 300
Facilities
Nearby Facilities
Barnstaple
✓✓✓✓Graded Park. Nearest site to Woolacombe's 3 mile beach. Set in beautiful countryside with scenic views overlooking the sea.

IT WILL HELP US TO CONTINUE PROVIDING THIS INFORMATION IF YOU WOULD KINDLY MENTION CADE'S WHEN REPLYING TO OUR ADVERTISERS

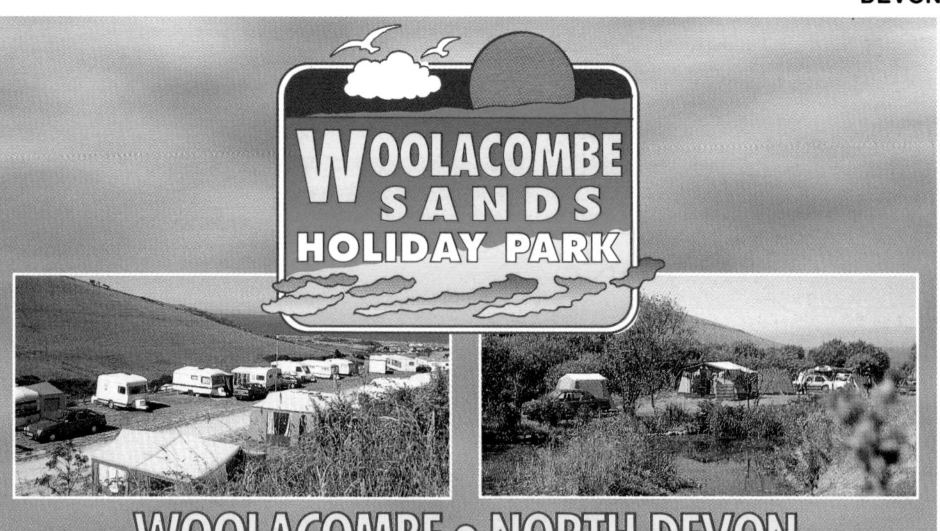

WOOLACOMBE • NORTH DEVON

Also available self-catering Chalets and Caravans with all amenities

THE NEAREST HOLIDAY PARK TO WOOLACOMBE BEACH

Set in beautiful countryside overlooking the sea and Woolacombe's fabulous Golden Sands. First class facilities for Tents and Tourers, which include Showers, Toilets, Wash-Basins, Hairdryers, Razor points, Launderette, Ironing room, Shop, Licensed Club, Bar Meals and Take-away, Nightly Entertainment (seasonal). **HEATED INDOOR SWIMMING POOL.**
Children have their own Woolly Bear Club, Games Room & Play Area.
Electric hook-ups available.
Booking is advisable especially in Peak Season.

Write for Brochure to: DEPT CG
WOOLACOMBE SANDS HOLIDAY PARK
BEACH ROAD, WOOLACOMBE, NORTH DEVON EX34 7AF.

TELEPHONE 01271 870569

AA

DORSET

BERE REGIS

Rowlands Wait Touring Park, Rye Hill, Bere Regis, Dorset, BH20 7LP.
Std: 01929 **Tel:** 471958
Std: 01929 **Fax:** 471958
Nearest Town/Resort Wareham
Directions At Bere Regis take road signposted to Wool/Bovington, about ¾ mile at top of Rye Hill turn right. Site 300yds.
Acreage 8 **Open** March **to** January
Access Good **Site** Lev/Slope
Sites Available **Total** 71
Facilities
Nearby Facilities
Wool
✓✓✓✓Graded Park. Situated in area of outstanding natural beauty. Within easy reach of coast, direct access from site into heath and woodland. Ideal walking, touring and the quiet family holiday. Rallies and Club Rallies welcome. Open Winter by arrangement. Countryside Discovery Member. David Bellamy Conservation Silver Award.

BLANDFORD

The Inside Park, Blandford, Dorset, DT11 9AD.
Std: 01258 **Tel:** 453719
Std: 01258 **Fax:** 459921
Nearest Town/Resort Blandford Forum
Directions 1¼ miles south west of Blandford on the road to Winterborne Stickland. Signposted from junction of A350 and A354 on Blandford bypass.
Acreage 13 **Open** Easter **to** October
Access Good **Site** Lev/Slope
Sites Available **Total** 100
Facilities
Nearby Facilities
✓✓✓✓✓Graded Park. Rural environment, ideal for touring, extensive wildlife.

BOURNEMOUTH

Cara Touring Park, Old Bridge Road, Iford, Bournemouth, Dorset, BH6 5RQ.
Std: 01202 **Tel:** 482121
Std: 01202 **Fax:** 482101
Nearest Town/Resort Bournemouth
Directions Just off the A35 between Bournemouth and Christchurch at Iford Bridge.
Acreage 6 **Open** All Year
Access Good **Site** Level
Sites Available **Total** 36
Facilities
Nearby Facilities
Bournemouth
✓✓✓✓✓Graded Park. Attractive setting adjoining the River Stour. Only ¾ mile from Bournemouth centre.

BOURNEMOUTH

Chesildene Caravan Park, 2 Chesildene Avenue, Bournemouth, Dorset, BH8 0DS.
Std: 01202 **Tel:** 513238
Std: 01202 **Fax:** 513238
Nearest Town/Resort Bournemouth.
Directions From Ringwood take the A338 southbound for approx. 6 miles, bear left off the A338 (signposted Bournemouth General Hospital) NB - DO NOT stay on the A338 and go over the flyover. At the roundabout turn right onto the A3060 Castle Lane West, at roundabout follow signs.
Acreage 1½ **Open** April **to** October
Access Good **Site** Level
Sites Available **Total** 35
Facilities
Nearby Facilities
Bournemouth.
Pets are welcome but not in August.

BOURNEMOUTH

St. Leonards Farm, Ringwood Road, West Moors, Ferndown, Dorset, BH22 0AQ.
Std: 01202 **Tel:** 872637
Std: 01202 **Fax:** 872637
Nearest Town/Resort Bournemouth
Directions On the A31 4 miles west of Ringwood, opposite Gulf Garage.
Acreage 12 **Open** April **to** September
Access Good **Site** Level
Sites Available
Facilities
Nearby Facilities
Bournemouth Central
✓✓✓✓Graded Park.

BRIDPORT

Binghams Farm Touring Caravan Park, Binghams Farm, Melplash, Bridport, Dorset, DT6 3TT.
Std: 01308 **Tel:** 488234
Nearest Town/Resort West Bay/Bridport.
Directions Turn off A35 in Bridport at the roundabout onto A3066, signposted Beaminster. In 1¼ miles turn left into Farm Road.
Acreage 5 **Open** All Year
Access Good **Site** Level
Sites Available **Total** 60
Facilities
Nearby Facilities
Dorchester
✓✓✓✓✓Graded Park. An Award Winning Park set in an area of outstanding natural beauty yet only 3 miles from the coast. An ideal base to explore Dorset. All modern heated facilities.

BRIDPORT

Eype House Caravan Park, Eype, Bridport, Dorset, DT6 6AL.
Std: 01308 **Tel:** 424903
Std: 01308 **Fax:** 424903
Nearest Town/Resort Bridport
Directions Signposted Eyes Mouth off the A35.
Acreage 4 **Open** Easter **to** 5 October
Site Sloping
Sites Available **Total** 20
Facilities
Nearby Facilities
Crewkerne/Weymouth
✓✓✓✓Graded Park. On a coastal path only 200 yards from the beach.

BRIDPORT

Freshwater Beach Holiday Park, Burton Bradstock, Bridport, Dorset.
Std: 01308 **Tel:** 897317
Std: 01308 **Fax:** 897336
Nearest Town/Resort Bridport.
Directions From Bridport take B3157 towards Weymouth site 2 miles on right.
Acreage 40 **Open** Easter **to** October
Access Good **Site** Level

OWN PRIVATE BEACH!

A Fine Family Park with Large Camping and Touring Fields

FREE ENTERTAINMENT NIGHTLY*

FRESHWATER BEACH HOLIDAY PARK

- Our Own Private Beach
- Heated Swimming Pools
- Club Complex with Licensed Restaurant & Bars
- Entertainment Nightly (*Whitsun-Mid Sept)
- Children's Activities & Amusements
- Sea Fishing & Horse/Pony Rides
- Supermarket & Take-away Foods
- Holiday Caravans for Hire
- High Level of Facilities & Amenities
- Fine Country and Seaside Walks
- Golf Course Adjoining Park
- Caravan Sales

Free colour brochure from: Mr C.C. Coads

FRESHWATER BEACH HOLIDAY PARK

Burton Bradstock, Near Bridport, Dorset DT6 4PT

TEL: 01308 897317 FAX:01308 897336

Website: http://www.wdi.co.uk/fresh/home.html e-mail:freshwater@wdi.co.uk

BRITISH GRADED HOLIDAY PARKS ✓✓✓✓

Sites Available **Total** 500
Facilities
Nearby Facilities
Dorchester
✓✓✓Graded Park. Own private beach. Free family entertainment. Good cliff walks. Golf course adjoining park.

BRIDPORT

Highlands End Farm Holiday Park, Eype, Bridport, Dorset, DT6 6AR.
Std: 01308. **Tel:** 422139
Std: 01308 **Fax:** 425672
Nearest Town/Resort Bridport.
Directions On approach to Bridport from east (Dorchester) on A35 turn left at roundabout, follow Bridport By-pass. Second roundabout take third exit signposted A35 West 1 mile turn left to Eype and follow signposts.
Acreage 8 **Open** March **to** October
Access Good **Site** Level
Sites Available **Total** 195
Facilities
Nearby Facilities
Axminsterr.
✓✓✓✓✓Graded Park. Exceptional views across Lyme Bay, 500 metres from the beach. Heated swimming pool, steam room and sauna. Tennis on site. All weather awning areas. E-Mail highlands@wdlh.co.uk

BRIDPORT

West Bay Holiday Park, West Bay, Bridport, Dorset, DT6 4HB.
Std: 01308 **Tel:** 422424
Std: 01308 **Fax:** 421371
Nearest Town/Resort Weymouth
Directions A35 from Dorchester. West Bay is towards the harbour.
Open Easter **to** End Oct
Access Good **Site** Level
Sites Available **Total** 131
Facilities
Nearby Facilities
Dorchester.
✓✓✓Graded Park. Riverside, next to the harbour.

CHARMOUTH

Manor Farm Holiday Centre, Manor Farm, Charmouth, Bridport, Dorset, DT6 6QL.
Std: 01297 **Tel:** 560226
Std: 01297 **Fax:** 560429
Nearest Town/Resort Charmouth.
Directions Come off the Charmouth bypass at east end Manor Farm is ¾ mile on right, in Charmouth.
Acreage 30 **Open** All year
Access Good **Site** Lev/Slope
Sites Available **Total** 345
Facilities
Nearby Facilities
Axminster.
✓✓✓Graded Park. Ten minutes level walk to beach, alongside river. In area of outstanding natural beauty. Ideal touring.

CHARMOUTH

Newlands Holidays, Charmouth, Dorset, DT6 6RB.
Std: 01297 **Tel:** 560259
Nearest Town/Resort Charmouth/Lyme Regis
Directions Turn off the A35 at the eastern exit for Charmouth, Newlands is situated a short distance on the left hand side.
Acreage 23
Access Good **Site** Terraced
Sites Available **Total** 200
Facilities
Nearby Facilities
Axminster
✓✓✓✓Graded Park. Situated in the Heritage Coast village of Charmouth, near Lyme Regis. Wonderful views and walks through National Trust land. A short stroll to the village centre and safe beach.

CHARMOUTH

Seadown Caravan Park, Bridge Road, Charmouth, Dorset, DT6 6QY.
Std: 01297 **Tel:** 560154
Nearest Town/Resort Lyme Regis/Charmouth
Directions From Bridport take the A35 towards Axminster and Honiton. Signposted for Charmouth, second turning left into Bridge Road.
Open All Year
Access Good **Site** Level
Sites Available **Total** 60
Facilities
Nearby Facilities
Axminster
Alongside the River Char with direct access to the beach and Heritage Coastal Path.

CHARMOUTH

Wood Farm Caravan & Camping Park, Axminster Road, Charmouth, Bridport, Dorset DT6 6BT.
Std: 01297. **Tel:** 560697
Std: 01297 **Fax:** 560697
Nearest Town/Resort Charmouth.
Directions On A35, ½ mile west Charmouth.
Acreage 12
Access Good **Site** Terraced
Sites Available **Total** 216
Facilities
Nearby Facilities
Axminster.
✓✓✓✓✓Graded Park. Beach ¾ mile. Country setting. Tennis on site. Indoor heated swimming pool.

CHIDEOCK

Golden Cap Holiday Park, Seatown, Chideock, Nr. Bridport, Dorset.
Std: 01308 **Tel:** 422139
Std: 01308 **Fax:** 425672
Nearest Town/Resort Bridport
Directions On approach to Bridport from east (Dorchester) follow A35 signs around Bridport by-pass. After 2 miles west of Bridport turn left for Seatown, at Chideock park is signposted.
Acreage 10 **Open** March **to** October
Access Good **Site** Level
Sites Available **Total** 120
Facilities
Nearby Facilities
Axminster
✓✓✓✓✓Graded Park. 100 metres from beach, overlooked by the famous Golden Cap cliff top. Indoor swimming pool available 5 minutes travelling time. All weather awning areas. Take-away food available. Unique location on the Heritage Coastline.

CHRISTCHURCH

Heathfield Caravan & Camping Park, Forest Road, Bransgore, Nr. Christchurch, Dorset, BH23 8LA.
Std: 01425 **Tel:** 672397
Nearest Town/Resort Christchurch/New Milton
Directions From the traffic lights at Lyndhurst drive 9 miles towards Christchurch on the A35. Turn right signposted Godwinscroft, then first right and the site is 200 yards on the left. From Christchurch turn left after the East Close Hotel, then first right and the site is 200 yards on the left.
Acreage 14 **Open** March **to** October
Access Good **Site** Level
Sites Available **Total** 200
Facilities
Nearby Facilities
Hinton Admiral
Well appointed site on the edge of the New Forest. Within easy reach of Bournemouth, Highcliffe and Mudeford beaches.

CHRISTCHURCH

Hoburne Park, Hoburne Lane, Christchurch, Dorset, BH23 4HU.
Std: 01425 **Tel:** 273379
Nearest Town/Resort Christchurch.
Directions From junction of A35 with A337 at Christchurch, take first exit left onto A337 towards Lymington and then left off next roundabout. Park entrance is 100yds on right.
Acreage 17 **Open** March **to** October
Access Good **Site** Level
Sites Available **Total** 285
Facilities
Nearby Facilities
Christchurch
✓✓✓✓✓Graded Park. Approx 8 miles from Bournemouth, close to sandy beaches, the New Forest, the Solent and the Isle of Wight. Caravan Holiday Park of the Year 1994, England for Excellence Awards (ETB).

CHRISTCHURCH

Longfield, Matchams Lane, Hurn, Christchurch, Dorset, BH23 6AW.
Std: 01202 **Tel:** 485214
Nearest Town/Resort Christchurch/ Bournemouth
Directions A338 into Bournemouth. Hurn road, Christchurch, Wessex Way.
Acreage 2½ **Open** All Year
Access Good **Site** Level
Sites Available **Total** 20
Facilities
Nearby Facilities
Christchurch

CHRISTCHURCH

Mount Pleasant Touring Park, Matchams Lane, Hurn, Christchurch, Dorset, BH23 6AW.
Std: 01202 **Tel:** 475474
Nearest Town/Resort Bournemouth
Directions From Ringwood take the A338, exit at the Christchurch/Airport signs. Follow signs for the Airport until you reach a mini roundabout, then follow camping signs.
Acreage 10 **Open** March **to** October
Access Good **Site** Level

Sites Available **Total** 150
Facilities
Nearby Facilities
Christchurch
✓✓✓✓✓ Graded Park. Exceptionally clean, "Excellent Graded" park. Closest camping to Bournemouth. Near to lovely forest walks.

CORFE CASTLE

Burnbake Campsite, Rempstone, Corfe Castle, Dorset, BH20 5JJ.
Std: 01929 **Tel:** 480570
Std: 01929 **Fax:** 480626
Nearest Town/Resort Swanage
Directions Between Corfe Castle and Studland just off the B3351. From Wareham take the A351 to Corfe Castle, turn left under the castle onto the Studland road, through the old railway arches, and take the third turning left signposted Rempstone.
Acreage 12 **Open** April **to** September
Site Lev/Slope
Sites Available **Total** 130
Facilities
Nearby Facilities
Wareham
A quiet, secluded site in woodlands with a stream. 4 miles from Studland with its three miles of sandy beach and excellent safe bathing. 4 miles from Swanage.

CORFE CASTLE

Knitson Tourers Site, Knitson Farm, Corfe Castle, Dorset, BH20 5JB.
Std: 01929 **Tel:** 425121
Nearest Town/Resort Swanage
Directions Take the A351 to Swanage outskirts, turn first left into Wash Pond Lane. Continue until the lane finishes at a T-Junction turn left. Site is approx. ½ mile further on, on the left hand side.
Acreage 5½ **Open** Easter **to** October
Site Lev/Slope
Sites Available **Total** 60
Facilities
Nearby Facilities
Wareham
Set in very beautiful countryside with many walks radiating from the field, including Swanage and Studland beaches.

CORFE CASTLE

The Woodland Camping Park, Glebe Farm, Bucknowle, Wareham, Dorset, BH20 5NS.
Std: 01929 **Tel:** 480280
Nearest Town/Resort Swanage/Wareham
Directions Take Church Knowle and Kimmeridge road off A351 at Corfe Castle ruins site ½ mile on right.
Acreage 6½ **Open** Easter **to** October
Site Lev/Slope
Sites Available **Total** 65
Facilities
Nearby Facilities
Direct access onto Purbeck Hills by public footpath. 3 beaches within 5 miles. A quiet family site. SAE for full information.

DORCHESTER

Camping & Caravanning Club Site, Station Road, Moreton, Near Dorchester, Dorset, DT2 8BB.
Std: 01305 **Tel:** 853801
Nearest Town/Resort Dorchester
Directions Take the A352 Dorchester ring road signposted to Wool and Wareham. At the first large roundabout take the B3390 to Crossways, go over the railway crossing and we are next to the Frampton Arms.
Acreage 7 **Open** 22 March **to** 27 Nov
Access Good **Site** Lev/Slope
Sites Available **Total** 130
Facilities
Nearby Facilities
Moreton
✓✓✓✓✓ Graded Park. Good fishing in the area. Ideal for touring Dorset.

DORCHESTER

Clay Pigeon Caravan Park, Wardon Hill, Evershot, Dorchester, Dorset.
Std: 01935 **Tel:** 83492
Nearest Town/Resort Dorchester.
Directions On A37 midway between Yeovil and Dorchester.
Acreage 3¼ **Open** All Year
Access Good **Site** Level
Sites Available **Total** 60
Facilities
Nearby Facilities
Dorchester
✓✓✓✓ Graded Park. Views over Dorset Downs. Ideal for touring. Lyme Bay and Weymouth close by. Separate 4¼ acre rally field.

DORCHESTER

Giants Head Caravan & Camping Park, Old Sherborne Road, Dorchester, Dorset.
Std: 01300 **Tel:** 341242
Nearest Town/Resort Dorchester
Directions From Dorchester avoiding by-pass, at top of town roundabout take Sherborne Road approx 500 yards fork right at Loaders Garage signposted.
Acreage 3 **Open** March **to** October
Access Good **Site** Lev/Slope
Sites Available **Total** 50
Facilities

Nearby Facilities
Dorchester.
✓✓✓ Graded Park. Ideal touring, wonderful views, good walking. Car is essential. Licensed.

DORCHESTER

Warmwell Country Touring Park, Warmwell, Nr. Dorchester, Dorset, DT2 8JE.
Std: 01305 **Tel:** 852313
Std: 01305 **Fax:** 852313
Nearest Town/Resort Weymouth
Directions From A31 Dorchester to Poole road take the B3390 signposted Warmwell.
Acreage 15 **Open** March **to** January
Access Good **Site** Level
Sites Available **Total** 190
Facilities
Nearby Facilities
Moreton
✓✓✓✓ Graded Park. Opposite major leisure attractions. Rallies welcome.

GILLINGHAM

Thorngrove Caravan & Camping Park, Common Mead Lane, Gillingham, Dorset, SP8 4RE.
Std: 01747 **Tel:** 822242
Std: 01747 **Fax:** 825966
Nearest Town/Resort Gillingham
Directions From the Gillingham relief road, take the B3081 signposted Wincanton. Take the second turning on the left signposted Kington Magna. Thorngrove is ¾ mile on the right.
Acreage 2½ **Open** All Year
Access Good **Site** Level
Sites Available **Total** 40
Facilities
Nearby Facilities
Gillingham
✓✓✓✓ Graded Park. Peacefully situated with a delightful view of rural Dorset. Modern purpose built facilities in individual rooms.

LULWORTH COVE

Durdle Door Holiday Park, Lulworth Cove, Wareham, Dorset, BH20 5PU.
Std: 01929 **Tel:** 400200
Std: 01929 **Fax:** 400260
Nearest Town/Resort Wareham
Directions Take the B3077 Wool to West Lulworth road, fork right in West Lulworth Village, entrance is at the top of the hill.
Acreage 45 **Open** March **to** October
Access Good **Site** Lev/Slope
Sites Available **Total** 193
Facilities
Nearby Facilities
Wool
✓✓✓✓ Graded Park. Unique cliff top position overlooking the famous landmark of Durdle Door.

LYME REGIS

Shrubbery Caravan Park, Rousdon, Lyme Regis, Dorset, DT7 3XW.
Std: 01297 **Tel:** 442227
Nearest Town/Resort Lyme Regis.
Directions 3 miles west of Lyme Regis on the A3052.
Acreage 10 **Open** March **to** November
Access Good **Site** Level
Sites Available **Total** 120
Facilities
Nearby Facilities
Axminster.
Quiet, level, sheltered site.

LYME REGIS

Uplyme Touring Park, Hook Farm, Gore Lane, Uplyme, Lyme Regis, Dorset, DT7 3UU.
Std: 01297 **Tel:** 442801
Nearest Town/Resort Lyme Regis
Directions Take the B3165, 1¼ miles north-west of Lyme Regis turn uphill into Gore Lane. In the village of Uplyme on the main Lyme Regis to Axminster road.
Acreage 6
Access Poor **Site** Sloping
Sites Available **Total** 100
Facilities
Nearby Facilities
Axminster
A quiet, rural site with good views. Ideal for walking.

LYME REGIS

Westhayes Caravan Park, Rousdon, Nr. Lyme Regis, Dorset, DT7 3RD.
Std: 01297 **Tel:** 23456
Std: 01297 **Fax:** 625079
Nearest Town/Resort Lyme Regis/ Seaton.
Directions Leave Axminster on A358 Seaton road, 3 miles turn left at Boshill Cross signposted Lyme Regis, site 1 mile on left.
Acreage 7½ **Open** All Year
Access Good **Site** Level
Sites Available **Total** 150
Facilities
Nearby Facilities
Axminster.
✓✓✓✓✓ Graded Park. Rallies welcome. Storage facilities. Static caravans for sale. Seasonal tourers.

OWERMOIGNE

Sandyholme Holiday Park, Moreton Road, Owermoigne, Nr. Dorchester, Dorset, DT2 8HZ.
Std: 01305 **Tel:** 852677
Nearest Town/Resort Dorchester/ Weymouth
Directions Situated off the A352 Dorchester/Wareham Road - 1 mile through the pretty village of Owermoigne.
Acreage 6 **Open** Easter **to** October
Access Good **Site** Level
Sites Available **Total** 65
Facilities
Nearby Facilities
Moreton
✓✓✓✓ Graded Park. Quiet family site in Hardy countryside, ideal touring spot with all facilities, situated between Lulworth Cove and Weymouth. Swimming pool nearby.

POOLE

Beacon Hill Touring Park, Blandford Road North, Poole, Dorset, BH16 6AB.
Std: 01202 **Tel:** 631631
Nearest Town/Resort Poole/Bournemouth
Directions Situated on the A350 ¼ mile north of the junction with the A35, between Poole and Blandford.
Acreage 30 **Open** Easter **to** September
Access Good **Site** level
Sites Available **Total** 170
Facilities
Nearby Facilities
Poole
✓✓✓✓ Graded Park. Partly wooded, lovely peaceful setting, scenic views. Proximity main routes. Ideal touring base for Bournemouth, New Forest and Dorset. Coarse fishing, tennis and childrens play areas on site. Take away meals and coffee shop in high season. Bellamy Conservation Award Park, AA 4 Pennants and ANWB Listed.

POOLE

Huntick Farm Caravans, Lytchett Matravers, Poole, Dorset, BH16 6BB.
Std: 01202 **Tel:** 622222
Nearest Town/Resort Poole
Directions Off the A350 Blandford to Poole road. Take the turning for Lytchett Matravers and at the Rose & Crown Public House turn down Huntick Road. The site is approx. ¾ mile on the right.

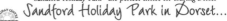

Acreage 3 **Open** Easter **to** September
Access Good **Site** Level
Sites Available **Total** 30
Facilities
Nearby Facilities
Poole
6 miles from the sea and within easy reach of ferry crossings to France. Many interesting places to visit nearby such as Corfe Castle, The Swannery at Abbotsbury, The Blue Pool and many famous gardens. Within easy reach of Hardy Country.

POOLE

Merley Court Touring Park, Merley, Wimborne, Nr Poole, Dorset, BH21 3AA.
Std: 01202 **Tel:** 881488
Std: 01202 **Fax:** 881484
Nearest Town/Resort Poole.

Acreage 20 **Open** March 1st **to** Jan 7th
Access Good **Site** Level
Sites Available **Total** 160
Facilities
Nearby Facilities
Poole.
✓✓✓✓✓Graded Park. AA 5 Pennant Premier park. Bournemouth 8 miles, Poole 4 miles, Purbeck and New Forest 7 miles. English Tourist Board Caravan Park of the Year 1991, Practical Caravan Magazine "Best Family Park" 1993 and 1997 and AA Campsite of the Year 1999. New Leisure Garden set in a beautifully landscaped walled garden, with croquet, petanque, beach volleyball, crazy golf and attractive gardens to explore.

POOLE

Organford Manor Caravans & Holidays, Organford, Poole, Dorset, BH16 6ES.
Std: 01202 **Tel:** 622202
Nearest Town/Resort Poole.
Directions Approaching from the Poole direction on the A35. At the Lytchett roundabout/junction of the A35/A351 continue on the A35 (signposted Dorchester) for ¼ mile. Take the first left, site first entrance on right.
Acreage 3 **Open** 15 March **to** October
Access Good **Site** Level
Sites Available **Total** 80
Facilities
Nearby Facilities
Poole/Wareham
✓✓✓Graded Park. Quiet, secluded site in wooded grounds of 11 acres. Seasonal site shop. House within 10 miles of good beaches from Bournemouth to Swanage. Facilities for the disabled limited, few motorcycles accepted at Proprietors discretion.

POOLE

Pear Tree Touring Park, Organford, Poole, Dorset, BH16 6LA.
Std: 01202 **Tel:** 622434
Std: 01202 **Fax:** 622434
Nearest Town/Resort Poole
Directions Take A35 Poole/Dorchester road. Turn onto A351 to Wareham at Lytchett Minster. Turn right within 1 mile signposted Organford. Second site on left hand side ½ mile.
Acreage 7½ **Open** April **to** October
Access Good **Site** Level
Sites Available **Total** 125
Facilities
Nearby Facilities
Wareham/Poole
✓✓✓✓✓Graded Park. Quiet, family, country park, centrally situated for Bournemouth, Poole and Swanage. The New Forest, the Purbeck Hills and the lovely sandy beaches at Sandbanks and Studland Bay are all within easy reach. Mobile fish and chip van.

POOLE

Rockley Park, Napier Road, Hamworthy, Poole, Dorset, BH15 4LZ.
Std: 0345 **Tel:** 753753
Nearest Town/Resort Poole
Directions From town centre go over lifting bridge and follow road to traffic lights. Turn left and follow signs for the park.
Open March **to** October
Access Good **Site** Sloping
Sites Available **Total** 75
Facilities
Nearby Facilities
Poole
✓✓✓✓✓Graded Park. Direct access to the beach. Kids Club and a full family entertainment programme. Watersports, bowling, multisports court and a Burger King on park. Boat storage facilities. Rose Award.

POOLE

Sandford Holiday Park, Holton Heath, Poole, Dorset, BH16 6JZ.
Std: 01202 **Tel:** 631600
Std: 01392 **Fax:** 445202
Nearest Town/Resort Poole
Directions Located on the A351 to Wareham which branches off the A35 5 miles west of Poole. Turn right at Holton Heath traffic lights by Texaco Petrol Station, park is on the left.
Acreage 60 **Open** Easter **to** October
Access Good **Site** Level
Sites Available **Total** 525
Facilities
Nearby Facilities
Wareham.
✓✓✓✓✓Graded Park. Set in beautiful woodland, within easy driving distance of Poole, Swanage, Sandbanks, Lulworth Cove, the New Forest, Corfe Castle and many superb family attractions.

POOLE

South Lytchett Manor Camping & Caravan Park, Dorchester Road, Lytchett Minster, Poole, Dorset, BH16 6JB.
Std: 01202 **Tel:** 622577
Nearest Town/Resort Poole
Directions From Poole take the A35 dual carriageway to the roundabout at the end. Take the third exit out, into and through Lytchett Minster and the site is situated on the left approx. 600 yards out of the village.
Acreage 11 **Open** April **to** October
Access Good **Site** Level
Sites Available **Total** 150
Facilities
Nearby Facilities

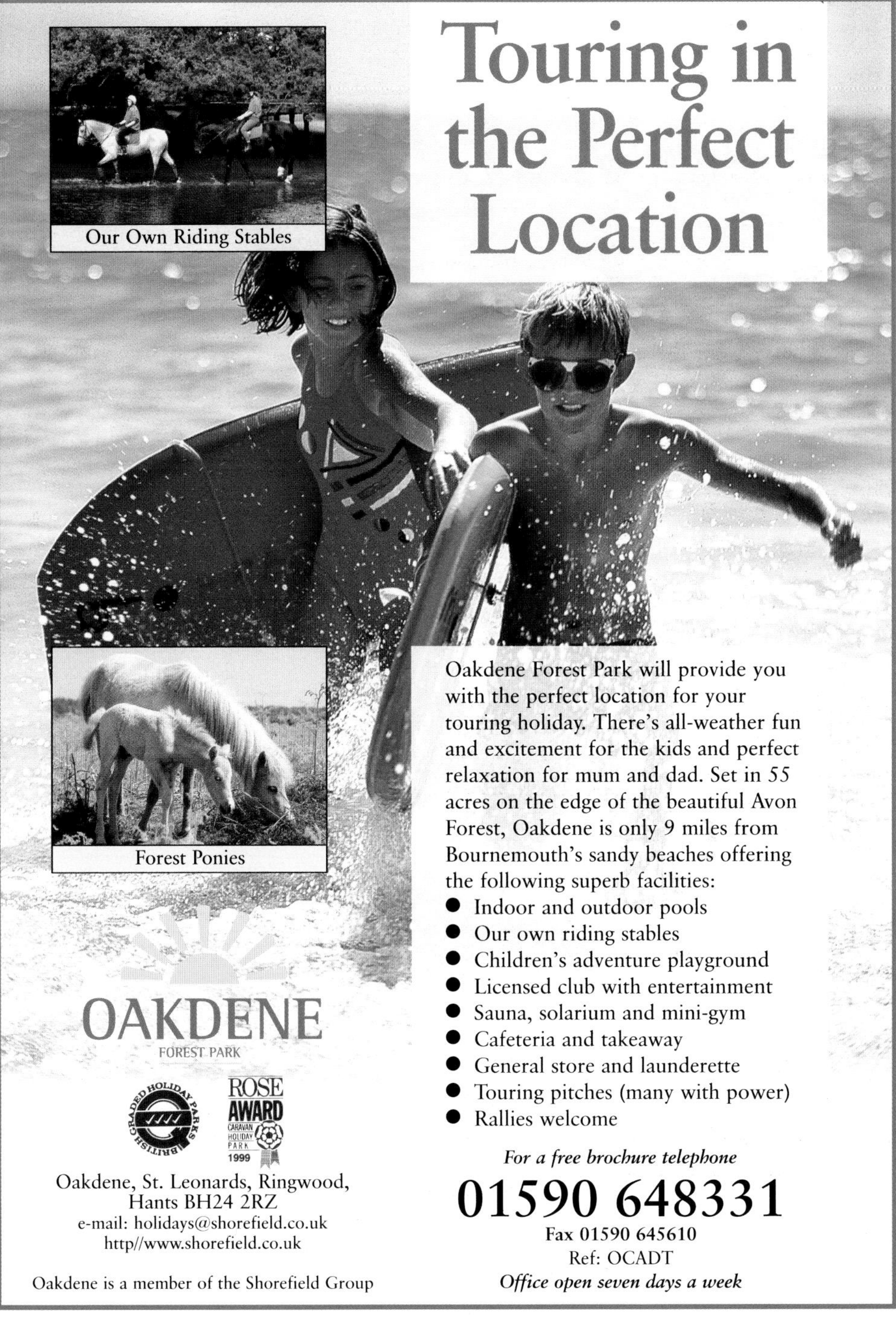
Touring in the Perfect Location
Our Own Riding Stables
Forest Ponies
Oakdene Forest Park will provide you with the perfect location for your touring holiday. There's all-weather fun and excitement for the kids and perfect relaxation for mum and dad. Set in 55 acres on the edge of the beautiful Avon Forest, Oakdene is only 9 miles from Bournemouth's sandy beaches offering the following superb facilities:
● Indoor and outdoor pools
● Our own riding stables
● Children's adventure playground
● Licensed club with entertainment
● Sauna, solarium and mini-gym
● Cafeteria and takeaway
● General store and launderette
● Touring pitches (many with power)
● Rallies welcome
OAKDENE
FOREST PARK
BRITISH GRADED HOLIDAY PARKS
ROSE AWARD
CARAVAN HOLIDAY PARK
1999
For a free brochure telephone
01590 648331
Fax 01590 645610
Ref: OCADT
Office open seven days a week
Oakdene, St. Leonards, Ringwood, Hants BH24 2RZ
e-mail: holidays@shorefield.co.uk
http//www.shorefield.co.uk
Oakdene is a member of the Shorefield Group

Poole
Popular, rural site situated in lovely parkland surroundings. Ideal base for exploring Poole Harbour, Bournemouth, Purbeck and beautiful beaches, sailing and wind surfing. AA 3 Pennants.

SHAFTESBURY

Blackmore Vale Caravan Park, Sherborne Causway, Shaftesbury, Dorset.
Std: 01747 **Tel:** 852573
Std: 01747 **Fax:** 851671
Nearest Town/Resort Shaftsbury
Open All Year
Access Good **Site** Level
Sites Available **Total** 50
Facilities
Nearby Facilities
Gillingham
Scenic views, ideal touring.

ST. LEONARDS

Camping International, 229 Ringwood Road, St. Leonards, Nr. Ringwood, Hants, BH24 2SD.
Std: 01202 **Tel:** 872817
Std: 01202 **Fax:** 861292
Nearest Town/Resort Bournemouth
Directions 2¼ miles west of Ringwood on A31.
Acreage 8 **Open** March **to** October
Access Good **Site** Level
Sites Available **Total** 205
Facilities
Nearby Facilities
Bournemouth.
✓✓✓✓Graded Park. New Forest, Bournemouth and coast, ideal touring.

ST. LEONARDS

Oakhill Holiday Park, 234 Ringwood Road, St. Leonards, Ringwood, Dorset, BH24 2SB.
Std: 01202 **Tel:** 876968
Nearest Town/Resort Ringwood
Directions 3½ miles west of Ringwood on A31.
Acreage 10 **Open** Easter/1 April **to** Oct
Access Good **Site** Level
Sites Available **Total** 80
Facilities
Nearby Facilities
Bournemouth
Within easy reach of the New Forest and Bournemouth.

ST. LEONARDS

Shamba Holiday Park, 230 Ringwood Road, St. Leonards, Ringwood, Dorset, BH24 2SB.
Std: 01202. **Tel:** 873302
Nearest Town/Resort Ringwood
Directions Just off the A31 midway between Ringwood and Wimborne.
Acreage 7 **Open** March **to** October
Access Good **Site** Level
Sites Available **Total** 150
Facilities
Nearby Facilities
Bournemouth.
✓✓✓Graded Park. Close to the New Forest and Bournemouth. AA 3 Pennants.

SWANAGE

Cauldron Barn Farm Caravan Park, Cauldron Barn Road, Swanage, Dorset, BH19 1QQ.
Std: 01929 **Tel:** 422080
Std: 01929 **Fax:** 427870
Nearest Town/Resort Swanage
Directions Turn left off Victoria Avenue into Northbrook Road, take the third left into Cauldron Barn Road.
Acreage 12 **Open** Mid March **to** Mid November
Access Good
Sites Available **Total** 40
Facilities
Nearby Facilities
Wareham
✓✓✓✓Graded Park. Nearest park to the beach and town, 15 minute walk. Ideal for walking, boating and golf.

SWANAGE

Flower Meadow Caravan Park, Haycrafts Lane, Swanage, Dorset, BH19 3EB.
Std: 01929 **Tel:** 480035
Nearest Town/Resort Swanage
Directions Take the A351 Wareham to Swanage road, 2½ miles beyond Corfe Castle turn right (south) at Harmans Cross crossroads. The site is 300 yards along on the left hand side.
Acreage 2 **Open** April **to** October
Access Good **Site** Lev/Slope
Sites Available **Total** 16
Facilities
Nearby Facilities
Wareham
300 yards from a steam railway station to Swanage or Corfe Castle. Near the beaches of Swanage and Studland. Walking in the Purbeck Hills.

SWANAGE

Herston Yards Farm, Wash Pond Lane, Swanage, Dorset, BH19 3DJ.
Std: 01929 **Tel:** 422932
Nearest Town/Resort Swanage.
Acreage 8 **Open** April **to** October

Access Good
Sites Available **Total** 80
Facilities
Nearby Facilities
Wareham.
Quiet, family site. Milk and eggs available. One shaver point available.

SWANAGE

Tom's Field Camping Site, Tom's Field Road, Langton Matravers, Nr. Swanage, Dorset.
Std: 01929 **Fax:** 427110
Nearest Town/Resort Swanage
Acreage 4 **Open** Easter **to** October
Site Lev/Slope
Sites Available **Total** 100
Facilities
Nearby Facilities
Wareham
The camp has a variety of fields and is well positioned amidst the Purbeck Hills in an area of outstanding natural beauty. Swanage, Corfe Castle and Studland all within easy reach. Access to coastal walk close by. Pets welcome on a lead.

SWANAGE

Ulwell Cottage Caravan Park, Ulwell, Swanage, Dorset, BH19 3DG.
Std: 01929 **Tel:** 422823
Nearest Town/Resort Swanage
Directions 1¼ miles from Swanage on Studland Road. Turn left by telephone box (left hand side) on side of road.
Open March **to** 7 January
Access Good **Site** Lev/Slope
Sites Available **Total** 70
Facilities
Nearby Facilities
Wareham
✓✓✓✓✓ Graded Park. Near sandy beaches, scenic walks and ideal for all water sports. Rose Award.

SWANAGE

Ulwell Farm Caravan Park, Ulwell, Swanage, Dorset, BH19 3DG.
Std: 01929 **Tel:** 422825
Nearest Town/Resort Swanage
Directions Approx. 1½ miles from Swanage on the road towards Studland and Sandbanks Chain Ferry. Park entrance is on the right 150 metres after the end of 30mph limit.
Acreage 2½ **Open** April **to** September
Access Good **Site** Sloping
Sites Available **Total** 50
Facilities
Nearby Facilities
Wareham
✓✓✓✓ Graded Park. Situated in an area of outstanding varied countryside and coastal scenery. Safe bathing and water sports nearby.

THREE LEGGED CROSS

Woolsbridge Manor Farm Caravan Park, Three Legged Cross, Wimborne, Dorset, BH21 6RA.
Std: 01202 **Tel:** 826369
Std: 01202 **Fax:** 813172
Nearest Town/Resort Ringwood
Directions Take the A31 west, 1 mile past Ringwood take the filter and follow signs for Three Legged Cross and Moors Valley Country Park. Caravan park is 2 miles along this road on the right hand side.
Acreage 7 **Open** Easter **to** October
Access Good **Site** Level
Sites Available **Total** 60
Facilities
Nearby Facilities
Bournemouth
✓✓✓✓ Graded Park. Quiet country location on a working farm, very spacious. Ideal and safe for families. Within walking distance of the Moors Valley Country Park and a pub with restaurant. Easy access to the South Coast attractions. AA 3 Pennants.

WAREHAM

Birchwood Tourist Park, North Trigon, Wareham, Dorset, BH20 7PA.
Std: 01929 **Tel:** 554763
Nearest Town/Resort Wareham
Directions From Bere Regis follow the A35 towards Poole. After approx 1 mile fork right to Wareham. Birchwood Park is the second park on the left after approx 3 miles.
Acreage 25 **Open** March **to** October
Access Good **Site** Level
Sites Available **Total** 175
Facilities
Nearby Facilities
Wareham
✓✓✓✓ Graded Park. Situated in Wareham Forest with direct access to forest walks. Ideal for touring the whole of Dorset.

WAREHAM

Manor Farm Caravan Park, 1 Manor Farm Cottage, East Stoke, Wareham, Dorset, BH20 6AW.
Std: 01929. **Tel:** Bindon Abbey 462870
Nearest Town/Resort Wareham/Lulworth Cove.
Directions From Wareham take the A352 to East Stoke. Turn left by redundant church and the park is ½ mile along the lane on the right.
Acreage 2½ **Open** Easter **to** September
Access Good **Site** Level
Sites Available **Total** 40
Facilities
Nearby Facilities
Wool/Wareham.
Flat, grass touring park on a working farm in a rural area of outstanding natural beauty, central for most of Dorset. Family run park with clean facilities. Resident Proprietors David & Gillian Topp. A.A. 3 Pennant, RAC Appointed - Alan Roger Good Sites Guide. No groups or singles.

WAREHAM

Ridge Farm Camping & Caravan Park, Barnhill Road, Ridge, Wareham, Dorset, BH20 5BG.
Std: 01929 **Tel:** 556444
Std: 01929 **Fax:** 556222
Nearest Town/Resort Wareham
Directions Approx. 1½ miles south of Wareham turn left in the village of Stoborough towards Ridge. Follow signs down Barnhill Road to Ridge Farm at the end of the lane.
Acreage 3½ **Open** March **to** October
Access Good **Site** Level
Sites Available **Total** 60
Facilities
Nearby Facilities
Wareham
Peaceful, family run site adjacent to a working farm and RSPB Reserve. In an area of outstanding natural beauty and ideally situated for the Purbeck Hills, Poole Harbour and the coast. Boat launching nearby.

WAREHAM

Wareham Forest Tourist Park, North Trigon, Wareham, Dorset, BH20 7NZ.
Std: 01929 **Tel:** 551393
Std: 01929 **Fax:** 551393
Nearest Town/Resort Wareham
Directions Located midway between Wareham and Bere Regis (off A35)
Open All Year
Access Good **Site** Level
Sites Available **Total** 200
Facilities
Nearby Facilities
Wareham
✓✓✓✓✓Graded Park. Forest and wild life.

WEYMOUTH

Bagwell Farm Touring Park, Bagwell Farm, Chickerell, Weymouth, Dorset.
Std: 01305. **Tel:** 782575
Nearest Town/Resort Weymouth.
Directions 4 miles from Weymouth, take the Bridport road, site entrance 500 yards past Victoria Inn on B3157.
Acreage 14 **Open** All Year
Access Good **Site** Lev/Slope
Sites Available **Total** 320
Facilities
Nearby Facilities
Weymouth.
✓✓✓✓Graded Park. Views of The Fleet and Chesil Beach. Campers shelter. Take-away food available.

WEYMOUTH

Chesil Beach Holiday Park, Weymouth, Dorset, DT4 9AG.
Std: 01305 **Tel:** 773233
Std: 01305 **Fax:** 781233
Nearest Town/Resort Weymouth
Directions Follow the A354 through Weymouth towards Portland. On the outskirts of Weymouth, Chesil Beach is on the right before the Causeway.
Acreage 19 **Open** May **to** September
Access Good **Site** Level
Sites Available **Total** 35
Facilities
Nearby Facilities
Weymouth
✓✓✓Graded Park. Situated overlooking the Fleet Lagoon to the Chesil Bank and the Portland Peninsula. On park facilities include indoor fun pool, 9 pin bowling and family clubroom.

WEYMOUTH

East Fleet Farm Touring Park, Fleet Lane, Chickerell, Weymouth, Dorset, DT3 4DW.
Std: 01305 **Tel:** 785768
Nearest Town/Resort Weymouth
Directions 3 miles west of Weymouth on the B3157, left at Chickerell T.A. Camp.
Acreage 20 **Open** 16 March **to** 15 Jan
Access Good **Site** Lev/Slope
Sites Available **Total** 210
Facilities

Nearby Facilities
Weymouth
✓✓✓✓Graded Park. On edge of Fleet Water. Area of outstanding natural beauty.

WEYMOUTH

Littlesea Holiday Park, Lynch Lane, Weymouth, Dorset, DT4 9DT.
Std: 01305 **Tel:** 774414
Std: 01305 **Fax:** 760338
Nearest Town/Resort Weymouth.
Directions From the outskirts of Weymouth turn right at the first and second roundabouts signposted Portland. At the third roundabout turn left signposted Chickerell, Portland. Go straight across the traffic lights and turn left into Lynch Lane. The Park is at the far end.
Acreage 11 **Open** 17 April **to** 30 Oct
Site Lev/Slope
Sites Available **Total** 265
Facilities
Nearby Facilities
Weymouth.
✓✓✓✓Graded Park. Pleasantly set on the sides of a small valley, overlooking The Fleet and Chesil Bank.

WEYMOUTH

Osmington Mills Holidays Ltd., Ranch House, Osmington Mills, Weymouth, Dorset, DT3 6HB.
Std: 01305 **Tel:** 832311
Std: 01305 **Fax:** 835251
Nearest Town/Resort Weymouth
Directions 5 miles east of Weymouth off the A353 Weymouth to Wareham road. Turn south at Osmington to Osmington Mills, ½ mile.
Acreage 14 **Open** Easter **to** October
Site Sloping
Sites Available **Total** 225
Facilities
Nearby Facilities
Weymouth
Set in a picturesque valley with gentle slopes. Overlooking sea views. We have available our own coarse fishing lake. Ideal situation for touring Dorset.

WEYMOUTH

Pebble Bank Caravan Park, 90 Camp Road, Wyke Regis, Weymouth, Dorset, DT4 9HF.
Std: 01305 **Tel:** 774844
Std: 01305 **Fax:** 774844
Nearest Town/Resort Weymouth
Directions From harbour roundabout up hill to mini roundabout, turn right onto Wyke Road. Camp Road is 1 mile at the apex of a sharp right hand bend, at the bottom of hill.
Acreage 7½ **Open** Easter/1 April **to** 4 Oct
Access Good **Site** Lev/Slope
Sites Available **Total** 140
Facilities
Nearby Facilities
Weymouth
✓✓✓Graded Park. You can also call us on: FREE PHONE 0500 242656.

WEYMOUTH

Portesham Dairy Farm Camp Site, Bramdon Lane, Portesham, Weymouth, Dorset, DT3 4HG.
Std: 01305 **Tel:** 871297
Std: 01305 **Fax:** 871297
Nearest Town/Resort Weymouth
Directions 7 miles from Weymouth on B3157 Coast road.
Acreage 3 **Open** 16 March **to** 31 Oct
Access Good **Site** Level
Sites Available **Total** 60
Facilities
Nearby Facilities
Weymouth
Ideal touring for Chesil area.

WEYMOUTH

Sea Barn Farm, Fleet, Weymouth, Dorset, DT3 4ED.
Std: 01305 **Tel:** 782218
Std: 01305 **Fax:** 775396
Nearest Town/Resort Weymouth.
Directions From Weymouth take the B3157 towards Bridport. Stay on this road until you reach a mini roundabout in Chickerell, turn left towards Fleet. After 1 mile turn left to Sea Barn Farm.
Acreage 10 **Open** Easter **to** 31 October
Site Level
Sites Available **Total** 250
Facilities
Nearby Facilities
Weymouth.
Panoramic views over Dorset coast and countryside. Tree sheltered beautiful walks to the Dorset Coastal Path. Adventure activities available on site.

WEYMOUTH

Seaview Holiday Park, Preston, Weymouth, Dorset, DT3 6DZ.
Std: 01305 **Tel:** 833037
Nearest Town/Resort Weymouth.
Directions Take the A353 from the centre of Weymouth, along the seawall to Preston. Seaview is ½ mile beyond the village, up the hill on the right.
Open Easter **to** October **Site** Sloping
Sites Available
Facilities
Nearby Facilities
Weymouth
✓✓✓✓Graded Park. Nestles on a hillside looking out over the charming Bowleaze Cove.

WEYMOUTH

Waterside Holiday Park, Bowleaze Cove, Weymouth, Dorset, DT3 6PP
Std: 01305 **Tel:** 833103
Std: 01305 **Fax:** 832830
Nearest Town/Resort Weymouth
Directions From Weymouth take the Preston Road along the seafront approx. 1 mile, take the road signposted Bowleaze Cove to Waterside Holiday Park.
Open 1st April **to** 31st October
Access Good **Site** Lev/Slope
Sites Available **Total** 120
Facilities
Nearby Facilities
Weymouth
✓✓✓✓✓Graded Park. Set in beautiful countryside close to the traditional seaside Town of Weymouth. Superb on-site facilities. Takeaway. Boat slipway.

WEYMOUTH

West Fleet Holiday Farm, Fleet, Weymouth, Dorset, DT3 4ED.
Std: 01305 **Tel:** 782218
Std: 01305 **Fax:** 775396
Nearest Town/Resort Weymouth.
Directions From Weymouth take the B3157 towards Bridport. At Chickerell turn left at the mini roundabout (the only one on that road), after 1 mile turn right to West Fleet Holiday Farm.
Acreage 12 **Open** Easter **to** 31 October
Site Level
Sites Available **Total** 250
Facilities
Nearby Facilities
Weymouth.
Dorset Heritage Coast, close to Fleet. Nature reserve. Extensive views of the coast and countryside. Many local attractions.

WEYMOUTH

Weymouth Bay Holiday Park, Preston, Weymouth, Dorset, DT3 6BQ.
Std: 01305 **Tel:** 832271
Std: 01305 **Fax:** 825101
Nearest Town/Resort Weymouth
Directions On the A353 Weymouth to Preston road, on the right about 10 minutes drive from Weymouth.
Open Easter **to** November
Access Good **Site** Level
Sites Available **Total** 50
Facilities
Nearby Facilities
Weymouth
✓✓✓✓Graded Park. Excellent indoor and outdoor swimming pools.

WIMBORNE

Camping & Caravanning Club Site, Sutton Hill, Woodlands, Wimborne, Dorset, BH21 6LF.
Std: 01202 **Tel:** 822763
Directions Take the A354 from Salisbury, after 13 miles turn onto the B3081, site is 1½ miles west of Verwood.
Open 22 March **to** 1 Nov
Site Lev/Slope
Sites Available **Total** 150
Facilities
Nearby Facilities
✓✓✓✓✓Graded Park. Close to the New Forest. Pool table and table tennis on site. 1½ miles from Moors Valley which is super for walking and cycling.

WIMBORNE

Charris Camping & Caravan Park, Candy's Lane, Corfe Mullen, Wimborne, Dorset, BH21 3EF.
Std: 01202 **Tel:** 885970
Nearest Town/Resort Wimborne
Directions A31 Wimborne bypass 1 mile west of Wimborne. Signs for entrance.
Acreage 3 **Open** March **to** October
Access Good **Site** Lev/Slope
Sites Available **Total** 45
Facilities
Nearby Facilities
Poole.
✓✓✓✓✓Graded Park. A.A. 3 Pennant, R.A.C. Approved, Caravan Club listed, Caravan and Camping Club listed. Good central site convienient for coast and New Forest. Poole 7½ miles, Bournemouth 8¼ miles. Good overnight stop for Cherbourg ferry. Cafe/restaurant close by.

WIMBORNE

Springfield Touring Park, Candys Lane, Corfe Mullen, Wimborne, Dorset, BH21 3EF.
Std: 01202 **Tel:** 881719
Nearest Town/Resort Wimborne
Directions 1¼ miles west of Wimborne just off main A31.
Acreage 3½ **Open** Mid March **to** October
Access Good **Site** Lev/Slope
Sites Available **Total** 45
Facilities
Nearby Facilities
Poole
✓✓✓✓✓Graded Park. Family run park, overlooking the Stour Valley. Free showers and awnings. Convenient for the coast, New Forest also ferry. Members of the BH and HPA - Highly Commended Practical Caravan (Dorset) 100 Best Family Parks UK 1996.

WOOL

Whitemead Caravan Park, East Burton Road, Wool, Dorset, BH20 6HG.
Std: 01929 **Tel:** 462241
Std: 01929 **Fax:** 462241
Nearest Town/Resort Wareham
Directions Off the A352 Wareham to Weymouth road. 5 miles west of Wareham and 5 miles north of Lulworth Cove.
Acreage 5 **Open** April **to** End October
Access Good **Site** Level
Sites Available **Total** 95
Facilities
Nearby Facilities
Wool
✓✓✓✓Graded Park. Woodland site with several secluded pitches.

DURHAM

BARNARD CASTLE

Bend Holm Farm Caravan Park, Eggleston, Barnard Castle, Co. Durham, DL12 0AX.
Std: 01833 **Tel:** 650457
Nearest Town/Resort Barnard Castle
Directions 7 miles from Barnard Castle heading northwest on the B6278 towards Stanhope.
Acreage 4½ **Open** March **to** October
Access Good **Site** Level
Sites Available **Total** 99
Facilities
Nearby Facilities
✓✓✓Graded Park.

BARNARD CASTLE

Camping & Caravanning Club Site, Dockenflatts Lane, Lartington, Barnard Castle, Co. Durham, DL12 9DG.
Std: 01833 **Tel:** 630228
Directions On approach from Scotch Corner take the second turn right for Middleton in Teesdale and Barnard Castle. On approach from Penrith take the B6277 to Middleton in Teesdale. In approx 1 mile take turn off left signposted Raygill Riding Stables. The site is 500 metres on the left.
Acreage 10 **Open** 22 March **to** 1 Nov
Site Level
Sites Available **Total** 90
Facilities
Nearby Facilities
✓✓✓✓✓Graded Park. Well placed for exploring the Pennines and the city of Durham. AA 4 Pennants.

BARNARD CASTLE

Pecknell Farm Caravan Site, Pecknell Farm, Lartington, Barnard Castle, Co. Durham, DL12 9DF.
Std: 01833 **Tel:** 638357
Nearest Town/Resort Barnard Castle
Directions 1½ miles from Barnard Castle on the B6277 to Lartington, we are the first farm on the right.
Acreage 1½ **Open** March **to** October
Access Good **Site** Level
Sites Available **Total** 15
Facilities
Nearby Facilities
Darlington
✓✓✓✓Graded Park. Ideal walking area, very attractive walk into historic Barnard Castle. Within easy reach of many attractions.

BARNARD CASTLE

Thorpe Hall, Wycliffe, Barnard Castle, Durham.
Std: 01833 **Tel:** Teesdale 627230
Nearest Town/Resort Barnard Castle.
Directions 5 miles east of Barnard Castle and 1½ miles north of A66 near Greta Bridge.
Acreage 2 **Open** March **to** October
Access Good **Site** Level
Sites Available **Total** 12
Facilities
Nearby Facilities
Darlington.
Near River Tees. Area of historic interest and of great beauty.

BARNARD CASTLE

West Roods, Mrs R Lowson, West Roods Working Farm, Boldron, Barnard Castle, County Durham, DL12 9SW.
Std: 01833 **Tel:** 690116
Nearest Town/Resort Barnard Castle
Directions A66 - Tebay 31½ miles, Penrith 36½ miles. Scotch Corner 13 miles, approx. 2½ miles East Bowes. Dual carriageway between Bowes and Barnard Castle. Do not enter Boldron, take sigboard for Lambhill, West Roods, Roods House. Turn in opposite electric pole and transformer.
Acreage 1 **Open** May **to** October
Access Poor **Site** Sloping
Sites Available **Total** 5
Facilities
Nearby Facilities
Darlington
✓✓✓Graded Park. Green countryside. On a very clear day with binoculars you can see the North Sea. Near to Bowes Museum, High Force Raby, Barnard Castle and Bowes Castle. Water dowsing taught. 1 tent and 1 superpitch. Children Welcome. NO PETS. Farmhouse B&B available.

BARNARD CASTLE

Winston Caravan Park, Winston, Darlington, Durham.
Std: 01325 **Tel:** 730228
Std: 01325 **Fax:** 730228
Nearest Town/Resort Barnard Castle.
Directions 5 miles east of Barnard Castle on A67.
Acreage 2 **Open** March **to** October
Access Good **Site** Level
Sites Available **Total** 20
Facilities
Nearby Facilities
Darlington.
✓✓✓✓Graded Park. Near to river. Within easy reach of many places of interest.

BISHOP AUCKLAND

Witton Castle Caravan & Camping Site, Witton Le Wear, Bishop Auckland, Co Durham, DL14 0DE.
Std: 01388 **Tel:** 488230
Std: 01388 **Fax:** 488008
Nearest Town/Resort Bishop Auckland
Directions On A68 signposted between Toft Hill and Witton le Wear.
Acreage 30 **Open** March **to** October
Access Good **Site** Lev/Slope
Sites Available **Total** 280
Facilities
Nearby Facilities
Bishop Auckland
Set in central Co Durham in an area of outstanding natural beauty.

CONSETT

Manor Park, The Caravan Park, Broadmeadows, Castleside, Consett, Co. Durham, DH8 9HD.
Std: 01207 **Tel:** 501000
Std: 01207 **Fax:** 582947
Nearest Town/Resort Consett
Directions Just off the A68, 3¼ miles south of Castleside (signposted Broadmeadows).
Acreage 7 **Open** April **to** October
Access Good **Site** Lev/Slope
Sites Available **Total** 40
Facilities
Nearby Facilities
Durham
✓✓✓✓Graded Park. Bordering a designated area of outstanding natural beauty.

DURHAM

Cocken Lodge Farm, Leamside, Durham, Co. Durham, DH4 6QP.
Std: 0191 **Tel:** 584 1053
Nearest Town/Resort Durham
Directions 2 miles off the A690 signed Leamside and Finchale Priory.
Acreage 3 **Open** All Year
Access Good **Site** Level
Sites Available **Total** 10
Facilities
Nearby Facilities
Durham

DURHAM

Finchale Abbey Farm, Finchale Abbey (Priory), Co. Durham, DH1 5SH.
Std: 0191 **Tel:** 386 6528
Std: 0191 **Fax:** 386 8593
Nearest Town/Resort Durham City
Directions Off the A1M north of Durham and head south onto the A167, over three roundabouts and at the fourth roundabout turn left (Arnison Centre) and follow signs for Finchale Priory.
Open All Year
Access Good **Site** Lev/Slope
Sites Available **Total** 80
Facilities
Nearby Facilities
Durham
Historic Site situated in a meander of the River Wear. Surrounded by beautiful countryside, overlooking the ruins of the Priory.

HARTLEPOOL

Ash Vale Holiday Park, Ash Vale, Easington Road, Hartlepool, Co. Durham, TS24 9RF.
Std: 01429 **Tel:** 862111
Std: 01429 **Fax:** 862111
Nearest Town/Resort Hartlepool
Directions Take the A179 off the A19, at the third roundabout turn first left, across the next roundabout and we are 300 yards on the left.
Acreage 6
Access Good **Site** Level
Sites Available **Total** 30
Facilities
Nearby Facilities
Hartlepool
✓✓✓Graded Park. 1 mile from a long sandy beach. 3 miles from Historic Ships Museum.

HARTLEPOOL

Crimdon Dene Caravan Park, Blackhall Rocks, Crimdon, Hartlepool, Co. Durham, TS27 4BN.
Std: 01429 **Tel:** 267801
Std: 01429 **Fax:** 261899
Nearest Town/Resort Hartlepool.
Directions From the A19 take the A179 Hartlepool road for 3 miles, then take the A1086 Blackhall road. After 2 miles turn right into the park next to the Seagull Pub.
Open April **to** October
Access Good **Site** Level
Sites Available
Facilities
Nearby Facilities
Hartlepool.
Near the beach with sea views. Large wooded dene and marina nearby.

MIDDLETON-IN-TEESDALE

Mickleton Mill Caravan Park, The Mill, Mickleton, Barnard Castle, Co. Durham, DL12 0LS.
Std: 01833 **Tel:** 640317
Std: 01833 **Fax:** 640317
Nearest Town/Resort Barnard Castle
Directions From the A66 take the B6277 towards Barnard Castle and Middleton-in-Teesdale. Follow this road to Mickleton and turn right just past the Blacksmiths Arms.
Acreage 6½ **Open** April **to** October
Access Fair **Site** Level
Sites Available **Total** 70
Facilities
Nearby Facilities
Darlington
Fishing on site.

TOW LAW

Viewley Hill Caravan & Camping Site, Viewley Hill Farm, Tow Law, Bishop Auckland, Co. Durham.
Std: 01388 **Tel:** 730308
Nearest Town/Resort Tow Law.
Directions 2 miles north of Tow Law. Turn off the A68 at Brown Horse Inn crossroad onto B6296 Wolsignham Road. Site is ½ mile on the right.
Acreage ¼ **Open** All Year
Access Good **Site** Level
Sites Available **Total** 5
Facilities
Nearby Facilities
Durham
Scenic views, 10 miles to Durham City.

WOLSINGHAM

Bradley Mill Caravan Park, Bradley Burn Farm, Wolsingham, Bishop Auckland, Co. Durham, DL13 3JH.
Std: 01388 **Tel:** 527285
Std: 01388 **Fax:** 527285
Nearest Town/Resort Wolsingham
Directions 2 miles east of Wolsingham on the A689 and 2 miles west of the A68/A689 junction.
Open April **to** October
Access Good **Site** Lev/Slope
Sites Available **Total** 12
Facilities
Nearby Facilities
Bishop Auckland
N.B. This is a STATIC holiday park with a few pitches available for tourers. Email - BradleyMill@bradleyburn.demm.co.uk

ESSEX

BATTLESBRIDGE

Hayes Farm Caravan Park, Hayes Chase, Burnham Road, Battlesbridge, Essex.
Std: 01245 **Tel:** 320309
Nearest Town/Resort Wickford.
Directions A132 to Burnham.
Acreage 26 **Open** End March **to** End October
Access Good **Site** Level
Sites Available **Total** 74
Facilities
Nearby Facilities
Wickford.
Alongside river.

BRENTWOOD

Camping & Caravanning Club Site, Warren Lane, Frog Street, Kelvedon Hatch, Near Brentwood, Essex, CM15 0JG.
Std: 01277 **Tel:** 372773
Nearest Town/Resort Brentwood
Directions Leave the M25 at junction 28 and take the A1023 towards Brentwood. Turn left onto the A128 to Ongar, the site is 3 miles on the right, signposted.
Acreage 12 **Open** 22 March **to** 1 Nov
Access Good **Site** Level
Sites Available **Total** 90
Facilities
Nearby Facilities
Brentwood
✓✓✓✓Graded Park. Peaceful site, good for country walks. 20 miles from the centre of London. Plenty of sporting activities within easy reach.

CLACTON-ON-SEA

Sacketts Grove, Jaywick Lane, Clacton-on-Sea, Essex, CO16 7BD.
Std: 01255 **Tel:** 427765
Std: 01255 **Fax:** 428752
Nearest Town/Resort Clacton-on-Sea
Directions Take the A12 from London or join the A120 at Colchester, A133 at Frating and follow signs for Sacketts Grove.
Acreage 6 **Open** Easter **to** Early October
Access Good **Site** Level
Sites Available **Total** 120
Facilities
Nearby Facilities
Clacton
1 mile from the beach. Riding school on site. Ideal for touring and camping.

CLACTON-ON-SEA

Tower Holiday Park, Jaywick, Clacton-on-Sea, Essex, CO15 2LF.
Std: 01255 **Tel:** 820372
Std: 01255 **Fax:** 820060
Nearest Town/Resort Clacton-on-Sea

Directions 3 miles west of Clacton. Head for Clacton sea front and turn right, proceed along the sea front and follow signs to Jaywick.
Acreage 5 **Open** March **to** October
Access Good **Site** Level
Sites Available **Total** 100
Facilities
Nearby Facilities
Clacton-on-Sea
✓✓✓Graded Park. Next to the beach with 24 hour access. Ideal base to visit Southern East Anglia.

CLACTON-ON-SEA

Valley Farm Caravan Park, Valley Road, Clacton-on-Sea, Essex, CO15 6LY.
Std: 01255 **Tel:** 422484
Std: 01255 **Fax:** 422484
Nearest Town/Resort Clacton-on-Sea
Directions 1¼ miles from Clacton Town Centre.
Open Mid March **to** End October
Access Good
Sites Available **Total** 38
Facilities
Nearby Facilities
Clacton-on-Sea
✓✓✓✓Graded Park. Part of a 50 acre holiday park. 10 minute stroll to local beaches.

COLCHESTER

Colchester Camping & Caravan Park, Cymbeline Way, Lexden, Colchester, Essex.
Std: 01206 **Tel:** 545551
Nearest Town/Resort Colchester
Directions From the A12 in any direction, follow tourist signs for caravan park into Colchester on the A133 Colchester central slip road.
Acreage 12 **Open** All Year
Access Good **Site** Level
Sites Available **Total** 251
Facilities
Nearby Facilities
Colchester
✓✓✓✓Graded Park. Close to Britains oldest town, convenient for ferry ports. Ideal for touring East Anglia.

COLCHESTER

Mill Farm Camping, Mill Farm, Harwich Road, Great Bromley, Colchester, Essex, CO7 7JQ.
Std: 01206 **Tel:** 250485
Std: 01206 **Fax:** 252040
Nearest Town/Resort Harwich
Directions Take the A12 to Colchester, then the A120 to Harwich, follow Mill Farm Camping signs.
Acreage 2 **Open** May **to** September
Access Fair **Site** Sloping
Sites Available **Total** 10
Facilities
Nearby Facilities
Wivenhoe
Peaceful and sheltered park. Within easy reach of Harwich Port.

HALSTEAD

Gosfield Lake Resort, Church Road, Gosfield, Nr Halstead, Essex, CO9 1UE.
Std: 01787 **Tel:** 475043
Std: 01787 **Fax:** 478528
Nearest Town/Resort Halstead
Directions A120, A131 and A1017 from Braintree, 5 miles A604, Sible Hedingham A1017.
Acreage 7 **Open** All Year
Access Good **Site** Level
Sites Available **Total** 25
Facilities
Nearby Facilities
Braintree.
✓✓Graded Park. Near a lake for water-skiing.

HARWICH

Dovercourt Caravan Park, Low Road, Harwich, Essex, CO12 3TZ.
Std: 01255 **Tel:** 243433
Std: 01255 **Fax:** 241673
Nearest Town/Resort Harwich
Directions Take the A120 to Harwich, at Ramsey junction turn right and follow the brown tourist board signs to Dovercourt Caravan Park.
Acreage 6 **Open** March **to** October
Access Good **Site** Level
Sites Available **Total** 60
Facilities
Nearby Facilities
Harwich International.
Close to a sandy beach and continental ferry port. Good base for exploration of Constable Country, Clacton-on-Sea and Roman Colchester.

MERSEA ISLAND

Fen Farm Camping & Caravan Site, Fen Farm, East Mersea, Colchester, Essex, CO5 8UA.
Std: 01206 **Tel:** 383275
Std: 01206 **Fax:** 386316
Nearest Town/Resort West Mersea
Directions Take the B1025 from Colchester, take the left fork onto Mersea Island. Take the first turn right past the Dog &

Pheasant Public House, signposted.
Acreage 5 **Open** March **to** September
Access Good **Site** Level
Sites Available **Total** 45
Facilities
Nearby Facilities
Colchester
√√√ Graded Park. Quiet, rural, family site by the beach and on an estuary. Close to a country park.

MERSEA ISLAND

Waldegraves Farm Holiday Park, Mersea Island, Colchester, Essex, CO5 8SE.
Std: 01206 **Tel:** 382898
Std: 01206 **Fax:** 385359
Nearest Town/Resort Mersea.
Directions From Colchester take B1025, 10 miles to West Mersea. Take left fork to East Mersea, second road to right.
Acreage 25 **Open** March **to** November
Access Good **Site** Level
Sites Available **Total** 60
Facilities
Nearby Facilities
Colchester.
√√√√ Graded Park. Grass park, surrounded by trees and lakes. Safe private beach, fishing and golf. Ideal family park. New swimming pool. Holiday homes for hire and sale.

ROYDON

Roydon Mill Leisure Park, Roydon, Essex, CM19 5EJ.
Std: 01279 **Tel:** 792777
Std: 01279 **Fax:** 792695
Nearest Town/Resort Roydon
Directions From the A414 between Harlow and the junction with the A10, follow brown and white tourist signs for "Roydon Mill Leisure Park".
Acreage 58 **Open** All Year
Access Good **Site** Level
Sites Available **Total** 140
Facilities
Nearby Facilities
Roydon
Riverside park with a 40 acre water-skiing lake, man-made beach and pool. Ideal base for visiting London from the adjacent railway station (35 minutes to Liverpool Street Station).

SHOEBURYNESS

East Beach Caravan Park, Leshome Ltd., Shoeburyness, Essex, SS3 9SG.
Std: 01702 **Tel:** 292466
Std: 01702 **Fax:** 290634
Nearest Town/Resort Southend-on-Sea.
Directions Take the A13 from Southend to Shoeburyness, at roundabout in Shoebury turn left into Elm Road. In ¾ mile at crossroads go straight into Blackgate Road, the site is 200yds on the right.
Acreage 9 **Open** 2nd Sat March **to** End Oct
Access Good **Site** Level
Sites Available **Total** 60
Facilities
Nearby Facilities
Shoeburyness.
√√√ Graded Park. 100yds from the beach, safe boating and bathing.

SOUTHEND-ON-SEA

Riverside Village Holiday Park, Wallasea Island, Rochford, Essex. SS4 2EY.
Std: 01702 **Tel:** 258297
Std: 01702 **Fax:** 258555
Nearest Town/Resort Southend
Directions From A127 through Rochford, follow caravan signs for Ashingdon then Wallasea Island. From Chelmsford left at Battlesbridge, past Hullbridge for Ashingdon then Wallasea.
Acreage 25 **Open** March **to** October
Access Good **Site** Level
Sites Available **Total** 60
Facilities
Nearby Facilities
Rochford
Alongside River Crouch, Nature reserve, picturesque inns with excellent food. Country walks. Boule pitch.

SOUTHMINSTER

Beacon Hill Leisure Park, St. Lawrence Bay, Southminster, Essex, CM0 7LP.
Std: 01621 **Tel:** 779248
Std: 01621 **Fax:** 778106
Nearest Town/Resort Southminster
Directions Head south from Maldon on the B1018, go through Mundon to Latchingdon then bear left towards St Lawrence Bay, site is signposted.
Acreage 45 **Open** March **to** October
Access Good **Site** Lev/Slope
Sites Available **Total** 130
Facilities
Nearby Facilities
Southminster
Situated on the Black Water Estuary with own slipway and beach. Beautiful green park with great views. Bird watching (SSSI). Ideal for water sports.

SOUTHMINSTER

Steeple Bay Holiday Park, Steeple, Nr. Southminster, Essex, CM0 7RS.
Std: 01621 **Tel:** 773991
Std: 01621 **Fax:** 773967
Nearest Town/Resort Southminster.
Directions Turn off the A12 onto the A414, then onto the B1010/B1012 to Latchingdon. At the mini-roundabout follow signs through Mayland, then Steeple Village. After the Blackwater Craft Shop turn left into a small lane. Steeple Bay is just past the farm.
Open Easter **to** Mid October
Access Good **Site** Level
Sites Available **Total** 61
Facilities
Nearby Facilities
√√√√ Graded Park. River setting. Touring guests are able to use our launching ramp for boats. Prices shown include 6 persons, awning and car.

ST. OSYTH

Hutleys Touring Park, St. Osyth Beach, St. Osyth, Essex, CO16 8TB.
Std: 01255 **Tel:** 820712
Std: 01255 **Fax:** 821442
Nearest Town/Resort Clacton-on-Sea.
Directions Take the A12 from Colchester, then the A133 to Clacton, then the B1027 to St. Osyth. Crossroads - to St Osyth Beach (2 miles).
Acreage 1 **Open** March **to** October
Access Good **Site** Level
Sites Available **Total** 18
Facilities
Nearby Facilities
Clacton-on-Sea.
Adjacent to the beach. Naturist beach nearby.

ST. OSYTH

The Orchards Holiday Village, Point Clear, St. Osyth, Clacton-on-Sea, Essex, CO16 8LJ.
Std: 01255 **Tel:** 820651
Std: 01255 **Fax:** 820184
Nearest Town/Resort Clacton.
Directions From Clacton-on-Sea take the B1027 (signposted Colchester). Turn left after Pumphill Station, over crossroads in St Osyth, 3 miles on to the park.
Open March **to** October
Access Good **Site** Level
Sites Available **Total** 71
Facilities
Nearby Facilities
Clacton
√√√√ Graded Park. Close to Colchester historic town. Kids Club and a full family entertainment programme. Beach access, water sports, golf, pitch'n'putt, fishing lakes, bars and take-away. Dogs are allowed but not in peak season. Bike hire available nearby.

GLOUCESTERSHIRE

BADMINTON

Petty France Farm Caravan & Camping Park, Badminton, South Gloucestershire, GL9 1AF.
Std: 01454 **Tel:** 238665
Acreage 1½ **Open** April **to** September
Access Good **Site** Level
Sites Available **Total** 12
Facilities
Nearby Facilities
Ideal touring.

BOURTON-ON-THE-WATER

Folly Farm, Nr. Bourton-on-the-Water, Cheltenham, Gloucestershire, GL54 3BY.
Std: 01451 **Tel:** 820285
Directions 2½ miles from Bourton-on-the-Water on the A436.
Acreage 3 **Open** All Year
Access Good **Site** Level
Sites Available **Total** 40
Facilities
Nearby Facilities
Europes largest domestic waterfowl and wildfowl conservation area of 50 acres.

CHELTENHAM

Beggars Roost, Bamfurlong Lane, Staverton, Nr. Cheltenham, Glos, GL51 6SL.
Std: 01242 **Tel:** 235324
Std: 01242 **Fax:** 235324
Nearest Town/Resort Cheltenham
Directions Leave M5 at junction 11 and turn towards Cheltenham. After ¾ mile turn left onto the B4063, site is 100 yards on the left.
Acreage 2 **Open** All Year
Access Good **Site** Level
Sites Available **Total** 40
Facilities
Nearby Facilities
Cheltenham
Situated between Cheltenham, Gloucester, Stroud and Tewkesbury. Ideal site for the Cotswolds. Very easy access to the motorway.

CHELTENHAM

Briarfields Caravan Park, Gloucester Road, Cheltenham, Gloucestershire, GL51 0SX.
Std: 01242 **Tel:** 235324
Std: 01242 **Fax:** 235324
Nearest Town/Resort Cheltenham
Directions Leave the M5 at junction 11 and turn towards Cheltenham. At large roundabout after ¾ mile, turn left onto the B4063, site is 100 yards on the left.
Acreage 6½ **Open** All Year
Access Good **Site** Level
Sites Available **Total** 85
Facilities
Nearby Facilities
Cheltenham
✓✓✓✓Graded Park. Ideal park for touring the Cotswolds and Forest of Dean.

CIRENCESTER

Cotswold Hoburne, Broadway Lane, South Cerney, Cirencester, GL7 5UQ.
Std: 01285 **Tel:** 860216
Std: 01285 **Fax:** 862106
Nearest Town/Resort Cirencester
Directions 4miles south of Cirencester on A419, follow signs to Cotswold Hoburne in the Cotswold Water Park.
Acreage 70 **Open** March **to** October
Access Good **Site** Level
Sites Available **Total** 302
Facilities
Nearby Facilities
Swindon
✓✓✓✓✓Graded Park. In the centre of the Cotswold Water Park - and ideal base for all watersports and nature lovers. Tennis on site.

CIRENCESTER

Mayfield Touring Park, Cheltenham Road, Perrotts Brook, Cirencester, GL7 7BH.
Std: 01285 **Tel:** 831301
Std: 01285 **Fax:** 831301
Nearest Town/Resort Cirencester
Directions On A435, 13miles Cheltenham and 2miles Cirencester.
Acreage 10 **Open** All Year
Access Good **Site** Lev/Slope
Sites Available **Total** 76
Facilities
Nearby Facilities
Kemble
✓✓✓✓Graded Park. Touring Cotswolds, castles, Abbey, Wildlife park, Local pub is five minutes walk - food suitable for children. 16 hard standing/grass pitches. Boar 6 acres of ground for recreation. Some 16 amp electric points.

COLEFORD

Bracelands - Forestry Commission, Christchurch, Forest of Dean, Coleford, Gloucestershire, GL16 7NN.
Std: 01594 **Tel:** 833376
Nearest Town/Resort Coleford
Directions At the crossroads of the A4136 and minor road at the Pike House Inn (1 mile north of Coleford), go north for ½ mile following campsite signs. Reception for Bracelands is at the Christchurch site.
Acreage 14 **Open** 1 March **to** 3 November
Access Good **Site** Level
Sites Available **Total** 520
Facilities
Nearby Facilities
Gloucester
Panoramic views over the magnificent countryside, Highmeadow Wood and the Wye Valley. Watch Peregrines at Symonds Yat, plus a host of outdoor activities.

COLEFORD

Chichester - Forestry Commission, Campsite Office, Christchurch, Coleford, Gloucestershire, GL16 7NN.
Std: 01594 **Tel:** 833376
Std: 01594 **Fax:** 833376
Nearest Town/Resort Coleford
Directions At the crossroads of the A4136 1 mile north of Coleford, go north for ½ mile following signs to the campsite. Reception is on the left.
Acreage 54¼ **Open** 1 March **to** 4 January
Access Good **Site** Lev/Slope
Sites Available **Total** 890
Facilities
Nearby Facilities
Gloucester
✓✓✓Graded Park. Located within the Royal Forest of Dean. Ideal for outdoor activities including walking, cycling, fishing, horse riding and bird watching.

COLEFORD

Woodlands - Forestry Commission, Christchurch, Forest of Dean, Coleford, Gloucestershire, GL16 7NN.
Std: 01594 **Tel:** 833376
Nearest Town/Resort Coleford
Directions At the crossroads of the A4136 and a minor road at Pike House Inn, 1 mile north of Coleford, go north for ½ mile following campsite signs. Reception for Woodlands is at Christchurch site.
Acreage 22 **Open** 1 March **to** 3 November
Access Good **Site** Level
Sites Available **Total** 90
Facilities
Nearby Facilities
Gloucester
A superbly wooded site with pitches set amongst trees. Ideal for a peaceful, tranquil break. Note : This site has NO toilets.

COLEFORD

Woodlands View Caravan & Camping Site, Sling, Nr. Coleford, Gloucestershire, GL16 8JA.
Std: 01594 **Tel:** 835127
Nearest Town/Resort Coleford
Directions Take the B4228 from Coleford towards Lydney and Chepstow, 2 miles.
Acreage 2 **Open** All Year
Access Good **Site** Lev/Slope
Sites Available **Total** 30
Facilities
Nearby Facilities
Lydney
Forest of Dean, ideal for hiking, rambling, cycling, canoeing or just walking. 1 hour from Weston-super-Mare, 20 minutes from Symonds Yat and 10 minutes to Clearwell Caves. Pubs within 10 and 20 minute walks.

DURSLEY

Hogsdown Farm Caravan & Camping Site, Lower Wick, Dursley, GL11 6OX.
Std: 01453 **Tel:** 810224
Nearest Town/Resort Gloucester
Directions Between junctions 13 & 14 of M5, 1mile off A38, 2miles from Berkeley.
Acreage 4 **Open** All Year
Access Good **Site** Level
Sites Available **Total** 40
Facilities
Nearby Facilities
Stroud
Ideal stopover north, south and touring Cotswolds Edge and Way Country, Severn Vale. Slimbridge Wild Fowl Trust, Berkeley castle, Jenner Museum, Western Burt Arboretum. Cotswold & Severn Way within 2miles. Oldbury power station, butterfly farm and rare animal farm. Also B+B.

GLOUCESTER

Red Lion Caravan & Camping Park, Wainlode Hill, Norton, GL2 9LW.
Std: 01452 **Tel:** 730251
Nearest Town/Resort Gloucester
Directions Off A38 at Norton, signposted Wainlode Hill, 5 miles Gloucester.
Acreage 12½ **Open** All Year
Access Good **Site** Level
Sites Available **Total** 90
Facilities
Nearby Facilities
Gloucester
✓✓✓Graded Park. Licensed Inn, hot and cold snacks. On banks of River Severn. Good fishing on site.

LECHLADE

Bridge House Campsite, Bridge House, Lechlade, GL7 3AG.
Std: 01367 **Tel:** 252348
Nearest Town/Resort Lechlade
Directions Lechlade A361 to Swindon. Opposite Riverside car park.
Acreage 3½ **Open** April **to** October
Site Level
Sites Available **Total** 51
Facilities
Nearby Facilities
Swindon
Ideal for touring Cotswolds and Upper Thames.

MORETON VALENCE

Gables Farm Caravan & Camping Site, Moreton Valence, GL2 7ND.
Std: 01452 **Tel:** 720331
Std: 01452 **Fax:** 720331
Nearest Town/Resort Gloucester
Directions On A38 6 miles from Gloucester. 2 miles from M5 junction 13.
Acreage 3 **Open** All Year
Access Good **Site** Level
Sites Available **Total** 40
Facilities
Nearby Facilities
Gloucester
Overnight or local touring. Wetlands Trust 6 miles. S.A.E. Gloucester docks and museums.

MORETON-IN-MARSH

Cross Hands Inn Caravan Park, Moreton-in-Marsh, GL56 0SP.
Std: 01608 **Tel:** 643106
Nearest Town/Resort Chipping Norton
Directions From Chipping Norton take the Worcester road A44. After 3 miles you will see the Inn on your right on the main A44 at the junction of A436.
Acreage 1¼ **Open** All Year
Access Good **Site** Level
Sites Available **Total** 18
Facilities
Nearby Facilities
Moreton-in-Marsh
Ideal touring site for the Cotswolds and only about 20 miles to Stratford-On-Avon.

SLIMBRIDGE

Tudor Caravanning & Camping Park, Sheperds Patch, Slimbridge, Gloucestershire.
Std: 01453 **Tel:** 890483
Nearest Town/Resort Dursley/Gloucester
Directions From Gloucester A38 south, after about 13 miles signposted to turn right (Slimbridge Wildfowl Trust). After 1¼ miles turn left through Tudor Arms car park.
Acreage 7¼ **Open** All Year
Access Good **Site** Level
Sites Available **Total** 75
Facilities
Nearby Facilities
Dursley
Sharpness Canal next property to Wildfowl Trust. AA 4 Pennants.

STROUD

Riverside Caravan Site, The George, Bristol Road, Cambridge, Gloucestershire, GL2 7AL.
Std: 01453 **Tel:** 890270
Nearest Town/Resort Gloucester
Directions Leave the M5 at junction 13 and turn onto the A38 (Bristol), 2¾ miles on the right hand side.
Acreage 2½ **Open** All Year
Access Good **Site** Level
Sites Available **Total** 29
Facilities
Nearby Facilities
Set on the banks of the River Cam. Within easy reach of the M5 holiday route.

TEWKESBURY
Camping & Caravanning Club Site, Brooklands Farm, Alderton, Nr. Tewkesbury, Gloucestershire, GL20 8NX.
Std: 01242 **Tel:** 620259
Nearest Town/Resort Tewkesbury
Directions 5 miles from junction 9 M5. take A46 Evesham road, continue to Teddington roundabout (approx. 3 miles) then follow B4077 Stow road for a further 3 miles past roundabout, site is on righthand side.
Acreage 20 **Open** 22 March **to** 1 Nov
Access Good **Site** Level
Sites Available **Total** 68
Facilities
Nearby Facilities
✓✓✓✓Graded Park. Site is situated around a small lake in 20 acres of farmland. Set amidst lovely Cotswold countryside. Multi-Service pitches. Fishing on site.

TEWKESBURY
Croft Farm Leisure & Water Park, Brendons Hardwick, Tewkesbury, GL20 7EE.
Std: 01684 **Tel:** 772321
Std: 01684 **Fax:** 773379
Nearest Town/Resort Tewkesbury
Directions 1½ miles north-east of Tewkesbury on B4080.
Acreage 10 **Open** 1 March **to** 1 January
Access Good **Site** Level
Sites Available **Total** 76
Facilities
Nearby Facilities
Ashchurch
✓✓✓Graded Park. Lakeside location with own watersports lake for sailing, windsurfing and canoeing.

TEWKESBURY
Dawleys Caravan Park, Owls Lane, Shuthonger, Tewkesbury, GL20 6EQ.
Std: 01684 **Tel:** 292622
Std: 01684 **Fax:** 292622
Nearest Town/Resort Cheltenham/ Gloucester
Directions A38 north from Tewkesbury, appromiately 2 miles on the left hand side. Or 1¼ miles south on A38 from M50 junction 1.
Acreage 3 **Open** 15 March **to** October
Access Fair **Site** Sloping
Sites Available **Total** 20
Facilities
Nearby Facilities
Cheltenham
Near ar river, secluded rural site, close to M5 and M50.

TEWKESBURY
Sunset View Caravan Park & Ostrich Farm, Church End Lane, Twyning, Tewkesbury, Gloucestershire, GL20 6EH.
Std: 01684 **Tel:** 292145
Std: 01684 **Fax:** 292145
Nearest Town/Resort Tewkesbury
Directions 2 miles north of Tewkesbury on the A38 to Worcester, turn right after the village of Shuthonger and before the car sales garage, 100 yards on the left hand side.
Acreage 2 **Open** All Year
Access Good **Site** Level
Sites Available **Total** 40
Facilities
Nearby Facilities
Tewkesbury
Ostrich farming on site, meat available to buy as well as other Ostrich goods including feather dusters and eggs.

WOTTON-UNDER-EDGE
Canons Court, Bradley Green, Wotton-under-Edge, Gloucestershire, GL12 7PN.
Std: 01453 **Tel:** 843128
Std: 01453 **Fax:** 844151
Nearest Town/Resort Wotton-under-Edge
Directions 1 mile north west of Wotton-under-Edge.
Acreage 2 **Open** Easter **to** October
Access Good **Site** Level
Sites Available **Total** 35
Facilities
Nearby Facilities
Gloucester
Countryside setting with a golf course on site. Licensed bar.

HAMPSHIRE

ANDOVER
Wyke Down Touring Caravan & Camping Park, Picket Piece, Andover, Hampshire.
Std: 01264 **Tel:** 352048
Std: 01264 **Fax:** 324661
Nearest Town/Resort Andover.
Directions International Camping Park Signs from A303 Trunk Road, follow signs to Wyke Down.
Acreage 7 **Open** All Year
Access Good **Site** Level
Sites Available **Total** 150
Facilities
Nearby Facilities
Andover.
✓✓✓Graded Park. Ideal touring area. Golf driving range. Country pub and restaurant.

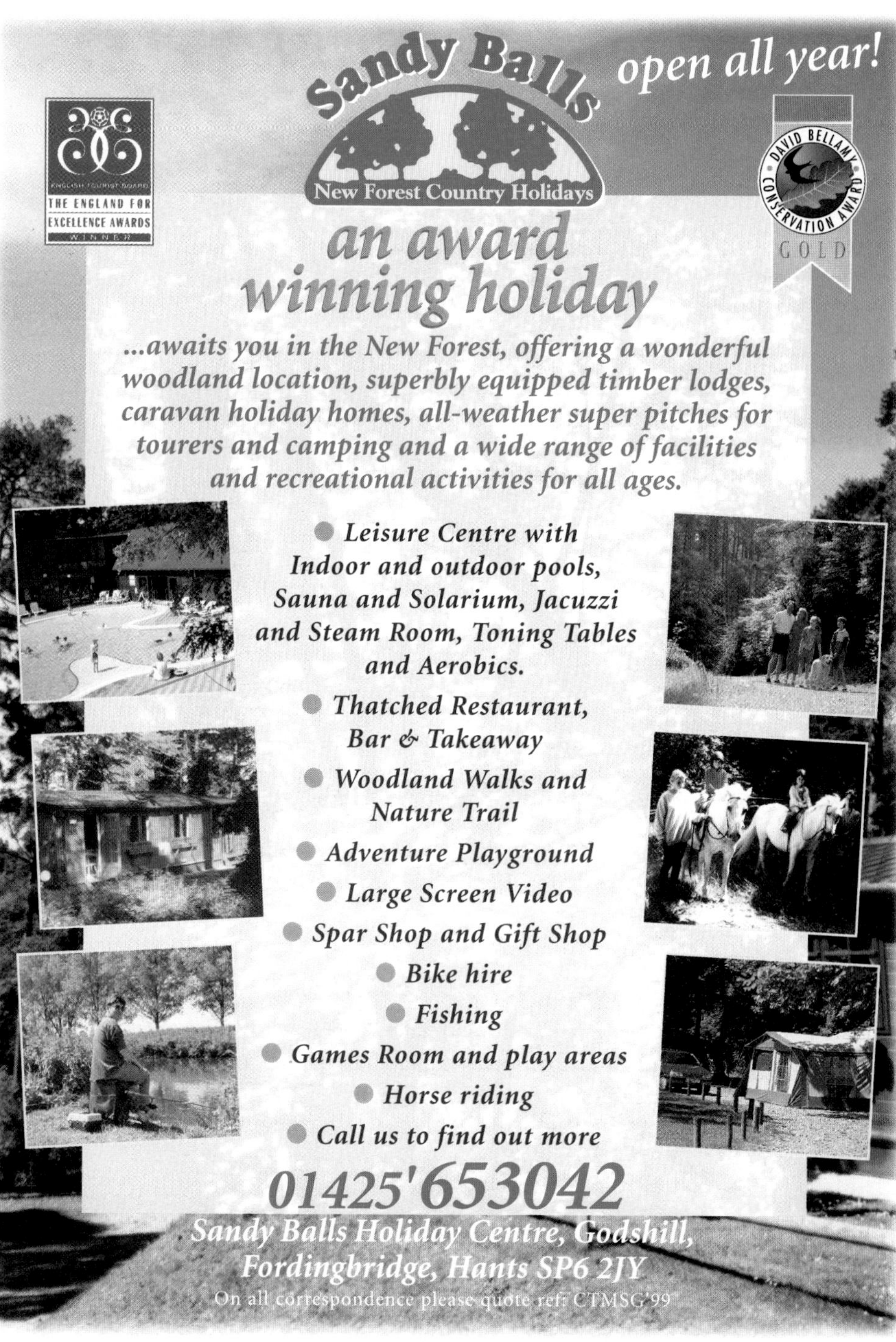

Sandy Balls
open all year!
New Forest Country Holidays
ENGLISH TOURIST BOARD
THE ENGLAND FOR EXCELLENCE AWARDS
WINNER
DAVID BELLAMY CONSERVATION AWARD
GOLD
an award winning holiday
...awaits you in the New Forest, offering a wonderful woodland location, superbly equipped timber lodges, caravan holiday homes, all-weather super pitches for tourers and camping and a wide range of facilities and recreational activities for all ages.
Leisure Centre with Indoor and outdoor pools, Sauna and Solarium, Jacuzzi and Steam Room, Toning Tables and Aerobics.
Thatched Restaurant, Bar & Takeaway
Woodland Walks and Nature Trail
Adventure Playground
Large Screen Video
Spar Shop and Gift Shop
Bike hire
Fishing
Games Room and play areas
Horse riding
Call us to find out more
01425'653042
Sandy Balls Holiday Centre, Godshill, Fordingbridge, Hants SP6 2JY
On all correspondence please quote ref: CTMSG'99

ASHURST

Ashurst Camp Site - Forestry Commission, Lyndhurst Road, Ashurst, Hampshire, SO42 2AA.
Std: 0131 314 **Tel:** 6100/6505
Nearest Town/Resort Lyndhurst.
Directions 5 miles southwest of Southampton on the A35, signposted.
Acreage 23 **Open** 25 March **to** 30 Sept
Access Good **Site** Level
Sites Available **Total** 280
Facilities
Nearby Facilities
Ashurst
√√√√√ Graded Park. Lightweight area on site for walkers and cyclists. 10 minutes walk to the shops in Ashurst Village.

BEAULIEU

Decoy Pond Farm, Beaulieu Road, Beaulieu, Brockenhurst, Hampshire, SO42 7YQ.
Std: 01703 **Tel:** 292652
Nearest Town/Resort Lyndhurst
Directions From Lyndhurst take the B3056, after crossing railway bridge, first on the left.
Acreage 5 **Open** March **to** October
Access Good **Site** Level
Sites Available **Total** 4
Facilities
Nearby Facilities
Beaulieu Road
Ideal for the New Forest.

BRANSGORE

Harrow Wood Farm Caravan Park, Poplar Lane, Bransgore, Nr. Christchurch, Dorset, BH23 8JE.
Std: 01425 **Tel:** 672487
Std: 01425 **Fax:** 672487
Nearest Town/Resort Christchurch/Bournemouth
Directions On the A35, 11 miles south-west of Lyndhurst turn right at the Cat & Fiddle Public House. Go 2 miles to Bransgore and turn first right after the school into Poplar Lane.
Acreage 6 **Open** 1 March **to** 6 January
Access Good **Site** Level
Sites Available **Total** 60
Facilities
Nearby Facilities
Hinton Admiral
√√√√√ Graded Park. Within easy reach of the New Forest and the sea.

BROCKENHURST

Aldridge Hill - Forestry Commission, Brockenhurst, Hampshire, SO42 7QD.
Std: 0131 **Tel:** 314 6100
Nearest Town/Resort Brockenhurst
Directions From Brockenhurst take the unclassified road (Ornamental Drive). The site is 1 mile on the right.
Acreage 22
Access Good **Site** Level
Sites Available **Total** 200
Facilities
Nearby Facilities
Brockenhurst
In a heathland clearing in the heart of the New Forest, on the edge of Oberwater Stream. Note : This site has NO toilets. Open 22 May to 2 June and 26 June to 1 Sept.

BROCKENHURST

Hollands Wood Camp Site - Forestry Commission, Lyndhurst Road, Brockenhurst, Hampshire, SO42 7QH.
Std: 0131 314 **Tel:** 6100/6505
Nearest Town/Resort Brockenhurst.
Directions ½ mile north of Brockenhurst on the A337, signposted.
Acreage 168 **Open** 25 March **to** 30 Sept
Access Good **Site** Level
Sites Available **Total** 600
Facilities
Nearby Facilities
Brockenhurst.
√√√√√ Graded Park. Sheltered site in an oak woodland. Special tenting areas. Brockenhurst Village nearby.

BROCKENHURST

Holmsley Camp Site - Forestry Commission, Forest Road, Holmsley, Christchurch, Dorset, BH23 7EQ.
Std: 0131 314 **Tel:** 6100/6505
Nearest Town/Resort Brockenhurst
Directions Turn west 8 miles southwest of Lyndhurst off the A35 and follow Holmsley Camp Site signs.
Acreage 89 **Open** 25 March **to** 3 Nov
Access Good **Site** Level
Sites Available **Total** 700
Facilities
Nearby Facilities
New Milton
√√√√ Graded Park. Coast within 5 miles. Shop and fast food takeaway on site.

BROCKENHURST

Roundhill Camp Site - Forestry Commission, Beaulieu Road, Brockenhurst, Hampshire, SO42 7QL.
Std: 0131 314 **Tel:** 6100/6505
Nearest Town/Resort Brockenhurst.
Directions On the B3055, 2 miles south east of Brockenhurst off the A337, signposted.
Acreage 156 **Open** 25 March **to** 29 Sept
Access Good **Site** Level
Sites Available **Total** 500
Facilities
Nearby Facilities
Brockenhurst.
√√√√ Graded Park. Motorcyclists' area on campsite available, also rally site.

CADNAM

Ocknell/Longbeech Campsite - Forestry Commission, Fritham, Nr. Lyndhurst, Hampshire, SO43 7NH.
Std: 0131 314 **Tel:** 6100/6505
Nearest Town/Resort Lyndhurst.
Directions From the A31 at Cadnam take the B3079, then the B3078 via Brook and Fritham.
Acreage 48 **Open** 25 March **to** 29 Sept
Access Good **Site** Level
Sites Available **Total** 480
Facilities
Nearby Facilities
√√√√ Graded Park. Two contrasting sites. Permits from Ocknell. Toilets at Ocknell.

FAREHAM

Dibles Park, Dibles Road, Warsash, Southampton, Hants, SO3 6SA.
Std: 01489 **Tel:** 575232
Nearest Town/Resort Fareham
Directions Turn left off the A27 (Portsmouth to Southampton) opposite Lloyds Bank into

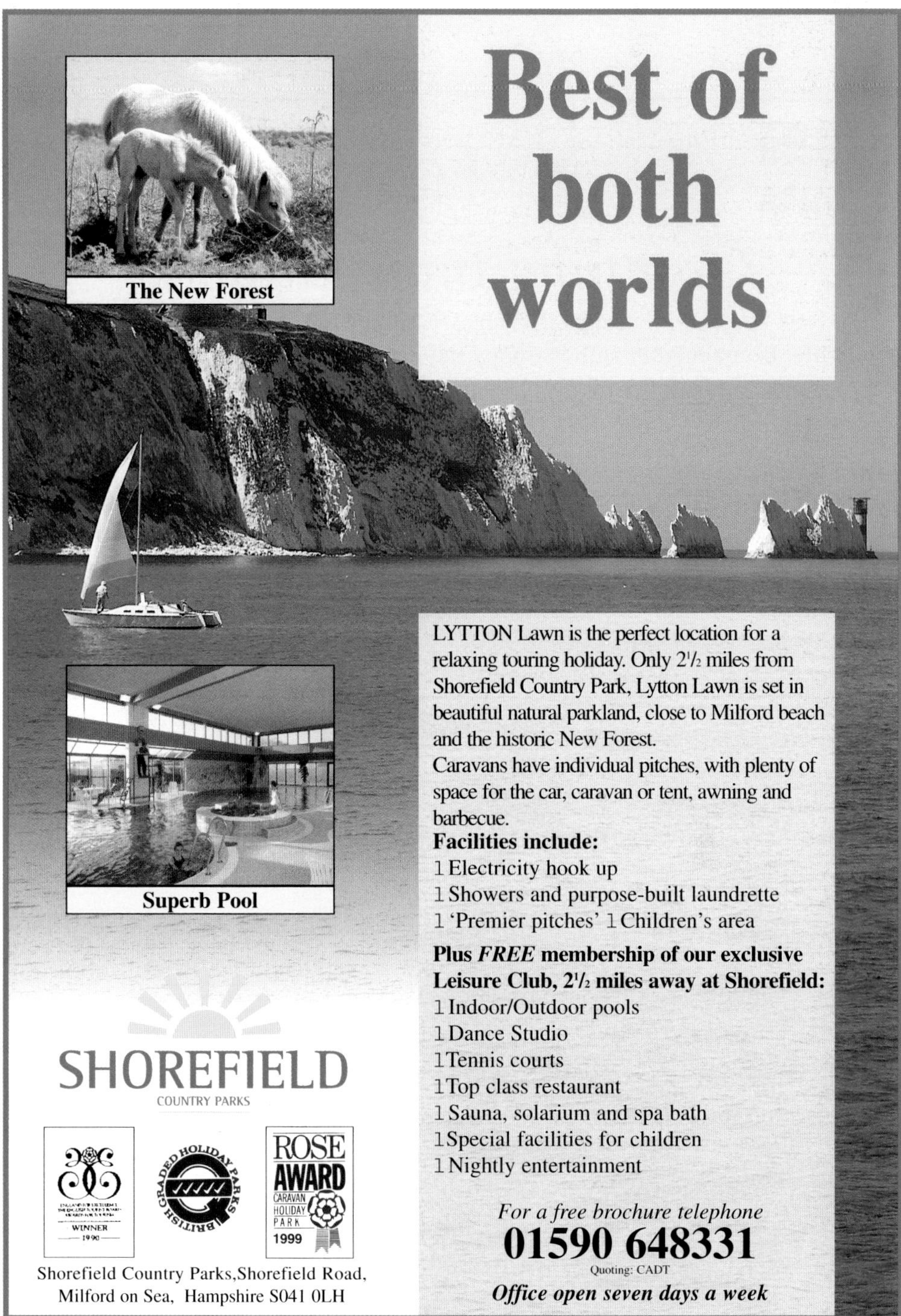
Best of both worlds
The New Forest
Superb Pool
LYTTON Lawn is the perfect location for a relaxing touring holiday. Only 2½ miles from Shorefield Country Park, Lytton Lawn is set in beautiful natural parkland, close to Milford beach and the historic New Forest.
Caravans have individual pitches, with plenty of space for the car, caravan or tent, awning and barbecue.
Facilities include:
1 Electricity hook up
1 Showers and purpose-built laundrette
1 'Premier pitches' 1 Children's area
Plus FREE membership of our exclusive Leisure Club, 2½ miles away at Shorefield:
1 Indoor/Outdoor pools
1 Dance Studio
1 Tennis courts
1 Top class restaurant
1 Sauna, solarium and spa bath
1 Special facilities for children
1 Nightly entertainment
For a free brochure telephone
01590 648331
Quoting: CADT
Office open seven days a week
SHOREFIELD
COUNTRY PARKS
WINNER
1990
GRADED HOLIDAY PARKS
BRITISH
ROSE AWARD
CARAVAN HOLIDAY PARK
1999
Shorefield Country Parks, Shorefield Road, Milford on Sea, Hampshire S041 0LH

Locks Road (sinposted Warsash). In about 1½ miles at the T-Junction turn right into Warsash Road, in about 300yds turn left into Fleet End Road. Take the first right and we are on the right.
Acreage ¾ **Open** Easter **to** October
Access Good **Site** Level
Sites Available **Total** 14
Facilities
Nearby Facilities
Swanwick
✓✓✓✓Graded Park. Shingle beach 1½ miles.

GOSPORT

Kingfisher Caravan Park, Browndown Road, Stokes Bay, Gosport, Hampshire, PO13 9BE.
Std: 01705 **Tel:** 502611
Std: 01705 **Fax:** 583583
Nearest Town/Resort Gosport
Directions Exit 11 off the M27, take the A32 to Gosport. After approx. 3 miles at Fort Brockhurst follow caravan signs to Stokes Bay.
Acreage 14 **Open** February **to** November
Access Good **Site** Level
Sites Available **Total** 100
Facilities
Nearby Facilities
Portsmouth Hard
✓✓✓✓Graded Park. Within easy reach of Portsmouth with ferries to the Continent and the Isle of Wight.

HAMBLE

Riverside Park, Satchell Lane, Hamble, Hampshire, SO31 4HR.
Std: 01703 **Tel:** 453220
Std: 01703 **Fax:** 453611
Nearest Town/Resort Southampton
Directions Leave the M27 at junction 8, follow signs for Hamble Village on the B3397 for approx. 2 miles, then turn left into Satchell Lane. Riverside is on the left hand side of Satchell Lane above Mercury Marina.
Acreage 2 **Open** March **to** October
Access Good **Site** Lev/Slight Slope
Sites Available **Total** 45
Facilities
Nearby Facilities
Hamble
✓✓✓✓Graded Park. Overlooking the River Hamble with a marina below the park. In the very pretty village of Hamble.

HAYLING ISLAND

Fishery Creek Caravan & Camping Park, Fishery Lane, Hayling Island, Hampshire, PO11 9NR.
Std: 01705 **Tel:** 462164
Std: 01705 **Fax:** 462164
Nearest Town/Resort Hayling Island
Directions Turn off the A27 at Havant, take the A3023 to Hayling Island. Turn left at the first roundabout and follow brown tourism signs to Fishery Creek, left after Mengham Town, left into Fishery Lane, park is at the end of the lane.
Acreage 8 **Open** March **to** October
Access Good **Site** Level
Sites Available **Total** 165
Facilities
Nearby Facilities
Havant
✓✓✓Graded Park. Alongside a beautiful tidal creek, offering peace and tranquility. Own slipway, short path to beach. Fishing on site. Caravan storage available all year round.

HAYLING ISLAND

Fleet Park, Yew Tree Road, Hayling Island, Hampshire, PO11 0QF.
Std: 01705 **Tel:** 463684
Nearest Town/Resort Havant/Southsea.
Directions Follow A3023 from Havant. Approx. 2 miles on Island turn left into Copse Lane then first right into Yew Tree Road.
Acreage 3 **Open** March **to** October
Access Good **Site** Level
Sites Available **Total** 75
Facilities
Nearby Facilities
Havant.
Quiet family site on a creek. Near Ferry Port. Portsmouth/Southsea, Isle of Wight. Easy touring for New Forest and Beaulieu.

HAYLING ISLAND

Lower Tye Camp Site, Copse Lane, Hayling Island, Hants, PO11 0QB.
Std: 01705 **Tel:** 462479
Std: 01705 **Fax:** 462479
Nearest Town/Resort Havant
Directions Exit the M27 or the A3M motorway at Havant. Follow the A3023 from Havant, turn left into Copse Lane. You will see the sign after being on Hayling Island for approx 1¼ miles.
Acreage 5 **Open** March **to** November
Access Good **Site** Level
Sites Available **Total** 150
Facilities
Nearby Facilities
Havant
Plunge pool on site. Near Portsmouth, Isle of Wight, Singlton Open Air Museum, Chichester, excellent beach, all water sports. £8 per unit for 2 people. Storage available and caravan parking with full use.

HAYLING ISLAND

Oven Camping Site, Manor Road, Hayling Island, Hampshire, PO11 0QX.
Std: 01705 **Tel:** 464695
Std: 01705 **Fax:** 462479
Nearest Town/Resort Havant.
Directions Exit M27 or the A37 at Havant. Take the A3023 from Havant, approx 3 miles after crossing bridge onto Hayling Island bear right at the roundabout. Site is on the left in 450yds.
Acreage 10 **Open** March **to** December
Access Good **Site** Level
Sites Available **Total** 330
Facilities
Nearby Facilities
Havant.
Heated swimming pool. Excellent touring area for Portsmouth, Chichester, New Forest etc. Safe, clean beaches, excellent for water sports. Caravan storage and on-site caravan parking. Rallies - special price. We accept motorcycles at our discretion.

LYNDHURST

Denny Wood - Forestry Commission, Near Lyndhurst, Hampshire.
Std: 0131 **Tel:** 314 6100/6505
Std: 0131 **Fax:** 334 0849
Nearest Town/Resort Lyndhurst
Directions Take the B3056 from Lyndhurst, the site is 2½ miles on the right.
Acreage 27 **Open** 25 March **to** 29 Sept
Access Good **Site** Level
Sites Available **Total** 170
Facilities
Nearby Facilities
Brockenhurst
Peaceful, grassland site among scattered oaks. New Forest ponies roam free around the site. Note : This site has NO toilets.

LYNDHURST

Matley Wood - Forestry Commission, Near Lyndhurst, Hampshire.
Std: 0131 **Tel:** 314 6100/6505
Std: 0131 **Fax:** 334 0849
Nearest Town/Resort Lyndhurst
Directions Take the B3056 from Lyndhurst, the site is 2 miles on the left. Reception for Matley Wood is at Denny Wood.
Acreage 5 **Open** 25 March **to** 29 Sept

Access Good **Site** Level
Sites Available **Total** 70
Facilities
Nearby Facilities
Brockenhurst
A small, secluded site within the natural woodland of the New Forest. Note : This site has NO toilets.

MILFORD-ON-SEA

Lytton Lawn, Lymore Lane, Milford-on-Sea, Hants, SO41 0TX.
Std: 01590 **Tel:** 648331
Std: 01590 **Fax:** 645610
Nearest Town/Resort Lymington
Directions From Lymington take the A337 towards Everton. Turn left onto the B3058 towards Milford-on-Sea and take the second left into Lymore Lane.
Acreage 4 **Open** March **to** 5 January
Access Good **Site** Lev/Slope
Sites Available **Total** 126
Facilities
Nearby Facilities
New Milton
✓✓✓✓✓Graded Park. Views of the Isle of Wight. 1 mile from the beach and 2 miles from the New Forest. FREE membership to the leisure club, restaurant, licensed club, colour TV, games room, indoor/outdoor swimming pools and tennis are available at our sister site Shorefield Country Park (2½ miles).

NEW MILTON

Bashley Park, Sway Road, New Milton, Hampshire.
Std: 01425 **Tel:** 612340
Std: 01425 **Fax:** 612602
Nearest Town/Resort New Milton.
Directions From A35 Lyndhurst/Bournemouth road, take B3055 signposted Sway. Over crossroads at 2¼ miles. Park is ½ mile on left.
Open March **to** October
Access Good **Site** Level
Sites Available **Total** 400
Facilities
Nearby Facilities
New Milton.
✓✓✓✓✓Graded Park. New Forest - 2 miles from beach, 10 miles Bournemouth. Own golf course and tennis. Many facilities. Rose Award for Excellence and England for Excellence Silver Award.

NEW MILTON

Setthorns Camp Site - Forestry Commission, Wootton, New Milton, Hampshire, BH25 5UA.
Std: 0131 314 **Tel:** 6100/6505
Nearest Town/Resort New Milton
Directions From Brockenhurst take the B3055 to Sway, after 2 miles take an unclassified signposted road to the site.
Acreage 60 **Open** All Year
Access Good **Site** Level
Sites Available **Total** 320
Facilities
Nearby Facilities
New Milton
✓✓✓✓✓Graded Park. Open woodland site with pitches nestling among pine and oak trees. This site has NO toilet facilities.

OWER

Green Pastures Farm, Ower, Romsey, Hampshire, SO51 6AJ.
Std: 01703 **Tel:** 814444
Nearest Town/Resort Romsey.
Directions Site is signposted from A36 and A3090 at Ower (exit 2 off M27 - signposted for Paultons Park).
Acreage 5 **Open** 15 March **to** 31 October
Access Good **Site** Level
Sites Available **Total** 45
Facilities
Nearby Facilities
Romsey.
✓✓✓Graded Park. A grassy site on family run farm, within easy reach of the New Forest. Paultons Park 1 mile, convenient for ferries from Portsmouth, Southampton and Lymington. Ample space for children to play. Separate toilet/shower room for the disabled.

RINGWOOD

Oakdene Forest Park, St. Leonards, Ringwood, Hampshire, BH24 7RZ.
Std: 01590 **Tel:** 648331
Std: 01590 **Fax:** 645610
Nearest Town/Resort Ringwood/Bournemouth
Directions 3 miles west of Ringwood off the A31 just past St Leonards Hospital.
Acreage 55 **Open** 1 Feb **to** 5 Jan
Access Good **Site** Level
Sites Available **Total** 200
Facilities
Nearby Facilities
Bournemouth
✓✓✓Graded Park. Bordering Avon Forest, surrounded by parkland and Forestry Commission land. 9 miles from Bournemouth beaches.

RINGWOOD

The Red Shoot Camping Park, Linwood, Nr. Ringwood, Hampshire, BH24 3QT.
Std: 01425 **Tel:** 473789
Std: 01425 **Fax:** 471558
Nearest Town/Resort Ringwood.
Directions Fron Ringwood take A338, 2 miles north of Ringwood take right turn signed Moyles Court and Linwood. Follow signs to Linwood.
Acreage 4 **Open** March **to** October
Access Good **Site** Lev/Slope
Sites Available **Total** 100
Facilities
Nearby Facilities
Brockenhurst.
✓✓✓✓Graded Park. Situated in a beautiful part of the New Forest. Half hour drive to Bournemouth coast, Salisbury and Southampton. Good pub adjacent. Mountain bike hire. Off peak tariff early and late season.

ROMSEY

Doctors Hill Farm Caravan & Camping Park, Sherfield English, Romsey, Hampshire, SO51 6FH.
Std: 01794 **Tel:** 340402
Std: 01794 **Fax:** 340402
Nearest Town/Resort Romsey.
Directions A31 towards Romsey and Winchester, just before you enter Romsey turn left onto the A27. In 4 miles turn right at Sherfield English crossroads. Park is 600yds on the right.
Acreage 10 **Open** March **to** November
Access Good **Site** Lev/Slope
Sites Available
Facilities
Nearby Facilities
✓✓✓Graded Park. Within easy reach of Salisbury, Southampton and the New Forest and the home of the late Lord Mountbatten. Special dog walk, pitch and putt. Lovely views of the surrounding countryside.

SOUTHSEA

Southsea Leisure Park, Melville Road, Southsea, Hampshire, PO4 9TB.
Std: 01705 **Tel:** 735070
Std: 01705 **Fax:** 821302
Nearest Town/Resort Portsmouth
Directions From M27/A27/A3M take southbound A2030 for 4 miles, turn left onto the A288 and follow signs.
Acreage 12 **Open** All Year
Access Good **Site** Level
Sites Available **Total** 216
Facilities
Nearby Facilities
Portsmouth Harbour
✓✓✓✓Graded Park. Located beside the beach at the quieter end of historic Portsmouth. Only 10 minutes from cross-channel ferries. Fully equipped, modern touring facilities.

ALWAYS REMEMBER TO BOOK IN PEAK SEASON

HEREFORDSHIRE

ABBEY DORE

The Neville Arms, Abbey Dore, Hereford, HR2 0AA.
Std: 01981 **Tel:** 240319
Nearest Town/Resort Hereford
Directions From Hereford take the A465 towards Abergavenny. At Pontrilas take the B4347 on the right, signposted Ewyas Harold. Stay on this road for 3 miles. Pub is on the left, site is on the right.
Acreage 1 **Open** April **to** November
Access Good **Site** Level
Sites Available **Total** 5
Facilities
Nearby Facilities
Hereford
Scenic views, ancient Abbey. On the edge of a common, plenty of walks. Licensed Pub.

BROMYARD

Boyce Caravan Park, Stanford Bishop, Bringsty, Bromyard, Herefordshire, WR6 5UB.
Std: 01885 **Tel:** 483439
Nearest Town/Resort Bromyard
Directions 3 miles east of Bromyard off the B4220. Follow official signs from the A44/ B4220 junction.
Acreage 4+ **Open** March **to** October
Access Good **Site** Level
Sites Available **Total** 24
Facilities
Nearby Facilities
✓✓✓✓✓Graded Park. Ideal for exploring the heart of England and the Welsh Marches etc.. Dogs are welcome by appointment only. Booking is advisable (evenings).

CRASWALL

Old Mill Caravan Park, Old Mill, Craswall, Herefordshire.
Std: 01981 **Tel:** 510226
Nearest Town/Resort Hereford.
Directions 8 miles off the A465 at Pandy.
Acreage 2 **Open** Easter **to** October
Access Good **Site** Level
Sites Available
Facilities
Nearby Facilities
Hereford.
Near Offas Dyke path, alongside river. Scenic views of the Black Mountains.

HAY-ON-WYE

Penlan Caravan Park, Penlan, Brilley, Hay-on-Wye, Herefordshire, HR3 6JW.
Std: 01497 **Tel:** 831485
Std: 01497 **Fax:** 831485
Nearest Town/Resort Hay-on-Wye
Directions From Kingston Church follow the Brilley to Whitney-on-Wye road for 4 miles. Look for National Trust signs on the left, turn sharp left into Apostles Lane, Penlan is first on the right.
Acreage 2½ **Open** Easter **to** October
Access Fair **Site** Lev/Slope
Sites Available **Total** 12
Facilities
Nearby Facilities
Hereford
✓✓✓Graded Park. Peaceful and relaxing site. Ideal for exploring Mid Wales and the black and white villages of Herefordshire. National Trust small holding.

HEREFORD

Camping & Caravanning Club Site, Hereford Racecourse, Roman Road, Hereford, Herefordshire, HR4 9QU.
Std: 01432 **Tel:** 272364
Nearest Town/Resort Hereford
Directions Turn left off the A49 (Ross to Leominster) onto the A4103 signposted Sutton Sugwas. Follow signs to the race course.
Acreage 5 **Open** 22 March **to** 27 Sept
Access Good **Site** Lev/Slope
Sites Available **Total** 60
Facilities
Nearby Facilities
Hereford
Located by the racecourse on the outskirts of the city. Border country, Wye Valley and a National Park. AA 3 Pennants.

HEREFORD

Cuckoo's Corner, Moreton-on-Lugg, Herefordshire, HR4 8AH.
Std: 01432 **Tel:** 760234
Nearest Town/Resort Hereford
Directions 4 miles north of Hereford on the A49, 100 yards beyond signpost Village Centre and Marden. Or 10 miles south of Leominster opposite advance sign Village Centre and Marden.
Acreage ½ **Open** All Year
Access Good **Site** Level
Sites Available **Total** 10
Facilities
Nearby Facilities
Hereford
✓✓✓Graded Park. Friendly family site with pleasant views. Archery and croquet on site. Farm animals and pet exercise area. Good touring area.

HEREFORD

Lucksall Caravan & Camping Park, 'Lucksall', Mordiford, Hereford, Herefordshire, HR1 4LP.
Std: 01432 **Tel:** 870213
Nearest Town/Resort Hereford
Directions On the B4224 5 miles from Hereford and 9 miles from Ross-on-Wye.
Acreage 9½ **Open** April **to** End October
Access Good **Site** Level
Sites Available **Total** 80
Facilities
Nearby Facilities
Hereford
✓✓✓✓Graded Park. Flat, riverside site with closecut grass. Peaceful and uncommercial.

HEREFORD

Upper Gilvach Farm, St. Margarets, Vowchurch, Hereford, Herefordshire.
Std: 01981 **Tel:** 510618
Nearest Town/Resort Hereford.
Directions 4 miles off the B4348.
Open Easter **to** October
Access Good **Site** Level
Sites Available **Total** 20
Facilities
Nearby Facilities
Hereford.

LEOMINSTER

Arrow Bank Caravan Park, Nun House Farm, Eardisland, Near Leominster, Herefordshire, HR6 9BG.
Std: 01544 **Tel:** 388312
Std: 01544 **Fax:** 388312
Nearest Town/Resort Leominster

Directions 6 miles west of Leominster, off the A44 Rhayadr/Brecon road.
Acreage 5 **Open** March **to** October
Access Good **Site** Level
Sites Available **Total** 34
Facilities
Nearby Facilities
Leominster
✓✓✓✓Graded Park. Peaceful, landscaped park in a beautiful "Black and White" village. Ideal holiday base.

ORLETON

Orleton Rise Holiday Home Park, Green Lane, Orleton, Ludlow, SY8 4JE.
Std: 01584 **Tel:** 831617
Nearest Town/Resort Ludlow/Leominster
Directions 5 miles south west of Ludlow off the B4361 towards Leominster. Turn off at the Maidenhead Inn (signposted), we are ½ mile along Green Lane.
Acreage 1 **Open** 14 March **to** 31 October
Access Good **Site** Level
Sites Available **Total** 15
Facilities
Nearby Facilities
Ludlow
Tranquility in the countryside.

PETERCHURCH

Poston Mill Park, Peterchurch, Golden Valley, Herefordshire, HR2 0SF.
Std: 01981 **Tel:** 550225
Std: 01981 **Fax:** 550885
Nearest Town/Resort Hereford
Directions On B4348. 11 miles from Hereford and 11 miles from Hay on Wye.
Acreage 20 **Open** All Year
Access Good **Site** Level
Sites Available **Total** 64
Facilities
Nearby Facilities
Hereford
✓✓✓✓✓Graded Park. Beautiful park, well maintained. On the banks of the River Dore. Adjacent to an excellent restaurant/bar. Highly recommended. TV Hook-ups. E-mail - Enquiries@poston-mill.co.uk

PETERCHURCH

The Bridge Inn, Michaelchurch Escley, Hereford, HR2 0JW.
Std: 01981 **Tel:** 510646
Nearest Town/Resort Hereford
Directions From Hereford take the A465 towards Abergavenny, turn right for Hay-on-Wye and Kingstone, go through Kingstone and turn right for Hay-on-Wye onto the B4347. After 4 miles turn left to Vowchurch and Michaelchurch, at T-Junction in the village turn left, 300 yards past the church turn left towards the pub.
Acreage ¼ **Open** April **to** September
Access Good **Site** Level
Sites Available **Total** 18
Facilities
Nearby Facilities
Hereford
Idyllic riverside location. Pub on site offering excellent food. Small camp shop for necessities. Enclosed childrens play area.

ROSS-ON-WYE

British Lion Inn, Fawley, Kings Caple, Herefordshire, HR1 4UQ.
Std: 01432 **Tel:** 840524
Std: 01432 **Fax:** 840404
Nearest Town/Resort Ross-on-Wye
Directions From the Wilton roundabout in Ross-on-Wye take the A49, second right. Drive for approx. 4 miles then take the next right after New Harp. Go over the bridge, British Lion is on the left after 1 mile.
Acreage 2 **Open** All Year
Access Good **Site** Sloping
Sites Available **Total** 20
Facilities
Nearby Facilities
Hereford
Near a disused railway line. Good walks. Pub food.

ROSS-ON-WYE

Broadmeadow Caravan Park, Broadmeadows, Ross-on-Wye, Herefordshire, HR9 7BH.
Std: 01989 **Tel:** 768076
Std: 01989 **Fax:** 566030
Nearest Town/Resort Ross-on-Wye
Directions Adjacent to the A40 Ross relief road. Access from Pancake roundabout off relief road turning into Ross. Take the first right opposite Wolf Tools into Ashburton Estate Road, then turn right by Safeway Supermarket.
Acreage 16 **Open** Easter/1st Apr **to** Oct
Access Good **Site** Level
Sites Available **Total** 150
Facilities
Nearby Facilities
Gloucester
✓✓✓✓✓Graded Park. Lake walks. Fishing on site. Only 5 minutes to the centre of Ross-on-Wye. Ideal touring and walking in the Wye Valley.

ROSS-ON-WYE

Lower Ruxton Farm, Kings Caple, Herefordshire, HR1 4TX.
Std: 01432 **Tel:** 840223
Nearest Town/Resort Ross-on-Wye.
Directions A49 from Ross-on-Wye, 1 mile turn right follow signs for Hoarwithy (Kings Caple 4 miles) across river bridge ½ mile sign to Ruxton second farm on right.
Acreage 8 **Open** Mid July **to** August
Site Level
Sites Available **Total** 20
Facilities
Nearby Facilities
Hereford.
Alongside river.

ROSS-ON-WYE

Yew Tree Inn Camping Site, Peterstow, Ross-on-Wye, Herefordshire, HR9 6JZ.
Std: 01989 **Tel:** 562815
Nearest Town/Resort Ross-on-Wye
Directions A49 Ross to Hereford road, 1½ miles on the right from roundabout.
Acreage 2 **Open** March **to** October
Access Good **Site** Lev/Slope
Sites Available **Total** 20
Facilities
Nearby Facilities
Hereford
Quiet, country park. Licensed pub with restaurant. Ideal for touring Symonds Yat etc..

WHITCHURCH

Doward Park Camp Site, Great Doward, Symonds Yat West, Near Ross-on-Wye, Herefordshire, HR9 6BP.
Std: 01600 **Tel:** 890438
Nearest Town/Resort Monmouth
Directions On the A40 between Ross-on-Wye and Monmouth. Turn off at Symonds Yat West and follow signs for The Doward.
Acreage 4 **Open** Easter **to** October
Access Good **Site** Level
Sites Available **Total** 40
Facilities
Nearby Facilities
Hereford
✓✓✓Graded Park. Very scenic and peaceful site with excellent, clean facilities. Close to the River Wye with woodland and river walks. Ideal base for touring the Wye Valley.

WHITCHURCH

Sterrett's Caravan Park, Symonds Yat (West), Near Ross-on-Wye, Herefordshire, HR9 6BY.
Std: 01594 **Tel:** 832888
Nearest Town/Resort Ross-on-Wye
Directions Take the A40 from Ross-on-Wye or Monmouth to Whitchurch. ½ mile from the A40 to Symonds Yat (West).
Acreage 5 **Open** March **to** October
Access Good **Site** Level
Sites Available **Total** 8
Facilities
Nearby Facilities
Hereford
✓✓✓✓Graded Park. Flat and grassy site, close to a river.

WHITCHURCH

Symonds Yat Caravan & Camping Limited, Symonds Yat West, Near Ross-on-Wye, Herefordshire, HR9 6BY.
Std: 01600 **Tel:** 890883/891069
Std: 01600 **Fax:** 890883
Nearest Town/Resort Monmouth
Directions A40, 7 miles to Ross-on-Wye and 4 miles to Monmouth. Park is ¼ mile from the A40.
Acreage 1 **Open** March **to** October
Access Good **Site** Level
Sites Available **Total** 35
Facilities
Nearby Facilities
Hereford
✓✓✓Graded Park. In an area of outstanding natural beauty, adjacent to the River Wye which is ideal for walking, canoeing and fishing. Good for touring the Forest of Dean.

HERTFORDSHIRE

BALDOCK

Ashridge Farm Touring Caravan Park, Ashridge Farm, 1 Ashwell Street, Ashwell, Baldock, Hertfordshire, SG7 5QF.
Std: 01462 **Tel:** 742527
Std: 01462 **Fax:** 742527
Nearest Town/Resort Baldock
Directions 3 miles east off Gate 10 A1(M). 1½ miles north west of the A505 Ashwell & Morden station turning.
Acreage 2½ **Open** All Year
Access Good **Site** Level
Sites Available **Total** 30
Facilities
Nearby Facilities
Ashwell & Morden
✓✓✓✓✓Graded Park. Peaceful park in a pleasant village with a host of services.

BALDOCK

Radwell Mill Lake, Radwell Mill, Baldock, Herts, SG7 5ET.
Std: 01462 **Tel:** 730253
Std: 01462 **Fax:** 733421
Nearest Town/Resort Baldock
Directions Junction 10 A1(M) then the A507, ½ mile towards Baldock take a lane signed "Radwell Only" to the lake and site.
Acreage 3 **Open** Easter **to** November
Access Good **Site** Level
Sites Available **Total** 20
Facilities
Nearby Facilities
Baldock
Quiet site with a lake and orchard. Good for bird watching.

HERTFORD

Camping & Caravanning Club Site, Mangrove Road (Not Ball Park), Hertford, Hertfordshire, SG13 8QF.
Std: 01992 **Tel:** 586696
Directions From the A10 follow the A414 Hertford signs to the next roundabout (Foxholes) and go straight across, after 200 yards turn left signposted Balls Park and Hertford University. Turn left at the T-Junction into Mangrove Road, go past Simon Balle School, University and Cricket Ground, site is 400 yards past the cricket club on the left.
Open 22 March **to** 1 Nov
Site Level
Sites Available **Total** 250
Facilities
Nearby Facilities
North & East Hertford
✓✓✓✓✓Graded Park. Set in acres of meadowland. 20 miles from London.

HODDESDON

Lee Valley Caravan Park, Essex Road, Dobbs Weir, Hoddesdon, Hertfordshire, EN11 0AS.
Std: 01992 **Tel:** 462090
Nearest Town/Resort Hoddesdon.
Directions Hoddesdon exit from A10 turn left at second roundabout.
Acreage 24 **Open** April **to** October
Access Good **Site** Level
Sites Available **Total** 100
Facilities
Nearby Facilities
Broxbourne.
✓✓✓✓Graded Park. A quiet riverside setting, fishing on site. Outdoor swimming pool and cafe/restaurant nearby.

WALTHAM CROSS

Camping & Caravanning Club Site, Theobalds Park, Bulls Cross Ride, Waltham Cross, Hertfordshire, EN7 5HS.
Std: 01992 **Tel:** 620604
Directions Leave the M25 at junction 25, take the A10 towards London keeping to the right hand side, turn right at the first set of traffic lights signposted Crews Hill. Turn right at the T-Junction (opposite Pied Bull), turn right behind the dog kennels, site is towards the top of the lane on the right.
Open 22 March **to** 1 Nov
Site Level
Sites Available **Total** 150
Facilities
Nearby Facilities
✓✓✓✓Graded Park. Tree-screened site. Only 13 miles from central London.

ISLE OF MAN

PEEL

Peel Camping Park, PTC6, Derby Road, Peel, Isle of Man.
Std: 01624 **Tel:** 842341
Std: 01624 **Fax:** 844010
Nearest Town/Resort Peel.
Directions A20 edge of town signposted.
Acreage 4 **Open** Mid May **to** Mid Sept
Access Good **Site** Level
Sites Available **Total** 100
Facilities
Nearby Facilities
3 miles T.T. course, near sea, central in island, cars and motorcycles free.

ISLE OF WIGHT

ATHERFIELD

Chine Farm Camping Site, Military Road, Atherfield Bay, I.O.W., PO38 2JH.
Std: 01983 **Tel:** 740228
Nearest Town/Resort Freshwater
Directions East of Freshwater 8 miles on the A3055 Coast Road.
Acreage 5 **Open** May **to** September
Access Good **Site** Level
Sites Available **Total** 80
Facilities
Nearby Facilities
✓✓✓Graded Park. Footpath to beach. Sea view. 3¼ miles Blackgang Chine.

BEMBRIDGE

Whitecliff Bay Holiday Park, Hillway, Whitecliff Bay, Bembridge, Isle of Wight, PO35 5PL.
Std: 01983 **Tel:** 872671
Nearest Town/Resort Sandown
Directions B3395 road to Sandown, follow signposts.
Acreage 15 **Open** April **to** October
Access Good **Site** Lev/Slope
Sites Available **Total** 450
Facilities
Nearby Facilities
Brading.
✓✓✓✓Graded Park. Situated in pleasant countryside adjoining Whitecliff Bay with sandy beach. Indoor pool and leisure centre, family owned and managed.

BRIGHSTONE

Grange Farm Caravan & Camping Site, Military Road, Brighstone Bay, Brighstone, Isle of Wight, PO30 4DA.
Std: 01983 **Tel:** 740296
Nearest Town/Resort BrighstoneNewport
Directions On coastal road A3055 midway from Freshwater to Chale (approx 5mls)
Acreage 2 **Open** March **to** End October
Access Good **Site** Level
Sites Available **Total** 60
Facilities
Nearby Facilities
✓✓✓Graded Park. Family run park on a small working farm with unusual farm animals. Situated on a cliff edge, south facing. Self catering accommodation also available. Pets are welcome if kept on leads. Restaurant and pubs nearby.

COWES

Comforts Farm Caravan & Camping Park, Comforts Farm, Pallance Road, Northwood, Cowes, Isle of Wight, PO31 8LS.
Std: 01983 **Tel:** 293888
Nearest Town/Resort Cowes.
Directions From Cowes take the A3020, turn right into The Gates Road at Plessey Radar Site. Turn left into Place Road, after ½ mile bear right into Pallance road. Farm entrance is on the right after passing Travellers Joy Public House.
Acreage 8¼ **Open** March **to** October
Access Good **Site** Lev/Slope
Sites Available **Total** 50
Facilities
Nearby Facilities
Horse riding on site.

COWES

Thorness Bay Holiday Park, Thorness, Isle of Wight, PO31 8NJ.
Std: 01983 **Tel:** 523109
Std: 01983 **Fax:** 822213
Nearest Town/Resort Newport.
Directions From Fishbourne, follow signs to Newport and turn off roundabout onto dual carriageway following signs for West Cowes then Yarmouth onto the A3054 (Forest Road) for approx 1 mile. Thorness Bay is signposted.
Open April **to** October
Access Good **Site** Sloping
Sites Available **Total** 120
Facilities
Nearby Facilities
✓✓✓✓Graded Park. Pools, riding stables, family club. On site facilities.

FRESHWATER

Heathfield Farm Camping Site, Heathfield Road, Freshwater, Isle Of Wight, PO40 9SH.
Std: 01983 **Tel:** 756756
Std: 01983 **Fax:** 752480
Nearest Town/Resort Freshwater
Directions 2 miles west of Yarmouth ferry port on the A3054.
Acreage 4 **Open** 1st May **to** 30 September
Access Good **Site** Level
Sites Available **Total** 60
Facilities
Nearby Facilities
✓✓✓✓Graded Park. Near beach with sea and open country views.

NETTLESTONE

Pondwell Camping & Chalets, Pondwell Hill, Nettlestone, Isle of Wight.
Std: 01983 **Tel:** 612330
Std: 01983 **Fax:** 613511
Nearest Town/Resort Ryde
Directions Signposted from Wightlink Fishbourne. Take A3054 to Ryde then A3055 turning left along B3350 to Seaview. Site is next to Wishing Well Pub.
Acreage 14 **Open** May **to** September
Access Good **Site** Level
Sites Available **Total** 200
Facilities
Nearby Facilities
Ryde
✓✓✓✓Graded Park. Set in countryside with scenic views, walking distance to sea.

NEWCHURCH

Southland Camping Park, Winford Road, Newchurch, Isle of Wight, PO36 0LZ.
Std: 01983 **Tel:** 865385
Std: 01983 **Fax:** 867663
Nearest Town/Resort Sandown/Shanklin.
Directions Newport to Sandown road A3056/A3055 through Arreton, after Fighting Cocks Public House take the second left. Continue along road for 1 mile, site is on the left.
Acreage 5¾ **Open** Easter **to** September
Access Good **Site** Level
Sites Available **Total** 100
Facilities
Nearby Facilities
Lake
✓✓✓✓✓Graded Park. Sheltered, secluded touring park, generous level pitches. Far reaching views over Arreton Valley.

RYDE

Beaper Farm Camping Site, Near Ryde, Isle of Wight, PO33 1QJ.
Std: 01983 **Tel:** 615210
Nearest Town/Resort Ryde
Directions On the A3055 2½ miles south of Ryde and 3 miles north of Sandown.
Acreage 13 **Open** April **to** October
Access Good **Site** Level
Sites Available **Total** 150
Facilities
Nearby Facilities
✓✓✓✓Graded Park. Centrally situated for the best beaches and touring the island.

SANDOWN

Adgestone Camping Park, Adgestone, Near Sandown, Isle of Wight, PO36 0HL.
Std: 01983 **Tel:** 403432/403989
Std: 01983 **Fax:** 404955
Nearest Town/Resort Sandown
Directions Turn off the A3055 at the Fairway by Manor House Pub in Lake, which is between Sandown and Shanklin, pass the golf course on the left, then turn right at the T-Junction, park is 200 metres on the right.
Acreage 17½ **Open** Easter **to** September
Access Good **Site** Level
Sites Available **Total** 200
Facilities
Nearby Facilities
Sandown
✓✓✓✓✓Graded Park. Beautiful countryside setting, ideal for walking. The River Yar borders the park for fishing, plus private pond fishing. Beach and Sandown Town 1½ miles. Please refer to our colour advertisement for further details.

GREAT VALUE HOLIDAYS

FERRY AND HOLIDAY PACKAGES AVAILABLE

OUTDOOR POOL * INDOOR POOL * CLUBS & ENTERTAINMENT

CAMPER GROUND FACILITIES INCLUDE:

Laundry ● Shop ● Toilets & Showers ● Electric hook-ups ● Super pitches

Prices are per person per night	ADULT	CHILD 5-13
LOW SEASON	£2.80	£1.90
+ PITCH FEE £1.00 PER NIGHT.		
HIGH SEASON	£3.90	£2.60
+ PITCH FEE £2.00 PER NIGHT.		

DEPT. C CC, BEMBRIDGE ISLE OF WIGHT, PO35 5PL

PHONE FOR FREE COLOUR BROCHURE

(24 HR.) 01983 872671

(FAX: 01983 872941)

SANDOWN

Camping & Caravanning Club Sandown, Cheverton Farm, Newport Road, Apse Heath, Sandown, Isle of Wight, PO36 9PJ.
Std: 01983 **Tel:** 866414
Nearest Town/Resort Sandown/Shanklin
Directions Road number 3056, 500 yards Sandown side of Apse Heath.
Acreage 5 **Open** 22 March **to** 27 Sept
Access Good **Site** Lev/Slope
Sites Available **Total** 47
Facilities
Nearby Facilities
Sandown.
√√√√Graded Park. Near beach, scenic views, country walks.

SANDOWN

Fairway Holiday Park, The Fairway, Sandown, Isle of Wight, PO36 9PS.
Std: 01983 **Tel:** 403462
Std: 01983 **Fax:** 405713
Nearest Town/Resort Sandown.
Directions Off Sandown/Shanklin road, into Fairway at Manor House Pub, Lake. Approx 1 mile from centre of Sandown.
Acreage 5½ **Open** March **to** September
Access Good **Site** Level
Sites Available **Total** 150
Facilities
Nearby Facilities
Sandown.
√√√√Graded Park. Picturesque location, with many facilities, relaxed, family atmosphere.

SANDOWN

Village Way Caravan & Camping Park, Newport Road, Apse Heath, Sandown, Isle of Wight, PO36 9PJ.
Std: 01983 **Tel:** 863279
Nearest Town/Resort Sandown
Directions From Newport take the A22 to Blackwater then the A3056 to Apse Heath. We are on the main A3056.
Open All Year
Access Good **Site** Level
Sites Available **Total** 14
Facilities
Nearby Facilities
√√√Graded Park. Near the beach. Beautiful country walks to the woods and within walking distance of a garden centre and Safeways. The Heights Leisure Centre is only a mile away.

SANDOWN

Cheverton Copse Caravan & Camping Park, Newport Road, Near Lake, Sandown, Isle of Wight, PO36 0JP.
Std: 01983 **Tel:** 403161
Std: 01983 **Fax:** 403161
Nearest Town/Resort Sandown.
Directions On the A3056 Newport/Sandown road, 1¼ miles west of Sandown.
Acreage 1 **Open** May **to** September
Access Good **Site** Sloping
Sites Available **Total** 26
Facilities
Nearby Facilities
Lake
√√√√Graded Park. Near to all amenities, ideal for touring with superb views.

SANDOWN

Queen Bower Dairy Caravan Park, Alverstone Road, Queen Bower, Sandown, Isle of Wight.
Std: 01983. **Tel:** 403840
Nearest Town/Resort Sandown.
Directions On the A3056 Newport to Sandown road, turn into Alverstone Road at Apse Heath crossroads. Park is 1 mile on the left.
Acreage 2¼ **Open** May **to** October
Access Good **Site** Level
Sites Available **Total** 20
Facilities
Nearby Facilities
Sandown.
Scenic views, ideal touring. Sell our own produced Dairy products (milk and cream). Public telephone ¼ mile.

SHANKLIN

Languard Camping Park, Languard Manor Road, Shanklin, Isle of Wight.
Std: 01983 **Tel:** 867028
Std: 01983 **Fax:** 865988
Nearest Town/Resort Shanklin.
Directions A3056 from Newport, ½ mile before Lake Town sign turn right up Whitecross Lane. 400 yards to site.
Acreage 5 **Open** May **to** September
Access Good **Site** Level
Sites Available **Total** 150
Facilities
Nearby Facilities
Shanklin.
√√√√Graded Park. Marked pitches.

SHANKLIN

Lower Hyde Holiday Village, Shanklin, Isle of Wight, PO37 7LL.
Std: 01983 **Tel:** 866131
Std: 01983 **Fax:** 862532
Nearest Town/Resort Shanklin.
Directions Approach Shanklin on the A3020, turn left at the traffic lights, go down the High Street and at Boots turn left into Regent Street. Take the first left, then turn right into Landguard Road. The park is on the left.
Acreage 8 **Open** 31 April **to** 16 October
Access Good **Site** Level
Sites Available **Total** 128
Facilities
Nearby Facilities
Shanklin.
✓✓✓✓Graded Park. Lies within some 55 acres of delightful wooded downland. Just outside Shanklin.

SHANKLIN

Ninham Country Holidays, Shanklin, Isle of Wight, PO37 7PL.
Std: 01983 **Tel:** 864243
Std: 01983 **Fax:** 868881
Nearest Town/Resort Shanklin.
Directions Signposted off Newport/ Sandown road (A3056). Site entrance is ¼ mile west of Safeway's on the left.
Acreage 10 **Open** May **to** September
Access Very Good **Site** Level
Sites Available **Total** 98
Facilities
Nearby Facilities
Shanklin.
✓✓✓✓Graded Park. Country park setting close to Islands premier seaside resort. Ferry inclusive "Package" holidays.

ST. HELENS

Carpenters Farm Camp Site, Carpenters Farm, St. Helens, Ryde, Isle of Wight, PO33 1YL.
Std: 01983 **Tel:** 872450
Nearest Town/Resort Sandown
Directions On the B3330, 3 miles from Sandown or Ryde.
Acreage 12½ **Open** End May **to** Oct
Access Good **Site** Sloping
Sites Available **Total** 70
Facilities
Nearby Facilities
✓✓✓Graded Park.

ST. HELENS

Nodes Point Holiday Park, St. Helens, Ryde, Isle of Wight, PO33 1YA.
Std: 01983 **Tel:** 872401
Directions Approach Ryde on the A3054 to join the A3055 in the town. At Bishop Lovett School (on the left), go straight ahead onto the B3330 to St. Helens/Bembridge/Nodes Point.
Acreage 16 **Open** 30 April **to** 1 October
Site Lev/Slope
Sites Available **Total** 240
Facilities
Nearby Facilities
Ryde.
✓✓✓✓Graded Park. Within 65 acres of parkland running down to the beach. Colour television in the bar.

VENTNOR

Appuldurcombe Gardens Caravan & Camping Park, Wroxall, Ventnor, I.O.W., PO38 3EP.
Std: 01983 **Tel:** 852597
Std: 01983 **Fax:** 856225
Nearest Town/Resort Ventnor.
Directions From Newport take the A3020, turn off towards Shanklin. Go through Godshill, turn right at Whiteley Bank roundabout towards Wroxall.
Acreage 4 **Open** April **to** October
Access Good **Site** Lev/Slope
Sites Available **Total** 100
Facilities
Nearby Facilities
Shanklin
✓✓✓✓✓Graded Park. Country setting with a stream. Ideal for walkers and cyclists.

YARMOUTH

The Orchards Holiday Caravan & Camping Park, Newbridge, Yarmouth, Isle of Wight, PO41 0TS.
Std: 01983 **Tel:** 531331
Std: 01983 **Fax:** 531666
Nearest Town/Resort Yarmouth.
Directions 4 miles east of Yarmouth and 6 miles west of Newport on B3401. Entrance opposite Newbridge Post Office.
Acreage 8 **Open** 20 February **to** 2 January
Access Good **Site** Lev/Slope
Sites Available **Total** 175
Facilities
Nearby Facilities
Lymington.
✓✓✓✓✓Graded Park. Good views of the Downs and Solent. Bookings inclusive of car ferries throughout season. Outdoor swimming pool from late May to early September, indoor swimming pool all season. Takeaway food and coarse fishing on site. Battery charging, small function/meeting room. Small rallies welcome. Ideal for rambling and cycling.

KENT

ASHFORD

Broadhembury Holiday Park, Steeds Lane, Kingsnorth, Ashford, Kent, TN26 1NQ.
Std: 01233 **Tel:** 620859
Std: 01233 **Fax:** 620859
Nearest Town/Resort Ashford
Directions Leave the M20 at junction 10, take the A2070 following signs for Kingsnorth. Turn left at the second cross-roads in the village.
Acreage 5 **Open** All Year
Access Good **Site** Level
Sites Available **Total** 60
Facilities
Nearby Facilities
Ashford
✓✓✓✓ Graded Park. Quiet, Award Winning park in Kentish countryside with every modern amenity. Central to many places of interest. Convenient for all Channel crossings.

ASHFORD

Dean Court Farm, Challock Lane, Westwell, Ashford, Kent, TN25 4NH.
Std: 01233. **Tel:** 712924
Nearest Town/Resort Ashford.
Directions Take A252 from Charing on A20 towards Canterbury for 3 miles. On reaching Challock, turn right signposted Westwell. Farm is 1 mile on the right.
Acreage 3 **Open** All Year
Access Good **Site** Sloping
Sites Available **Total** 30
Facilities
Nearby Facilities
Charing.
Quiet, very good walking on North Downs Way and good for touring. Good stop-over site for channel ports, Folkestone and Dover.

BIDDENDEN

Spilland Farm Holiday & Tourist Park, Benenden Road, Biddenden, Kent.
Std: 01580 **Tel:** 291379
Std: 01580 **Fax:** 291379
Nearest Town/Resort Biddenden/ Tenterden.
Directions A262 from Biddenden, 1 mile fork right, park ¼ mile on right.
Acreage 6 **Open** April **to** September
Access Good **Site** Sloping
Sites Available **Total** 65
Facilities
Nearby Facilities
Headcorn.
Centre for tourists, castles etc., yet 15 miles to coast at Rye. 4 miles grass airfield, flying lessons, parachuting. No motor caravans accepted.

BIDDENDEN

Woodlands Park, Tenterden Road, Biddenden, Ashford, Kent.
Std: 01580 **Tel:** 291216
Std: 01580 **Fax:** 291216
Nearest Town/Resort Tenterden/Leeds Castle.
Directions On A262, 3 miles north of Tenterden. 15 miles south of Maidstone.
Acreage 10 **Open** March **to** October
Access Good **Site** Level
Sites Available **Total** 100
Facilities
Nearby Facilities
Headcorn.
Quiet, country site. Ideal for tourist centre.
E-mail: woodlandsp@aol.con

BIRCHINGTON

Quex Caravan Park, Park Road, Birchington, Kent, CT7 0BL.
Std: 01843 **Tel:** 841273
Std: 01227 **Fax:** 740585
Nearest Town/Resort Margate/ Ramsgate.
Directions Follow road signs to Margate. When in Birchington turn right at mini roundabout (signposted Margate). Approximately 100yds after roundabout take the first turning on the right and then right again as directed by Tourist Board signs.
Acreage 3 **Open** 7 March **to** 7 November
Access Good **Site** Level
Sites Available **Total** 50
Facilities
Nearby Facilities
Birchington.
✓✓✓✓ Graded Park. Ideal base for touring Thanet and Canterbury areas.

BIRCHINGTON

St. Nicholas Camping Site, Court Road, St. Nicholas at Wade, Nr. Birchington, Kent, CT7 0NH.
Std: 01843 **Tel:** 847245
Nearest Town/Resort Birchington/ Margate
Directions Village signposted off the A299 and off the A28 near Birchington.
Open March **to** October
Access Good **Site** Level
Sites Available **Total** 70
Facilities
Nearby Facilities
Birchington
Ideal touring, central to Five Towns, Margate, Ramsgate, Herne Bay, Broadstairs and Canterbury.

BIRCHINGTON

Thanet Way Caravan Co., Frost Farm, Frost Lane, St. Nicholas-at-Wade, Birchington, Kent, CT7 0NA.
Std: 01843 **Tel:** 847219
Nearest Town/Resort Minis Bay.
Directions From the M2 take the A299 for 17 miles to St Nicholas roundabout, turn back on the A299, ¼ mile signposted.
Open March **to** October
Access Good **Site** Lev/Slope
Sites Available **Total** 10
Facilities
Nearby Facilities
Birchington.
✓✓✓Graded Park. Quiet country site, 1½ miles from beach. Walking.

BIRCHINGTON

Two Chimneys Caravan Park, Shottendane Road, Birchington, Thanet, Kent.
Std: 01843 **Tel:** 841068/843157
Std: 01843 **Fax:** 843157/848676
Nearest Town/Resort Margate.
Directions 1½ miles Birchington, turn right into park lane at Birchington Church, left fork "RAF Manston". First left onto B2049 site ½ mile on right.
Acreage 10 **Open** March **to** October
Access Good **Site** Level
Sites Available **Total** 90
Facilities
Nearby Facilities
Birchington.
✓✓✓✓Graded Park. Country site, ideal touring centre, 3 miles Margate, 13 miles Canterbury. Sauna, solarium and spa bath. Tennis court on site.

CANTERBURY

Camping & Caravanning Club Site, Bekesbourne Lane, Canterbury, Kent, CT3 4AB.
Std: 01227 **Tel:** 463216
Directions From Canterbury follow the A257 towards Sandwich, turn right opposite the golf course.
Acreage 20 **Open** All Year
Site Lev/Slope
Sites Available **Total** 210
Facilities
Nearby Facilities
Canterbury
✓✓✓✓Graded Park. Close to Canterbury and within easy reach of the Channel ports.

CANTERBURY

Red Lion Caravan Park, Old London Road, Dunkirk, Near Canterbury, Kent, ME13 9LL.
Std: 01227 **Tel:** 750661
Nearest Town/Resort Canterbury.
Directions 5 miles - Take the A2 London bound, turn off at park sign ¼ mile for Dunkirk. 3 miles - At the end of the M2 (junction 7) take the A2 Canterbury bound. Immediately take park sign 3 miles for Dunkirk.
Acreage 1 **Open** All Year
Access Good **Site** Level
Sites Available **Total** 25
Facilities
Nearby Facilities
Canterbury
Orchard and country routes, gardens to visit, Canterbury city, Dover 15 miles, beaches 5 miles, Channel Tunnel 17 miles. Cafe/restaurant in the adjoining pub.

CANTERBURY

Royal Oak Camping, 114 Sweech Gate, Broad Oak, Canterbury, Kent, CT2 0QP.
Std: 0227 **Tel:** 710448
Nearest Town/Resort Canterbury/Herne Bay
Directions North Lane Canterbury or the A28 Margate road. North Lane is direct to the site, keep straight. A28 Margate road, Sturry, Herne Bay, top of hill first left into Sweech Gate. 500yds on the right to site.
Acreage 2 **Open** March **to** October
Access Good **Site** Level
Sites Available **Total** 40
Facilities
Nearby Facilities
Sturry
Quiet site, busy pub with lunchtime food. 10 minutes to the beach and city.

CANTERBURY

Yew Tree Caravan Park, Stone Street, Petham, Canterbury, Kent, CT4 5PL.
Std: 01227 **Tel:** 700306
Std: 01227 **Fax:** 700306
Nearest Town/Resort Canterbury.
Directions 4 miles south of Canterbury on the B2068, turn right by the Chequers Public House, park entrance is on the left hand side.
Acreage 2 **Open** March **to** October
Access Good **Site** Lev/Slope
Sites Available **Total** 45
Facilities
Nearby Facilities
Canterbury East
✓✓✓✓Graded Park. Small picturesque park overlooking the Chartham Downs. Scenic views, large swimming pool, ideal touring base.

CHATHAM

Woolmans Wood Tourist Caravan & Camping Park, Maidstone Road, Bridgewood, Chatham, Kent, ME5 9SB.
Std: 01634 **Tel:** 867685
Nearest Town/Resort Rochester/ Chatham
Directions Leave the M2 at junction 2, M20 at junction 6. A229 then the B2097, park is ¼ mile on the right hand side.
Acreage 5 **Open** All Year
Access Good **Site** Level
Sites Available **Total** 60
Facilities
Nearby Facilities
Chatham
✓✓✓✓Graded Park. Rochester - Charles Dickens Centre. Chatham Dockyard, Leeds Castle, Rochester Castle and Cathedral.

DEAL

Clifford Park Caravans, Clifford Park, Thompson Close, Walmer, Deal, Kent, CT14 7PB.
Std: 01304 **Tel:** 373373
Nearest Town/Resort Deal.
Directions A258, Deal 1 mile and Dover 5 miles.

Acreage ¼ **Open** March **to** 30 October
Access Good **Site** Level
Sites Available **Total** 15
Facilities
Nearby Facilities
Walmer
Ideal touring area for day trips to France or the beaches.

DEAL

Leisurescope Holiday Caravan Park, Golf Road, Deal, Kent, CT14 6RG.
Std: 01304 **Tel:** 363332
Nearest Town/Resort Deal
Directions If approaching from the A2 take the A258 to Deal. Follow road onto the seafront heading north, follow seafront road. At T-Junction turn right into Golf Road, go past the golf clubhouse to Leisurescope.
Acreage 2½ **Open** March **to** October
Access Good **Site** Level
Sites Available **Total** 55
Facilities
Nearby Facilities
Deal
✓✓✓✓Graded Park. 300yds from the sea, scenic views, walking and cycling. Fishing and golf. Quiet and peaceful park. Chequers Restaurant and Bar now open opposite park.

DOVER

Hawthorn Farm, Martin Mill, Dover, Kent, CT15 5LA.
Std: 01304 **Tel:** 852658
Std: 01304 **Fax:** 853417
Nearest Town/Resort Dover
Directions Martin Mill is approx. 3 miles from Dover, signposted along the main A258 towards Deal.
Acreage 27 **Open** March **to** October
Access Good **Site** Level
Sites Available **Total** 250
Facilities
Nearby Facilities
Martin Mill
✓✓✓✓✓Graded Park. Beautiful Award Winning park in a quiet and peaceful location. Superb toilet and shower facilities.

DOVER

Sutton Vale Country Club & Holiday Park, Vale Road, Sutton-By-Dover, Kent, CT15 5DH.
Std: 01304 **Tel:** 374155
Std: 01304 **Fax:** 381132
Nearest Town/Resort Deal/Dover
Directions Off the A2 London to Dover road, 4 miles from Dover and 4 miles from Deal.
Acreage 7 **Open** March **to** January
Access Good **Site** Level
Sites Available **Total** 100
Facilities
Nearby Facilities
Deal/Dover
✓✓✓✓Graded Park. Set in open countryside.

EASTCHURCH

Warden Springs Caravan Park, Warden Point, Eastchurch, Sheppey, Kent, ME12 4HF.
Std: 01795 **Tel:** 880216
Std: 01795 **Fax:** 880218
Nearest Town/Resort Sheerness
Directions M20 junction 7 or M2 junction 5 to the A249. A249 to Sheppey, B2231 to Eastchurch.
Acreage 2 **Open** March **to** October
Access Good **Site** Sloping
Sites Available **Total** 48
Facilities
Nearby Facilities
Sheerness
✓✓✓✓Graded Park. Near beach, scenic views, fishing.

FAVERSHAM

Painters Farm Caravan & Camping Site, Painters Forstal, Ospringe, Faversham, Kent, ME13 0EG.
Std: 01795 **Tel:** 532995
Nearest Town/Resort Faversham
Directions Turn south off the A2 at Faversham signposted Painters Forstal/Eastling. 1½ miles down a No Through road at Forstal.
Acreage 3 **Open** March **to** October
Access Good **Site** Level
Sites Available **Total** 45
Facilities
Nearby Facilities
Faversham
Pleasant orchard setting. Convenient for the coast and Channel Ports.

FOLKESTONE

Black Horse Farm Caravan Club Site, 385 Canterbury Road, Densole-Swingfield, Folkestone, Kent, CT18 7BG.
Std: 01303 **Tel:** 892665
Nearest Town/Resort Folkestone.
Directions Park is on the A260 2 miles from the junction with the A20 towards Canterbury.
Acreage 6½ **Open** January **to** December
Access Good **Site** Level
Sites Available **Total** 110
Facilities
Nearby Facilities

Folkestone.
√√√√Graded Park. Ideal centre for touring east Kent. Telephone 9a.m.-8p.m. Convenient for Channel ferries.

FOLKESTONE

Camping & Caravanning Club Site, The Warren, Folkestone, Kent, CT19 6PT.
Std: 01303 **Tel:** 255093
Directions From the M2 and Canterbury on the A260 take a left turn at the roundabout into Hill Road, Folkestone. Go straight over the crossroads into Wear Bay Road, turn second left past Martello Tower, site is ½ mile on the right.
Open 22 March **to** 27 Sept
Site Level
Sites Available **Total** 82
Facilities
Nearby Facilities
Folkestone
√√√Graded Park. Just a short walk to the beach. On a clear day you can see France.

FOLKESTONE

Little Satmar Holiday Park, Winehouse Lane, Capel-le-Ferne, Nr. Folkestone, Kent, CT18 7JF.
Std: 01303 **Tel:** 251188
Std: 01303 **Fax:** 251188
Nearest Town/Resort Folkestone
Directions Travelling towards Folkestone on the A20 from Dover, exit left signposted Capel-le-Ferne onto the B2011. After 1 mile turn right into Winehouse Lane.
Acreage 6 **Open** March **to** October
Access Good
Sites Available **Total** 40
Facilities
Nearby Facilities
Folkestone
Quiet, secluded park. Convenient for Channel ports and Tunnel.

HERNE BAY

Southview Camping, Southview, Maypole Lane, Hoath, Canterbury, Kent.
Std: 01227 **Tel:** 860280
Nearest Town/Resort Canterbury
Directions Well signed from the A299 at Herne Bay or the A28 near Canterbury.
Acreage 3 **Open** All Year
Access Good **Site** Level
Sites Available **Total** 45
Facilities
Nearby Facilities
Herne Bay
Very central location for Canterbury and the beautiful beaches of Thanet. Public telephone 100yds. Pets welcome by arrangement only.

LEYSDOWN-ON-SEA

Priory Hill, Wing Road, Leysdown, Isle of Sheppey, Kent, ME12 4QT.
Std: 01795 **Tel:** 510267
Std: 01795 **Fax:** 510267
Nearest Town/Resort Leysdown-on-Sea
Directions M25, M20 or M2 onto the A249 to Sheppey, then the B2231 to Leysdown, bear right into Wing Road.
Acreage 1½ **Open** March **to** October
Access Good **Site** Level
Sites Available **Total** 55
Facilities
Nearby Facilities
Sheerness
√√√√Graded Park. Super sea views. Pitch and putt coarse. Adjacent to a coastal park, seaside.

MAIDSTONE

Pine Lodge Touring Park, Ashford Road, Hollingbourne, Kent, ME17 1XH.
Std: 01622 **Tel:** 730018
Std: 01622 **Fax:** 734498
Nearest Town/Resort Maidstone
Directions Leave the M20 at junction 8, onto the A20 roundabout, turn off towards Bearsted and Maidstone. Pine Lodge is on the left after approx. 1 mile.
Acreage 7 **Open** All Year
Access Good **Site** Level
Sites Available
Facilities
Nearby Facilities
√√√√√Graded Park. Ideal for exploring the Kent countryside. Leeds Castle. Only 1 hour from London and convenient for ferries and The Channel Tunnel.

MARDEN

Tanner Farm Touring Caravan & Camping Park, Tanner Farm, Goudhurst Road, Marden, Kent, TN12 9ND.
Std: 01622 **Tel:** 832399
Std: 01622 **Fax:** 832472
Nearest Town/Resort Maidstone/Tunbridge Wells
Directions From the A262 or A229 onto the B2079. Midway between the village of Marden and Goudhurst.
Acreage 15 **Open** All Year
Access Good **Site** Level
Sites Available **Total** 100
Facilities
Nearby Facilities
√√√√√Graded Park. Peaceful, secluded park in the centre of a 150 acre farm. Shire horses kept.

MINSTER

Wayside Caravan Park, Way Hill, Minster, Nr. Ramsgate, Kent, CT12 4HP.
Std: 01843 **Tel:** 821272
Std: 01843 **Fax:** 822668
Nearest Town/Resort Ramsgate
Directions 3 miles from Ramsgate and ½ mile from Minster.
Open March **to** October
Access Good **Site** Level
Sites Available **Total** 5
Facilities
Nearby Facilities
Minster
✓✓✓✓Graded Park. Country setting, close to the village and beaches.

NEW ROMNEY

Marlie Farm Holiday Village, Dymchurch Road, New Romney, Kent, TN28 8UE.
Std: 01797 **Tel:** 363060
Nearest Town/Resort Dymchurch/ Folkestone
Directions ¼ mile east of New Romney on the main coast road A259.
Acreage 120 **Open** March **to** October
Access Good **Site** Level
Sites Available **Total** 350
Facilities
Nearby Facilities
Ideal touring base for South East England. Indoor leisure complex with pool, sauna and bubble spa. Club House with FREE entertainment.

RAMSGATE

Manston Caravan & Camping Park, Manston Court Road, Manston, Ramsgate, Kent.
Std: 01843 **Tel:** 823442
Nearest Town/Resort Ramsgate.
Directions From the M2 follow the A299 and join the A253 towards Ramsgate. Turn left onto the B2048 then first right onto the B2190 towards KIA. Turn right onto the B2050 across the airfield passing the entrance to KIA. Take the first turning right into Manston Court Road, park is 500 yards on the right.
Acreage 7 **Open** April **to** October
Access Good **Site** Level
Sites Available **Total** 100
Facilities
Nearby Facilities
Ramsgate
✓✓✓✓Graded Park. Quiet, family park. Motorcycles are sometimes accepted.

RAMSGATE

Pine Meadow Touring Park, Spratling Court Farm, Manston, Ramsgate, Kent, CT12 5AN.
Std: 01843 **Tel:** 587770
Nearest Town/Resort Ramsgate
Directions From A256 junction take B2050 west towards Manston village, in 300 yards turn right, signposted Greensole Lane Pine Meadow.
Acreage 3 **Open** April **to** September
Access Good **Site** Level
Sites Available **Total** 40
Facilities
Nearby Facilities
Ramsgate
✓✓✓✓Graded Park. Sheltered rural site, 10 minutes from Margate, Broadstairs and Ramsgate (Sally Line Terminal). Golf practise centre on site.

SANDWICH

Sandwich Leisure Park, Woodnesborough Road, Sandwich, Kent, CT13 0AA.
Std: 01304 **Tel:** 612681
Std: 01227 **Fax:** 273512
Nearest Town/Resort Sandwich
Directions Follow brown tourist signs, ½ mile from the town centre.
Acreage 10 **Open** March **to** October
Access Good **Site** Level
Sites Available **Total** 120
Facilities
Nearby Facilities
Sandwich
✓✓✓✓Graded Park. Ideal touring base for East Kents beaches and towns of historic interest, Dover, Canterbury and many other seaside areas.

SEVENOAKS

Camping & Caravanning Club Site, Stynants Bottom, Seal, Sevenoaks, Kent, TN15 0ET.
Std: 01732 **Tel:** 762728
Directions From Sevenoaks take the A25 towards Borough Green, turn left just after the Crown Point Inn which is on the right, go down a narrow lane to Stynants Bottom, site is on the left.
Acreage 4 **Open** 22 March **to** 1 Nov
Site Lev/Slope
Sites Available **Total** 58
Facilities
Nearby Facilities
Sevenoaks/Borough Green
✓✓✓✓Graded Park. On National Trust land, surrounded by woodland for walks.

SEVENOAKS

East Hill Farm Caravan Park, East Hill, Near Otford, Sevenoaks, Kent, TN15 6YD.
Std: 01959 **Tel:** 522347
Nearest Town/Resort Sevenoaks
Directions Please telephone for directions.
Acreage 6 **Open** April **to** October
Access Good **Site** Level
Sites Available **Total** 30
Facilities
Nearby Facilities
Otford

SEVENOAKS

Gate House Wood Touring Park, Ford Lane, Wrotham Heath, Sevenoaks, Kent, TN15 7SD.
Std: 01732 **Tel:** 843062
Nearest Town/Resort Maidstone/ Sevenoaks
Directions From Maidstone take the M20 and exit at junction 3 onto the M26, within ½ mile take junction 2A. At the roundabout take the A20 signposted Maidstone, continue straight through the traffic lights at Wrotham Heath and take the first turn left signposted Trottiscliffe. After 50 yards turn left into Ford Lane and the park is 100 yards on the left.
Acreage 3½ **Open** All Year
Access Good **Site** Level
Sites Available **Total** 60
Facilities
Nearby Facilities
Borough Green
✓✓✓✓✓Graded Park. Conveniently situated for Channel ports and sightseeing in South East London (45 minutes by train). Many country pubs, restaurants and take-away nearby.

SHEERNESS

Sheerness Holiday Park, Halfway Road, Minster-on-Sea, Sheerness, Kent, ME12 3AA.
Std: 01795 **Tel:** 662638
Nearest Town/Resort Sheerness.
Directions From M20 or M2 take the A249 towards Sheerness, then the A250 into the town. We are ½ mile from the town centre.
Acreage 20 **Open** Easter **to** October
Access Good **Site** Level
Sites Available **Total** 86
Facilities
Nearby Facilities
Sheerness.
✓✓✓Graded Park. A Haven Holiday Park.

WEST KINGSDOWN

'To The Woods', Botsom Lane, West Kingsdown, Nr. Sevenoaks, Kent TN15 6BN.
Std: 01322. **Tel:** Farningham 863751
Std: 01322 **Fax:** 863751
Nearest Town/Resort West Kingsdown.
Directions A20 West Kingsdown facing London Clearways Cafe on left next turning Botsom Lane.
Acreage 3 **Open** All year
Access Poor **Site** Level
Sites Available **Total** 40
Facilities
Nearby Facilities
Swanley.
Easy access via Swanley to centre of London. Margate, Dover etc., only 1 hour by car. Winter and all year caravan storage available.

WHITSTABLE

Primrose Cottage Caravan Park, Golden Hill, Whitstable, Kent, CT5 3AR.
Std: 01277 **Tel:** 273694
Nearest Town/Resort Whitstable.
Directions On A299, 1 mile east of Whitstable roundabout.
Acreage ½ **Open** March **to** October
Access Good **Site** Level
Sites Available **Total** 10
Facilities
Nearby Facilities
Whitstable.

WHITSTABLE

Seaview Caravan Park, St Johns Road, Whitstable, Kent, CT5 2RV.
Std: 01227 **Tel:** 792246
Std: 01227 **Fax:** 792247
Nearest Town/Resort Whitstable
Directions From the A299 follow signs for Swalecliffe. Between Whitstable and Herne Bay.
Open April **to** October
Access Good **Site** Level
Sites Available
Facilities
Nearby Facilities
Swalecliffe
On the beach with a clunhouse, family and games room.

WROTHAM

Thriftwood Caravan Park, Plaxdale Green Road, Stansted, Nr. Wrotham, Kent.
Std: 01732 **Tel:** 822261
Std: 01732 **Fax:** 822261
Nearest Town/Resort Sevenoaks
Directions On A20 on top of Wrotham Hill, 3¼ miles south of Brands Hatch, exit 2 off M20 signposted with international camping signs.
Acreage 10 **Open** March **to** January
Access Good **Site** Level
Sites Available **Total** 150
Facilities
Nearby Facilities
Borough Green
✓✓✓✓✓Graded Park. 35 minutes by train to London, convenient for southern ports. Free colour brochure on request.

LANCASHIRE

BENTHAM

Riverside Caravan Park, Wenning Avenue, Bentham, Lancaster, Lancashire.
Std: 015242 **Tel:** 61272
Std: 015242 **Fax:** 62163
Nearest Town/Resort Bentham.
Directions Follow caravan signs off the B6480 at the Black Bull Hotel in Bentham.
Acreage 10 **Open** March **to** October
Access Good **Site** Level
Sites Available **Total** 60
Facilities
Nearby Facilities
Bentham.
Free fishing for trout and sea trout adjacent to the site. Electric points for tourers.

BLACKPOOL

Gillett Farm Caravan Park, Peel Road, Nr. Blackpool, Lancs, FY4 5JU.
Std: 01253 **Tel:** 761676
Nearest Town/Resort Blackpool.
Directions Blackpool junction 4 on M55 turn left to Kirkham 400yds to traffic lights. Turn right and immediate left into Peel Road. 350yds second site on the right.
Acreage 12 **Open** March **to** October
Access Good **Site** Slightly Sloping
Sites Available **Total** 76
Facilities
Nearby Facilities
Blackpool
✓✓✓✓Graded Park. Within easy reach of Blackpool, Lytham St Annes and Fleetwood.

BLACKPOOL

High Moor Farm, Singleton Road, Weeton, Preston, Lancashire, PR4 3JJ.
Std: 01253 **Tel:** 836273
Nearest Town/Resort Blackpool.
Directions Leave the M55 at junction 3 and head north towards Fleetwood, after 3 miles turn left, after 1 mile at T-Junction turn left and we are 1 mile on the left opposite Weeton Army Base.
Acreage 3 **Open** March **to** October
Access Good **Site** Level
Sites Available **Total** 60
Facilities
Nearby Facilities
Kirkham.
Well sheltered, family run site, within the centre of the Fylde. Within easy reach of the south lakes and the West Yorkshire Moors.

BLACKPOOL

Mariclough - Hampsfield, Preston New Road, Peel, Blackpool, Lancs.
Std: 01253 **Tel:** 761034
Nearest Town/Resort Blackpool.
Directions M55 junction 4, first left onto the A583. Go through traffic lights, site 200yds on the left.
Acreage 2 **Open** Easter **to** November
Access Good **Site** Level
Sites Available **Total** 50
Facilities
Nearby Facilities
Blackpool/Kirkham
Flat, mowed grass, sheltered park. Off license. Please telephone before 8pm.

BLACKPOOL

Marton Mere Holiday Village, Mythop Road, Blackpool, Lancashire, FY4 4XN.
Std: 01253 **Tel:** 767544
Nearest Town/Resort Blackpool
Directions Take the A583 towards Blackpool, turn right at Clifton Arms traffic lights onto Mythop Road, park is 150 yards on the left.
Acreage 93 **Open** March **to** November
Access Good **Site** Level
Sites Available **Total** 431
Facilities
Nearby Facilities
✓✓✓✓Graded Park. A sanctuary for birds and wildlife with spectacular views. Kids Club, family entertainment, bowling, tennis, amusements and crazy golf.

BLACKPOOL

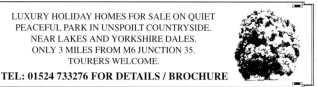

Pipers Height Caravan & Camping Park, Peel Road, Peel, Blackpool, Lancashire.
Std: 01253 **Tel:** 763767
Nearest Town/Resort Blackpool.
Directions Exit M55 junction 4 take the first turning left on the A583. At the first set of lights turn right then sharp left. Site is first on the right. Site ½ mile from the M55.
Acreage 11 **Open** March **to** October
Access Good **Site** Level
Sites Available **Total** 150
Facilities
Nearby Facilities
Blackpool

BLACKPOOL

Richmond Hill Caravan Park, 352 St. Anne's Road, Blackpool, Lancashire.
Std: 01253 **Tel:** 344266
Nearest Town/Resort Blackpool.
Directions We are situated in Blackpool south shore. Near Airport.
Acreage 1 **Open** March **to** October
Access Good **Site** Level
Sites Available **Total** 15
Facilities
Nearby Facilities
Blackpool South.
Near beach, theatres, piers, pleasure beach.

BLACKPOOL

Sunset Park, Sower Carr Lane, Hambleton, Poulton-le-Fylde, Blackpool, Lancashire, FY6 9EQ.
Std: 01253 **Tel:** 700222
Std: 01253 **Fax:** 701756
Nearest Town/Resort Blackpool.
Directions M55 junction 3 onto the A585. First traffic lights turn left, second traffic lights bear right, next set of traffic lights turn right onto the A588. After village of Hambleton turn right.
Acreage 2 **Open** April **to** October
Access Good **Site** Level
Sites Available **Total** 30
Facilities
Nearby Facilities
Poulton-le-Fylde.
✓✓✓✓Graded Park. Rural site. Sunset Club with a licensed bar. Family room, sauna and spa, course fishing. Blackpool and Fleetwood nearby.

BLACKPOOL

Under Hill Farm, Under Hill Farm, Peel, Blackpool, Lancashire, FY4 5JS.
Std: 01253 **Tel:** 763107
Nearest Town/Resort Blackpool.
Directions 3 miles east of Blackpool on the A583 and ½ mile from the M55 junction 4.
Acreage 4 **Open** Easter **to** October
Access Good **Site** Sloping
Sites Available **Total** 40
Facilities
Nearby Facilities
Blackpool.
Near the beach and Pleasure Beach attractions. Ideal touring.

CARNFORTH

Bolton Holmes Farm, Bolton-le-Sands, Carnforth, Lancashire, LA5 8ES.
Std: 01524 **Tel:** 732854
Nearest Town/Resort Lancaster/ Morecambe.
Directions Travel north on A6. Take first left after Royal Hotel, Mill Lane, Bolton-le-Sands.
Open April **to** September
Access Good **Site** Sloping
Sites Available **Total** 30
Facilities
Nearby Facilities
Carnforth.
Scenic views. On shore side.

CARNFORTH

Capernwray House, Capernwray, Carnforth, Lancs, LA6 1AE.
Std: 01524 **Tel:** 732363
Std: 01524 **Fax:** 732363
Nearest Town/Resort Carnforth/Kirby Lonsdale.
Directions Leave the M6 junction 35 and follow signs for Over Kellet. At the village green turn left signposted Capernwray. Site is 2 miles on the right.
Acreage 5¼ **Open** March **to** October
Access Good **Site** Lev/Slope
Sites Available **Total** 60
Facilities
Nearby Facilities
Carnforth
✓✓✓✓Graded Park. Near a canal, beautiful scenery and good walking. 10 minutes to the beach. Swimming pool around the corner.

CARNFORTH

Holgate's Caravan Parks Ltd., Cove Road, Silverdale, Nr. Carnforth, Lancashire, LA5 0SH.
Std: 01524 **Tel:** 701508
Std: 01524 **Fax:** 701580
Nearest Town/Resort Morecambe.
Directions 5 miles northwest of Carnforth, between Silverdale and Arnside.
Acreage 10 **Open** 22 Dec **to** 3 Nov
Access Good **Site** Lev/Slope
Sites Available **Total** 70
Facilities
Nearby Facilities
Silverdale.
✓✓✓✓✓Graded Park. On Morecambe Bay. In area of outstanding natural beauty. Spa bath, sauna, steam room, licensed lounge bar. Restricted facilities during Winter months. AA Campsite of the Year Award 1995/96, Regional Winner for Northern England.

CARNFORTH

Morecambe Lodge Caravan Park, Shore Lane, Bolton-le-Sands, Carnforth, Lancs, LA5 8JP.
Std: 01524 **Tel:** 823260/824361
Nearest Town/Resort Morecambe/ Lancaster.
Directions A6 north from Lancaster, 4 miles to Bolton-le-Sands, turn left onto coastal road A5105 at traffic lights. 200yds turn right by the first house and follow this road to the beach. Site is on the left before the beach.

Acreage 1¼ **Open** March **to** October
Access Good **Site** Level
Sites Available **Total** 25
Facilities
Nearby Facilities
Carnforth
Direct access to the beach, peaceful with beautiful views of lakes, hills. Noted for spectacular sunsets. Pressure reduced water and sewage hook-ups.

CARNFORTH

Old Hall Caravan Park, Capernwray, Carnforth, Lancashire, LA6 1AD.
Std: 01524 **Tel:** 733276
Std: 01524 **Fax:** 734488
Nearest Town/Resort Carnforth
Directions Leave the M6 at junction 35, go to Over Kellet. Turn left in the village of Over Kellet and the park is 1½ miles on the right.
Open 1 March **to** 10 January
Access Good **Site** Level
Sites Available **Total** 38
Facilities
Nearby Facilities
Carnforth
✓✓✓✓✓Graded Park. Quiet, peaceful, woodland retreat.

CARNFORTH

Sandside Caravan & Camping Park, The Shore, Bolton-le-Sands, Carnforth, Lancashire LA5 8JS.
Std: 01524 **Tel:** 822311
Std: 01524 **Fax:** 822311
Nearest Town/Resort Carnforth
Directions A6 from junc 35 (M6) through Carnforth, turn right at Little Chef in Bolton Le Sands.
Acreage 6 **Open** March **to** October
Access Good **Site** Lev/Slope
Sites Available **Total** 130
Facilities
Nearby Facilities
Carnforth.
✓✓✓Graded Park. Scenic views on shoreside overlooking Morecambe Bay, ideal touring lakes and dales. Easy walk to a local restaurant and country pubs. Beautifully kept parks.

CARNFORTH

Woodclose Caravan Park, Casterton, Carnforth, Lancashire, LA6 2SE.
Std: 015242 **Tel:** 71597
Nearest Town/Resort Kirkby Lonsdale.
Directions ½ mile south east of Kirkby Lonsdale on the A65.
Acreage 9½ **Open** March **to** October
Access Good **Site** Level
Sites Available **Total** 120
Facilities
Nearby Facilities
Oxenholme.
Close to the Lake District, Yorkshire Dales and the seaside.

CLITHEROE

Camping & Caravanning Club Site, Edisford Road, Clitheroe, Lancashire, BB7 3LA.
Std: 01200 **Tel:** 425294
Directions Nearest main road is the A59. From the west follow the A671 into Clitheroe. Look for the signpost indicating a left turn to Longridge/Sports Centre, turn into Greenacre Road approx 25 metres beyond the pelican crossing. Continue until the T-Junction at Edisford Road, turn left and continue past the church on the right, look for the Sports Centre on the right and car park opposite.
Acreage 6 **Open** 22 March **to** 1 Nov
Site Lev/Slope
Sites Available **Total** 80
Facilities
Nearby Facilities
Clitheroe
✓✓✓✓Graded Park. In the Ribble Valley, on the banks of a river.

CLITHEROE

Three Rivers Country Park, Eaves Hall Lane, West Bradford, Clitheroe, Lancs, BB7 3JG.
Std: 01200 **Tel:** 423523
Std: 01200 **Fax:** 442383
Nearest Town/Resort Clitheroe
Directions A59 Clitheroe North turning, through the village to a T-Junction and turn left. Go past the Three Mile Stones Pub on the left, go round the s-bend and take the first turn right. ½ mile along this lane on the right is Three Rivers.
Acreage 45 **Open** All Year
Access Good **Site** Level
Sites Available **Total** 80
Facilities
Nearby Facilities
Clitheroe
✓✓✓Graded Park. Forest and the Trough of Boland. Explore picturesque villages, Clitheroe Castle and Ingleton Waterfalls. Easy driving distance to the Yorkshire Dales and Skipton.

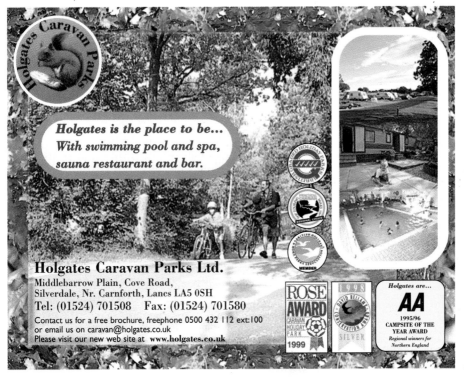

CROSTON

Royal Umpire Touring Park, Southport Road, Croston, Lancs, PR5 7JB.
Std: 01772 **Tel:** 600257
Std: 01772 **Fax:** 600662
Nearest Town/Resort Chorley
Directions 6 miles west of Chorley and 10 miles east of Southport on the A581, between the A49 and the A59. Across from Highfield Restaurant.
Acreage 12 **Open** All Year
Access Good **Site** Level
Sites Available **Total** 200
Facilities
Nearby Facilities
Croston
✓✓✓✓Graded Park. On the edge of the River Lostock, fly fishing in the village. 100 yards from a restaurant. Only 3 miles from Camelot Theme Park. Not far from Blackpool and South Lakes.

GARSTANG

Claylands Caravan Park, Cabus, Garstang, Nr. Preston, Lancashire, PR3 1AJ.
Std: 01524 **Tel:** 791242
Std: 01524 **Fax:** 792406
Nearest Town/Resort Blackpool
Directions Leave the M6 at junction 32, 8 miles north by-pass Garstang. Signpost off the A6, 2 miles north of Garstang traffic lights.
Acreage 10 **Open** March **to** November
Access Good **Site** Level
Sites Available **Total** 60
Facilities
Nearby Facilities
Preston
✓✓✓Graded Park. Well stocked fishing lakes for coarse fishing.

GARSTANG

Six Arches Caravan Park, Scorton, Garstang, Lancashire, PR3 1AL.
Std: 01524 **Tel:** 791683
Nearest Town/Resort Garstang
Directions Leave the M6 at junction 33 and follow the A6 south towards Garstang for 4 miles. Turn left just before the Little Chef into Station Lane, park is at the bottom of the lane.
Acreage 16 **Open** March **to** October
Access Good **Site** Level
Sites Available **Total** 16
Facilities
Nearby Facilities
Lancaster
✓✓✓Graded Park. Riverside park. Within easy reach of Blackpool, Lake District, Morecambe and the Trough of Scotland.

GISBURN

Todber Caravan Park, Burnley Road, Gisburn, Clitheroe, Lancashire, BB7 4JJ.
Std: 01200 **Tel:** 445322
Nearest Town/Resort Nelson/Clitheroe.
Directions On A682, Nelson, 1½ miles from A59 at Gisburn (A59 Preston to Skipton Road.
Acreage 4 **Open** March **to** October
Access Good **Site** Lev/Slope
Sites Available **Total** 100
Facilities
Nearby Facilities
Ideal touring Yorkshire Dales, Bronte country, good views Ribble Valley.

GREAT ECCLESTON

Meadowcroft & Queensgate Caravan Parks, Garstang Road, Great Eccleston, Nr. Blackpool, Lancs, PR3 0ZQ.
Std: 01995 **Tel:** 670266
Nearest Town/Resort Blackpool
Directions Leave the M55 at junction 3 onto the A585 to the traffic lights. Turn right onto the A586, first caravan park on the right and opposite.
Acreage 5 **Open** March **to** October
Access Good **Site** Level
Sites Available **Total** 98
Facilities
Nearby Facilities
Poulton-le-Fylde/Preston

GREAT HARWOOD

Harwood Bar Caravan Park, Mill Lane, Great Harwood, Nr. Blackburn, Lancashire, BB6 7UQ.
Std: 01254 **Tel:** 884853
Nearest Town/Resort Blackburn/Accrington
Directions From Blackburn follow signs to Clayton Le Moors on the A678. Go past the turning for Clayton Le Moors Centre and turn right, before the Renault Garage, at the caravan tourism sign.
Open February **to** December
Access Good **Site** Level
Sites Available **Total** 35
Facilities
Nearby Facilities
Great Harwood
✓✓✓Graded Park. Perfect base for for the forests of Pendle and Bowland with areas of beauty. Peace and quiet. 7 golf courses, fishing and walking in the surrounding area.

HEYWOOD

Gelder Wood Country Park, Ashworth Road, Heywood, Rochdale, Lancashire, OL11 5UP.
Std: 01706 **Tel:** 364858
Std: 01706 **Fax:** 364858
Nearest Town/Resort Heywood
Directions Leave the M62 at junction 18 onto the M66 (signposted Bury). At the second exit left (junction 2) turn right onto the A58 (signposted Heywood). Go into Heywood and at Morrison's Supermarket on the left turn left into Bamford Road, at T-Junction turn left (Bury and Rochdale road). After 100 yards turn right into Ashworth Road, go over the bridge, up the hill 800 yards, site is on the right opposite the Scout Camp.
Open March
Access Good **Site** Level
Sites Available **Total** 34
Facilities
Nearby Facilities
Rochdale/Bury Metro
✓✓✓Graded Park. Set between two rivers and surrounded by trees on three sides. Part of the smallest village in England.

LANCASTER

Cockerham Sands Country Park, Cockerham, Lancaster, Lancashire, LA2 0BB.
Std: 01524 **Tel:** 751387
Std: 01524 **Fax:** 752275
Nearest Town/Resort Lancaster
Directions Leave M6 at Junction 33, take the A6 signposted Garstang/Glasson Dock for 1¼ miles. Turn right onto Cockerham Road and follow signs for Cockerham/Glasson Dock. Proceed for 2 miles into Cockerham Village, turn right following signs for Glasson/Thurnham Hall. After 2¼ miles turn left at Thurnham Hall and follow lane to the end, 3 miles.
Open March **to** October
Access Good **Site** Level
Sites Available **Total** 9
Facilities
Nearby Facilities
Lancaster
✓✓✓✓Graded Park.

LANCASTER

Crook O'Lune Caravan Park, Caton Road, Caton, Lancaster, Lancashire, LA2 9HP.
Std: 01524 **Tel:** 770216
Std: 01524 **Fax:** 771694
Nearest Town/Resort Lancaster/Morecambe
Directions Leave the M6 at junction 34 and follow the Kirkby Lonsdale road, 2 miles on the right.
Acreage 3 **Open** February **to** November
Access Good **Site** Level
Sites Available **Total** 23
Facilities
Nearby Facilities
Lancaster
✓✓✓✓Graded Park. Alongside the River Lune. Close to Lancaster and Morecambe and only 30 minutes from the Lake District.

LANCASTER

Laundsfield Caravan Site, Stoney Lane, Galgate, Near Lancaster, Lancashire.
Std: 01524 **Tel:** 751763
Nearest Town/Resort Lancaster
Open March **to** October
Access Good **Site** Level
Sites Available **Total** 20
Facilities
Nearby Facilities
Lancaster
Quiet site. Near to a canal marina, bowling and pubs. Country walks in the area. 1½ miles to Lancaster University.

LANCASTER

Marina Luxury Holiday Park, Conder Green, Glasson Dock, Nr. Lancaster, Lancashire, LA2 0BP.
Std: 01524 **Tel:** 751787
Std: 01524 **Fax:** 751436
Nearest Town/Resort Lancaster
Directions Leave the M6 at junction 33 and follow signs to Lancaster/Glasson Dock. In Galgate follow signs to Glasson Dock, Marina is on the left before entering the village.
Acreage ½ **Open** 1 March **to** 4 January
Access Good **Site** Level
Sites Available **Total** 15
Facilities
Nearby Facilities
Lancaster
✓✓✓✓Graded Park. Next to the village of Glasson Dock with its boating marina, only 5 minutes from historical Lancaster. Haven for watersports.

LANCASTER

Mosswood Caravan Park, Crimbles Lane, Cockerham, Lancaster, Lancashire, LA2 0ES.
Std: 01524 **Tel:** 791041
Std: 01524 **Fax:** 792444
Nearest Town/Resort Lancaster
Directions Leave the M6 at junction 33, take the A6 heading south then the second right to Cockerham. Follow the A588 west for 1 mile and there is a Mosswood sign at the top of Crimbles Lane.
Acreage 25 **Open** March **to** October
Access Good **Site** Level
Sites Available **Total** 30
Facilities
Nearby Facilities
Lancaster
✓✓✓✓✓Graded Park. Ideal location mid-way between Blackpool and Morecambe. Fishing, parachuting and microlight flying are all available near to our park which abounds wildlife.

LANCASTER

Wyreside Lakes Fishery, Duchy of Lancaster Estate, Bay Horse, Nr. Lancaster, Lancashire, LA2 9DG.
Std: 01524 **Tel:** 792093
Nearest Town/Resort Lancaster
Directions Leave the M6 North at junction 33, turn left at the roundabout then first left into Hamson Lane. Follow Fishery signs to Wyreside Lake Fishery, approx. 2 miles.
Acreage 500 **Open** All Year
Access Good **Site** Level
Sites Available **Total** 250
Facilities
Nearby Facilities
Lancaster
✓✓✓Graded Park. 13 lakes in 500 acres in the Duchy of Lancaster Estate.

LONGRIDGE

Beacon Fell View Caravan Park, Higher Road, Longridge, Nr. Preston, Lancashire, PR3 2TY.
Std: 01772 **Tel:** 785434
Std: 01772 **Fax:** 784204
Directions Leave M6 at junction 32, take Garstang signs onto the A6. At traffic lights turn right, follow to Longridge. DO NOT take the sign for Beacon Fell. At Longridge go across the roundabout, keep left at the White Bull. Park is 1 mile on the right.
Open March **to** October
Site Level
Sites Available **Total** 100
Facilities
Nearby Facilities
Preston.
✓✓✓✓Graded Park. Scenic views of Ribble Valley. Ideal centre for touring.

LYTHAM ST. ANNES

Eastham Hall Caravan Park, Saltcoates Road, Lytham St. Annes, Lancashire, FY8 4LS.
Std: 01253 **Tel:** 737907
Nearest Town/Resort Lytham St. Annes.
Directions Leave Lytham centre on the A584 coast road towards Preston. Through traffic lights at the junction with Dock Road and Lorne Street and at the mini roundabout turn left. Go over the railway bridge, turn right at the next mini roundabout and the site is ½ mile on the right.
Acreage 20 **Open** March **to** October
Access Good **Site** Level
Sites Available **Total** 120
Facilities
Nearby Facilities
Lytham
✓✓✓Graded Park. Quiet, rural site yet close to lovely Lytham St Annes, miles of beach with bustling Blackpool only 15 minutes away. Dogs allowed on leads.

MORECAMBE

Broadfields Caravan & Camping Site, 276 Oxcliffe Road, Morecambe, Lancashire, LA3 3EH.
Std: 01524 **Tel:** 410278
Nearest Town/Resort Morecambe
Acreage 2 **Open** 1 March **to** 4 January
Access Good **Site** Level
Sites Available **Total** 10
Facilities
Nearby Facilities
Near the beach, promenade and fair. Swimming pool nearby.

MORECAMBE

Glen Caravan Park, Westgate, Morecambe, Lancashire, LA3 3EL.
Std: 01524 **Tel:** 423896
Nearest Town/Resort Morecambe.
Directions In Morecambe itself close to promenade, Regent Road and Westgate.
Acreage ½ **Open** March **to** October
Access Good **Site** Level
Sites Available **Total** 10
Facilities
Nearby Facilities
15 minutes walk Morecambe Promenade.

MORECAMBE

Greendales Farm, Carr Lane, Middleton, Morecambe, Lancashire, LA3 3LH.
Std: 01524 **Tel:** 852616
Nearest Town/Resort Morecambe
Directions Junction 34 off the M6, follow signs for Morecambe then Middleton. Turn down Carr Lane, site is on the left ½ mile down road to house and site is at the rear.
Acreage 2 **Open** All Year
Access Good **Site** Lev/Slope
Sites Available **Total** 20
Facilities
Nearby Facilities
Morecambe
Near Middleton Sands with its large beach. Close to the Lake District, Blackpool and Morecambe.

MORECAMBE

Melbreak Camp Site, Carr Lane, Middleton, Nr. Morecambe, Lancashire.
Std: 01524 **Tel:** 852430
Nearest Town/Resort Morecambe.
Directions Take A589 out of Morecambe. Follow signs to Middleton. Turn right by church. Site ½ mile on left.
Acreage 1½ **Open** March **to** October
Access Good **Site** Level
Sites Available **Total** 50
Facilities
Nearby Facilities
Morecambe.
✓✓✓Graded Park. Site is ½ mile from Middleton Sands and 3 miles from seaside attractions of Morecambe.

MORECAMBE

Ocean Edge Leisure Park, Moneyclose Lane, Heysham, Lancashire, LA3 2XA.
Std: 01524 **Tel:** 855657
Nearest Town/Resort Morecambe/Lancaster.
Directions M6 junction 34, follow signs for Port of Heysham, site signed from 2 miles.
Acreage 20 **Open** March **to** October
Access Good **Site** Level
Sites Available **Total** 100+
Facilities
Nearby Facilities
Morecambe.
Coastal site with bars, entertainment, kiddies disco, amusements and day-time activities. A complete family park. Ideal touring centre. Holiday Home hire and sales.

MORECAMBE

Regent Leisure Park, Westgate, Morecambe, Lancashire, LA3 3DF.
Std: 01524 **Tel:** 413940
Std: 01524 **Fax:** 832247
Nearest Town/Resort Morecambe
Directions Leave the M6 at junction 34 and follow the A589 over the River Lune. Turn left at the third roundabout and the park is approximately 1 mile on the left.
Acreage 15 **Open** March **to** January
Access Good **Site** Level
Sites Available **Total** 23
Facilities
Nearby Facilities
Lancaster
✓✓✓✓✓Graded Park. ½ mile from the promenade with magnificent views over Morecambe Bay. Rose Award.

MORECAMBE

Venture Caravan Park, Langridge Way, Westgate, Morecambe, Lancashire, LA4 4TQ.
Std: 01524 **Tel:** 412986
Std: 01524 **Fax:** 422029
Nearest Town/Resort Morecambe
Open All Year
Access Good **Site** Level
Sites Available
Facilities
Nearby Facilities
Morecambe

ORMSKIRK

Abbey Farm Caravan Park, Dark Lane, Ormskirk, Lancashire, L40 5TX.
Std: 01695 **Tel:** 572686
Std: 01695 **Fax:** 572686
Nearest Town/Resort Southport
Directions From the M6 junction 27 onto the A5209 to Newburgh and Parbold. After 4½ miles turn left onto the B5240 and turn immediate right into Hobcross Lane. Site is 1½ miles on the right.
Acreage 6 **Open** All Year
Access Good **Site** Level
Sites Available **Total** 104
Facilities
Nearby Facilities
Ormskirk
✓✓✓✓Graded Park. Peace and quiet in a rural setting. Ideal touring centre. Family bathroom available. Off license on site. A Countryside Discovery Park, David Bellamy Environment Award and Merseyside Caravan Park of the Year 1995.

ORMSKIRK

Hurlston Hall Country Caravan Park, Southport Road, Scarisbrick, Ormskirk, Lancashire, L40 8HB.
Std: 01704 **Tel:** 841064
Std: 01704 **Fax:** 841700
Nearest Town/Resort Southport
Directions Leave the M6 at junction 26 and join the M58. Leave the M58 at junction 3 and follow the A570 towards Southport, go through Ormskirk, Hurlston Hall is 3 miles outside Ormskirk.
Acreage 6 **Open** Easter **to** October
Access Good **Site** Level
Sites Available **Total** 60
Facilities
Nearby Facilities
Ormskirk
✓✓✓✓Graded Park. Hurlston Hall sits beside a private lake and Hurlston Brook. It also has an 18 hole golf course with driving range and clubhouse on site.

PILLING

Glenfield Caravan Park, Smallwood Hey Road, Pilling, Nr. Blackpool, Lancashire, PR3 6HE.
Std: 01253 **Tel:** 790782
Nearest Town/Resort Blackpool
Directions In the village of Pilling just off the A588 Lancaster to Blackpool main road. 10 miles from Lancaster and Blackpool.
Acreage 2 **Open** March **to** October
Access Good **Site** Level
Sites Available **Total** 8
Facilities
Nearby Facilities
Poulton-le-Fylde
✓✓✓✓Graded Park. Flat site on the coast. Ideal for walking and cycling.

PREESALL

Maaruig Caravan Park, 71 Pilling Lane, Preesall, Poulton-le-Fylde, Lancashire, FY6 0HB.
Std: 01253 **Tel:** 810404
Nearest Town/Resort Blackpool
Directions Leave the M55 at junction 3, onto the A585 towards Fleetwood. At the third set of traffic lights turn right onto the A588. Follow Knott End (B5377) up to the T-Junction, turn left then the first right into Pilling Lane.
Acreage 1 **Open** 1 March **to** 4 January
Access Good **Site** Level
Sites Available **Total** 28
Facilities
Nearby Facilities
Poulton-le-Fylde
Quiet site, near the beach.

SOUTHPORT

Riverside Leisure Centre Limited, Southport New Road, Banks, Southport, Merseyside, PR9 8DF.
Std: 01704 **Tel:** 228886
Std: 01704 **Fax:** 505886
Nearest Town/Resort Southport
Directions 5 miles from Southport on the A565.
Open March **to** 7 January
Access Good **Site** Level
Sites Available **Total** 300+
Facilities
Nearby Facilities
Southport
Situated by a rover, fishing permitted. 10 minutes by car to the beach, Southport town and funfair. Ideal for touring.

THORNTON

Kneps Farm Holiday Park, River Road, Thornton-Cleveleys, Blackpool, Lancashire, FY5 5LR.
Std: 01253 **Tel:** 823632
Std: 01253 **Fax:** 863967
Nearest Town/Resort Blackpool.
Directions 5 miles north north east of Blackpool. From the M55 junction 3 take the A585 Fleetwood road to the River Wyre Hotel on the left, turn right at the roundabout onto the B5412 signposted Little Thornton. Turn right after the school into Stanah Road which leads to River Road.
Acreage 3½ **Open** March **to** Mid Nov
Access Good **Site** Level
Sites Available **Total** 70
Facilities
Nearby Facilities
Poulton-le-Fylde.
✓✓✓✓✓Graded Park. Situated adjacent to the Stanah Amenity and Picnic Area, forming part of the River Wyre Estuary Country Park. A rural retreat close to Blackpool.

WARTON

Sea View Caravan Park, Bank Lane, Warton, Lancashire, PR4 1TD.
Std: 01772 **Tel:** 679336
Std: 01772 **Fax:** 679336
Nearest Town/Resort Lytham St Annes
Directions Follow Lytham St Annes signs from the M6 junction 29, M610 onto the A584. Go through Freckleton to Warton, turn left at the art shop into Bank Lane. The park is the second on the right near the estuary.
Acreage 6 **Open** March **to** October
Access Good **Site** Level
Sites Available **Total** 80
Facilities
Nearby Facilities
Lytham St Annes
River walks. 2 miles from the beach at Lytham. Line Dancing only 1 mile away.

LEICESTERSHIRE

CASTLE DONINGTON

Donington Park Farmhouse Hotel, Melbourne Road, Isley Walton, Near Castle Donington, Leicestershire, DE74 2RN.
Std: 01332 **Tel:** 862409
Std: 01332 **Fax:** 862364
Nearest Town/Resort Castle Donington
Directions Leave the M1 at junction 24, go past East Midlands Airport on the A453. 1½ miles after the airport take the Melbourne Road at Isley Walton, site is ½ mile on the right hand side.
Acreage 7 **Open** March **to** December
Access Good **Site** Lev/Slope
Sites Available **Total** 60
Facilities
Nearby Facilities
Derby
✓✓✓Graded Park. At Donington Motor Racing Circuit. Ideal for Southern Derbyshire and the Peak District.

LUTTERWORTH

Kilworth Caravan Park, Lutterworth Road, North Kilworth, Nr. Lutterworth, Leics, LE17 6JE.
Std: 01858 **Tel:** 880597
Nearest Town/Resort Lutterworth/Mkt Harborough
Directions Leave the M1 at junction 20 and turn onto the A4304 towards Market Harborough, approx 3½ miles. You will see the first set of chevrons 2 miles after Walcote, left hand bend, at the bottom sign on the right to the site.
Acreage 12 **Open** All Year
Access Good **Site** Lev/Slope
Sites Available **Total** 45
Facilities
Nearby Facilities
Market Harborough
Lake for fishing. Golf course nearby. Ideal for touring places of interest. AA 3 Pennants.

MARKET BOSWORTH

Bosworth Water Trust, Far Cotton Lane, Market Bosworth, Leics, CV13 6PD.
Std: 01455 **Tel:** 291876
Nearest Town/Resort Market Bosworth
Directions From Hinckley A447, left onto the B585 to Market Bosworth. From Nuneaton A444 and cross the A5, right onto the B585 to Market Bosworth.
Acreage 5 **Open** All Year
Access Good **Site** Level
Sites Available **Total** 20
Facilities
Nearby Facilities
Hinckley
Battlefields of Market Bosworth, Twycross Zoo and steam railway.

LINCOLNSHIRE

ALFORD

Woodthorpe Hall Leisure Park, Woodthorpe, Nr. Alford, Lincs, LN13 0DD.
Std: 01507 **Tel:** 450294
Nearest Town/Resort Alford
Directions Situated on the B1370 between Alford and Withern. From Louth take the A157 and from Alford take the A1104.
Acreage 10 **Open** March **to** January
Access Good **Site** Level
Sites Available **Total** 100
Facilities
Nearby Facilities
Skegness
Adjacent facilities include golf, fishing, a garden centre and an Aquafil centre. The Lincolnshire Wolds and coastal resorts within easy reach.

BARTON-UPON-HUMBER

Silver Birches Tourist Park, Silver Birches, Waterside Road, Barton-Upon-Humber, North Lincolnshire, DN18 5BA.
Std: 01652 **Tel:** 632509
Nearest Town/Resort Hull/Cleethorpes
Directions From the A15 or A1077, follow Humber Bridge Viewing Area signs to Waterside Road, site is just past the Sloop public house.
Acreage 1¼ **Open** April **to** October
Access Good **Site** Level
Sites Available **Total** 24
Facilities
Nearby Facilities
Barton-Upon-Humber
Next to Barton clay pits. Ideal for touring.

BOSTON

Orchard Park, Frampton Lane, Hubberts Bridge, Boston, Lincolnshire, PE20 3QU.
Std: 01205 **Tel:** 290328
Std: 01205 **Fax:** 290247
Nearest Town/Resort Boston
Directions Take the A52 from Boston, in 3 miles at 'Four Cross Roads' Pub turn right onto the B1192. Park is on the right in about ¼ mile.
Acreage 12 **Open** March **to** October
Access Good **Site** Level
Sites Available **Total** 60
Facilities
Nearby Facilities
Hubberts bridge
✓✓✓Graded Park. Angling lake on site.

BOSTON

Pilgrims Way Camping Park, Church Green Road, Fishtoft, Boston, Lincolnshire.
Std: 01205 **Tel:** 366646
Nearest Town/Resort Boston/Skegness
Directions Take the A52 Boston to Skegness road, 1 mile out of town turn right at Ball House Pub, follow signs to camping park.
Acreage 1 **Open** Easter **to** End September
Access Good **Site** Level
Sites Available **Total** 20
Facilities
Nearby Facilities
Boston
Quiet park. 20 minutes from Skegness. Close to Bowling, swimming and historical sites. AA 4 Pennants De Lux.

BOSTON

White Cat Caravan & Camping Park, Shaw Lane, Old Leake, Boston, Lincolnshire.
Std: 01205 **Tel:** 870121
Nearest Town/Resort Boston/Skegness.
Directions 8 miles from Boston on the A52 Skegness road. At Old Leake follow signs to a right turn into Shaw Lane, site is 300 yards on the left.
Acreage 2½ **Open** Mid March **to** Mid Nov
Sites Available **Total** 40
Facilities
Nearby Facilities
Boston.
Ideal touring for Fens, wild life marshes, Skegness resort. Permanent tourer sites available.

CHAPEL ST LEONARDS

Robin Hood Leisure Park, South Road, Chapel St Leonards, Skegness, Lincolnshire, PE24 5TR.
Std: 01754 **Tel:** 874444
Std: 01754 **Fax:** 874648
Nearest Town/Resort Skegness
Directions 7 miles north of Skegness on the A52 turn right signposted Chapel St Leonards onto Trunch Lane. In ½ mile on both sides of the road.
Acreage 41 **Open** 15 March **to** 31 October
Access Good **Site** Level
Sites Available **Total** 125
Facilities
Nearby Facilities
Skegness
✓✓✓✓Graded Park. 100 yards from a long sandy beach. Ideal for children with playgrounds and Childrens Club. Heated swimming pool, superb theatre club, shopping complex and amusements.

CLEETHORPES

Thorpe Park Holiday Centre, Thorpe Park, Humberston, Cleethorpes, North East Lincolnshire, DN36 4HG.
Std: 01472 **Tel:** 813395
Nearest Town/Resort Cleethorpes
Directions From the M180 take the A180 and follow signs for Grimsby and Cleethorpes. In Cleethorpes town centre follow signs for the park.
Open March **to** October
Access Good **Site** Level
Sites Available **Total** 85
Facilities
Nearby Facilities
Cleethorpes
✓✓✓✓Graded Park. Next to Pleasure Island. Near the beach. Kids Club and a full family entertainment programme. Fishing lake, pets corner, crazy golf and a mini park train.

CONINGSBY

Orchard Caravans, Witham Bank, Chapel Hill, Conningsby, Lincs, LN4 4PZ.
Std: 01526 **Tel:** 342414
Directions 1½ miles along Riverbank Road off the A153 Sleaford to Horncastle road. Near Tattershall Bridge.
Acreage 2½ **Open** March **to** October
Access Good **Site** Level
Sites Available **Total** 45
Facilities
Nearby Facilities
Secluded site running alongside the River Witham. Ideal base for touring.

HOLBEACH

Delph Bank Touring Caravan & Camping Park, Main Street, Fleet Hargate, Holbeach, Nr. Spalding, Lincs, PE12 8LL.
Std: 01406 **Tel:** 422910
Std: 01406 **Fax:** 422910
Nearest Town/Resort Holbeach
Directions From Kings Lynn take the A17,

Turn left in the village of Fleet Hargate. From Spalding take the A151 to Holbeach, continue a further 3 miles to Fleet Hargate, turn right just before the A151 joins the A17.
Acreage 3 **Open** 1 March **to** 31 October
Access Good **Site** Level
Sites Available **Total** 45
Facilities
Nearby Facilities
Kings Lynn
Ideal for touring. Sandringham House and grounds. Convenient for Lincolnshire and Norfolk coastal resorts. Public telephone, restaurant and childrens play area nearby. AA 3 Pennants.

HOLBEACH

Whaplode Manor Caravan Park, Whaplode Manor, Saracens Head, Holbeach, Lincs.
Std: 01406 **Tel:** 422837
Std: 01406 **Fax:** 426824
Nearest Town/Resort Holbeach
Directions Just off the A17, 3 miles north of Holbeach.
Acreage 2 **Open** Easter **to** November
Access Good **Site** Level
Sites Available **Total** 20
Facilities
Nearby Facilities
Spalding
Quiet country. Licensed bar.

HORNCASTLE

Ashby Park, West Ashby, Nr Horncastle, Lincs, LN9 5PP.
Std: 01507 **Tel:** 527966
Nearest Town/Resort Horncastle.
Directions 1¾ miles north of Horncastle between the A153 and the A158.
Acreage 54 **Open** All Year
Access Good **Site** Level
Sites Available **Total** 80
Facilities
Nearby Facilities
Lincoln
Six fishing lakes, pub and restaurant ½ mile, swimming pool 1¾ miles. 23 miles to the coast. Holiday caravans for sale.

HUTTOFT

Jolly Common, Jolly Common Lane, Huttoft, Alford, Lincolnshire, LN13 9RW.
Std: 01507 **Tel:** 490236
Nearest Town/Resort Mablethorpe/ Skegness
Directions Take the A52 south from Mablethorpe and turn first left in the village of Huttoft, after ¾ miles turn first right, site is 200 yards on the left.
Acreage 9 **Open** 15 March **to** October
Access Good **Site** Level
Sites Available **Total** 55
Facilities
Nearby Facilities
Skegness
1 mile from a sandy beach.

INGOLDMELLS

Country Meadows Holiday Park, Anchor Lane, Ingoldmells, Skegness, Lincs, PE25 1LZ.
Std: 01754 **Tel:** 874455
Std: 01754 **Fax:** 874125
Nearest Town/Resort Skegness
Directions On the A52 4 miles north of Skegness. ¾ mile out of Ingoldmells Village turn right into Anchor Lane, go 1 mile down toward the sea and the site is on the left hand side.
Acreage 10 **Open** March **to** October
Access Good **Site** Level
Sites Available **Total** 200
Facilities
Nearby Facilities
Skegness
✓✓✓✓Graded Park. 5 minutes walk from the beach.

INGOLDMELLS

Hardy's Touring Site, Sea Lane, Ingoldmells, Skegness, Lincs, PE25 1PG.
Std: 01754 **Tel:** 874071
Nearest Town/Resort Skegness/ Ingoldmells
Directions Take the A52 north from Skegness to Ingoldmells. At the Ship Inn in Ingoldmells turn right down Sea Lane, towards the sea. Site is ½ mile on the right.
Acreage 5 **Open** Easter **to** October
Access Good **Site** Level
Sites Available **Total** 112
Facilities
Nearby Facilities
Skegness
5 minutes walk from the beach. 10 minutes from an animal farm and near Fantasy Island.

INGOLDMELLS

Valetta Farm Caravan Site, Mill Lane, Addlethorpe, Skegness, Lincs.
Std: 01754 **Tel:** 763758
Nearest Town/Resort Skegness.
Directions Turn left off the A158 (Horncastle to Skegness road) in Burgh-le-Marsh at the signpost Ingoldmells and Addlethorpe. Follow signposts for Ingoldmells for 3 miles, turn right by disused mill into Mill Lane. Site is on the left in 150yds.

Acreage 2 **Open** 25 March **to** 20 October
Access Good **Site** Level
Sites Available **Total** 35
Facilities
Nearby Facilities
Skegness
1 mile from the beach, quite a pretty site in the country.

LINCOLN

Hartsholme Country Park, Skellingthorpe Road, Lincoln, Lincolnshire, LN6 0EY.
Std: 01522 **Tel:** 686264
Nearest Town/Resort Lincoln.
Directions 2½ miles south west of Lincoln city centre. Signposted from the A46 on the B1378.
Acreage 2½ **Open** March **to** October
Access Good **Site** Level
Sites Available **Total** 50
Facilities
Nearby Facilities
Lincoln.
✓✓✓Graded Park. Set amongst mature woodland with a large picturesque lake, as well as open grassland. Adjacent to Award Winning nature reserve.

LINCOLN

Oakhill Leisure, Thurlby Moor, Swinderby, Lincolnshire, LN6 9QG.
Std: 01522 **Tel:** 868771
Std: 01522 **Fax:** 868771
Nearest Town/Resort Lincoln/Newark
Directions Take the A46 signed Lincoln or Newark to Bassingham or Thurlby. At the T-Junction turn right, go round the S bend and infront of you there is a sign for Oakhill Leisure, turn right and the entrance is 25 yards.
Acreage 5 **Open** All Year
Access Good **Site** Level
Sites Available **Total** 6
Facilities
Nearby Facilities
Lincoln/Newark
✓✓✓✓Graded Park. Ideal touring.

LONG SUTTON

Foremans Bridge Caravan Park, Sutton St James, Nr. Spalding, Lincolnshire.
Std: 01945 **Tel:** 440346
Std: 01945 **Fax:** 440346
Nearest Town/Resort Spalding/Kings Lynn/Wisbech
Directions From the A17 take the B1390 to Sutton St James, site is on the left after 2 miles.
Acreage 2¼ **Open** March **to** November
Access Good **Site** Level
Sites Available **Total** 40
Facilities
Nearby Facilities
Spalding/Kings Lynn
✓✓✓✓✓Graded Park. 40 minutes away from the beach, fishing alongside park. Ideal for touring the Fens. Six holiday statics for hire also. 2 miles to a restaurant.

LOUTH

Manby Caravan Park, Manby Middlegate, Nr. Louth, Lincolnshire, LN11 8SX.
Std: 01507 **Tel:** 328232
Std: 01507 **Fax:** 328232
Nearest Town/Resort Louth/Mablethorpe
Directions From Louth pick up the B1200 off the A16 bypass. Proceed for 3½ miles and look for the Rix Petrol Station, site is behind it.
Acreage 5 **Open** March **to** October
Access Good **Site** Level
Sites Available **Total** 100
Facilities
Nearby Facilities
Grimsby/Skegness
✓✓✓✓Graded Park. 20 minutes from the beach. Indoor swimming pool in club, temporary membership available.

MABLETHORPE

Camping & Caravanning Club Site, Highfield, 120 Church Lane, Mablethorpe, Lincolnshire, LN12 2NU.
Std: 01507 **Tel:** 472374
Directions On the outskirts of Mablethorpe, on the A1104, just after the 'Welcome to Mablethorpe' sign, petrol station on the right turn into Church Lane, drive 800 yards to the end of the lane. The site is on the right hand side.
Open 22 March **to** 27 Sept
Site Level
Sites Available **Total** 105
Facilities
Nearby Facilities
Cleethorpes
✓✓✓✓Graded Park. Just 1 mile from the sea.

MABLETHORPE

Dunes Holivan Estate, Quebec Road, Mablethorpe, Lincolnshire, LN12 1QH.
Std: 01507 **Tel:** 473327
Std: 01507 **Fax:** 473327
Nearest Town/Resort Mablethorpe
Directions Go into Mablethorpe on the A1104, up to the pullover and turn left into Quebec Road. After ¾ mile turn into the caravan park.
Acreage 10 **Open** Easter **to** October
Access Good **Site** Level

Sites Available **Total** 25
Facilities
Nearby Facilities
Skegness/Grimsby
Adjacent to dunes and beaches. E-mail: holivans@enterprise.net

MABLETHORPE

Golden Sands Holiday Centre, Quebec Road, Mablethorpe, Lincs, LN12 1QJ.
Std: 01507 **Tel:** 472671/477871
Std: 01507 **Fax:** 472066
Nearest Town/Resort Mablethorpe
Directions From Mablethorpe town centre, follow the sea front road to the North end for Golden Sands.
Acreage 23 **Open** 26 March **to** 29 Oct
Access Good **Site** Level
Sites Available **Total** 400
Facilities
Nearby Facilities
Skegness
✓✓✓✓Graded Park. Next to rolling dunes and the finest sandy beach for miles.

MABLETHORPE

Mermaid Park - East Lindsey District Council, Seaholme Road, Mablethorpe, Lincolnshire, LN12 2NX.
Std: 01507 **Tel:** 473273
Std: 01507 **Fax:** 473273
Nearest Town/Resort Mablethorpe
Directions 600 yards from the A52.
Open Mid March **to** Mid October
Access Good **Site** Level
Sites Available **Total** 200
Facilities
Nearby Facilities
Skegness
Level walk to the beach and town centre with its indoor sports centre.

MABLETHORPE

Trusthorpe Springs Leisure Park, Mile Lane, Trusthorpe, Mablethorpe, Lincolnshire, LN12 2QQ.
Std: 01507 **Tel:** 441384
Std: 01507 **Fax:** 441333
Nearest Town/Resort Mablethorpe
Directions On the outskirts of Mablethorpe, signposted from all main roads.
Acreage 6 **Open** March **to** November
Access Good **Site** Level
Sites Available **Total** 125
Facilities
Nearby Facilities
Skegness
✓✓✓Graded Park. Large club and heated swimming pool.

MABLETHORPE

Willows Caravan Park, Maltby le Marsh, Near Mablethorpe, Lincolnshire, LN13 0JS.
Std: 01507 **Tel:** 450244
Std: 01507 **Fax:** 450450
Nearest Town/Resort Mablethorpe
Directions On the A1104 Mablethorpe to Alford road, 1 mile from Mablethorpe Town Centre.
Acreage 32 **Open** 15 March **to** 30 November
Access Good **Site** Level
Sites Available **Total** 40
Facilities
Nearby Facilities
Skegness

Quiet, secluded, well maintained park set in 32 acres, yet only 1 mile from the town centre. Large, well-stocked fishing lake and 9 hole golf course. Good central location for local resorts and activities.

MARKET DEEPING

Tallington Lakes, Barholm Road, Tallington, Stamford, Lincolnshire.
Std: 01778 **Tel:** 347000
Std: 01778 **Fax:** 346213
Nearest Town/Resort Stamford.
Directions Off the A1 at Stamford, through the centre following signs. A16 Spalding/ Market Deeping for 6 miles. Go through the village of Tallington, over the level crossing and take the first left (farm shop on the corner). Entrance is 600yds on the right.
Acreage 250 **Open** All Year
Access Good **Site** Level
Sites Available **Total** 135
Facilities
Nearby Facilities
Stamford
Tallington Lakes is a watersports centre offering some of the best water-skiing, jetskiing, sailing and wind-surfing in the country.

MARKET DEEPING

The Deepings Caravan & Camping Park, Outgang Road, Market Deeping, Lincolnshire, PE6 8LQ.
Std: 01778 **Tel:** 344335
Std: 01778 **Fax:** 344394
Nearest Town/Resort Market Deeping.
Directions Park is 2 miles from Market Deeping, on the A16 Spalding road. Take the first left after The Goat Inn.
Open February **to** December
Access Good **Site** Level
Sites Available **Total** 90
Facilities
Nearby Facilities
Peterborough
Fishing on park.

MARKET RASEN

The Rother Camp Site, Gainsborough Road, Middle Rasen, Nr. Market Rasen, Lincolnshire, LN8 3JU.
Std: 01673 **Tel:** 842433
Nearest Town/Resort Market Rasen.
Directions 1½ miles west of Market Rasen, on east side of A631/A46 junction. Site at rear of Rother.
Acreage 2 **Open** March **to** October
Access Good **Site** Level
Sites Available **Total** 45
Facilities
Nearby Facilities
Market Rasen.
Tree and hedge screened. Natural, relaxed country site. Good overnight stop and touring centre.

MARKET RASEN

Walesby Woodland Caravan Park, Walesby Road, Market Rasen, Lincolnshire.
Std: 01673 **Tel:** 843285
Nearest Town/Resort Market Rasen.
Directions In Market Rasen, take the B1203 to Tealby. After ¾ mile, turn left onto unclassified road to Walesby. ¼ mile on the left, enter lane. Site entrance 150 yards on right, signposted.
Acreage 2½ **Open** March **to** 1st November
Access Good **Site** Level
Sites Available **Total** 60
Facilities
Nearby Facilities
Market Rasen.
Ideal sight seeing. Lincoln 16 miles. Set in forestry land, many walks. Total peace yet close to town. 20 miles from beach. A.A. 3 Pennant, R.A.C. Appointed, Calor Gas Runner-up Green Award 1993 and E.M.T.B. Best of Tourism Awards 1995 Caravan Park of the Year Winner.

METHERINGHAM

The White Horse Inn & Caravan Park, Dunston Fen, Metheringham, Lincoln, Lincs, LN4 3AP.
Std: 01526 **Tel:** 398341
Std: 01526 **Fax:** 398341
Nearest Town/Resort Lincoln
Directions Take the B1188 to Dunston Village, go through the village following River Witham signs. 5 miles to the river and White Horse Inn.
Acreage 3 **Open** February **to** December
Access Good **Site** Level
Sites Available **Total** 15
Facilities
Nearby Facilities
Metheringham
Very quiet riverside site with fishing. Open farmland. Traditional pub for meals 7 nights a week.

NORTH SOMERCOTES

Lakeside Park, North Somercotes, Nr. Louth, Lincolnshire, LN11 7RB.
Std: 01507 **Tel:** 358428
Std: 01507 **Fax:** 358135
Nearest Town/Resort Mablethorpe
Directions Located on the A1031 Grimsby to Mablethorpe coast road.
Acreage 15 **Open** 15 March **to** 30 December
Access Good **Site** Level
Sites Available **Total** 150
Facilities
Nearby Facilities
Cleethorpes
Set within acres of pine forests. Ideal for visiting local coastal resorts and the Lincolnshire Wolds. Seal Sanctuary nearby.

SCUNTHORPE

Brookside Caravan & Camping Park, Stather Road, Burton-Upon-Stather, Scunthorpe, Lincolnshire, DN15 9DH.
Std: 01724 **Tel:** 721369
Nearest Town/Resort Scunthorpe
Directions B1430 from Scunthorpe Town centre to Burton-Upon-Stather (4 miles) turn left in front of Sheffield Arms public house. Down the hill past the Ferry Boat Inn, entrance to park 100yds further on right - signposted.
Acreage 6 **Open** All Year
Access Good **Site** Level
Sites Available **Total** 20
Facilities
Nearby Facilities
Scunthorpe
Set in an area of outstanding beauty, enjoying scenic views over the River Trent, ideal base for touring, fishing, walking and cycling.

SKEGNESS
Hill View Fishing Lakes & Touring Caravan Park, Skegness Road (A52), Hogsthorpe, Nr. Skegness, Lincs, PE24 5NR.
Std: 01754 **Tel:** 872979
Directions On the A52, 7 miles from Skegness towards Mablethorpe.
Acreage 2¼ **Open** 15 March **to** 30 Oct
Access Good **Site** Level
Sites Available **Total** 60
Facilities
Nearby Facilities
Skegness
Ideal touring, three well stocked fishing lakes.

SKEGNESS
Manor Farm Caravan Park, Sea Road, Anderby, Skegness, Lincolnshire, PE24 5YB.
Std: 01507 **Tel:** 490372
Nearest Town/Resort Anderby Creek
Directions From Alford take the A1104 and turn onto the A1111 to Bilsby. Turn right onto the B1449 then left onto the A52, take the first right into Anderby. After 1½ miles turn left, site access is 100 yards on the left.
Acreage 3 **Open** 1 March
Access Good **Site** Level
Sites Available **Total** 15
Facilities
Nearby Facilities
Skegness
A quiet, secluded park, near the beach. Many local attractions within easy reach. AA 3 Pennants.

SKEGNESS
North Shore Holiday Centre, Roman Bank, Skegness, Lincolnshire.
Std: 01754 **Tel:** 763815
Std: 01754 **Fax:** 761323
Nearest Town/Resort Skegness.
Directions A52 towards Mablethorpe, 500yds from the A158 junction.
Open April **to** October
Access Good **Site** Level
Sites Available **Total** 250
Facilities
Nearby Facilities
Skegness.
✓✓✓✓Graded Park. Near the beach. Pitch & Putt, Miniature Golf, tennis, bowls and boule all on site.

SKEGNESS
Richmond Holiday Centre, Richmond Drive, Skegness, Lincolnshire, PE25 3TQ.
Std: 01754 **Tel:** 762097
Std: 01754 **Fax:** 765631
Nearest Town/Resort Skegness
Directions Follow signs to the coach station on Richmond Drive, we are approx. 600 yards past the coach station on the right.
Acreage 50 **Open** March **to** November
Access Good **Site** Level
Sites Available **Total** 200
Facilities
Nearby Facilities
Skegness
✓✓✓✓Graded Park. Level, grassy, well drained site with internal roads. 10 minute walk to the town centre and a 15 minute walk the beach. Bookings available for three nights plus.

SKEGNESS
Riverside Caravan Park, Wainfleet Bank, Wainfleet, Skegness, Lincolnshire, PE24 4ND.
Std: 01754 **Tel:** 880205
Nearest Town/Resort Skegness.
Directions A52 Boston to Skegness. Turn left onto the B1195 to Wainfleet All Saints and follow brown signs.
Acreage 1.4 **Open** 15th March **to** October
Access Good **Site** Level
Sites Available **Total** 30
Facilities
Nearby Facilities
Wainfleet.
Alongside a river for fishing and boating. Beach 6 miles.

SKEGNESS
Royal Oak Caravan Park, Roman Bank, Skegness, Lincolnshire, PE25 1QP.
Std: 01754 **Tel:** 764270
Std: 01754 **Fax:** 760224
Nearest Town/Resort Skegness
Directions On the main road, half way between Skegness and Ingoldmells.
Open March **to** November
Access Good **Site** Level
Sites Available
Facilities
Nearby Facilities
Skegness
✓✓✓✓✓Graded Park. Near the beach.

SKEGNESS
Skegness Water Leisure Park, Walls Lane, Skegness, Lincolnshire, PE25 1JF.
Std: 01754 **Tel:** 769019
Std: 01754 **Fax:** 612511
Nearest Town/Resort Skegness/ Ingoldmells
Directions Conveniently situated 3 miles north of Skegness just off the A52, 400 yards from Butlins. Once you reach the outskirts of Skegness follow the brown information signs.
Acreage 133 **Open** 6 March **to** 30 October
Access Good **Site** Level
Sites Available **Total** 200
Facilities
Nearby Facilities
Skegness
✓✓✓Graded Park. Near the beach, fishing lake and water-skiing lake. Near Funcoast World (Butlins).

SKEGNESS
Southview Leisure Park, Burgh Road, Skegness, Lincolnshire, PE25 2LA.
Std: 01754 **Tel:** 764893
Std: 01754 **Fax:** 768455
Nearest Town/Resort Skegness
Directions A158 Skegness to Lincoln road.
Open All Year
Access Good **Site** Level
Sites Available **Total** 100
Facilities
Nearby Facilities
Skegness
Super pitches.

SLEAFORD
Low Farm Touring Park, Spring Lane, Folkingham, Sleaford, Lincolnshire, NG34 0SJ.
Std: 01529 **Tel:** 497322
Nearest Town/Resort Sleaford
Directions 9 miles south of Sleaford on the A15. Go through village, turn right opposite the petrol station.
Acreage 2¼ **Open** Easter **to** October
Access Good **Site** Lev/Slope
Sites Available **Total** 36
Facilities
Nearby Facilities
Sleaford
✓✓✓Graded Park.

STICKNEY
Midville Caravan Park, Midville, Stickney, Boston, Lincolnshire, PE22 8HW.
Std: 01205 **Tel:** 270316
Std: 01205 **Fax:** 270316
Nearest Town/Resort Boston/Skegness.
Directions Turn east from the A16 at Stickney (which is north of Boston) for 2 miles. At bridge turn left for ¼ mile, park is next to Duke of Wellington Pub.
Acreage 3½ **Open** March **to** November
Access Good **Site** Level
Sites Available **Total** 24
Facilities
Nearby Facilities
Boston
Fishing adjacent. Licensed pub and weekend entertainment adjacent to park.

SUTTON-ON-SEA
Cherry Tree Site, Huttoft Road, Sutton-on-Sea, Lincs, LN12 2RU.
Std: 01507 **Tel:** 441626
Nearest Town/Resort Sutton-on-Sea.
Directions Take the A52 from Sutton-on-Sea, 1¼ miles on the left hand side. Entrance via a lay-by. Tourist Board signs on road.
Acreage 3 **Open** March **to** October
Access Good **Site** Level
Sites Available **Total** 60
Facilities
Nearby Facilities
Skegness
Beach, golf course and Lincolnshire Wolds.

SUTTON-ON-SEA
Kirkstead Holiday Park, North Road, Trusthorpe, Sutton-on-Sea, Lincolnshire, LN12 2QD.
Std: 01507 **Tel:** 441483
Nearest Town/Resort Sutton-on-Sea
Directions Take the A52 coast road from Sutton to Mablethorpe, turn off left at Trusthorpe. Signposted from the A52.
Acreage 6 **Open** March **to** 1 December
Access Good **Site** Level
Sites Available **Total** 60
Facilities
Nearby Facilities
Skegness
✓✓✓Graded Park. 10 minute walk to the beach. Clubhouse, new shower block. Familys welcome. Fishing.

SWINESHEAD
The Plough, Swineshead Bridge, Nr. Boston, Lincs, PE20 3PT.
Std: 01205 **Tel:** 820300
Nearest Town/Resort Boston
Directions From Sleaford on the A17 towards Kings Lynn, 10 miles.
Acreage 1½ **Open** March **to** September
Access Good **Site** Level
Sites Available **Total** 8
Facilities
Nearby Facilities

Swineshead
Alongside a river. 30 miles from Skegness, 7 miles from Boston and 10 miles from Sleaford and Spalding.

TATTERSHALL

Willow Holt Caravan & Camping Park, Lodge Road, Tattershall, Lincolnshire, LN4 4JS.
Std: 01526 **Tel:** 343111
Std: 01526 **Fax:** 345391
Nearest Town/Resort Lincoln/Boston
Directions Take the A153 Sleaford/ Skegness road, in Tattershall turn at the market place onto the B1192 (signposted Woodhall Spa). In 1½ miles site is on the left. Good wide entrance.
Acreage 25 **Open** 15 March **to** 31 October
Access Good **Site** Level
Sites Available **Total** 100
Facilities
Nearby Facilities
Peaceful site, all level pitches, abundant wildlife. Ten acres of fishing lakes on site, free for 1998 to site occupants.

WAINFLEET ALL SAINTS

Swan Lake, Culvert Road, Wainfleet, Skegness, Lincolnshire, PE24 4NJ.
Std: 01754 **Tel:** 881456
Std: 01754 **Fax:** 881456
Nearest Town/Resort Skegness.
Directions Signposted from the A52, 1½ miles from Wainfleet.
Acreage 7½ **Open** March **to** November
Access Good **Site** Level
Sites Available **Total** 30
Facilities
Nearby Facilities
Wainfleet
Country setting, around a lake and near a river. 10 minutes to Skegness. Minicom No. 01754 881456.

WOODHALL SPA

Bainland Country Park, Horncastle Road, Woodhall Spa, Lincolnshire, LN10 6UX.
Std: 01526 **Tel:** 352903
Std: 01526 **Fax:** 353730
Nearest Town/Resort Woodhall Spa
Directions Situated on the B1191, 1½ miles from Woodhall Spa towards Horncastle. Just before petrol station.
Acreage 12 **Open** All Year
Access Good **Site** Level
Sites Available **Total** 150
Facilities
Nearby Facilities
Metheringham
✓✓✓✓✓Graded Park. Situated on the edge of the Wolds, surrounded by woodland. Ideally central for touring this delightful county. Golf and tennis on site.

WOODHALL SPA

Camping & Caravanning Club Site, Wellsyke Lane, Kirkby-on-Bain, Woodhall Spa, Lincolnshire, LN10 6YU.
Std: 01526 **Tel:** 352911
Directions From Sleaford or Horncastle take the A153 to Haltham. At the garage turn onto the side road, go over the bridge then turn left towards Kirkby-on-Bain. At the first turn right (Kirkby Lane) opposite Ebrington Arms, after 1 mile you will see Camping & Caravanning Club signs.
Open 22 March **to** 1 Nov
Site Level
Sites Available **Total** 110
Facilities
Nearby Facilities
Metheringham
✓✓✓✓✓Graded Park. A nature lovers dream with woodpeckers, kestrels and kingfishers often seen from the site.

LONDON

ACTON

Tent City Acton, Old Oak Common Lane, East Acton, London, W3 7DP.
Std: 0181 **Tel:** 743 5708
Std: 0181 **Fax:** 749 9074
Nearest Town/Resort London
Directions From the A40 turn onto Old Oak Common Lane, go under the bridge and Tent City is on the right.
Acreage 3 **Open** 1 June
Site Level
Sites Available **Total** 200
Facilities
Nearby Facilities
East Acton Underground
A young and lively campsite with excellent access to Central London via the tube. On site entertainment and a great atmosphere.

CHINGFORD

Lee Valley Campsite, Sewardstone Road, Chingford, London, E4 7RA.
Std: 0181 **Tel:** 529 5689
Std: 0181 **Fax:** 559 4070
Nearest Town/Resort Chingford
Directions Leave M25 at junction 26, fol-

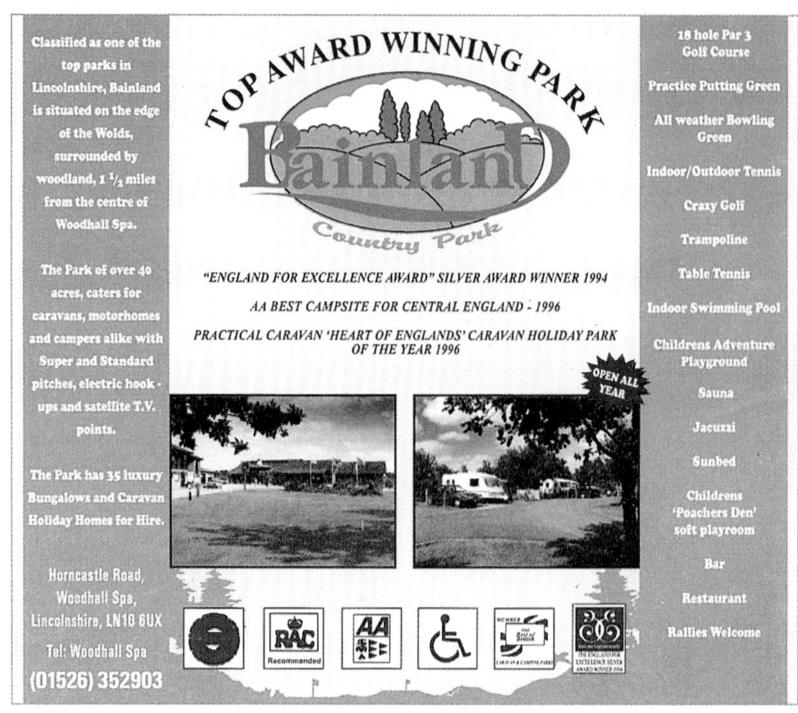

low signs for Waltham Abbey, turn left at traffic lights, site is 2 miles on right.
Acreage 12 **Open** Easter **to** October
Access Good **Site** Lev/Slope
Sites Available **Total** 200
Facilities
Nearby Facilities
Chingford.
✓✓✓✓✓Graded Park. Ideal for touring London. Nearest London Underground Station Walthamstow Central.

EDMONTON

Lee Valley Leisure Complex (Picketts Lock), Meridian Way, Edmonton, London, N9 0AS.
Std: 0181 **Tel:** 803 6900
Std: 0181 **Fax:** 884 4975
Directions Signposted from the A406 and from junction 25 off the M25 onto the A10, situated on the A1055.
Acreage 6 **Open** All Year
Access Good **Site** Level
Sites Available **Total** 160
Facilities
Nearby Facilities
Lower Edmonton.
✓✓✓✓Graded Park. Good base for London. Golf course on site and other facilities include squash, badminton, table tennis, roller skating, creche, sauna and a cinema.

HACKNEY

Tent City Hackney, Millfields Road, Hackney, London, E5 0AR.
Std: 0181 **Tel:** 985 7656
Std: 0181 **Fax:** 749 9074
Nearest Town/Resort London.
Directions From Dover A2 Blackwall Tunnel A102 (Clapton/Hackney direction). Kenworthy Road, Davbenay Road, Mandeville Street, go over Cow Bridge where Mandeville Street meets Millfields Road.
Acreage 3 **Open** 18 June **to** 30 August
Access Good **Site** Level
Sites Available **Total** 200
Facilities
Nearby Facilities
Pleasant, peaceful site, very close to central London. Alongside a canal. Free cooking facilities etc.. Swimming pool ¼ mile and indoor climbing nearby. E-Mail tentcity@btinternet.com

LEYTON

Lee Valley Cycle Circuit Campsite, Lee Valley Cycle Circuit, Temple Mills Lane, Leyton, London, E15 2EN.
Std: 0181 **Tel:** 534 6085
Std: 0181 **Fax:** 536 0959
Directions A102(M) north from Blackwall Tunnel, follow sign for 'Leyton' onto A106 and then signs to Lee Valley Sports Centre.
Acreage 4 **Open** April **to** October
Access Good **Site** Level
Sites Available **Total** 120
Facilities
Underground-Leyton.

✓✓Graded Park. Camp site is part of 40 acre landscaped parkland, only 4 miles from the City of London.

LOUGHTON

The Elms Caravan & Camping Park, Lippitts Hill, High Beech, Loughton, IG10 4AW.
Std: 0181 **Tel:** 508 3749
Std: 0181 **Fax:** 502 0016/508 3749
Nearest Town/Resort Loughton
Directions Leave the M25 at junction 26 and follow signs to Waltham Abbey (A121). Turn left at traffic lights (A112) for 1 mile, take the third turning left beside the Plough Pub, then ½ mile to Lippitts Hill.
Acreage 3 **Open** March **to** October
Access Good **Site** Level
Sites Available **Total** 50
Facilities
Nearby Facilities
Loughton
✓✓✓Graded Park. In the conservation area of Epping Forest. Ideal base for London. Free bus service to and from the station.

MANCHESTER

HYDE

Camping & Caravanning Club Site, Crowden, Hadfield, Hyde, Greater Manchester, SK14 7HZ.
Std: 01457 **Tel:** 866057
Directions On the A628 Manchester to Barnsley road, in Crowden follow signs for car park, Youth Hostel and camp site. Camp site is approx. 300 yards from the main road.
Open 22 March **to** 1 Nov
Site Sloping
Sites Available **Total** 45
Facilities
Nearby Facilities
Hadfield/Glossop
✓✓✓✓✓Graded Park. In the heart of the Peak District National Park, close to the Pennine Way.

LITTLEBOROUGH

Hollingworth Lake Caravan Park, Round House Farm, Rakewood, Littleborough, OL15 0AT.
Std: 01706 **Tel:** 378661
Nearest Town/Resort Rochdale
Directions Leave the M62 at junction 21, Milnrow B6255. Follow Hollingworth Lake Country Park signs to the Fish Pub. Take Rakewood Road, then the second on the right.
Acreage 3 **Open** All Year
Access Good **Site** Level
Sites Available **Total** 45
Facilities
Nearby Facilities
Littleborough
✓✓✓Graded Park. Near a large lake that covers 120 acres.

MERSEYSIDE

SOUTHPORT

Brooklyn Park & Country Club, Gravel Lane, Banks, Southport, Merseyside, PR9 8BU.
Std: 01704 **Tel:** 228534
Std: 01704 **Fax:** 228534
Nearest Town/Resort Southport.
Directions Off the A565 at Banks roundabout, 1 mile Southport.
Open March **to** 7 January
Access Good **Site** Level
Sites Available **Total** 100
Facilities
Nearby Facilities
Southport
Prices include entry into Country Club with live entertainment most weekends and bar food. 1 mile outside Southport with its many attractions. Beach, botanical gardens, Lord Street shopping and theatres.

SOUTHPORT

Leisure Lakes, Mere Brow, Tarleton, Preston, PR4 6JX.
Std: 01772 **Tel:** 813446
Std: 01772 **Fax:** 816250
Nearest Town/Resort Southport
Directions 6 miles outside Southport on the Southport to Preston road, A565.
Acreage 10 **Open** All Year
Access Good **Site** Level
Sites Available **Total** 86
Facilities
Nearby Facilities
Southport
35 acres of lakes, surrounded by woodland.

NORFOLK

ACLE

Broad Farm Trailer Park, Fleggburgh, Burgh St. Margaret, Great Yarmouth, Norfolk, NR29 3AF.
Std: 01493 **Tel:** 369273
Nearest Town/Resort Great Yarmouth
Directions Midway between Acle and Caister-on-Sea, on the A1064.
Acreage 24 **Open** Easter **to** September
Access Good **Site** Level
Sites Available **Total** 482
Facilities
Nearby Facilities
Acle
Ideally situated for touring Norfolk and visiting the Norfolk Broads.

ATTLEBOROUGH

Oak Tree Caravan Park, Norwich Road, Attleborough, Norfolk, NR17 2JX.
Std: 01953 **Tel:** 455565
Nearest Town/Resort Attleborough
Acreage 5 **Open** All Year
Access Good **Site** Level
Sites Available **Total** 30

Facilities
Nearby Facilities
Attleborough
Centrally based in Norfolk, ideal for touring.

BLAKENEY

Long Furlong Cottage Caravan Park, Blakeney-Saxlingham Road, Wiveton, Nr. Holt, Norfolk, NR25 7DD.
Std: 01263 **Tel:** 740833
Nearest Town/Resort Blakeney/Holt.
Directions From Holt turn off right at Sharrington (A148). Follow signs to 1 mile outside Langham, then turn right at the crossroads (signposted By Road). Site is approx. 5 miles from Holt.
Acreage 2
Access Good **Site** Lev/Slope
Sites Available **Total** 34
Facilities
Nearby Facilities
Sheringham.
ADULTS ONLY. Sheltered and well drained site set in an apple orchard. Central position for local attractions. Number of dogs accepted are limited.

CAISTER-ON-SEA

Grasmere Caravan Park, Bultitudes Loke, Yarmouth Road, Caister-on-Sea, Great Yarmouth, Norfolk, NR30 5DH.
Std: 01493 **Tel:** 720382
Nearest Town/Resort Great Yarmouth.
Directions Enter Caister from roundabout near Yarmouth Stadium at Yarmouth end of bypass. After ½ mile turn sharp left just past Esso garage.
Acreage 2 **Open** April **to** Mid October
Access Good **Site** Level
Sites Available **Total** 46
Facilities
Nearby Facilities
Great Yarmouth.
✓✓✓Graded Park. ½ mile from beach, 3 miles to centre of Great Yarmouth. Advance bookings taken for touring site pitches. Each pitch with it's own electric, water tap and foul water drain.

CAWSTON

Haveringland Hall Caravan Park, Cawston, Norwich, Norfolk, NR10 4PN.
Std: 01603 **Tel:** 871302
Std: 01603 **Fax:** 871302
Nearest Town/Resort Aylsham
Acreage 50 **Open** March **to** October
Access Good **Site** Lev/Slope
Sites Available **Total** 65
Facilities
Nearby Facilities
Norwich
Private 14 acre course fishing lake on site, permits available from the office. Park situated 10 miles from Norwich, 18 miles from the coast and the Norfolk Broads are only 10 miles away.

CLIPPESBY

Clippesby Holidays, Clippesby, Nr. Gt. Yarmouth, Norfolk, NR29 3BL.
Std: 01493 **Tel:** 367800
Std: 01493 **Fax:** 367809
Nearest Town/Resort Acle
Directions Turn down the lane opposite the Clippesby Village sign which is on the B1152 between Acle (A1064) and Potter Heigham (A149). Then turn into the first drive on the right, 500yds signposted.
Acreage 34 **Open** Easter W/end & May **to** September
Access Good **Site** Level
Sites Available **Total** 100
Facilities
Nearby Facilities
Acle
✓✓✓✓✓Graded Park. A quiet family-owned park in the grounds of Clippesby Hall in Broadlands National Park - great cycling country! Its sheltered glades provide a haven both for birds and for campers. Attractive courtyard and woodland cottages (up to ETB 4 Keys Commended). Lots of family things to do. Awards for commitment to people, to quality and the environment. Send for colour brochure of camping and touring and for cottages. E-mail: clippesby.hols@virgin.net

CROMER

Camping & Caravanning Club Site, Holgate Lane, West Runton, Cromer, Norfolk, NR27 9NW.
Std: 01263 **Tel:** 837544
Directions Take the A148 from Kings Lynn, on approaching West Runton turn left at the Roman Camp Inn, site entrance is ½ mile long and is right at the crest of the hill, opposite National Trust sign.
Open 22 March **to** 1 Nov
Site Lev/Slope
Sites Available **Total** 225
Facilities
Nearby Facilities
West Runton
✓✓✓✓Graded Park. Good views over the surrounding countryside. Just 1 mile from the sea.

CROMER

Forest Park Caravan Site Limited, Northrepps Road, Cromer, Norfolk, NR27 0JR.
Std: 01263 **Tel:** 513290
Std: 01263 **Fax:** 511992
Nearest Town/Resort Cromer.
Directions Take coast road B1159 south,

WoodHill Park
Peaceful & Friendly
SET BETWEEN CROMER & SHERINGHAM IN PRETTY NORTH NORFOLK
Award winning Woodhill is one of Norfolk's finest parks. Set in countryside overlooking the sea, you will find peace and tranquillity. Developed to the highest standards our peaceful park specialises in touring and camping, with multi-service and super size hook-up pitches, superb toilet & cleansing facilities and a spares section in our shop. Our coastal park is operated to the highest standards by our trained and caring staff.
We also hire a small fleet of luxury holiday caravans which overlook the sea, boasting heating, satellite/teletext TV, barbecue and many other extras.
WE THINK YOU'LL FIND AS MANY DO, YOU WILL RETURN.
Send for brochure to Mrs. C. Hill
WOODHILL PARK
CROMER ROAD, EAST RUNTON, CROMER, NORFOLK NR27 9PX.
Telephone: 01263 512242
BRITISH GRADED HOLIDAY PARKS
EXCELLENT
ROSE AWARD
CARAVAN HOLIDAY PARKS
NORTH NORFOLK DISTRICT COUNCIL
AWARD OF EXCELLENCE WINNER

in approx 1 mile fork right onto Northrepps Road. Site entrance is approx ½ mile on the left.
Acreage 85 **Open** 15 March **to** October
Access Good **Site** Sloping
Sites Available **Total** 330
Facilities
Nearby Facilities
Cromer.
✓✓✓Graded Park. Park is at the apex of a fabulous touring area, with beach close to hand and golf club adjoining.

CROMER

Ivy Farm Holiday Park, 1 High Street, Overstrand, Nr. Cromer, Norfolk, NR27 0PS.
Std: 01263 **Tel:** 579239
Nearest Town/Resort Cromer
Directions Take the coast road from Cromer towards Mundesley and Overstrand is the next village. Pass the church on the left, pass the garden centre on the right, turn next left into Carr Lane. Entrance is half way down on the right.
Acreage 4 **Open** 20 March **to** 31 October
Access Good **Site** Lev/Slope
Sites Available **Total** 43
Facilities
Nearby Facilities
Cromer
✓✓✓✓Graded Park. Just a 2 minute walk to the beach. Country walks.

CROMER

Laburnum Caravan Park, Water Lane, West Runton, Cromer, Norfolk, NR27 9QP.
Std: 01263 **Tel:** 837473
Std: 01692 **Fax:** 402136
Nearest Town/Resort Sheringham
Directions 1½ miles from Sheringham turn left by the Village Inn.
Acreage 13 **Open** March **to** October
Sites Available **Total** 180
Facilities
Nearby Facilities
West Runton
✓✓✓✓Graded Park. Gently sloping, cliff top site.

CROMER

Manor Farm Caravan & Camping Site, Manor Farm, East Runton, Cromer, Norfolk, NR27 9PR.
Std: 01263 **Tel:** 512858
Std: 01263 **Fax:** 512858
Nearest Town/Resort Cromer
Directions 1½ miles west of Cromer, turn off the A148 at signpost 'Manor Farm'.
Acreage 16 **Open** Easter **to** October
Access Good **Site** Lev/Slope
Sites Available **Total** 130
Facilities
Nearby Facilities
Cromer
Panoramic sea and woodland views. Spacious, quiet, family run farm site. Ideal for families. Separate field for dog owners.

CROMER

Roman Camp & Caravan Park, West Runton, Nr. Cromer, Norfolk, NR27 9ND.
Std: 01263 **Tel:** 837256
Nearest Town/Resort Cromer/Sheringham.
Directions Cromer to King's Lynn. A148 right to West Runton. Cromer to Sheringham. A149 left at West Runton.
Acreage 1 **Open** Easter **to** 1 October
Access Good **Site** Level
Sites Available **Total** 12
Facilities
Nearby Facilities
West Runton.
Near beach, scenic views.

CROMER

Seacroft Camping & Caravan Park, Runton Road, Cromer, Norfolk, NR27 9NJ.
Std: 01263 **Tel:** 511722
Nearest Town/Resort Cromer.
Directions 1 mile west of Cromer on A149 coast road.
Acreage 5 **Open** 20th March **to** October
Access Good **Site** Gently Sloping
Sites Available **Total** 118
Facilities
Nearby Facilities
Cromer.
✓✓✓✓Graded Park. Well screened camping area divided by rows of shrubs. Fine sea views.

CROMER

Woodhill Camping & Caravan Park, Cromer Road, East Runton, Cromer, Norfolk, NR27 9PX.
Std: 01263 **Tel:** 512242
Std: 01263 **Fax:** 515326
Nearest Town/Resort Cromer
Directions Set between East and West Runton on the seaside of the A149 Cromer to Sheringham road.
Acreage 32 **Open** April **to** October
Access Good **Site** Lev/Slope
Sites Available **Total** 390
Facilities
Nearby Facilities
West Runton
✓✓✓✓✓Graded Park. Peaceful and tranquil, set in countryside overlooking the sea, developed to highest standards. Multi-service and super size hook-up pitches. Spares section in shop. Rose Award.

DISS

Farm Meadow Caravan & Camping Park, Banham Zoo, The Grove, Banham, Norwich, Norfolk, NR16 2HE.
Std: 01953 **Tel:** 888370
Std: 01953 **Fax:** 888427
Nearest Town/Resort Diss
Directions Banham is situated between Attleborough and Diss on the B1113 Norwich to Bury St Edmunds road. Follow the brown tourist signs.
Acreage 13 **Open** All Year
Access Good **Site** Level
Sites Available **Total** 113
Facilities
Nearby Facilities
Diss
✓✓✓✓✓Graded Park. Banham Zoo.

DISS

Willows Camping & Caravan Park, Diss Road, Scole, Norfolk.
Std: 01379 **Tel:** Diss 740271
Nearest Town/Resort Diss.
Directions 200yds off the A140 roundabout at Scole in the direction of Diss on the A1066.

Acreage 4 **Open** May **to** September
Access Good **Site** Level
Sites Available **Total** 32
Facilities
Nearby Facilities
Diss.

FAKENHAM

Crossways, Holt Road (A148), Little Snoring, Fakenham, Norfolk, NR21 0AX.
Std: 01328 **Tel:** 878335
Std: 01328 **Fax:** 878335
Nearest Town/Resort Fakenham.
Directions On A148 3 miles from Fakenham towards Cromer.
Acreage 1¼ **Open** Easter **to** October
Access Good **Site** Level
Sites Available **Total** 27
Facilities
Nearby Facilities
Kings Lynn
8 miles from coast, ideal for touring North Norfolk.

FAKENHAM

Fakenham Racecourse Caravan & Camping Site, The Racecourse, Fakenham, Norfolk, NR21 7NY.
Std: 01328 **Tel:** 862388
Std: 01328 **Fax:** 855908
Nearest Town/Resort Fakenham.
Directions On approaching Fakenham from all directions, follow "Campsite" and international caravan/camping signs, they all refer to this site.
Acreage 11½ **Open** All Year
Access Good **Site** Level
Sites Available **Total** 150
Facilities
Nearby Facilities
King's Lynn.
✓✓✓✓Graded Park. Immaculate facilities in beautiful countryside. Heated toilets, Cable TV (8 channels free of charge) all pitches. Ideally situated for visiting Norfolk's stately homes, bird and wildlife sanctuaries, rural life museums, coastal resorts and other attractions too numerous to mention. There is something for EVERYONE in the Fakenham area.

FAKENHAM

The Old Brick Kilns, Little Barney Lane, Barney, Fakenham, Norfolk, NR21 0NL.
Std: 01328 **Tel:** 878305
Std: 01328 **Fax:** 878948
Nearest Town/Resort Fakenham.
Directions From the A148 Fakenham/Cromer road, turn right onto the B1354 (Aylsham), 6 miles from Fakenham. Follow the tourist board signs (caravan park) to Barney then Little Barney.
Acreage 7 **Open** 15th March **to** October
Access Good **Site** Lev/Slope
Sites Available **Total** 60
Facilities
Nearby Facilities
Kings Lynn
✓✓✓✓✓Graded Park. Quiet, secluded, sheltered, family park. Ideal centre for visiting the many attractions and activities in North Norfolk. E-mail: enquire@old-brick-kilns.co.uk

GREAT HOCKHAM

Puddledock Farm, Great Hockham, Thetford, Norfolk, IP24 1PA.
Std: 01953 **Tel:** 498455
Nearest Town/Resort Thetford
Directions From Thetford take the A1075 for 5 miles, go 100 yards past the picnic site and turn left at sign 83 (Forestry Commission Fire Route sign), follow signs.
Acreage 5 **Open** All Year
Access Good **Site** Level
Sites Available **Total** 30
Facilities
Nearby Facilities
Thetford
Next to Thetford Forest, ideal for walking, cycling, bird and animal watching.

GREAT YARMOUTH

Blue Sky Holiday Park, Burgh Road, Bradwell, Gt. Yarmouth, Norfolk, NR31 9ED.
Std: 01493 **Tel:** 781234
Std: 01493 **Fax:** 782233
Nearest Town/Resort Great Yarmouth
Directions Take Burgh Road at junction of A12/A143. Blue Sky Park is 1½ miles down road on left.
Acreage 7 **Open** April **to** October
Access Good **Site** Level
Sites Available **Total** 240
Facilities
Nearby Facilities
Great Yarmouth
✓✓✓✓Graded Park. Centrally situated for sandy beaches at Great Yarmouth and for touring the Norfolk Broads and Coastline.

GREAT YARMOUTH

Bureside Holiday Park, Boundary Farm, Oby, Nr. Great Yarmouth, Norfolk, NR29 3BW.
Std: 01493 **Tel:** 369233
Nearest Town/Resort Great Yarmouth
Directions From Acle take the A1064 over the bridge, then first left after Acle Bridge and follow caravan and tent signs to Oby.
Acreage 12 **Open** Spring Bank End May **to** Mid Sept

Access Good **Site** Level
Sites Available **Total** 170
Facilities
Nearby Facilities
Acle
Situated in unspoilt broadland, launching slipway, 3½ miles of river fishing, carp and tench lake. Heated swimming pool and play area.

GREAT YARMOUTH

Burgh Castle Marina & Caravan Park, Nr. Great Yarmouth, Norfolk, NR31 9PZ.
Std: 01493 **Tel:** 780331
Std: 01493 **Fax:** 780163
Nearest Town/Resort Gorleston-on-Sea
Directions A143. At 2 miles southwest from Gorleston roundabout fork right for Belton and Burgh Castle then ¾ mile turn right and entrance ¾ mile on the left.
Acreage 15 **Open** All Year
Access Good **Site** Level
Sites Available **Total** 60
Facilities
Nearby Facilities
Great Yarmouth.
Own salt water harbour, slipway, pontoons, boat park, public bar. Licensed pub.

GREAT YARMOUTH

Cherry Tree Holiday Park, Mill Road, Burgh Castle, Great Yarmouth, Norfolk, NR31 9QR.
Std: 01493 **Tel:** 780024
Std: 01493 **Fax:** 780457
Nearest Town/Resort Great Yarmouth.
Directions Close to the A143 from Beccles to Great Yarmouth, 4 miles south west of Great Yarmouth and 2 miles from the seaside town of Gorleston.
Acreage 33 **Open** March **to** October
Access Good **Site** Level
Sites Available **Total** 24
Facilities
Nearby Facilities
Great Yarmouth.
✓✓✓✓Graded Park. Set in a picturesque orchard in the delightful East Anglian countryside, on the edge of the beautiful Norfolk Broads bordering England's newest National Park. Wildlife parks and the beach of Norfolk Coast.

GREAT YARMOUTH

Liffens Holiday Park, Burgh Castle, Great Yarmouth, Norfolk, NR31 9QB.
Std: 01493 **Tel:** 780357
Std: 01493 **Fax:** 782383
Nearest Town/Resort Great Yarmouth.
Directions From Great Yarmouth follow signs for Lowestoft A12. After third roundabout look for sign for Burgh Castle. Follow for 2 miles to T-junction turn right, follow tourist signs to Liffens.
Acreage 12 **Open** Easter **to** October
Access Good **Site** Level
Sites Available **Total** 150
Facilities
Nearby Facilities
Great Yarmouth.
✓✓✓✓Graded Park. Family holiday park close to old Roman fortress yet 10 minutes from Gt. Yarmouth. 2 bars/entertainment/cabaret. 2 heated pools. Play area amusements. Free colour brochure.

GREAT YARMOUTH

Rose Farm Touring & Camping Park, Stepshort, Belton, Great Yarmouth, Norfolk, NR31 9JS.
Std: 01493 **Tel:** 780896
Std: 01493 **Fax:** 780896
Nearest Town/Resort Gorleston
Directions From Great Yarmouth on new bypass take the A143 to Beccles, through Bradwell up to the small dual carriageway. Turn right into new road signposted Belton and Burgh Castle. Down new road first right at Stepshort, site is first on right.
Acreage 6 **Open** All Year
Access Good **Site** Level
Sites Available **Total** 80
Facilities
Nearby Facilities
Great Yarmouth
✓✓✓✓Graded Park. A clean site in peaceful surroundings.

GREAT YARMOUTH

Sunfield Holiday Park, Station Road, Belton, Great Yarmouth, Norfolk, NR31 9NB.
Std: 01493 **Tel:** 781234
Nearest Town/Resort Great Yarmouth
Directions From Great Yarmouth follow A143, turn right off duel carriageway to Belton. Once in Belton follow brown tourist site signs.
Acreage 16 **Open** April **to** October
Access Good **Site** Level
Sites Available **Total** 150
Facilities
Nearby Facilities
Great Yarmouth
✓✓✓✓Graded Park. The ideal base for touring the Norfolk Coast and countryside. Also close to Great Yarmouth. Rose Award.

NORTH NORFOLK

KELLING HEATH

A UNIQUE HOLIDAY EXPERIENCE

A DAVID BELLAMY AWARD WINNING PARK
"The best lowland pond I have seen in years"

Stay in 250 acres of woodland and heather

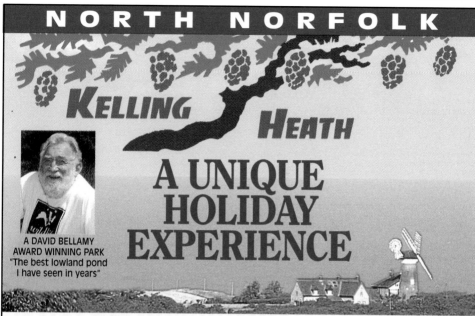

North Norfolk, an area with beautiful views, historic towns, pretty villages and, rich in wildlife. **Relax** and stay at Kelling Heath, situated in an area of outstanding natural beauty you only have to step out from your accommodation to enjoy miles of woodland walks through this natural wildlife reserve. The parks elevated location also commands magnificent views of the coast and sea.

Turn North at Site sign at Bodham on A148, or turn South off A149 at Weybourne Church.

Our excellent range of on park facilities include:-

- Pitches for Touring Caravans and Tents
- Electric Hook-ups ✧ Nature & Trim Trails
- Tennis Courts ✧ Woodland Walks
- Cycle Routes
- Children's Adventure Playgrounds

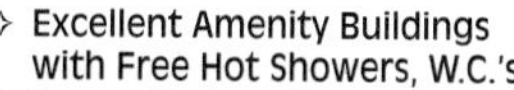

- Excellent Amenity Buildings with Free Hot Showers, W.C.'s
- Luxury Holiday Homes for Hire
- Holiday Homes for Sale

Kelling Village Square with:

- Village Store
- Licensed Bars, Bar Meals, Entertainment and Take-away
- Heated Leisure Pool
- Launderette and Ironing Room
- Family Fun Centre

Booking is advisable at all times.

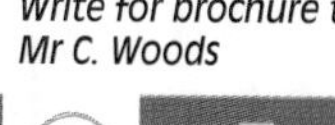

ROSE AWARD
BRITISH GRADED HOLIDAY PARKS
EXCELLENT
CALOR Gas
BEST HOLIDAY PARK IN BRITAIN 1998

Write for brochure to Mr C. Woods

WEYBOURNE, HOLT, NORFOLK NR25 7HW ☎ 01263 588181

BROAD FARM
TRAILER PARK

pitches for
TOURING CARAVANS
DORMOBILES & TENTS

Fleggburgh
Burgh St. Margaret
Great Yarmouth
Norfolk
NR29 3AF

For details + brochure
Tel: Great Yarmouth
(01493) 369273
Office Hours:
9am-5pm

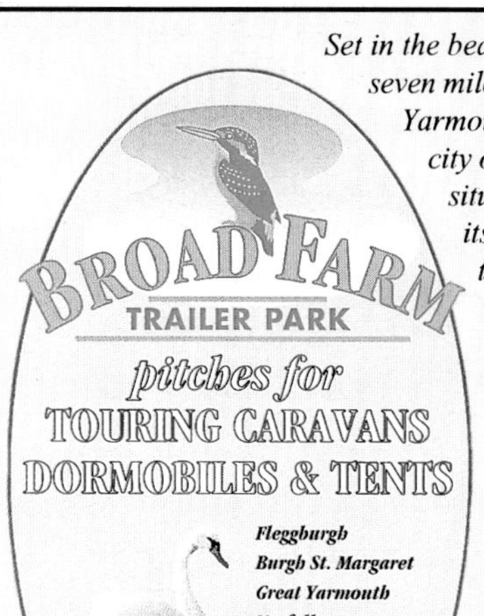

Set in the beautiful Norfolk countryside, just seven miles from the seaside resort of Gt. Yarmouth, and 15 miles from the historic city of Norwich. This site is ideally situated for touring Norfolk and seeing its many attractions, which include the beautiful Norfolk Broads.

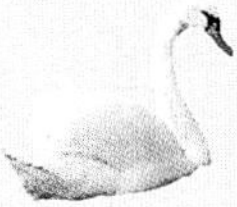

We are situated midway between Acle and Caister-On-Sea, on the A1064.

Pets welcome

Holiday caravans also for hire.
Tel: (01493) 748594

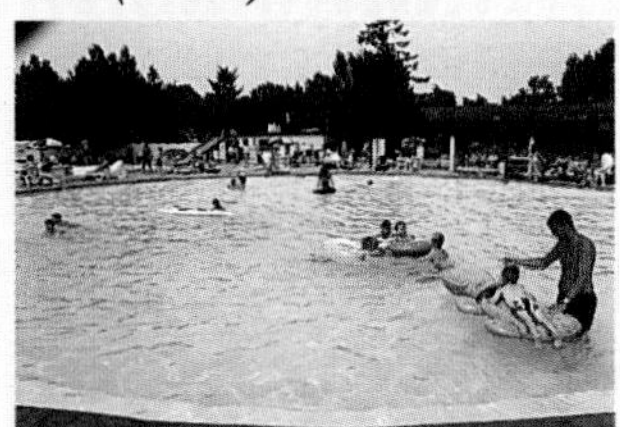

Facilities

Self service shop. Off licence. Calor & Camping gaz. Chip shop. Free heated fun pool. Free children's play area. Free entertainment & dancing. Licenced bar. Amusements. Pool. Grill Room. Launderette. Toilet / Shower Blocks all with constant FREE hot water. Electric hook-ups. Telephone kiosk.

Facilities will be open according to demand.

O.A.P. half price during low season.

TENTING, TOURING & SELF CATERING

FOR GREAT FUN & GREAT VALUE...

English Tourist Board

ROSE AWARD CARAVAN HOLIDAY PARK

BRITISH GRADED HOLIDAY PARKS

RAC

LIFFENS
THE FAMILY OWNED HOLIDAY PARK

Liffen's family owned Holiday Park near the busy seaside resort of Gt.Yarmouth but close to the picturesque Norfolk Broads is packed with fun!

With swimming, tennis, crazy golf, bars, kids club and outstanding on-site facilities too numerous to mention as well as all the fun of the beach with amusements and shows just 10 minutes away, why holiday anywhere else?

Luxury self catering Caravans & Chalets with showers & colour TV. Beautiful grassed park for tents, tourers and motorhomes, (with FREE showers and hot water). Electric hook-ups available.

Make Liffen's Holiday Park your holiday choice this year for a truly fun packed family holiday!

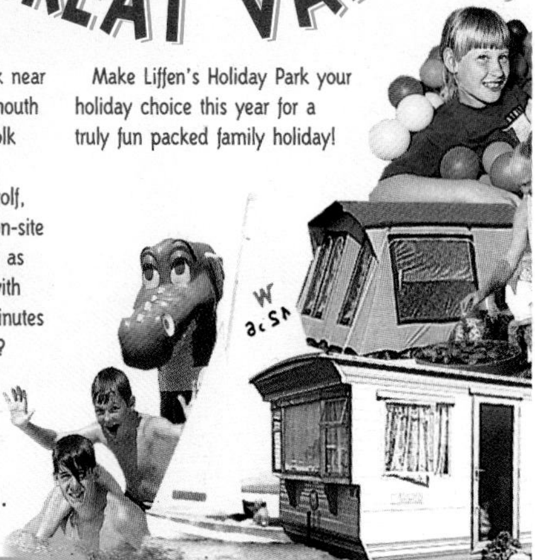

...CALL GREAT YARMOUTH 01493 780357

Liffen's Holiday Park, Burgh Castle, Gt.Yarmouth, Norfolk NR31 9QB. **24hr Brochure Hotline - quote CADE T99**

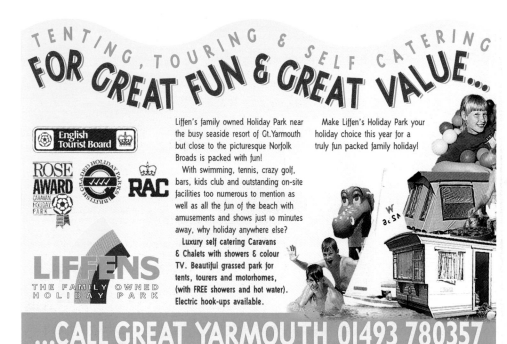

GREAT YARMOUTH

The Grange Touring Park, Yarmouth Road, Ormesby St. Margaret, Great Yarmouth, Norfolk, NR29 3QG.
Std: 01493 **Tel:** 730306
Std: 01493 **Fax:** 730188
Nearest Town/Resort Great Yarmouth
Directions At the junction of the A149 and the B1159, 3 miles north of Great Yarmouth.
Acreage 3½ **Open** Easter **to** End Sept
Access Good **Site** Level
Sites Available **Total** 70
Facilities
Nearby Facilities
Great Yarmouth
✓✓✓✓Graded Park. Very convenient for Great Yarmouth, the beach and the Norfolk Broads.

GREAT YARMOUTH

Vauxhall Holiday Park, 8 Acle New Road, Great Yarmouth, Norfolk, NR30 1TB.
Std: 01493 **Tel:** 857231
Std: 01493 **Fax:** 331122
Nearest Town/Resort Great Yarmouth
Directions Situated on approach to Great Yarmouth on A47 from Norwich.
Acreage 20 **Open** Easter then **to** Mid May-Sept
Access Good **Site** Level
Sites Available **Total** 256
Facilities
Nearby Facilities
Great Yarmouth
✓✓✓✓Graded Park. Ideal centre for attractions of Great Yarmouth and for exploring the famous Norfolk Broads.

GREAT YARMOUTH

Wild Duck Holiday Park, Howards Common, Belton, Great Yarmouth, Norfolk, NR31 9NE.
Std: 01493 **Tel:** 780268
Std: 01493 **Fax:** 782308
Nearest Town/Resort Great Yarmouth.
Directions Take the A47 to Great Yarmouth, then the A143 to Beccles, a couple of hundred yards on the dual carriageway turn right at the sign for Belton. Wild Duck is on the right hand side.
Acreage 60 **Open** March **to** November
Access Good **Site** Level
Sites Available **Total** 165
Facilities
Nearby Facilities
Great Yarmouth.
Set in 60 acres of unspoilt woodland. Ideal holiday base for golf, fishing, unspoilt beaches of the Norfolk Coast and beautiful riverside villages. Greyhound, horse and car racing nearby.

GREAT YARMOUTH

Willowcroft Camping & Caravan Park, Staithe Road, Repps with Bastwick, Potter Heigham, Norfolk, NR29 5JU.
Std: 01692 **Tel:** 670380
Std: 01692 **Fax:** 670380
Nearest Town/Resort Potter Heigham.
Directions 10 miles from Great Yarmouth on the Potter Heigham road, into Church Road, then Staithe Road.
Acreage 2 **Open** All Year
Access Good **Site** Level
Sites Available **Total** 44
Facilities
Nearby Facilities
Acle.

Quiet park, just a two minute walk to a river for fishing. Excellent for walks and bikes etc..

HADDISCOE

Pampas Lodge, Beccles Road, Haddiscoe, Norfolk.
Std: 01502 **Tel:** Aldeby 677265
Std: 01502 **Fax:** 677265
Nearest Town/Resort Beccles.
Directions A143 Beccles/Great Yarmouth, centre of village.
Acreage 3 **Open** March **to** October
Access Good **Site** Level
Sites Available **Total** 40
Facilities
Nearby Facilities
Haddiscoe.
1 mile to a river.

HARLESTON

Little Lakeland Caravan Park, Wortwell, Harleston, Norfolk, IP20 0EL.
Std: 01986 **Tel:** 788646
Nearest Town/Resort Harleston
Directions Turn off A143 (Diss to Lowestoft) at roundabout signposted Wortwell. In village turn right about 300 yards after Bell P.H. at bottom of lane turn right into site.
Acreage 4 **Open** March **to** October
Access Good **Site** Level
Sites Available **Total** 40
Facilities
Nearby Facilities
Diss.
✓✓✓✓Graded Park. Half acre fishing lake, site library.

HEMSBY

Long Beach Caravan Park, Hemsby, Great Yarmouth, Norfolk, NR29 4JD.
Std: 01493 **Tel:** 730023
Std: 01493 **Fax:** 730188
Nearest Town/Resort Great Yarmouth.
Directions Take A149 north from Great Yarmouth, then B1159 on roundabout on Caister bypass. At Hemsby turn right on Beach Road, then second left at King's Loke signposted Longbeach.
Acreage 2 **Open** Easter **to** October
Access Good **Site** Level
Sites Available **Total** 40
Facilities
Nearby Facilities
Great Yarmouth.
30 acres private sandy beach. Ten minutes drive to Great Yarmouth.

HEMSBY

Newport Caravan Park (Norfolk) Ltd., Newport Road, Hemsby, Great Yarmouth, Norfolk, NR29 4NW.
Std: 01493 **Tel:** 730405
Nearest Town/Resort Great Yarmouth.
Directions Take the A149 from Great Yarmouth, B1159 follow signs for Hemsby/ Winterton-on-Sea, turn right to Newport Road.
Open Easter **to** End October
Access Good **Site** Level
Sites Available **Total** 90
Facilities
Nearby Facilities
Great Yarmouth.
✓✓✓✓Graded Park. 500yds from the beach, 6 miles from Great Yarmouth. Convenient base for visiting the Broads, North Norfolk and Norwich.

HORSEY

Waxham Sands Holiday Park, Warren Farm, Horsey, Nr. Great Yarmouth, Norfolk, NR29 4EJ.
Std: 01692 **Tel:** 598325
Nearest Town/Resort Great Yarmouth.
Directions Site is situated on the B1159 coast road 12 miles from Great Yarmouth.
Acreage 100 **Open** Spring Bank Holiday **to** End Sept
Access Good **Site** Level
Sites Available **Total** 200
Facilities
Nearby Facilities
Acle.
Adjacent to the beach and nature reserve. ¼ mile from the Broads.

HUNSTANTON

Heacham Beach Holiday Park, South Beach Road, Heacham, Hunstanton, Norfolk, PE31 7BD.
Std: 01485 **Tel:** 570270
Std: 01485 **Fax:** 572055
Nearest Town/Resort Hunstanton.
Directions A149 from King's Lynn to Hunstanton and Heacham is the first village after Snettisham. Turn left at the sign for Heacham Beaches and left about ½ mile along this road.
Acreage 26 **Open** 31 March **to** 31 October
Site Level
Sites Available **Total** 20
Facilities
Nearby Facilities
Kings Lynn
✓✓✓✓Graded Park.

HUNSTANTON

Manor Park Holiday Village, Manor Road, Hunstanton, Norfolk, PE36 5AZ.
Std: 01485 **Tel:** 532300
Std: 01485 **Fax:** 533881
Nearest Town/Resort Hunstanton
Directions At the southern end of Hunstanton.
Open March **to** October
Access Good **Site** Level
Sites Available **Total** 64
Facilities
Nearby Facilities
Kings Lynn
✓✓✓✓Graded Park.

HUNSTANTON

Searles Holiday Centre, South Beach, Hunstanton, Norfolk, PE36 5BB.
Std: 01485 **Tel:** 534211
Std: 01485 **Fax:** 533815
Nearest Town/Resort Hunstanton.
Directions South of Hunstanton on B1161 off A149.
Acreage 50 **Open** Easter **to** October
Access Good **Site** Level
Sites Available **Total** 250
Facilities
Nearby Facilities
King's Lynn.
✓✓✓✓✓Graded Park. Caravans over 17 feet in length by arrangement. Air-Conditioned club. Beach 150 metres. AA Best Campsite Midlands 1998/99.

HUNSTANTON

The Orchards Caravan Park, Heacham, King's Lynn, Norfolk, PE31 7HG.
Std: 01485 **Tel:** 570327
Nearest Town/Resort Hunstanton.
Directions Turn off the A149 at the traffic

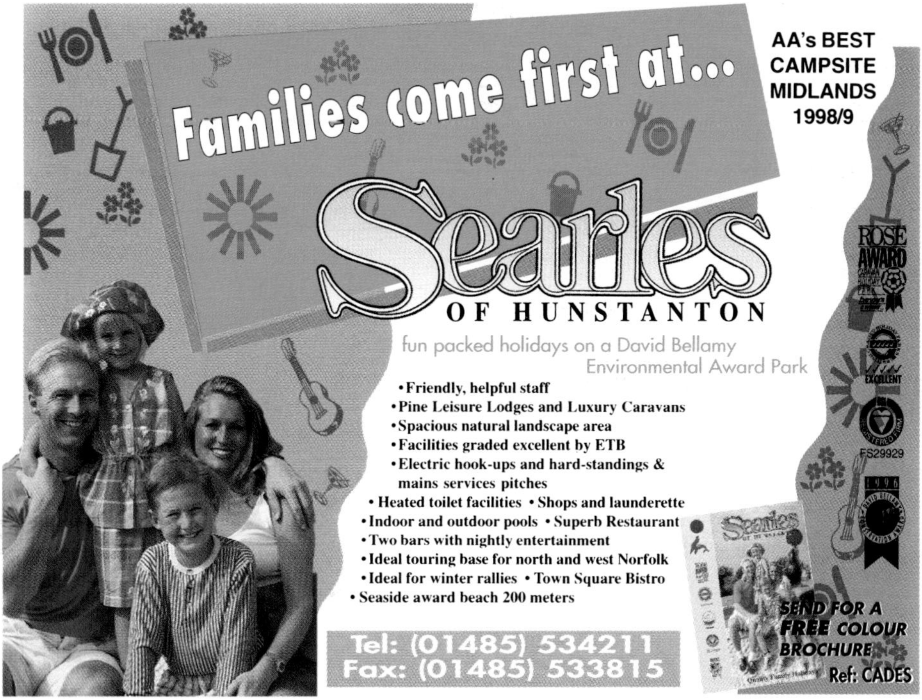

Families come first at...

AA's BEST CAMPSITE MIDLANDS 1998/9

Searles OF HUNSTANTON

fun packed holidays on a David Bellamy Environmental Award Park

- Friendly, helpful staff
- Pine Leisure Lodges and Luxury Caravans
- Spacious natural landscape area
- Facilities graded excellent by ETB
- Electric hook-ups and hard-standings & mains services pitches
- Heated toilet facilities • Shops and launderette
- Indoor and outdoor pools • Superb Restaurant
- Two bars with nightly entertainment
- Ideal touring base for north and west Norfolk
- Ideal for winter rallies • Town Square Bistro
- Seaside award beach 200 meters

Tel: (01485) 534211
Fax: (01485) 533815

ROSE AWARD

EXCELLENT

FS29929

SEND FOR A FREE COLOUR BROCHURE Ref: CADES

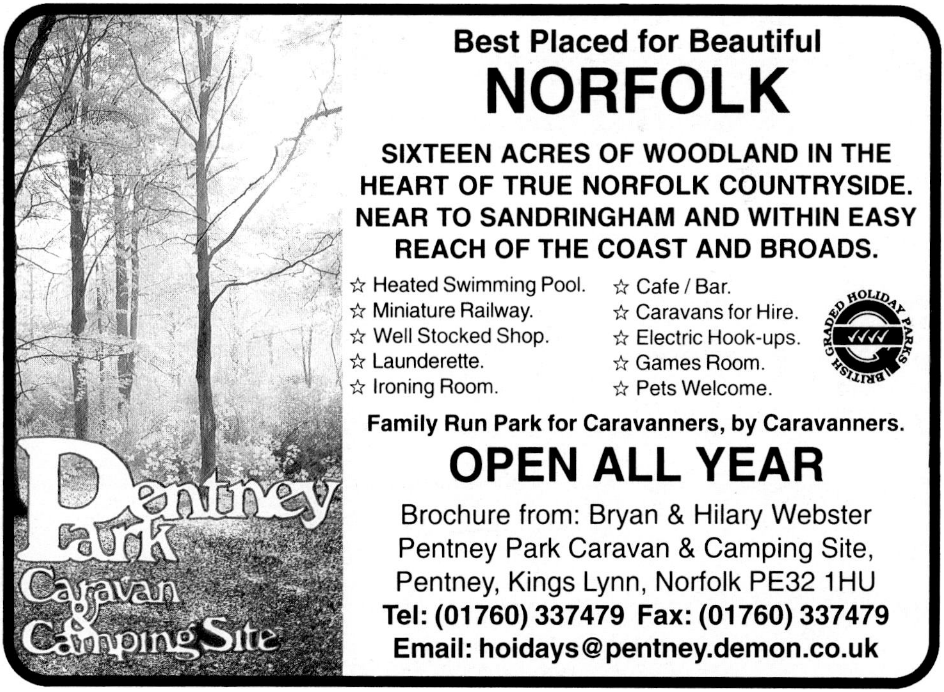

Best Placed for Beautiful

NORFOLK

SIXTEEN ACRES OF WOODLAND IN THE HEART OF TRUE NORFOLK COUNTRYSIDE. NEAR TO SANDRINGHAM AND WITHIN EASY REACH OF THE COAST AND BROADS.

☆ Heated Swimming Pool.
☆ Miniature Railway.
☆ Well Stocked Shop.
☆ Launderette.
☆ Ironing Room.
☆ Cafe / Bar.
☆ Caravans for Hire.
☆ Electric Hook-ups.
☆ Games Room.
☆ Pets Welcome.

Family Run Park for Caravanners, by Caravanners.

OPEN ALL YEAR

Brochure from: Bryan & Hilary Webster
Pentney Park Caravan & Camping Site,
Pentney, Kings Lynn, Norfolk PE32 1HU
Tel: (01760) 337479 Fax: (01760) 337479
Email: hoidays@pentney.demon.co.uk

island (signed Heacham - DO NOT follow Heacham Beaches signs). Go through Heacham Village and the entrance is next to the public hall. MOTORCARAVANS ONLY.
Acreage 1 **Open** All Year
Access Good **Site** Level
Sites Available **Total** 18
Facilities
Nearby Facilities
King's Lynn.
In the centre of a seaside village in beautiful West Norfolk. Next door to a licensed club, near a public telephone. Please make cheques payable to J PIGNEY.

KINGS LYNN

Gatton Water Touring Caravan & Camping Site, Hillington, Nr. Sandringham, Kings Lynn, Norfolk, PE31 6BJ.
Std: 01485 **Tel:** 600643
Nearest Town/Resort Kings Lynn
Directions 8 miles from Kings Lynn on the A148 (Kings Lynn/Cromer road).
Acreage 24 **Open** April **to** October
Access Good **Site** Level
Sites Available **Total** 90
Facilities
Kings Lynn
Most pitches overlook a lake. Fishing on site. ADULTS ONLY (except for Seasonal Pitches).

KINGS LYNN

Kings Lynn Caravan & Camping Park, Parkside House, New Road, North Runcton, Kings Lynn, Norfolk, PE33 0QR.
Std: 01553 **Tel:** 840004
Nearest Town/Resort Kings Lynn
Directions 1½ miles from the A17, A47, A10 and A149 main Kings Lynn Hardwick roundabout. Take the A47 towards Swaffham and take the first right at North Runcton.
Acreage 3½ **Open** All Year
Access Good **Site** Level
Sites Available **Total** 35
Facilities
Nearby Facilities
Kings Lynn
Situated in a beautiful parkland setting with mature trees. Well situated for Kings Lynn, inland market towns, the North Norfolk coast, watersports and good pubs. Tesco's nearby.

KINGS LYNN

Pentney Lakes Leisure Park, Common Road, East Winch, Kings Lynn, Norfolk, PE32 1JT.
Std: 01760 **Tel:** 338668
Std: 01760 **Fax:** 338668
Nearest Town/Resort Kings Lynn
Directions Take A47 from Kings Lynn to Norwich. 6 miles to East Winch, large brown direction signs, turn right in to Common Road, site 2 miles.
Acreage 285 **Open** All Year
Access Good **Site** Level
Sites Available **Total** 100
Facilities
Nearby Facilities
Kings Lynn
Leisure Park including fishing, water skiing, jet skiing, windsurfing, sailing, walking and wildlife site no. 532, 160 acres of water.

KINGS LYNN

Pentney Park Caravan & Camping Site, Pentney, King's Lynn, Norfolk. PE32 1HU.
Std: 01760 **Tel:** 337479
Std: 01760 **Fax:** 338118
Nearest Town/Resort King's Lynn.
Directions Situated on A47 midway between Kings Lynn and Swaffham, entrance 150 yards from junction of B1153 with A47.
Acreage 16 **Open** All Year
Access Good **Site** Level
Sites Available **Total** 200
Facilities
Nearby Facilities
King's Lynn.
✓✓✓✓Graded Park. Ideal touring base set in woodland and clearings, easy reach of coast and Broadlands.

MUNDESLEY

Sandy Gulls New Cliff Top Touring Park, Cromer Road, Mundesley, Norfolk, NR11 8DF.
Std: 01263 **Tel:** 720513
Nearest Town/Resort Cromer.
Directions South along the coast road for 4 miles.
Acreage 2½ **Open** Easter **to** October
Access Good **Site** Level
Sites Available **Total** 40
Facilities
Nearby Facilities
Cromer.
Cliff top location, near to the Broads National Park.

NORTH WALSHAM

Two Mills Touring Park, Scarborough Hill, Yarmouth Road, North Walsham, Norfolk, NR28 9NA.
Std: 01692 **Tel:** 405829
Std: 01692 **Fax:** 405829
Nearest Town/Resort North Walsham
Directions Follow Hospital signs passing the Police Station on route. 1 mile on the left from the town centre.
Acreage 6 **Open** 1 March **to** 3 January
Access Good **Site** Level
Sites Available **Total** 59
Facilities
Nearby Facilities
North Walsham
✓✓✓✓✓Graded Park. ADULTS ONLY.

NORWICH

Camping & Caravanning Club Site, Martineau Lane, Norwich, Norfolk, NR1 2HX.
Std: 01603 **Tel:** 620060
Directions From the A47 join the A146 towards the city centre. At the traffic lights turn left, at the next set of traffic lights under low bridge to the Cook Public House turn left, site is on the right in 150 yards.
Open 22 March **to** 1 Nov
Site Level
Sites Available **Total** 50
Facilities
Nearby Facilities
Thorpe
✓✓✓Graded Park. Close to Norwich and within easy reach of the Norfolk Broads. Fishing on site. 3 miles from Norwich Cathedral and Colmans Mustard.

NORWICH

Swans Harbour Caravan & Camping Park, Barford Road, Marlingford, Norwich, Norfolk.
Std: 01603 **Tel:** 759658
Nearest Town/Resort Norwich.
Directions Turn off the B1108 (Norwich to Watton road). 3 miles past Southern Bypass turn right signposted Marlingford. Follow brown tourist signs to the site.
Acreage 4 **Open** All Year
Access Good **Site** Level
Sites Available **Total** 30
Facilities
Nearby Facilities
Wymondham
Alongside a river with own fishing rights.

POTTER HEIGHAM

Causeway Cottage Caravan Park, Bridge Road, Potter Heigham, Nr. Great Yarmouth, Norfolk, NR29 5JB.
Std: 01692 **Tel:** 670238
Nearest Town/Resort Great Yarmouth
Directions Potter Heigham is between Great Yarmouth and Norwich. Turn off the A149 at Potter Heigham, we are 250yds from the river and old bridge.
Acreage 1 **Open** March **to** October

Access Good **Site** Level
Sites Available **Total** 5
Facilities
Nearby Facilities
Great Yarmouth
250yds from river, shops and hotels. Fishing, boating and walking. 6 miles from Golden Sands beach.

PULHAM ST. MARY

Waveney Valley Holiday Park, Airstation Farm, Pulham St Mary, Diss, Norfolk, IP21 4QF.
Std: 01379 **Tel:** 741228
Std: 01379 **Fax:** 741228
Nearest Town/Resort Harleston
Directions Take A140 at Scole, travel north for 3 miles. Turn right into Dickleborough and at the church turn right, 2 miles on take the first turn left then first left again.
Open April **to** October
Access Good **Site** Level
Sites Available **Total** 25
Facilities
Nearby Facilities
Diss
Licensed pub on site.

REEDHAM

Reedham Ferry Touring Park, Reedham Ferry, Norwich, Norfolk, NR13 3HA.
Std: 01493 **Tel:** 700429
Std: 01493 **Fax:** 700999
Nearest Town/Resort Acle
Directions Turn off the A47 (Norwich to Great Yarmouth road) at Acle onto the B1140. Go all the way to Reedham, over the railway bridge, large road sign to Reedham Ferry.
Acreage 4 **Open** Easter **to** End October
Access Good **Site** Level
Sites Available **Total** 20
Facilities
Nearby Facilities
Reedham
✓✓✓Graded Park. Quietness and tranquility.

SANDRINGHAM

Camping & Caravanning Club Site, The Sandringham Estate, Double Lodges, Sandringham, Norfolk, PE35 6EA.
Std: 01485 **Tel:** 542555
Directions From the A148 Kings Lynn to Cromer road, turn left onto the B1440 signposted West Newton and follow signs indicating tents and caravan to reach the site. From the A149 Hunstanton to Kings Lynn road, turn left at sign indicating tent and caravan, travel for ½ mile to crossroads and turn right, take second turn on the left to camp site.
Open 22 Feb **to** 29 Nov
Site Level
Sites Available **Total** 250
Facilities
Nearby Facilities
Kings Lynn
✓✓✓✓✓Graded Park. In the grounds of the Royal Estate. Just a few miles from beaches.

SCRATBY

Green Farm Caravan Park, Scratby, Great Yarmouth, Norfolk, NR29 3NW.
Std: 01493 **Tel:** 730440
Nearest Town/Resort Great Yarmouth
Directions 4 miles north of Great Yarmouth on the B1159.
Acreage 20 **Open** 26 March **to** October
Access Good **Site** Level
Sites Available **Total** 200
Facilities
Nearby Facilities
Great Yarmouth
✓✓✓✓✓Graded Park. Near the beach.

SCRATBY

Scratby Hall Caravan Park, Scratby, Great Yarmouth, Norfolk, NR29 3PH.
Std: 01493 **Tel:** 730283
Nearest Town/Resort Great Yarmouth
Directions Approx. 5 miles north of Great Yarmouth, off the B1159, signed.
Acreage 4½ **Open** Easter **to** Mid October
Access Good **Site** Level
Sites Available **Total** 108
Facilities
Nearby Facilities
Great Yarmouth
✓✓✓✓Graded Park. Quiet, rural site. Approx. ½ mile from the beach.

SEA PALLING

Golden Beach Holiday Centre, Beach Road, Sea Palling, Norwich, Norfolk, NR12 0AL.
Std: 01692 **Tel:** 598269
Nearest Town/Resort Stalham
Directions Follow the coast road to Stalham then follow caravan and camping signs to Sea Palling. Turn down Beach Road, site is on the left 200 yards from the beach.
Acreage 7 **Open** March **to** 1 November
Access Good **Site** Level
Sites Available **Total** 50
Facilities
Nearby Facilities
Wroxham
✓✓✓✓Graded Park. Family site with a family atmosphere, 200 yards from the beach. New toilets.

SHERINGHAM

Beeston Regis Caravan Park Limited, Cromer Road, West Runton, Cromer, Norfolk, NR27 9NG.
Std: 01263 **Tel:** 823614
Nearest Town/Resort Sheringham
Directions From Sheringham take the A149 coast road towards Cromer. After ¾ mile you will see the main entrance to the park on the left hand side, opposite Beeston Hall School.
Acreage 44 **Open** March **to** October
Access Good **Site** Level
Sites Available **Total** 440
Facilities
Nearby Facilities
West Runton
Cliff top position in an area of outstanding natural beauty. Direct access to a sandy beach. Excellent shower block.

SHERINGHAM

Kelling Heath Holiday Park, Weybourne, Nr. Sheringham, Norfolk, NR25 7HW.
Std: 01263 **Tel:** 588181
Std: 01263 **Fax:** 588599
Nearest Town/Resort Sheringham
Directions Turn north at site sign at Bodham on the A148 or turn south off the A149 at Weybourne Church.
Acreage 75 **Open** 19th March **to** October
Access Good **Site** Level
Sites Available **Total** 300
Facilities
Nearby Facilities
Sheringham
√√√√√Graded Park. A 250 acre estate of woodland and heather, with magnificent views of the Weybourne coastline. Rose Award.

SHERINGHAM

Woodlands Caravan Park, Holt Road, Upper Sheringham, Sheringham, Norfolk, NR26 8TU.
Std: 01263 **Tel:** 823802
Nearest Town/Resort Sheringham.
Directions 4 miles east of Holt, off the A148.
Acreage 20 **Open** March **to** October
Access Good **Site** Lev/Slope
Sites Available **Total** 286
Facilities
Nearby Facilities
√√√√Graded Park. Surrounded by woodlands on two sides, fields and trees on the remaining two sides. In an area of outstanding natural beauty. Indoor 25mtr swimming pool and complex. Bar meals available. 216 electric hook-ups.

SNETTISHAM

Diglea Caravan & Camping Park, Beach Road, Snettisham, Norfolk, PE31 7RA.
Std: 01485 **Tel:** 541367
Nearest Town/Resort Hunstanton.
Directions Take the A149 Kings Lynn to Hunstanton road. Turn left at the sign marked Snettisham Beach, park is on the left after 1½ miles.
Acreage 6 **Open** April **to** October
Access Good **Site** Level
Sites Available **Total** 200
Facilities
Nearby Facilities
King's Lynn.
√√√Graded Park. Peaceful, family run park in a rural setting. Beach and RSPB sanctuary close by. Rally field available.

STANHOE

The Rickels Caravan & Camping Site, Bircham Road, Stanhoe, Kings Lynn, Norfolk, PE31 8PU.
Std: 01485 **Tel:** 518671
Std: 01485 **Fax:** 518969
Nearest Town/Resort Hunstanton.
Directions From Kings Lynn take the A148 to Hillington, turn left onto the B1153 to Great Bircham. Fork right onto the B1155 to the crossroads, straight over. Site is 100yds on the left.
Acreage 2¼ **Open** March **to** October
Access Good **Site** Lev/Slope
Sites Available **Total** 30
Facilities
Nearby Facilities
Kings Lynn
√√√√Graded Park. Local beaches, stately homes, Sandringham and market towns. Childrens Television. Dogs 50p per night, short dog walk.

SWAFFHAM

Breckland Meadows Touring Park, Lynn Road, Swaffham, Norfolk, PE37 7AY.
Std: 01760 **Tel:** 721246
Nearest Town/Resort Kings Lynn/Hunstanton.
Directions Take the A47 from Kings Lynn to Swaffham, approx 15 miles. Take the first exit off the dual carriageway, site is ¼ mile before Swaffham town centre.
Acreage 2½ **Open** 20 March **to** 31 October
Access Good **Site** Level
Sites Available **Total** 30
Facilities
Nearby Facilities
Kings Lynn
Central for touring, ideal for walking Swaefas Way and Peddars Way. New amenity block for 1999. 16 amp electrics to all pitches.

THETFORD

The Dower House Touring Park, East Harling, Norwich, Norfolk, NR16 2SE.
Std: 01953 **Tel:** 717314
Std: 01953 **Fax:** 717843
Nearest Town/Resort Norwich
Directions From Thetford take A1066 East for 5 miles, fork left at camping sign onto unclassified road, site on left after 2 miles signposted.
Acreage 20 **Open** 20th March **to** October
Access Good **Site** Level
Sites Available **Total** 160
Facilities
Nearby Facilities
Harling Road.
√√√√Graded Park. Set in Thetford Forest, the site is spacious and peaceful. Although we have a bar, we have no amusement arcade or gaming machines.

THETFORD

Thorpe Woodlands - Forestry Commission, Shadwell, Thetford, Norfolk, IP24 2RX.
Std: 01842 **Tel:** 751042
Nearest Town/Resort Thetford
Directions Take the A1066 from Thetford, after 5 miles bear left to East Harling. The site is ¼ mile on the left.
Open End March **to** End Oct
Access Good **Site** Level
Sites Available **Total** 138
Facilities
Nearby Facilities
Thetford
In Thetford Forest Park, on the banks of the River Thet. A good base for visiting the Norfolk Broads. Note : This site has NO toilets.

WELLS NEXT THE SEA

Pinewoods Holiday Park, Beach Road, Wells Next the Sea, Norfolk, NR23 1DR.
Std: 01328 **Tel:** 710439
Std: 01328 **Fax:** 711060
Nearest Town/Resort Wells Next the Sea
Directions Situated 1 mile from Wells Quay off the A149 (coast road) OR approach Wells by the B1105 from Fakenham.
Acreage 40 **Open** March **to** October
Access Good **Site** Level
Sites Available **Total** 200
Facilities
Nearby Facilities
√√√√Graded Park. Beaside a beach and Pine woods, in a National Nature Reserve. A charming harbour town. Ideal centre to tour North Norfolk.

NORTHAMPTONSHIRE

NORTHAMPTON

Billing Aquadrome Ltd., Crow Lane, Great Billing, Northampton, Northamptonshire, NN3 9DA.
Std: 01604 **Tel:** 408181
Std: 01604 **Fax:** 784412
Nearest Town/Resort Northampton
Directions Leave the M1 at junction 15, fully AA signposted from there.
Acreage 235 **Open** March **to** November
Access Good **Site** Level
Sites Available **Total** 755
Facilities
Nearby Facilities
Northampton
✓✓✓✓Graded Park. Funfair, bars and restaurants. Lakes for fishing, sailing, boating and jet-skiing.

NORTHUMBERLAND

BAMBURGH

Glororum Caravan Park, Glororum, Bamburgh, Northumberland, NE69 7AW.
Std: 01668 **Tel:** 214457
Directions Caravan Park 1 mile from Bamburgh on Adderstone (B1341) or from A1 take B1341 Adderstone towards Bamburgh, 4 miles.
Open April **to** October
Access Good **Site** Level
Sites Available **Total** 100
Facilities
Nearby Facilities
Berwick-upon-Tweed.
✓✓✓✓Graded Park. Caravan Park is set in peaceful surroundings. Nearby lovely beach. Within easy reach of Holy Island, Farne Islands. Cheviots. No single sex parties.

BEADNELL

Beadnell Links Ltd., Beadnell Harbour, Beadnell, Chathill, Northumberland, NE67 5BU.
Std: 01665 **Tel:** 720993
Nearest Town/Resort Beadnell.
Directions B1340 to Beadnell, thereafter signed.
Open April **to** October
Access Good **Site** Level
Sites Available **Total** 20
Facilities
Nearby Facilities
Chathill.
✓✓✓✓Graded Park. Site near beach.

BEADNELL

Camping & Caravanning Club Site, Beadnell, Chathill, Northumberland, NE67 5BX.
Std: 01665 **Tel:** 720586
Directions From south leave the A1 and follow the B1430 signposted Seahouses. At Beadnell ignore signs for Beadnell Village, site is on the left after the village, just beyond the left hand bend. From north leave the A1 and follow the B1342 via Bamburgh and Seahouses, site is on the right just before Beadnell Village.
Acreage 14 **Open** 22 March **to** 27 Sept
Site Level
Sites Available **Total** 150
Facilities
Nearby Facilities
✓✓✓✓Graded Park. 2 miles of sandy beach just over the road.

BEADNELL

Swinhoe Links Caravan Park, Beadnell Bay, Beadnell, Northumberland, NE67 5BW.
Std: 01665 **Tel:** 720589
Nearest Town/Resort Beadnell/ Seahouses.
Directions 1½ miles south of Seahouses on the B1340.
Acreage 12 **Open** April **to** 1 November
Access Good **Site** Level
Sites Available **Total** 20
Facilities
Nearby Facilities
Chathill.
Next to a quality beach in an area of outstanding natural beauty. Sport, natural and cultural history in abundance.

BELLINGHAM

Brown Rigg Caravan & Camping Park, Tweed House, Brown Rigg, Bellingham, Hexham, Northumberland, NE48 2JY.
Std: 01434 **Tel:** 220175
Std: 01434 **Fax:** 220175
Nearest Town/Resort Bellingham/ Hexham
Directions Take the A69 signposted Hexham, ½ mile west turn onto the A6079 Acomb/Bellingham road. Then take the B6318 to Chollerford, B6320 signposted Bellingham 12 miles. We are ½ mile south of Bellingham.
Acreage 5½ **Open** Wk before Easter **to** 31 Oct
Access Good **Site** Level
Sites Available **Total** 60
Facilities
Nearby Facilities

Hexham

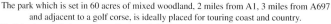

✓✓✓✓Graded Park. Pennine Way borders the site. Salmon and Trout fishing in the North Tyne ½ mile. Bellingham Golf Course, Hadrians Wall, Kielder Water and Forest 9 miles.

BELLINGHAM

Demesne Farm Campsite, Demesne Farm, Bellingham, Hexham, Northumberland, NE48 2BS.
Std: 01434 **Tel:** 220107/220258
Nearest Town/Resort Hexham
Directions 17 miles from Hexham on the B6320. Drive into the centre of Bellingham Village and turn left at Lloyds Bank, we are 50 yards on the right next to the garage.
Acreage 2 **Open** March **to** January
Access Good **Site** Lev/Slope
Sites Available **Total** 30
Facilities
Nearby Facilities
Hexham
✓✓✓Graded Park. On the Pennine Way for nice walks. Near Kielder Water, the Roman Wall and many other places of interest. Shops, pubs, cafe and a fish and chip shop in the village. Good golf course nearby.

BERWICK-UPON-TWEED

Berwick Holiday Centre, Magdalene Fields, Berwick-upon-Tweed, Northumberland, TD15 1NE.
Std: 01289 **Tel:** 307113
Std: 01281 **Fax:** 331700
Nearest Town/Resort Berwick-upon-Tweed.
Directions Signposted on the A1 from both north and south. You will find signs directing you to Berwick Holiday Centre in the town. (5 minutes walk from the centre).
Open March **to** November
Access Good **Site** Level
Sites Available **Total** 36
Facilities
Nearby Facilities
Berwick-upon-Tweed
✓✓✓✓Graded Park. Superb coastal location, within easy walking distance of Berwick-upon-Tweed. Access to the beach. Excellent rail links, Elizabethan walls and local heritage. Kids Club and a full family entertainment programme. Outdoor bowling green, bike hire and a childrens soft play area. Next door to a golf course.

BERWICK-UPON-TWEED

Haggerston Castle, Beal, Northumberland, TD15 2PA.
Std: 01289 **Tel:** 381333
Nearest Town/Resort Berwick-upon-Tweed
Directions On A1, 7 miles south of Berwick-upon-Tweed.
Open 9 March **to** November
Access Good **Site** Level
Sites Available **Total** 159
Facilities
Nearby Facilities
Berwick
✓✓✓✓✓Graded Park. Situated in an area of great heritage interest. Lots of on park facilities. Kids Club and farm. A full family entertainment programme. Golf, horse riding, tennis, bowls, boating, bikes and heated swimming pools. Rose Award and David Bellamy Conservation Award.

BERWICK-UPON-TWEED

Ord House Caravan Park, East Ord, Berwick-upon-Tweed, Northumberland, TD15 2NS.
Std: 01289 **Tel:** 305288
Std: 01289 **Fax:** 330832
Nearest Town/Resort Berwick-upon-Tweed.
Directions Take East Ord road from bypass, follow caravan signpost.
Acreage 42 **Open** March **to** Early Jan
Access Good **Site** Lev/Slope
Sites Available **Total** 60
Facilities
Nearby Facilities
Berwick-upon-Tweed.
✓✓✓✓✓Graded Park. Sheltered tree lined estate with 18th century mansion house containing a licenced club.

EMBLETON

Camping & Caravanning Club Site, Dunstan Hill, Dunstan, Alnwick, Northumberland, NE66 3TQ.
Std: 01665 **Tel:** 576310
Directions Travelling north on the A1 take the B1340 signposted Seahouses, follow to the T-Junction at Christon Bank and turn right, take the next right signpost Embleton turn right at the crossroads then first left signposted Craster. Travelling south on the A1 take the B6347 through Christon Bank, take a right turn to Embleton, turn right at the crossroads, then first left signposted Craster, site is 1 mile on the left.
Acreage 10 **Open** 22 March **to** 1 Nov
Site Level
Sites Available **Total** 150
Facilities
Nearby Facilities
Berwick/Alnmouth
✓✓✓✓Graded Park. 1 mile from the coast. Access to Dunstanburgh Castle from the site.

HALTWHISTLE

Camping & Caravanning Club Site, Burnfoot Park Village, Haltwhistle, Northumberland, NE49 0JP.
Std: 01434 **Tel:** 320106
Directions Follow signs from the new by-pass.
Open 22 March **to** 1 Nov
Site Level
Sites Available **Total** 60
Facilities
Nearby Facilities
Haltwhistle
✓✓✓✓Graded Park. On the banks of the River South Tyne for fishing on site. Close to the Pennine Way.

HALTWHISTLE

Seldom Seen Caravan Park, Haltwhistle, Northumberland, NE49 0NE.
Std: 01434 **Tel:** 320571
Nearest Town/Resort Haltwhistle
Directions Off the A69 east of Haltwhistle, signposted.
Open March **to** January
Access Good **Site** Level

Sites Available **Total** 20
Facilities
Nearby Facilities
Haltwhistle
Central touring area, Roman wall. David Bellamy Award 1997.

HALTWHISTLE

Yont the Cleugh, Coanwood, Haltwhistle, Northumberland.
Std: 01434 **Tel:** 320274
Nearest Town/Resort Haltwhistle.
Directions Signposted 4½ miles from A69 at Haltwhistle.
Acreage 5 **Open** March **to** January
Access Good **Site** Level
Sites Available **Total** 30
Facilities
Nearby Facilities
Haltwhistle.
✓✓✓✓Graded Park. Rural site. Scenic views. Near main Roman Wall site.

HEXHAM

Barrasford Park Caravan & Camping Site, 1 Front Drive, Barrasford Park, Nr. Hexham, Northumberland, NE48 4BE.
Std: 01434 **Tel:** 681210
Nearest Town/Resort Hexham
Directions Take the A69 to Corbridge, turn onto the A68 to Jedburgh. Barrasford Park is signposted 8 miles north of Corbridge on the A68.
Acreage 2 **Open** April **to** October
Access Good **Site** Sloping
Sites Available **Total** 30
Facilities
Nearby Facilities
Hexham
✓✓✓Graded Park. Set in a 60 acre woodland park, 6 miles from Hadrian's Wall.

HEXHAM

Causey Hill Caravan Park, Hexham, Northumberland, NE46 2JN.
Std: 01434 **Tel:** 604647
Std: 01434 **Fax:** 604647
Nearest Town/Resort Hexham
Directions On the racecourse road at High Yarridge.
Acreage 7½ **Open** April **to** October
Access Good **Site** Sloping
Sites Available **Total** 135
Facilities
Nearby Facilities
Hexham
✓✓✓✓Graded Park.

HEXHAM

Fallowfield Dene Caravan Park, Acomb, Nr. Hexham, Northumberland, NE46 4RP.
Std: 01434 **Tel:** 603553
Std: 01434 **Fax:** 601252
Nearest Town/Resort Hexham.
Directions North off the A69 onto the B6379 to Acomb.
Acreage 17½ **Open** April **to** October
Access Fair **Site** Lev/Slope
Sites Available **Total** 165
Facilities
Nearby Facilities
Hexham.
✓✓✓✓Graded Park. Near to Hadrian's Wall. Ideal touring.

HEXHAM

Riverside Leisure, Tyne Green, Hexham, Northumberland, NE46 3RY.
Std: 01434 **Tel:** 604705
Std: 01434 **Fax:** 606217
Nearest Town/Resort Hexham
Acreage 6 **Open** March **to** January
Access Good **Site** Level
Sites Available **Total** 30
Facilities
Nearby Facilities
Hexham
✓✓✓✓✓Graded Park. Wildlife conservation park.

HEXHAM

Springhouse Farm Caravan Park, Slaley, Hexham, Northumberland.
Std: 01434 **Tel:** 673241
Nearest Town/Resort Hexham
Open March **to** October
Access Good **Site** Sloping
Sites Available **Total** 20
Facilities
Nearby Facilities
Hexham Station
Quiet, surrounded by forest. Panoramic views, excellent country walks.

KIELDER

Kielder Campsite - Forestry Commission, Kielder, Hexham, Northumberland, NE48 1EP.
Std: 01434 **Tel:** 250291
Nearest Town/Resort Kielder
Directions The site is 500 yards north of Kielder Village, on the right hand side.
Acreage 10 **Open** 24 March **to** 2 Oct
Access Good **Site** Level
Sites Available **Total** 70
Facilities
Nearby Facilities
Hexham
✓✓✓Graded Park. Attractive riverside setting in Kielder Forest Park, close to Kielder Water. Just a few miles from the Scottish Border.

MORPETH

Forget-Me-Not Caravan Park, Croftside, Longhorsley, Morpeth, Northumberland, NE65 8QY.
Std: 01670 **Tel:** 788364
Nearest Town/Resort Morpeth
Directions From the A1 take the A697 to Longhorsley, turn left in Longhorsley towards Netherwitton, park is 1¼ miles on the right.
Acreage 20+ **Open** March **to** October
Access Good **Site** Level
Sites Available **Total** 60
Facilities
Nearby Facilities
Morpeth
On the edge of a national park, ideal touring. 7 miles from the beach.

MORPETH

Percy Wood Caravan Park, Swarland, Nr. Morpeth, Northumberland, NE65 9JW.
Std: 01670 **Tel:** 787649
Std: 01670 **Fax:** 787034
Nearest Town/Resort Alnwick.
Directions From the A1 turn off to Swarland and follow caravan signs.
Acreage 60 **Open** March **to** Janurary
Access Good **Site** Lav/Slope
Sites Available **Total** 80
Facilities
Nearby Facilities
Morpeth.
✓✓✓✓✓Graded Park. Ideal base for touring coast and country. Adjacent to a golf course and forest walks. Rose Award.

OTTERBURN

Border Forest Caravan Park, Cottonshope Burnfoot, Nr. Otterburn, Northumberland, NE19 1TF.
Std: 01830 **Tel:** 520259
Nearest Town/Resort Jedburgh/Hexham
Directions Adjacent to A68 - 17 miles to Jedburgh, 28 miles to Hexham, 38 miles to Newcastle.
Acreage 3 **Open** 1st March **to** 31st October
Access Good **Site** Level
Sites Available **Total** 36
Facilities
Nearby Facilities
Hexham
Surrounded by Cottonshope, Burn and River Rede. Ideal walking and touring base. 6 miles south of the Scottish Border at Carter Bar. Situated in Border Forest Park.

ROTHBURY

Clennell Hall, Alwinton, Morpeth, Northumberland, NE65 7BG.
Std: 01669 **Tel:** 650341
Nearest Town/Resort Rothbury
Directions From Rothbury take the B6341 for 4 miles, turn right signed Alwinton. Go through Harbottle Village, continue for 2 miles, after second bridge turn right signposted Clennell Hall.
Acreage 14 **Open** March **to** January
Access Good **Site** Level
Sites Available **Total** 50
Facilities
Nearby Facilities
Morpeth
Situated in the Border Country of the Cheviot Hills. Set in the grounds of Clennell Hall, a 16th century, Grade 2, Listed building. Rallies welcome.

ROTHBURY

Coquetdale Caravan Park, Whitton, Rothbury, Morpeth, Northumberland.
Std: 01669 **Tel:** 620549
Nearest Town/Resort Rothbury.
Directions ½ mile southwest of Rothbury on road to Newtown.
Acreage 1½ **Open** Easter **to** October
Access Good **Site** Level
Sites Available **Total** 50
Facilities
Nearby Facilities
Morpeth.
Beautiful views. Ideal situation for touring Borders and coast. All units are strictly for families and couples only.

SEAHOUSES

Seafield Caravan Park, Seafield Road, Seahouses, Northumberland, NE68 7SP.
Std: 01665 **Tel:** 720628
Std: 01665 **Fax:** 720088
Nearest Town/Resort Seahouses
Directions B1340 east off the main A1 to the coast.
Acreage 1 **Open** March **to** January
Access Good **Site** Level
Sites Available **Total** 20
Facilities
Nearby Facilities
Chathill
✓✓✓✓Graded Park. In the centre of the village, near to a beach, scenic views and the harbour.

WOOLER

Highburn House Caravan & Camping Park, Wooler, Northumberland, NE71 6EE.
Std: 01668 **Tel:** 281344/281839
Nearest Town/Resort Wooler.
Directions Off A1 take A697 to Wooler town centre, at the top of Main Street take left turn, 400 metres on left is our site.
Acreage 12 **Open** April **to** December
Access Good **Site** Level
Sites Available **Total** 100
Facilities
Nearby Facilities
Berwick.
Stream runs through middle of site, beautiful view over hills and valley.

WOOLER

Riverside Caravan Park, Wooler, Northumbria, NE71 6EE.
Std: 01668 **Tel:** 281447
Std: 01668 **Fax:** 282142
Nearest Town/Resort Wooler.
Directions From Newcastle follow signs for Morpeth, then Coldstream, thus joining the A697 to Wooler. From Scotland take the A697 from Coldstream to Wooler. Riverside lies on the south-east outskirts of the town.
Open Easter to End October
Sites Available **Total** 55
Facilities
Nearby Facilities
✓✓✓✓Graded Park. Situated on the edge of Northumbria National Park.

NOTTINGHAMSHIRE

CARLTON-ON-TRENT

Carlton Manor Caravan Park, Ossington Road, (off A1), Carlton-on-Trent, Nr. Newark, Nottinghamshire.
Std: 01530 **Tel:** 835662
Nearest Town/Resort Newark.
Directions A1 north towards Doncaster. Site is 7 miles north of Newark. Signposted on the A1.
Acreage 2 **Open** April **to** October
Access Good **Site** Level
Sites Available **Total** 22
Facilities
Nearby Facilities
Newark.
We do allow individual motor cyclists, but not groups. Spotless toilets and clean site. Warden on site at all times. Emergency phone on site at Wardens. Hotel opposite open all day for food and drink etc.. Doctor in village. Train spotting on site. Shops and fishing in village. Pubs, library, hairdressers etc. all nearby. Shop (Co-Op) open between 8am and 8pm. You can also call us on MOBILE 07970 649093.

HOLME PIERREPONT

Holme Pierrepont Caravan & Camping Park, National Water Sports Centre, Adbolton Lane, Nottingham, NG12 2LU.
Std: 0115 **Tel:** 982 4721
Std: 0115 **Fax:** 945 5213
Nearest Town/Resort Nottingham
Directions Follow brown National Water Sports signs. 1½ miles from Trent Bridge off the A52 to Grantham.
Acreage 28 **Open** April **to** October
Access Good **Site** Level
Sites Available **Total** 330+
Facilities
Nearby Facilities
Nottingham
Next to the River Trent in 270 acres of parkland with a Nature Reserve. 100 pitches available on the Rally field.

KIRKLINGTON

Robin Hood View Caravan Park, Middle Plantation Farm, Belle Eau Park, Kirklington, Newark, Notts, NG22 8TY.
Std: 01623 **Tel:** 870361
Std: 01623 **Fax:** 870361
Nearest Town/Resort Southwell
Directions From the A614/A617 traffic island travel east for 1½ miles (Kirklington to Newark) and follow official road signs.
Acreage 5 **Open** All Year
Access Good **Site** Level
Sites Available **Total** 50
Facilities
Nearby Facilities
Newark/Mansfield
Set in beautiful rolling countryside away from the traffic. Ideal touring.

MANSFIELD

Sherwood Forest Caravan Park, Nr. Edwinstowe, Mansfield, Nottinghamshire, NG21 9HW.
Std: 0800 **Tel:** 146505
Std: 01623 **Fax:** 824637
Nearest Town/Resort Nottingham
Directions From the B6030 at Old Clipstone, take the turning on the sharp bend towards Warsop. The park entrance is ¾ mile on the left. On the A6075 between Mansfield and Edwinstowe take the turning to Old Clipstone.

Acreage 22 **Open** February **to** November
Access Good **Site** Level
Sites Available **Total** 180
Facilities
Nearby Facilities
Mansfield
Royal Oak at Nottingham, Legend of Robin Hood. Coarse fishing nearby and our own boating lake. Countryside walks in the surrounding area.

NEWARK

Milestone Caravan Park, North Road, Cromwell, Newark, Notts, NG23 6JE.
Std: 01636 **Tel:** 821244
Std: 01636 **Fax:** 822256
Nearest Town/Resort Newark
Directions A1 south take the signpost for Cromwell, site is ½ mile on the left. A1 north take the signpost for Cromwell Doll Museum, over the flyover and the site is on the left in 500 yards.
Acreage 4½ **Open** All Year
Access Good **Site** Level
Sites Available **Total** 60
Facilities
Nearby Facilities
Newark
✓✓✓✓Graded Park. Level, grass site at the side of a trout lake. Coarse fishing in the village. A short distance to Sherwood Forest.

NOTTINGHAM

Manor Farm, Thrumpton, Nottinghamshire, NG11 0AX.
Std: 0115 **Tel:** 983 0341
Std: 0115 **Fax:** 983 0341
Nearest Town/Resort Nottingham.
Directions From M1 junction 24, take the A453 Nottingham south, in 3 miles turn left. In 100 yds turn right. At next junction turn left, site immediately on right.
Acreage 3 **Open** All Year
Access Good **Site** Level
Sites Available **Total** 12
Facilities
Nearby Facilities
Nottingham.
Good walks, fishing in the village on River Trent. We charge a small extra fee for electric and awnings. We only have 1 flush2 toilets and 2 showers. We are able to cater for very large mobile homes as our gateways are so wide.

NOTTINGHAM

Thornton's Holt Camping Park, Stragglethorpe, Radcliffe-on-Trent, Notts, NG12 2JZ.
Std: 0115 **Tel:** 933 2125
Std: 0115 **Fax:** 933 3318
Nearest Town/Resort Nottingham.
Directions 3 miles east of Nottingham turn south of A52 towards Cropwell Bishop. Park is ¼ mile on left.
Acreage 15 **Open** All Year
Access Good **Site** Level
Sites Available **Total** 90
Facilities
Nearby Facilities
Radcliffe-on-Trent
✓✓✓Graded Park. Only 3 miles from Nottingham. Ideal base for touring Sherwood Forest and the Vale of Belvoir. Pub and restaurant nearby.

TUXFORD

Greenacres Touring Park, Lincoln Road, Tuxford, Newark, Nottinghamshire, NG22 0JW.
Std: 01777 **Tel:** 870264
Std: 01777 **Fax:** 872512
Nearest Town/Resort Retford.
Directions From A1 (north or south) follow signs. Park is on the left 250yds after Fountain Public House.
Acreage 4 **Open** March **to** October
Access Good **Site** Level
Sites Available **Total** 67
Facilities
Nearby Facilities
Retford.
✓✓✓Graded Park. Ideal for night halt or for touring Robin Hood country.

TUXFORD

Orchard Park, Marnham Road, Tuxford, Newark, Notts, NG22 0PY.
Std: 01777 **Tel:** 870228
Nearest Town/Resort Retford
Directions 1¼ miles south east of A1, off A6075 Lincoln Road, turn right in ¾ mile onto the Marnham Road - site on right in ¾ mile.
Acreage 5¼ **Open** March **to** October
Access Good **Site** Level
Sites Available **Total** 50
Facilities
Nearby Facilities
Retford
Peaceful location, ideal for Sherwood Forest and many attractions river fishing 3 miles.

WORKSOP

Riverside Caravan Park, Worksop Cricket Club, Central Avenue, Worksop, Notts, S80 1ER.
Std: 01909 **Tel:** 474118
Nearest Town/Resort Worksop.
Directions At the roundabout on the junction with the A57/A60 Mansfield, follow international site signs towards the town centre.
Acreage 4¼ **Open** All Year
Access Good **Site** Level
Sites Available **Total** 45
Facilities
Nearby Facilities
Worksop.
✓✓✓✓Graded Park. Ideal for touring Notts, Derbys and South Yorks areas. Few miles to the M1 and A1 roads.

OXFORDSHIRE

BANBURY

Barnstones Caravan Site, Barnstones, Main Street, Great Bourton, Nr Banbury, Oxon.
Std: 01295 **Tel:** 750289
Nearest Town/Resort Banbury
Directions Leave Banbury on the A423 to Southam, in 3 miles turn right signposted Great Bourton. Site entrance is 100yds on the right.
Acreage 3 **Open** All Year
Access Good **Site** Level
Sites Available **Total** 50
Facilities
Nearby Facilities
Banbury
Cotswolds, Oxford, Stratford-upon-Avon and Warwick Castle. 40 pitches are hard standing with a grass area for awnings.

BANBURY

Bo Peep Farm Caravan Park, Aynho Road, Adderbury, Near Banbury, Oxon, OX17 3NP.
Std: 01295 **Tel:** 810605
Std: 01295 **Fax:** 810605
Nearest Town/Resort Banbury
Directions Take the A4260 south from Banbury for 3 miles. At Adderbury turn left onto the B4100 towards Aynho, site is ½ mile on the right.
Acreage 7 **Open** March **to** November
Access Good **Site** Level
Sites Available **Total** 88
Facilities
Nearby Facilities
Banbury
Graded Park. Quiet, elegant and restful park with a ½ mile driveway. Farm walks over 70 acres including woods and riverside. Central for Oxford, Stratford, Blenheim, Warwick, etc..

BLETCHINGDON

Diamond Farm Caravan & Camping Park, Islip Road, Bletchington, Oxford, Oxon, OX5 3DR.
Std: 01869 **Tel:** 350909
Std: 01869 **Fax:** 350918
Nearest Town/Resort Oxford
Directions A34 from Oxford towards the M40. After 4 miles turn left onto B4027, site is 1 mile on the left.
Acreage 3½ **Open** All Year
Access Good **Site** Level
Sites Available **Total** 37
Facilities
Nearby Facilities
Islip
Ideal centre for Oxford, Blenheim Palace and the Cotswolds.

CHIPPING NORTON

Camping & Caravanning Club Site, Chipping Norton Road, Chadlington, Chipping Norton, Oxon, OX7 3PE.
Std: 01608 **Tel:** 641993
Directions Take the A44 or the A361 to Chipping Norton. Pick up the A361 Burford road, turn left at the crossroads and the site is 150 yards. From Burford stay on the A361 and turn right at the sign for Chadlington.
Open 22 March **to** 1 Nov
Site Lev/Slope
Sites Available **Total** 75
Facilities
Nearby Facilities
Graded Park. Perfect for exploring the Cotswolds. 11 miles from Blenheim Palace.

CHIPPING NORTON

Churchill Heath Caravan Park, Kingham, Chipping Norton, Oxon, OX7 6UJ.
Std: 01608 **Tel:** 658317
Std: 01608 **Fax:** 659231
Nearest Town/Resort Chipping Norton.
Directions 6 miles from Stow-on-the-Wold, 4 miles from Chipping Norton on the B4450.
Acreage 6 **Open** All Year
Access Good **Site** Level
Sites Available **Total** 50
Facilities
Nearby Facilities
Kingham
Bourton-on-the-Water, ideal touring. In the centre of the Cotswolds.

HENLEY-ON-THAMES

Swiss Farm International Camping, Marlow Road, Henley-on-Thames, Oxfordshire, RG9 2HY.
Std: 01491 **Tel:** 573419
Std: 01491 **Fax:** 573419
Nearest Town/Resort Henley-on-Thames.
Directions ½ mile north of Henley on Marlow road A4155.
Acreage 14 **Open** March **to** October
Access Good **Site** Sloping
Sites Available **Total** 180
Facilities
Nearby Facilities
Henley.
Graded Park. Beautiful old bridge town famous for its Regatta. Fishing on site.

OXFORD

Cassington Mill Caravan Park, Eynsham Road, Cassington, Witney, Oxford, OX8 1DB.
Std: 01865 **Tel:** 881081
Std: 01865 **Fax:** 884167
Nearest Town/Resort Oxford
Directions A40 west of Oxford, 3 miles on left. A40 east, 1 mile from Eynsham on the right.
Acreage 4 **Open** April **to** October
Access Good **Site** Level
Sites Available **Total** 83
Facilities
Nearby Facilities
Oxford
✓✓✓Graded Park. River, close to Oxford and Blenheim Palace. Boating on site.

OXFORD

Oxford Camping International, 426 Abingdon Road, Oxford, Oxfordshire, OX1 4XN.
Std: 01865 **Tel:** 246551
Nearest Town/Resort Oxford.
Directions South side of Oxford take A4144 to City centre, 100yds (90 metres) on left to the rear of Touchwoods Outdoor Life Centre, signposted.
Acreage 5 **Open** All Year
Access Good **Site** Level
Sites Available **Total** 129
Facilities
Nearby Facilities
Oxford.
✓✓✓✓✓Graded Park. Historic city 1¼ miles, River Thames ½ mile, ideal touring centre.

WALLINGFORD

Bridge Villa International Camping & Caravan Park, Crowmarsh Gifford, Wallingford, Oxfordshire, OX10 8HB.
Std: 01491 **Tel:** 836860
Std: 01491 **Fax:** 839103
Nearest Town/Resort Wallingford
Directions A4130/500 metres.
Acreage 4 **Open** 1 February **to** 31 December
Access Good **Site** Level
Sites Available **Total** 111
Facilities
Nearby Facilities
Cholsey
Within 400 metres of River Thames.

WITNEY

Hardwick Parks, Downs Road, Standlake, Nr. Witney, Oxon, OX8 7PZ.
Std: 01865 **Tel:** 300501
Std: 01865 **Fax:** 300037
Nearest Town/Resort Witney.
Directions A415 Witney to Abingdon road, signposted 4 miles out of Witney on the main road.
Acreage 40 **Open** April **to** October
Access Good **Site** Level
Sites Available **Total** 250
Facilities
Nearby Facilities
Oxford.
✓✓✓Graded Park. On the edge of the Cotswolds. Ideal for all watersports, two lakes on park for fishing, sailing, boating, jet-skiing and water-skiing.

WITNEY

Lincoln Farm Park, High Street, Standlake, Nr Witney, Oxon, OX8 7RH.
Std: 01865 **Tel:** 300239
Nearest Town/Resort Witney.
Directions 5½ miles southeast Witney on the A415 to Abingdon.
Acreage 7¼ **Open** March **to** November
Access Good **Site** Level
Sites Available **Total** 87
Facilities
Nearby Facilities
Oxford.
✓✓✓✓✓Graded Park. Situated in the heart of classic Oxfordshire Village. Private leisure club with swimming pool, spa pool and sauna. Member of Best of British Caravan and Camping Parks. Advance booking recommended.

SHROPSHIRE

BISHOPS CASTLE

Cwnd House Farm, Wentnor, Bishops Castle, Shropshire.
Std: 01588 **Tel:** Linley 650237
Nearest Town/Resort Church Stretton.
Directions Cwnd House Farm is on Longden Pulverbatch road from Shrewsbury (13 miles) Bishops Castle is southwest. From Craven Arms take the A489 to Lydham Heath, turn right, site is about 1 mile past the Inn on the Green on the right.
Acreage 2 **Open** May **to** October
Access Good **Site** Level
Sites Available **Total** 10
Facilities
Nearby Facilities
Church Stretton.
Farm site with scenic views, Ideal touring centre.

BISHOPS CASTLE

Daisy Bank Caravan Park, Snead, Bishops Castle, Salop, SY15 6EB.
Std: 01588 **Tel:** 620471
Nearest Town/Resort Bishops Castle
Directions Situated on the A489, between Lydham and Church Stoke.
Acreage 4 **Open** February **to** November
Access Good **Site** Lev/Slope
Sites Available **Total** 40
Facilities
Nearby Facilities
✓✓✓✓✓Graded Park. Situated in the heart of the Camlad Valley, scenic views. Fenced off dog walk. Ideal touring and walking.

BISHOPS CASTLE

The Green Caravan Park, Wentnor, Bishops Castle, Shropshire, SY9 5EF.
Std: 01588 **Tel:** 650605
Nearest Town/Resort Bishops Castle.
Directions From A5 Shrewsbury, take the A488 south to the A489 (19 miles). At Lydham turn left onto the A489 for ¾ mile. Turn left at caravan signpost, park is 3 miles on the left.
Open Easter **to** October
Access Good **Site** Level
Sites Available **Total** 140
Facilities
Nearby Facilities
Craven Arms.
Picturesque, riverside site in an area of outstanding natural beauty. Superb walking in the countryside. Central for touring.

BRIDGNORTH

Stanmore Hall Touring Park, Stourbridge Road, Bridgnorth, Shropshire.
Std: 01746 **Tel:** 761761
Nearest Town/Resort Bridgnorth
Directions 1¼ miles from Bridgnorth on A458 to Stourbridge.
Acreage 6 **Open** All Year
Access Good **Site** Level
Sites Available **Total** 120
Facilities
Nearby Facilities
Wolverhampton
✓✓✓✓✓Graded Park. Sited around lake and amongst trees, ideal site for Severn Valley Railway and Iron Bridge museums. Motorcycles accepted but families only.

CHURCH STRETTON

Small Batch, Little Stretton, Church Stretton, Shropshire.
Std: 01694 **Tel:** 723358
Nearest Town/Resort Church Stretton.
Directions A49 south, 1¼ miles turn right onto the B4370. Take the second left, at T-Junction turn right up to site through stream.
Acreage 1½ **Open** Easter **to** End Sept
Access Good **Site** Level
Sites Available **Total** 40
Facilities
Nearby Facilities
Church Stretton
Scenic views and ideal touring.

CLUN

Bush Farm, Clunton, Craven Arms, Shropshire, SY7 0HU.
Std: 01588 **Tel:** 660330
Std: 01588 **Fax:** 660225
Nearest Town/Resort Clun/Bishops Castle/Ludlow
Directions From the A49 at Craven Arms turn west onto the B4368 signposted Clun, 7 miles into Clunton. Turn left at the Crown Inn, go over a small bridge and turn immediately left. Continue for 500 yards to Bush Farm at the end of the road.
Acreage 2½ **Open** Good Friday **to** 31 October
Access Good **Site** Level
Sites Available **Total** 55
Facilities
Nearby Facilities
Craven Arms
On the banks of the River Clun, very peaceful. NO games for children. Ideal base for walking and cycling.

CRAVEN ARMS

Kangaroo Inn, Aston-on-Clun, Nr. Craven Arms, Shropshire, SY7 8EW.
Std: 01588 **Tel:** 660263
Nearest Town/Resort Craven Arms
Directions Turn into the Clun Road off the A49 and we are 2½ miles on the left.
Open All Year
Access Good **Site** Level
Sites Available **Total** 18
Facilities
Nearby Facilities
Broome
In the heart of the beautiful Clun Valley, with local walks. Close to Historic Ludlow, Ironbridge and Shrewsbury - The perfect place to discover Shropshire.

CRAVEN ARMS

Kevindale, Broome, Craven Arms, Salop, SY7 0NT.
Std: 01588 **Tel:** 660326
Nearest Town/Resort Craven Arms
Directions From Craven Arms which is situated on the A49 Hereford to Shewsbury road, take the B4368 Clun/Bishops Castle road in 2 miles take B4367 Knighton road 1¼ miles turn right into Broome Village.
Acreage 2 **Open** All Year
Access Good **Site** Level
Sites Available **Total** 12
Facilities
Nearby Facilities
Broome
Scenic views, near village inn with good food, close to Mid Wales Border, ideal walking.

ELLESMERE

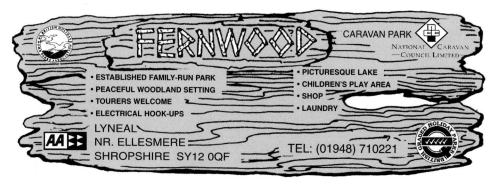

Fernwood Caravan Park, Lyneal, Nr. Ellesmere, Shropshire.
Std: 01948 **Tel:** 710221
Std: 01948 **Fax:** 710324
Nearest Town/Resort Ellesmere.
Directions A495 from Ellesmere signposted Whitchurch. In Welshampton, right turn on B5063 signed Wem. Over canal bridge right sign Lyneal.
Acreage 7 **Open** March **to** November
Access Good **Site** Lev/Slope
Sites Available **Total** 60
Facilities
Nearby Facilities
Wem.
✓✓✓✓✓Graded Park. 40 acres of woodland open to caravanners. Lake with wildfowl and coarse fishing.

KINNERLEY

Cranberry Moss Camping & Caravan Park, Kinnerley, Oswestry, Shropshire, SY10 8DY.
Std: 01743 **Tel:** 741444
Nearest Town/Resort Oswestry.
Directions 8 miles south east of Oswestry and 11 miles north west of Shrewsbury. Leave A5 for B4396, site 300yds on the left. Signposted on the A5.
Acreage 4 **Open** April **to** October
Access Good **Site** Level
Sites Available **Total** 60
Facilities
Nearby Facilities
Shrewsbury.
✓✓✓✓Graded Park. Ideal touring. Country park, walks.

LUDLOW

Westbrook Park, Little Hereford, Ludlow, Shropshire, SY8 4AU.
Std: 01584 **Tel:** 711280
Std: 01584 **Fax:** 711460
Nearest Town/Resort Ludlow
Directions 3 miles west of Tenbury Wells on the A456, enter the village of Little Hereford. Turn left after passing over River Teme bridge, travel 300yds and turn left onto the park.
Acreage 6 **Open** All Year
Access Good **Site** Level
Sites Available **Total** 38
Facilities
Nearby Facilities
Ludlow
In a pretty orchard on the banks of the River Teme, ½ mile of fishing. On well maintained quality park. Short walk to the local inn for good food.

MINSTERLEY

The Old School Caravan Park, The Old School, Shelve, Minsterley, Shrewsbury, Shropshire, SY5 0JQ.
Std: 01588 **Tel:** 650410
Nearest Town/Resort Shrewsbury
Directions On the A5 at Shrewsbury turn onto the A488 and travel south for 16 miles. We are on the left past the More Arms Pub. 6 miles north of Bishops Castle along the A488.
Acreage 1½ **Open** March **to** October
Access Good **Site** Level
Sites Available **Total** 12
Facilities
Nearby Facilities
Shrewsbury
✓✓✓✓Graded Park. A small, family run caravan park in the Shropshire hills. Within easy reach of of the legendary Stiper Stones and Longmynd. Good walking, biking and fishing nearby.

MUCH WENLOCK

Mill Farm Holiday Park, Hughley, Nr Shrewsbury, Shropshire.
Std: 01746 **Tel:** 785208/785255
Nearest Town/Resort Much Wenlock.
Directions Telford take the A4169 to Much Wenlock. Then take the A458 to Harley, turn left to Hughley. Follow Hughley and caravan signs to Hughley.
Acreage 15 **Open** March **to** October
Access Good **Site** Level
Sites Available **Total** 45
Facilities
Nearby Facilities
Church Stretton
Peaceful site alongside brook in an area of outstanding natural beauty. Fishing and riding. David Bellamy Gold Award.

NESSCLIFFE

Royal Hill Camping Site, Royal Hill, Edgerley, Kinnerley, Oswestry, Salop, SY10 8ES.
Std: 01743 **Tel:** 741242
Nearest Town/Resort Oswestry
Directions 3 miles from the A5 at Nesscliffe. Follow Pentre Melverley signs.
Acreage 2 **Open** April **to** October
Access Good **Site** Level
Sites Available **Total** 25
Facilities
Nearby Facilities
Licensed pub.

SHREWSBURY

Bridge Inn Campsite, Bridge Inn, Dorrington (A49), Shrewsbury, Shropshire.
Std: 01743 **Tel:** 718209
Nearest Town/Resort Shrewsbury.
Directions 5 miles south of Shrewsbury on the A49.
Acreage 2 **Open** All Year
Access Good **Site** Lev/Slope
Sites Available **Total** 24
Facilities
Nearby Facilities
Shrewsbury.
Scenic views, alongside brook.

SHREWSBURY

Cartref Caravan & Camping Site, Cartref, Fords Heath, Nr. Shrewsbury, Shropshire.
Std: 01743 **Tel:** 821688
Directions From Shrewsbury bypass A5 trunk road take the A458 Welshpool West. 2 miles to Ford Village, turn south at Ford, follow camp signs.
Acreage 1½ **Open** Easter **to** October
Access Good **Site** Level
Sites Available **Total** 25+
Facilities
Nearby Facilities
Shrewsbury.
Ideal touring, overnight stop. One holiday caravan for hire. Peaceful countryside.

SHREWSBURY

Oxon Touring Park, Welshpool Road, Bicton Heath, Shrewsbury, Shropshire, SY3 5FB.
Std: 01743 **Tel:** 340868
Nearest Town/Resort Shrewsbury
Directions 1¼ miles from the town centre on the A458, adjacent to Oxon Park and Ride.
Acreage 25 **Open** All Year
Access Good **Site** Level
Sites Available **Total** 130
Facilities
Nearby Facilities
Shrewsbury
✓✓✓✓✓ Graded Park. Well landscaped, level site adjoining local Park and Ride facilities, in a rural situation. Ideal for visiting Shrewsbury and the Welsh border counties. Motorcycles accepted, but families only.

TELFORD

Camping & Caravanning Club Site, Ring Bank, Haughton, Telford, Shropshire, TF6 6BU.
Std: 01743 **Tel:** 709334
Nearest Town/Resort Shrewsbury
Directions 2½ miles through Shawbury on the A53, turn left signed Haughton/U. Magna. Site is on the right in 1½ miles.
Acreage 18 **Open** 22 March **to** 1 Nov
Access Good **Site** Lev/Slope
Sites Available **Total** 160
Facilities
Nearby Facilities
Shrewsbury
✓✓✓✓ Graded Park. Set on an ancient Iron Age hill fort, with panoramic views. Close to Shrewsbury and Ironbridge Gorge.

TELFORD

Severn Gorge Caravan Park, Bridgnorth Road, Tweedale, Telford, Shropshire, TF7 4JB.
Std: 01952 **Tel:** 684789
Std: 01952 **Fax:** 684789
Nearest Town/Resort Telford
Directions From the M54 junction 4, follow signs (A442) for Kidderminster for 1 mile. Then take the A442 signposted Kidderminster to the first roundabout Brockton roundabout 4 miles. Follow brown Severn Gorge caravan Park signposts, 1 mile to the site.
Acreage 16 **Open** All Year
Access Good **Site** Level
Sites Available **Total** 170
Facilities
Nearby Facilities
Telford
✓✓✓✓ Graded Park. Ironbridge, Gorge and museums.

WEM

Lower Lacon Caravan Park, Wem, Shropshire, SY4 5RP.
Std: 01939 **Tel:** 232376
Std: 01939 **Fax:** 233606
Nearest Town/Resort Wem
Directions 1 mile from Wem on the B5065. From the A49 then the B5065, 3 miles.
Acreage 48 **Open** All Year
Access Good **Site** Level
Sites Available **Total** 270
Facilities
Nearby Facilities
Wem
✓✓✓ Graded Park.

WHITCHURCH

Green Lane Farm Caravan & Camping Site, Green Lane Farm, Prees, Whitchurch, Shropshire, SY13 2AH.
Std: 01948 **Tel:** 840460
Nearest Town/Resort Whitchurch.
Directions 4¼ miles south south east of Whitchurch. Turn right off the A41 (Whitchurch to Newport) onto the A442 signposted Telford. In 150yds turn right at the crossroads (signposted Prees).
Acreage 3 **Open** March **to** October
Access Good **Site** Level
Sites Available **Total** 20
Facilities
Nearby Facilities
Prees
Unspoilt North Shropshire, close to Hawkstone Park Follies and Golf Course.

WHITCHURCH

Roden View Caravan & Camping, Roden View, Dobsons Bridge, Whixall, Whitchurch, Shropshire, SY13 2QL.
Std: 01948 **Tel:** 710320
Nearest Town/Resort Wem
Directions From Shrewsbury Wem Church turn left after second garage, then turn right for Northwood Mill, at the next T-Junction turn left then right, 2½ miles to the next T-Junction turn left. ½ mile the house is on the right before Dobsons Bridge.
Acreage 4½ **Open** March **to** October
Access Good **Site** Level
Sites Available **Total** 5
Facilities
Nearby Facilities
Wem
Near to the Shropshire Onion, Canal Whikall Moss. 5 miles from Ellesmere, Shropshire's Lake District. There is a washing machine available for use.

SOMERSET

BATH

Bath Marina & Caravan Park, Brassmill Lane, Bath, Somerset, BA1 3JT.
Std: 01225 **Tel:** 428778
Std: 01225 **Fax:** 428778
Nearest Town/Resort Bath
Directions 2 miles west of Bath on the A4 at Newbridge, turn left at the Murco garage into Brassmill Lane, take the first turning on the right.
Acreage 4 **Open** All Year
Access Good **Site** Level
Sites Available **Total** 88
Facilities
Nearby Facilities
Bath
✓✓✓✓✓Graded Park. Alongside a river, picturesque. 3 min walk from park and ride bus.

BATH

Bury View, Corston Fields, Bath, Somerset, BA2 9HD.
Std: 01225. **Tel:** 873672
Nearest Town/Resort Bath.
Directions 5 miles from Bath, situated on A39 Wells road.
Acreage 1¼ **Open** All Year
Access Good **Site** Level
Sites Available **Total** 15
Facilities
Nearby Facilities
Bath
Quiet countryside site, close to Bath.

BREAN SANDS

Holiday Resort Unity at Unity Farm, Coast Road, Brean Sands, Somerset.
Std: 01278 **Tel:** 751235
Std: 01278 **Fax:** 751539
Nearest Town/Resort Burnham-on-Sea.
Directions Leave M5 at junction 22. Follow signs for Berrow and Brean, site on right 4½ miles from M5.
Acreage 150 **Open** Easter **to** October
Access Good **Site** Level
Sites Available **Total** 600
Facilities
Nearby Facilities
Weston-super-Mare.
✓✓✓✓Graded Park. 200yds from 7 mile beach, own leisure centre with 30 fun fair attractions, pool complex with 3 giant water slides, 18 hole golf course, lake for fishing, horse riding and 10 Pin Bowling. Family entertainment - end of May to end of Sept. Special offers for young families and OAPs in June and Sept.

BREAN SANDS

Northam Farm Caravan & Touring Park, Brean, Nr. Burnham-on-Sea, Somerset.
Std: 01278 **Tel:** 751244/751222
Std: 01278 **Fax:** 751150
Nearest Town/Resort Burnham-on-Sea.
Directions M5 Junction 22. Follow signs to Brean, ¼ mile past Leisure Park on righthand side.
Acreage 20 **Open** Easter **to** October
Access Good **Site** Level
Sites Available **Total** 350
Facilities
Nearby Facilities
Weston-super-Mare.
✓✓✓✓Graded Park. Ideal base for seeing Somerset. 200 metres to safe sandy beach. Family entertainment within easy walking distance. Excellent facilities, fishing lake on park. Take-away food. Indoor and outdoor swimming pools nearby. Seagull Inn nearby. AA 3 Pennants.

BREAN SANDS

Warren Farm Touring Park, Brean Sands, Burnham-on-Sea, Somerset, TA8 2RP.
Std: 01278 **Tel:** 751227
Std: 01278 **Fax:** 751033
Nearest Town/Resort Burnham-on-Sea.
Directions Leave M5 at junction 22, follow signs to Burnham-on-Sea, Berrow and Brean on the B3140. Site is 1¼ miles past the leisure centre.
Acreage 50 **Open** April **to** Mid October
Access Good **Site** Level
Sites Available **Total** 500
Facilities
Nearby Facilities
Weston-super-Mare.
✓✓✓✓Graded Park. Flat, grassy, family park with excellent facilities. 100 metres from 5 miles of sandy beach.

BRIDGWATER

Mill Farm Caravan & Camping Park, Fiddington, Bridgwater, Somerset, TA5 1JQ.
Std: 01278 **Tel:** 732286
Std: 01278 **Fax:** 732286
Nearest Town/Resort Bridgwater.
Directions Leave the M5 at junction 23 or 24, through Bridgwater, take the A39 west for 6 miles. Turn right to Fiddington, then follow camping signs.
Acreage 12 **Open** All Year
Access Good **Site** Level
Sites Available **Total** 250
Facilities
Nearby Facilities
Bridgwater.
✓✓✓✓Graded Park. Free boating, canoe and trampoline hire on site. Walking, riding and fishing. Quantock Hills 2 miles. Beach 4 miles. Exmoor, Cheddar Gorge, Wookey Caves within easy reach. Tourist Information Room. Free swimming and paddling pools and luxury indoor heated pools. Children's pony rides on site. Off licence, licensed club in peak season, large sandpit, Splash Pool. Free hot showers and 3 new toilet blocks. Holiday cottage to let.

BRIDGWATER

The Fairways International Touring Caravan & Camping Park, Bath Road, Bawdrip, Bridgwater, Somerset, TA7 8PP.
Std: 01278 **Tel:** 685569
Std: 01278 **Fax:** 685569
Nearest Town/Resort Bridgwater
Directions 3¾ miles on Glastonbury side of Bridgwater. 1½ miles off M5 junction 23 at junction A39 and B3141.
Acreage 5¾ **Open** 1st March **to** 15th Nov
Access Good **Site** Level
Sites Available **Total** 200

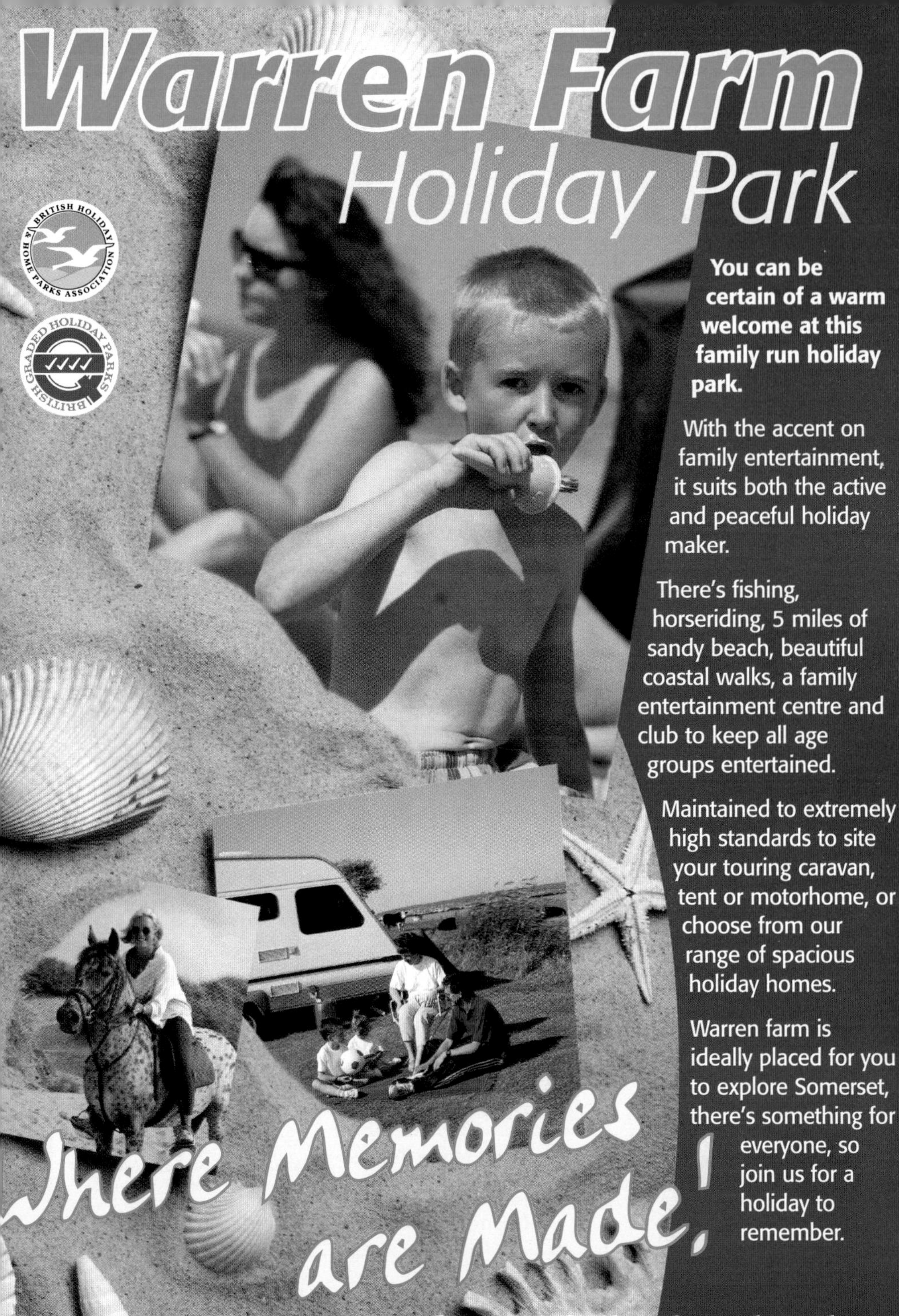
Warren Farm
Holiday Park
BRITISH HOLIDAY & HOME PARKS ASSOCIATION
BRITISH GRADED HOLIDAY PARKS
You can be certain of a warm welcome at this family run holiday park.
With the accent on family entertainment, it suits both the active and peaceful holiday maker.
There's fishing, horseriding, 5 miles of sandy beach, beautiful coastal walks, a family entertainment centre and club to keep all age groups entertained.
Maintained to extremely high standards to site your touring caravan, tent or motorhome, or choose from our range of spacious holiday homes.
Warren farm is ideally placed for you to explore Somerset, there's something for everyone, so join us for a holiday to remember.
Where Memories are Made!
Telephone 01278 751227 for our full colour brochure
Brean Sands, Nr Burnham-on-Sea, Somerset TA8 2RP

Facilities
Nearby Facilities
Bridgwater
✓✓✓✓Graded Park. Ideal for touring Somerset. Off Licence. Winner of "Loo of the Year Award" 1994, 1995, 1996 & 1997.

BRUTON

Batcombe Vale Caravan & Camping Park, Batcombe, Shepton Mallet, Somerset, BA4 6BW.
Std: 01749 **Tel:** 830246
Nearest Town/Resort Bruton
Directions Access must be off the B3081 between Bruton and Evercreech from where it is well signed.
Acreage 7 **Open** May **to** September
Access Good **Site** Level
Sites Available **Total** 32
Facilities
Nearby Facilities
Bruton
Own secluded valley of lakes and wild gardens. Near Longleat, Stourhead and Glastonbury. Fishing and boats.

BURNHAM-ON-SEA

Burnham Touring Park, B.A.S.C. Sportsground, Stoddens Road, Burnham-on-Sea, Somerset, TA8 1NZ.
Std: 01278 **Tel:** 751235
Std: 01278 **Fax:** 751539
Nearest Town/Resort Burnham-on-Sea
Directions Leave the M5 at junction 22 Burnham-on-Sea, at roundabout by Tescos turn right and park is on the right ¾ mile, entrance over the cattle grid. Park Managed by Holiday Resort Unity (telephone as above).
Acreage 23 **Open** All Year
Access Good **Site** Level
Sites Available **Total** 40
Facilities
Nearby Facilities
Highbridge
Quiet park with good views. 1 mile from the town centre and beach. Suits the self contained caravanner. Warden on site May to October. Swimming pool 1 mile.

BURNHAM-ON-SEA

Burnham-on-Sea Holiday Village, Marine Drive, Burnham-on-Sea, Somerset, TA8 1LA.
Std: 01278 **Tel:** 783391
Std: 01278 **Fax:** 793776
Nearest Town/Resort Burnham-on-Sea
Directions Leave the M5 at junction 22, turn left at the roundabout onto the A38 to Highbridge. Continue over the mini roundabout and railway bridge, turn next left onto the B3139 to Burnham-on-Sea. Turn left at the Elf Garage into Marine Drive and the park is 400 yards on the left.
Acreage 95 **Open** March **to** November
Access Good **Site** Level
Sites Available **Total** 75
Facilities
Nearby Facilities
Highbridge
✓✓✓✓Graded Park. Near the beach. Fishing, golf and tennis on park. Cafe bar and two entertainment venues.

BURNHAM-ON-SEA

Diamond Farm Caravan & Touring Park, Diamond Farm, Weston Road, Brean, Nr Burnham-on-Sea, Somerset.
Std: 01278 **Tel:** 751263
Nearest Town/Resort Burnham-on-Sea
Directions M5 junction 22, follow signs to Brean, ½ mile past leisure park turn right to Lympsham/Weston-super-Mare. Diamond Farm is 800yds on the left hand side.
Acreage 6 **Open** April **to** 15 October
Access Good **Site** Level
Sites Available **Total** 100
Facilities
Nearby Facilities
Weston-super-Mare
✓✓✓✓Graded Park. A quiet, family site alongside River Axe and only 800yds from the beach. River fishing available on site.

BURNHAM-ON-SEA

Home Farm Holiday Park & Country Club, Edithmead, Burnham-on-Sea, Somerset, TA9 4HD.
Std: 01278 **Tel:** 788888
Std: 01278 **Fax:** 780113
Nearest Town/Resort Burnham-on-Sea
Directions Home Farm is situated just ¼ of a mile from the M5 junction 22 and the A38. Signposted from the B3140 into Burnham-on-Sea.
Acreage 44 **Open** All Year
Access Good **Site** Level
Sites Available **Total** 800
Facilities
Nearby Facilities
Highbridge
✓✓✓✓Graded Park. Outdoor heated swimming pool and fishing lakes on site. Near the beach.

BURNHAM-ON-SEA

Southfield Farm Caravan Park, Brean, Nr. Burnham-on-Sea, Somerset TA8 2RL.
Std: 01278 **Tel:** 751233
Nearest Town/Resort Burnham-on-Sea.
Directions 4 miles north along coast road from Burnham-on-Sea (well signposted). Site is in Brean village.
Acreage 10 **Open** Spring Bank Holiday **to** September
Access Good **Site** Level
Sites Available
Facilities
Nearby Facilities
Weston-super-Mare.
Adjacent beach, good centre for touring Somerset. Local entertainments nearby.

CHARD

"The Beeches", Catchgate Lane, Wambrook, Chard, Somerset, TA20 3PS.
Nearest Town/Resort Chard
Directions 1 mile from Chard on the A30 turn right Form, pass bungalow on the left go up the lane 500 yards, name is on the gate on the right.
Acreage 5 **Open** All Year
Access Good **Site** Level
Sites Available **Total** 5
Facilities
Nearby Facilities
Axminster/Crewkerne
Unspoilt countryside with lovely walks. Ideal touring. Good food at the pubs in Wambrook, Combe, St Nichols and Wadeford. 30 minute drive to Seaton, Beer, Lyme Regis etc..

CHARD

Alpine Grove Touring Park, Forton, Chard, Somerset, TA20 4HD.
Std: 01460 **Tel:** 63479
Nearest Town/Resort Chard.
Directions Turn left off the A30 Crewkerne to Chard road onto the B3167 (Axminster). In 1½ miles at the crossroads turn right onto the B3162 signposted Forton. Site is on the right in about ½ mile.
Acreage 7½ **Open** Easter **to** End September
Access Good **Site** Level
Sites Available **Total** 40
Facilities
Nearby Facilities
Axminster
✓✓✓✓Graded Park. Pretty woodland site, set amongst oak trees and Rhododendrons. Superb point from which to travel the South and South West coast. Numerous places of interest to visit nearby, only 2 miles from Cricket St Thomas Wildlife Park. Shingle and sandy beach 11 miles. All weather pitches.

CHARD

South Somerset Holiday Park, The Turnpike, Howley, Chard, Somerset, TA20 3EA.
Std: 01460 **Tel:** 62221/66036
Std: 01460 **Fax:** 66246
Nearest Town/Resort Chard
Directions 3 miles west of Chard on the A30.
Acreage 7 **Open** All Year
Access Good **Site** Level
Sites Available **Total** 110
Facilities
Nearby Facilities
Crewkerne
Scenic views and ideal touring. AA 4 Pennants.

CHEDDAR

Broadway House Holiday, Touring Caravan & Camping Park, Cheddar, Somerset.
Std: 01934 **Tel:** 742610
Std: 01934 **Fax:** 744950
Nearest Town/Resort Cheddar Gorge.
Directions Exit 22 (M5) 8 miles. Follow brown tourist signs for Cheddar Gorge. We are midway between Cheddar and Axbridge on the A371.
Acreage 25 **Open** March **to** November
Access Good **Site** Level
Sites Available **Total** 400
Facilities
Nearby Facilities
Weston-super-Mare.
✓✓✓✓✓Graded Park. Centrally situated in wonderful touring area, i.e. Wells, Bristol and Weston-super-Mare.

CHEDDAR

Bucklegrove Caravan & Camping Park, Rodney Stoke, Cheddar, Somerset, BS27 3UZ.
Std: 01749 **Tel:** 870261
Std: 01749 **Fax:** 870101
Nearest Town/Resort Wells/Cheddar
Directions Midway Between Wells and Cheddar on the A371.
Open March **to** November
Access Good **Site** Lev/Slope
Sites Available **Total** 125
Facilities
Nearby Facilities
Weston Super Mare
✓✓✓✓✓Graded Park. Ideal touring centre on the south side of the Mendip Hills with scenic views and walking.

CHEDDAR

Froglands Farm Caravan & Camping Park, Froglands Farm, Cheddar, Somerset.
Std: 01934 **Tel:** 742058
Nearest Town/Resort Cheddar/Weston-super-Mare
Directions On main A371, 150yds past village church.
Acreage 4 **Open** Easter **to** October
Access Good **Site** Level
Sites Available **Total** 68
Facilities
Nearby Facilities
Weston-super-Mare
Walking distance, village shops, pubs, Gorge and Caves. AA 3 Pennants.

CHEDDAR

Longbottom Farm, Shipham, Winscombe, Somerset, BS25 1RW.
Std: 01934 **Tel:** 743166
Nearest Town/Resort Cheddar
Directions Take the A38 to Shipham on the Cheddar road take Charterhouse Road, 1 mile on the left hand side.
Acreage 3 **Open** All Year
Access Good **Site** Level
Sites Available **Total** 16
Facilities
Nearby Facilities
Yatton
Open space, Black Down.

CHEDDAR

Splott Farm, Blackford, Near Wedmore, Somerset, BS28 4PD.
Std: 01278 **Tel:** 641522
Nearest Town/Resort Burnham-on-Sea/Cheddar
Directions Leave M5 at junction 22, 2 miles to Highbridge, take B3139 Highbridge/Wells road, about 5 miles.
Acreage 4¼ **Open** March **to** September
Access Good **Site** Gentle Slope
Sites Available **Total** 20
Facilities
Nearby Facilities
Highbridge
Views of Mendip Hills (and Quantocks), very peaceful site, ideal touring. Weston-super-Mare, Wells, Cheddar, Burnham-on-Sea, Wookey. Very rural area.

CLEVEDON

Warrens Holiday Park, Colehouse Lane, Clevedon, Somerset, BS21 6TQ.
Std: 01275 **Tel:** 871666
Nearest Town/Resort Weston-super-Mare.
Directions M5 junction 20, follow road towards Congresbury for 1 mile.
Acreage 8 **Open** March **to** January
Access Good **Site** Level
Sites Available **Total** 100
Facilities
Nearby Facilities
Yatton
Fishing.

CONGRESBURY

Oak Farm Touring Park, Weston Road, Congresbury, Somerset, BS49 5EB.
Std: 01934 **Tel:** 833246
Nearest Town/Resort Weston-super-Mare
Directions 4 miles from junc. 21 on M5, on the A370 midway between Bristol and Weston Super Mare.
Open 31st Mar **to** October
Access Good **Site** Level
Sites Available **Total** 27
Facilities
Nearby Facilities
Yatton

CROWCOMBE

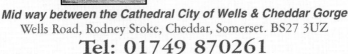

Quantock Orchard Caravan Park, Crowcombe, Nr. Taunton, Somerset, TA4 4AW.
Std: 01984 **Tel:** 618618
Std: 01984 **Fax:** 618618
Nearest Town/Resort Minehead
Directions Just off the A358 Taunton to Minehead road, towards Crowcombe Steam Railway Station. 10 miles from the M5 junction 25 Taunton.
Acreage 3½ **Open** All Year
Access Good **Site** Level
Sites Available **Total** 75
Facilities
Nearby Facilities
Taunton
✓✓✓✓✓Graded Park. Located in a designated area of outstanding natural beauty in the Quantock Hills. Close to Exmoor and the coast.

DULVERTON

Lakeside Touring Caravan Park, Higher Grants, Exbridge, Dulverton, Somerset, TA22 9BE.
Std: 01398 **Tel:** 324068
Nearest Town/Resort Dulverton
Directions Leave the M5 junction 27. Take the A361 towards Barnstaple, turn right onto A396 at first roundabout. Turn left at the next roundabout, straight on at the Black Cat and stay on the A396. Park is 3 miles on the left hand side.

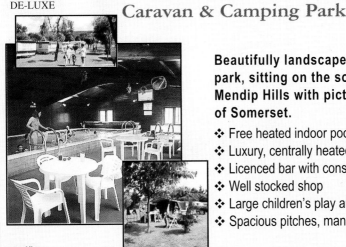

Quantock Orchard Caravan Park

The small, clean and friendly park for Touring Caravans & Camping in the beautiful Quantock Hills.

Situated at the foot of the glorious Quantock Hills, this small, quiet, family-run park is close to Exmoor and the coast in the perfect location for touring Somerset and North Devon. Our full facilities include: Immaculate timber and tiled washing facilities with free showers (AA award for excellence winners 97/98) - Large en-suite bathroom - Full laundry facilities - Mother and baby room - Dish washing room with microwave (free use) - Beautiful heated swimming pool - Good children's play area - Games room / TV room with Sky TV - Level individual pitches, most with hook-ups, some hardstanding - Tastefully landscaped, plenty of flowers - Level tent paddock - Mountain bike hire. Quality without quantity in a designed area of outstanding natural beauty. Dogs welcome on leads. Riding, Fishing, Steam Railway, Good Pub Food - all nearby.

AA De-Luxe

Open all year

Send for colour brochure and price guide to:

Mr & Mrs E. C. Biggs, QUANTOCK ORCHARD CARAVAN PARK, Crowcombe, Taunton, Somerset TA4 4AW Tel: (01984) 618618

Acreage 4 **Open** 1 March **to** 31 October
Access Good **Site** Lev/Slope
Sites Available **Total** 50
Facilities
Nearby Facilities
✓✓✓✓Graded Park. Lovely views, ideal for touring Exmoor. Dog walking field.

EAST BRENT

Dulhorn Farm Holiday Park, Weston Road, Lympsham, Weston-super-Mare, North Somerset, BS24 0JQ.
Std: 01934 **Tel:** 750298
Std: 01934 **Fax:** 750913
Directions From Weston-super-Mare take the A370 Bridgwater road. Site is on the right approx 4½ miles. From the M5 junction 22 take the A38 for Bristol, at the second island bear left, A370 Weston-super-Mare, site is on the left.
Acreage 1½ **Open** March **to** October
Access Good **Site** Level
Sites Available **Total** 45
Facilities
Nearby Facilities
Weston-super-Mare
✓✓✓Graded Park.

EXFORD

Downscombe Farm Campsite, Downscombe Farm, Exford, Nr. Minehead, Somerset, TA24 7NP.
Std: 01643 **Tel:** 831239
Std: 01458 **Fax:** 833618
Nearest Town/Resort Porlock
Directions 1 mile from Exford. Take the Porlock road, after ½ mile fork left, after ½ mile campsite is on the left.
Acreage 10 **Open** April **to** October
Access Good **Site** Level
Sites Available **Total** 60
Facilities
Nearby Facilities
Taunton
Very peaceful site beside the River Exe. Level meadows with wooded hills either side

EXFORD

Westermill Farm, Exford, Minehead, Somerset, TA24 7NJ.
Std: 01643 **Tel:** 831238
Std: 01643 **Fax:** 831660
Nearest Town/Resort Exford.
Directions Leave Exford on Porlock Road. After ½ mile fork left. Continue for 2 miles past another campsite until "Westermill" seen on tree, fork left.
Acreage 6 **Open** All Year
Access Poor **Site** Level
Sites Available **Total** 60
Facilities
Nearby Facilities
Taunton
✓✓✓Graded Park. Beautiful, secluded site beside a river for fishing. Fascinating 500 acre farm with Waymarked walks. Centre Exmoor National Park. Log cottages and farmhouse cottage for hire. Holder of the Gold David Bellamy Award for Conservation. Free hot showers.

GLASTONBURY

The Old Oaks Touring Park, Wick Farm, Wick, Glastonbury, Somerset, BA6 8JS.
Std: 01458 **Tel:** 831437
Nearest Town/Resort Glastonbury
Directions From Glastonbury take the A361 Shepton Mallet road. In 2 miles turn left signposted Wick 1, site is on the left in 1 mile.
Acreage 2½ **Open** March **to** October
Access Good **Site** Lev/Slope
Sites Available **Total** 40
Facilities
Nearby Facilities
Castle Cary
✓✓✓✓✓Graded Park. A family run park offering excellent centrally heated facilities in an outstanding environment.

HIGHBRIDGE

Greenacre Place Touring Caravan Park, Bristol Road, Edithmead, Highbridge, Somerset, TA9 4HA.
Std: 01278 **Tel:** 785227
Nearest Town/Resort Burnham-on-Sea
Acreage 1 **Open** March **to** November
Access Good **Site** Level
Sites Available **Total** 10
Facilities
Nearby Facilities
Highbridge
✓✓✓Graded Park. Small, peaceful caravan park with easy access. Short drive to sandy beaches. Ideally placed for touring Somerset.

ILMINSTER

Thornleigh Caravan Park, Hanning Road, Horton, Ilminster, Somerset, TA19 9QH.
Std: 01460 **Tel:** 53450
Std: 01460 **Fax:** 53450
Nearest Town/Resort Ilminster
Directions A303 West Ilminster, take the A358 signposted Chard. ¼ mile turn right signposted Horton and Broadway. Site on the left opposite the filling station, ¾ mile.
Acreage 1¼ **Open** March **to** October
Access Good **Site** Level
Sites Available **Total** 20
Facilities
Nearby Facilities
Crewkerne
Flat site in a village location, ideal for touring Somerset and Devon. Sauna and solarium on site. 6 miles to Cricket St Thomas Wildlife Park. National Trust properties nearby. New shower block for 1997. Holiday chalet also to let.

LANGPORT

Thorney Lakes Caravan Site, Thorney Farm, Muchelney, Langport, Somerset, TA10 0DW.
Std: 01458 **Tel:** 250811
Nearest Town/Resort Langport
Directions Turn off the A303 dual carriageway signposted Martock, Ash and Kingsbury Episcopi. Follow signs to Kingsbury Episcopi, at the T-Junction in the village turn right, site is 1 mile on the right.
Acreage 7 **Open** March **to** November
Access Good **Site** Level
Sites Available **Total** 14
Facilities
Nearby Facilities
Yeovil/Taunton

Beautiful secluded site for tents and dormobiles beside the upper reaches of the River Exe, in the centre of Exmoor National Park.
Four way marked walks over 500 acre working farm.
2½ miles of shallow river for fishing and bathing.
Information Centre and small Shop.
Farm holiday cottages for hire, one to 4 key commended. Free hot showers and hot water with dishwashing and laundry. A site and farm to enjoy in the most natural way.
Pets welcome - childrens paradise.

Phone or write for a free colour brochure:

Mrs. K. Edwards, Westermill Farm, Exford, Nr. Minehead, Somerset. TA24 7NJ.

Telephone: (01643) 831238 Fax: (01643) 831660

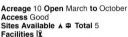

✓✓✓Graded Park. Site is an orchard on Somerset Moors. Ideal for walking and cycling. Fishing on site.

MARTOCK

Southfork Caravan Park, Parrett Works, Martock, Somerset, TA12 6AE.
Std: 01935 **Tel:** 825661
Std: 01935 **Fax:** 825122
Nearest Town/Resort Martock/Yeovil.
Directions Situated 2 miles north west of A303 (between Ilchester and Ilminster). From A303 east of Ilminster, at roundabout take first exit signposted South Petherton and follow camping signs. From A303 west of Ilchester, after Cartgate roundabout (junction with A3088 to Yeovil) take exit signposted Martock and follow camping signs.
Acreage 2 **Open** All Year
Access Good **Site** Level
Sites Available ⋏ ⊕ ⊖ **Total** 30
Facilities
Nearby Facilities
⇌ Yeovil
✓✓✓✓Graded Park. Set in open countryside near River Parrett. Numerous places of interest nearby for all age groups. Ideal base for touring. 3 static caravans for hire.

MINEHEAD

Blagdon Farm, Wheddon Cross, Minehead, Somerset, TA24 7ED.
Std: 01643 **Tel:** 841280
Nearest Town/Resort Minehead.
Directions From Taunton take the A358 Minehead road then the B3224 signposted Raleghs Cross. At Wheddon Cross take the Exford road for ¾ miles, farm is 100 yards on Drapers Way.
Acreage 10 **Open** March **to** October
Access Good
Sites Available ⋏ ⊕ **Total** 5
Facilities
Nearby Facilities
⇌ Taunton
Quiet, rural site with outstanding views of the moor. 1 mile from Dunkery and 8 miles from Minehead.

MINEHEAD

Blue Anchor Park, Blue Anchor, Nr. Minehead, Somerset, TA24 6JT.
Std: 01643 **Tel:** 821360
Nearest Town/Resort Minehead
Directions From A39 at Williton, travel west for 4 miles to Carhampton and turn right onto B3191 signposted Blue Anchor. Park is 1¼ miles on right.
Acreage 29 **Open** March **to** October
Access Good **Site** Level
Sites Available ⊕ ⊖ **Total** 103
Facilities
Nearby Facilities
⇌ Minehead
✓✓✓✓✓Graded Park. On waters edge, an ideal base from which to explore Exmoor and this beautiful coastline.

MINEHEAD

Camping & Caravanning Club Site, North Hill, Minehead, Somerset, TA24 5SF.
Std: 01643 **Tel:** 704138
Nearest Town/Resort Minehead
Directions From the town centre go towards the sea front, turn left into Blenheim Road, left into Martlett Road, left around the War Memorial into St Michaels Road. Go past the church into Moor Road and the site is on the right.
Acreage 3¾ **Open** 22 March **to** 27 Sept
Site Sloping
Sites Available ⋏ ⊖ **Total** 60
Facilities
Nearby Facilities
⇌ Minehead
✓✓✓✓Graded Park. Views over Blue Anchor Bay, good for walking. West Somerset Steam Railway, Exmoor, Carriage Driving Championships and a Cycling Festival. NO caravans allowed.

MINEHEAD

Minehead & Exmoor Caravan Park, Porlock Road, Minehead, Somerset, TA24 8SN.
Std: 01643 **Tel:** 703074
Nearest Town/Resort Minehead.
Directions 1 mile west of Minehead, official signposts on the A39.
Acreage 3 **Open** 1 March **to** 22 October
Access Good **Site** Level
Sites Available ⋏ ⊕ ⊖ **Total** 50
Facilities
Nearby Facilities
⇌ Minehead.
1 mile from the centre of Minehead, near the beach and all local attractions.

MINEHEAD

Totterdown Farm Camp Site, Mr & Mrs B.T. Halse, Totterdown Farm, Timberscombe, Minehead, Somerset, TA24 7TA.
Std: 01643 **Tel:** 841317
Nearest Town/Resort Minehead.
Directions Take the A396 Tiverton Road from Dunster for 2 miles. Farm in layby on the left before Timberscombe Village.

Acreage 8 **Open** Mid July **to** Mid Sept
Access Good **Site** Level
Sites Available **Total** 15
Facilities
Nearby Facilities
Taunton.
Quiet, rural site with beautiful views of Exmoor. Near the River Avil. 1 mile from Dunster Castle and 6 miles from Minehead beach.

PORLOCK

Burrowhayes Farm Caravan & Camping Site & Riding Stables, West Luccombe, Porlock, Nr. Minehead, Somerset, TA24 8HU.
Std: 01643 **Tel:** 862463
Nearest Town/Resort Minehead.
Directions 5 miles west of Minehead on A39, left hand turning to West Luccombe, site ¼ mile on the right.
Acreage 8 **Open** 15 March **to** 31 October
Access Good **Site** Lev/Slope
Sites Available **Total** 140
Facilities
Nearby Facilities
Taunton.
✓✓✓✓Graded Park. Real family site set in glorious National Trust scenery on Exmoor. Ideal for walking. Riding on site.

PORLOCK

Porlock Caravan Park, Highbank, Porlock, Nr. Minehead, Somerset, TA24 8NS.
Std: 01643 **Tel:** 862269
Std: 01643 **Fax:** 862269
Nearest Town/Resort Minehead
Directions A39 from Minehead to Lynton, take the B3225 in Porlock to Porlock Weir. Site signposted.
Acreage 3½ **Open** Mid March **to** October
Access Good **Site** Level
Sites Available **Total** 40
Facilities
Nearby Facilities
Taunton
✓✓✓✓Graded Park. Scenic views, Ideal touring and walking.

REDHILL (BRISTOL)

Brook Lodge Touring Caravan & Camping Park, Brook Lodge Farm, Cowslip Green, Redhill, Somerset, BS40 5RD.
Std: 01934 **Tel:** 862311
Nearest Town/Resort Bristol/Bath
Directions From the historic city of Bristol take the A38 south west for 7 miles, park is signposted on the left. From the M5 junction 19 take the A369, then the B3129, then the B3130, then right onto the A38, 6 miles. From the A368 at Churchill take the A38 north, park is on the right in 3½ miles.
Acreage 3½ **Open** March **to** October
Access Good **Site** Mostly Level
Sites Available **Total** 29
Facilities
Nearby Facilities
✓✓✓Graded Park. Beautiful grounds with trees, lawns and garden. Trout fishing at Blagdon Lake 2 miles, hot air ballooning by arrangement nearby and a dry ski slope 3 miles. Bird life and walks. Swimming pool available in July and August. Rural non-tourist area. Ideal for touring. AA 3 Pennants.

SHEPTON MALLET

Greenacres Camping, Barrow Lane, North Wootton, Nr. Shepton Mallet, Somerset, BA4 4HL.
Std: 01749 **Tel:** 890497
Nearest Town/Resort Wells
Directions From Wells take the A39, turn left at Brownes Garden Centre. Site signposted in the village.
Acreage 4¼ **Open** April **to** October
Site Level
Sites Available **Total** 30
Facilities
Nearby Facilities
Castle Cary
An award winning family site. Peacefully set within sight of Glastonbury Tor.

SHEPTON MALLET

Manleaze Caravan Park, Cannards Grave, Shepton Mallet, Somerset, BA4 4LY.
Std: 01749 **Tel:** 342404
Nearest Town/Resort Shepton Mallet
Directions 1 mile south of Shepton Mallet on the junction of the A371 and the A37.
Acreage 1 **Open** All Year
Access Good **Site** Level
Sites Available **Total** 25
Facilities
Nearby Facilities
Castle Cary

SHEPTON MALLET

Old Down Caravan & Camping Park, Old Down House, Emborough, Bath, Somerset, BA3 4SA.
Std: 01761 **Tel:** 232355
Std: 01761 **Fax:** 232619
Nearest Town/Resort Midsomer Norton.
Directions From Shepton Mallet head north on the A37 towards Bristol. After 6 miles turn right onto the B3139. Old Down Inn is on the left, site entrance is 50 yards along on your right.
Acreage 4 **Open** April **to** October
Access Good **Site** Level
Sites Available **Total** 30
Facilities
Nearby Facilities
Bath
Ideal for family games.

SHEPTON MALLET

Phippens Farm, Stoke St. Michael, Oakhill, Nr. Bath, Somerset.
Std: 01749 **Tel:** 840395
Nearest Town/Resort Shepton Mallet.
Directions A367 Bath/Shepton Mallet road. Turn into Stoke St. Michael road in village of Oakhill sit on right hand side (1½ miles).
Acreage 7 **Open** Easter **to** September
Access Good **Site** Level
Sites Available
Facilities
Nearby Facilities
Frome
Good touring area. Longleat, Bath, Cheddar, Wookey Hole, Bristol, Wells, etc.

SPARKFORD

Long Hazel International Caravan & Camping Park, High Street, Sparkford, Near Yeovil, Somerset, BA22 7JH.
Std: 01963 **Tel:** 440002
Std: 01963 **Fax:** 440002
Nearest Town/Resort Yeovil/Sherborne
Directions From Wincanton take the A303 to the end of Sparkford by-pass. At the roundabout turn left into Sparkford Village, site is approx. 400 yards on the left.
Acreage 3½ **Open** March **to** December
Access Good **Site** Level
Sites Available **Total** 75
Facilities
Nearby Facilities
Yeovil/Sherborne
✓✓✓✓✓Graded Park. Full disabled shower unit. Near to an inn and restaurant. Ideal for touring or an overnight halt. Haynes Motor Museum and Fleet Air Arm Museum nearby. 3 static caravans available.

STREET

Bramble Hill Camping Site, Bramble Hill, Walton, Nr. Street, Somerset, BA16 9RQ.
Std: 01458 **Tel:** 442548
Nearest Town/Resort Street
Directions A39 1 mile from Street, 2 miles from Glastonbury.
Acreage 3½ **Open** April **to** September
Access Good **Site** Level
Sites Available
Facilities
Nearby Facilities
Castle Cary/Taunton
Quiet site. Caravan storage also available. Ideal site for visiting Clarks Village - 1 mile. Few seasonal pitches available. Near to Sainsburys, restaurants and swimming pools (1 mile).

TAUNTON

Ashe Farm Caravan & Camp Site, Ashe Farm, Thornfalcon, Taunton, Somerset, TA3 5NW.
Std: 01823 **Tel:** 442567
Std: 01823 **Fax:** 443372
Nearest Town/Resort Taunton.
Directions 4 miles southeast Taunton on A358, turn right at 'Nags Head' towards West Hatch, ¼ mile on right.
Acreage 7 **Open** April **to** October
Access Good **Site** Level
Sites Available **Total** 30
Facilities
Nearby Facilities
Taunton.
✓✓✓✓Graded Park. Ideal touring centre, easy reach of Quantock and Blackdown Hills.

TAUNTON

Holly Bush Park, Culmhead, Taunton, Somerset, TA3 7EA.
Std: 01823 **Tel:** 421515
Std: 01823 **Fax:** 421885
Nearest Town/Resort Taunton
Directions From Taunton follow signs for the Racecourse and Corfe on the B3170, 3½ miles from Corfe turn right at crossroads towards Wellington. Turn right at the next T-Junction, site is 200yds on the left.
Acreage 2¼ **Open** All Year
Access Good **Site** Level
Sites Available **Total** 40
Facilities
Nearby Facilities
Taunton.
✓✓✓✓Graded Park. Area of Outstanding Natural Beauty.

TAUNTON

Tanpits Cider Farm, Caravan & Camping Site, Dyers Lane, Bathpool, Taunton, Somerset, TA2 8BZ.
Std: 01823 **Tel:** 270663
Nearest Town/Resort Taunton

Directions Leave the M5 at junction 25 and follow tourist camping signs. From Taunton take the A38 Bridgwater road signed with brown tourist signs.
Open March **to** November
Access Good **Site** Level
Sites Available **Total** 20
Facilities
Nearby Facilities
Taunton
✓✓Graded Park. Within walking distance of a canal. Approx. 5 miles from the Quantock Hills. Close to supermarkets, cinema, bowling alley, pubs and fast food restaurants.

WATCHET

Doniford Bay Holiday Park, Watchet, Somerset, TA23 0TJ.
Std: 01984 **Tel:** 632423
Nearest Town/Resort Watchet
Directions Leave the M5 at exit 24. Follow Minehead signs on the A39 until you reach West Quantoxhead. Fork right after St. Audries Garage to Doniford Bay, the park is signposted.
Acreage 5 **Open** April **to** 2 November
Site Sloping
Sites Available **Total** 75
Facilities
Nearby Facilities
Taunton
✓✓✓✓Graded Park. Overlooking the sea.

WELLS

Ebborlands Camping Grounds, Ebborlands Farm, Wookey Hole, Nr Wells, Somerset.
Std: 01749 **Tel:** 672550
Std: 01749 **Fax:** 672550
Nearest Town/Resort Wells
Directions Wells - Unclassified road to Wookey Hole, approx 2 miles and past caves, on road marked Unsuitable for Charabangs.
Acreage 2 **Open** May **to** October
Access Good **Site** Sloping
Sites Available **Total** 20
Facilities
Nearby Facilities
Castle Cary
Near Wookey Hole Caves and Mendip Hills.

WELLS

Haybridge Caravan Park, Haybridge Farm, Haybridge, Wells, Somerset, BA5 1AJ.
Nearest Town/Resort Wells
Directions On the main A371 Wells to Cheddar road, just outside the Wells boundary.
Acreage 4 **Open** All Year
Access Good **Site** Lev/Slope
Sites Available **Total** 35
Facilities
Nearby Facilities
Bristol
Close to Wells and Wookey Hole Caves, ideal touring position.

WELLS

Homestead Park, Wookey Hole, Wells, Somerset, BA5 1BW.
Std: 01749 **Tel:** 673022
Nearest Town/Resort Wells.
Directions Leave Wells by A371 towards Cheddar, turn right for Wookey Hole. Site 1¼ miles on left in village.
Acreage 2 **Open** Easter **to** October
Access Good **Site** Level
Sites Available **Total** 55
Facilities
Nearby Facilities
Bristol/Bath
✓✓✓✓Graded Park. Sheltered on bank of River Axe, Wookey Hole Caves, National Trust Area, Mendip Hills, walking, climbing. Leisure centre nearby.

WELLS

Mendip Heights Camping & Caravan Park, Priddy, Wells, Somerset, BA5 3BP.
Std: 01749 **Tel:** 870241
Std: 01749 **Fax:** 870241
Nearest Town/Resort Cheddar/Wells.
Directions On A39 north from Wells, turn left at Green Ore crossroads onto B3135 towards Cheddar and follow campsite signs.
Acreage 4¼ **Open** March **to** 15 Nov
Access Good **Site** Level
Sites Available **Total** 90
Facilities
Nearby Facilities
Bristol/Bath/Weston-super-Mare
✓✓✓✓Graded Park. Peaceful, rural park in an area of outstanding natural beauty. Ideal for touring and walking. Near Cheddar, Wookey Hole and Wells. Activities available - see our main advertisement. Pets welcome if kept on leads.

WESTON-SUPER-MARE

Ardnave Holiday Park, Kewstoke, Weston-super-Mare, Somerset, BS22 9XJ.
Std: 01934 **Tel:** 622319
Nearest Town/Resort Weston-super-Mare.
Directions Off motorway M5 at junction 21 follow signs to Kewstoke.
Acreage ½ **Open** March **to** October
Access Good **Site** Level
Sites Available **Total** 12
Facilities
Nearby Facilities
Weston-super-Mare.
✓✓✓✓Graded Park. Near Beach.

WESTON-SUPER-MARE

Country View Caravan Park, 29 Sand Road, Sand Bay, Weston-super-Mare, Somerset, BS22 9UJ.
Std: 01934 **Tel:** 627595
Nearest Town/Resort Weston-super-Mare
Directions 4 miles north of Weston-super-Mare along the coast road. Leave the M5 at junction 21 and follow all signs for Sand Bay.
Acreage 4½ **Open** March **to** October
Access Good **Site** Level
Sites Available **Total** 120
Facilities
Nearby Facilities
Weston-super-Mare
✓✓✓✓Graded Park. 300 yards from the beach. National Trust headland and woods.

WESTON-SUPER-MARE

Purn International Holiday Park, A370 Bridgwater Road, Bleadon, Weston-super-Mare, Somerset, BS24 0AN.
Std: 01934 **Tel:** 812342
Std: 01934 **Fax:** 812342
Nearest Town/Resort Weston Super Mare
Directions From North leave M5 at junction 21 take signs for Weston and Hospital. At Hospital roundabout turn left onto the A370, we are on the right in 1 mile, next to the Anchor Inn. From South leave M5 junction 22 take signs for Weston on the left next to the Anchor Inn on A370.
Acreage 11 **Open** March **to** 7th Nov
Access Good **Site** Level
Sites Available **Total** 60
Facilities
Nearby Facilities
Weston Super Mare
✓✓✓✓Graded Park. Nearest Park to Weston, Licensed club with entertainment and dancing. Childrens Prize Bingo with Uncle Darren. RAC Appointed 4 Ticks and AA 3 Pennants.

WESTON-SUPER-MARE

West End Farm Caravan & Camping Park, Locking, Weston-super-Mare, Somerset, BS24 8RH.
Std: 01934 **Tel:** 822529
Nearest Town/Resort Weston-super-Mare
Directions Leave the M5 at junction 21 and follow signs for Weston-super-Mare, follow the signs for International Helicopter Museum and turn right immediately after Helicopter Museum and follow signs for site.
Access Good **Site** Level
Sites Available
Facilities
Nearby Facilities
Weston-super-Mare
✓✓✓✓Graded Park. Ideal for touring.

WESTON-SUPER-MARE

Weston Gateway Tourist Park, Westwick, Weston-super-Mare, Somerset, BS24 7TF.
Std: 01934 **Tel:** 510344
Nearest Town/Resort Weston-super-Mare.
Directions From the M5 junction 21, follow signs for Westwick approx. ¾ miles. From Weston-super-Mare take the A370 to the motorway interchange then follow signs to Westwick.
Acreage 15 **Open** March **to** November
Access Good **Site** Level
Sites Available **Total** 175
Facilities
Nearby Facilities
Weston-super-Mare.
✓✓✓✓Graded Park. Ideal, sheltered park with many famous tourist attractions within easy driving distance.

WILLITON

Home Farm Holiday Centre, St. Audries Bay, Williton, Somerset.
Std: 01984 **Tel:** 632487
Std: 01984 **Fax:** 634687
Nearest Town/Resort Williton / Watchet
Directions Leave M5 at Junction 23, follow A39 towards Minehead for 17 miles. At West Quantoxhead take first right turn after St. Audries Garages (signposted Blue Anchor, Doniford and Watchet) B3191 take first right turning in ½ mile to our drive.
Open All Year
Access Good **Site** Terraced
Sites Available **Total** 30
Facilities
Nearby Facilities
Taunton.
✓✓✓✓Graded Park. Private beach, good base for touring Exmoor. West Somerset Railway - 2 miles.

WINSCOMBE

Netherdale Caravan & Camping Site, Bridgwater Road, Sidcot, Winscombe, Somerset, BS25 1NH.
Std: 01934 **Tel:** 843481/843007
Nearest Town/Resort Cheddar.
Directions From Weston-super-Mare follow A371 to join A38 at Sidcot corner, site ¼ mile south. From Wells and Cheddar follow A371 westwards to join A38 a mile south of site.
Acreage 3½ **Open** March **to** October
Access Good **Site** Lev/Slope
Sites Available **Total** 25.
Facilities
Nearby Facilities
Weston-super-Mare.
Excellent walking area, footpath from site to valley and Mendip Hills adjoining. Good views. Ideal touring centre for Somerset. Many historical places and beaches within easy reach of site. Only individual motorcycles accepted, not groups. Dry ski slope - 3 miles.

WINSFORD

Halse Farm Caravan & Tent Park, Halse Farm, Winsford, Minehead, Somerset, TA24 7JL.
Std: 01643 **Tel:** 851259
Std: 01643 **Fax:** 851592
Nearest Town/Resort Dulverton.
Directions Turn off the A396 (Tiverton to Minehead road) to Winsford. In Winsford take small road in front of Royal Oak Inn. 1 mile up hill and over cattle grid, our entrance is immediately on the left.
Acreage 3 **Open** March **to** End October
Access Good **Site** Lev/Slope
Sites Available **Total** 44
Facilities
Nearby Facilities
Taunton
✓✓✓✓Graded Park. In Exmoor National Park, on working farm with beautiful views. For those who enjoy peaceful countryside. Quality heated toilet block and FREE showers. David Bellamy Silver Conservation Award.

STAFFORDSHIRE

CHEADLE

Hales Hall Caravan Park, Oakamoor Road, Cheadle, Staffordshire.
Std: 01538 **Tel:** 753305
Nearest Town/Resort Cheadle.
Directions Take the B5417 from Cheadle, signposted Oakamoor. Site is ¾ mile on the left.
Acreage 8 **Open** Easter **to** November
Access Good **Site** Sloping
Sites Available **Total** 50
Facilities
Nearby Facilities
Stoke-on-Trent.
4 miles to Alton Towers, Peak District, Wedgwood and other potteries and Gladstone Pottery Museum.

CHEADLE

Quarry Walk Park, Coppice Lane, Cheadle, Staffs, ST10 1RQ.
Std: 01538 **Tel:** 723495
Nearest Town/Resort Cheadle
Directions Take the A522 to Cheadle, turn left at the Crown Pub, go over the crossroads and turn right.
Acreage 46 **Open** All Year
Access Good **Site** Level
Sites Available **Total** 40
Facilities
Nearby Facilities
Stoke-on-Trent
✓✓✓✓Graded Park. Individually sited in 46 acres of a beautiful conservation area and woodland. Natural sun spot with a variety of wildlife.

CHEADLE

Star Caravan & Camping Park, Nr. Alton Towers, Stoke-on-Trent, Staffs, ST10 3DW.
Std: 01538 **Tel:** 702219/702256
Nearest Town/Resort Cheadle
Directions Situated off the B5417, ¾ mile from Alton Towers.
Acreage 50 **Open** 1 Feb **to** 31 Dec
Access Good **Site** Lev/Slope
Sites Available **Total** 188
Facilities
Nearby Facilities
Stoke
✓✓✓Graded Park. Situated in the centre of beautiful countryside within 9 miles of Leek, Uttoxeter and Ashbourne Town. Within easy reach of the Peak District and Dovedale. Cafe/Restaurant nearby. 6 static caravans for hire, please contact Mrs Brindley on 01538 702564. Large rally fields always available. Motorcycles are welcome.

LEEK

Camping & Caravanning Club Site, Blackshaw Grange, Blackshaw Moor, Leek, Staffs, ST13 8TL.
Std: 01538 **Tel:** 300285
Directions Just 2 miles from Leek on the

A53 Leek to Buxton road. The site is located 200 yards past the sign for 'Blackshaw Moor' on the left hand side.
Open All Year
Site Level
Sites Available **Total** 60
Facilities
Nearby Facilities
Stoke
√√√√Graded Park. On the edge of the Peak District. Ideal for visiting Alton Towers.

LEEK

Glencote Caravan Park, Churnet Valley, Station Road, Cheddleton, Nr. Leek, Staffs, ST13 7EE.
Std: 01538 **Tel:** 360745
Std: 01538 **Fax:** 361788
Nearest Town/Resort Leek
Directions 3¼ miles south of Leek off the A520 (Stone to Leek road).
Acreage 6 **Open** April **to** October
Site Level
Sites Available **Total** 50
Facilities
Nearby Facilities
Stoke-on-Trent.
√√√√√Graded Park. Situated in the heart of Churnet Valley. Steam Railway Centre and canalside pub close by, near to Alton Towers. Six static caravans for hire all with Rose Award 1999. David Bellamy Gold Award for Conservation and Practical Caravan 100 Top Parks 1998.

LONGNOR

Longnor Wood Over 50's Caravan & Camping Park, Longnor, Nr. Buxton, Derbyshire, SK17 0LD.
Std: 01298 **Tel:** 83648
Nearest Town/Resort Buxton
Directions A515 from Buxton, 7 miles to Longnor. From Longnor follow caravan site signs for 1½ miles.
Acreage 11 **Open** Easter **to** October
Access Good **Site** Lev/Slope
Sites Available **Total** 47
Facilities
Nearby Facilities
Buxton
Ideal location for walking and tourist attractions, Chatsworth and Blue John Mines.

RUGELEY

Camping & Caravanning Club Site, Old Youth Hostel, Cannock Chase, Wandon, Rugeley, Staffs, WS15 1QW.
Std: 01889 **Tel:** 582166
Directions Take the A460 to Hednesford, turn right at signpost Rawnsley/Hazelslade, then turn first left, site is ½ mile past the golf club.
Acreage 5 **Open** 22 March **to** 1 Nov
Site Lev/Slope
Sites Available **Total** 59
Facilities
Nearby Facilities
Rugeley Town
√√√√√Graded Park. On the edge of Cannock Chase.

RUGELEY

Silvertrees Caravan Park, Stafford Brook Road, Rugeley, Staffordshire, WS15 2TX.
Std: 01889 **Tel:** 582185
Std: 01889 **Fax:** 582185
Nearest Town/Resort Rugeley.
Directions From A51 take unclassified road towards Penkridge at traffic lights After two miles turn right by a white fence, entrance 100 yards on left.
Acreage 10 **Open** April **to** October
Access Good **Site** Lev/Slope
Sites Available **Total** 100
Facilities
Nearby Facilities
Rugeley.
√√√√√Graded Park. Set on Cannock Chase, a designated area of outstanding natural beauty. Tennis on site. 18 miles from Alton Towers.

RUGELEY

Tackeroo - Forestry Commission, Birches Valley, Rugeley, Staffordshire, WS15 2UQ.
Std: 01889 **Tel:** 586593
Nearest Town/Resort Rugeley
Directions In the centre of Cannock Chase on the Penkridge to Rugeley road. Join the A34 Cannock to Stafford road east of junctions 12 and 13 of the M6. Turn east 1 mile north of Huntingdon for Rugeley, site is 2 miles on the right.
Acreage 3 **Open** All Year
Access Good **Site** Level
Sites Available **Total** 70
Facilities
Nearby Facilities
Penkridge
The wide open spaces of Cannock Chase are ideal for walking, cycling, orienteering and relaxing. Ideal stopover site, just off the M6. Note : This site has NO toilets.

TAMWORTH

Drayton Manor Park, Nr. Tamworth, Staffordshire, B78 3TW.
Std: 01827 **Tel:** 287979
Std: 01827 **Fax:** 288916
Nearest Town/Resort Fazeley.
Directions M42 junction 9, A4091 main road passes entrance. 3 miles from junction 9. B5404 at Fazeley ¼ mile.
Acreage 4 **Open** Easter **to** October
Access Good **Site** Level
Sites Available **Total** 75
Facilities
Nearby Facilities
Tamworth.
Within a 250 acre theme park and zoo (admission inclusive to both for all occupants and vehicles up to 4 per unit). Take-aways and bars, garden centre. 100 rides, games and attractions. Only one dog per unit is permitted. Childrens play area and swimming pool locally. Licensed bar with T.V. and Gas available locally.

TRENTHAM

Trentham Gardens Caravan Park, Trentham Gardens, Trentham, Stoke-on-Trent, Staffordshire, ST4 8AX.
Std: 01782 **Tel:** 657519
Std: 01782 **Fax:** 644536
Nearest Town/Resort Stoke-on-Trent
Directions 2 minutes from the M6 junction 15, follow signs.
Acreage 35 **Open** All Year
Access Good **Site** Sloping
Sites Available **Total** 250
Facilities
Nearby Facilities
Stoke-on-Trent
√√√Graded Park. Set in 750 acres of ancestral woodland. Near potteries and Alton Towers.

WATERHOUSES

The Cross Inn Caravan Park, Cauldon Low, Stoke-on-Trent, Staffs, ST10 3EX.
Std: 01538 **Tel:** 308338
Std: 01538 **Fax:** 308767
Nearest Town/Resort Leek
Directions On the A523 Leek to Ashbourne road, turn right at Waterhouses and go 3 miles to crossroads (A52) and turn right, site is 10 yards on the right.
Acreage 2 **Open** March **to** November
Access Good **Site** Level
Sites Available **Total** 36
Facilities
Nearby Facilities
Stoke
√√√Graded Park. Pub with restaurant on site, meals served every lunch and evening. Carvery Saturday evening and all day Sunday.

SUFFOLK

BECCLES

Waveney River Centre, Burgh-St-Peter, Nr. Beccles, Suffolk.
Std: 01502 **Tel:** 677343
Nearest Town/Resort Lowestoft/Great Yarmouth
Directions Signpost at Haddiscoe on the A143.
Acreage 5 **Open** Easter **to** October
Access Good **Site** Lev/Slope
Sites Available **Total** 30
Facilities
Nearby Facilities
Beccles
Overlooking River Waveney.

BUNGAY

Outney Meadow Caravan Park, Outney Meadow, Bungay, Suffolk, NR35 1HG.
Std: 01986 **Tel:** 892338
Nearest Town/Resort Bungay
Directions Entrance is signposted from the junction of the A143 and A144 at Bungay.
Acreage 6 **Open** Easter **to** October
Access Good **Site** Level
Sites Available **Total** 45
Facilities
Nearby Facilities
Beccles
✓✓✓✓Graded Park. Beside the River Waveney and common.

BURY ST EDMUNDS

The Dell Touring Park, Beyton Road, Thurston, Bury St Edmunds, Suffolk, IP31 3RB.
Std: 01359 **Tel:** 270121
Nearest Town/Resort Bury St Edmunds
Directions Take A14 eastbound 6 miles from Bury follow Thurston signs.
Open All Year
Access Good **Site** Level
Sites Available **Total** 100
Facilities
Nearby Facilities
Thurston
✓✓✓Graded Park. Ideal for touring East Anglia. 1 hour from Cambridge, Norwich and coast.

DARSHAM

Haw-Wood Farm Caravan & Camping Park, Darsham, Suffolk, IP17 3QT.
Std: 01986 **Tel:** 784248
Nearest Town/Resort Lowestoft.
Directions Approx. 30 miles north of Ipswich on the A12. Turn right 1 mile after Darsham level crossing at the Little Chef. Caravan park is ¼ mile on the right.
Acreage 7 **Open** April **to** October
Access Good **Site** Level
Sites Available **Total** 90
Facilities
Nearby Facilities
Darsham
Near the beach, ideal touring and bird watching. Peaceful and quiet.

DUNWICH

Cliff House, Minsmere Road, Dunwich, Saxmundham, Suffolk, IP17 3DQ.
Std: 01728 **Tel:** 648282
Std: 01728 **Fax:** 648282
Nearest Town/Resort Southwold
Directions From A12, at Blythburgh or Yoxford, follow signs to Dunwich Heath.
Acreage 30 **Open** April/Easter **to** Oct
Access Good **Site** Level
Sites Available **Total** 87
Facilities
Nearby Facilities
Yoxford
✓✓✓Graded Park. Beach frontage, adjoining National Trust and Minsmere Bird Reserve. Suffolk Heritage Coast.

EYE

Honeypot Camp & Caravan Park Wortham, Eye, Suffolk, IP22 1PW.
Std: 01379 **Tel:** 783312
Std: 01379 **Fax:** 783292
Nearest Town/Resort Diss
Directions Four miles south west of Diss, on south side A143, towards Bury St. Edmunds.
Acreage 6½ **Open** April **to** September
Access Good **Site** Level
Sites Available **Total** 35
Facilities
Nearby Facilities
Diss
✓✓✓Graded Park. Highly recommended family run inland touring site, Norfolk/Suffolk centre, Steam Museum 2 miles. Quiet and peaceful surroundings. Fishing on site. Lakeside pitches. Free colour illustrated brochure. Established over 30 years.

FELIXSTOWE

Suffolk Sands Holiday Park, Carr Road, Felixstowe, Suffolk, IP11 8TS.
Std: 01394 **Tel:** 273434
Std: 01394 **Fax:** 671269
Nearest Town/Resort Felixstowe
Directions Take the A14 into Felixstowe and turn right at the first roundabout. Go straight across the next roundabout, continue along Walton Avenue to the traffic lights. Turn right and after 200yds bear right into Carr Road. The park is on the left.
Acreage 3 **Open** Easter **to** November
Access Good **Site** Level
Sites Available **Total** 49
Facilities
Nearby Facilities
✓✓✓✓Graded Park. Situated right by the seafront.

HALESWORTH

The Garage, St. Lawrence, Beccles, Suffolk.
Std: 01986 **Tel:** Ilketshall 781241
Nearest Town/Resort Halesworth.
Directions Situated on A144, 3½ miles north Halesworth, 5½ miles south Bungay.
Acreage 1 **Open** March **to** October
Access Good **Site** Level
Sites Available **Total** 12
Facilities
Nearby Facilities
Halesworth.
Ideal touring centre. Situated in rural area, 12 miles coast.

IPSWICH

Low House Touring Caravan Centre, Low House, Bucklesham Road, Foxhall, Ipswich, Suffolk, IP10 0AU.
Std: 01473 **Tel:** 659437
Std: 01473 **Fax:** 659880
Nearest Town/Resort Ipswich/Felixstowe
Directions Turn off the A14 Ipswich Ring Road (South) via slip road onto the A1156 (signposted East Ipswich). In 1 mile turn right (signposted), in ½ mile turn right signposted Bucklesham. Site is on the left in ¼ mile.
Acreage 3½ **Open** All Year
Access Good **Site** Level
Sites Available **Total** 30
Facilities
Nearby Facilities
Ipswich
✓✓✓Graded Park. Camp in a beautiful garden packed with ornamental trees and plants, arches and bower doves, rabbits, bantams and guinea fowl. Wildlife all around. Ornamental Tree Walk and Pets Corner. Heated toilet and shower block. Electric hook-ups available on ALL pitches. Mobile shop on Thursday mornings only. Temporary membership for the sports centre opposite.

IPSWICH

Orwell Meadows Leisure Park, Priory Lane, Ipswich, Suffolk, IP10 0JS.
Std: 01473 **Tel:** 726666
Std: 01473 **Fax:** 721441
Nearest Town/Resort Ipswich.
Directions From A14 towards Felixstowe take first exit after Orwell Bridge, at roundabout turn left and first left again then follow signs.
Acreage 17
Access Good **Site** Level
Sites Available **Total** 80
Facilities
Nearby Facilities
Ipswich
✓✓✓✓Graded Park. A quiet, family run park, ideally situated for touring beautiful Suffolk. Adjacent to the Orwell Country Park. Forest and river walks.

IPSWICH

Priory Park, Ipswich, Suffolk, IP10 0JT.
Std: 01473 **Tel:** 727393
Std: 01473 **Fax:** 278372
Nearest Town/Resort Ipswich.
Directions Travelling east along A14 Ipswich southern by-pass take first exit after River Orwell Road bridge, turn left towards Ipswich following caravan/camping signs. 300yards from by-pass on left, follow signs to Priory Park.
Acreage 100 **Open** Easter **to** End October
Access Good **Site** Level
Sites Available **Total** 75
Facilities
Nearby Facilities
Ipswich.
Superb historic setting. Frontage onto River Orwell. Magnificent south facing panoramic views. 9 hole golf course and hard tennis court within the park grounds. Club adventure play area, nature trails, access to foreshore. Holiday lodges for hire. Holiday Homes for sale.

KESSINGLAND

Camping & Caravanning Club Site, Suffolk Wildlife Park, Whites Lane, Kessingland, Suffolk, NR33 7SL.
Std: 01502 **Tel:** 742040
Nearest Town/Resort Lowestoft
Directions From London on the A12, leave at roundabout in Kessingland following Wildlife Park signs. Turn right through park entrance.
Acreage 6½ **Open** 22 March **to** 1 Nov
Access Good **Site** Level
Sites Available **Total** 90
Facilities
Nearby Facilities
Lowestoft
✓✓✓✓Graded Park. Next to Suffolk Wildlife Park. Set in a quiet seaside resort, close to Great Yarmouth.

LEISTON

Cakes & Ale, Abbey Lane, Leiston, Suffolk.
Std: 01728 **Tel:** 831655
Std: 01473 **Fax:** 736270
Nearest Town/Resort Leiston/Aldeburgh.
Directions Leave A12 taking B1121 Saxmundham, Benhall, Sternfield in Saxmundham take B1119 signposted Leiston proceed for 3 miles then take byroad left following signs to park.
Acreage 45 **Open** April **to** October
Access Good **Site** Level
Sites Available **Total** 100
Facilities
Nearby Facilities
Saxmundham.
2 miles best beach in area. Excellent base for coastal Suffolk, Southwold, Dunwich, Minsmere, Aldeburgh. Tennis courts, table tennis, golf driving range and practice nets, volley and soft ball on park.

LOWESTOFT

Azure Seas Caravan Park, The Street, Corton, Lowestoft, Suffolk.
Std: 01502 **Tel:** 731403
Std: 01502 **Fax:** 730958
Nearest Town/Resort Lowestoft.
Directions From A12 2 miles north of Lowestoft, turn least on Long Lane. Park at junction with The Street.
Acreage 10 **Open** Easter **to** Mid Oct
Access Good **Site** Level
Sites Available **Total** 30
Facilities
Nearby Facilities
Lowestoft.
Adjoining beach. Very convenient for Pleasurewood Hills Theme Park. Cafe/restaurant and licensed club adjoining.

LOWESTOFT

Beach Farm Residential & Holiday Park Ltd., Arbor Lane, Pakefield, Lowestoft, Suffolk, NR33 7BD.
Std: 01502 **Tel:** 572794
Std: 01502 **Fax:** 572794
Nearest Town/Resort Lowestoft
Directions Main roundabout Kessingland Lowestoft A12, fourth exit from Lowestoft first exit.
Acreage 5 **Open** March **to** October
Access Good **Site** Level
Sites Available **Total** 35
Facilities
Nearby Facilities
Lowestoft
✓✓✓Graded Park. ¼ mile from the beach. Close to all amenities. Club, heated pool and a fast food restaurant on park.

LOWESTOFT

Broad View Caravans, Marsh Road, Oulton Broad, Suffolk, NR32 3PW.
Std: 01502 **Tel:** 565587
Nearest Town/Resort Lowestoft
Directions From Beccles A146 into Oulton Broad. At traffic lights bear left over railway bridge, Marsh Road is on the left. Very sharp so continue to roundabout and come back round then into Marsh Road.
Acreage 1 **Open** April **to** October
Access Good **Site** Level
Sites Available **Total** 15
Facilities
Nearby Facilities
Oulton Broad South
Alongside the Broads, fishing and boating. Licensed club nearby.

LOWESTOFT

Chestnut Farm Caravan Site, Gisleham, Lowestoft, Suffolk, NR33 8EE.
Std: 01502 **Tel:** 740227
Nearest Town/Resort Lowestoft
Directions 3 miles south of Lowestoft off the A12 at Kessingland (Suffolk Wildlife Park roundabout). Turn west signposted Rushmore/Mutford/Gisleham, take the second left and then the first drive on the left.
Acreage 3 **Open** Easter **to** October
Access Good **Site** Level
Sites Available **Total** 20
Facilities
Nearby Facilities
Oulton Broad/Lowestoft
River fishing on the farm, good cycling area.

LOWESTOFT

Heathland Beach Caravan Park, London Road, Kessingland, Suffolk, NR33 7PJ.
Std: 01502 **Tel:** 740337
Std: 01502 **Fax:** 742355
Nearest Town/Resort Lowestoft
Directions 1 mile north of Kessingland off the B1437, 3 miles south of Lowestoft on the A12.
Acreage 8 **Open** April **to** October
Access Good **Site** Level
Sites Available **Total** 106
Facilities
Nearby Facilities
Lowestoft
✓✓✓✓✓Graded Park. Surrounded by farmland near the beach.

LOWESTOFT

Kessingland Beach Holiday Park, Beach Road, Kessingland, Lowestoft, Suffolk, NR33 7RN.
Std: 01502 **Tel:** 740636
Std: 01502 **Fax:** 740907
Nearest Town/Resort Lowestoft
Directions Take the A12 Ipswich to Lowestoft road, 4 miles from Lowestoft. Take Kessingland Beach beach exit from roundabout (Whites Lane) and follow road for approx. 1½ miles to the beach.
Acreage 65 **Open** March **to** November
Access Good **Site** Level
Sites Available **Total** 90
Facilities
Nearby Facilities
Lowestoft
✓✓✓✓Graded Park. Situated alongside the

beach - access from park. Horse racing, sea and river fishing, Pleasurewood Hills Family Theme Park, Heritage Coast, Norfolk Broads and Great Yarmouth.

LOWESTOFT

Pakefield Caravan Park, Arbor Lane, Pakefield, Lowestoft, Suffolk, NR33 7BQ.
Std: 01502 **Tel:** 561136/511884
Nearest Town/Resort Lowestoft.
Directions 2 miles south of Lowestoft off A12.
Open April **to** October
Access Good **Site** Level
Sites Available **Total** 20
Facilities
Nearby Facilities
Lowestoft/Oulton Broad
✓✓✓Graded Park. Right beside beach yet only minutes walk from main shopping area. Ideal for touring the Broads.

LOWESTOFT

White House Farm, Gisleham, Lowestoft, Suffolk, NR33 8DX.
Std: 01502 **Tel:** 740248
Std: 01502 **Fax:** 740248
Nearest Town/Resort Lowestoft
Directions Take the A12 Ipswich road, at Safeways roundabout turn to Gisleham, after 1½ miles at the church turn left and White House Farm is 300 yards on the left.
Acreage 4½ **Open** April **to** October
Access Good **Site** Level
Sites Available **Total** 40
Facilities
Nearby Facilities
Oulton Broad
Very quiet farm with walks and private fishing. Near sandy and golden beaches and the Norfolk Broads.

NAYLAND

Rushbanks Farm, Wiston, Nayland, Suffolk, CO6 4NA.
Std: 01206 **Tel:** 262350
Nearest Town/Resort Colchester.
Directions 7 miles north west of Colchester off the A134.
Acreage 4 **Open** May **to** October
Access Good **Site** Level
Sites Available **Total** 20
Facilities
Nearby Facilities
Colchester
Peaceful, riverside site, suitable for boating and fishing. You can also telephone us on 01787 375691.

NEWMARKET

Camping & Caravanning Club Site, Rowley Mile Racecourse, Newmarket, Suffolk, CB8 8JL.
Std: 01638 **Tel:** 663235
Directions From the A1304 follow signs to the racecourse. Drive down the Rowley Mile which is signposted to the site, keeping the grandstand on your left.
Open 22 March **to** 20 Sept
Site Level
Sites Available **Total** 90
Facilities
Nearby Facilities
Newmarket
✓✓✓Graded Park. Located on the racecourse. Horse racing May to October. 1½ miles from the Horse Racing Museum and close to Newmarket town. AA 3 Pennants.

SAXMUNDHAM

Whitearch Touring Park, Main Road, Benhall, Saxmundham, Suffolk, IP17 1NA.
Std: 01728 **Tel:** 604646
Nearest Town/Resort Saxmundham
Directions Just off the main A12 junction with the B1121 at the Ipswich end of Saxmundham by-pass.
Acreage 14½ **Open** April **to** October
Access Good **Site** Level
Sites Available **Total** 30
Facilities
Nearby Facilities
Saxmundham
✓✓✓Graded Park. Fishing and tennis on site. Suffolk coast, Snape Maltings Concert Hall, Minsmere Bird Reserve, American Theme Park and castles.

SUDBURY

Willowmere Caravan Park, Bures Road, Little Cornard, Sudbury, Suffolk, CO10 0NN.
Std: 01787 **Tel:** 375559
Std: 01787 **Fax:** 375559
Nearest Town/Resort Sudbury
Directions Leave Sudbury on the B1508 to Bures and Colchester, 1 mile from Sudbury.
Acreage 2 **Open** Easter **to** 1 October
Access Good **Site** Level
Sites Available **Total** 40
Facilities
Nearby Facilities
Sudbury
✓✓✓✓Graded Park. Quiet, country park near a river.

WOODBRIDGE

Forest Camping Tangham, Tangham Campsite, Butley, Woodbridge, Suffolk, IP12 3NF.
Std: 01394 **Tel:** 450707
Nearest Town/Resort Woodbridge
Directions Take the A1152 off the A12 on the Woodbridge bypass. Fork left at roundabout in Bromeswell then straight onto the B1084 towards Orford. After 4 miles turn right into forest.
Acreage 7 **Open** April **to** 10 January
Access Good **Site** Level
Sites Available **Total** 90
Facilities
Nearby Facilities
Melton
✓✓✓Graded Park. Near to Orford Castle and Aldeburgh. Cycling in the forest.

WOODBRIDGE

Sandlings Centre, Lodge Road, Hollesley, Woodbridge, Suffolk.
Std: 01394 **Tel:** 411202
Std: 01394 **Fax:** 411422
Nearest Town/Resort Woodbridge.
Directions Take A1152 off A12 passed Woodbridge across Milton traffic lights and onto B1083 Bawdsey Road, turn left at T junction, Shottisham. Drive out of Village 1¼ miles on left.
Acreage 4 **Open** March **to** January
Site Level
Sites Available **Total** 65
Facilities
Nearby Facilities
Woodbridge.
✓✓✓Graded Park. Natural History Information Centre on site. Ideal area for walking, bird watching, etc. NO Touring caravans accepted.

WOODBRIDGE

The Moon and Sixpence, Newbourne Road, Waldringfield, Woodbridge, Suffolk, IP12 4PP.
Std: 01473 **Tel:** 736650
Std: 01473 **Fax:** 736270
Nearest Town/Resort Woodbridge
Directions Turn off A12, Ipswich Eastern By-Pass, onto unclassified road signposted Waldringfield, Newbourn. Follow caravan direction signs.
Acreage 5 **Open** April **to** October
Access Good **Site** Level
Sites Available **Total** 75
Facilities
Nearby Facilities
Woodbridge
Picturesque location. Sheltered, terraced site. Own private lake and sandy beach.

TO ENSURE ACCURACY ALL INFORMATION IN THIS GUIDE IS UPDATED ANNUALLY

SURREY

CHERTSEY

Camping & Caravanning Club Site, Bridge Road, Chertsey, Surrey, KT16 8JX.
Std: 01932 **Tel:** 562405
Directions Leave the M5 at junction 11 and follow the A317 to Chertsey. At the roundabout take the first exit to the traffic lights and go straight across to the next set of traffic lights, turn right and after 400 yards turn left into the site.
Open All Year
Site Level
Sites Available **Total** 200
Facilities
Nearby Facilities
Chertsey
✓✓✓✓Graded Park. On the banks of the River Thames, fishing on site. Close to London. AA 4 Pennants.

FARNHAM

Tilford Touring Camping & Caravan Park, The Old Barn, Upper Street Farm, Tilford, Farnham, Surrey, GU10 2BN.
Std: 01252 **Tel:** 792199
Std: 01252 **Fax:** 781027
Nearest Town/Resort Farnham
Directions Head south from Farnham Railway Station, take the right fork over crossing, 3 miles to Tilford Village. Pass the village green 1 mile, turn left down the lane beside the Hankley Pub, signposted.
Acreage 4 **Open** All Year
Access Good **Site** Level
Sites Available **Total** 80
Facilities
Nearby Facilities
Farnham

HAMBLEDON

The Merry Harriers, Hambledon, Surrey.
Std: 01428 **Tel:** Wormley 682883
Nearest Town/Resort Godalming.
Directions Leave Godalming on B2130 and follow Hambledon signs approx. 4 miles.
Acreage 1 **Open** All Year
Access Good **Site** Level
Sites Available **Total** 25
Facilities
Nearby Facilities
Witley.
Unspoilt countryside, opposite country pub.

LINGFIELD

Longacres Caravan & Camping Park, Newchapel Road, Lingfield, Surrey, RH7 6LE.
Std: 01342 **Tel:** 833205
Std: 01342 **Fax:** 834307
Nearest Town/Resort East Grinstead.
Directions From the M25 junction 6 take the A22 south towards East Grinstead. At Newchapel roundabout turn left onto the B2028 towards Lingfield. Site is on the right in 700yds.
Acreage 18 **Open** All Year
Access Good **Site** Lev/Slope
Sites Available **Total** 60
Facilities
Nearby Facilities
Lingfield
✓✓✓✓Graded Park. Quad bikes, BMX and skateboard facilities, fishing and tourist information on site. Ideal to visit London, Surrey, Kent and Sussex.

SUSSEX

ARUNDEL

Maynards Caravan & Camping Park, Crossbush, Arundel, West Sussex, BN18 9PQ.
Std: 01903 **Tel:** 882075
Nearest Town/Resort Arundel/Littlehampton
Directions ¾ mile from Arundel on A27, turn left into car park of Beefeater Pub & Restaurant going east on Worthing/Brighton road.
Acreage 3 **Open** All Year
Access Good **Site** Level
Sites Available **Total** 70
Facilities
Nearby Facilities
Arundel
Very central for touring. 3 miles to sea, ¾ mile to river. Arundel Castle and Bird Sanctuary. 24 hour shop adjacent.

ARUNDEL

Ship & Anchor Marina, Heywood & Bryett Ltd., Ford, Arundel, West Sussex, BN18 0BJ.
Std: 01243 **Tel:** 551262
Nearest Town/Resort Arundel/Littlehampton.
Directions From the A27 at Arundel, follow road signposted to Ford for 2 miles. Site is on the left after level-crossing at Ford.
Acreage 12 **Open** March **to** October
Access Good **Site** Level
Sites Available **Total** 160
Facilities
Nearby Facilities
Ford.
✓✓✓✓Graded Park. Beside the River Arun with a public house on site. 3 miles to beaches. Advance booking is advisable for hook-ups and groups.

BATTLE

Brakes Coppice Park, Forewood Lane, Crowhurst, East Sussex, TN33 9AB.
Std: 01424 **Tel:** 830322
Std: 01424 **Fax:** 830322
Nearest Town/Resort Battle.
Directions Turn right off the A2100 (Battle to Hastings road) 2 miles from Battle. Follow signs to Crowhurst, 1¼ miles turn left into site.
Acreage 3¼ **Open** March **to** October
Access Good **Site** Sloping
Sites Available **Total** 30
Facilities
Nearby Facilities
Crowhurst
Secluded, 11 acre, woodland park with level pitches. Fishing on site.

BATTLE

Crowhurst Park, Battle, East Sussex, TN33 0SL.
Std: 01424 **Tel:** 773344
Std: 01424 **Fax:** 775727
Nearest Town/Resort Battle.
Directions Situated on the A2100 2 miles south of Battle towards Hastings.
Acreage 4 **Open** 1 April **to** 28 October
Access Good **Site** Slight Slope
Sites Available **Total** 65
Facilities
Nearby Facilities
Battle
✓✓✓✓✓Graded Park. Within the grounds

of a 17th Century estate, in an area of outstanding natural beauty. Tennis on site. Holiday Park of the Year 1997.

BATTLE

Senlac Park Touring Caravan Site, Main Road, Catsfield, Nr Battle, East Sussex, TN33 9DU.
Std: 01424 **Tel:** 773969
Nearest Town/Resort Battle/Hastings.
Directions From Battle take A271, after about 1½ miles pass the Squirrel Public House on the left then turn left (B2204). Site is on the left hand side.
Acreage 5 **Open** March **to** October
Access Good **Site** Level
Sites Available **Total** 32
Facilities
Nearby Facilities
Battle
20 acre site in an area of outstanding natural beauty. Many historic features nearby. "1066 Country". Beach 7 miles. Ideal touring base.

BEXHILL-ON-SEA

Cobbs Hill Farm Caravan & Camping Park, Watermill Lane, Bexhill-on-Sea, East Sussex, TN39 5JA.
Std: 01424 **Tel:** 213460
Nearest Town/Resort Bexhill-on-Sea.
Directions From Bexhill take the A269, turn right into Watermill Lane. Site is 1 mile on the left.
Acreage 7 **Open** April **to** October
Access Good **Site** Level
Sites Available **Total** 45
Facilities
Nearby Facilities
Bexhill-on-Sea
✓✓✓✓Graded Park. Quiet countryside, on a small farm. Large tent field at peak times.

BILLINGHURST

Limeburners (Camping) Ltd., Limeburners, Newbridge, Billinghurst,Sussex, RH14 9JA.
Std: 01403 **Tel:** 782311
Nearest Town/Resort Billinghurst
Directions 1½ miles west of billinghurst on A272, turn left on B2133 150yds onleft.
Open April **to** October
Access Good **Site** Level
Sites Available **Total** 40
Facilities
Nearby Facilities
Public house attached, lunch time and evening food.

BOGNOR REGIS

Copthorne Caravan Park, Rose Green Road, Bognor Regis, Sussex, PO21 3ER.
Std: 01243 **Tel:** 262408
Nearest Town/Resort Bognor Regis
Directions 2 miles from Bognor, take B2166 and turn left at third roundabout. Copthorne is approx 200 metres on the right nearly opposite Esso garage.
Acreage 6 **Open** April **to** September
Access Good **Site** Level
Sites Available **Total** 4-6
Facilities
Nearby Facilities
Bognor Regis
Established 1945 - 1995. Mainly static park with a small touring field. Ideal access to Chichester, Goodwood and South Downs.

BOGNOR REGIS

The Lillies Nursery & Caravan Park, Yapton Road, Barnham, Bognor Regis, Sussex, PO22 0AY.
Std: 01243 **Tel:** 552081
Nearest Town/Resort Bognor Regis
Directions From Bognor Regis take the A29 to Eastergate, turn right at the War Memorial onto the B2233, 5 miles.
Acreage 2 **Open** March **to** October
Access Good **Site** Level
Sites Available **Total** 10
Facilities
Nearby Facilities
Barnham
✓✓✓Graded Park. Quiet, secluded site within walking distance of Barnham Railway Station where theres a direct line to all main local attractions.

BOLNEY

Aurora Ranch Caravan Site, London Road, Bolney, Haywards Heath, West Sussex, RH17 5RL.
Std: 01444 **Tel:** 881597
Nearest Town/Resort Brighton
Directions Take the A23 from Crawley, 10 miles.
Acreage 9 **Open** March **to** October
Access Good **Site** Lev/Slope
Sites Available **Total** 63
Facilities
Nearby Facilities
Haywards Heath
Ideal touring centre for the National Trust properties etc..

CHICHESTER

Bell Caravan Park, Bell Lane, Birdham, Nr. Chichester, Sussex.
Std: 01243 **Tel:** 512264
Nearest Town/Resort Chichester.
Directions From Chichester take the A286 towards Wittering for approx. 4 miles. At Birdham turn left into Bell Lane, site is 500yds on the left.
Acreage ¼ **Open** March **to** October
Access Good **Site** Level
Sites Available **Total** 15
Facilities
Nearby Facilities
Chichester
✓✓Graded Park.

CHICHESTER

Camping & Caravanning Club Site, 345 Main Road, Southbourne, Emsworth, Hampshire, PO10 8JH.
Std: 01243 **Tel:** 373202
Nearest Town/Resort Emsworth
Directions On the A259 from Chichester, site is on the right at sign Southbourne.
Acreage 3 **Open** All Year
Access Good **Site** Level
Sites Available **Total** 58
Facilities
Nearby Facilities
Southbourne
✓✓✓✓✓Graded Park. 500 yards through a footpath to the beach. Ideal touring, well placed for visiting the Sussex Downs and south coast resorts. Close to the City of Portsmouth.

CHICHESTER

Goodwood Racecourse Caravan Park, Singleton, Chichester, West Sussex, PO18 0PS.
Std: 01243 **Tel:** 755033
Nearest Town/Resort Chichester
Directions Take the A286 from Chichester or the A285 from Petworth to Goodwood Racecourse, entrance is signposted.
Acreage 2½ **Open** Mid June **to** Mid September
Access Good **Site** Level
Sites Available **Total** 61
Facilities
Nearby Facilities
Chichester
✓✓✓✓Graded Park. Easy access to Goodwood House, Downlands Museum, Chichester and South Downs Way. Park is closed on race days. Also open Easter and May Bank Holidays.

CHICHESTER

Red House Farm, Bookers Lane, Earnley, Chichester, Sussex, PO20 7JG.
Std: 01243 **Tel:** 512959
Std: 01243 **Fax:** 514216
Nearest Town/Resort Bracklesham Bay.
Directions From Chichester turn south on A286 signposted "Witterings". 5 miles south turn left opposite Birdham Garage towards Bracklesham Bay, ¼ mile turn left again into Bookers Lane, site is on the left.
Acreage 4 **Open** Easter **to** October
Access Good **Site** Level
Sites Available **Total** 100
Facilities
Nearby Facilities
Chichester.
In countryside, quiet and spacious. 1 mile from beach and shops. Childrens adventure playground. Camping Gaz only. We do NOT have electric hook-ups.

CHICHESTER

Southern Leisure Lakeside Village, Vinnetrow Road, Chichester, West Sussex, PO20 6LB.
Std: 01243 **Tel:** 787715
Std: 01243 **Fax:** 533643
Nearest Town/Resort Chichester
Directions From the A27 at the roundabout where the A259 to Bognor Regis crosses the A27, take the exit for Pagham.
Open March **to** October
Access Good **Site** Level
Sites Available **Total** 1500
Facilities
Nearby Facilities
Chichester
✓✓✓Graded Park. Situated among several lakes, good for wind surfing, water skiing and fishing. Evening entertainment in peak season. Heated outdoor swimming pool. Takeaway food available. You can also telephone us on : 0345 508508.

CROWBOROUGH

Camping & Caravanning Club Site, Goldsmith Recreation Ground, Crowborough, Sussex, TN6 2TN.
Std: 01892 **Tel:** 664827
Directions Take the A26 turn off into the entrance to 'Goldsmiths Ground' signposted leisure centre, at the top of the road turn right into site lane.
Acreage 13 **Open** 1 Feb **to** 20 Dec
Site Lev/Slope
Sites Available **Total** 88
Facilities
Nearby Facilities
✓✓✓✓Graded Park. On the edge of Ashdown Forest. Adjacent to a sports centre. AA 4 Pennants.

DIAL POST

Honeybridge Park, Honeybridge Lane, Dial Post, Nr. Horsham, West Sussex, RH13 8NX.
Std: 01403 **Tel:** 710923
Std: 01403 **Fax:** 710923
Nearest Town/Resort Worthing
Directions 1 mile south of Dial Post on the A24 (London- Worthing Road). Follow brown internationl signs from the A24 Horsham to Worthing trunk road, by Old Barn Nursery.
Acreage 15 **Open** All Year
Access Good **Site** Level
Sites Available **Total** 100
Facilities
Nearby Facilities
Horsham
✓✓✓✓Graded Park. A spacious 15 acre park, nestling within the peace and quiet of an area of outstanding natural beauty. Heated amenitiy block; free showers (incl. disabled), washing-up facilities and laundry. Seasonal pitches and storage available.

EAST WITTERING

The Gees, 127 Stocks Lane, East Wittering, Nr. Chichester, West Sussex, PO20 8NY.
Std: 01243 **Tel:** 670223
Nearest Town/Resort Chichester
Directions From Chichester take the Wittering and Bracklesham Bay turn off, in 5 miles take the Bracklesham bay road and the camp site is situated by Lively Lady Pub.
Acreage 1 **Open** March **to** October
Access Good **Site** Level
Sites Available **Total** 28
Facilities
Nearby Facilities
150 yards from a safe beach. Country walks and good local village shopping. Opposite RBL Club and 100 yards from the local pub.

EASTBOURNE

Fairfields Farm Camping & Caravan Park, Eastbourne Road, Westham, Pevensey, East Sussex, BN24 5NG.
Std: 01323 **Tel:** 763165
Nearest Town/Resort Eastbourne.
Directions On B2191, signposted on the east side of Eastbourne and off the A27 in the village of Westham.
Acreage 3 **Open** April **to** October
Access Good **Site** Level
Sites Available **Total** 60
Facilities
Nearby Facilities
Pevensey/Westham
A clean, well kept site on a small family farm. Only 2 miles from the sea and 3 miles from Eastbourne town centre.

GRAFFHAM

Camping & Caravanning Club Site, Great Bury, Graffham, Petworth, West Sussex, GU28 0QJ.
Std: 01798 **Tel:** 867476
Directions From Petworth take the A285, pass Badgers Pub on the left and the BP Garage on the right, take the next right turn signposted Selham Graffham (with brown camping sign), follow signs to site. From Chichester take the A285 through Duncton and turn left signposted Selham Graffham (with brown camping sign).
Open 22 March **to** 1 Nov
Site Sloping
Sites Available **Total** 90
Facilities
Nearby Facilities
Chichester
✓✓✓✓Graded Park. Set in 20 acres of woodland with many walks.

HAILSHAM

The Old Mill Caravan Park, Chalvington Road, Golden Cross, Hailsham, East Sussex, BN27 3SS.
Std: 01825 **Tel:** Chiddingly 872532
Nearest Town/Resort Hailsham/ Eastbourne
Directions 4 miles north west of Hailsham. Turn left off the A22 just before Golden Cross Inn car park. Site is 150yds on the right of Chalvington Road.
Acreage 2 **Open** April **to** October
Access Good **Site** Level
Sites Available **Total** 26
Facilities
Nearby Facilities
Polegate
Ideal touring for beach, downland and countryside. Static holiday caravans sold and sited. Static caravan for hire.

HASTINGS

Carters Farm, Elm Lane, Pett, Nr. Hastings, East Sussex, TN35 4JD.
Std: 01424 **Tel:** Pett 813206/812244
Nearest Town/Resort Hastings.
Directions On A259 towards Rye, right turn for Pett at Gustling, signposted after that.
Acreage 12 **Open** Easter **to** October
Access Good **Site** Lev/Slope
Sites Available **Total** 100
Facilities
Nearby Facilities
Hastings.
Farm site, family run, few restrictions, family run.

HASTINGS

Shearbarn Holiday Park, Barley Lane, Hastings, East Sussex, TN35 5DX.
Std: 01424 **Tel:** 716474/423583
Std: 01424 **Fax:** 718740

Nearest Town/Resort Hastings
Directions From the A259 Hastings seafront travelling towards Rye/Folkestone, turn right into Harold Road, right again into Gurth Road and left into Barley Lane. Reception is on the right in ¼ mile.
Acreage 17 **Open** March **to** 15 January
Access Good **Site** Lev/Slope
Sites Available **Total** 450
Facilities
Nearby Facilities
Hastings
✓✓✓✓Graded Park. Good views of the sea and country. Adjacent to Hastings Country Park. 20 minute walk to Hastings and the seafront.

HASTINGS

Stalkhurst Camping & Caravan Site, Stalkhurst Cottage, Ivyhouse Lane, Hastings, Sussex.
Std: 01424 **Tel:** 439015
Std: 01424 **Fax:** 439015
Nearest Town/Resort Hastings.
Directions From Hastings take A259 towards Rye, turn left onto B2093. In ½ mile turn right into Ivyhouse Lane. From the A21 take the B2093 for 2½ miles, turn left into Ivyhouse Lane.
Acreage 2¼ **Open** March **to** 15 January
Access Good **Site** Level
Sites Available **Total** 33
Facilities
Nearby Facilities
Hastings.
✓✓✓Graded Park. 2½ miles to beach. Ideal touring site.

HENFIELD

Downsview Caravan Park, Bramlands Lane, Woodmancote, Near Henfield, West Sussex, BN5 9TG.
Std: 01273 **Tel:** 492801
Std: 01273 **Fax:** 495214
Nearest Town/Resort Brighton.
Directions Signed off the A281 in the village of Woodmancote. 2½ miles east of Henfield and 6½ miles north of Brighton.
Acreage 4 **Open** 1 April/Easter **to** 31 Oct
Access Good **Site** Level
Sites Available
Facilities
Nearby Facilities
Brighton/Hassocks.
✓✓✓✓Graded Park. Specialists in peace and quiet. Near to Brighton and South Downs. NO playgrounds or discos etc. Waste water hook-ups available.

HENFIELD

Farmhouse Caravan & Camping Site, Tottington Drive, Small Dole, Henfield, Sussex, BN5 9XZ.
Std: 01273 **Tel:** 493157
Nearest Town/Resort Brighton.
Directions Turn first left off A2037 (Henfield/ Upperbeeding). After Small Dole sign into Tottington Drive, farm at end.
Acreage 4 **Open** February **to** November
Access Good **Site** Level
Sites Available **Total** 35
Facilities
Nearby Facilities
Shoreham.
Small farm site near South Downs. Beach 5 miles, Brighton and Worthing 10 miles.

HENFIELD

Harwoods Farm, West End Lane, Henfield, West Sussex.
Std: 01273 **Tel:** 492820
Nearest Town/Resort Horsham/Brighton.
Directions From Henfield village on A281 turn opposite White Hart pub. 2 miles into West End lane, signposted in Henfield Highstreet.
Acreage 1¾ **Open** Easter **to** October
Access Good **Site** Level
Sites Available **Total** 35
Facilities
Nearby Facilities
Horsham/Brighton.
Small, sheltered site near River Adur, Established since 1964. Miles of walking along river and local footpaths. Limited fishing available. Booking advised Bank Holidays. (2) Deep earth closets. No youth clubs. Only individual motorcycles accepted, not groups. No trailer caravans.

HORAM

Horam Manor Touring Park, Horam, Nr. Heathfield, East Sussex, TN21 0YD.
Std: 01435 **Tel:** 813662
Nearest Town/Resort Heathfield/ Eastbourne
Directions On A267, 3 miles south of Heathfield, 10 miles north of Eastbourne.
Acreage 7 **Open** March **to** October
Access Good **Site** Sloping
Sites Available **Total** 90
Facilities
Nearby Facilities
Eastbourne
✓✓✓✓Graded Park. A tranquil rural setting, but with plenty to do on the estate, and many places to visit.

HORAM

Horam Woodland View Touring Park, Horebeech Lane, Horam, Heathfield, East Sussex, TN21 0HR.
Std: 01435 **Tel:** 813597
Nearest Town/Resort Hailsham
Directions Off A267 Heathfield to Hailsham Road, at Horam take road opposite Merrydown Wine Company ¼ mile down is site entrance.
Open Easter **to** October
Access Good **Site** Level
Sites Available **Total** 25
Facilities
Nearby Facilities
Small quiet site, pretty countryside, good walks, many places to visit.

LEWES

Bluebell Holiday Park, The Broyle, Shortgate, Ringmer, Lewes, East Sussex, BN8 6PJ.
Std: 01825 **Tel:** 840407
Nearest Town/Resort Lewes/Brighton
Directions A27 to Lewes, A26 turn off to B2192. 3 miles from Ringmer on the B2192. From the A22, 2 miles from Halland behind the Bluebell Inn.
Acreage 1 **Open** April **to** October
Access Good **Site** Level
Sites Available **Total** 20
Facilities
Nearby Facilities
Lewes/Uckfield

LITTLEHAMPTON

Rutherford's Touring Park, Cornfield Close, Worthing Road, Littlehampton, BN17 6LD.
Std: 01903 **Tel:** 714240
Std: 01903 **Fax:** 732461
Nearest Town/Resort Littlehampton
Directions The site is situated on the A259 Worthing to Bognor Regis, between two Body Shop roundabouts. 3 miles from Arundel.
Acreage 6½ **Open** All Year
Access Good **Site** Level
Sites Available **Total** 80
Facilities
Nearby Facilities
Littlehampton
1½ to sandy beach. 1 mile to River Arun.

LITTLEHAMPTON

White Rose Touring Park, Mill Lane, Wick, Nr. Littlehampton, West Sussex, BN17 7PH.
Std: 01903 **Tel:** 716176
Std: 01903 **Fax:** 732671

Nearest Town/Resort Littlehampton
Directions From Arundel (A27) take A284 south. Mill Lane on left 1½ miles from A27/ A284 Junction, just past Six Bells public house.
Acreage 6 **Open** 15th March **to** 15th January
Access Good **Site** Level
Sites Available **Total** 127
Facilities
Nearby Facilities
Arundel
Ideal location for countryside and beach. 2 miles from Arundel Castle. Credit card telephone bookings accepted (essential for Bank Holidays and peak periods).

PEVENSEY

Camping & Caravanning Club Site, Normans Bay, Pevensey, East Sussex, BN24 6PR.
Std: 01323 **Tel:** 761190
Nearest Town/Resort Eastbourne
Directions From Bexhill take the A259 (Eastbourne), after roundabout turn left at traffic lights, left at signpost Beachlands, site is straight on.
Acreage 12 **Open** 22 March **to** 1 Nov
Access Good **Site** Level
Sites Available **Total** 200
Facilities
Nearby Facilities
Eastbourne
✓✓✓✓Graded Park. Site is next to its own beach (where the Normans landed). Watersports, fishing and table tennis on site. Close to Eastbourne. AA 4 Pennants.

PEVENSEY BAY

Bay View Caravan & Camping Park, Old Martello Road, Pevensey Bay, Nr. Eastbourne, East Sussex, BN24 6DX.
Std: 01323 **Tel:** 768688
Std: 01323 **Fax:** 769637
Nearest Town/Resort Eastbourne
Directions 2 miles from Eastbourne centre off the A259.
Acreage 3¼ **Open** Easter **to** October
Access Good **Site** Level
Sites Available **Total** 49
Facilities
Nearby Facilities
Pevensey Bay
✓✓✓✓✓Graded Park. Scenic views, next to a beach. Ideal for touring. 1998 South East England Tourism Awards - WINNER - Caravan Park of the Year.

POLEGATE

Peel House Farm Caravan Park, Sayerlands Lane (B2104), Polegate, East Sussex, BN26 6QX.
Std: 01323 **Tel:** 845629
Nearest Town/Resort Hailsham/Eastbourne
Directions Off the A22 at South Hailsham roundabout. Turn right at mini roundabout by the BP Station onto the B2104 signposted Pevensey. We are on the right ½ mile after Cuckoo Trail Crossing.
Acreage 3 **Open** April/Easter **to** End Oct
Access Good **Site** Level
Sites Available **Total** 20
Facilities
Nearby Facilities
Polegate
✓✓✓✓Graded Park. Quiet, rural site with views over the Downs. Footpath and Cuckoo Trail for walking and cycling. Many places to visit nearby. Small shop and garden produce.

RYE

Camber Sands Leisure Park, Lydd Road, Camber, Rye, Sussex, TN31 7RT.
Std: 01797 **Tel:** 225555
Std: 01797 **Fax:** 225756
Nearest Town/Resort Rye
Directions Take the A259 out of Rye to the east. After 1 mile turn right following signs to Camber, continue through the village. The park is well signposted and easy to find at the eastern end of Camber.
Acreage 8 **Open** March **to** November
Access Good **Site** Level
Sites Available **Total** 60
Facilities
Nearby Facilities
Rye
✓✓✓✓Graded Park. Alongside the Award Winning famous Camber Sands beach.

RYE

The Cock Horse Inn, Main Street, Peasmarsh, East Sussex, TN31 6YD.
Std: 01797 **Tel:** 230281
Nearest Town/Resort Rye.
Directions 4 miles west of Rye on the A268.
Acreage 1 **Open** March **to** 30 October
Access Good **Site** Level
Sites Available **Total** 5
Facilities
Nearby Facilities
Rye.
Easy touring for Rye, Hastings, Camber and Romney Marsh.

SEAFORD

Buckle Caravan Park, Marine Parade, Seaford, East Sussex, BN25 2QR.
Std: 01323 **Tel:** 897801
Nearest Town/Resort Seaford
Directions Between Newhaven and

Seaford, just off the A259.
Acreage 8 **Open** March **to** 2 January
Access Good **Site** Level
Sites Available **Total** 150
Facilities
Nearby Facilities
Bishopstone
Adjoining beach. Newhaven Ferry 2 miles, Brighton 12 miles and Eastbourne 8 miles. Dogs are welcome.

SEDLESCOMBE

Whydown Farm Tourist Caravan Park, Whydown Farm, Crazy Lane, Sedlescombe, East Sussex, TN33 0QT.
Std: 01424 **Tel:** 870147
Nearest Town/Resort Battle/Hastings
Directions Travelling south on A21, turn left into Crazy Lane, 100 yds past junction A21/ B2244, opposite Black Brooks Garden Centre.
Acreage 3 **Open** 1 March **to** 31 Oct
Access Good **Site** Level
Sites Available **Total** 36
Facilities
Nearby Facilities
Battle
Ideal touring, 15 minutes to the beach. Countryside and Hastings.

SELSEY

Warner Farm Touring Park, Warner Lane, Selsey, West Sussex, PO20 9EL.
Std: 01243 **Tel:** 604499
Std: 01243 **Fax:** 604499
Nearest Town/Resort Chichester
Directions From the A27 Chichester take the B2145 to Selsey. On entering Selsey turn right into School Lane. Follow signs for Warner Farm Touring Park.
Acreage 10 **Open** March **to** October
Access Good **Site** Level
Sites Available **Total** 200
Facilities
Nearby Facilities
Chichester.
✓✓✓✓✓Graded Park. Near beach.

SLINDON

Camping & Caravanning Club Site, Slindon Park, Nr. Arundel, Sussex, BN18 0RG.
Std: 01243 **Tel:** 814387
Directions From Chichester take the A27 towards Fontwell, turn left into Brittons Lane (second turn left after the B2233 on the right), then take the second turn right to Slindon, site is on this road.
Open 22 March **to** 27 Sept
Site Level
Sites Available **Total** 46
Facilities
Nearby Facilities
Arundel/Barnham
✓✓✓Graded Park. Within the National Trust property of Slindon Park. Interesting walks around the camp site.

UCKFIELD

Honeys Green Farm Caravan Park, Easons Green, Framfield, Uckfield, East Sussex, TN22 5RE.
Std: 01825 **Tel:** 840334
Nearest Town/Resort Uckfield/Lewes
Directions Turn off A22 (Uckfield - Eastbourne) at Halland roundabout onto B2192 signposted Blackboys/Heathfield, site ¼ mile on left.
Acreage 2 **Open** Easter **to** October
Access Good **Site** Level
Sites Available **Total** 22
Facilities
Nearby Facilities
Uckfield/Lewes
✓✓✓Graded Park. Small peaceful rural park, coarse fishing lake, walks.

WASHINGTON

Washington Caravan & Camping Park, London Road, Washington, West Sussex, RH20 4AT.
Std: 01903 **Tel:** 892869
Nearest Town/Resort Worthing
Directions 2 miles from Storrington, 4 miles from Steyning and 8 miles from Worthing on the A283 and the A24.
Acreage 4½ **Open** All Year
Access Good **Site** Sloping
Sites Available **Total** 90
Facilities
Nearby Facilities
Worthing - Pulborough
✓✓✓✓✓Graded Park. Own riding school on site.

WEST WITTERING

Nunnington Farm Camping Site, Nunnington Farm, West Wittering, West Sussex, PO20 8LZ.
Std: 01243 **Tel:** 514013 No Booking
Nearest Town/Resort Chichester.
Directions 7 miles south of Chichester on the A286 - B2179. 200yds before village on left, look for signs.
Acreage 4½ **Open** Easter **to** Mid October
Access Good **Site** Level
Sites Available **Total** 125
Facilities
Nearby Facilities
Chichester.
Near the beach.

WEST WITTERING

Wicks Farm Camping Park, Redlands Lane, West Wittering, Chichester, Sussex, PO20 8QD.
Std: 01243 **Tel:** 513116
Std: 01243 **Fax:** 511296
Nearest Town/Resort West Wittering/ Chichester.
Directions From Chichester A286 for Birdham. Then B2179 for West Wittering.
Acreage 2¼ **Open** April **to** October
Access Good **Site** Level
Sites Available **Total** 40
Facilities
Nearby Facilities
Chichester.
✓✓✓✓✓Graded Park.

WINCHELSEA

Rye Bay Caravan Park, Pett Level Road, Winchelsea Beach, Sussex, TN36 4NE.
Std: 01797 **Tel:** 226340
Std: 01797 **Fax:** 224699
Nearest Town/Resort Rye.
Directions 3 miles west of Rye and 7 miles east of Hastings.
Open March **to** October
Access Good
Sites Available **Total** 70
Facilities
Nearby Facilities
Rye
Direct frontage to the beach.

WISBOROUGH GREEN

Bat & Ball, Newpound Lane, Wisborough Green, West Sussex, RH14 0EH.
Std: 01403 **Tel:** 700313
Nearest Town/Resort Billinghurst.
Directions From Billinghurst (A29) take the A272 west for Petworth. After 2 miles turn right onto the B2133 for Guildford. Site is 1 mile on the left hand side.
Acreage 3 **Open** All Year
Access Good **Site** Level
Sites Available **Total** 40
Facilities
Nearby Facilities
Billingshurst.
Good views, walking and touring. Very close to a river.

TYNE & WEAR

SOUTH SHIELDS

Lizard Lane Caravan Park, Lizard Lane, Marsden, South Shields, Tyne & Wear, NE34 7AB.
Std: 0191 **Tel:** 454 4982
Nearest Town/Resort South Shields
Directions Take the coast road from South Shields to Marsden and the camp site.
Open March **to** Last Weekend Oct
Access Good **Site** Sloping
Sites Available **Total** 70
Facilities
Nearby Facilities
South Shields
✓✓✓Graded Park. Near the beach. Ideal for touring Scotland, Yorkshire and the Lakes. Childrens play area for up to 8 years.

WARWICKSHIRE

BIDFORD-ON-AVON

Cottage of Content, Barton, Bidford-on-Avon, Warwicks, B50 4NP.
Std: 01789 **Tel:** 772279
Nearest Town/Resort Bidford-on-Avon.
Directions 1 mile from Bidford follow Honeybourne road for ¾ mile. Turn left at crossroads signposted Barton, situated on bend in ¼ mile.
Acreage 2 **Open** March **to** October
Access Good **Site** Sloping
Sites Available **Total** 25
Facilities
Nearby Facilities
Stratford-upon-Avon.

LONG COMPTON

Mill Farm, Long Compton, Shipston-on-Stour, Warwickshire.
Std: 01608 **Tel:** 684663
Nearest Town/Resort Moreton-on-Marsh.
Directions Turn off A3400 west for Barton-on-the-Heath. Site on right in ½ mile.
Acreage 3 **Open** March **to** October
Access Good **Site** Level
Sites Available **Total** 10
Facilities
Nearby Facilities
Moreton-in-Marsh.
Fringe of the Cotswolds.

RUGBY

Lodge Farm, Bilton Lane, Long Lawford, Rugby, Warwickshire, CV23 9DU.
Std: 01788 **Tel:** 560193
Std: 01788 **Fax:** 550603
Nearest Town/Resort Rugby

Directions Take the A428 from Rugby towards Coventry. After 1½ miles turn left at Sheaf & Sickle, site is 400 yards on the left.
Acreage 2½ **Open** Easter **to** End October
Access Good **Site** Level
Sites Available **Total** 35
Facilities
Nearby Facilities
Rugby

SHIPSTON-ON-STOUR

Parkhill Farm, Idlicote Road, Halford, Shipston on Stour, Warks.
Std: 01608 **Tel:** 662492
Nearest Town/Resort Shipston on Stour
Directions A429 Fosse Way to Halford, turn for Idlicote road ½ mile on fork.
Acreage 5 **Open** Easter **to** October
Access Good **Site** Lev/Slope
Sites Available
Facilities
Nearby Facilities
Moreton in Marsh
By River Stour.

SOUTHAM

Holt Farm, (N.G. & A.C. Adkins), Southam, Leamington Spa, CV33 0NJ.
Std: 01926 **Tel:** 812225
Directions From Southam By-Pass, follow camping and caravan signs. Site is 3 miles from Southam off Priors Marston, Priors Hardwick Road.
Acreage 1½ **Open** March **to** End October
Access Good **Site** Level
Sites Available **Total** 45
Facilities
Nearby Facilities
Leamington Spa.
Ideal touring centre for Mid Warwickshire. Near canal.

STRATFORD-UPON-AVON

Dodwell Park, Evesham Road, Stratford-upon-Avon, Warwickshire, CV37 9SR.
Std: 01789 **Tel:** 204957
Std: 01926 **Fax:** 336476
Nearest Town/Resort Stratford-upon-Avon.
Directions 2 miles southwest of Stratford on B439 (formerly the A439)- Not the race-course site.
Acreage 2 **Open** All Year
Access Good **Site** Lev/Slope
Sites Available **Total** 50
Facilities
Nearby Facilities
Stratford-upon-Avon.
√√√√Graded Park. Shakespeare Theatre and Cotswolds.

STRATFORD-UPON-AVON

Island Meadow Caravan Park, Aston Cantlow, Warwickshire, B95 6JP.
Std: 01789 **Tel:** 488273
Std: 01789 **Fax:** 488273
Nearest Town/Resort Stratford-upon-Avon.
Directions From the A46 or the A3400 follow signs for Aston Cantlow Village. Park is ½ mile west of the village in Mill Lane.
Acreage 3 **Open** March **to** October
Access Good **Site** Level
Sites Available **Total** 34
Facilities
Nearby Facilities
Wilmcote
√√√√Graded Park. Small, quiet island with fishing, adjacent to a picturesque village. Ideal centre for Shakespeare Country.

STRATFORD-UPON-AVON

Riverside Caravan Park, Tiddington Road, Stratford-upon-Avon, Warwickshire, CV37 7AG.
Std: 01789 **Tel:** 292312
Nearest Town/Resort Stratford-upon-Avon
Directions On the B4086 1¼ miles from the town centre, just before entering Tiddington Village.
Acreage 8 **Open** April **to** October
Access Good **Site** Lev/Slope
Sites Available **Total** 90
Facilities
Nearby Facilities
Stratford-upon-Avon
Alongside river, close to Shakespeare House.

STUDLEY

Outhill Caravan Park, Outhill, Studley, Warwicks, B80 7DY.
Std: 01527 **Tel:** 852160
Nearest Town/Resort Henley-in-Arden
Directions From A435 (Birmingham to Evesham road) turn towards Henley-in-Arden on A4189. Take third turning to the right (approx 1¼ miles), check in at Outhill Farm (first on left).
Acreage 11 **Open** April **to** October
Access Good **Site** Level
Sites Available **Total** 15
Facilities
Peace and quiet.

WOLVEY

Wolvey Caravan Park, "Villa Farm", Wolvey, Warwickshire, LE10 3HF.
Std: 01455 **Tel:** 220493/220630
Nearest Town/Resort Hinckley
Directions Leave the M6 at junction 2 then take the B4065 and follow Wolvey signs. Leave the M69 at junction 1 and follow signs for Wolvey and camping signs.
Acreage 8 **Open** All Year
Access Good **Site** Level
Sites Available **Total** 110
Facilities
Nearby Facilities
Hinckley
A quiet site, ideally situated to explore the many places of interest in the Midlands.

WEST MIDLANDS

HALESOWEN

Camping & Caravanning Club Site, Fieldhouse Lane, Romsley, Halesowen, West Midlands, B62 0NH.
Std: 01562 **Tel:** 710015
Nearest Town/Resort Halesowen
Directions Travelling northwest on the M5, leave at junction 3 onto the A456. Then take the B4551 to Romsley, turn right at Sun Hotel, take signpost for Bell End Broughton on the left, take the next left and left again and the site is straight ahead.
Acreage 6½ **Open** 24 March **to** 3 November
Access Good **Site** Lev/Slope
Sites Available **Total** 120
Facilities
Nearby Facilities
Bromsgrove
√√√√Graded Park. In the heart of the West Midlands. Ideal for walkers and cyclists. Close to Dudley Castle and Zoo. AA 4 Pennants.

MERIDEN

Somers Wood Caravan & Camping Park, Somers Road, Meriden, Coventry, West Midlands, CV7 7PL.
Std: 01676 **Tel:** 522978
Std: 01676 **Fax:** 522978
Nearest Town/Resort Solihull
Directions Leave the M42 at junction 6, take the A45 to Coventry. Immediately on the left pick up signs for the A452 Leamington. Down to roundabout and turn right onto the A452 signed Leamington/Warwick, at the next roundabout turn left into Hampton Lane. Site is ½ mile on the left hand side.
Acreage 4 **Open** All Year
Access Good **Site** Level
Sites Available **Total** 48
Facilities
Nearby Facilities
Hampton-in-Arden
Adjacent to a golf course with clubhouse. Approx. 3 miles from the N.E.C. Birmingham. Fishing adjacent.

SUTTON COLDFIELD

Camping & Caravanning Club Site, Kingsbury Water Park, Bodymoor Heath Lane, Sutton Coldfield, West Midlands, B76 0DY.
Std: 01827 **Tel:** 874101
Directions Leave the M42 at junction 9 and take the B4097 towards Kingsbury. At the roundabout turn left and continue past the main entrance to the water park, go over the motorway and turn next right, follow lane for ½ mile to the site.
Open 22 March **to** 1 Nov
Site Level
Sites Available **Total** 120
Facilities
Nearby Facilities
Tamworth
√√√Graded Park. Surrounding the site are the 600 acres of Kingsbury Water Park.

WILTSHIRE

CALNE

Blackland Lakes Holiday & Leisure Centre, Stockley Lane, Calne, Wiltshire, SN11 0NQ.
Std: 01249 **Tel:** 813672
Std: 01249 **Fax:** 811346
Nearest Town/Resort Calne
Directions Signposted east of Calne from the A4.
Acreage 17 **Open** All Year
Access Good **Site** Mostly Level
Sites Available **Total** 180
Facilities
Nearby Facilities
Chippenham
Rural, natural, scenic, sheltered paddocks. 3 small lakes for super coarse fishing. 20 x 10m covered swimming pool. Catering and licensed bar for groups. Take-away food available. 120 electric hook-ups (increased supply for 1997 - 10 amp). 15 Super Pitches. AA 4 Pennants.

CASTLE EATON

Second Chance Caravan Park, Nr. Marston Meysey, Wltshire, SN6 6SN.
Std: 01285 **Tel:** 810675
Nearest Town/Resort Castle Eaton/ Fairford

Directions Between Swindon and Cirencester on the A419. Turn off at the Fairford/Latton signpost and caravan park signs. Proceed approx. 3 miles then turn right at the Castle Eaton signpost. We are on the right.
Acreage 2 **Open** March **to** November
Access Good **Site** Level
Sites Available **Total** 26
Facilities
Nearby Facilities
Swindon
Riverside location, private fishing and access for your own canoe, to explore upper reaches of Thames. Ideal base for touring the Cotswolds. A.A. 2 Pennants and RAC.

CHIPPENHAM

Piccadilly Caravan Site, Folly Lane West, Lacock, Chippenham, Wiltshire, SN15 2LP.
Std: 01249 **Tel:** 730260
Nearest Town/Resort Chippenham/Melksham.
Directions Turn right off A350 Chippenham/Melksham Road,5 miles south of Chippenham, close to Lacock. Signposted to Gastard (with caravan symbol), site is after the Nurseries.
Acreage 2½ **Open** April **to** October
Access Good **Site** Level
Sites Available **Total** 40
Facilities
Nearby Facilities
Chippenham.
✓✓✓✓✓Graded Park. Close National Trust village of Lacock. Ideal touring centre.

DEVIZES

Bell Caravan & Camping Site, Andover Road, Lydeway, Devizes, Wiltshire, SN10 3PS.
Std: 01380 **Tel:** 840230
Std: 01380 **Fax:** 840137
Nearest Town/Resort Devizes.
Directions 3 miles south east of Devizes on Andover A342 road.
Acreage 3 **Open** April **to** 1 October
Access Good **Site** Level
Sites Available **Total** 30
Facilities
Nearby Facilities
Pewsey.
✓✓✓✓Graded Park. Ideal touring, Stonehenge, Avebury and Bath. Off License.

DEVIZES

Camping & Caravanning Club Site, Sells Green, Nr Seend, Devizes, Wiltshire, SN12 6RN.
Std: 01203 **Tel:** 694995
Directions Take the A365 from Melksham, turn right down the lane beside Three Magpies Public House, site is on the right.
Open All Year
Site Level
Sites Available **Total** 90
Facilities
Nearby Facilities
Bordering the Kennett & Avon Canal, fishing on site.

MALMESBURY

Burton Hill Caravan & Camping Park, Arches Lane, Burton Hill, Malmesbury, Wiltshire.
Std: 01666 **Tel:** 822585
Std: 01666 **Fax:** 822585
Nearest Town/Resort Malmesbury.
Directions Turn off the A429 Chippenham road into Arches Lane, opposite Malmesbury Hospital. ½ mile south of Malmesbury.
Acreage 1½ **Open** April **to** November
Access Good **Site** Level
Sites Available **Total** 30
Facilities
Nearby Facilities
Chippenham.
✓✓✓Graded Park. A quiet site on the edge of Cotswolds. Dogs welcome.

MARLBOROUGH

Hill-View Caravan Park, Oare, Marlborough, Wiltshire.
Std: 01672 **Tel:** 563151
Nearest Town/Resort Marlborough.
Directions On A345, 6 miles south of Marlborough on Pewsey/Amesbury road.
Open Easter **to** September
Access Good **Site** Level
Sites Available **Total** 10
Facilities
Nearby Facilities
Pewsey.
✓✓✓✓Graded Park. Place of historic interest and scenic views. SAE for enquiries. Booking is advisable.

MARLBOROUGH

Postern Hill - Forestry Commission, Postern Hill, Marlborough, Wiltshire, SN8 4ND.
Std: 01672 **Tel:** 515195
Nearest Town/Resort Marlborough
Directions 1 mile south of Marlborough on the A346. Just 10 miles from the M4 junction 15.
Acreage 28½ **Open** Mid Mar **to** 20 Oct
Access Good **Site** Level
Sites Available **Total** 170
Facilities
Nearby Facilities
Marlborough
In the heart of Savernake Forest, the ideal site for exploring historic Wiltshire including Stonehenge and Salisbury Cathedral.

NETHERHAMPTON

Coombe Caravan Park, Coombe Nurseries, Race Plain, Netherhampton, Salisbury, Wilts, SP2 8PN.
Std: 01722 **Tel:** 328451
Std: 01722 **Fax:** 328451
Nearest Town/Resort Salisbury
Directions Take A36-A30 Salisbury - Wilton road, turn off at traffic lights onto A3094 Netherhampton - Stratford Tony road, cross on bend following Stratford Tony road, 2nd left behind racecourse, site on right, signposted.
Acreage 3 **Open** All Year
Access Good **Site** Level
Sites Available **Total** 48
Facilities
Nearby Facilities
Salisbury
Adjacent to racecourse (flat racing), ideal touring, lovely views.

ORCHESTON

Stonehenge Touring Park, Orcheston, Near Shrewton, Wiltshire.
Std: 01980 **Tel:** 620304
Std: 01980 **Fax:** 621121
Nearest Town/Resort Salisbury
Directions On A360 11 miles Salisbury, 11 miles Devizes.
Acreage 2 **Open** All Year
Access Good **Site** Level
Sites Available **Total** 30
Facilities
Nearby Facilities
Salisbury.
✓✓✓✓Graded Park. Stonehenge 5 miles, Salisbury plain, easy reach Bath and the New Forest. Take Away Food. AA 3 Pennants.

SALISBURY

Camping & Caravanning Club Site, Hudson's Field, Castle Road, Salisbury, Wiltshire, SP1 3RR.
Std: 01722 **Tel:** 320713
Directions 1½ miles from Salisbury or 7 miles from Amesbury on the A345. Hudson's Field is a large open field next to Old Sarum.
Acreage 4½ **Open** 22 March **to** 1 Nov
Site Lev/Slope
Sites Available **Total** 150
Facilities
Nearby Facilities
Salisbury
✓✓✓✓Graded Park. ¼ mile from Old Sarum Castle and 1 mile from Salisbury Cathedral. Plenty to do in the local area.

SALISBURY

Summerlands Caravan Park, Rockbourne Road, Coombe Bissett, Salisbury, Wiltshire, SP5 4LP.
Std: 01722 **Tel:** 718259
Nearest Town/Resort Salisbury
Directions Turn left off the A354 (Salisbury to Blandford road) 1½ miles past Coombe Bissett church at the signpost Rockbourne, Roman Villa. After 300 yards turn left at the park sign, ¾ mile down a gravel road.
Open April **to** October
Access Good **Site** Level
Sites Available
Facilities
Nearby Facilities
Salisbury
Panoramic views, 450' contour line, facing south in the midst of the rolling chalk downs of Wiltshire. Ideal for walkers and cyclists. Within easy reach of Salisbury, Stone Henge and the New Forest. Gas is available at the village shop.

TILSHEAD

Brades Acre, Tilshead, Salisbury, Wiltshire, SP3 4RX.
Std: 01980 **Tel:** Shrewton 620402
Nearest Town/Resort Salisbury/Devizes.
Directions A360, 10 miles to Devizes, 13 miles to Salisbury.
Acreage 1½ **Open** All Year
Access Good **Site** Level
Sites Available **Total** 35
Facilities
Nearby Facilities
Salisbury.
Touring for Stonehenge, Salisbury Cathedral, Wilton and Longleat Houses. Avebury, Orcheston riding.

WESTBURY

Woodland Park, Brokerswood, Nr. Westbury, Wiltshire, BA13 4EH.
Std: 01373 **Tel:** 822238
Std: 01373 **Fax:** 858474
Nearest Town/Resort Westbury/Trowbridge.

Directions 4 miles Westbury, 5 miles Trowbridge, 5 miles Frome, left off A361 Southwick onto unclassified 1¼ miles on left, turn at Standerwick on A36.
Acreage 1 **Open** All Year
Access Good **Site** Level
Sites Available **Total** 30
Facilities
Nearby Facilities
Westbury.
Site adjoins an 80 acre area of forest open to the public together with a museum, lake, Narrow Gauge Railway, etc.

WHITEPARISH

Hillcrest Campsite, Southampton Road, Whiteparish, Nr Salisbury, Wilts, SP5 2QW.
Std: 01794 **Tel:** 884471
Std: 01794 **Fax:** 884471
Nearest Town/Resort Salisbury
Directions 8 miles from Salisbury on A36. Travelling towards Southampton, one mile from A27 junction at Brickworth Garage on left.
Acreage 3 **Open** All Year
Access Good **Site** Lev/slop
Sites Available **Total** 35
Facilities
Nearby Facilities
Salisbury
√√√√Graded Park. Central to Salisbury, Winchester, New Forest. Ideal for overnight stop before channel crossing.

WORCESTERSHIRE

EVESHAM

Evesham Vale Caravan Park, Yessell Farm, Boston Lane, Charlton, Near Evesham, Worcestershire, WR11 6RD.
Std: 01386 **Tel:** 860377
Nearest Town/Resort Evesham
Directions From Evesham take the A44, after approx. 1½ miles turn right for Charlton. Park is on the left hand side after approx. ¾ mile.
Acreage 6 **Open** April **to** October
Access Good **Site** Level
Sites Available **Total** 70
Facilities
Nearby Facilities
Evesham
On the Blossom Trail route, near a river for fishing. Central for the Cotswolds, Stratford, Worcester, etc..

EVESHAM

Ranch Caravan Park, Station Road, Honeybourne, Nr. Evesham, Worcestershire, WR11 5QG.
Std: 01386 **Tel:** 830744
Std: 01386 **Fax:** 833503
Nearest Town/Resort Evesham.
Directions From Evesham take B4035 to Badsey and Bretforton. Turn left to Honeybourne. At village crossroads take Bidford direction, site on left in 400 yards.
Acreage 48 **Open** March **to** November
Access Good **Site** Level
Sites Available **Total** 120
Facilities
Nearby Facilities
Evesham.
√√√√√Graded Park. Situated in meadow land in Vale of Evesham on north edge of Cotswolds. Meals available in licensed club.

EVESHAM

Weir Meadow Holiday & Touring Park, Lower Leys, Evesham, Worcestershire.
Std: 01386. **Tel:** 442417
Std: 01386 **Fax:** 442417
Nearest Town/Resort Evesham.
Directions On A44, 500 yards south of town centre.
Acreage 10 **Open** April **to** October
Access Good **Site** Level
Sites Available **Total** 65
Facilities
Nearby Facilities
Evesham.
√√√√√Graded Park. In the centre of Evesham. Own River Avon frontage, boat moorings. One dog only allowed. Free fishing on site for patrons only. Site shop selling ice-cream and caravan accessories. Hire caravan available for the disabled. We also hire Rose Award Caravans and chalets.

GREAT MALVERN

Camping & Caravanning Club Site, Blackmore Camp Site No. 2, Hanley Swan, Worcestershire, WR8 0EE.
Std: 01684 **Tel:** 310280
Nearest Town/Resort Worcester
Directions Take the A38 to Upton-on-Severn, turn north over the river bridge, turn second left then first left signposted Hanley Swan. Site is on the right after 1 mile.
Acreage 12 **Open** 22 March **to** 27 Nov
Access Good **Site** Level
Sites Available **Total** 200
Facilities
Nearby Facilities
Worcester
√√√√Graded Park. Close to the River Severn. Situated in the Malvern Hills, ideal walking country. Close to the market towns of Ledbury, Tewkesbury and Evesham.

HARTLEBURY

Shorthill Caravan & Camping Centre, Crossway Green, Worcester Road, Hartlebury, Worcestershire, DY13 9SH.
Std: 01299 **Tel:** 250571
Nearest Town/Resort Stourport-on-Severn
Directions Take the A449 Kidderminster to Worcester road. At garage island go straight over, 200 yards to the Little Chef Restaurant, site is at the rear of the restaurant.
Acreage 3 **Open** All Year
Access Good **Site** Level
Sites Available **Total** 50
Facilities
Nearby Facilities
Hartlebury
Ideal touring site with outdoor swimming and paddling pools and a childrens play area. Inland pleasure/leisure resort, funfair etc., 3 miles.

KIDDERMINSTER

Camping & Caravanning Club Site, Brown Westhead Park, Wolverley, Nr. Kidderminster, Worcestershire, DY10 3PX.
Std: 01562 **Tel:** 850909
Directions From Kidderminster take the A449 to Wolverhampton, turn left at the traffic lights onto the B4189 signposted Wolverley. Look for brown camping sign and turn right, the site entrance is on the left hand side.
Open 22 March **to** 1 Nov
Site Lev/Slope
Sites Available **Total** 119
Facilities
Nearby Facilities
√√√√Graded Park. A quiet village site. Table tennis on site. Just 2 miles from Kidderminster and the Severn Valley Railway.

MALVERN

Kingsgreen Caravan Park, Berrow, Near Malvern, Worcestershire, WR13 6AQ.
Std: 01531 **Tel:** 650272
Nearest Town/Resort Ledbury/Malvern
Directions From Ledbury take the A417 towards Gloucester. Go over the M50 then take the first turning left to the Malvern Park,

we are 1 mile on the right. OR M50 Southbound junction 2, turn left onto the A417, in 1 mile turn left to the Malverns.
Acreage 3 **Open** 1 March **to** End October
Access Good **Site** Level
Sites Available **Total** 45
Facilities
Nearby Facilities
Ledbury/Malvern
Beautiful walks on the Malvern Hills and Malvern with its famous Elgar Route. Historic Black and White timber towns. Tewkesbury and Upton-on-Severn. Fishing on site.

MALVERN

The Robin Hood, Castle Morton, Near Malvern, Worcestershire, WR13 6BS.
Std: 01684 **Tel:** 833212
Nearest Town/Resort Malvern/Ledbury
Directions The B4208 Worcester to Gloucester road.
Open All Year
Access Good **Site** Level
Sites Available **Total** 15
Facilities
Nearby Facilities
Malvern/Ledbury
Situated at the foot of the Malvern Hills, ideal for walking, riding and cycling.

MALVERN

Three Counties Park, Sledge Green, Berrow, Nr. Malvern, Worcestershire, WR13 6JW.
Std: 01684 **Tel:** Birtsmorton 833439
Std: 01684 **Fax:** 833439
Nearest Town/Resort Tewkesbury
Directions From Tewkesbury take A438 Ledbury road for 6 miles.
Acreage 2 **Open** April **to** October
Access Good **Site** Level
Sites Available **Total** 50
Facilities
Nearby Facilities
Tewkesbury
Malvern Hills, Rivers Severn and Avon. Walking, boating, and historic sights.

SHRAWLEY

Lenchford Caravan Park, Shrawley, Worcestershire, WR6 6TB.
Std: 01905 **Tel:** Worcester 620246
Nearest Town/Resort Worcester
Directions Take A443 Worcester/Tenbury road. At Holt Heath crossroads, take B4196 to Stourport. Signpost in ¾ mile on right.
Acreage 2 **Open** All Year
Access Good **Site** Level
Sites Available **Total** 12
Facilities
Nearby Facilities
Worcester.

STOURPORT-ON-SEVERN

Lickhill Manor Caravan Park, Lickhill Manor, Stourport-on-Severn, Worcestershire, DY13 8RL.
Std: 01299 **Tel:** 871041/822024
Std: 01299 **Fax:** 824998
Nearest Town/Resort Stourport-on-Severn.
Directions From Stourport town centre proceed 1 mile along Lickhill Road, turn left at sign and follow lane.
Acreage 9 **Open** All Year
Access Good **Site** Level
Sites Available **Total** 120
Facilities
Nearby Facilities
Kidderminster.
✓✓✓✓✓Graded Park. Alongside river, fishing rights held. Walks through unspoilt Wyre Forest. West Midlands Safari Park, Severn Valley Railway.

STOURPORT-ON-SEVERN

Lincomb Lock Caravan Park, Lincomb Lock, Titton, Stourport-on-Severn, Worcestershire, DY13 9QR.
Std: 01299 **Tel:** 823836
Nearest Town/Resort Stourport-on-Severn
Directions 1 mile from Stourport on the A4025 turn right at park signs. Or approaching from the A4025 at Cross Way Green, after 1 mile turn left at park signs.
Acreage 1 **Open** 1 March **to** 6 January
Access Good **Site** Level
Sites Available **Total** 14
Facilities
Nearby Facilities
Kidderminster.
✓✓✓Graded Park. Alongside a river. Local attractions to suit all ages including West Midlands Safari Park, Severn Railway, Riverside Amusements, ancient Wyre Forest and local museums.

WORCESTER

Ketch Caravan Park, Bath Road, Worcester, Worcs, WR5 3HW.
Std: 01905 **Tel:** 820430
Nearest Town/Resort Worcester
Directions Leave the M5 at junction 7 and take the main A38 Worcester to Tewkesbury road for 1¾ miles.
Acreage 3 **Open** April **to** End October
Access Good **Site** Level
Sites Available **Total** 32
Facilities
Nearby Facilities
Worcester
On the River Severn.

WORCESTER

Mill House Caravan & Camping Site, Mill House, Hawford, Worcestershire.
Std: 01905 **Tel:** 451283
Std: 01905 **Fax:** 754143
Nearest Town/Resort Worcester.
Directions A449 Worcester to Kidderminster.
Acreage 8½ **Open** Easter **to** October
Access Good **Site** Level
Sites Available **Total** 150
Facilities
Nearby Facilities
Shrubhill/Worcester
Please note motocycles are not allowed into field.

YORKSHIRE (EAST)

BARMBY MOOR

The Sycamores Camping & Caravan Park, Feoffe Common Lane, Barmby Moor, East Yorkshire, YO4 5HS.
Std: 01759 **Tel:** 388838
Nearest Town/Resort York/Bridlington
Directions From York take the A1079 (York to Hull road) east for approx. 7 miles, turn sharp left before the Esso Filling Station signposted Yapham, we are 200 yards on the right hand side.
Acreage 3 **Open** March **to** November
Access Good **Site** Level
Sites Available **Total** 36
Facilities
Nearby Facilities
York
✓✓✓✓Graded Park. York City Centre and a gliding club nearby.

BARMSTON

Barmston Beach Caravan Park, Sands Lane, Barmston, Nr. Driffield, East Yorkshire, YO25 8PJ.
Std: 01262 **Tel:** 468202
Directions Take A165 from Bridlington to Hull. The turning to Barmston Beach is signposted about six miles South of Bridlington.
Open March **to** November
Access Good **Site** Level
Sites Available **Total** 8
Facilities
Nearby Facilities
Bridlington
✓✓✓✓Graded Park. Barmston Beach is right next to the beach. Bridlington is a bustling resort with an attractive old harbour. Ideal for touring the Yorkshire beauty spots and popular resorts. part of Haven Holidays.

BEVERLEY

Lakeminster Park, Hull road, Beverley, East Yorkshire, HU17 0PN.
Std: 01482 **Tel:** 882655
Std: 01482 **Fax:** 882655
Nearest Town/Resort Beverley
Directions One mile from main Hull to Beverley road on the 1174.
Open All Year
Access Good **Site** Level
Sites Available **Total** 50
Facilities
Nearby Facilities
Beverley & Hull
on site two ponds well stocked with fish. Bar with food also takeaway. 14 miles from Hornsea.

BRANDES BURTON

Dacre Lakeside Park, Brandes Burton, Driffield, East Yorkshire, YO25 8RT.
Std: 01964 **Tel:** 543704
Std: 01964 **Fax:** 544040
Nearest Town/Resort Beverley
Directions From the A1 or M1 take the M62 then the A63 to South Cave. Turn off after junction 38 onto the A1079. Go by Beverley onto the A1035, then onto the A165.
Acreage 10 **Open** March **to** October
Access Good **Site** Level
Sites Available **Total** 120
Facilities
Nearby Facilities
Beverley
✓✓✓✓✓Graded Park. 8 acre lake for fishing, wind surfing and sailing. E-mail: dacresurf@aol.com

BRIDLINGTON

Shirley Caravan Park, Jewison Lane, Bridlington, East Yorkshire, YO16 5YG.
Std: 01262 **Tel:** 676442
Std: 01262 **Fax:** 676442
Nearest Town/Resort Bridlington
Directions From roundabout on A165 take B1255 to Flamborough for 2 miles. Jewison Lane is on the left and site is on the left after the level crossing.
Acreage 25 **Open** March **to** November
Access Good **Site** Level
Sites Available **Total** 46
Facilities
Nearby Facilities
Bridlington

BRIDLINGTON

South Cliff Caravan Park, Wilsthorpe, Bridlington, East Yorkshire, YO15 3QN.
Std: 01262 **Tel:** 671051
Std: 01262 **Fax:** 605639
Nearest Town/Resort Bridlington
Directions 1½ miles south of Bridlington on the A165.
Open March **to** November
Access Good **Site** Level
Sites Available **Total** 200
Facilities
Nearby Facilities
Bridlington
✓✓✓✓Graded Park. Easy access to award winning, sandy beaches.

BRIDLINGTON

The Poplars, 45 Jewison Lane, Sewerby, Bridlington, East Yorkshire, YO15 1DX.
Std: 01262 **Tel:** 677251
Nearest Town/Resort Bridlington
Directions Take B1255 towards Flamborough, after 2 miles turn left off the second leg of Z bend.
Acreage 1¼ **Open** All Year
Access Good **Site** Level
Sites Available **Total** 30
Facilities
Nearby Facilities
Bridlington
Family owned pub/restaurant next door. family room with free entertainment. Also motel on site.

HORNSEA

Longbeach Leisure Park, South Cliff, Hornsea, East Yorkshire, HU18 1TL.
Std: 01964 **Tel:** 532506
Std: 01964 **Fax:** 536846
Nearest Town/Resort Hornsea
Acreage 50 **Open** March **to** October
Access Good **Site** Level
Sites Available **Total** 50
Facilities
Nearby Facilities
Hull
✓✓✓✓Graded Park. By the sea with direct access. 400 metres from a leisure centre with swimming pool. Freshwater and sea fishing. 9 hole golf course on park.

HORNSEA

Springfield Caravan Park, Atwick Road, Hornsea, East Yorkshire.
Std: 01964 **Tel:** 532112
Std: 01964 **Fax:** 535530
Nearest Town/Resort Hornsea
Directions Leave Hornsea on main Bridlington road, site ¼ mile on top of hill.
Acreage 2 **Open** Easter **to** End October
Access Good **Site** Level
Sites Available **Total** 30
Facilities
Nearby Facilities
Beverley
Views of the bay.

LITTLE WEIGHTON

Louvain, Rowley Road, Little Weighton, East Yorkshire, HU20 3XJ.
Std: 01482 **Tel:** 848249
Nearest Town/Resort Beverley
Directions From M62 then A63. At South cave crossroads turn right (Beverley Road) keep on this road for approx 3 miles, turn left at signpost Little Weighton & Rowley.
Acreage 1½ **Open** All Year
Access Good **Site** Level
Sites Available **Total** 5
Facilities
Nearby Facilities
Hull
Old Town Beverley. Ideal touring.

ROOS

Sand-le-Mere Caravan Park, Seaside Lane, Tunstall, Roos, Nr. Hull, East Yorkshire, HU12 0JQ.
Std: 01964 **Tel:** 670403
Std: 01964 **Fax:** 671099
Nearest Town/Resort Withernsea
Directions From Hull to Preston heading north on the A1033. Burton Pidsea, Roos to Tunstall to the sea.
Acreage 3 **Open** March **to** 31 December
Access Good **Site** Level
Sites Available **Total** 40
Facilities
Nearby Facilities
Hull
✓✓✓Graded Park. Natural slope to the beach. Fresh water fishing. Heated swimming pool and jacuzzi.

RUDSTON

Thorpe Hall Caravan & Camping Site, Rudston, Driffield, East Yorkshire, YO25 4JE.
Std: 01262 **Tel:** 420393
Std: 01262 **Fax:** 420588
Nearest Town/Resort Bridlington
Directions 4½ miles from Bridlington on the B1253.
Acreage 4½ **Open** March **to** October
Access Good **Site** Level
Sites Available **Total** 90
Facilities
Nearby Facilities
Bridlington
✓✓✓✓Graded Park. Countryside site with our own fishery. Ideally placed for touring.

SKIPSEA

Far Grange Park Skipsea, Driffield, East Yorkshire, YO25 8SY.
Std: 01262 **Tel:** 468293/468248
Std: 01262 **Fax:** 468648
Nearest Town/Resort Hornsea
Directions 4¼ miles north of Hornsea on B1242.
Open March **to** October
Access Good **Site** Level
Sites Available **Total** 180
Facilities
Nearby Facilities
Bridlington
✓✓✓✓✓Graded Park. Clifftop location with superb views of Bridlington Bay.

SKIPSEA

Mill Farm Country Park, Mill Lane, Skipsea, East Yorkshire, YO25 8SS.
Std: 01262 **Tel:** 468211
Nearest Town/Resort Hornsea
Directions The A165 Hull to Bridlington Road, at Beeford take B1249 to Skipsea. At crossroads turn right, then first left up Cross Street which leads on to Mill Lane, site is on the right.
Acreage 6 **Open** 1st March **to** 10th October
Access Good **Site** Level
Sites Available **Total** 56
Facilities
Nearby Facilities
Bridlington
Farm walk, beach nearby. RSPB sites at Bempton and Hornsea. Good centre for many places of local interest. Many facilities nearby including an indoor swimming pool ½ mile away.

SKIPSEA

Skipsea Sands Holiday Park, Mill Lane, Skipsea, East Yorkshire, YO25 8TZ.
Std: 01262 **Tel:** 468210
Std: 01262 **Fax:** 468454
Nearest Town/Resort Hornsea
Directions Off the B1242 Hornsea to Bridlington road. In Skipsea Village follow signs into Cross Street then into Mill Lane, park is 1 mile from the village.
Acreage 8 **Open** March **to** November
Access Good **Site** Level
Sites Available **Total** 60
Facilities
Nearby Facilities
Bridlington
✓✓✓✓Graded Park. Coastal park with full facilities for a pleasant family holiday.

SKIPSEA

Skirlington Leisure Park, Low Skirlington, Skipsea, Driffield, East Yorkshire, YO25 8SY.
Std: 01262 **Tel:** 468213/466
Std: 01262 **Fax:** 468105
Nearest Town/Resort Bridlington
Directions 3 miles north of Hornsea on the B1242.
Acreage 30 **Open** March **to** October
Access Good **Site** Level
Sites Available **Total** 300
Facilities
Nearby Facilities
Bridlington

SOUTH CAVE

Waudby Caravan and Camping Park, Brough Road, South Cave, East Yorkshire, HU15 2DB.
Std: 01430 **Tel:** 422523
Std: 01430 **Fax:** 424777

Nearest Town/Resort Hull/Beverley
Directions Situated 12 miles west of Hull off A63. From east depart A63 at South Cave, park opposite petrol station. From west depart A63 South Cave, right at top opposite petrol station.
Acreage 1 **Open** April **to** 6th January
Access Good **Site** Level
Sites Available **Total** 20
Facilities
Nearby Facilities
Brough
Scenic Walks on Yorkshire Dales. Near to Humber Bridge and Beverley.

STAMFORD BRIDGE

Weir Camping Park, Stamford Bridge, East Yorkshire, YO41 1AN.
Std: 01759 **Tel:** 371377
Std: 01759 **Fax:** 371377
Nearest Town/Resort York
Directions Off A166 7miles north-west of Pocklington, 7miles east of York.
Acreage 2 **Open** March **to** October
Access Good **Site** Lev/Slope
Sites Available **Total** 60
Facilities
Nearby Facilities
✓✓✓✓Graded Park.

WILBERFOSS

Fangfoss Old Station Caravan Park, Fangfoss, East Yorkshire, YO4 5QB.
Std: 01759 **Tel:** 380491
Nearest Town/Resort York
Directions The A1079 towards Hull. 7miles to Wilberfoss, signposted left to Fangfoss.
Acreage 4 **Open** March **to** October
Access Good **Site** Level
Sites Available **Total** 45
Facilities
Nearby Facilities
York
✓✓✓Graded Park. Peaceful country park, easy access to Wolds, coast, moors, York etc..

WITHERNSEA

Seathorne Holiday Village, North Road, Withernsea, East Yorkshire, HU19 2BS.
Std: 01964 **Tel:** 612189
Std: 01964 **Fax:** 612189
Nearest Town/Resort Hornsea
Directions From Hull go straight down Queen Street, turn left into Hull Road, turn right into North Road at the lighthouse.
Open 1 March **to** 31 December
Access Good **Site** Level
Sites Available
Facilities
Nearby Facilities
Hull
Close to the beach and amusements.

YORKSHIRE (NORTH)

AYSGARTH

Little Cote Site, West Burton, Aysgarth, North Yorkshire, DL8 4JY.
Std: 01969 **Tel:** 663450
Directions From the A684 Aysgarth/ Northallerton road, 2 miles east of Aysgarth take the B6160 to West Burton, fork left Walden for ¾ mile.
Acreage 2 **Open** March **to** October
Access Good **Site** Lev/Slope
Sites Available **Total** 20
Facilities
Northallerton
Small, quiet site alongside a river. Own car essential. Ideal touring.

AYSGARTH

Street Head Caravan Park, Newbiggin, Bishopdale, Leyburn, North Yorks, DL8 3TE.
Std: 01969 **Tel:** 663472
Std: 01969 **Fax:** 663571
Nearest Town/Resort Aysgarth
Directions From the A684 Leyburn to Hawes road, take the B6160 Kettlewell to Skipton road for 1½ miles. Site is on the right adjacent to Street Head Inn.
Acreage 4½ **Open** March **to** October
Access Good **Site** Lev/Slope
Sites Available **Total** 80
Facilities
Nearby Facilities
Northallerton
Small, quiet, well appointed site, in the heart of the Yorkshire Dales National Park.

AYSGARTH

Westholme Caravan & Camping Park, Aysgarth, Leyburn, North Yorks, DL8 3SP.
Std: 01969 **Tel:** 663268
Nearest Town/Resort Leyburn/Hawes.
Directions Follow the A684 from Leyburn towards Hawes, turn left in 7½ miles just before Aysgarth.
Acreage 22 **Open** March **to** October
Access Good **Site** Level
Sites Available **Total** 75
Facilities
Nearby Facilities
Darlington.
✓✓✓✓Graded Park. Alongside stream, scenic views, ideal touring centre. Fishing.

BARDEN

Howgill Lodge, Barden, Nr. Skipton, North Yorkshire, BD23 6DJ.
Std: 01756 **Tel:** 720655
Nearest Town/Resort Bolton Abbey
Directions Turn off B6160 at Barden Tower, site 1 mile on right.
Acreage 4 **Open** April **to** October
Access Narrow **Site** Terraced
Sites Available **Total** 30
Facilities
Nearby Facilities
Skipton.
✓✓✓✓Graded Park. Beautiful views, ideal for walking or touring.

BEDALE

Pembroke Caravan Park, 19 Low Street, Leeming Bar, Northallerton, North Yorkshire, DL7 9BW.
Std: 01677 **Tel:** 422652
Nearest Town/Resort Bedale.
Directions A1 Leeming Services, right onto A684 to Leeming Bar. Keep left, crossroads into Leases Road. ½ mile on the right.
Acreage 1¼ **Open** March **to** October
Access Good **Site** Slight Slope
Sites Available **Total** 25
Facilities
Nearby Facilities
Northallerton.
✓✓✓Graded Park. Between the Yorkshire Dales and North Yorks Moors. Take-away food available.

BENTHAM

Riverside Caravan Park, Wenning Avenue, Bentham, Nr. Lancaster, North Yorkshire.
Std: 015242 **Tel:** 61272
Std: 015242 **Fax:** 62163
Nearest Town/Resort Bentham.
Directions Off B6480 at Black Bull Hotel in Bentham and right before crossing river.
Acreage 9 **Open** March **to** October
Access Good **Site** Level
Sites Available **Total** 30
Facilities
Nearby Facilities
Bentham.
✓✓✓✓Graded Park. Riverside site, ideal for touring, with free fishing.

BOROUGHBRIDGE

Camping & Caravanning Club Site, Bar Lane, Roecliffe, Boroughbridge, North Yorkshire, YO51 9LS.
Std: 01423 **Tel:** 322683
Directions From junction 48 aim north and

southbound slip roads, follow signs for Bar Lane Industrial Estate and Roecliffe Village. Site entrance is ¼ mile from the roundabout.
Open All Year
Site Level
Sites Available **Total** 80
Facilities
Nearby Facilities
✓✓✓✓Graded Park. On the banks of the River Ure for fishing. Table tennis and pool table on site. Close to the Yorkshire Dales.

BOROUGHBRIDGE

Old Hall Caravan Park, Langthorpe, Boroughbridge, York, North Yorkshire, YO5 9BZ.
Std: 01423 **Tel:** 322130
Nearest Town/Resort Boroughbridge
Directions From Boroughbridge follow the B6265 towards Ripon (A1), pass the Anchor Pub on the left hand side, 200 yards further on turn left to Langthorpe, Skelton and Newby Hall. Park is second on the right.
Open April **to** October
Access Good **Site** Level
Sites Available **Total** 20
Facilities
Nearby Facilities
Knaresborough
✓✓✓✓Graded Park. Small countryside park. Ideal centre for York, Harrogate and The Moors.

CLAPHAM

Laughing Gravy, Flying Horse Shoe Hotel, Clapham, North Yorkshire, LA2 8ES.
Std: 015242 **Tel:** 51229
Std: 015242 **Fax:** 51229
Nearest Town/Resort Clapham
Directions Take the A65 from Settle to Ingleton, turn left after the sign marked Flying Horse Shoe.
Acreage 3½ **Open** March **to** November
Access Good **Site** Level
Sites Available **Total** 45
Facilities
Nearby Facilities
Clapham
Magnificent countryside, famous walks, potholes and mountains.

EASINGWOLD

Alders Caravan Park, Home Farm, Alne, York, North Yorkshire, YO61 1TB.
Std: 01347 **Tel:** 838722
Std: 01347 **Fax:** 838722
Nearest Town/Resort York
Directions 9 miles north of York on the A19, turn left. Or south of Easingwold on the A19, turn right. Alders is 2¼ miles in the centre of the village in Monk Green.
Acreage 6 **Open** March **to** October
Access Good **Site** Level
Sites Available **Total** 40
Facilities
Nearby Facilities
York
✓✓✓✓✓Graded Park. On a working farm, in historic parkland where visitors may enjoy peace and tranquility. York (on bus route), Moors, Dales and coast nearby.

EASINGWOLD

Hollybrook Touring Caravan Park, Penny Carr Lane, Off Stillington Road, Easingwold, York, YO6 3EU.
Std: 01347 **Tel:** 821906
Nearest Town/Resort York
Directions From A19 (York/Thirsk) turn right on entering Easingwold. Signpost-ed Stillington ¼ mile turn right, into narrow lane, site on right.
Acreage 2 **Open** March **to** December
Access Good **Site** Level
Sites Available **Total** 30
Facilities
Nearby Facilities
York
Ideal touring centre, North Yorks Moors, Dales, East Coast Resorts Owned by Caravanners. ADULTS ONLY.

FILEY

Blue Dolphin Holiday Centre, Gristhorpe Bay, Filey, North Yorkshire, YO14 9PU.
Std: 01723 **Tel:** 515155
Std: 01723 **Fax:** 512059
Nearest Town/Resort Scarborough
Directions Turn off the A165 Scarborough to Bridlington road, 2 miles north of Filey.
Acreage 30 **Open** Easter **to** End October
Access Good **Site** Lev/Slope
Sites Available **Total** 431
Facilities
Nearby Facilities
Filey
✓✓✓✓Graded Park. Extensive facilities on park. Close to Scarborough and North Yorkshire Moors National Park.

FILEY

Muston Grange Caravan Park, Muston Road, Filey, North Yorkshire, YO14 0HU.
Std: 01723 **Tel:** 512167
Nearest Town/Resort Filey
Directions On the A1039 south of Filey, site entrance is on the left 100yds before the junction with the A165.
Acreage 10 **Open** Late March **to** October
Access Good **Site** Lev/Slope
Sites Available **Total** 220
Facilities
Nearby Facilities
Filey
Pleasant walk to a five mile stretch of beach, 5 minute walk to a golf course. Ideally situated for visiting Scarborough, Bridlington and North Yorkshire Moors.

FILEY

Orchard Farm Holiday Village, Hunmanby, Filey, North Yorkshire, YO14 0PU.
Std: 01723 **Tel:** 891582
Std: 01723 **Fax:** 891582
Nearest Town/Resort Filey
Directions Turn off the A165 signposted Hunmanby, go under the railway bridge and the entrance is on the right.
Acreage 14 **Open** All Year
Access Good **Site** Sloping
Sites Available **Total** 85
Facilities
Nearby Facilities
Hunmanby
✓✓✓✓✓Graded Park. Well sheltered, family park with full amenities including bar, take-away food and entertainment. Fishing and boating on site. Close to sandy beaches. Bus route nearby. AA 4 Pennants.

FILEY

Primrose Valley Holiday Centre, Primrose Valley, Near Filey, North Yorkshire, YO14 9RF.
Std: 01723 **Tel:** 513771
Std: 01723 **Fax:** 513777
Nearest Town/Resort Filey
Directions Take the A165 Scarborough to Bridlington road. You will see our signpost about a mile from the Filey turn-off.
Acreage 170 **Open** March **to** October
Site Lev/Slope
Sites Available **Total** 90
Facilities
Nearby Facilities
Filey
✓✓✓✓Graded Park. Situated on a cliff top with access to a large sandy beach. Excellent facilities include swimming pools and evening entertainment.

FILEY

Reighton Sands Holiday Park, Reighton Gap, Nr. Filey, North Yorks, YO14 9SJ.
Std: 01723 **Tel:** 890476
Nearest Town/Resort Filey
Directions We are signposted opposite the garage at Reighton, on the A165 Filey to Bridlington road, and are located just 1 mile off this road.
Acreage 110 **Open** 19 Mar **to** End Oct
Access Good **Site** Lev/Slope
Sites Available **Total** 327
Facilities
Nearby Facilities
Filey
✓✓✓✓Graded Park. On a cliff top with access to a beach.

GRASSINGTON

Fold Farm, Kettlewell, Skipton, North Yorkshire, BD23 5RH.
Std: 01756 **Tel:** 760886
Std: 01756 **Fax:** 760464
Nearest Town/Resort Skipton
Directions On the B6160 to Skipton.
Acreage 1½ **Open** All Year
Sites Available
Facilities
Nearby Facilities
Skipton
Ideal walking and touring.

GRASSINGTON

Hawkswick Cote Caravan Park, Arncliffe, Skipton, North Yorkshire, BD23 5PX.
Std: 01756 **Tel:** 770226
Std: 01756 **Fax:** 770327
Nearest Town/Resort Skipton.
Directions Take the B6265 Skipton to Threshfield road, at Threshfield take the B6160 to Kilnsey, after Kilnsey bear left to Arncliffe. Park is 1½ miles on the left.
Open 6 March **to** 14 November
Access Good **Site** Level
Sites Available **Total** 50
Facilities
Nearby Facilities
Skipton.
Yorkshire Dales walking area and climbing at Kilnsey Crag.

GRASSINGTON

Threaplands Camping & Caravan Park, Threaplands House, Cracoe, Nr. Skipton, North Yorks, BD23 6LD.
Std: 01756 **Tel:** 730248
Nearest Town/Resort Skipton
Directions 6 miles from Skipton on the B6265 to Cracoe. ¼ mile past Cracoe keep going straight on, site is ¼ mile on the left.
Acreage 8 **Open** March **to** October
Access Good **Site** Level

Sites Available **Total** 30
Facilities

Nearby Facilities
Skipton
Scenic views. Ideal for touring and walking.

GRASSINGTON

Wood Nook Caravan Park, Skirethorns, Threshfield, Skipton, North Yorks, BD23 5NU.
Std: 01756 **Tel:** 752412
Std: 01756 **Fax:** 752412
Nearest Town/Resort Grassington
Directions From Skipton take the B6265 to Threshfield then the B6160 for 100yds. Turn left after garage into Skirethorns Lane, signposts at 600yds and 300yds entrance clearly marked Wood Nook on the left.
Acreage 3 **Open** March **to** October
Access Good **Site** Level
Sites Available **Total** 48
Facilities
Nearby Facilities
Skipton
✓✓✓✓Graded Park. Quiet, secluded, ideal for touring and walking.

GUISBOROUGH

Tockets Mill, Skelton Road, Guisborough, North Yorkshire, TS14 6QA.
Std: 01287 **Tel:** 610182
Std: 01287 **Fax:** 610182
Nearest Town/Resort Guisborough/ Saltburn
Directions 1 mile out of Guisborough on A173, Whitby Coast Road,
Acreage 38 **Open** March **to** October
Access Good **Site** Level
Sites Available **Total** 50
Facilities
Nearby Facilities
Saltburn

HARROGATE

Bilton Park, Village Farm, Bilton Lane, Harrogate, North Yorkshire, HG1 4DH.
Std: 01423 **Tel:** 863121
Nearest Town/Resort Harrogate.
Directions On the A59 in Harrogate between the A661 and the A61. Turn at Dragon Inn and site is 1 mile down Bilton Lane.
Acreage 8 **Open** April **to** October
Access Good **Site** Level
Sites Available **Total** 25
Facilities
Nearby Facilities
Harrogate.
River. Conference and Exhibition town. Ideal touring.

HARROGATE

Ripley Caravan Park, Ripley, Harrogate, North Yorks, HG3 3AU.
Std: 01423 **Tel:** 770050
Std: 01423 **Fax:** 770050
Nearest Town/Resort Harrogate
Directions From Harrogate take A61 to Ripon after 3 miles at Ripley roundabouttake B6165 Knaresborough Road site 300 yards on left.
Acreage 18 **Open** Easter **to** October
Access Good **Site** Level
Sites Available **Total** 100
Facilities
Nearby Facilities
Harrogate
✓✓✓✓Graded Park. Ideal site for touring Dales, Harrogate and York. A level and quiet family site. David Bellamy Bronze Conservation Award and AA 5 Pennants.

HARROGATE

Rudding Holiday Park, Follifoot, Harrogate, North Yorkshire.
Std: 01423 **Tel:** 870439
Std: 01423 **Fax:** 870859
Nearest Town/Resort Harrogate.
Directions 3 miles south of Harrogate between A61 Leeds/Harrogate road and A661 Wetherby/Harrogate road.
Acreage 30 **Open** March **to** October
Access Good **Site** Level
Sites Available **Total** 141
Facilities
Nearby Facilities
Harrogate.
✓✓✓✓✓Graded Park. Set in 50 acres of parkland, peaceful Yorkshire countryside. Heated swimming pool, 18 hole golf course and driving range.

HARROGATE

Shaws Trailer Park, Knaresborough Road, Harrogate, North Yorkshire, HG2 7NE.
Std: 01423 **Tel:** 884432
Nearest Town/Resort Harrogate
Directions On the A59, opposite Harrogate General Hospital, 50yds south of Ford garage.
Acreage 11 **Open** All Year
Access Good **Site** Level
Sites Available **Total** 200
Facilities
Nearby Facilities
Starbeck
✓✓✓✓Graded Park. A quiet and peaceful park. Ideal for touring Yorkshire Dales, spa town of Harrogate (1 mile) and gardens, Knaresborough (4 miles) and historic York. Health centre next door and a bus stop at the gateway.

HARROGATE

The Yorkshire Hussar Inn Holiday Caravan Park, Markington, Harrogate, Yorkshire, HG3 3NR.
Std: 01765 **Tel:** 677327
Nearest Town/Resort Harrogate/Ripon.
Directions 1 mile west of A61 (Harrogate/ Ripon road). Ripon 5 miles. Harrogate 7 miles.
Acreage 5 **Open** April **to** October
Access Good **Site** Level
Sites Available **Total** 40
Facilities
Nearby Facilities
Harrogate.
Ideal touring centre. Site at rear of Inn. Garden setting in village. Ideal touring centre for the Dales. Fountains Abbey 1¼ miles. Holiday vans for hire.

HAWES

Bainbridge Ings Caravan & Camping Site, Hawes, North Yorkshire, DL8 3NU.
Std: 01969 **Tel:** 667354
Nearest Town/Resort Hawes.
Directions Approaching Hawes from Bainbridge on the A684 turn left at the signpost marked Gayle and we are 300yds on at the top of the hill.
Acreage 3¼ **Open** April **to** October
Access Good **Site** Level
Sites Available **Total** 80
Facilities
Nearby Facilities
Garsdale.
✓✓✓Graded Park. A quiet, clean, family run site with beautiful views and only ½ mile from Hawes. Motorcycles are accepted but not in large groups.

HAWES

Honeycott Caravan Park, Ingleton Road, Hawes, North Yorkshire, DL8 3LH.
Std: 01969 **Tel:** 667310
Nearest Town/Resort Hawes
Directions ¼ mile out of Hawes on the B6255 Hawes to Ingleton road.
Acreage 2½ **Open** March **to** October
Access Good **Site** Lev/Slope
Sites Available **Total** 46
Facilities
Nearby Facilities
Garsdale
✓✓✓Graded Park. On the Pennine Way, ideal for walking, fishing, local attractions and touring. Within the Dales National Park area. Short steep hill into park.

HAWES

Shaw Ghyll Farm, Simonstone, Hawes, North Yorkshire.
Std: 01969 **Tel:** 667359
Std: 01969 **Fax:** 667894
Nearest Town/Resort Hawes.
Directions 2 miles north of Hawes following the Muker road.
Acreage 2½ **Open** March **to** October
Access Good **Site** Level
Sites Available **Total** 30
Facilities
Nearby Facilities
Quiet sheltered site, ideal for walks and families, pleasant aspect, river and lovely scenic walks.

HELMSLEY

Foxholme Touring Caravan Park, Harome, Helmsley, York, North Yorkshire, YO62 5JG.
Std: 01439 **Tel:** 770416
Std: 01439 **Fax:** 771744
Nearest Town/Resort Helmsley.
Directions A170 towards Scarborough ½ mile turn right to Harome, turn left at church, through village, follow caravan signs.
Acreage 6 **Open** Easter **to** October
Access Good **Site** Level
Sites Available **Total** 60
Facilities
Nearby Facilities
Malton.
✓✓✓✓✓Graded Park. Ideal touring area. Near National Park, Abbeys, Herriot country. Use of an indoor swimming pool in a hotel in Harome.

HELMSLEY

Golden Square Caravan Park, Oswaldkirk, York, North Yorkshire.
Std: 01439 **Tel:** 788269
Std: 01439 **Fax:** 788236
Nearest Town/Resort Helmsley.
Directions 2 miles south of Helmsley. First right off the B1257 to Ampleforth.
Acreage 10 **Open** March **to** October
Access Good **Site** Level
Sites Available **Total** 110
Facilities
Nearby Facilities
Thirsk/Malton
✓✓✓✓✓Graded Park. Secluded site with magnificent views of North Yorkshire Moors. Regional Winner Loo of the Year Award. De-Lux all service pitches. Seasonal pitches and storage compound.

HELMSLEY

Wombleton Caravan Park, Moorfield Lane, Wombleton, Kirbymoorside, North Yorks.
Std: 01751 **Tel:** 431684
Nearest Town/Resort Kirbymooorside/ Helmsley
Directions Leave Helmsley by A170 for 4 miles, turn right for Wombleton go through Wombleton ½ mile on left
Acreage 6 **Open** March **to** October
Access Good **Site** Level
Sites Available **Total** 78
Facilities
Nearby Facilities
Malton
✓✓✓✓✓Graded Park. Ideal touring, scenic view, near Yorkshire Dales National Parks and Herriot country. Seasonal pitches available.

HELMSLEY

Wren's of Ryedale, Gale Lane, Nawton, North Yorkshire.
Std: 01439 **Tel:** 771260
Std: 01439 **Fax:** 771260
Nearest Town/Resort Scarborough/York
Directions Leave Helmsley by A170. 2½ miles to Beadlam, pass White Horse Inn and church on left, in 50 yards turn right. Site 700 yards down lane.
Acreage 3½ **Open** April **to** October
Access Good **Site** Level
Sites Available **Total** 45
Facilities
Nearby Facilities
Malton.
✓✓✓✓Graded Park. Attractive, quiet, family run site. Situated on edge of Yorkshire Moors National Park. Very good centre for touring.

INGLETON

The Goat Gap Inn, Clapham, North Yorkshire, LA2 8JB.
Std: 015242 **Tel:** 41230
Std: 015242 **Fax:** 41230
Nearest Town/Resort Settle
Directions On the north side of the A65, 1 mile east of Ingleton.
Acreage 10 **Open** All Year
Access Good **Site** Level
Sites Available **Total** 40
Facilities
Nearby Facilities
Clapham
Ideal walking and touring. Half way between the Dales and lakes, within sight of three peaks.

INGLETON

The Trees Caravan Park, Westhouse, Ingleton, North Yorkshire.
Std: 015242 **Tel:** 41511
Nearest Town/Resort Ingleton.
Directions From Ingleton, travel 1¼ miles along the A65 towards Kirkby Lonsdale (about ¼ mile past the A687 junction - Country Harvest). Turn left at signpost for Lower Westhouse, site is on the left in 50yds.
Acreage 3 **Open** April **to** October
Access Good **Site** Level
Sites Available **Total** 29
Facilities
Nearby Facilities
Bentham
Set in beautiful country scenery. Ideal for walking and touring. Mountains, caves and waterfalls nearby.

KNARESBOROUGH

Allerton Park Caravan Park, Allerton Mauleverer, Nr. Knaresborough, North Yorks, HG5 0SE.
Std: 01423 **Tel:** 330569
Std: 01759 **Fax:** 371377
Nearest Town/Resort Knaresborough
Directions A59 York to Harrogate road, ½ mile east of Aim.
Acreage 17 **Open** 1 February **to** 3 January
Access Good **Site** Level
Sites Available **Total** 45
Facilities
Nearby Facilities
Harrogate
✓✓✓✓✓Graded Park. Woodland park with plenty of wildlife and walks.

KNARESBOROUGH

Kingfisher Caravan & Camping Park, Low Moor Lane, Farnham, Knaresborough, North Yorks, HG5 9DQ.
Std: 01423 **Tel:** 869411
Nearest Town/Resort Knaresborough
Directions From Knaresborough take the A6055. In 1¼ miles turn left to Farnham Village, in Farnham turn left, park is approx. 1 mile on the left.
Acreage 10 **Open** March **to** October
Access Good **Site** Level
Sites Available **Total** 50
Facilities
Nearby Facilities
Knaresborough
✓✓✓Graded Park. Ideal touring base for the Dales, convenient for Harrogate and York. Adjacent to private fishing and a golf range.

LEYBURN

Constable Burton Hall Caravan Park, Constable Burton, Near Leyburn, North Yorkshire, DL8 5LJ.
Std: 01677 **Tel:** 450428
Nearest Town/Resort Leyburn
Directions From the A1 take the A684 in a westerly direction for 9 miles. Park is on the right after the village.
Acreage 10 **Open** April **to** October
Access Good **Site** Lev/Slope
Sites Available **Total** 120
Facilities
Nearby Facilities
Northallerton
✓✓✓✓✓Graded Park.

MALTON

Ashfield Caravan Park, Kirby Misperton, Malton, North Yorkshire, YO17 0UU.
Std: 01653 **Tel:** 668555
Nearest Town/Resort Pickering
Directions 1½ miles off the A169 Malton to Pickering road.
Open March **to** October
Access Good **Site** Level
Sites Available **Total** 44
Facilities

Nearby Facilities
Malton
✓✓✓Graded Park. Pub on site.

MALTON
Castle Howard Caravan & Camping Site, Coneysthorpe, York, North Yorkshire, YO6 7DD.
Std: 01653 **Tel:** 648366
Std: 01653 **Fax:** 648529
Nearest Town/Resort Malton
Directions 15 miles north east of York, off the A64 road to Scarborough. Follow signs to Castle Howard.
Acreage 17 **Open** March **to** October
Access Good **Site** Level
Sites Available **Total** 70
Facilities
Nearby Facilities
Malton
✓✓✓✓Graded Park. Site is on a private estate with views. Within walking distance of Castle Howard and Great Lake.

MASHAM
Black Swan Caravan & Camping Site, Rear of Black Swan Hotel, Fearby, Masham, Ripon, North Yorkshire.
Std: 01765 **Tel:** 689477
Std: 01765 **Fax:** 689477
Nearest Town/Resort Masham.
Directions Turn left off A6108 800yds past filling station. Site is 2 miles on the left hand side at the rear of the Black Swan in Fearby.
Acreage 2 **Open** March **to** October
Access Good **Site** Level
Sites Available **Total** 50
Facilities
Nearby Facilities
Northallerton.
✓✓✓✓Graded Park. Small site overlooking Burn Valley in beautiful countryside. Ideal for walking.

MUKER
Usha Gap Caravan & Camp Site, Usha Gap, Muker, Richmond, North Yorkshire, DL11 6DW.
Std: 01748 **Tel:** 886214
Nearest Town/Resort Hawes
Acreage 1 **Open** All Year
Access Good **Site** Level
Sites Available **Total** 24
Facilities
Nearby Facilities
Darlington
Alongside a small river. Shops and a pub ¼ mile. Ideal touring and good walking.

NORTHALLERTON
Hutton Bonville Caravan Park, Hutton Bonville, Northallerton, North Yorkshire, DL7 0NR.
Std: 01609 **Tel:** 881416
Std: 01609 **Fax:** 881416
Nearest Town/Resort Northallerton
Directions 4 miles north of Northallerton on the A167.
Acreage 3 **Open** Easter **to** October
Access Good **Site** Level
Sites Available **Total** 75
Facilities
Nearby Facilities
Northallerton

OSMOTHERLEY
Cote Ghyll Caravan Park, Osmotherley, Northallerton, North Yorks, DL6 3AH.
Std: 01609 **Tel:** 883425
Nearest Town/Resort Northallerton
Directions Leave A19 at junction of A684 Northallerton turnoff. Follow Osmotherley signs to village, then caravan signs uphill from village cross. Entrance ½ mile on right.
Open April **to** October
Access Good **Site** Sloping
Sites Available **Total** 77
Facilities
Nearby Facilities
North Yorkshire Moors, ideal touring.

PATELEY BRIDGE
Heathfield Caravan Park, Ramsgill Road, Pateley Bridge, Harrogate, North Yorkshire, HG3 5PY.
Std: 01423 **Tel:** 711652
Nearest Town/Resort Pateley Bridge
Directions In Pateley turn onto Low Wath Road at the filling station, after 1 mile turn left, 100 metres turn left again and the park is 100 metres.
Acreage 12 **Open** Beg. March **to** End Oct
Access Good **Site** Sloping
Sites Available **Total** 188
Facilities
Nearby Facilities
Harrogate
Secluded wooded valley with a stream and pleasant views.

PATELEY BRIDGE
Manor House Farm Caravan Site, Summerbridge, Nr Harrogate, North Yorks, HG3 4JS.
Std: 01423 **Tel:** 780322
Nearest Town/Resort Harrogate.
Directions From Harrogate take the A61 to Ripley, then the B6165 to Pateley Bridge. We are 5 miles from Ripley.
Open March **to** October
Access Good **Site** Level
Sites Available **Total** 60
Facilities
Nearby Facilities
Harrogate.
Quiet site near the River Nidd. Ideal touring.

PATELEY BRIDGE
Riverside Caravan Site, Pateley Bridge, Harrogate, N.Yorks, HG3 5HL.
Std: 01423 **Tel:** 711383/711320
Nearest Town/Resort Harrogate/Ripon
Directions From Harrogate take B6165, in Pateley Bridge go over river and turn right, site is ¼ mile up Ramsgill road.
Acreage 4½ **Open** April **to** October
Access Good **Site** Level
Sites Available
Facilities
Nearby Facilities
Harrogate
Alongside river, scenic views, ideal touring and walking.

PATELEY BRIDGE
Studfold Farm Caravan & Camping Site, Studfold Farm, Lofthouse, Harrogate, North Yorkshire, HG3 5SG.
Std: 01423 **Tel:** 755210
Nearest Town/Resort Harrogate/Ripon
Directions Take the B6265 to Pateley Bridge, then take beach road to Lofthouse 7 miles. ½ mile past bear left signposted Stean.
Acreage 2 **Open** April **to** October
Access Good **Site** Level
Sites Available **Total** 20
Facilities
Nearby Facilities
Harrogate.
Ideal walking country, beautiful scenery. Near How Stean Gorge. Good centre for touring the Dales.

PATELEY BRIDGE
Westfield, Westfield Farm, Heathfield, Pateley Bridge, Harrogate, North Yorks.
Std: 01423 **Tel:** 711410
Nearest Town/Resort Pateley Bridge.
Directions From Pateley Bridge 1 mile turn left to Heathfield after 100yds turn left to continue on this road through Heathfield caravan site. We are the third site.
Acreage 3 **Open** April **to** October
Access Single Track. **Site** Lev/Slope
Sites Available
Facilities
Nearby Facilities
Harrogate.
Small farm site along stream in quiet Yorkshire Dales location. Holiday chalet for hire.

PICKERING
Overbrook Caravan Park, Malton Gate, Thornton-le-Dale, Nr Pickering, North Yorks, YO18 7SE.
Std: 01751 **Tel:** 474417
Nearest Town/Resort Pickering.
Directions From A1 follow A64 to A169, 4 miles turn right to Thornton Dale, follow road for 3½ miles. The site is opposite the village road sign Thornton Dale, turn right into the railway station.
Acreage 3 **Open** March **to** October
Access Good **Site** Level
Sites Available **Total** 50
Facilities
Nearby Facilities
Malton
In one of North Yorkshires prettiest villages. Lovely views, Beck runs through the site. Ideal for touring and walking. SORRY this park is unsuitable for children.

PICKERING
Spiers House Campsite - Forestry Commission, Cropton, Pickering, North Yorks, YO18 8ES.
Std: 01751 **Tel:** 417591
Nearest Town/Resort Pickering
Directions Take A170 westwards from Pickering and at Wrelton turn north to Cropton, continue from there on the Rosedale Road for 1 mile where site is signposted at the edge of Cropton Forest.
Acreage 10 **Open** End March **to** End Sept
Access Good **Site** Lev/Slop
Sites Available **Total** 150
Facilities
Nearby Facilities
Malton
✓✓✓✓Graded Park. Site located in an extensive open grassland area and there are several way-marked walks in the adjoining forest. An ideal base to explore the surrounding moors and coast.

PICKERING
The Black Bull Caravan Park, Malton Road, Pickering, North Yorkshire, YO18 8EA.
Std: 01751 **Tel:** 472528
Nearest Town/Resort Pickering
Directions 1 mile south of Pickering on the Malton road, behind The Black Bull Public House.
Acreage 4 **Open** Easter **to** October
Access Good **Site** Level
Sites Available **Total** 36
Facilities
Nearby Facilities
Malton
Ideal base for touring the North Yorkshire Moors.

PICKERING
Upper Carr Chalet & Touring Park, Upper Carr Lane, Malton Road, Pickering, North Yorks, YO18 7JP.
Std: 01751 **Tel:** 473115
Std: 01751 **Fax:** 475325
Nearest Town/Resort Pickering
Directions 1½ miles south of Pickering on the A169, opposite the Black Bull Inn.
Acreage 6 **Open** March **to** October
Access Good **Site** Level
Sites Available **Total** 80
Facilities
Nearby Facilities
Malton
√√√√√Graded Park. Quiet, level, country park. Playground, Pets Corner, cycle hire, nature trail and a Family History Reserach Library. Please phone for a brochure. David Bellamy Gold Conservation Award, White Rose Award Winner Holiday Caravan Park 1998.

PICKERING
Vale of Pickering Caravan Park, Carr House Farm, Allerston, Pickering, North Yorkshire, YO18 7PQ.
Std: 01723 **Tel:** 859280
Std: 01723 **Fax:** 850060
Nearest Town/Resort Scarborough
Directions From Pickering take the A170 to Allerston, turn right opposite Cayley Arms Hotel, due south 1¼ miles.
Acreage 8 **Open** Mid March **to** End October
Access Good **Site** Level
Sites Available **Total** 120
Facilities
Nearby Facilities
Malton
√√√√√Graded Park. Superb play area and games area. Mobile Fish & Chip van.

RICHMOND
Brompton-on-Swale Caravan Park, Brompton-on-Swale, Richmond, North Yorkshire, DL10 7EZ.
Std: 01748 **Tel:** 824629
Std: 01748 **Fax:** 824629
Nearest Town/Resort Richmond
Directions Exit A1 at Catterick A6136. Follow B6271 to Richmond and drive through Brompton-on-Swale. Park on left 1 mile out of Brompton. 1¼ miles south east of Richmond.
Acreage 10 **Open** March **to** End October
Access Good **Site** Level
Sites Available **Total** 150
Facilities
Nearby Facilities
Darlington/Northallerton
√√√√√Graded Park. Situated in a peaceful natural setting on the banks of the River Swale which provides fishing and walks. Mobile fish and chips.

RICHMOND
Fox Hall Caravan Park, Ravensworth, Nr. Richmond, North Yorkshire, DL11 7JZ.
Std: 01325 **Tel:** 718344
Nearest Town/Resort Richmond
Directions From Scotch Corner take the A66 and travel for 5 miles, take the first turning left to Ravensworth. Site is 300yds on the right.
Acreage 3½ **Open** April **to** October
Access Good **Site** Level
Sites Available **Total** 10
Facilities
Nearby Facilities
Darlington
Wooded site.

RICHMOND
Swaleview Caravan Park, Reeth Road, Richmond, North Yorkshire.
Std: 01748 **Tel:** 823106
Nearest Town/Resort Richmond.
Directions On A6108, 3 miles west town.
Acreage 4 **Open** March **to** October
Access Good **Site** Level
Sites Available **Total** 50
Facilities
Nearby Facilities
Darlington.
Beautiful area in National Park by side of River Swale. Central for coasts and lakes.

RICHMOND
Tavern House Caravan Park, Newsham, Nr. Richmond, North Yorkshire, DL11 7RA.
Std: 01833 **Tel:** 621223
Nearest Town/Resort Barnard Castle/Richmond
Directions 7 miles west from Scotch Corner on the A66 turn left, 1 mile into the middle of the village, on the left.
Acreage 1½ **Open** March **to** October
Access Good **Site** Lev/Slope
Sites Available **Total** 8
Facilities
Nearby Facilities
Darlington
√√√Graded Park. Walking, fishing and historic towns.

RIPON
Gold Coin Farm, Galphay, Ripon, North Yorks, HG4 3NJ.
Std: 01765 **Tel:** 658508
Nearest Town/Resort Ripon
Directions Take Pateley Bridge road from Ripon (B6265) turning right after 1 mile.
Acreage ¼ **Open** April **to** October
Access Good **Site** Lev/Slope
Sites Available
Facilities
Harrogate
Scenic views, ideal touring, Lightwater Valley.

RIPON
River Laver Holiday Park, Studley Road, Ripon, North Yorkshire, HG4 2QR.
Std: 01765 **Tel:** 690508
Std: 01748 **Fax:** 811393
Nearest Town/Resort Ripon
Directions From the A1 take the A61 to Ripon following signs for Fountains Abbey. The park is situated off the B6265 1 mile from Ripon Market Square.
Acreage 5 **Open** March **to** December
Access Good **Site** Level
Sites Available **Total** 50
Facilities
Nearby Facilities
Thirsk/Harrogate
√√√√√Graded Park. Quiet, peaceful, privately owned park. Ideal base for the Yorkshire Dales. Many television locations nearby and Fountains Abbey. Lightwater Valley Theme Park within 3 miles.

RIPON
Riverside Meadows Country Caravan Park, Ure Bank Top (Dept. No. I), Ripon, North Yorkshire, HG4 1JD.
Std: 01765 **Tel:** 602964
Std: 01765 **Fax:** 604045
Nearest Town/Resort Ripon
Directions Take the A61 south from Ripon Town Centre, ½ mile.
Acreage 28 **Open** March **to** October
Access Good **Site** Lev/Slope
Sites Available **Total** 400

Facilities
Nearby Facilities
Harrogate
Countryside park alongside a river. Ideal for touring the Yorkshire Dales. Pets are welcome by arrangement.

RIPON

Sleningford Watermill, North Stainley, Ripon, North Yorks, HG4 3HQ.
Std: 01765 **Tel:** 635201
Nearest Town/Resort Ripon
Directions 5½ miles N.W. of Ripon (turning at clock tower) onto A6108, between North Stainley and West Tanfield. Or by following Lightwater Valley signs which is 1½ miles along the same road.
Acreage 14 **Open** Easter **to** October
Access Good **Site** Level
Sites Available **Total** 80
Facilities
Nearby Facilities
✓✓✓✓Graded Park. Picturesque riverside, fly fishing and canoeing access, quiet rural site, birds, wildflowers etc. Ideal for touring Herriot country and Dales.

RIPON

Woodhouse Farm Caravan & Camping Park, Winksley, Nr. Ripon, North Yorkshire, HG4 3PG.
Std: 01765 **Tel:** 658309
Std: 01765 **Fax:** 658882
Nearest Town/Resort Ripon.
Directions Take B6265 from Ripon 3½ miles. Right at the Winksley/Grantley signpost. Follow site signs for 2¼ miles.
Acreage 20 **Open** April **to** October
Access Good **Site** Level
Sites Available **Total** 160
Facilities
Nearby Facilities
Harrogate.
✓✓✓✓Graded Park. An attractive, quiet, country site with excellent facilities. Ideal for touring Yorkshire Dales. On site coarse fishing lake. SAE for Brochure.

ROBIN HOOD'S BAY

Middlewood Farm Holiday Park, Middlewood Lane, Fylingthorpe, Near Whitby, North Yorkshire, YO22 4UF.
Std: 01947 **Tel:** 880414
Std: 01947 **Fax:** 880414
Nearest Town/Resort Whitby
Directions Scarborough to Whitby A171 road. 3 miles south of Whitby take the Fylingthorpe/Robin Hood's Bay road. At Fylingthorpe Post Office turn onto Middlewood Lane, park is 500 yards on the left.
Acreage 4
Access Good **Site** Level
Sites Available **Total** 150
Facilities
Nearby Facilities
Whitby
✓✓✓✓✓Graded Park. Super luxury toilet facilities with FREE hot showers, dish washing, laundry and private bathrooms for hire. Telephone, adventure playground. A walkers, artists and wildlife paradise. Magnificent panoramic views. Close to the BEACH and a PUB. Rose Award Park.

SCARBOROUGH

Arosa Caravan & Camping Park, Ratten Row, Seamer, Scarborough, North Yorkshire, YO12 4QB.
Std: 01723 **Tel:** 862166
Std: 01723 **Fax:** 862166
Nearest Town/Resort Scarborough
Directions 4 miles from Scarborough on the A64.
Acreage 4½ **Open** 1 March **to** 4 January
Access Good **Site** Level
Sites Available **Total** 92
Facilities
Nearby Facilities
Seamer
✓✓✓✓Graded Park. Ideal touring.

SCARBOROUGH

Blue Dolphin Holiday Centre, Gristhorpe Bay, Filey, North Yorks, YO14 9PU.
Std: 01723 **Tel:** 515155
Std: 01723 **Fax:** 512059
Nearest Town/Resort Filey
Directions Off the A165 between Scarborough and Filey.
Acreage 30 **Open** Easter **to** 1st wk Oct
Access Good **Site** Sloping
Sites Available **Total** 410
Facilities
Nearby Facilities
Filey
Overlooking the Yorkshire Wolds.

SCARBOROUGH

Brown's Caravan Park, Mill Lane, Cayton Bay, Scarborough, North Yorkshire, YO11 3NN.
Std: 01723 **Tel:** 582303
Nearest Town/Resort Scarborough.
Directions 3 miles south of Scarborough just off A165.
Acreage ¼ **Open** April **to** September
Access Good **Site** Level
Sites Available **Total** 35
Facilities
Nearby Facilities
Close to beach. Ideal touring centre for North Yorkshire Moors.

SCARBOROUGH

Cayton Village Caravan Park, D1 Mill Lane, Cayton Bay, Scarborough, North Yorks, YO11 3NN.
Std: 01723 **Tel:** 583171
Nearest Town/Resort Scarborough
Directions On the A165, 3 miles south of Scarborough turn inland at Cayton Bay. The park is on the right hand side in ½ mile. From the A64 take the B1261 signposted Filey. At Cayton take the second left at the Blacksmiths Arms onto Mill Lane, the park is on the right hand side.
Acreage 11 **Open** Easter **to** October
Access Good **Site** Level
Sites Available **Total** 200
Facilities
Nearby Facilities
½ mile from the beach. 150 yards to the village inns, fish shop and bus service. 4 acre dog walk. Family bathroom. Winter Telephone Number - 01904 624630.

SCARBOROUGH

Crows Nest Caravan Park, Gristhorpe, Filey, North Yorkshire.
Std: 01723 **Tel:** 582206
Std: 01723 **Fax:** 582205
Nearest Town/Resort Filey/Scarborough.
Directions Off A165 north of Filey, south of Scarborough.
Acreage 12 **Open** March **to** October
Access Good **Site** Lev/Slope
Sites Available
Facilities
Nearby Facilities
Scarborough.
✓✓✓✓✓Graded Park. AA 4 Pennants.

SCARBOROUGH

Flower of May Holiday Park, Lebberston Cliff, Scarborough, North Yorks. YO11 3NU.
Std: 01723 **Tel:** 584311/582324
Std: 01723 **Fax:** 581361
Nearest Town/Resort Scarborough.
Directions 3 miles south of Scarborough off A165 signposted at roundabout.
Acreage 13 **Open** Easter **to** October
Access Good **Site** Level
Sites Available **Total** 300
Facilities
Nearby Facilities

≠ Scarborough
✓✓✓✓✓Graded Park. Winner AA Best Holiday Park Northern England 95. Family run park with superb facilities. Exciting new playground, luxury leisure centre with indoor pool and golf. Family bars. Supermarket. Pets are welcome by arrangement.

SCARBOROUGH

Jacobs Mount Caravan & Camping Site, Stepney Road, Scarborough, North Yorks, YO12 5NL.
Std: 01723 **Tel:** 361178
Std: 01723 **Fax:** 361178
Nearest Town/Resort Scarborough
Directions 2 miles west of Scarborough on the A170 Thirsk Road.
Acreage 5 **Open** March **to** October
Access Good **Site** Lev/Slope
Sites Available **Total** 56
Facilities
Nearby Facilities
≠ Scarborough
✓✓✓✓✓Graded Park. Set in Mature woodland in beautiful countryside, yet only 2 miles from Scarborough beaches and attractions. Bar with family room. Touring caravan rallies catered for off-peak. Rose Award RAC Appointed, AA 3 Pennants and Caravan Club Listed.

SCARBOROUGH

Jasmine Caravan Park, Cross Lane, Snainton, Scarborough, North Yorkshire, YO13 9BE.
Std: 01723 **Tel:** 859240
Std: 01723 **Fax:** 859240
Nearest Town/Resort Scarborough/Pickering.
Directions Turn off the A170 in Snainton Village opposite junior school, ¾ mile signposted.
Acreage 4 **Open** March **to** Janurary
Access Good **Site** Level
Sites Available **Total** 70
Facilities
Nearby Facilities
≠ Scarborough.
✓✓✓✓✓Graded Park. "In Bloom" and David Bellamy Conservation Award Winning peaceful park, situated in an area providing pursuits for all ages and tastes. Personal supervision. SAE.

SCARBOROUGH

Lebberston Touring Caravan Park, Manor View Road, Lebberston, Scarborough, North Yorks, YO11 3PB.
Std: 01723 **Tel:** 585723
Nearest Town/Resort Scarborough/Filey
Directions From A64 or A165 take B1261 to Lebberston and follow signs.
Acreage 7½ **Open** March **to** October
Access Good **Site** Lev/Slope
Sites Available **Total** 125
Facilities
Nearby Facilities
≠ Scarborough.
Quiet, country site, situated on farm. Most pitches on outside overlooking Yorkshire Wolds, Vale of Pickering. Dogs on lead, dog area. Individual pitches. Trailer tents accepted. AA 3 Pennants.

SCARBOROUGH

Scalby Close Park, Burniston Road, Scarborough, North Yorkshire, YO13 0DA.
Std: 01723 **Tel:** 365908
Nearest Town/Resort Scarborough
Directions 2 miles north of Scarborough's North Bay, signed 400 yards.
Acreage 3 **Open** March **to** October
Access Good **Site** Level
Sites Available **Total** 42
Facilities
Nearby Facilities
≠ Scarborough
✓✓✓✓Graded Park. Sheltered, tree lined, level pitches. Ideal for touring North Yorkshire Moors and the coast. Near to Scarborough.

SCARBOROUGH

Scalby Manor Caravan & Camping Park, Field Lane, Station Road, Scalby, Scarborough, North Yorkshire, YO13 0DA.
Std: 01723 **Tel:** 366212
Nearest Town/Resort Scarborough.
Directions Located 2 miles north of Scarborough Town Centre on the coast road to Whitby, A165. Follow signposts to Burniston/Whitby.
Acreage 20 **Open** Easter **to** October
Access Good
Sites Available **Total** 375
Facilities
Nearby Facilities
≠ Scarborough.
✓✓✓✓Graded Park. The site offers an ideal touring base for the North Yorkshire National Park and Moors and yet only 2 miles from the resort of Scarborough.

SCARBOROUGH

Spring Willows Touring Park, Main Road, Staxton, Scarborough, North Yorks, YO12 4SB.
Std: 01723 **Tel:** 891505
Nearest Town/Resort Scarborough.
Directions Exit the A64 at Staxton onto the A1039 to Filey. Entrance is on the right in 100yds.
Acreage 10 **Open** March **to** December
Access Good **Site** Level
Sites Available **Total** 184
Facilities
Nearby Facilities
✓✓✓✓✓Graded Park. Childrens Club during school holidays, FREE entertainment. Ideal for touring.

SELBY

Oakmere Caravan Park & Fishery, Hill Farm, Skipwith, Selby, North Yorkshire, YO8 5SN.
Std: 01757 **Tel:** 288910
Std: 01757 **Fax:** 288910
Nearest Town/Resort York
Directions Take the A19 south from York, Escrick 5 miles turn left, 5 miles to Skipwith. M62 from East or West, leave at Howden and follow signs for York, Skipwith signed from the A63.
Acreage 3 **Open** 1 March **to** 1 November
Access Good **Site** Level
Sites Available **Total** 25
Facilities
Nearby Facilities
≠ York
✓✓✓✓Graded Park. Set in rural countryside, 3 lakes for coarse fishing. Near the City of York.

SETTLE

Knight Stainforth Hall, Stainforth, Settle, North Yorkshire.
Std: 01729 **Tel:** 822200
Std: 01729 **Fax:** 823387
Nearest Town/Resort Settle.
Directions A65 Settle/Kendal. Turn opposite Settle High School. 2½ miles along Stackhouse Lane.
Acreage 6 **Open** March **to** October
Access Good **Site** Sloping
Sites Available **Total** 100
Facilities
Nearby Facilities
≠ Settle.
✓✓✓✓✓Graded Park. Riverside site, near to potholes. Ideal walking and touring.

SKIPTON

Lower Heights Farm, Silsden, Keighley, North Yorkshire, BD20 9HW.
Std: 01535 **Tel:** 653035
Nearest Town/Resort Skipton
Directions 1 mile from Silsden off A6034.

Acreage 2 **Open** Easter **to** November
Access Good **Site** Level
Sites Available **Total** 5
Facilities
Nearby Facilities
Keighley.
Scenic views. Yorkshire Dales and Bronte Country.

SLINGSBY

Camping & Caravanning Club Site, Railway Street, Slingsby, North Yorkshire, YO6 7AA.
Std: 01653 **Tel:** 628335
Nearest Town/Resort Slingsby
Directions From Slingsby take Railway Street through the village for approx. ¼ mile to the camp.
Open 22 March **to** 1 Nov
Access Good **Site** Level
Sites Available **Total** 60
Facilities
Nearby Facilities
Malton
✓✓✓✓Graded Park. Situated between the towns of Helmsley and Malton, in the North Yorkshire Moors. Close to York, Scarborough and Bridlington.

SLINGSBY

Robin Hood Caravan & Camping Park, Green Dyke Lane, Slingsby, North Yorkshire.
Std: 01653 **Tel:** 628391
Nearest Town/Resort Malton
Directions From Malton take B1257 westwards 6 miles to Slingsby. Turn right and right again.
Acreage 4 **Open** March **to** October
Access Good **Site** Level
Sites Available **Total** 48
Facilities
Nearby Facilities
Malton.
✓✓✓✓Graded Park. Sheltered site, Ideal touring site for North Yorkshire Moors, coast, Ryedale, Castle Howard and York. A.A. 3 Pennants. A family run site with modern, fully tiled and cubicled wash room.

THIRSK

Beechwood Caravan Park, South Kilvington, Thirsk, North Yorkshire, YO7 2LZ.
Std: 01845 **Tel:** 522348
Nearest Town/Resort Thirsk
Directions Take the A61 north from Thirsk, South Kilvington is 1½ miles. Caravan site is on the left on entering the village.
Acreage 1½ **Open** March **to** October
Access Good **Site** Level
Sites Available **Total** 30
Facilities
Nearby Facilities
Northallerton
Ideal base to explore the Moors and Dales of North Yorkshire. The historic city of York, the spa town of Harrogate and many National Trust sites are within easy reach.

THIRSK

Nursery Caravan Park, Rainton, Thirsk, North Yorkshire, YO7 3PG.
Std: 01845 **Tel:** 577277
Nearest Town/Resort Thirsk
Directions From Thirsk take the A19 south, then onto the A168 to Topcliffe, go through the village, over the bridge and turn sharp right to Rainton. ½ mile to the T-Junction and turn right, the park is ½ mile on the right.
Acreage 5 **Open** March **to** October
Access Good **Site** Level
Sites Available **Total** 72
Facilities
Nearby Facilities
Thirsk
✓✓✓✓✓Graded Park. Ideal for touring the Yorkshire Dales, abbeys and castles. Only 40 minutes away from York. We are approx. 1 hours drive from the coast, Filey, Whitby and Scarborough.

THIRSK

Quernhow Caravan & Camp Site, Great North Road (A1), Near Sinderby, Thirsk, North Yorkshire, YO7 4LG.
Std: 01845 **Tel:** 567221
Nearest Town/Resort Thirsk
Directions Adjacent to the A1 (northbound), 3 miles north of the junction of the A1 and the A61, behind the Quernhow Cafe.
Acreage 4 **Open** All Year
Access Good **Site** Level
Sites Available **Total** 40
Facilities
Nearby Facilities
Thirsk
✓✓✓Graded Park. Ideal site for visiting the Dales or North Yorkshire Moors. Pine holiday chalet available for weekly rent, suitable for a disabled person and helper.

THIRSK

Sowerby Caravan Park, Sowerby, Thirsk, North Yorkshire, YO7 3AG.
Std: 01845 **Tel:** 522753
Nearest Town/Resort Thirsk
Directions From Thirsk go through Sowerby towards Dalton, the park is ½ mile south of Sowerby on the right.
Acreage 1½ **Open** March **to** October
Access Good **Site** Level
Sites Available **Total** 25
Facilities
Nearby Facilities
Thirsk
Alongside a river. Ideal location for touring.

THIRSK

York House Caravan Park, Balk, Thirsk, North Yorkshire, YO7 2AQ.
Std: 01845 **Tel:** 597495
Nearest Town/Resort Thirsk
Directions From Thirsk take the A19 towards York, after approx. 2 miles take a left turn for Bagby/Balk/Kilburn. Continue through Balk Village and at the T-Junction turn right, continue down hill for approx. 500 yards, park is on the left.
Acreage 14 **Open** April **to** October
Access Good **Site** Level
Sites Available **Total** 80
Facilities
Nearby Facilities
Thirsk
✓✓✓Graded Park. At the foot of Hambleton Hills, overlooked by White Horse of Kilburn. A stream runs through the park. Ideal walking location.

WHITBY

"Serenity" Touring Caravan & Camping Park, High Street, Hinderwell, Whitby, North Yorks, TS13 5JH.
Std: 01947 **Tel:** 841122
Nearest Town/Resort Whitby.
Directions Take B1266 off A171 Whitby to Guisborough Moor road. To T-Junction turn left onto A174. 1 mile Hinderwell. Site entrance in village on left signed "Serenity".
Acreage 3 **Open** March **to** October
Access Good **Site** Level
Sites Available **Total** 20
Facilities
Nearby Facilities
Whitby.
A very quiet, sheltered and secure site with lovely country views. ½ mile from the sea. Marvellous coastal, country and moorland walks. Village shops, public telephone and pubs all nearby.

WHITBY

Burnt House Holiday Park, Ugthorpe, Nr. Whitby, North Yorks, YO21 2BG.
Std: 01947 **Tel:** 840448
Nearest Town/Resort Whitby
Directions 8½ miles north of Whitby on A171, towards Guisborough, signposted Ugthorpe Village.
Acreage 7 **Open** March **to** October
Access Good **Site** Level
Sites Available **Total** 99
Facilities
Nearby Facilities
Whitby
Ideal base for touring coast or countryside, 4 miles to beach. Fully serviced static caravans for sale. Holiday cottage to let.

WHITBY

Grouse Hill Touring Caravan & Camping Park, Fylingdales, Whitby, North Yorkshire, YO22 4QH.
Std: 01947 **Tel:** 880543
Nearest Town/Resort Scarborough/ Whitby
Directions 12 miles from Scarborough and 8 miles from Whitby. Signed off the A171 just north of the Flask Inn.
Open Easter **to** 1st Tues Oct
Access Good **Site** Lev/Slope
Sites Available **Total** 175
Facilities
Nearby Facilities
Expansive views of woodland and moorland. Ideal for families. Close to moorland walks. AA 3 Pennants.

WHITBY

Northcliffe Holiday Park, High Hawsker, Whitby, North Yorkshire.
Std: 01947 **Tel:** 880477
Std: 01947 **Fax:** 880972
Nearest Town/Resort Whitby.
Directions South from Whitby 3 miles, turn left B1447 to Robin Hood's Bay.
Open Mid March **to** End Oct
Access Good
Sites Available **Total** 30
Facilities
Nearby Facilities
Whitby.
✓✓✓✓✓Graded Park. Luxury Award Winning park with panoramic sea views. Woodland Shop/cafe/take-away. New childrens play park.

WHITBY

Sandfield House Farm Caravan Park, Sandsend Road, Whitby, North Yorkshire, YO21 3SR.
Std: 01947 **Tel:** 602660
Nearest Town/Resort Whitby
Directions 1 mile north of Whitby on the A174 coast road. Opposite Whity Golf Course.
Acreage 12 **Open** March **to** October
Access Good **Site** Level
Sites Available **Total** 50
Facilities
Nearby Facilities
Whitby
✓✓✓✓✓Graded Park. Sea views, ¼ mile from sandy beach (2 miles long). Set in undulating countryside.

WHITBY

Whitby Holiday Village, Saltwick Bay, Whitby, North Yorks, YO22 4JX.
Std: 01947 **Tel:** 602664
Nearest Town/Resort Whitby
Directions As you approach Whitby, look for signs directing you to Whitby Abbey. Follow Green Lane to the T-Junction, turn right then look for caravan signs.
Acreage 14 **Open** 31 March **to** October
Site Sloping
Sites Available **Total** 250
Facilities
Nearby Facilities
Whitby
✓✓✓✓Graded Park. Overlooks Saltwick Bay.

WHITBY

York House Caravan Park, Hawsker, Whitby, North Yorkshire.
Std: 01947 **Tel:** 880354
Nearest Town/Resort Whitby.
Directions 3 miles south of Whitby on the A171, signposted.
Acreage 4¼ **Open** March **to** October
Access Good **Site** Lev/Slope
Sites Available **Total** 59
Facilities
Nearby Facilities
Whitby
Scenic views of the sea, Whitby and North Yorkshire Moors.

YORK

Camping & Caravanning Club Site, Bracken Hill, Sheriff Hutton, York, North Yorkshire, YO6 1QG.
Std: 01347 **Tel:** 878660
Directions From York follow signposts for Earswick Strensall, keep left at the filling station and Ship Inn, site is second on the right.
Acreage 10 **Open** 22 March **to** 1 Nov
Site Level
Sites Available **Total** 88
Facilities
Nearby Facilities
✓✓✓✓✓Graded Park. Close to the city of York and 6 miles from Castle Howard and Waterworld.

YORK

Chestnut Farm Caravan Park, Acaster Malbis, York, North Yorkshire, YO2 1UQ.
Std: 01904 **Tel:** 704676
Std: 01904 **Fax:** 704676
Nearest Town/Resort York
Directions Take the A64 towards York, turn left at sliproad to Copmanthorpe and Acaster Malbis, over the flyover, and left into Copmanthorpe. Follow signs to Acaster Malbis.
Acreage 5 **Open** April **to** End October
Access Good **Site** Level
Sites Available **Total** 81
Facilities
Nearby Facilities
York
✓✓✓✓✓Graded Park. Family run park in a pretty village by a river. 3½ miles from York. Ideal for touring the Dales, Moors and coast.

YORK

Goosewood Caravan Park, Sutton-on-the-Forest, York, YO61 1ET.
Std: 01347 **Tel:** 810829
Nearest Town/Resort York
Directions From the A1237 take the B1363 north. Pass the Haxby-Wigginton junction and in 2 miles take next right and follow signs.
Open 27 March **to** 31 October
Access Good **Site** Level
Sites Available **Total** 75
Facilities
Nearby Facilities
York
✓✓✓✓✓Graded Park. Set in woodland with our own lake.

YORK

Moor End Farm, Acaster, Malbis, York, North Yorkshire, YO2 1UQ.
Std: 01904 **Tel:** 706727
Std: 01904 **Fax:** 706727
Nearest Town/Resort York.
Directions Off A64 going west turn off at Copmanthorpe and follow symbols and Acaster signs to village.
Acreage 1 **Open** April 1st **to** October
Access Good **Site** Level
Sites Available **Total** 15
Facilities
Nearby Facilities
York.
✓✓✓✓Graded Park. A working farm and small friendly site. Dish washing facilities.

YORK

Moorside Caravan Park, Lords Moor Lane, Strensall, York, North Yorkshire, YO3 5XF.
Std: 01904 **Tel:** 491865
Nearest Town/Resort York
Directions Take the A1237, then take the Strensall turn and head towards Flaxton.
Open Easter **to** October
Access Good **Site** Level
Sites Available **Total** 50
Facilities
Nearby Facilities
York
✓✓✓✓✓Graded Park. NO CHILDREN. Fishing lake on site. Near York Golf Course.

YORK

Mount Pleasant Holiday Park & Park Homes Estate, Acaster Malbis, York, North Yorkshire, YO23 2UA.
Std: 01904 **Tel:** 707078
Std: 01904 **Fax:** 700888
Nearest Town/Resort York
Directions From the A64 York ringroad take the Bishopthorpe/Racecourse exit and head into Bishopthorpe Village. Turn right in the village towards Acaster Airfield, at the next T-Junction turn left and then left again before the boatyard. Park is on the right hand side after 200 metres.
Acreage 20 **Open** March **to** October
Access Good **Site** Level
Sites Available **Total** 72
Facilities
Nearby Facilities
York
✓✓✓Graded Park. Quiet park with top quality touring pitches and self catering accommodation. Ideally placed for the historical city of York and its many attractions.

YORK

Naburn Lock Caravan & Camping Park, Naburn, York, North Yorkshire, YO1 4RU.
Std: 01904 **Tel:** 728697
Std: 01904 **Fax:** 728697
Nearest Town/Resort York
Directions Take the A19 from York, before the by-pass turn right onto the B1222, go through Naburn and we are ½ mile on the right.
Acreage 7 **Open** March **to** 6 November
Access Good **Site** Level
Sites Available **Total** 100
Facilities
Nearby Facilities
York
✓✓✓✓Graded Park. Ideal for York, the Yorkshire Dales, Moors and coast. Service bus and River Bus to York. Fishing and riding on site.

YORK

Shieling Adult Only Caravan Site, Shieling, Wheldrake Lane, Crockey Hill, York, North Yorkshire, YO19 4SH.
Std: 01904 **Tel:** 659271
Nearest Town/Resort York
Directions From the A64 York by-pass leave at junction signed the A19 Selby (South). After 1 mile turn left into Wheldrake Lane, site is on the left.
Acreage 4 **Open** March **to** October
Access Good **Site** Level
Sites Available **Total** 10
Facilities
Nearby Facilities
York
✓✓✓✓✓Graded Park. Peace and tranquility, no children and no pets. Bus service past the site to York every 15 minutes. Ideal touring centre.

YORK

Swallow Hall Caravan Park, Swallow Hall, Crockey Hill, York, North Yorkshire, YO19 4SG.
Std: 01904 **Tel:** 448219
Std: 01904 **Fax:** 448219
Nearest Town/Resort York.
Directions A19 6-8 miles.
Acreage 5 **Open** Easter **to** October
Access Good **Site** Level
Sites Available **Total** 35
Facilities
Nearby Facilities
York.
Golf and tennis on site.

YORKSHIRE (SOUTH)

BARNSLEY

Greensprings Touring Park, Rockley Lane, Worsbrough, Barnsley, South Yorks, S75 3DS.
Std: 01226 **Tel:** 288298
Std: 01226 **Fax:** 288298
Nearest Town/Resort Barnsley.
Directions Junction 36 on M1. A61 to Barnsley, take left turn after ¼ mile signed to Pilley. Site is 1 mile along this road.
Acreage 4 **Open** April **to** October
Access Good **Site** Lev/Slope
Sites Available **Total** 60
Facilities
Nearby Facilities
Barnsley.
Country site, well wooded, pleasant walks. Convenient from M1. Ideal location for Sheffield venues. TV Hook-up.

ROTHERHAM

Thrybergh Country Park, Doncaster Road, Thrybergh, Rotherham, South Yorkshire, S65 4NU.
Std: 01709 **Tel:** 850353
Std: 01709 **Fax:** 851532
Nearest Town/Resort Rotherham
Directions Thrybergh Country Park is conveniently situated 5 miles from the A1(M) and M1 and 3 miles from the M18 on the main Rotherham to Doncaster road the A630. The entrance is well signposted from both directions.
Acreage 1 **Open** All Year
Access Good **Site** Level
Sites Available **Total** 18
Facilities
Nearby Facilities
Rotherham
The caravan site forms an integral part of the country park along with the reservoir providing fly fishing. A circular walk of 1¾ miles. Improved access to showers and toilets.

SHEFFIELD

Fox Hagg Farm, Lodge Lane, Rivelin, Sheffield, South Yorkshire, S6 5SN.
Std: 0114 **Tel:** 230 5589
Nearest Town/Resort Sheffield.
Directions Off the A57
Acreage 2 **Open** April **to** October
Access Good **Site** Level
Sites Available **Total** 60
Facilities
Nearby Facilities
Sheffield.
Outskirts of Peak District. Ideal touring, scenic views. Post Office. Nature walks. Wash room.

YORKSHIRE (WEST)

BINGLEY

Harden & Bingley Caravan Park, Goit Stock Lane, Harden, Bingley, West Yorkshire, BD16 1DF.
Std: 01535 **Tel:** 273810
Nearest Town/Resort Bingley
Directions From Bingley take the B6429, at the mini-roundabout in Harden Village turn left signposted Wilsden, just before the bridge turn right into Goit Stock Lane.
Acreage 1 **Open** April **to** October
Access Poor **Site** Lev/Slope
Sites Available **Total** 21
Facilities
Nearby Facilities
Bingley
✓✓✓✓Graded Park. Quiet, peaceful valley beside a trout beck. Lovely walks through woodland, Fairy Glen Waterfall.

HEBDEN BRIDGE

Pennine Camp & Caravan Site, High Greenwood House, Heptonstall, Hebden Bridge, West Yorkshire, HX7 7AZ.
Std: 01422 **Tel:** 842287
Nearest Town/Resort Hebden Bridge
Directions From Hebden Bridge take Heptonstall road then follow tent and caravan signs.
Open April **to** October
Site Lev/Slope
Sites Available **Total** 50
Facilities
Nearby Facilities
Hebden Bridge

HOLMFIRTH

Holme Valley Camping & Caravan Park, Thongsbridge, Holmfirth, West Yorkshire, HD7 2TD.
Std: 01484 **Tel:** 665819
Std: 01484 **Fax:** 663870
Nearest Town/Resort Holmfirth
Directions 6 miles south of Huddersfield in valley bottom off the A6042, halfway between Honley and Holmfirth.
Acreage 4½ **Open** All Year
Access Good **Site** Level
Sites Available **Total** 62
Facilities
Nearby Facilities
Brockholes
✓✓✓✓Graded Park. In the heart of 'Last of the Summer Wine' Country, on the fringe of the Peak District National Park. On-site angling. Recipient of David Bellamy Gold Conservation Award.

KEIGHLEY

Upwood Holiday Park, Blackmoor Road, Oxenhope, Keighley, West Yorkshire, BD22 9SS.
Std: 01535 **Tel:** 644242
Std: 01535 **Fax:** 643254
Nearest Town/Resort Haworth
Directions From Keighley take the A629 to Haworth, bear left onto the A6033 just be-

fore Haworth. Take the next left onto Brow Top Road, then turn right into Blackmoor Road and follow for 1½ miles to the park.
Open March **to** October
Access Good **Site** Level
Sites Available **Total** 60
Facilities
Nearby Facilities
Keighley
We are in Bronte Country, overlooking Haworth with some fantastic views of the surrounding countryside.

LEEDS

Moor Lodge Caravan Park, Blackmoor Lane, Bardsey, Leeds, West Yorkshire, LS17 9DZ.
Std: 01937 **Tel:** 572424
Nearest Town/Resort Leeds.
Directions From Leeds 8 miles along the A58 Wetherby. Turn left signposted Shadwell/Harewood, follow lane right fork, over two crossroads, bottom of hill on right.
Acreage 8 **Open** All Year
Access Good **Site** Level
Sites Available **Total** 12
Facilities
Nearby Facilities
Leeds
✓✓✓✓ Graded Park. Local fishing, good rural location. Ideal touring.

LEEDS

Roundhay Caravan & Camping Site, Elmete Lane, Roundhay, Leeds, West Yorkshire, LS8 2LG.
Std: 0113 **Tel:** 265 2354
Nearest Town/Resort Leeds.
Directions A58 from the city centre (4¼ miles). A6120 from west to A58 junction. A1 to A58 from north. A1 and M62 from south and east.
Acreage 7 **Open** April **to** November
Access Good **Site** Level
Sites Available **Total** 60
Facilities
Nearby Facilities
Leeds City
✓✓✓ Graded Park. Roundhay Park with Tropical World. Temple Newsam House, Kirkstall Abbey and many other places of interest. Royal Armeries now open.

SILSDEN

Dales Bank Holiday Park, Low Lane, Silsden, Keighley, West Yorkshire, BD20 9JH.
Std: 01535 **Tel:** 653321/656523
Nearest Town/Resort Silsden
Directions Signed from the Police Station. Silsden to Addingham road (called Bolton Road) turn left into Cringles Lane. Keep left for 2 miles.
Acreage 5 **Open** April **to** October
Access Good **Site** Level
Sites Available **Total** 52
Facilities
Nearby Facilities
Steeton
Ideal for Bronte's Country, Craven Dales and Bolton Abbey Industrial Museum. Bowling area on site.

WAKEFIELD

Nostell Priory Holiday Home Park, Nostell, Wakefield, West Yorkshire, WF4 1QD.
Std: 01924 **Tel:** 863938
Nearest Town/Resort Wakefield
Directions A638 Wakefield to Doncaster road, 5 miles from Wakefield, entrance is in the village of Foulby.
Acreage 4 **Open** April **to** September
Access Good **Site** Level
Sites Available **Total** 60
Facilities
Nearby Facilities
Fitzwilliam
✓✓✓✓✓ Graded Park. Nostell Priory Stately Home owned by the National Trust. A lake for fishing (extra charge).

WETHERBY

Haighfield Caravan Park, 5 Blackmoor Lane, Bardsey, West Yorkshire, LS17 9DY.
Std: 01937 **Tel:** 574658
Std: 01937 **Fax:** 574658
Nearest Town/Resort Wetherby/Leeds
Directions From Leeds take the A58 towards Wetherby, stay on the main road until Bardsey Village. Turn left into Bardsey and stay on the main village road, site is ¾ mile on the left.
Acreage 10 **Open** All Year
Access Good **Site** Level
Sites Available **Total** 30+
Facilities
Nearby Facilities
Leeds
Ideal spot for television locations such as Heartbeat and Emmerdale. York, Ripon, Dales, Harewood and the Royal Armouries Leeds. Close to the market towns of Knaresborough and Harrogate.

WETHERBY

Maustin Caravan Park, Kearby with Netherby, Nr. Wetherby, West Yorkshire, LS22 4DP.
Std: 0113 **Tel:** 288 6234
Std: 0113 **Fax:** 288 6234
Nearest Town/Resort Harrogate/Wetherby.
Directions A61 three right turns, after crossing River Wharfe at bottom of Harewood Bank. A1 from Wetherby through Sicklinghall to Kearby.
Acreage 2 **Open** March **to** October
Access Good **Site** Level
Sites Available **Total** 13
Facilities
Nearby Facilities
✓✓✓✓✓ Graded Park. Quiet site, suits couples. Flat green bowling. Harewood House nearby. Good touring centre. NCC Member, Welcome Host.

WALES

BRIDGEND

PORTHCAWL

Brodawel Camping Park, Brodawel House, Moor Lane, Nottage, Porthcawl, Bridgend.
Std: 01656 **Tel:** 783231
Std: 01656 **Fax:** 783231
Nearest Town/Resort Porthcawl.
Directions Leave the M4 at junction 37, turn onto the A4229 for Porthcawl for 2 miles, signposted Moor Lane.
Acreage 5 **Open** April **to** October
Access Good **Site** Level
Sites Available **Total** 100
Facilities
Nearby Facilities
Pyle
Convenient to all beaches, very central for touring area. Off Licence. Designer village Wales 8 miles.

PORTHCAWL

Happy Valley Caravan Park, Wig Fach, Porthcawl, Bridgend, CF32 0NG.
Std: 01656 **Tel:** 782144
Std: 01656 **Fax:** 782146
Nearest Town/Resort Porthcawl
Directions 2 miles east of Porthcawl on the A4106.
Acreage 9 **Open** April/Easter **to** Sept
Access Good **Site** Level
Sites Available **Total** 100
Facilities
Nearby Facilities
Bridgend
On the Heritage Coast, good central base for touring.

CAERPHILLY

ABERCARN

Cwmcarn Forest Drive Visitor Centre & Campsite, Cwmcarn, Risca, Caerphilly, NP1 7FA.
Std: 01495 **Tel:** 272001
Std: 01495 **Fax:** 272001
Nearest Town/Resort Newport
Directions Leave the M4 at junction 28 and drive north on the A467 towards Risca then Brynmawr. After approx. 7 miles the signs for Cwmcarn Forest Drive & Campsite will be seen.
Acreage 4 **Open** March **to** November
Access Good **Site** Lev/Slope
Sites Available **Total** 40
Facilities
Nearby Facilities
Newport
✓✓✓✓Graded Park. In a beautiful, peaceful, wooded valley with a fishing lake and exceptional hill and woodland walking. Spectacular 7 mile forest drive. Central to many attractions. 3 hard standings available. Visitor Centre providing gifts and refreshments. Restaurant seasonal weekends only.

BLACKWOOD

Pen y Fan Caravan & Leisure Park, Manmoel Road, Oakdale, Blackwood, Caerphilly, NP2 0HY.
Std: 01495 **Tel:** 226636
Std: 01495 **Fax:** 227778
Nearest Town/Resort Caerphilly
Directions Leave the M4 at junction 28 and take the A467. Follow signs to Brynmawr, at the traffic lights at Crumlin turn left, follow signs to Pen y Fan Pond.
Acreage 20 **Open** All Year
Access Good **Site** Level
Sites Available **Total** 72
Facilities
Nearby Facilities
Newport
Beautiful views. Central to most South East Wales tourist attractions.

CARDIGANSHIRE (CEREDIGION)

ABERAERON

Aeron Coast Caravan Park, North Road, Aberaeron, Ceredigion, SA46 0JF.
Std: 01545 **Tel:** 570349
Nearest Town/Resort Aberaeron.
Directions Main coastal road A487 on northern edge of Aberaeron. Filling station at entrance.
Acreage 8 **Open** Easter **to** End October
Access Good **Site** Level
Sites Available **Total** 50
Facilities
Nearby Facilities
Aberystwyth
✓✓✓✓Graded Park. Aberaeron is a recognised beauty spot. Picturesque harbour, coastal and river walks. Only 200yds from shops.

ABERPORTH

Caerfelin Caravan Park, Aberporth, Ceredigion.
Std: 01239 **Tel:** 810540
Nearest Town/Resort Aberporth.
Directions Turn off A487 at Blaenannerch onto B433, enter village of Aberporth. Turn right at St. Cynwyls Church, park 200 yards on left.
Acreage 2 **Open** April **to** September
Access Good **Site** Lev/Slope
Sites Available **Total** 25
Facilities
Nearby Facilities
Carmarthen.
Well sheltered site overlooking sea. Some five minutes walk to sandy beaches.

ABERPORTH

Llety Caravan Park, Tresaith, Aberporth, Cardigan, Ceredigion, SA43 2ED.
Std: 01239 **Tel:** 810354
Std: 01239 **Fax:** 811731
Nearest Town/Resort Aberporth
Directions From Aberystwyth take the A487 and turn off towards Aberporth onto the B4333. Take the coastal road towards Tresaith where the park is situated ½ mile on the left.
Acreage 12 **Open** March **to** October
Access Good **Site** Lev/Slope
Sites Available **Total** 50
Facilities
Nearby Facilities
Aberporth
✓✓✓✓Graded Park. Family run park in an ideal location with panoramic views of Cardigan Bay. Only a 5 minute walk to the beach, shop, restaurant and local inn.

ABERPORTH

Maes Glas Caravan Park, Penbryn, Sarnau, Llandysul, Ceredigion, SA44 6QE.
Std: 01239 **Tel:** 654268
Std: 01239 **Fax:** 654268
Nearest Town/Resort Llangrannog
Directions Turn off the A487 between Cardigan and New Quay in the village of Sarnau by the old church, signposted Penbryn. Follow the road down for ¾ mile to the telephone box, at next junction bear left and the park entrance is on the right.
Acreage 4 **Open** March **to** October
Access Good **Site** Level
Sites Available **Total** 10
Facilities
Nearby Facilities
Aberystwyth
✓✓✓✓Graded Park. Near Penbryn beach.

ABERPORTH

Pilbach Caravan Park, Bettws Ifan, Aberporth, Ceredigion.
Std: 01239 **Tel:** 851434
Std: 01239 **Fax:** 851434
Nearest Town/Resort Aberporth.
Directions From A487 take B4333 (Newcaste Emlyn road). first left, first right, first left.
Acreage 15 **Open** March **to** October
Access Good **Site** Level
Sites Available **Total** 65
Facilities
Nearby Facilities
Aberystwyth.
✓✓✓✓✓Graded Park. Dragon Award Park and Bellamy Bronze Award.

ABERYSTWYTH

Aberystwyth Holiday Village, Penparcau Road, Aberystwyth, Ceredigion.
Std: 01970 **Tel:** 624211
Std: 01970 **Fax:** 611536
Nearest Town/Resort Aberystwyth.
Directions Take A487 out of Aberystwyth,

south ½ mile.
Acreage 6 **Open** March **to** October
Access Good **Site** Level
Sites Available **Total** 152
Facilities
Nearby Facilities
Aberystwyth.
Panoramic views of Aberystwyth, Cardigan Bay and the Rheidol Valley.

ABERYSTWYTH

Glan-Y-Mor Leisure Park, Clarach Bay, Nr. Aberystwyth, Ceredigion, SY23 3DT.
Std: 01970 **Tel:** 828900
Std: 01970 **Fax:** 828890
Nearest Town/Resort Aberystwyth
Directions Turn off the A487 following signs for Clarach 1 mile north of Aberystwyth or at Bow Street. Park entrance is on the sea front.
Acreage 12 **Open** March **to** November
Access Good **Site** Lev/Slope
Sites Available **Total** 160
Facilities
Nearby Facilities
Aberystwyth
✓✓✓✓✓Graded Park. Sea front location with many facilities. High quality indoor leisure centre, ten-pin bowling and childrens activities. Dogs are not allowed during school holidays.

ABERYSTWYTH

Morfa Bychan Holiday Park, Aberystwyth, Ceredigion, SY23 4QQ.
Std: 01970 **Tel:** 617254
Std: 01970 **Fax:** 617254
Nearest Town/Resort Aberystwyth
Directions Take the A487 south from Aberystwyth, after ½ mile signposted to the right, but this is NOT suitable for touring caravans who should continue for 2½ miles and turn right at the second sign. Follow signs for 1½ miles.
Acreage 5 **Open** March **to** October
Access Good **Site** Sloping
Sites Available **Total** 50
Facilities
Nearby Facilities
Aberystwyth
100 acre park overlooking Cardigan Bay with our own private beach. Heated swimming pool, water hook-ups.

ABERYSTWYTH

Ocean View, North Beach, Clarach Bay, Aberystwyth, Ceredigion.
Std: 01970 **Tel:** 623361
Nearest Town/Resort Aberystwyth.
Directions Take the A487 Aberystwyth to Machynlleth toad. Turn into Bow Street for Clarach Bay. Follow road to the beach. Ocean View is on the right.
Open March **to** October
Access Good **Site** Level
Sites Available **Total** 24
Facilities
Nearby Facilities
Aberystwyth.
✓✓✓✓Graded Park. Small select park, short walk to popular beach. Glorious views, ideal touring area of magic Mid-Wales.

BORTH

Brynowen Holiday Village, Borth, Near Aberystwyth, Ceredigion, SY24 5LS.
Std: 01970 **Tel:** 871366
Std: 01970 **Fax:** 871125
Nearest Town/Resort Borth
Directions Turn off the A487 between Aberystwyth and Machynlleth onto the B4353. The entrance to Brynowen is 100 yards from the southern end of Borth seafront.
Acreage 1 **Open** April **to** September
Access Good **Site** Level
Sites Available **Total** 24
Facilities
Nearby Facilities
Borth
Spectacular views across Cardigan Bay and the River Dovey to Cader Idris and the Cambrian Mountains. Ideal base to explore this spectacular area.

BORTH

Brynrodyn Caravan & Leisure Park, Borth, Ceredigion, SY24 5NR.
Std: 01970 **Tel:** 871472
Std: 01970 **Fax:** 871472
Nearest Town/Resort Borth
Directions Take the Clarach road out of Borth at the Lifeboat Station. The park is at the top of the hill on the right.
Open March **to** January
Access Good **Site** Level
Sites Available
Facilities
Nearby Facilities
Borth
✓✓✓✓Graded Park. On a cliff top overlooking the sea. Beach is at the base of the park. Wildlife and walks abundant. New purpose built toilets and showers. Dragon Award Park.

BORTH

Cambrian Coast Holiday Park, Borth, Ceredigion, SY24 5JU.
Std: 01970 **Tel:** 871233
Std: 01970 **Fax:** 871124
Nearest Town/Resort Borth
Directions Adjoining the sea front. Turn off the A487 Machynlleth to Aberystwyth road onto the B4353 Borth road. Entrance to the site is 1¼ miles north of Borth Village.
Open March **to** October
Access Good **Site** Level
Sites Available
Facilities
Nearby Facilities
Borth
✓✓✓✓Graded Park. Near the beach and adjacent to a golf course and a nature reserve. Ideal touring base.

BORTH

Glanlerry Caravan Park, Borth, Ceredigion, SY24 5LU.
Std: 01970 **Tel:** 871413
Nearest Town/Resort Borth
Open April **to** October
Access Good **Site** Level
Sites Available
Facilities
Nearby Facilities
Borth
Sheltered touring area, alongside a river bank with spectacular scenery. Beach ½ mile.

BORTH

The Mill House Caravan & Camping Park, Dolybont, Borth, Ceredigion, West Wales, SY24 5LX.
Std: 01970 **Tel:** 871481
Nearest Town/Resort Borth.
Directions On Aberystwyth/Machynlleth road A487, turn west at Rhydypennau Garage corner (between Talybont and Bow Street) onto B4353 through Llandre. Proceed 1 mile, on Borth B4353 stop under railway bridge by the white railings, fork right into Dolybont Village singposted. First right before hump-back bridge in Village.
Acreage 7 **Open** Easter **to** October
Access Good **Site** Level
Sites Available **Total** 40
Facilities
Nearby Facilities
Borth.
Delightful site beside stream, own fishing and river swimming. 1 mile Borth seaside, safe bathing, rock pools and sand hills.

BORTH

Ty Craig Holiday Park, Llancynfelin, Nr. Borth, Cerdigion, SY20 8PU.
Std: 01970 **Tel:** 832339
Nearest Town/Resort Borth.
Directions 2 miles off the A487 at Trer'ddol onto the B4353. On the left hand side of road by the church.
Acreage 2 **Open** March **to** October
Access Good **Site** Level
Sites Available **Total** 20
Facilities
Nearby Facilities
Near to beach for swimming and surfing. Near to mountains for walking and hiking.

CARDIGAN

Allt-y-Coed, St. Dogmaels, Cardigan, Ceredigion.
Std: 01239 **Tel:** 612673
Nearest Town/Resort Cardigan.
Directions Cardigan/St. Dogmaels/Poppit Sands coast road from Poppit Sands, past Youth Hostel for 1 mile. Over the cattle grid and follow coastal footpath signs. Ordanance Survey Grid Ref : (Sheet 145) 135 495.
Acreage 2 **Open** All Year
Access Good **Site** Level
Sites Available
Facilities
Nearby Facilities
Fishguard.
Pembrokeshire coast path goes past the site. Dolphins, seals, falcons, rare birds, wild flowers and panoramic views. Long and short term parking for walks along the coastal path. Ample parking. You can also contact us on Mobile Telephone 0421 658900.

CARDIGAN

Blaenwaun Farm, D J Davies, Mwnt, Cardigan, Ceredigion, SA43 1QF.
Std: 01239 **Tel:** 612165
Nearest Town/Resort Cardigan
Directions 4 miles from Cardigan, follow sings for Mwnt, north west of Cardigan Town.
Acreage 10 **Open** Easter **to** September
Access Good **Site** Level
Sites Available **Total** 30
Facilities
Nearby Facilities
Carmarthen
Overlooking Cardigan Bay, within walking distance of sandy beach of Mwnt. Dolphins in the bay. Coastal walks. Coarse fishing lake - free.

CARDIGAN

Brongwyn Mawr Caravan Park, Brongwyn Mawr, Penparc, Cardigan, Ceredigion, SA43 1SA.
Std: 01239 **Tel:** 613644
Std: 01239 **Fax:** 613644
Nearest Town/Resort Cardigan
Directions 2½ miles north of Cardigan on the A487, turn left at the crossroads in Penparc signed Mwnt and Ferwig. Gos straight across the next crossroads and the park is the next lane on the right.
Acreage 2 **Open** March **to** October
Access Good **Site** Level
Sites Available **Total** 20
Facilities
Nearby Facilities
Aberystwyth/Carmarthen
✓✓✓✓Graded Park. Secluded park in the countryside. Ideal location to explore, discover and enjoy. Only 2½ miles from a beautiful beach where you can sometimes see the Dolphins.

CARDIGAN

Patch Caravan Park, Gwbert-on-Sea, Cardigan, Ceredigion.
Std: 01239 **Tel:** 613241
Std: 01239 **Fax:** 615391
Nearest Town/Resort Cardigan.
Directions 2 miles from Cardigan on the Gwbert road.
Open Easter **to** October
Access Good **Site** Level
Sites Available **Total** 12
Facilities
Nearby Facilities
Carmarthen.
In sand dunes right on the sea shore. Superb for sailing.

CARDIGAN

Penralltllyn Caravan Park, Cilgerran, Cardigan, Ceredigion, SA43 2PR.
Std: 01239 **Tel:** 682350
Nearest Town/Resort Cardigan
Directions A484 Cardigan to Carmarthen, Llechryd Bridge (sign on bridge), cross bridge and follow for 1½ miles (no turning off). Large sign on the top of farm lane - camp site.
Acreage ½ **Open** Easter **to** October
Access Good **Site** Level
Sites Available **Total** 20
Facilities
Nearby Facilities
CarmarthenHaverfordwest
Quiet site with a pond for canoeing. Farm animals. Plenty of walks, old railway line (closed). Preseli Mountains, various beaches.

CARDIGAN

Ty-Gwyn Farm Caravan Park, Ty-Gwyn, Mwnt, Cardigan, Ceredigion, SA43 1QH.
Std: 01239 **Tel:** 614518
Nearest Town/Resort Cardigan
Directions 5 miles north west of Cardigan. Leave the A487 at Cardigan onto the B4548 Gwbert and Mwnt road and follow signs to Mwnt.
Acreage 5 **Open** March **to** October
Access Good **Site** Lev/Slope
Sites Available **Total** 30
Facilities
Nearby Facilities
Carmarthen
Farm site with scenic views. Near the to Award Winning Mwnt beach. 5 minute walk (approx.) to see the seals and dolphins in the bay.

DEVILS BRIDGE

Erwbarfe Caravan Site, Devils Bridge, Aberystwyth, Ceredigion, SY23 3JR.
Nearest Town/Resort Aberystwyth.
Directions On the A4120 midway between Ponterwyd and Devils Bridge, off the A44.
Acreage 5 **Open** March **to** October
Access Good **Site** Level
Sites Available **Total** 25
Facilities
Nearby Facilities
Aberystwyth.
Ideal location for walking, fishing and touring Mid Wales.

DEVILS BRIDGE

The Woodlands Caravan Park, Devils Bridge, Aberystwyth, Ceredigion, SY23 3JW.
Std: 01970 **Tel:** 890233
Std: 01970 **Fax:** 890233
Nearest Town/Resort Devils Bridge
Directions 12 miles East of Aberystwyth on A4120 in Devils Bridge village and 300yds from bridge. Or 3 miles south west of Ponterwyd, turn off A44 at Ponterwyd.
Acreage 8 **Open** Easter **to** October
Access Good **Site** Level
Sites Available **Total** 60
Facilities
Nearby Facilities
Devils Bridge
Quiet country site adjoining farm. Ideal for walking, bird watching touring, fishing.

LAMPETER

Hafod Brynog Caravan Park, Ystrad Aeron, Felinfach, Lampeter, Ceredigion, SA48 7PG.
Std: 01570 **Tel:** 470084
Nearest Town/Resort Aberearon
Directions On the main A482 Lampeter to Aberaeron road, 6 miles from both. Site entrance is opposite the church and next to the pub in the village of Ystrad Aeron.
Acreage 8 **Open** March **to** October
Access Good **Site** Lev/Slope
Sites Available **Total** 30
Facilities
Nearby Facilities
Aberystwyth
A quiet site with beautiful views. 6 miles from Cardigan Bay. Ideal for coastal and inland touring, or just relaxing.

LAMPETER

Moorlands Caravan Park, Llangyby, Nr Lampeter, Ceredigion.
Std: 01570 **Tel:** 493543
Nearest Town/Resort Lampeter
Directions 4½ miles approx. on the A485 Lampeter to Tregaron road.
Acreage 2 **Open** Easter **to** October
Access Good **Site** Level
Sites Available **Total** 10
Facilities
Nearby Facilities
Aberystwyth
Ideal touring centre, 12 miles from Cardigan Bay. You can also call us on Mobile 0836 333107.

LLANARTH

Llain Activity Centre, Llanarth, Ceredigion, SA47 0PZ.
Std: 01545 **Tel:** 580127
Std: 01545 **Fax:** 580697
Nearest Town/Resort New Quay
Directions Take the A487 south from Aberaeron towards Cardigan. After the village of Llwncelyn take a right hand turn to Cei Bach.
Acreage 1 **Open** March **to** October
Sites Available **Total** 10
Facilities
Nearby Facilities
Aberystwyth
On site outdoor activities with qualified staff (May to September).

LLANDYSUL

Camping & Caravanning Club Site, Llwynhelyg, Cross Inn, Llandysul, Ceredigion, SA44 6LW.
Std: 01545 **Tel:** 560029
Directions From the A487 Cardigan to Aberystwyth road, at Synod Inn turn left onto the A486 signposted New Quay. After 2 miles in the village of Cross Inn turn left after the Penrhiwgated Arms Pub, site is on the right after approx. ¾ miles.
Acreage 13½ **Open** 22 March **to** 1 Nov
Site Lev/Slope
Sites Available **Total** 90
Facilities
Nearby Facilities
Aberystwyth
Near to golden beaches, forests and lakes.

LLANON

Woodlands Caravan Park, Llanon, Nr. Aberystwyth, Ceredigion, SY23 5LX.
Std: 01974 **Tel:** 202342
Nearest Town/Resort Aberaeron
Directions 5 miles north of Aberaeron on the A487, turn left at the sign.
Acreage 4 **Open** April **to** October
Access Good **Site** Level
Sites Available **Total** 80
Facilities
Nearby Facilities
Aberystwyth
Tree screened site with a small river. 250 yards from the beach, 300 yards from the main road.

LLANRHYSTUD

Pengarreg Caravan Park, Llanrhystud, Ceredigion, SY23 5DJ.
Std: 01974 **Tel:** 202247
Nearest Town/Resort Aberystwyth/ Aberaeron
Directions On the A487 in the village of Llanrhystud opposite Shell Garage.
Acreage 7 **Open** March **to** 2 January
Access Good **Site** Level
Sites Available **Total** 100
Facilities
Nearby Facilities
Aberystwyth
Two touring fields, one on the sea front. A river runs through the camp for fishing, boating ramp. 196 acres of scenic hills and farmland for walking.

NEW QUAY

Cei Bach Country Club, Parc-Y-Brwcs, Cei Bach, Newquay, Ceredigion, SA45 9SL.
Std: 01545 **Tel:** 580237
Std: 01545 **Fax:** 580237
Nearest Town/Resort New Quay
Directions From the A487 take the B4342 for New Quay. Follow the road to Quay-West and Cambrian Hotel crossroads, take the road signed for Cei Bach.
Acreage 3 **Open** Easter **to** End Sept
Access Poor **Site** Lev/Slope
Sites Available **Total** 60
Facilities
Nearby Facilities
Aberystwyth
Great views of the coast line, safe sandy beach. Coastal walk to Aberaeron.

NEW QUAY

Frondeg Caravan Park, Gilfachreda, Nr. New Quay, Ceredigion, SA45 9SP.
Std: 01545 **Tel:** Llanarth 580491
Nearest Town/Resort New Quay.
Directions Take A487 from Aberystwyth to Llanarth, then take the B4342 to New Quay for approx. 1 mile to Gilfachreda Village.
Acreage 1 **Open** Easter **to** October
Access Good **Site** Level
Sites Available **Total** 10
Facilities
Nearby Facilities
Aberystwyth.
Quiet, secluded site near a small river leading to safe, sandy bathing beaches, 10 minutes walk. New Quay harbour town, 2 miles by road.

NEW QUAY

Pantgwyn, Synod, Llandysul, Ceredigion, SA44 6JN.
Std: 01545 **Tel:** 580320
Nearest Town/Resort Aberaeron
Directions South of Aberystwyth on the A487 between the villages of Synod Inn and Plwmp.
Acreage 4 **Open** April **to** September
Access Fair **Site** Lev/Slope
Sites Available
Facilities
Nearby Facilities
Aberystwyth
Part of the Heritage Coast, near many sandy beaches. Ideal touring.

NEW QUAY

Wern Mill Camping Site, Gilfachrheda, New Quay, Ceredigion, SA45 9SP.
Std: 01545 **Tel:** 580699
Nearest Town/Resort New Quay.
Directions From Aberystwyth take the A487 via Aberaeron to Llanarth. Gilfachrheda is located 1½ miles from Llanarth on the B4342 to New Quay road.
Acreage 2½ **Open** Easter **to** October
Access Good **Site** Level
Sites Available **Total** 50
Facilities
Nearby Facilities
Aberystwyth.
✓✓✓Graded Park. Very sheltered site, ½ mile from two sandy beaches. Ideal centre for touring mid Wales. Idyllic walks. Family site. No motorcycles.

SARNAU

Brynawelon Touring Caravan Park, Sarnau, Llandysul, Ceredigion, SA44 6RE.
Std: 01239 **Tel:** 654584
Nearest Town/Resort Cardigan.
Directions Travelling north on A487 take a right turn at Sarnau crossroads, site is 550yds on the left.
Acreage 2 **Open** April **to** October
Access Good **Site** Level
Sites Available **Total** 30
Facilities
Nearby Facilities
Carmarthen.
✓✓✓Graded Park. 2 miles to Penbryn Beach. Rural surroundings, quiet family site.

SARNAU

Manorafon Caravan Park, Sarnau, Llandysul, Ceredigion, SA44 6QH.
Std: 01239 **Tel:** 810564
Std: 01239 **Fax:** 810564
Nearest Town/Resort Cardigan
Directions Take the A487 north from Cardigan for 7 miles to Tanyagroes, go through the village, second road on the left signed Penbryn/Tresaith. After ½ mile take the first right, after ¾ mile turn second left, we are 200 yards on the right.
Acreage 1½ **Open** Easter **to** October
Access Average **Site** Sloping
Sites Available **Total** 15
Facilities
Nearby Facilities
Carmarthen
Set in a wooded valley, good for families. ¾ mile from Penbryn beach. Ideal camping and touring for birdwatchers, golfers and walkers.

SARNAU

Talywerydd Touring Caravan Park, Penbryn Sands, Sarnau, Llandysul, Ceredigion, SA44 6QY.
Std: 01239 **Tel:** 810322
Nearest Town/Resort Cardigan
Directions From Cardigan take the second Penbryn turn off the A487. From Aberystwyth take the second Penbryn turn off the A487. Talywerydd is 500yds on the left.
Acreage 4 **Open** March **to** End October
Access Good **Site** Level
Sites Available **Total** 40
Facilities
Nearby Facilities
Aberystwyth
✓✓✓✓Graded Park. Family site with scenic views over Cardigan Bay. 2 miles from Penbryn Beach. Covered heated swimming pool.

TREGARON

Aeron View Caravan Park, Blaenpennal, Aberystwyth, Ceredigion.
Std: 01974 **Tel:** 251488
Std: 01974 **Fax:** 251488
Nearest Town/Resort Blaenpennal
Directions 1 mile west off A485 Aberystwyth to Tregaron road, 4 miles north west of Tregaron.
Acreage 2 **Open** April **to** October
Access Good **Site** Level
Sites Available **Total** 24
Facilities
Nearby Facilities
Aberystwyth
Quiet, inland site in the middle of a Red Kite birdwatching area. Midway between holiday Aberystwyth and historic Lampeter.

CARMARTHENSHIRE

CARMARTHEN

Coedhirion Farm Parc, Coedhirion, Llanddarog, Carmarthen, Carmarthenshire, SA32 8BH.
Std: 01267 **Tel:** 275666
Nearest Town/Resort Carmarthen.
Directions 9 miles west of the M4 junction 49, just off the A48 dual carriageway, 6 miles east of Carmarthen.
Acreage 5 **Open** Easter **to** Christmas
Access Good **Site** Level
Sites Available **Total** 20
Facilities
Nearby Facilities
Carmarthen.
Quiet, convenient, woodland site.

CARMARTHEN

Sunrise Bay Holiday Park, Llansteffan, Carmarthen, Carmarthenshire, SA33 5LP.
Std: 01267 **Tel:** 241394
Nearest Town/Resort Carmarthen
Directions 1 mile west of Carmarthen on the A40, turn south onto the B4312. After 7 miles, on entering Llansteffan turn sharp left. Follow road to the car park and the site entrance is signposted.
Open April **to** October
Access Good **Site** Level
Sites Available **Total** 6
Facilities
Nearby Facilities
Carmarthen
✓✓✓✓Graded Park. Magnificent views of Norman Castle and Towy Estuary. 250 yards from the beach. Lovely walks. Ideal touring centre.

CLYNDERWEN

Derwenlas, Clynderwen, Carmarthenshire, SA66 7SU.
Std: 01437 **Tel:** 563504
Nearest Town/Resort Narberth
Directions 3 to 3½ miles north of Narberth on the A478.
Open April **to** September
Access Good **Site** Level
Sites Available **Total** 8
Facilities
Nearby Facilities
Clynderwen

CROSS HANDS

Black Lion Caravan & Camping Park, 78 Black Lion Road, Gorslas, Cross Hands, Llanelli, Carmarthenshire, SA14 6RU.
Std: 01269 **Tel:** 845365
Std: 01269 **Fax:** 831882
Nearest Town/Resort Llanelli
Directions At the end of the M4 continue on the A48 to Cross Hands, turn right to Llandeilo. Within ½ mile at Gorslas turn a sharp right and the site is within ½ mile on the right hand side.
Acreage 12 **Open** Easter **to** October
Access Good **Site** Lev/Slope
Sites Available **Total** 40
Facilities
Nearby Facilities
Llanelli
✓✓✓Graded Park. Wales Botanical Garden nearby. Ideal for touring South and West Wales. Web Address: www.caravansite.com

KIDWELLY

Carmarthen Bay Touring & Camping, Tanylan Farm, Kidwelly, Carmarthenshire, SA17 5HJ.
Std: 01267 **Tel:** 267306
Nearest Town/Resort Kidwelly
Directions In Kidwelly turn left at the Spar Supermarket, take the coastal road to Ferryside for approx. 1 mile and turn right at the duck pond.
Acreage 4 **Open** Easter **to** End Sept
Access Good **Site** Level
Sites Available **Total** 50
Facilities
Nearby Facilities
Kidwelly
✓✓✓Graded Park. Level ground on this working dairy farm. 200 yards from the beach.

LAUGHARNE

Ants Hill Caravan Park, Laugharne, Carmarthenshire, SA33 4QN.
Std: 01994 **Tel:** 427293
Std: 01994 **Fax:** 427293
Nearest Town/Resort Carmarthen
Directions From the M4 to Carmarthen, follow the A40 towards St Clears. Turn off onto the A4066 for Laugharne and Pendine, site is the first turning left before the signpost for Laugharne.
Acreage 6½ **Open** Easter **to** October
Access Good **Site** Level
Sites Available **Total** 60
Facilities
Nearby Facilities
Carmarthen
✓✓✓Graded Park. Ideal for inland and coastal touring. Historic township with its Circa 12th Castle and Dylan Thomas' Boat House. Near the famous sands of Pendine.

LLANDDEUSANT

Cross Inn & Black Mountain Caravan Park, Cross Inn, Llanddeusant, Llangadog, Carmarthenshire.
Std: 01550 **Tel:** 740621
Nearest Town/Resort Llandovery
Directions Take the A40 from Llandovery to Trecastle, turn right to Llanddeusant, site is on the right in 9 miles. From the B4069 Bryamman to Llangadog road, turn over the bridge opposite the Three Horseshoes and continue for 3 miles.
Acreage 5 **Open** All Year
Access Good **Site** Lev/Slope
Sites Available **Total** 40
Facilities
Nearby Facilities
Llangadog
✓✓✓Graded Park. In an area of outstanding natural beauty in the Brecon Beacons National Park, superb walking.

LLANDOVERY

Camping & Caravanning Club Site, Rhandirmwyn, Llandovery, Carmarthenshire, SA20 0NT.
Std: 01550 **Tel:** 760257
Directions From the A483 in Llandovery, take the road signed Rhandirmwyn for 7 miles. Turn left at the Post Office in Rhandirmwyn, signposted.
Acreage 11 **Open** 22 March **to** 1 Nov
Access Good **Site** Level
Sites Available **Total** 90
Facilities
Nearby Facilities
Llandovery
✓✓✓✓✓Graded Park. Situated on the banks of the Afon Tywi. Ideal for hill walking and fishing. Close to Rhayader Days.

LLANDOVERY

Erwlon Caravan & Camping Park, Erwlon, Llandovery, Carmarthenshire, SA20 0RD.
Std: 01550 **Tel:** 720332
Nearest Town/Resort Llandovery.
Directions ½ mile east of Llandovery on the A40 towards Brecon.
Acreage 5 **Open** April **to** October
Access Good **Site** Level
Sites Available **Total** 40
Facilities
Nearby Facilities
Llandovery.
✓✓✓✓Graded Park. Alongside a river. Convenient for Brecon Beacons, South Wales valleys and coastline. Ideally located for touring South Wales.

LLANGADOG

Abermarlais Caravan Park, Nr Llangadog, Carmarthenshire, SA19 9NG.
Std: 01550 **Tel:** 777868
Nearest Town/Resort Llandovery.
Directions 6 miles west of Llandovery and 6 miles east of Llandeilo on the A40.
Acreage 16 **Open** 15 March **to** 1 Nov
Access Good **Site** Lev/Slope
Sites Available **Total** 88
Facilities
Nearby Facilities
Llangadog
✓✓✓✓✓Graded Park. Alongside river with scenic views.

LLANGADOG

Pont Aber Inn, Gwynfe, Llanddeusant, Llangadog, Carmarthenshire, SA19 9TA.
Std: 01550 **Tel:** 740202
Nearest Town/Resort Llandovery/Llandielo
Directions Take the A4069 from Llangadog towards Brynaman, 4 miles out of Llangadog.
Acreage 2 **Open** All Year
Access Good **Site** Level
Sites Available
Facilities
Nearby Facilities
Llangadog
Site runs alongside a river.

LLANWRDA

Maesbach Caravan Park, Ffarmers, Llanwrda, Carmarthenshire, SA19 8EX.
Std: 01558 **Tel:** 650650
Nearest Town/Resort Lampeter.
Directions From A40 turn onto the A482 (Llandello or Llandovery). Turn right to Ffarmers, north of Pumpsaint, turn right at Drovers Inn in Ffarmers.
Acreage 2½ **Open** March **to** October
Access Good **Site** Sloping
Sites Available **Total** 20
Facilities
Nearby Facilities
Llanwrda
Local walking and bird life.

NEWCASTLE EMLYN

Afon Teifi Caravan & Camping Park, Pentrecagal, Newcastle Emlyn, Carmarthenshire, SA38 9HT.
Std: 01559 **Tel:** 370532
Nearest Town/Resort Newcastle Emlyn
Directions On the A484 2 miles east of Newcastle Emlyn.
Acreage 6½ **Open** All Year
Access Good **Site** Level
Sites Available **Total** 110
Facilities
Nearby Facilities
Carmarthen
✓✓✓✓✓Graded Park. Situated by the River Teifi in the beautiful Teifi Valley. Only 20 minutes from numerous Cardigan Bay beaches. Ideal touring centre.

NEWCASTLE EMLYN

Cenarth Falls Holiday Park, Cenarth, Newcastle Emlyn, Carmarthenshire, SA38 9JS.
Std: 01239 **Tel:** 710345
Nearest Town/Resort Newcastle Emlyn
Directions 3 miles west of Newcastle Emlyn on the A484. Cross Cenarth Bridge and travel for ¼ mile, turn right at directional signs for the park.
Acreage 2 **Open** March **to** November
Access Good **Site** Level
Sites Available **Total** 30
Facilities
Nearby Facilities
Carmarthen
✓✓✓✓✓Graded Park. Ideal touring location for the coast and countryside. Near a National Park. Awarded AA Campsite of the Year for Wales 1997 and Daffodil Award.

NEWCASTLE EMLYN

Dolbryn Farm, Capel Iwan Road, Newcastle Emlyn, Carmarthenshire, SA38 9LP.
Std: 01239 **Tel:** 710683
Nearest Town/Resort Newcastle Emlyn.
Directions Turn left off the A484 Carmarthen to Cardigan road at Newcastle Emlyn signposted leisure centre & swimming pool. Follow camping signs for 1½ miles.
Acreage 4 **Open** Easter **to** October
Access Good **Site** Lev/Slope
Sites Available **Total** 40
Facilities
Nearby Facilities
Carmarthen.
✓✓✓Graded Park. Idyllic country site with stream, lakes, hills, etc..

PENDINE

Pendine Sands Holiday Park, Pendine, Nr Carmarthen, Carmarthenshire, SA33 4NZ.
Std: 01994 **Tel:** 453398
Nearest Town/Resort Tenby.
Directions Take the A40 from carmarthen towards St Clears. Pendine/Pentywyn signposted to the left along the A4066, continue for 8 miles, pass through the village of Laugharne, park is 5 miles further on the right hand side.
Open March **to** October
Access Good **Site** Level
Sites Available **Total** 40
Facilities
Nearby Facilities
Carmarthen
√√√√Graded Park. 7 miles of golden sands adjacent to the park, coastal scenery. Kids Club and a full family entertainment programme.

PUMPSAINT

Penlanwen, Pumpsaint, Llanwrda, Carmarthenshire, SA19 8RR.
Std: 01558 **Tel:** 650667
Nearest Town/Resort Lampeter.
Directions 7 miles northwest of Llandovery, take A40, turn right onto A482 at Llanwrda, past Bridgend Inn on left and look for site signs.From Lampeter take A482 for 8 miles to Pumpsaint.
Acreage 3 **Open** All Year
Access Good **Site** Level
Sites Available **Total** 20
Facilities
Nearby Facilities
Llandovery.
Scenic views, guided tour of gold mines with cafe and shop. Pony trekking, ideal for families.

RED ROSES

South Carvan Caravan Park, Tavernspite, Whitland, Carmarthenshire, SA34 0NL.
Std: 01834 **Tel:** 831451
Nearest Town/Resort Whitland
Directions From St. Clears take A477 to Tenby at Red Roses turn right 1¾ miles down road into village of Tavernspite.
Acreage 15 **Open** April **to** September
Access Good **Site** Level
Sites Available **Total** 65
Facilities
Nearby Facilities
Whitland.

ST. CLEARS

Parciau Bach Caravan Park, Afon Lodge, St. Clears, Carmarthenshire, SA33 4LG.
Std: 01994 **Tel:** 230647
Nearest Town/Resort St. Clears.
Directions From St. Clears traffic lights take Llanboidy Road. In a 100 yards fork right, then first right, first right.
Acreage 5 **Open** March **to** December
Access Good **Site** Lev/Slope
Sites Available **Total** 35
Facilities
Nearby Facilities
√√√√Graded Park. Beautiful tranquil site, ideal touring. T.V. Hook-up.

WHITLAND

The Old Vicarage Caravan Park, Red Roses, Whitland, Carmarthenshire, SA34 0PG.
Std: 01834 **Tel:** 831637
Std: 01834 **Fax:** 831637
Nearest Town/Resort Tenby
Directions On the A477 at the junction with the B4314 Pendine road, between St. Clears and Tenby.
Acreage 3 **Open** March **to** End January
Access Good **Site** Level
Sites Available **Total** 17
Facilities
Nearby Facilities
Whitland
√√√Graded Park. 3 miles from Pendine beach, close to many attractions. Ideal for touring South West Wales.

CONWY

ABERGELE

Gwrych Towers Camp, Llandulas Road, Abergele, Conwy, LL22 8ET.
Std: 01745 **Tel:** 832109
Nearest Town/Resort Abergele
Directions ¼ mile from Abergele on the B5443. Main entrance to Gwrych Castle. Office is in the right hand tower. Ask for Mr or Miss Dutton.
Acreage 3 **Open** Spring Bank Hol **to** Early Sept
Access Good **Site** Level
Sites Available
Facilities
Nearby Facilities
Abergele
Near the beach, shops and golf links. Central for touring coastal resorts and enjoying the lovely mountain scenery.

ABERGELE

Henllys Farm Camping & Touring Site, Towyn Road, Towyn, Abergele, Conwy.
Std: 01745 **Tel:** 351208
Nearest Town/Resort Rhyl.
Directions On A548 south side, near Towyn.
Acreage 11 **Open** Whitsun **to** September
Access Good **Site** Level
Sites Available **Total** 280
Facilities
Nearby Facilities
Rhyl.
√√√√Graded Park. ½ mile from beach.

ABERGELE

Hunters Hamlet Touring Park, Sirior Goch Farm, Betws-Yn-Rhos, Abergele, Conwy, LL22 8PL.
Std: 01745 **Tel:** 832237
Std: 01745 **Fax:** 832237
Nearest Town/Resort Abergele
Directions From Abergele take the A548 Llanrwst road for 2¾ miles, at first crossroads turn right towards Betws-Yn-Rhos on the B5381 and the site is on the left in ½ mile.
Acreage 2 **Open** 21 March **to** 312 October
Access Good **Site** Sloping
Sites Available **Total** 23
Facilities
Nearby Facilities
Abergele/Pensarn
√√√√√Graded Park. Ideal for the coast and country. Lots to do and see. Superpitches and a family bathroom. Mini site shop.

ABERGELE

Ty Mawr Holiday Park, Towyn Road, Towyn, Abergele, Conwy, LL22 9HG.
Std: 01745 **Tel:** 832079
Nearest Town/Resort Abergele.
Directions On the A548 between Rhyl and Abergele, ½ mile west of Towyn.
Acreage 27
Access Good **Site** Level
Sites Available **Total** 485
Facilities
Nearby Facilities
Abergele.
√√√√Graded Park. A short distance from the sandy beach of Colwyn Bay, close to Snowdonia.

BETWS-Y-COED

Cwmlanerch Caravan Park, Betws-y-Coed, Conwy, LL24 0BG.
Std: 01690 **Tel:** 710363
Nearest Town/Resort Betws-y-Coed
Directions From Betws-y-Coed take the B5106 road and we are 1 mile on the right.
Acreage 2 **Open** March **to** October
Access Good **Site** Level
Sites Available **Total** 16
Facilities
Nearby Facilities
Betws-y-Coed
✓✓✓Graded Park. Alongside a river, close to wooded hillside with many varied walks. Convenient for all of North Wales attractions and the scenic village of Betws-y-Coed with its quality shops and restaurants.

BETWS-Y-COED

Riverside Caravan & Camping Park, Old Church Road, Betws-y-Coed, Conwy, LL24 0BA.
Std: 01690 **Tel:** 710310
Std: 01690 **Fax:** 710826
Nearest Town/Resort Betws-y-Coed.
Directions Enter Betws-y-Coed over Waterloo Bridge. Take first right after passing "Little Chef" Filling Station.
Acreage 3¼ **Open** 14 March **to** October
Access Good **Site** Level
Sites Available **Total** 120
Facilities
Nearby Facilities
Betws-y-Coed.
Alongside river, adjacent to golf course. Ideally based as centre for touring Snowdonia.

BETWS-Y-COED

Rynys Farm Camping Site. Rynys Farm, Near Betws-Y-Coed, Llanrwst, Conwy.
Std: 01690 **Tel:** 710218
Nearest Town/Resort Betws-y-Coed.
Directions 2 miles south of Betws-y-Coed Left by Conway Falls, 200yds from A5.
Acreage 6 **Open** All Year
Access Good **Site** Level
Sites Available
Facilities
Nearby Facilities
Betws-y-Coed.
Very scenic and peaceful site with excellent clean facilities. Central for touring.

BETWS-Y-COED

Tanaeldroch Farm, Dolwyddelan, Conwy, LL25 0LZ.
Std: 01690 **Tel:** 750225
Nearest Town/Resort Betws-y-Coed.
Directions Take the A470 from Betws-y-Coed towards Blaenau Ffestiniog. Site is 2½ miles on the left.
Acreage 8 **Open** All Year
Access Good **Site** Level
Sites Available **Total** 20
Facilities
Nearby Facilities
Pont-y-Pant.
Alongside a river with scenic views. Ideal touring.

COLWYN BAY

Bron-Y-Wendon Touring Caravan Park, Wern Road, Llanddulas, Colwyn Bay, Conwy, LL22 8HG.
Std: 01492 **Tel:** 512903
Std: 01492 **Fax:** 512903
Nearest Town/Resort Colwyn Bay.
Directions Follow the A55 into North Wales and take the Llanddulas junction (A547). Follow the tourist information signs to the park.
Acreage 8 **Open** 21 March **to** 30 October
Access Good **Site** Lev/Slope
Sites Available **Total** 130
Facilities
Nearby Facilities
Colwyn Bay
✓✓✓✓✓Graded Park. All pitches have coastal views. 300yds to beach. Site is ideal for seaside and touring. Daffodil Award.

COLWYN BAY

Dinarth Hall, Rhos-on-Sea, Colwyn Bay, Conwy.
Std: 01492 **Tel:** 548203
Nearest Town/Resort Rhos on Sea
Directions A55 to Rhos-on-Sea then B5115.
Acreage 4 **Open** Easter **to** October
Access Good **Site** Level
Sites Available **Total** 90
Facilities
Nearby Facilities
Colwyn Bay.
✓✓✓Graded Park. Close to sea and within reach of Snowdonia.

CONWY

Conwy Touring Park, Conwy, LL32 8UX.
Std: 01492 **Tel:** 592856
Std: 01492 **Fax:** 580024
Nearest Town/Resort Conwy.
Acreage 70 **Open** Easter
Access Good **Site** Level
Sites Available **Total** 300
Facilities
Nearby Facilities
Conwy
✓✓✓Graded Park. Scenic views, ideal for touring Snowdonia. Special Offers.

CONWY

Tyn Terfyn Touring Caravan Park, Tal Y Bont, Conwy, LL32 8YX.
Std: 01492 **Tel:** 660525
Nearest Town/Resort Conwy.
Directions From Conwy travel 5 miles (approx) on the B5106 until road sign for Tal-y-Bont. First house on the left after sign.
Acreage 2 **Open** 14 March **to** October
Access Good **Site** Level
Sites Available **Total** 15
Facilities
Nearby Facilities
Scenic views, good walking, fishing and boating. Ideal touring location.

LLANDUDNO

Penrhyn Hall Farm Caravan Park, Penrhyn Bay, Llandudno, Conwy, LL30 3EE.
Std: 01492 **Tel:** 549207
Nearest Town/Resort Llandudno
Directions From the A55, take the Rhos-on-Sea exit onto the B5115, follow road for approx. 2 miles. Entrance to park is second exit off the roundabout before going up the hill to Llandudno.
Open 20 March **to** 1 November
Access Good **Site** Lev/Slope
Sites Available **Total** 10
Facilities
Nearby Facilities
Llandudno
✓✓✓✓✓Graded Park. Beaches, golf courses, cruises, castle, ski slope, theatre, museums, mines, zoo, markets, shopping centres and cable cars all within 5 miles.

LLANRWST

Bodnant Caravan Park, Nebo Road, Llanrwst, Conwy, LL26 0SD.
Std: 01492 **Tel:** 640248/640683
Nearest Town/Resort Llanrwst.
Directions Entrance by 30 mile limit on Nebo Road. From Betws-y-Coed (A470). Sharp right at first crossroads to B5427, Nebo road.
Acreage 4 **Open** March **to** October
Access Good **Site** Level

Sites Available **Total** 58
Facilities
Nearby Facilities
Llanrwst.
✓✓✓✓Graded Park. Lovely scenery, small, quiet, clean site. Ideal touring centre. 24 times Winner of Wales in Bloom. 8 multi service pitches. 2 holiday caravans and a cottage also for hire.

LLANRWST

Glyn Farm Caravans, Trefriw, Nr. Llanrwst, Conwy, LL27 0RZ.
Std: 01492 **Tel:** 640442
Nearest Town/Resort Llanrwst.
Directions Follow the A470 to Llanrwst, over hump bridge onto the B5106 Betws-y-Coed to Conwy road. Trefriw is 1¼ miles from Gwydr Castle. Turn right opposite woollen mills, site 200yds.
Open March **to** October
Access Good **Site** Level
Sites Available **Total** 28
Facilities
Nearby Facilities
Llanrwst.
✓✓✓✓✓Graded Park. Very centrally situated for Snowdonia and the sea. Beautiful country, lovely walks and ideal touring. Small family run site.

LLANRWST

Maenan Abbey Caravan Park, Maenan, Nr. Llanrwst, Conwy, LL26 0UL.
Std: 01492 **Tel:** 660630
Nearest Town/Resort Llanrwst
Directions From the A55 follow signs for Llanrwst, approx. 4 miles along the A470.
Acreage 6 **Open** March **to** October
Access Good **Site** Level
Sites Available **Total** 26
Facilities
Nearby Facilities
Llanrwst
✓✓✓✓✓Graded Park. Quiet, rural park.

PENMAENMAWR

Trwyn Yr Wylfa Farm, Trwyn Yr Wylfa, Penmaenmawr, Conwy, LL34 6SF.
Std: 01492 **Tel:** 622357
Nearest Town/Resort Penmaenmawr.
Directions Leave A55 at roundabout for Penmaenmawr. Turn by Mountain View Hotel, farm is ¼ mile east.
Acreage 10 **Open** Spring Bank Holiday **to** End Aug
Site Level
Sites Available **Total** 100
Facilities
Nearby Facilities
Penmaenmawr.
In Snowdonia National Park, secluded.

PENMAENMAWR

Woodlands Camping Park, Pendyffrin Hall, Penmaenmawr, Conwy, LL34 6UF.
Std: 01492 **Tel:** 623219
Nearest Town/Resort Penmaenmawr/Conwy.
Directions 200yds off A55 expressway between Conwy and Penmaenmawr.
Acreage 9 **Open** March **to** October
Site Level
Sites Available **Total** 100
Facilities
Nearby Facilities
Penmaenmawr.
✓✓✓✓Graded Park. Situated in Snowdonia National Park area. Ideal touring centre. Short walk to the beach. S.A.E. for details. Families and couples only.

TREFRIW

Plas Meirion Caravan Park, Gower Road, Trefriw, Conwy, LL27 0RZ.
Std: 01492 **Tel:** 640247
Std: 01492 **Fax:** 640247
Nearest Town/Resort Betws-y-Coed
Directions On the B5106 Betws-y-Coed to Conwy road, in Trefriw turn directly opposite Woollen Mill, site is 300 metres on the left.
Acreage 2 **Open** Easter **to** End October
Access Good **Site** Level
Sites Available **Total** 5
Facilities
Nearby Facilities
Llandudno Junction
✓✓✓✓Graded Park. Quiet, family run site in an attractive garden setting.

DENBIGHSHIRE

CORWEN

Glan Ceirw Caravan Park, Ty Nant, Corwen, Denbighshire, LL21 0RF.
Std: 01490 **Tel:** 420346
Nearest Town/Resort Corwen/Betws-y-Coed.
Directions Between Corwen and Betws-y-Coed just off the A5. Coming from Betws-y-Coed take the second right after Cerrigydrudion over a small bridge and 300yds along the lane. From Corwen turn left after Glan Ceirn signs over a small bridge, 300yds on the left.
Acreage 1 **Open** March **to** October
Access Good **Site** Level
Sites Available **Total** 10
Facilities
Nearby Facilities
Ruabon.
Picturesque site bordering Snowdonia National Park. Trout fishing on site. Ideal for touring North and West Wales.

CORWEN

Hendwr Caravan Park, Llandrillo, Corwen, Denbighshire, LL21 0SN.
Std: 01490 **Tel:** 440210
Nearest Town/Resort Corwen/Bala.
Directions From Corwen (A5) take the B4401 for 4 miles, turn right at sign Hendwr. Site is on the right in ¼ mile. From Bala take the A494 for 1½ miles, turn right onto the B4401 via Llandrillo. Site is 1 mile north on the left.
Acreage 2¼ **Open** April **to** October
Access Good **Site** Level
Sites Available **Total** 60
Facilities
Nearby Facilities
Ruabon.
Alongside a river, good walking, pony trekking and fishing. Wonderful views and an excellent touring centre for North Wales.

CORWEN

Y Felin Caravan Park, Llandrillo, Corwen, Denbighshire, LL21 0TD.
Std: 01490 **Tel:** 440333
Nearest Town/Resort Bala.
Directions A5 to Corwen, take the B4401 into Llandrillo Village, keep left after the church, park in 500yds on the left.
Acreage 2 **Open** Easter **to** October
Access Good **Site** Level
Sites Available
Facilities
Nearby Facilities
Wrexham
Very quiet and private, alongside a river.

DENBIGH

Station House Caravan Park, Bodfari, Denbigh, Denbighshire, LL16 4DA.
Std: 01745 **Tel:** 710372
Std: 01745 **Fax:** 710372
Nearest Town/Resort Denbigh.
Directions From the A541 Mold to Denbigh road, turn onto the B5429 in the direction of Tremeirchion. Site is immediately on the left by cream house.
Acreage 2 **Open** April **to** October
Access Good **Site** Level
Sites Available **Total** 26
Facilities
Nearby Facilities
Rhyl
Attractive site with scenic views. Ideal touring centre. Offa's Dyke path 400yds. Close to two inns (400yds).

LLANGOLLEN

"Eirianfa" Riverside Holiday Park, Berwyn Road, Llangollen, Denbighshire.
Std: 01978 **Tel:** 860919
Std: 01978 **Fax:** 860919
Nearest Town/Resort Llangollen
Directions Going north on the A5, 1 mile from the traffic lights in Llangollen.
Acreage 2 **Open** All Year
Access Good **Site** Level
Sites Available **Total** 30
Facilities
Nearby Facilities
Wrexham
✓✓✓✓Graded Park. River fishing, white water canoeing and rafting. Mountain bike hire.

LLANGOLLEN

Tower Farm, Tower Road, Llangollen, Denbighshire, LL20 8TE.
Std: 01978 **Tel:** 860798
Nearest Town/Resort Llangollen
Open March **to** October
Access Good **Site** Sloping
Sites Available **Total** 70
Facilities
Nearby Facilities
Ruabon
Alongside a canal and the River Dee. Steam trains, canoeing, fishing. Dr Who for children. Ideal for hikers.

LLANGOLLEN

Wern Isaf Farm, Llangollen, Denbighshire.
Std: 01978 **Tel:** 860632
Nearest Town/Resort Llangollen
Directions Up behind Bridgend Hotel over canal bridg turn right into Wern road first farm on right.
Acreage 4 **Open** Easter **to** October
Access Good **Site** Lev/Slope
Sites Available **Total** 40
Facilities
Nearby Facilities
Ruabon
✓✓✓Graded Park. Scenic views, ideal walking, touring.

PRESTATYN

Lido Beach Holiday Park, Central Beach, Off Bastion Road, Prestatyn, Denbighshire, LL19 7EU.
Std: 01745 **Tel:** 855626
Nearest Town/Resort Prestatyn
Directions Entering Prestatyn on the A548 from Queensferry, turn right at T.A. Barracks into Bastion Road. We are the fourth turning on the left.
Open March **to** 29 September
Access Good **Site** Level
Sites Available **Total** 44
Facilities
Nearby Facilities
Prestatyn
✓✓✓✓Graded Park. Superb seaside location with a relaxed, friendly atmosphere. Pitch & Putt, tennis, bowling and play area on park. Next door to Nova Leisure Centre, indoor pool and cafe/restaurant nearby. Gas available nearby. 400yds to the town of Prestatyn, 10 minutes drive to the resort town of Rhyl.

PRESTATYN

Nant Mill Farm Caravan & Tenting Park, Nant Mill, Prestatyn, Denbighshire, LL19 9LY.
Std: 01745 **Tel:** 852360
Nearest Town/Resort Prestatyn.
Directions ½ mile east of Prestatyn on A548 coast road.
Acreage 5 **Open** Easter **to** October
Access Good **Site** Lev/Slope
Sites Available **Total** 150
Facilities
Nearby Facilities
Prestatyn.
✓✓✓✓Graded Park. Near town shops. ½ mile beach, ideal to tour north Wales. Hotel bar meals 200yds.

PRESTATYN

Presthaven Sands Holiday Park, Gronant, Prestatyn, Denbighshire, LL19 9TT.
Std: 01745 **Tel:** 856471
Nearest Town/Resort Prestatyn
Directions Take the A548 out of Prestatyn towards Gronant. The park is signposted left, then entrance is ½ mile afurther on the right.
Acreage 12 **Open** Easter **to** November
Access Good **Site** Level
Sites Available **Total** 100
Facilities
Nearby Facilities
Prestatyn.
Alongside 2 miles of beaches and sand dunes. Very flat park.

PRESTATYN

Tan-Y-Don Caravan Park, 263 Victoria Road, Prestatyn, Denbighshire, LL19 7UT.
Std: 01745 **Tel:** 853749
Std: 01745 **Fax:** 854147
Nearest Town/Resort Prestatyn/Rhyl
Directions Main A548 coast road between Prestatyn and Rhyl, opposite Ffrith Beach.
Open March **to** November
Access Good **Site** Level
Sites Available **Total** 7
Facilities
Nearby Facilities
Prestatyn
✓✓✓✓✓Graded Park. Near to Ffrith Beach, Festival Gardens and an indoor bowls centre. Ideal for touring Wales.

RUTHIN

Parc Farm Caravan Park, Grianrhyd Road, Llanarmon-Yn-Ial, Near Mold, Denbighshire, CH7 4QW.
Std: 01824 **Tel:** 780666
Std: 01824 **Fax:** 780700
Nearest Town/Resort Ruthin/Mold
Directions From Mold on the A494 signed Ruthin, after approx. 5 miles turn left onto the B5430 Llanarmon-Yn-Ial road. After 2½ miles passing the sign for the village, Parc Farm is the next turning on the right and is signposted at the entrance.
Acreage 46 **Open** March **to** October
Access Good **Site** Lev/Slope
Sites Available **Total** 20
Facilities
Nearby Facilities
Wrexham
Fantastic scenery and lovely views of Moel Fammau. Go walking near Offa's Dyke Footpath and Loggerheads Country Park. Central for Chester, Llangollen, Ruthin, Mold, etc..

RUTHIN

Three Pigeons Inn, Graigfechan, Ruthin, Denbighshire, LL15 2EU.
Std: 01824 **Tel:** 703178
Std: 01824 **Fax:** 703178
Nearest Town/Resort Ruthin
Directions A525 from Wrexham or the A494 from Mold, in Ruthin.
Open April **to** October
Access Good **Site** Level
Sites Available
Facilities
Nearby Facilities
Wrexham
Attached to a good pub. Ideal walking.

ST. ASAPH

Penisar Mynydd Caravan Park, Caerwys Road, Rhuallt, St. Asaph, Denbighshire, LL17 0TY.
Std: 01745 **Tel:** 582227
Std: 01745 **Fax:** 582227
Nearest Town/Resort Rhyl/Prestatyn.
Directions Signposted in both directions off the A55(T) with brown and white caravan signs. Travelling from the Chester direction along the A55(T), take the first turning right (crossing the central reservation) 1 mile past Sundawn Nurseries and Tea Pot Cafe. If you are unfortunate to miss the turning, continue for 2 miles down the hill and take the B5429 Tefnant Road and follow the A55 Chester road back up the hill and take first turning left at the top to our site, ½ mile on the right hand side. The site is protected by a HEIGHT BARRIER so please call in at reception prior to driving into the site.
Open April **to** October
Access Good **Site** Lev/Slope
Sites Available **Total** 30
Facilities
Nearby Facilities
Rhyl/Prestatyn.
Ideal base for Rhyl and Prestatyn, within easy reach of North Wales attractions. Ideal stopover for Holyhead Port.

FLINTSHIRE

HOLYWELL

Misty Waters Country Lodge & Caravan Park, Dyserth Road, Lloc, Flintshire, CH8 8RQ.
Std: 01352 **Tel:** 720497
Nearest Town/Resort Rhyl
Directions Turn off the A55 (Chester to Conway) dual carriageway via the slip road and turn right onto the A5151 signed Prestatyn. Within ¾ mile at the roundabout turn right signed Holywell, site is on the left in 200 yards at the first stone house.
Acreage 16 **Open** All Year
Access Good **Site** Lev/Slope
Sites Available **Total** 36
Facilities
Nearby Facilities
Flint
✓✓✓Graded Park. Ideal for beaches, pony treking, riding, walking, touring, golf and fishing. Three Crown Park.

MOLD

Fron Farm Caravan & Camping Site, Fron Farm, Hendre, Mold, Flintshire, CH7 5QW.
Std: 01352 **Tel:** 741217
Nearest Town/Resort Mold/Holywell
Directions A541 between Denbigh and Mold, take sign for Rhes-Y-Cae. Fron Farm

is the third turning on the right including farm lanes.
Acreage 5 **Open** April **to** October
Access Good **Site** Lev/Slope
Sites Available **Total** 25
Facilities
Nearby Facilities
Flint/Chester
Farm site with animals to see and scenic views. Lovely walks. Ideal touring.

QUEENSFERRY

Greenacres Farm Park, Mancot, Deeside, Flintshire, CH5 2AZ.
Std: 01244 **Tel:** 531147
Std: 01244 **Fax:** 531147
Nearest Town/Resort Hawarden
Directions Head for Queensferry on the A550, Take a slip road for Queensferry, at roundabout follow signs for 'Farm Park'.
Acreage 3 **Open** April **to** September
Access Good **Site** Level
Sites Available **Total** 50
Facilities
Nearby Facilities
Hawarden/Shotton
Field adjacent to a farm park. Site fee includes entry into the farm where there is a petting zoo, childrens rides and entertainment.

GWYNEDD

ABERDARON

Caerau Farm, Aberdaron, Pwllheli, Gwynedd, LL53 8BG.
Std: 01758 **Tel:** 760237
Nearest Town/Resort Pwllheli.
Directions Pwllheli to Abersoch road, take the B4413 at Llanbedrog. Aberdaron is in about 14 miles, site is on the left before entering Aberdaron.
Acreage 2½ **Open** March **to** October
Access Good **Site** Lev/Slope
Sites Available **Total** 62
Facilities
Nearby Facilities
Pwllheli.
A quiet site in an area of natural beauty. Near beach, good walking area. Good views of the sea and mountains. Dogs are welcome if kept on a lead. Motorcycles on appointment.

ABERDARON

Mur Melyn Camping Site, Mur Melyn, Aberdaron, Pwllheli, Gwynedd, LL53 8LW.
Std: 01758 **Tel:** 760522
Nearest Town/Resort Pwllheli.
Directions Take A499 west from Pwllheli, then fork onto to B4413 at Llanbedrog about 3 miles before Aberdaron take Whistling Sand road. Turn left at Pen-y-Bont House to site ½ mile.
Acreage 2½ **Open** Whitsun **to** September
Access Good **Site** Level
Sites Available **Total** 60
Facilities
Nearby Facilities
Pwllheli.
Near beach, scenic views, ideal touring, river nearby, ideal for Wales.

ABERDARON

Tir Glyn Farm, Uwchmynydd, Aberdaron, Pwllheli, Gwynedd, LL53 8DA.
Std: 01758 **Tel:** 760248
Nearest Town/Resort Aberdaron/Abersoch
Directions Pwllheli to Abersoch road, take the B4413 at Llanbedrog to Aberdaron. In Aberdaron Village turn right on the bridge signed Uwchmynydd, keep left all the way, first farm on the left.
Acreage 3 **Open** May **to** October
Access Good **Site** Lev/Slope
Sites Available **Total** 30
Facilities
Nearby Facilities
Pwllheli
Surrounded by National Trust land, overlooking the sea for scenic views. Near beaches.

ABERSOCH

Bryn Bach Caravan & Camping Site, Tyddyn Talgoch, Bwlch Tocyn, Abersoch, Gwynedd, LL53 7BT.
Std: 01758 **Tel:** 712285
Std: 01758 **Fax:** 712285
Nearest Town/Resort Abersoch
Directions Continue from the A499 in Abersoch at signpost Sarnbach, after approx. 1¼ miles turn left signposted Bwlch Tocyn. After ¾ miles turn into Hardcore Lane and the site is on the left.
Acreage 2½ **Open** March **to** October
Access Good **Site** Lev/Slope
Sites Available **Total** 55
Facilities
Nearby Facilities
Pwllheli
✓✓✓ Graded Park. Fishing, sailing, windsurfing, skiing, golf, horse riding, Go-Karting in Pwllheli and shooting. Two beaches.

ABERSOCH

Bryn Cethin Bach Caravan Park, Lon Garmon, Abersoch, Pwllheli, North Wales, LL53 7UL.
Std: 01758 **Tel:** 712719
Nearest Town/Resort Abersoch
Directions Take the A499 from Pwllheli to Abersoch. Fork right at Abersoch Land & Sea Garage, park is ½ mile up the hill on the right.
Acreage 3 **Open** March **to** October
Access Good **Site** Level
Sites Available **Total** 15
Facilities
Nearby Facilities
Pwllheli
✓✓✓✓✓ Graded Park. ½ mile from the beach and harbour. Fishing lakes for residents. Heated free showers and toilets.

ABERSOCH

Deucoch Camping & Touring Site, Sarn Bach, Abersoch, Pwllheli, Gwynedd, LL53 7LD.
Std: 01758 **Tel:** 713293
Nearest Town/Resort Abersoch.
Directions Take Sarn Bach road out of Abersoch, continue on main road to Sarn Bach. Turn right in the square.
Acreage 5 **Open** March **to** October
Access Good **Site** Level
Sites Available **Total** 65
Facilities
Nearby Facilities
Pwllheli
✓✓✓✓✓ Graded Park. Near the beach, ideal touring and scenic views. Dogs are allowed on leads. Cafe/restaurant, public telephone and licensed club nearby.

ABERSOCH

Sarnlys, Sarn Bach, Abersoch, Pwllheli, Gwynedd.
Std: 01758 **Tel:** 712956
Nearest Town/Resort Pwllheli.
Directions 1½ miles from Abersoch on A499.
Open Easter **to** October
Sites Available
Facilities
Nearby Facilities
Pwllheli.
Overlooking bay, six minutes walk to the beach.

ABERSOCH

Tan-y-Bryn Farm, Tan-y-Bryn, Sarn Bach, Abersoch, Gwynedd.
Std: 01758 **Tel:** Abersoch 712093
Nearest Town/Resort Abersoch.
Directions 1½ miles south of Abersoch on Sarn Bach road.
Acreage 2 **Open** Mid May **to** Mid Sept
Access Good **Site** Lev/Slope
Sites Available
Facilities
Nearby Facilities
Pwllheli.
Very popular seaside resort.

ABERSOCH

The Warren Touring Park, Abersoch, Pwllheli, Gwynedd, LL53 7AA.
Std: 01758 **Tel:** 712043
Std: 01758 **Fax:** 712998
Nearest Town/Resort Abersoch.
Directions 1 mile east of Abersoch on A499.
Acreage 9 **Open** Easter **to** September
Site Lev/Slope
Sites Available **Total** 75
Facilities
Nearby Facilities
Pwllheli.
✓✓✓✓✓Graded Park.

ABERSOCH

Tyn-y-Mur Camping Site, Abersoch, Gwynedd, LL53 7UL.
Std: 0175 871 **Tel:** 2328
Nearest Town/Resort Abersoch.
Directions A499 Pwllheli to Abersoch, on approaching Abersoch turn right at Land & Sea Services Garage, is then 1 mile on lefthand side.
Acreage 3 **Open** March **to** October
Access Good **Site** Level
Sites Available **Total** 90
Facilities
Nearby Facilities
Pwllheli.
✓✓✓✓✓Graded Park. Superb, uninterrupted panoramic coastal views of Abersoch Bay and Hell's Mouth. Only allowed 1 pet per unit.

ARTHOG

Garthyfog Camping Site, Garthyfog Farm, Arthog, Gwynedd, LL39 1AX.
Std: 01341 **Tel:** Fairbourne 250338
Nearest Town/Resort Barmouth/ Dolgellau
Directions A493, 6 miles from Dolgellau, left by Village hall, look for signs on righthand side.
Acreage 2 **Open** All Year
Site Lev/Slope
Sites Available **Total** 20
Facilities
Nearby Facilities
Morfa Mawddach.
2 miles from Fairbourne, safe bathing, sandy beach and shops. Beautiful scenery, panoramic views. 300 yards from main road, sheltered from wind. Mains cold water. Plenty of room for children to play around the farm, rope-swing, little stream, etc. 2 static caravans to let.

ARTHOG

Graig-Wen, Arthog, Gwynedd, LL39 1BQ.
Std: 01341 **Tel:** 250482/250900
Std: 01341 **Fax:** 250482
Nearest Town/Resort Fairbourne.
Directions Between Dolgellau and Fairbourne on the A493.
Acreage 42
Access Good **Site** Lev/Slope
Sites Available
Facilities
Nearby Facilities
Land reaching down to estuary with scenic views, woodlands and pastures. Ideal for bird watchers and walkers.

BALA

Bryn Melyn Country Holiday Park, Llandderfel, Bala, Gwynedd, LL23 7RA.
Std: 01678 **Tel:** 530212
Nearest Town/Resort Bala
Directions From A5 turn at Corwen onto the B4401 and continue for 7¼ miles.
Acreage 40 **Open** March **to** October
Access Good **Site** Lev/Terraced
Sites Available **Total** 20
Facilities
Nearby Facilities
Ruabon
Snowdonia National Park, Bala Lake Water Sports. Fishing on site.

BALA

Camping & Caravanning Club Site, Crynierth Caravan Park, Cefn-Ddwysarn, Bala, Gwynedd, LL23 7LN.
Std: 01678 **Tel:** 530324
Nearest Town/Resort Bala
Directions From the A5 turn onto the A494 to Bala. At signpost Cefn-Ddwysarn turn right before the red phone box, site is 400 yards on the left.
Acreage 4 **Open** 22 March **to** 25 Oct
Access Good **Site** Level
Sites Available **Total** 50
Facilities
Nearby Facilities
Wrexham
✓✓✓✓✓Graded Park. Situated on the edge of Snowdonia National Park. 4 miles from Bala Lake. Good for watersports. Ideal touring site.

BALA

Glanllyn Caravan & Camping Park, Bala, Gwynedd, LL23 7ST.
Std: 01678 **Tel:** 540227
Nearest Town/Resort Bala
Directions 3 miles south west of Bala on the A494, situated on the left alongside Bala Lake.
Acreage 14 **Open** Easter **to** October
Access Good **Site** Level
Sites Available **Total** 100
Facilities
Nearby Facilities
Wrexham
✓✓✓✓Graded Park. Level parkland with trees. Alongside a lake and river, large launching area for sailing.

BALA

Pen Y Bont Touring & Camping Park, Llangynog Road, Bala, Gwynedd, LL23 7PH.
Std: 01678 **Tel:** 520549
Std: 01678 **Fax:** 520006
Nearest Town/Resort Bala.
Directions ½ mile from Bala on B4391 to Llangynog.
Acreage 6 **Open** April **to** October
Access Good **Site** Level
Sites Available **Total** 85
Facilities
Nearby Facilities
Ruabon.
✓✓✓✓Graded Park. Nearest park to Bala (10 minute walk) and next to a sailing club. NEW Free showers, separate vanity cubicles and washing areas all under cover. AA 4 Pennants.

BALA

Pen Y Garth Caravan & Camping Park. Rhos y Gwaliau, Bala, Gwynedd, LL23 7ES.
Std: 01678 **Tel:** 520485
Std: 01678 **Fax:** 520485
Directions Take B4391 Bala to Llangynog road. 1½ miles from Bala fork right to Rhos-Y-Gwaliau. Site in 600yds.
Acreage 20 **Open** March **to** October
Access Good **Site** Level
Sites Available **Total** 63
Facilities
Nearby Facilities
Ruabon
✓✓✓✓Graded Park. Picturesque setting with superb views. Bala Lake, Sailing, Windsurfing, Snowdonia National Park, good touring centre. Barbecue and picnic area, 3 acre field for recreation or dog walks. AA 3 Pennants and Dragon Award for holiday caravans (for hire).

BALA

Ty-Isaf Camping Site, Ty-Isaf, Bala, Gwynedd, LL23 7PP.
Std: 01678 **Tel:** 520574
Nearest Town/Resort Bala

Directions 2½ miles southeast of Bala, on B4391 road near the telephone kiosk and post box.
Acreage 2 **Open** 1 April/Easter **to** Oct
Access Good **Site** Level
Sites Available **Total** 30
Facilities
Nearby Facilities
Ruabon
Working farm, alongside a stream. Near the beach. Leisure Centre in Bala.

BALA

Tyn Cornel Camping & Caravan Park, Frongoch, Bala, Gwynedd, LL23 7NU.
Std: 01678 **Tel:** 520759
Std: 01678 **Fax:** 520759
Nearest Town/Resort Bala.
Directions Leave Bala on the A4212 Porthmadog road, turn left after 4 miles over river bridge.
Acreage 1¼ **Open** Mid March **to** Mid Oct
Access Good **Site** Level
Sites Available **Total** 37
Facilities
Nearby Facilities
Llangollen.
Next to National White Water Centre on the River Tryweryn. Canoeing and white water rafting available.

BANGOR

Dinas Farm Camping & Touring Site, Halfway Bridge, Tregarth, Bangor, Gwynedd, LL57 4NB.
Std: 01248 **Tel:** 364227
Nearest Town/Resort Bangor.
Directions 3 miles south of Bangor and 2 miles north of Bethesda on the A5, at Halfway Bridge towards Tregarth then first left.
Acreage 5 **Open** Easter (March) **to** October
Access Good **Site** Level
Sites Available **Total** 35
Facilities
Nearby Facilities
Bangor.
Farm site on the banks of the Ogwen River. On Bethesda to Bangor bus route. Centrally situated for the beaches and mountains.

BARMOUTH

Bellaport Touring Site, Bellaport, Tal-y-Bont, Nr. Barmouth, Gwynedd, LL43 2BX.
Std: 01341 **Tel:** 247338
Nearest Town/Resort Barmouth
Directions 4 miles north of Barmouth towards Tal-y-Bont, turn sharp right at 40mph limit sign leaving Tal-y-Bont, at the top of the lane.
Acreage 1½ **Open** 31 March **to** 31 October
Access Good **Site** Level
Sites Available **Total** 22
Facilities
Nearby Facilities
Dyffryn Ardudwy
✓✓✓Graded Park. Quiet farm site with beautiful views over Cardigan Bay. 1 mile from the beach. Access to lovely mountain walks.

BARMOUTH

Hendre Mynach Touring Caravan & Camping Park, Barmouth, Gwynedd.
Std: 01341 **Tel:** 280262
Std: 01341 **Fax:** 280586
Nearest Town/Resort Barmouth
Directions ¼ mile north of Barmouth on the A496 Barmouth to Harlech road.
Acreage 10 **Open** March **to** October
Access Good **Site** Level
Sites Available **Total** 245
Facilities
Nearby Facilities
Barmouth
✓✓✓✓✓Graded Park. 100yds from the beach, ½ mile from town centre. An excellent base for beach and mountain walks. A courtesy bus can take you to the nearest pub that has a childrens room.

BARMOUTH

Islawrffordd Caravan Park, Tal-y-bont, Nr. Barmouth, Gwynedd, LL43 2AQ.
Std: 01341 **Tel:** 247269
Std: 01341 **Fax:** 247269
Nearest Town/Resort Barmouth
Directions From Barmouth heading north on the A496 coast road, take the first left after Tal-y-Bont name plate (approx. 3½ miles), we are the last park on the left hand side.
Open April **to** October
Access Good **Site** Level
Sites Available **Total** 200
Facilities
Nearby Facilities
Tal-y-Bont
✓✓✓✓Graded Park. Next to the beach. Ideal base for touring North and Mid Wales coast.

BARMOUTH

Moelfre View Caravan Park, Talybont, Nr. Barmouth, Gwynedd, LL43 2AQ.
Std: 01341 **Tel:** 247100
Std: 01341 **Fax:** 242637
Nearest Town/Resort Barmouth
Directions A496 Barmouth to Harlech coast road, turn left to the beach just before the village of Talybont.
Acreage 3 **Open** March **to** January
Access Good **Site** Level
Sites Available **Total** 54
Facilities
Nearby Facilities
Talybont
Scenic views, near a safe sandy beach, ideal for all water sports. Boat launching facility nearby.

BARMOUTH

Sunnysands Holiday Park, Talybont, Nr. Barmouth, Gwynedd, LL43 2LQ.
Std: 01341 **Tel:** 247301
Std: 01341 **Fax:** 242637
Nearest Town/Resort Barmouth
Directions 3½ miles from Barmouth on the seaward side of the A496. 7 miles from Harlech.
Acreage 1½ **Open** 1 March **to** 16 November
Access Good **Site** Level
Sites Available **Total** 25
Facilities
Nearby Facilities
Barmouth
Situated on the edge of a safe, sandy beach, recently awarded the Blue Flag. Ideal base for exploring Snowdonia National Park, and only 7 miles from Harlech with its castle and other attractions.

BEDDGELERT

Beddgelert - Forestry Commission, Beddgelert, Gwynedd, LL55 4UU.
Std: 01766 **Tel:** 890288
Nearest Town/Resort Beddgelert
Directions 2 miles north of Beddgelert Village on the A4085.
Acreage 23½ **Open** All Year
Access Good **Site** Level
Sites Available **Total** 280
Facilities
Nearby Facilities
In the heart of Snowdonia, within walking distance of Snowdon itself. Walking, cycling and canoeing also nearby.

BETHESDA

Ogwen Bank Caravan Park, Bethesda, Gwynedd, LL57 3LQ.
Std: 01248 **Tel:** 600486
Std: 01248 **Fax:** 600559
Nearest Town/Resort Bangor.
Directions Follow the A5 signposted for Betwys-y-Coed. Park is situated on the right just after the village of Bethesda.

Open March **to** October
Access Good **Site** Lev/Slope
Sites Available
Facilities
Nearby Facilities
Bangor
✓✓✓Graded Park. Set in ancient woodlands, alongside a river and waterfalls. All individual pitches are level.

CAERNARFON

Bryn Gloch Caravan & Camping Park, Betws Garmon, Caernarfon, Gwynedd, LL54 7YY.
Std: 01286 **Tel:** 650216
Std: 01286 **Fax:** 650216
Nearest Town/Resort Caernarfon.
Directions 4½ miles south west of Caernarfon on A4085. Site on right opposite Betws Garmon church.
Acreage 12 **Open** All Year
Access Good **Site** Level
Sites Available **Total** 150
Facilities
Nearby Facilities
Bangor.
✓✓✓✓✓Graded Park. Fishing, scenic views, ideal touring centre. Family owned and operated. AA 4 Pennants. Award winning site.

CAERNARFON

Cadnant Valley Camping & Caravan Park, Llanberis Road, Caernarfon, Gwynedd, LL55 2DF.
Std: 01286 **Tel:** 673196
Nearest Town/Resort Caernarfon.
Directions ¼ mile from Caernarfon Castle on A4086 signposted for Llanberis. Entrance on left 150yds after roundabout opposite the school. Drive slowly, easy to overshoot entrance.
Acreage 4¼ **Open** 14 March **to** 31 Oct
Access Good **Site** Level
Sites Available **Total** 69
Facilities
Nearby Facilities
Bangor.
✓✓✓✓Graded Park. Beautiful peaceful valley with attractive stream and trees. Everything clean and well maintained, terraced. Ideal touring centre. Swimming pool nearby.

CAERNARFON

Challoner Camping Site, Erw Hywel, Llanrug, Caernarfon, Gwynedd, LL55 2AJ.
Std: 01286 **Tel:** 672985
Nearest Town/Resort Caernarfon.
Directions A4086 from Caernarfon, 3 miles to Llanberis ½ mile west of Llanrug.
Acreage 2 **Open** March **to** October
Access Good **Site** Level
Sites Available **Total** 35
Facilities
Nearby Facilities
Bangor.
Flat dry, touring, view of Angelesey. Quiet, flat site, very central for Snowdonia Mountains and the sea.

CAERNARFON

Glan Gwna Holiday Park, Caethro, Caernarfon, Gwynedd, LL55 2SG.
Std: 01286 **Tel:** 673456
Std: 01286 **Fax:** 673456
Nearest Town/Resort Caernarfon.
Directions 1¼ mile from Caernarfon on A4085.
Acreage 5 **Open** Easter **to** October
Access Good **Site** Lev/Slope
Sites Available **Total** 100
Facilities
Nearby Facilities
Bangor.
Lakes, river, fishing.

CAERNARFON

Llyn-y-Gele Caravan Park, Pontllyfni, Caernarfon, Gwynedd, LL54 5EL.
Std: 01286 **Tel:** 660283/660289
Nearest Town/Resort Caernarfon.
Directions Take the A487 out of Caernarfon for 2 miles, onto the A499 for 4 miles. Entrance to the site is the first right by garage and shop in the village of Pontllyfni.
Acreage 4 **Open** Easter **to** October
Access Good **Site** Level
Sites Available **Total** 30
Facilities
Nearby Facilities
Bangor.
Panoramic views of Snowdonia range. 5 minute walk to a beach with safe bathing. Fishing ¼ mile. Ideal location for touring Snowdonia.

CAERNARFON

Plas Gwyn Caravan Site, Plas Gwyn, Llanrug, Caernarfon, Gwynedd, LL53 2AQ.
Std: 01286 **Tel:** 672619
Std: 01286 **Fax:** 672619
Nearest Town/Resort Caernarfon.
Directions 3 miles from Caernarfon on the A4086, signposted on right.
Acreage 4 **Open** March **to** October
Access Good **Site** Level
Sites Available **Total** 70
Facilities
Nearby Facilities
Bangor.
✓✓✓✓✓Graded Park. Snowdonia Mountains 3 miles, beach 2 miles, leisure complex ¾ mile Natural beauty within National Park Area. Dragon Award hire caravans. En-suite bed and breakfast available in the house.

CAERNARFON

Rhyd-y-Galen Caravan Park, Rhyd-y-Galen, Bethel, Caernarfon, Gwynedd, LL55 3PS.
Std: 01248 **Tel:** 670110
Nearest Town/Resort Caernarfon
Directions Signposted 1½ miles east of Caernarfon on the B4366.
Acreage 3 **Open** Easter **to** October
Access Good **Site** Lev/Slope
Sites Available **Total** 35
Facilities
Nearby Facilities
Bangor
Ideal touring site for North Wales. Outdoor pursuit centre within 1½ miles. Beaches, mountains and forest within low mileage.

CAERNARFON

Riverside Camping, Caer Glyddyn, Pontrug, Caernarfon, Gwynedd, LL55 2BB.
Std: 01286 **Tel:** 678781
Std: 01286 **Fax:** 677223
Nearest Town/Resort Caernarfon.
Directions 2 miles out of Caernarfon on the righthand side of the A4086 (Llanberis road).
Acreage 4½ **Open** Easter **to** October
Access Good **Site** Level
Sites Available **Total** 55
Facilities
Nearby Facilities
Bangor.
✓✓✓Graded Park. The campsite is bordered on two sides by a lovely river which is suitable for paddling and bathing. An ideal area for touring. Dogs on leads at all times. Toilet and shower facilities for the disabled.

CAERNARFON

Twll Clawdd, Llanrug, Caernarfon, Gwynedd, LL55 2AZ.
Std: 01286 **Tel:** 672838
Nearest Town/Resort Caernarfon
Directions We are on the A4086 Llanberis to Caernarfon road, we are on the right by speed sign just past the Spar Shop in Llanrug.
Open March **to** October
Access Good **Site** Level

WHEN YOU DISCOVER BRYNTEG HOLIDAY PARK. . . .

Brynteg Holiday Park is truly unique. Set in wooded grounds, overlooking superb countryside in idyllic North Wales the park offers a world of fun and enjoyment for the whole family. Whether you want to get away from it all with a good book and your fishing rod or dance the night away in the club Brynteg has it all, including a fantastic leisure complex with heated indoor pool. Situated within easy distance of Caernarfon and Conway Castles and Snowdonia National Park, Brynteg is a firm favourite with the outdoor lover. Enjoy a quiet stroll amidst the most breathtaking scenery North Wales has to offer.

You Discover North Wales

One of the few parks to have been awarded the coveted Daffodil Award.

01286 871374

BRYNTEG
Holiday Park

LLANRUG, NEAR CAERNARFON, GWYNEDD, LL55 4RF

GLAN GWNA HOLIDAY PARK

GLAN GWNA IS AN ENCHANTING HOLIDAY VILLAGE hidden amongst the woods and meadows of an old country estate within easy reach of historic castles, golden beaches, lakes and breath taking mountain walks.

Glan Gwna has many amenities including excellent coarse and game fishing on four lakes and the River Seiont. Horse riding on site. Tennis Court.

Heated (Outdoor) Swimming pool, Poolside bar with meals.
CARAVANS AND CHALETS FOR HIRE ON SITE AND FOR SALE

Directions to site: 1·5 miles from Caernarfon on A4085
Bookings essential Bank Holidays & Summer Months

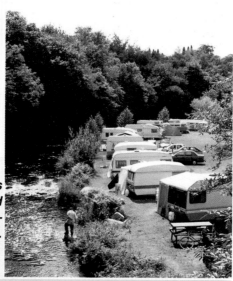

Sites Available **Total** 40
Facilities
Nearby Facilities
Bangor
In the heart of Snowdonia, 4 miles from the beach. Ideal touring.

CAERNARFON

Tyn-yr-Onnen Mountain Farm Caravan & Camping Park, Waunfawr, Caernarfon, Gwynedd, LL55 4AX.
Std: 01286 **Tel:** 650281
Std: 01286 **Fax:** 650043
Nearest Town/Resort Caernarfon
Directions A4085 Caernarfon (A487) to Beddgelert, left at Waunfawr village church/chip shop, signposted from that point.
Acreage 4¼ **Open** 1st May Holiday **to** Sept
Access Good **Site** Lev/Slope
Sites Available **Total** 70
Facilities
Nearby Facilities
Bangor
✓✓✓✓Graded Park. A working farm at the foot of a mountain, secluded and peaceful, ideal touring and walking base. Colour brochure only on receiving a S.A.E.. AA 3 Pennants.

CAERNARFON

White Tower Caravan Park, Llandwrog, Caernarfon, Gwynedd, LL54 5UH.
Std: 01286 **Tel:** 830649
Nearest Town/Resort Caernarfon
Directions From Caernarfon follow the A487 Porthmadog road for approx ¼ mile, go past the Pioneer Supermarket, straight ahead at the roundabout and take the first turning on the right. We are 3 miles on the right.
Acreage 3 **Open** March **to** October
Access Good **Site** Level
Sites Available **Total** 52
Facilities
Nearby Facilities
✓✓✓✓✓Graded Park. 2½ miles beach, 3¼ miles Caernarfon. Splendid views of Snowdon. Central for touring Llyn Peninsula, Anglesey and Snowdonia.

CLYNNOG FAWR

Aberafon Camping Site, Gyrn Goch, Caernarfon, Gwynedd, LL54 5PN.
Std: 01286 **Tel:** 660295
Std: 01286 **Fax:** 660582
Nearest Town/Resort Caernarfon
Directions From Caernarfon take the A499 towards Pwllheli. 1 mile after Clynnog Fawr on the right hand side.
Acreage 15 **Open** April **to** October
Access Poor **Site** Level
Sites Available **Total** 150
Facilities
Nearby Facilities
Pwllheli
Private beach. Boat launching available. Take-away food.

CRICCIETH

Cae-Canol Caravan & Camping, Criccieth, Gwynedd.
Std: 01766 **Tel:** 522351
Nearest Town/Resort Criccieth.
Directions Take the B4411 from Criccieth, 2 miles. Also 2½ miles from the A487 towards Criccieth.
Acreage 3 **Open** April **to** October
Access Very Good **Site** Level
Sites Available **Total** 25
Facilities
Nearby Facilities
Criccieth.
Sheltered, grassy site. Private trout fishing available for caravanners and campers. Delightful riverside walk nearby. Ideal for touring.

CRICCIETH

Camping & Caravanning Club Site, Tyddyn Sianel, Llanystumdwy, Criccieth, Gwynedd, LL52 0LS.
Std: 01766 **Tel:** 522855

Nearest Town/Resort Criccieth
Directions From Criccieth take the A497 and turn second right signposted Llanstumdwy, site is on the right.
Acreage 4 **Open** 22 March **to** 1 Nov
Access Good **Site** Sloping
Sites Available **Total** 60
Facilities
Nearby Facilities
Criccieth
✓✓✓✓Graded Park. Situated just outside Criccieth with scenic coastal views. Nearby attractions include Ffestiniog Railway and Snowdonia National Park.

CRICCIETH

Eisteddfa Caravan & Camping Site, Eisteddfa Lodge, Pentrefelin, Criccieth, Gwynedd, LL52 0PT.
Std: 01766 **Tel:** 522696
Nearest Town/Resort Criccieth.
Directions On the A497 Porthmadog to Criccieth road, 1½ miles north east of Criccieth. Entrance is at the west end of Pentrefelin beside the Plas Gwyn Hotel.
Acreage 11 **Open** March **to** October
Access Good **Site** Lev/Slope
Sites Available **Total** 145
Facilities
Nearby Facilities
Criccieth.

CRICCIETH

Llwynbugeilydd, Criccieth, Gwynedd, LL52 0PN.
Std: 01766 **Tel:** 522235
Nearest Town/Resort Criccieth
Directions First site on the B4411, 1 mile north of Criccieth off the A497. From Caernarfon on the A487 turn right after Bryncir onto the B4411, the site is on the left in 3½ miles.
Acreage 6 **Open** Easter **to** 31st October
Access Good **Site** Level
Sites Available **Total** 45
Facilities
Nearby Facilities
Criccieth
✓✓✓✓Graded Park. Within 10 minutes walking distance to beach and shops. Fine views of Cardigan Bay and Snowdonia. Hand driers. Restaurants and pubs 1 mile. AA 2 Pennants.

CRICCIETH

Muriau Bach, Rhoslan, Criccieth, Gwynedd, LL52 0NP.
Std: 01766 **Tel:** 530642
Nearest Town/Resort Criccieth
Directions Coming from Porthmadog on the A487, turn left onto the B4411. Fourth entrance on the left over a cattle grid, with a drive leading up to the site.
Acreage 1¼ **Open** March **to** October
Access Good **Site** Level
Sites Available **Total** 30
Facilities
Nearby Facilities
Criccieth
Attractive, clean, level site, central to all places of interest. Commanding the best views in the area, nice walks nearby. Cycle track nearby that leads to Caernarfon. One static caravan with all mod cons, sleeps four, terms reasonable. Rock climbing at Tremadog.

CRICCIETH

Mynydd-Du Caravan & Camping Site, Mynydd-Du, Criccieth, Gwynedd, LL52 0PS.
Std: 01766 **Tel:** 522533
Nearest Town/Resort Criccieth.
Directions On the A497, 3 miles west of Porthmadog and 1 mile east of Criccieth.
Acreage 5½ **Open** April **to** October
Access Good **Site** Level
Sites Available **Total** 80
Facilities
Nearby Facilities
Criccieth.
Superb views of the Snowdonia range of hills and Cardigan Bay. 1 mile from the beach. Central for places of interest including castles.

CRICCIETH

Tyddyn Cethin Caravan & Camping Site, Rhoslan, Criccieth, Gywnedd, LL52 0NF.
Std: 01766 **Tel:** 522149
Nearest Town/Resort Criccieth
Directions Situated on the B4411 Caernarfon road approx. 1½ miles from Criccieth.
Acreage 10 **Open** March **to** October
Access Good **Site** Level
Sites Available **Total** 50
Facilities
Nearby Facilities
Criccieth
✓✓✓✓Graded Park. Quiet, family site on the banks of the River Dwyfor.

CRICCIETH

Tyddyn Morthwyl, Criccieth, Gwynedd.
Std: 01766 **Tel:** 522115
Nearest Town/Resort Criccieth.
Directions 1½ miles north of Criccieth on

B4411 main road to Caernarfon.
Acreage 6 **Open** March **to** October
Access Good **Site** Level
Sites Available **Total** 40
Facilities
Nearby Facilities
Criccieth.
Central for mountains of Snowdonia and beaches of Lleyn Peninsula. Level and sheltered with mountain views.

DINAS DINLLE

Morfa Lodge Caravan Park, Dinas Dinlle, Near Caernarfon, Gwynedd, LL54 5TP.
Std: 01286 **Tel:** 830205
Std: 01286 **Fax:** 831329
Nearest Town/Resort Caernarfon
Directions Take the A487 south from Caernarfon which leads onto the A499. 7 miles from Caernarfon turn for Dinas Dinlle, turn right at the far end of Beach Road.
Acreage 15 **Open** March **to** October
Access Good **Site** Level
Sites Available **Total** 220
Facilities
Nearby Facilities
Bangor
✓✓✓✓Graded Park. ¼ mile from Dinas Dinlle beach, central for touring Snowdonia, Anglesey and Lleyn Peninsula.

DOLGELLAU

Dolgamedd Camping & Caravan Site, Dolgamedd, Bontnewydd, Dolgellau, Gwynedd.
Std: 01341 **Tel:** 422624
Std: 01341 **Fax:** 422624
Nearest Town/Resort Dolgellau
Directions 3 miles from Dolgellau towards Bala, turn right for Brithdir and continue over the bridge and we are 30 yards on the left.
Acreage 6 **Open** Easter/1 April **to** End Oct
Access Good **Site** Level
Sites Available **Total** 100
Facilities
Nearby Facilities
Machynlleth/Barmouth
Alongside the River Wnion, good for Salmon fishing. Way-marked riverside and woodland walks. Camp fires and BBQ sites.

DOLGELLAU

Llwyn-Yr-Helm Farm, Brithdir, Dolgellau, Gwynedd, LL40 2SA.
Std: 01341 **Tel:** 450254
Nearest Town/Resort Dolgellau
Directions Take minor road at telephone kiosk off the B4416 which is a loop road from A470 to A494, Dolgellau 4 miles.
Acreage 2½ **Open** Easter **to** End October
Site Level
Sites Available **Total** 25
Facilities
Nearby Facilities
Machynlleth
Friendly, quiet small farm site with scenic views, ideal for walking, touring and sandy beaches. Milk and eggs available. Well behaved pets welcome.

DOLGELLAU

Tanyfron Camping & Caravan Park, Arran Road, Dolgellau, Gwynedd, LL40 2AA.
Std: 01341 **Tel:** 422638
Std: 01341 **Fax:** 422638
Nearest Town/Resort Dolgellau.
Directions From Welshpool take A470, turn for Dolgellau by ARC Depot, off A470. ¼ mile on left - Dolgellau straight on ½ mile from site.
Acreage 3¼ **Open** All Year
Access Good **Site** Level
Sites Available **Total** 43
Facilities
Nearby Facilities
Barmouth.
✓✓✓✓Graded Park. 10 miles beach, scenic views, walking, touring, fishing, walking distance of town. TV hook-ups to touring pitches. En-suite B&B available. Snowdonia National Park Award 1993. Wales in Bloom Award Winners 1996.

DOLGELLAU

Vanner Abbey Farm Caravan Park, Llanelltyd, Dolgellau, Gwynedd, LL40 2HE.
Std: 01341 **Tel:** 422854
Nearest Town/Resort Dolgellau
Directions Follow the A470 north of Dolgellau for 2 miles and follow "Cymer Abbey" signs to the farm.
Open Easter **to** October
Access Good **Site** Level
Sites Available
Facilities
Nearby Facilities
Barmouth
Alongside a river, 4 miles from the beach. Ideal for walking and fishing.

DYFFRYN ARDUDWY

Dyffryn Seaside Estate, Dyffryn Ardudwy, Gwynedd, LL44 2HD.
Std: 01341 **Tel:** 247220
Std: 01341 **Fax:** 247622
Nearest Town/Resort Barmouth
Directions On the A494 north from Barmouth, after 5 miles turn left at the church just north of Talybont.
Acreage 11 **Open** April **to** September
Site Level
Sites Available **Total** 200
Facilities

Nearby Facilities
Dyffryn Ardudwy
Near a sandy beach.

DYFFRYN ARDUDWY

Murmur-yr-Afon Touring Caravan & Camping Site, Dyffryn Ardudwy, Gwynedd, LL44 2BE.
Std: 01341 **Tel:** 247353
Std: 01341 **Fax:** 247353
Nearest Town/Resort Barmouth
Directions Take the A496 coast road from Barmouth towards Harlech. Site entrance is 100yds from the Power Garage in Dyffryn Village on the right hand side.
Acreage 4 **Open** March **to** October
Access Good **Site** Level
Sites Available **Total** 47
Facilities
Nearby Facilities
✓✓✓✓Graded Park. 1 mile from beach. Set in sheltered and natural surroundings, 100yds from village and shops, petrol stations and licensed premises.

FFESTINIOG

Llechrwd, Maentwrog, Blaenau Ffestiniog, Gwynedd.
Std: 01766 **Tel:** Maentwrog 590240
Directions On the A496. Blaenau Ffestiniog 3 miles, Porthmadog 8 miles.
Acreage 5 **Open** Easter **to** October
Access Good **Site** Lev/Slope
Sites Available
Facilities
Nearby Facilities
Blaenau Ffestiniog.
✓✓✓Graded Park. Riverside camp.

HARLECH

Beach Road Caravan Park, Beach Road, Harlech, Gwynedd, LL46 2UG.
Std: 01766 **Tel:** 780328
Nearest Town/Resort Harlech
Directions 10 miles north of Barmouth on the A496, turn left at Queens Hotel along Beach Road.
Acreage 3½ **Open** March **to** October
Access Good **Site** Level
Sites Available **Total** 10
Facilities
Nearby Facilities
Harlech
✓✓✓✓Graded Park. Small, quiet site landscaped with trees, flower beds and shrubs.

HARLECH

Min-y-Don Caravan Park & Camping Sites, Min-y-Don, Beach Road, Harlech, Gwynedd, LL46 2UG.
Std: 01766 **Tel:** 780286
Nearest Town/Resort Harlech
Directions Follow the A496 main coast road to Lower Harlech and turn into Beach Road opposite Queens Hotel. Site approx. 500 metres.
Open Easter **to** October
Access Good **Site** Level
Sites Available **Total** 60
Facilities
Nearby Facilities
Harlech
5 and 10 minute walks to the beach, swimming pool, Swings Golf Course, Harlech Town and 12th Century Castle. Ideal base for touring Snowdonia.

HARLECH

Woodlands Caravan Park, Harlech, Gwynedd, LL46 2UE.
Std: 01766 **Tel:** 780419
Std: 01766 **Fax:** 780419
Nearest Town/Resort Harlech
Directions Leave A496 at Harlech railway crossing, site signposted at crossing at foot of castle.
Acreage 2 **Open** March **to** October
Access Good **Site** Level
Sites Available **Total** 37
Facilities
Nearby Facilities
Harlech
✓✓✓✓✓Graded Park. Near beach, shops and golfcourse. Harlech Castle adjacent. Swimming pool nearby. Ideal touring.

LLANBEDROG

Bolmynydd Caravan & Camping Park, Contact Address: Refail, Llanbedrog, Pwllheli, Gwynedd, LL53 7NP.
Std: 01758 **Tel:** 740511
Nearest Town/Resort Llanbedrog
Directions Follow the A499 from Pwllheli to Llanbedrog for 3½ miles. Continue towards Abersoch (on the A499) for ½ mile and take the first left after Llanbedrog Riding Centre (by the red post box). Site is ½ mile on the left.
Acreage 2 **Open** Easter **to** End September
Access Poor **Site** Level
Sites Available **Total** 48
Facilities
Nearby Facilities
Pwllheli
✓✓✓✓✓Graded Park. 5 minutes walk to the beach and nearest pub. Adjacent to 500 acres of moorland with beautiful hill and coastal footpaths. Panoramic views of Llyn Peninsula, Snowdonia and coast. New facilities.

LLANBEDROG

Refail Caravan & Camping Park, Refail, Llanbedrog, Pwllheli, Gywnedd, LL53 7NP.
Std: 01758 **Tel:** 740511
Nearest Town/Resort Pwllheli
Directions Follow A499 from Pwllheli to Llanbedrog turn right onto B4413 at LLanbedrog, site situated 500 metres on the right hand side.
Acreage 1¾ **Open** Easter **to** October
Access Good **Site** Level
Sites Available **Total** 33
Facilities
Nearby Facilities
Pwllheli
✓✓✓✓✓Graded Park. Two mins from beach, scenic views, shops and 2 pubs. Pets welcome if kept on leads. WTB Welcome Host Gold Award, RAC Approved and Caravan & Camping Club Approved.

LLANBERIS

Snowdon View Caravan Park, Brynrefail, Nr. Llanberis, Caernarfon, Gwynedd, LL55 3PD.
Std: 01286 **Tel:** 870349
Nearest Town/Resort LLanberis.
Directions 5 miles east of Caernarfon on the A4086, then turn north on the B4547 Bangor road for ¾ mile. We are situated on the right.
Acreage 12 **Open** March **to** January
Access Good **Site** Level
Sites Available **Total** 218
Facilities
Nearby Facilities
Scenic views, lake 300 yards away. Ideal touring, walking, fishing, boating and climbing area. Bar meals now available.

NANT PERIS

Snowdon House, Gwastadnant, Nant Peris, Llanberis Pass, Gwynedd, LL55 4UL.
Std: 01286 **Tel:** 870356
Nearest Town/Resort Llanberis/Betws-y-Coed
Directions A4086 from Capel Curig to Llanberis.
Acreage ¼ **Open** All Year
Access Good **Site** Level
Sites Available **Total** 20
Facilities
Nearby Facilities

Bangor

Ideal for climbing, rambling and walks. Main attraction is Mount Snowdon and within easy reach of the seaside. £2.50 per person per night. Web Site: http://www.harleys.force9.co.uk/Snowdon-House/

PORTHMADOG

Black Rock Camping Park, Morfa Bychan, Porthmadog, Gwynedd.
Std: 01766 **Tel:** 513919
Nearest Town/Resort Porthmadog.
Directions After croosing Toll, turn left at Woolworths, and continue down the A492 to Black Rock Sands. Continue for 3 miles approx, and bear right.
Acreage 9 **Open** March **to** October
Access Good **Site** Level
Sites Available **Total** 150
Facilities
Nearby Facilities
Porthmadog.
✓✓✓Graded Park. Adjacent to beach, ideal base for sightseeing, climbing, walking and water activities. Pets are welcome, but only one per unit.

PORTHMADOG

Garreg Goch Caravan Park, Black Rock Sands, Morfa Bychan, Porthmadog, Gwynedd, LL49 9YD.
Std: 01766 **Tel:** 512210
Nearest Town/Resort Porthmadog.
Directions Turn off A487 in Porthmadog, at Woolworths, follow signs for Morfa Bychan for 2 miles, turn left at sign for park.
Acreage 5 **Open** March **to** October
Access Good **Site** Level
Sites Available **Total** 24
Facilities
Nearby Facilities
Porthmadog
✓✓✓✓Graded Park. Near sandy beach, scenic views. Ideal for touring places of interest.

PORTHMADOG

Greenacres Holiday Park, Black Rock Sands, Morfa Bychan, Porthmadog, Gwynedd, LL49 9YB.
Std: 0345 **Tel:** 125931
Std: 01766 **Fax:** 512084
Nearest Town/Resort Porthmadog
Directions After going over the toll bridge at Porthmadog, go along the high street and turn between the Post Office and Woolworths. ¼ mile on through the village of Morfa Bychan, take the right fork to Black Rock Sands, Greenacres is about 2 miles.
Open March **to** October
Access Good **Site** Level
Sites Available **Total** 71
Facilities
Nearby Facilities
Porthmadog
✓✓✓Graded Park. Near the beach with scenic views. New sport and leisure facilities including bike hire, bowling and Pitch & Putt. Kids Club and a full family entertainment programme. Ideal touring. Dragon Award.

PORTHMADOG

Gwyndy Caravan Park, Black Rock Sands, Morfa Bychan, Porthmadog, Gwynedd, LL49 9YB.
Std: 01766 **Tel:** 512047
Std: 01766 **Fax:** 512047
Nearest Town/Resort Porthmadog
Directions In Porthmadog turn at Woolworths to Black Rock Sands follow the road into the village of Morfa Bychan past the petrol station and little supermarket, turn first left and then second right into road leading into caravan park, exactly 2 miles from Porthmadog.
Acreage 5 **Open** March **to** October
Access Good **Site** Level
Sites Available **Total** 20
Facilities
Nearby Facilities
Porthmadog
Select family run park, just a few minutes from the beach, with backdrop of mountain views. Ideal for touring the Snowdonia area.

PORTHMADOG

Sound of the Sea, Morfa Bychan, Porthmadog, Gwynedd, LL49 9YB.
Std: 01766 **Tel:** 513076
Nearest Town/Resort Porthmadog
Directions In Porthmadog turn at Woolworths to Black Rock Sands, follow signs for Morfa Bychan, go past the petrol station and and Spar, turn first left then second right into the road that leads into the caravan park, exactly 2 miles.
Open 31 March **to** 31 October
Access Good **Site** Level
Sites Available **Total** 4
Facilities
Nearby Facilities
Porthmadog
Near a sandy beach, scenic views. Own leisure park 200 yards.

PORTHMADOG

Ty Bricks Caravan Site, Traeth Mawr, Porthmadog, Gwynedd, LL49 9PP.
Std: 01766 **Tel:** 512597
Nearest Town/Resort Porthmadog.
Acreage 5 **Open** March **to** October
Access Good **Site** Level
Sites Available **Total** 8
Facilities
Nearby Facilities
Porthmadog.
Small, quiet site, very scenic views.

PORTHMADOG

Tyddyn Adi Camping Park, Morfa Bychan, Porthmadog, Gwynedd, LL49 9YW.
Std: 01766 **Tel:** 512933
Nearest Town/Resort Porthmadog
Directions From Porthmadog take the Morfa Bychan road 2¼ miles. Follow to the end of village and there is a large red sign on the right.
Acreage 28 **Open** Easter **to** October
Access Good **Site** Level
Sites Available **Total** 200
Facilities
Nearby Facilities
Porthmadog.
Close to Porthmadog attractions and ¼ mile from Black Rock Sands. Ideal for touring.

PORTHMADOG

Tyddyn Llwyn Caravan Park & Campsite, Black Rock Road, Porthmadog, Gwynedd, LL49 9UR.
Std: 01766 **Tel:** 512205
Std: 01766 **Fax:** 512205
Nearest Town/Resort Porthmadog.
Directions On high street turn by the Post Office signposted golf course and Black Rock Sands. Park is on the right in under ¼ mile. Verge signs on left.
Acreage 52 **Open** March **to** October
Access Good **Site** Lev/Slope
Sites Available **Total** 150
Facilities
Nearby Facilities
Porthmadog.
✓✓✓ Graded Park. Only 2 miles from Black Rock Sands. In a sheltered valley beneath Moel Y Gest mountain with beautiful wooded scenery.

PWLLHELI

Abererch Sands Holiday Centre, Pwllheli, Gwynedd, LL53 6PJ.
Std: 01758 **Tel:** 612327
Nearest Town/Resort Pwhelli
Directions A497 Portmadog to Pwllheli road, 2 miles before Pwllheli.
Open March **to** October
Access Good **Site** Level
Sites Available
Facilities
Nearby Facilities
Abererch Halt
Near beach, scenic views, safe swimming.

PWLLHELI

Rhosfawr Nurseries Touring Caravan & Camping Park, Rhosfawr, Y Ffor, Pwllheli, Gwynedd, LL53 6YA.
Std: 01766 **Tel:** 810545
Nearest Town/Resort Pwllheli
Directions 2 miles from Y Ffor on the B4354 Nefyn road, telephone box on the left, we are just a bit further along on the right.
Acreage 2 **Open** March **to** End October
Access Good **Site** Level
Sites Available **Total** 20
Facilities
Nearby Facilities
Pwllheli
✓✓✓ Graded Park. Situated in the centre of the beautiful Llyn Peninsula. Ideal for touring.

TALSARNAU

Barcdy Touring Caravan & Camping Park, Talsarnau, Gwynedd, LL47 6YG.
Std: 01766 **Tel:** 770736
Nearest Town/Resort Harlech.
Directions From Bala A4212 to Trawsfynydd. A487 to Maentwrog. At Maentwrog left onto A496, signposted Harlech. Site 4 miles.
Acreage 12 **Open** April **to** October
Access Good **Site** Lev/Slope
Sites Available **Total** 78
Facilities
Nearby Facilities
Talsarnau.
✓✓✓✓ Graded Park. Walks from site to nearby mountains and lakes. Ideal touring Snowdonia.

TYWYN

Cwmrhwyddfor Campsite, Talyllyn, Tywyn, Gwynedd, LL36 9AJ.
Std: 01654 **Tel:** 761286/761380
Nearest Town/Resort Dolgellau.
Directions Situated on the A487 between Dolgellau and Machynlleth, at foot of Cader Idris mountain, right at the bottom of Talyllyn pass, a white house under the rocks.
Acreage 6 **Open** All Year
Access Good **Site** Level
Sites Available **Total** 30
Facilities
Nearby Facilities
Machynlleth.
Very central for Tywyn, Aberdovey, Barmouth. The site runs alongside a stream. Ideal for the mountains and sea. All kept very clean, excellent reputation. TV reception on site. Public telephone and Cafe/Restaurant nearby. Prices on application.

TYWYN

Tynllwyn Caravan & Camping Park, Bryncrug, Tywyn, Gwynedd, LL36 9RD.
Std: 01654 **Tel:** 710370
Std: 01654 **Fax:** 710370
Nearest Town/Resort Tywyn
Directions Leave Tywyn on the A493, turn off right onto the B4405, turn first right off and go up the lane, site is on the left.
Open March **to** October
Access Good **Site** Level
Sites Available **Total** 78
Facilities
Nearby Facilities
Tywyn
✓✓✓✓ Graded Park. Talyllyn Narrow Gauge Railway runs alongside the site. Only 2½ miles from the beach. Excellent for walkers.

TYWYN

Waenfach Caravan Site, Waenfach, Llanegryn, Tywyn, Gwynedd, LL36 9SB.
Std: 01654 **Tel:** Tywyn 710375
Nearest Town/Resort Tywyn.
Directions 3 miles north of Tywyn on the A493.
Open Easter **to** October
Access Good
Sites Available **Total** 20
Facilities
Nearby Facilities
Tywyn.
Small site on a working farm. 3 miles from the sea.

TYWYN

Ynysymaengwyn Caravan Park, The Lodge, Tywyn, Gwynedd, LL36 9RY.
Std: 01654 **Tel:** 710684
Std: 01654 **Fax:** 710684
Nearest Town/Resort Tywyn
Directions Take the A493 from Tywyn to Dolgellau, we are the second caravan park on the left.
Acreage 4 **Open** April **to** October
Access Good **Site** Level
Sites Available **Total** 80
Facilities
Nearby Facilities
✓✓✓✓ Graded Park. In the grounds of an old manor house with a river at the bottom of the site for fishing. Near to the beach and shops. Woodland walks.

ISLE OF ANGLESEY

AMLWCH

Plas Eilian, Llaneilian, Amlwch, Anglesey, LL68 9LS.
Std: 01407 **Tel:** Amlwch 830323
Nearest Town/Resort Amlwch.
Directions Follow coastal road from Bangor for about 18 miles. Turn right by garage, continue straight until you reach the church.
Acreage 3 **Open** April **to** October
Access Good **Site** Level
Sites Available **Total** 18
Facilities
Nearby Facilities
Bangor.

AMLWCH

Point Lynas Caravan Park, Llaneilian, Amlwch, Anglesey, LL68 9LT.
Std: 01407 **Tel:** 831130
Std: 01248 **Fax:** 852423
Nearest Town/Resort Amlwch.
Directions Turn off the A5025 at Anglesey Mowers towards the sea. Follow signs for Llaneilian/Porth Eilian. Pass the phone box, entrance is 300yds on the the left.
Acreage 1¼ **Open** Late March **to** October
Access Good **Site** Level

Sites Available **Total** 15
Facilities
Nearby Facilities
Bangor
✓✓✓✓✓Graded Park. 200yds from Porth Eilian Cove.

AMLWCH

Tyn Rhos, Penysarn, Amlwch, Anglesey, LL69 9YR.
Std: 01407 **Tel:** 830574
Nearest Town/Resort Amlwch.
Directions A5025 turn off bypass to village of Penysarn. Take the first right after Y Bedol Public House and cross the cattle grid. 100yds up the drive.
Acreage 2 **Open** Easter **to** September
Access Good **Site** Level
Sites Available **Total** 30
Facilities
Nearby Facilities
Bangor
✓✓✓Graded Park. Near the village shops, post office and inn. Sports centre, beaches and swimming all 2 miles. Cafe/restaurant and licensed club within 200yds.

BEAUMARIS

Kingsbridge Caravan Park, Llanfaes, Beaumaris, Anglesey, LL58 8LR.
Std: 01248 **Tel:** 490636
Nearest Town/Resort Beaumaris.
Directions 1¼ miles past Beaumaris Castle. At crossroads turn left, 400yds to the site.
Acreage 9 **Open** March **to** October
Access Good **Site** Level
Sites Available **Total** 48
Facilities
Nearby Facilities
Bangor.
Fishing, scenic views, historical sites. Ideal for touring and bird watching. Brochure sent on request.

BENLLECH

Ad Astra Caravan Park, Brynteg, Nr. Benllech, Anglesey, LL78 7JH.
Std: 01248 **Tel:** Tynygongl 853283
Nearest Town/Resort Benllech.
Directions Turn left up the hill from Benllech Village square on B5108. Drive 1½ miles to California Inn, turn left onto B5110. Park is 500 yards on right hand side.
Acreage 3 **Open** March **to** October
Access Good **Site** Level
Sites Available
Facilities
Nearby Facilities
Bangor.
Scenic views, ideal base for touring.

BENLLECH

Bodafon Caravan & Camping Park, Bodafon, Benllech, Anglesey, LL74 8RU.
Std: 01248 **Tel:** 852417
Nearest Town/Resort Benllech Bay.
Directions A5025 through Benllech, ¼ mile on left.
Acreage 2 **Open** March **to** October
Access Good **Site** Lev/Slope
Sites Available **Total** 50
Facilities
Nearby Facilities
Bangor.
Near to beach (¾ mile), good views, quiet family site. Ideal touring.

BENLLECH

Bwlch Holiday Park, Tynygongl, Benllech Bay, Anglesey.
Std: 01248 **Tel:** Tynygongl 852914
Nearest Town/Resort Benllech Bay.
Directions A5025. Menai Bridge to Benllech 8 miles, turn left B5110. 1 miles.
Acreage 12 **Open** March **to** October
Access Good **Site** Level
Sites Available **Total** 12
Facilities
Nearby Facilities
Bangor.
Near beach, ideal touring, golf, riding (nearby).

BENLLECH

Clai Mawr Caravan Park, Pentraeth, Anglesey, LL75 8DX.
Std: 01248 **Tel:** 450629/450467
Nearest Town/Resort Benllech
Directions Travel on the A5/A55 turn onto the A5052. Go through the village of Pentraeth towards Benllech, pass The Bull Public House and take the third turning on the right signed Clai Mawr Caravan Park.
Acreage 1 **Open** March **to** October
Access Good **Site** Lev/Slope
Sites Available **Total** 8
Facilities
Nearby Facilities
Bangor
✓✓✓Graded Park. Overlooking bays and near the beach. Ideal touring.

BENLLECH

Garnedd Touring Caravan & Tent Park. Lon Bryn Mair, Brynteg, Anglesey, LL78 8QA.
Std: 01248 **Tel:** 853240
Nearest Town/Resort Benllech.
Directions From mainland Wales take A5 over Brittania Bridge. Keep on A5, then A5025 signed Amlwch/Benllech. Pass through Pentraeth then turn left at lay-by onto unclassified road signed Llanbedrgoch. In exactly 2 miles turn left at T junction, in 100yds take first left onto Lon Bryn Mair. Site is the third on lane in ½ mile at orange signs.
Acreage 5 **Open** Easter **to** September
Access Good **Site** Level
Sites Available **Total** 35
Facilities
Nearby Facilities
Bangor.
1½ miles to beach. Very clean toilet facilities. Superb views. Farm, dairy, garden produce. No dogs. Spin dryer and socket for ladies hair-dryers etc. Washroom for clothes and crockery. Couples preferred, children by arrangement.

BENLLECH

Plas Uchaf Caravan & Camping Park, Benllech Bay, Benllech, Anglesey, LL74 8NU.
Std: 01407 **Tel:** 763012
Nearest Town/Resort Benllech.
Directions ¼ mile from Benllech, signposted just after fire station on the B5108.
Acreage 9 **Open** March **to** October
Access Good **Site** Level
Sites Available **Total** 80
Facilities
Nearby Facilities
Bangor
Well sheltered, family park, under a mile from the beach. Tarmac roads, close mown grass, picnic tables, street lighting, freezers etc..

BRYNSIENCYN

Fron Caravan & Camping Site, Brynsiencyn, Anglesey, LL61 6TX.
Std: 01248 **Tel:** 430310
Std: 01248 **Fax:** 430310
Nearest Town/Resort Llanfairpwllgwyn.
Directions At start of Llanfairpwllgwyn turn left onto A4080 to Brysiencyn follow road through village site is on the right ¼ mile after village.
Acreage 5¼ **Open** Easter **to** September
Access Good **Site** Level
Sites Available **Total** 70
Facilities
Nearby Facilities
Bangor.
✓✓✓✓✓Graded Park. Ideal for touring Angelsey and North Wales.

LLANFWROG

Penrhyn Bay Caravan Park, Llanfwrog, Holyhead, Anglesey, LL65 4YG.
Std: 01407 **Tel:** 730496
Nearest Town/Resort Holyhead/Valley
Directions Take the A5 to Valley, turn right at the traffic lights through Llanfachraeth Village then turn first left for Llanfwrog. At the village turn left up hill by signpost for Penrhyn, keep on this road to the end.
Acreage 15 **Open** Easter **to** October
Access Good **Site** Level
Sites Available **Total** 60
Facilities
Nearby Facilities
Valley
✓✓✓✓Graded Park. Quiet, family site in an area of outstanding natural beauty. Long stretch of sandy beach and plenty of coastal walks. Indoor heated swimming pool. Clean, heated toilets and showers.

MARIANGLAS

Home Farm Caravan Park, Marianglas, Anglesey, LL73 8PH.
Std: 01248 **Tel:** 410614
Std: 01248 **Fax:** 410900
Nearest Town/Resort Moelfre
Directions Follow A5025 from bridge through Bennlech, keep left at roundabout, on left.
Acreage 20 **Open** April **to** October
Access Good **Site** Level
Sites Available **Total** 61
Facilities
Nearby Facilities
Bangor.
✓✓✓✓✓Graded Park. Peaceful, scenic, near to several beaches, ideal for familes.

MOELFRE

Capel Elen Caravan Park, Lligwy, Dulas, Anglesey, LL70 9PQ.
Std: 01248 **Tel:** 410670
Std: 01248 **Fax:** 410670
Nearest Town/Resort Benllech.
Directions Take the A5025 after bridge onto Anglesey. 11 miles, through Benllech to village of Brynrefail, turn right at craft shop. Park is 300yds on the left.
Acreage 2 **Open** March **to** October
Access Good **Site** Sloping
Sites Available **Total** 18
Facilities
Nearby Facilities
Bangor.
Quiet, family run site, ½ mile from beach. Well kept, short grass, showers and toilets.

MOELFRE

Melin Rhos Caravan Park, Lligwy Bay, Dulas, Amlwch, Anglesey, LL70 9HQ.
Std: 01248 **Tel:** 410213
Nearest Town/Resort Benllech
Directions From Menai Bridge take the A5025, turn left at Moelfre roundabout, turn right at the bottom of the hill, we are 1 mile down the lane.
Open Easter **to** October
Access Good **Site** Level
Sites Available **Total** 23
Facilities
Nearby Facilities
Bangor
Quiet site, near the beach. Local walks and sea fishing.

MOELFRE

Tyddyn Isaf Camping & Caravan Park, Lligwy Bay, Dulas, Anglesey, LL70 9PQ.
Std: 01248 **Tel:** 410203
Std: 01248 **Fax:** 410667
Nearest Town/Resort Benllech
Directions Take the A5025 from Britannia Bridge, go through Benllech approx. 8 miles, continue to Moelfre Island via left staying on the main road to Brynrefail Village. Turn right opposite the telephone box and International camping sign, we are ½ mile on the right down the lane.
Acreage 16 **Open** March **to** October
Access Good **Site** Sloping
Sites Available **Total** 80
Facilities
Nearby Facilities
Bangor
✓✓✓✓Graded Park. Family run park with a private footpath to a fine, sandy beach. "Loo of the Year" Winner, AA 4 Pennants, Welcome Host Award and Dragon Award.

NEWBOROUGH

Awelfryn Caravan Park, Newborough, Anglesey, LL61 6SG.
Std: 01248 **Tel:** 440230
Nearest Town/Resort Bangor
Directions On the A4080 from Britannia Bridge take a left by a tall column, and follow the A4080 through to Newborough. Turn left at the crossroads for Beach Road, site is on the left after ¼ mile.
Acreage 2 **Open** 1 April/Easter **to** 30 Sept
Access Good **Site** Lev/Slope
Sites Available **Total** 24
Facilities
Nearby Facilities
Bangor
Beauty spot on the edge of Forestry Commission land. 1½ miles from the beach. Llanddwyn Island.

PENTRAETH

Rhos Caravan Park, Rhos Farm, Pentraeth, Anglesey, North Wales, LL75 8DZ.
Std: 01248 **Tel:** 450214
Nearest Town/Resort Red Wharf Bay.
Directions Through Pentraeth on A5025 main road. Site entrance on left 1 mile north of Pentraeth.
Acreage 6 **Open** March **to** October
Access Good **Site** Level
Sites Available **Total** 40
Facilities
Nearby Facilities
Bangor.
Near beach and central location for Anglesey, good views of Snowdonia.

RHOSNEIGR

Bodfan Farm, Rhosneigr, Anglesey, LL64 5XA.
Std: 01407 **Tel:** 810563
Nearest Town/Resort Rhosneigr.
Directions Turn left off A5 onto A4080. Site 1½ miles on.
Acreage 12 **Open** April **to** September
Access Good **Site** Lev/Slope
Sites Available **Total** 80
Facilities
Nearby Facilities
Rhosneigr.
Near beach, lake and river. Scenic views. Ideal touring. Next door to a primary school.

RHOSNEIGR

Plas Caravan Park, Llanfaelog, Rhosneigr, Anglesey, LL63 5TU.
Std: 01407 **Tel:** 810234
Std: 01407 **Fax:** 810234
Nearest Town/Resort Rhosneigr
Directions On the A5 go through Gwalchmai, turn left onto the A4080. Continue until you reach the village of Llanfaelog, turn right at the Post Office and general stores, park is ½ mile on the right hand side.
Open Mid-March **to** End October
Access Good **Site** Level
Sites Available **Total** 30
Facilities
Nearby Facilities
Rhosneigr
✓✓✓Graded Park. Sheltered site in a rural setting, within walking distance to the beach.

RHOSNEIGR

Shoreside Camp & Caravan Park, Station Road, Rhosneigr, Anglesey, LL64 5QX.
Std: 01407 **Tel:** 810279
Nearest Town/Resort Rhosneigr
Directions A4080 Rhosneigr, opposite the golf club.
Acreage 6 **Open** Easter **to** October
Access Good **Site** Lev/Slope
Sites Available **Total** 100
Facilities
Nearby Facilities
Rhosneigr
Riding centre on site, bowling and tennis. Near the beach and opposite a golf club. 10 miles from Holyhead, day trips to Dublin.

RHOSNEIGR

Ty Hen, Station Road, Rhosneigr, Anglesey, LL64 5QZ.
Std: 01407 **Tel:** 810331
Std: 01407 **Fax:** 810331
Nearest Town/Resort Rhosneigr
Directions Take the A5 across Anglesey, turn left onto the A4080 for Aberfraw. Turn right at Llanfaelog Post Office, Ty Hen is next to the Railway Station, up the drive ½ mile.
Acreage 50 **Open** April **to** October
Access Good **Site** Level
Sites Available **Total** 41
Facilities
Nearby Facilities
Rhosneigr
✓✓✓✓Graded Park. On the banks of a 65 acre lake, good for fishing. Two premier beaches, golf and sub-aqua. Dragon Award.

TREARDDUR BAY

Bagnol Caravan Park, Ravenspoint Road, Trearddur Bay, Anglesey, LL65 2AZ.
Std: 01407 **Tel:** 860223
Std: 01407 **Fax:** 860223
Nearest Town/Resort Holyhead
Directions Take the A5 across Anglesey, at Valley crossroads turn left onto the B4545. 3 miles to Trearddur Bay, first left Ravenspoint Road to the caravan park signed on the left.
Acreage 10 **Open** March **to** November
Access Good **Site** Level
Sites Available **Total** 60
Facilities
Nearby Facilities
Holyhead
Near the beach, all sailing and watersports facilities, leisure centre and golf course.

TREARDDUR BAY

Gwynfair Caravan Park, Ravenspoint Road, Trearddur Bay, Nr. Holyhead, Anglesey, LL65 2AX.
Std: 01407 **Tel:** 860289
Nearest Town/Resort Holyhead
Acreage 2 **Open** March **to** October
Access Good **Site** Level
Sites Available **Total** 39
Facilities
Nearby Facilities
Holyhead

TREARDDUR BAY

Valley of the Rocks Camping & Caravan Park, Porthdafarch Road, Trearddur Bay, Anglesey, LL65 2LL.
Std: 01407 **Tel:** 765787
Nearest Town/Resort Holyhead.
Directions Follow the expressway and continue on the A5 to Valley. At the first set of traffic lights turn left onto the B4545 to Trearddur Bay, turn left at the garage and follow the road for 2 miles. Turn right at Porthdafarch Road, park is 300 yards on the right.
Open March **to** October
Access Good **Site** Lev/Slope
Sites Available **Total** 30
Facilities
Nearby Facilities
Holyhead.

VALLEY

Bodowyr Caravan Park, Bodowyr, Bodedern, Anglesey, LL65 3SS.
Std: 01407 **Tel:** 741171
Nearest Town/Resort Holyhead
Directions Follow the A5(T) from Holyhead to Caergeiliog, at staggered crossroads turn left towards Bodedern. Bodowyr is the first turning on the left. Site has international camping signs from the A5 junction.
Open March **to** October
Access Good **Site** Level
Sites Available **Total** 30
Facilities
Nearby Facilities
Valley
✓✓✓Graded Park. Very handy for ferries to Ireland. Close to beaches and a wide range of sporting facilities.

VALLEY
Pen-Y-Bont Farm, Valley, Holyhead, Anglesey, LL65 3EY.
Std: 01407 **Tel:** 740481
Nearest Town/Resort Holyhead
Directions 1 mile from Valley on the B4545, turn left at the traffic lights on Treaddur Bar Road, at Four Mile Bridge.
Acreage 3 **Open** Whitsun **to** October
Access Good **Site** Level
Sites Available
Facilities
Nearby Facilities
Valley

MERTHYR TYDFIL
MERTHYR TYDFIL
Grawen Caravan & Camping Park, Cwm-Taf, Cefn Coed, Merthyr Tydfil, CF48 2HS.
Std: 01685 **Tel:** 723740
Std: 01685 **Fax:** 723740
Nearest Town/Resort Merthyr Tydfil
Directions Easy access along the A470 Brecon Beacons road, 2 miles from Cefn Coed and 4 miles from Merthyr Tydfil. 2 miles off the A465 Heads of the Valleys road, ¼ mile from the reservoir.
Acreage 3½ **Open** April **to** 30 October
Access Good **Site** Level
Sites Available **Total** 50
Facilities
Nearby Facilities
Merthyr Tydfil
✓✓✓Graded Park. Picturesque mountain, forest and reservoir walks inside the Brecon Beacons National Park. A wealth of history can be found in the town of Merthyr Tydfil and the Valleys.

MONMOUTHSHIRE
ABERGAVENNY
Aberbaiden Caravan & Camping Park, Gilwern, Nr. Abergavenny, Monmouthshire.
Std: 01873 **Tel:** Gilwern 830157
Nearest Town/Resort Abergavenny.
Directions A465 Head of the Valleys road, site adjacent to the Gilwern roundabout.
Acreage 9 **Open** April **to** October
Access Good. **Site** Lev/Slope.
Sites Available **Total** 60
Facilities
Nearby Facilities
Abergavenny.
Situated in the National Park, very close to the Black Mountains and the Brecon Beacons.

ABERGAVENNY
Clydach Gorge, Station Road, Clydach, Nr. Abergavenny, Monmouthshire, NP7 0LL.
Std: 01633 **Tel:** 644856
Std: 01633 **Fax:** 644800
Nearest Town/Resort Abergavenny
Directions Take the A465 from Abergavenny to Brynmawr.
Acreage 2 **Open** April **to** September
Access Good **Site** Level
Sites Available **Total** 25
Facilities
Nearby Facilities
✓✓Graded Park. Mountain walking. Woodlands, river and vineyard in Abergavenny.

ABERGAVENNY
Pyscodlyn Farm Caravan & Camping Site, Llanwenarth Citra, Abergavenny, Monmouthshire, NP7 7ER.
Std: 01873 **Tel:** 853271
Std: 01873 **Fax:** 853271
Nearest Town/Resort Abergavenny.
Directions Situated on A40 to Brecon. 2 miles west of Abergavenny, approx 50 metres past telephone box on the left.
Acreage 4¼ **Open** 1 April **to** 31 Oct
Access Good. **Site** Level.
Sites Available **Total** 60
Facilities
Nearby Facilities
Abergavenny.
✓✓✓Graded Park. Ideal walking area, set in picturesque Usk Valley, in Black Mountain area.

MONMOUTH
Bridge Caravan Park & Camping Site, Dingestow, Monmouth, Monmouthshire, NP5 4DY.
Std: 01600 **Tel:** 740241
Nearest Town/Resort Monmouth
Directions 4 miles west of Monmouth.
Acreage 4 **Open** Easter **to** October
Access Good **Site** Level
Sites Available **Total** 123
Facilities
Nearby Facilities
Abergavenny
✓✓✓✓Graded Park. Riverside site with free fishing. Easy access.

MONMOUTH
Glen Trothy Caravan Park, Mitchel Troy, Monmouth, Monmouthshire, NP5 4BD.
Std: 01600 **Tel:** 712295
Std: 01600 **Fax:** 712295
Nearest Town/Resort Monmouth.
Directions From north M5, M50 then A40 taking the left turn after the traffic lights and before reaching road tunnel. From East Gloucester, A40 Ross on Wye,A40 Monmouth. From south and southeast M4 Severn Bridge, A466 Chepstow, Tintern and Monmouth turning left at traffic lights onto A40.
Acreage 6½ **Open** 1 March **to** 31 October
Access Good **Site** Level
Sites Available **Total** 184
Facilities
Nearby Facilities
Aberganenny
Alongside river, ideal touring. Public house and restaurant next door. No arrivals between 1-2pm.

MONMOUTH
Monmouth Caravan Park, Rockfield Road, Monmouth, Monmouthshire, NP5 3BA.
Std: 01600 **Tel:** 714745
Std: 01600 **Fax:** 716690
Nearest Town/Resort Monmouth
Directions Take the B4233 Rockfield Road, we are ¼ mile, opposite the fire and ambulance station.
Acreage 3¾ **Open** March **to** October
Access Good **Site** Level
Sites Available **Total** 40
Facilities
Nearby Facilities
Hereford
✓✓✓✓Graded Park. Set in an area of outstanding natural beauty. Ideal touring.

MONMOUTH
Monnow Bridge Caravan Site, Drybridge Street, Monmouth, Monmouthshire, NP5 3AD.
Std: 01600 **Tel:** 714004
Nearest Town/Resort Monmouth
Directions In the town.
Open All Year
Access Good **Site** Level
Sites Available **Total** 12
Facilities
Nearby Facilities
Newport
On the banks of the River Monnow, fishing on site.

USK
Chainbridge Caravan Park, Chainbridge Inn, Kemeys Commander, Nr. Usk, Monmouthshire, NP5 1PP.
Std: 01873 **Tel:** 880243
Nearest Town/Resort Abergavenny/Usk
Directions Main road from Usk to Abergavenny.
Acreage 3 **Open** March **to** October
Access Good **Site** Level
Sites Available **Total** 30
Facilities
Nearby Facilities
Newport
Riverside site for fishing. Big screen TV. Usk Valley walk and riverside dining area.

NEATH PORT TALBOT
PORT TALBOT
Afan Argoed Countryside Centre, Afan Forest Park, Cynonville, Port Talbot, Neath Port Talbot, SA13 3HG.
Std: 01639 **Tel:** 850564
Std: 01639 **Fax:** 850446
Nearest Town/Resort Port Talbot/Neath
Directions Leave the M4 at junction 40 and follow the A4107 for 6 miles. Call in at the Countryside Centre for keys.
Open April **to** October
Access Good **Site** Level
Sites Available **Total** 10
Facilities
Nearby Facilities
Port Talbot/Neath
In a forest park for peace and quiet, cycling, walking and bird watching.

NEWPORT
NEWPORT
Pentre-Tai Farm, Rhiwderin, Newport, South Wales, NP1 9RQ.
Std: 01633 **Tel:** 893284
Std: 01633 **Fax:** 893284
Nearest Town/Resort Newport
Directions Leave the M4 at junction 28 and take the A467, at the next roundabout take the A468 for approx. 1 mile. Turn right immediately after "Rhiwderin Inn" and go straight through the village and on down lane. Farm is on the left.
Acreage 5 **Open** March **to** October
Access Good **Site** Lev/Slope
Sites Available **Total** 5
Facilities
Nearby Facilities
Newport
Ideal for visiting Cardiff and the Welsh castles. Useful stopover for Irish ferry. Good pub nearby. B&B also available (WTB 2 Crown Highly Commended).

PEMBROKESHIRE

AMROTH

Meadow House Holiday Park, Amroth, Pembrokeshire.
Std: 01834 **Tel:** 812438
Nearest Town/Resort Saundersfoot
Directions From Carmarthen take the A477 past Folly Cross, turn left at the signpost for Amroth and Wisemans Bridge. Pass Summerhill Village and park is on the left hand side.
Acreage 25 **Open** March **to** October
Access Good **Site** Level
Sites Available **Total** 60
Facilities
Nearby Facilities
Kilgetty
Overlooking the sea. Coastal footpath to Amroth and Wisemans Bridge beaches.

AMROTH

Pantglas Farm, Tavernspite, Whitland, Pembrokeshire, SA34 0NS.
Std: 01834 **Tel:** 831618
Nearest Town/Resort Amroth
Directions A477 towards Tenby take the B4314 at Red Roses crossroads to Tavernspite 1¼ miles, take the middle road at the village pump. Pantglas is ½ mile down on the left.
Acreage 8 **Open** Easter **to** October
Access Good **Site** Level
Sites Available **Total** 75
Facilities
Nearby Facilities
Whitland.
✓✓✓✓Graded Park. A quiet, secluded, family run caravan and camping park. Super play area for kids. High standard toilet and shower facilities. Caravan storage available for £2.50 weekly. Short walk to village shop. Easy reach of Tenby, Saundersfoot and Amroth.

ANGLE

Castle Farm Camping Site, Castle Farm, Angle, Nr. Pembroke, Pembrokeshire, SA71 5AR.
Std: 01646 **Tel:** 641220
Nearest Town/Resort Pembroke/Angle.
Directions Pembroke to Angle, approx 10 miles. Camping field directly behind village church and the school.
Acreage 2 **Open** Easter **to** October
Access Good **Site** Sloping
Sites Available **Total** 25
Facilities
Nearby Facilities
Pembroke.
Overlooking East Angle Bay, a walk to sandy beach of West Angle Bay. Scenic views. Near to telephone, cafe/restaurant, licensed club and childrens play area.

BROAD HAVEN

Creampots Touring Caravan & Camping Park, Havenway, Broad Haven, Haverfordwest, Pembrokeshire, SA62 3TU.
Std: 01437 **Tel:** 781776
Nearest Town/Resort Broad Haven
Directions Take B4131 Broad Haven road from Haverfordwest to Broadway (5 miles). Turn left and Creampots is the SECOND site on the right (600yds).
Acreage 7 **Open** Easter **to** October
Access Good **Site** Level
Sites Available **Total** 72
Facilities
Nearby Facilities
Haverfordwest
✓✓✓✓Graded Park. Ideal touring base, 1½ miles from safe, sandy beach and coastal path at Broad Haven.

FISHGUARD

Fishguard Bay Caravan Park, Dinas Cross, Newport, Pembrokeshire, SA42 0YD.
Std: 01348 **Tel:** 811415
Std: 01348 **Fax:** 811425
Nearest Town/Resort Fishguard
Directions Take A478 Cardigan road from Fishguard for 1½ miles. Turn left at sign.
Acreage 5 **Open** March **to** December
Access Good **Site** Lev/Slope
Sites Available **Total** 50
Facilities
Nearby Facilities
Fishguard
✓✓✓✓Graded Park. Superb cliff top location offering excellent views and walks along this 'Heritage' coast of Pembrokeshire.

FISHGUARD

Gwaun Vale Holiday Touring Park, LLanychaer, Fishguard, Pembrokeshire, SA65 9TA.
Std: 01348 **Tel:** 874698
Nearest Town/Resort Fishguard.
Directions From Fishguard take the B4313 Gwaun Valley/Llanychaer Road for 1¼ miles, touring park on the right hand side.
Acreage 2 **Open** March **to** 9th January
Access Good **Site** Level
Sites Available **Total** 31
Facilities
Nearby Facilities
Fishguard.
✓✓✓✓Graded Park. Ideal touring park, peaceful and quiet, with beautiful views, walks and within easy reach of beaches. AA 3 pennants.

FISHGUARD

Tregroes Park, Fishguard, Pembrokeshire, SA65 9QF.
Std: 01348 **Tel:** 872316
Nearest Town/Resort Fishguard
Directions 1 mile south of Fishguard on the A40 take unclassified road signed Manorowen and large caravan sign. Tregroes is 200 yards from the A40.
Acreage 5 **Open** April **to** October
Access Good **Site** Lev/Slope
Sites Available **Total** 45
Facilities
Nearby Facilities
Fishguard
✓✓Graded Park. 2 miles from a National Park and the coast for beautiful views and walks. Fishguard Harbour, fast ferry route for Ireland day trips. Ideal touring.

HAVERFORDWEST

Nolton Cross Caravan Park, Nolton, Haverfordwest, Pembrokeshire, SA62 3NP.
Std: 01437 **Tel:** 710701
Nearest Town/Resort Haverfordwest
Directions Take the A487 from Haverfordwest towards St Davids, after 5 miles at Simpson Cross turn left for Nolton, follow for 1 mile to the next crossroads and turn left, entrance is 100 yards on the right.
Acreage 1½ **Open** March **to** October
Access Good **Site** Level
Sites Available **Total** 5
Facilities
Nearby Facilities
Haverfordwest
✓✓✓✓Graded Park. Set in open countryside. 1½ miles from the coast.

HAVERFORDWEST

Redlands Touring Caravan Park, Little Haven, Haverfordwest, Pembrokeshire, SA62 3SJ.
Std: 01437 **Tel:** 781300
Std: 01437 **Fax:** 781093
Nearest Town/Resort Little Haven.
Directions 6½ miles southwest of Haverfordwest, on B4327 Dale Road.
Acreage 5 **Open** Easter **to** October
Access Good **Site** Level
Sites Available **Total** 60
Facilities
Nearby Facilities
Haverfordwest.
✓✓✓✓Graded Park. Small well run site in Pembrokeshire Natural Park, within easy reach of coastal park and superb sandy beaches.

HAVERFORDWEST

Scamford Caravan Park, Keeston, Haverfordwest, Pembrokeshire, SA62 6HN.
Std: 01437 **Tel:** 710304
Std: 01437 **Fax:** 710304
Nearest Town/Resort Newgale.
Directions From Haverfordwest take the A487 towards St. Davids. In approx. 4¼ miles turn right at Keeston, then follow signs for Scamford Caravan Park.
Open April **to** October
Access Good **Site** Level
Sites Available **Total** 5
Facilities
Nearby Facilities
Haverfordwest.
✓✓✓✓✓Graded Park. Ideal location for many beaches, coast path, Preseli Hills, Milford Haven Waterway, etc..

HAVERFORDWEST

The Rising Sun Inn, St. David's Road, Pelcomb Bridge, Haverfordwest, Pembrokeshire, SA62 6EA.
Std: 01437 **Tel:** 765171
Nearest Town/Resort Haverfordwest
Directions From Haverfordwest take the A487 road to St Davids. After approx. 1¼ miles at Pelcomb Bridge turn left, site is on the corner.
Acreage 2½ **Open** Easter **to** October
Access Good **Site** Lev/Slope
Sites Available **Total** 25
Facilities
Nearby Facilities
Haverfordwest
✓✓✓✓Graded Park. 5/7 miles from many lovely beaches. Ideal centre for touring, bird watching, golf, etc..

KILGETTY

Masterland Farm Touring Caravan & Tent Park, Broadmoor, Kilgetty, Pembrokeshire, SA68 0RH.
Std: 01834 **Tel:** 813298
Std: 01834 **Fax:** 814408
Nearest Town/Resort Tenby
Directions After Carmarthen take main A40 to St. Clears, then take the A477 to Broadmoor. Turn right at Cross Inn Public House, Masterland Farm is 300yds on your right.
Acreage 8 **Open** March **to** October
Access Good **Site** Level
Sites Available **Total** 38
Facilities
Nearby Facilities
Kilgetty.
✓✓✓✓Graded Park. Ideal touring, close to leisure parks etc..

KILGETTY

Ryelands Caravan Park, Ryelands Lane, Kilgetty, Pembrokeshire.
Std: 01834 **Tel:** 812369
Nearest Town/Resort Saundersfoot/Tenby.
Directions Turn left after railway bridge in Kilgetty into Ryelands Lane. Site in ½ mile on the right.
Acreage 5 **Open** March **to** 30 October
Access Good **Site** Lev/Slope
Sites Available **Total** 45
Facilities
Nearby Facilities
Kilgetty
Set in open countryside with views to the west, north and east.

LITTLE HAVEN

Hasguard Cross Caravan Park, Hasguard Cross, Haverfordwest, Pembrokeshire, SA62 3SL.
Std: 01437 **Tel:** 781443
Std: 01437 **Fax:** 781443
Nearest Town/Resort Little Haven
Directions B4327 out of Haverfordwest 7 miles on the Dale road. Turn right Hasguard crossroads. Site entrance 100 yards on right.
Acreage 3¼ **Open** All Year
Access Good **Site** Level
Sites Available **Total** 60
Facilities
Nearby Facilities
Haverfordwest.
✓✓✓✓Graded Park. Near many beaches nearest 1¼ miles.

LITTLE HAVEN

Howelston Caravan & Camping Site, Littlehaven, Haverfordwest, Pembrokeshire.
Std: 01437 **Tel:** 781253
Nearest Town/Resort Haverfordwest
Directions Off B4327 6 miles S.W. of Haverfordwest, turn right at Hasgaurd crossroads and right again in ¼ mile. Site on left in ½ mile.
Acreage 5 **Open** April **to** September
Access Good **Site** Lev/Slope
Sites Available **Total** 60
Facilities
Nearby Facilities
Haverfordwest
1 mile from nearest beach. Site overlooking St. Brides Bay. Freezing and dish washing facilities. Cafe nearby.

LITTLE HAVEN

South Cockett Caravan & Camping Park, Broadway, Little Haven, Haverfordwest, Pembrokeshire, SA62 3TU.
Std: 01437 **Tel:** 781296/781760
Std: 01437 **Fax:** 781296
Nearest Town/Resort Broad Haven
Directions From Haverfordwest take B4341 road for Broad Haven for about 6 miles, turn left at official camping signs, site 300yds.
Acreage 6 **Open** Easter **to** October
Access Good **Site** Level
Sites Available **Total** 75
Facilities
Nearby Facilities
Haverfordwest
Scenic views, ideal touring, near beach, coastal path nearby.

MANORBIER

Park Farm Caravans, Manorbier, Tenby, Pembrokeshire.
Std: 01834 **Tel:** 871273 (Site Office)
Nearest Town/Resort Tenby
Directions 5 miles west of Tenby on A4139 take second turning left for Manorbier.
Acreage 7 **Open** Easter **to** October
Access Good **Site** Level
Sites Available **Total** 70
Facilities
Nearby Facilities
Manorbier
Footpath to beach. For ENQUIRIES please telephone 01646 672583.

MARLOES

East Hook Farm, Marloes, Haverfordwest, Pembrokeshire, SA62 3BJ.
Std: 01646 **Tel:** 636291
Nearest Town/Resort Haverfordwest
Open All Year
Access Good **Site** Level
Sites Available **Total** 30
Facilities
Nearby Facilities
Haverfordwest
Within walking distance of two beaches. Riding on site. The Boat to Skomer and Skokholm nearby.

MILFORD HAVEN

Sandy Haven Caravan Park, Herbrandston, Nr. Milford Haven, Pembrokeshire, SA73 2AL.
Std: 01646 **Tel:** 698844
Nearest Town/Resort Milford Haven
Directions Take the Dale Road from Milford Haven, turn left at Herbrandston School and follow the village road down to the beach.
Acreage 1 **Open** Easter **to** September
Access Good **Site** Lev/Slope
Sites Available **Total** 20
Facilities
Nearby Facilities
Milford Haven
Very quiet and uncommercialised site, alongside a beautiful beach and sea estuary. Ideal family holidays, boating, windsurfing, canoeing, etc.. You can also call our Answerphone on 01646 698083.

MYNACHLOG-DDU

Trefach Country Pub & Caravan Park, Mynachlog-Ddu, Clynderwen, Pembrokeshire, SA66 7RU.
Std: 01994 **Tel:** 419225
Std: 01994 **Fax:** 419221
Nearest Town/Resort Crymmych
Directions 1½ miles off A478 at Glandy Cross Inn.
Acreage 18 **Open** March **to** October
Access Good **Site** Lev/Slope
Sites Available **Total** 70
Facilities
Nearby Facilities
Clynderwen.
✓✓✓Graded Park. In the Preseli Hills, good walking and pony trekking. Central for touring West Wales.

NARBERTH

Dingle Caravan Park, The Dingle, Jesse Road, Narberth, Pembrokeshire, SA67 7DP.
Std: 01834 **Tel:** 860482
Std: 01834 **Fax:** 860482
Nearest Town/Resort Narberth
Directions 2 miles from the A40 roundabout at Pembleyin.
Acreage 3 **Open** March **to** October
Access Good **Site** Level
Sites Available **Total** 30
Facilities
Nearby Facilities
Narberth
Ideal location, central to all of the Pembrokeshire coastline. 40 minutes from Fishguard Ferry.

NARBERTH

Noble Court Caravan Park, Redstone Road, Narberth, Pembrokeshire, SA67 7ES.
Std: 01834 **Tel:** 861191
Std: 01834 **Fax:** 861484
Nearest Town/Resort Narberth.
Directions ½ mile north of Narberth on B4313 road and ½ mile south of A40 on B4313.
Acreage 20 **Open** March **to** November
Access Good **Site** Lev/Slope
Sites Available **Total** 92
Facilities
Nearby Facilities
Narberth.
✓✓✓✓✓Graded Park. Conveniently situated for travel to all Pembrokeshire beaches and countryside also Pembrokeshire National Park. Quiet family caravan park with amenities for all ages.

NARBERTH

Wood Office Caravan & Tent Park, Cold Blow, Narberth, Pembrokeshire, SA67 8RR.
Std: 01834 **Tel:** 860565
Nearest Town/Resort Narberth.
Directions A40 through Narberth onto the A478 towards Tenby, turn off onto the B4315 at Templeton.
Acreage 5 **Open** Easter **to** October
Access Good **Site** Level
Sites Available **Total** 45
Facilities
Nearby Facilities
Narberth.
Near beaches and one of the closest caravan parks to Oakwood, Folly Farm and Herons Brook.

NEWPORT

'Morawelon', Parrog, Newport, Pembrokeshire, SA42 0RW.
Std: 01239 **Tel:** 820565
Nearest Town/Resort Fishguard/Cardigan.
Directions A487 from Fishguard, 7 miles to Newport. A487 from Cardigan, 12 miles to Newport. Turn down road signposted Parrog Beach or Parrog at the western end of town. Morawelon is the last house at the

end of the road by the quay wall.
Acreage 5 **Open** Easter **to** Mid Oct
Access Good **Site** Lev/Slope
Sites Available **Total** 85
Facilities
Nearby Facilities
Fishguard.
✓✓✓Graded Park. Direct access to the beach and sea, scenic views over the bay, ideal centre for Windsurfers, sailing etc. Canoe hire available, Salmon river fishing and coastal path walking. All accessable from the site. Boat park by the quay wall. Tourist Board Verified.

NEWPORT

Llwyngwair Manor, Newport, Pembrokeshire.
Std: 01239 **Tel:** 820498
Nearest Town/Resort Newport.
Directions 1 mile from Newport on the A487 to Cardigan.
Open March **to** November
Access Good **Site** Level
Sites Available **Total** 80
Facilities
Nearby Facilities
Fishguard.
✓✓✓✓Graded Park. 1 mile from sandy beach. 55 acres of parkland in Pembrokeshire Coast National Park, alongside the River Nevern. Tennis on site.

PEMBROKE

Upper Portclew Farm, Freshwater East, Pembrokeshire, Dyfed.
Std: 01646 **Tel:** Lamphey 672112
Nearest Town/Resort Freshwater East.
Directions 3 miles southeast of Pembroke.
Acreage 3 **Open** Whitsun **to** 10 Sept
Site Level
Sites Available
Facilities
Nearby Facilities
Lamphey.
Near beach, National Park.

SAUNDERSFOOT

Mill House Caravan Park, Pleasant Valley, Stepaside, Saundersfoot, Pembrokeshire, SA67 8LN.
Std: 01834 **Tel:** 812069
Nearest Town/Resort Saundersfoot
Directions Take the A40 from Carmarthen to St. Clears. Take the A477 trunk road towards Tenby for approx. 10 miles and turn left to Stepaside. Pass over a bridge and turn left again under the bridge and drive 300 yards to Pleasant Valley.
Acreage 2½ **Open** March **to** October
Access Good **Site** Level
Sites Available **Total** 16
Facilities
Nearby Facilities
Kilgetty
✓✓✓✓Graded Park. Riverside setting located in a beautiful wooded valley, quiet sunny position. Walk to the beach and Coastal Path. Large childrens safe recreational area. Only one hard standing.

SAUNDERSFOOT

Moreton Farm Leisure Park, Moreton, Saundersfoot, Pembrokeshire, SA69 9EA.
Std: 01834 **Tel:** 812016
Nearest Town/Resort Tenby/Saundersfoot
Directions From St. Clears o the A477, turn left onto A478 for Tenby. Site is on left 1¼ miles, opposite chapel.
Acreage 12 **Open** March **to** December
Access Good **Site** Level
Sites Available **Total** 60
Facilities
Nearby Facilities
Saundersfoot
✓✓✓✓Graded Park. 1 mile of safe golden beach. Own fishing lake. Dragon Award.

SAUNDERSFOOT

Moysland Farm Camping Site, Tenby Road, Saundersfoot, Pembrokeshire, SA69 9DS.
Tel: Saundersfoot 812455
Nearest Town/Resort Saundersfoot/Tenby
Directions M4 to Kilgetty, turn left to Tenby. Site is on right hand side of road before New Hedges roundabout.
Acreage 4 **Open** Whitsun **to** September
Access Good **Site** Level
Sites Available **Total** 40
Facilities
Nearby Facilities
Tenby
Beach ¼ mile, ideal centre for touring. Tents for hire.

SAUNDERSFOOT

Sunnyvale Holiday Park, Valley Road, Saundersfoot, Pembrokeshire, SA69 9BT.
Std: 01348 **Tel:** 872462
Std: 01348 **Fax:** 872351
Nearest Town/Resort Tenby
Directions Take the A478 to Tenby, proceed through Pentlepoir and take a left turn into Valley Road, Sunnyvale is 300 yards down on the left hand side.
Acreage 5 **Open** March **to** October
Access Good **Site** Lev/Slope
Sites Available **Total** 50
Facilities
Nearby Facilities
Saundersfoot
✓✓✓✓Graded Park. Near Tenby, Saundersfoot and numerous golden sandy beaches. Pitches from just £3 per night.

SAUNDERSFOOT

Trevayne Farm, Saundersfoot, Pembrokeshire, SA69 9DL.
Std: 01834 **Tel:** 813402
Nearest Town/Resort Saundersfoot/Tenby
Directions A40 to St. Clears A477 to Kilgetty. A478 towards Tenby, approx 2½ miles from Tenby turn left for Saundersfoot, right for New Hedges and left again for Trevayne ¾ mile.
Acreage 7 **Open** Easter **to** October
Access Good **Site** Level
Sites Available **Total** 100
Facilities
Nearby Facilities
Tenby
Situated on coast with lovely sandy beach and scenery. 25 electricity hook-ups available for touring caravans.

ST. DAVIDS

Caerfai Bay Caravan & Tent Park, St. Davids, Pembrokeshire, SA62 6QT.
Std: 01437 **Tel:** 720274
Std: 01437 **Fax:** 720274
Nearest Town/Resort St. Davids.
Directions Turn off the A487 (Haverfordwest to St. Davids road) in St. Davids at the Caerfai signpost. Entrance to the park is at the end of the road, ¼ mile on the right.
Open April **to** October
Access Good **Site** Lev/Slope
Sites Available **Total** 80
Facilities
Nearby Facilities
Haverfordwest
✓✓✓✓Graded Park. Magnificent sea views and coastal scenery. 200yds from award winning Caerfai bathing beach. Immediately adjacent to Pembrokeshire Coastal Path. A short walk into Britain's smallest city, St Davids, with its magnificent Cathedral.

ST. DAVIDS

Camping & Caravanning Club Site, Dwr Cwmwdig, Berea, St Davids, Haverfordwest, Pembrokeshire, SA62 6DW.
Std: 01348 **Tel:** 831376
Directions Travelling south on the A487, in Croesgoch turn right at Glyncheryn Farmers Stores. After approx. 1 mile turn right signposted Abereiddy, at the crossroads turn left and the site is 75 yards on the left hand side.
Acreage 4 **Open** 22 March **to** 27 Sept
Site Sloping
Sites Available **Total** 40
Facilities
Nearby Facilities
Fishguard
✓✓✓✓✓Graded Park. Just 1 mile from the beach and Pembrokeshires Coastal Path. Close to Britains smallest cathedral city.

ST. DAVIDS

Hendre Eynon Camp Site, Hendre Eynon, St. Davids, Pembrokeshire, SA62 6DB.
Std: 01437 **Tel:** 720474
Nearest Town/Resort St. Davids
Directions 2 miles from St. Davids on an unclassified road to Llanrhian.
Acreage 7 **Open** Easter **to** October
Access Good **Site** Level
Sites Available **Total** 85
Facilities
Nearby Facilities
Fishguard
✓✓✓✓Graded Park. Just below the Coastal Trail at Carn Penberry. Superb facilities. Ideal site for walkers and birdwatchers.

ST. DAVIDS

Nine Wells Caravan & Camping Park, Nine Wells, Solva, Nr. Haverfordwest, Pembrokeshire, SA62 6UH.
Std: 01437 **Tel:** 721809
Nearest Town/Resort Haverfordwest.
Directions From Haverfordwest take A487 to Solva. ¼ mile past Solva turn left at Nine Wells. Site clearly signposted.
Acreage 4½ **Open** Easter **to** October
Access Good **Site** Lev/Slope
Sites Available **Total** 70
Facilities
Nearby Facilities
Haverfordwest.
Sandy beach ¾ mile. Walk the coastal footpath to Solva. About 5 minute walk to cove and coastal footpath and Iron Age Fort, down National Trust Valley.

ST. DAVIDS

Park Hall Camping Park, Maerdy Farm, Penycwm, Haverfordwest, Pembrokeshire.
Std: 01437 **Tel:** 721606/721282
Std: 01437 **Fax:** 721606
Nearest Town/Resort Haverfordwest.
Directions 12 miles from Haverfordwest on the A487 and 6 miles from St. Davids. Turn at the 14th Signal Regiment Brawdy.
Acreage 7 **Open** March **to** October
Access Good **Site** Level

Sites Available **Total** 100
Facilities
Nearby Facilities
Haverfordwest.
Near beach, scenic views. Ideal touring, fishing on private lake.

ST. DAVIDS

Prendergast Caravan & Camping Park, Cartlett Lodge, Trefin, Haverfordwest, Pembrokeshire, SA62 5AL.
Std: 01348 **Tel:** 831368
Nearest Town/Resort St. Davids/ Fishguard.
Directions From Haverfordwest take A40 towards Fishguard, until Letterston. Turn left on B4331 until you reach A487. Turn left for St. Davids in about 2½ miles. Turn right by sign for Trefin.
Acreage ½ **Open** April **to** September
Access Good **Site** Lev/Slope
Sites Available **Total** 12
Facilities
Nearby Facilities
Haverfordwest
✓✓✓Graded Park. Lovely walks along coastal path.

ST. DAVIDS

Rhos-y-Cribed, St. Davids, Haverfordwest, Pembrokeshire, SA62 6RR.
Std: 01437 **Tel:** 720336
Nearest Town/Resort St. Davids
Directions Take the Porthclais road out of St Davids down to the harbour. Farm is signposted near the car park.
Access Good **Site** Level
Sites Available
Facilities
Nearby Facilities
Haverfordwest
Views of St Davids, the cathedral and St Brides Bay. Near the harbour and coastal path.

ST. DAVIDS

Tretio Caravan & Camping Park, St Davids, Pembrokeshire, SA62 6DE.
Std: 01437 **Tel:** 781359/720270
Nearest Town/Resort St. Davids
Directions From St Davids keep left at St Davids R.F.C. and continue straight on for 3 miles, signpost pointing right, park is 300 yards.
Acreage 3 **Open** March **to** November
Access Good **Site** Level
Sites Available **Total** 20
Facilities
Nearby Facilities
Haverfordwest
✓✓✓✓Graded Park. Set in a national park with beautiful views. 1½ miles from the beach and ½ mile from coastal path. Own 9 hole pitch 'n' putt course on 4 acres adjoining.

TENBY

Buttyland, Manorbier, Tenby, Pembrokeshire, SA70 7SN.
Std: 01834 **Tel:** 871278
Nearest Town/Resort Tenby
Directions Take the A4139 west from Tenby for 6 miles. Turn right by Chapel with red cross, 400yds down the road on the right hand side.
Acreage 10 **Open** Easter **to** End September
Access Good **Site** Level
Sites Available **Total** 53
Facilities
Nearby Facilities
Manorbier Beach and the Blue Flag beach of Tenby. Ideal touring.

TENBY

Cross Park Holiday Centre, Broad Moor, Kilgetty, Tenby, Pembrokeshire, SA68 0RS.
Std: 01834 **Tel:** 813205/811244
Std: 01834 **Fax:** 814300
Nearest Town/Resort Tenby
Directions At Kilgetty roundabout follow the A477 west for 1 mile to Broad Moor, turn right at the Cross Inn Pub and we are 150 yards along on the left.
Acreage 11 **Open** 4 April **to** October
Access Good **Site** Level
Sites Available **Total** 50
Facilities
Nearby Facilities
Tenby
✓✓✓✓✓Graded Park. 11 acres of landscaped gardens and lawns surrounded by mature trees and colourful shrubs. Family club with free entertainment.

TENBY

Hazelbrook Caravan Park, Sageston, Nr. Tenby, Pembrokeshire, SA70 8SY.
Std: 01646 **Tel:** 651351
Std: 01646 **Fax:** 651595
Nearest Town/Resort Tenby
Directions Turn off the A477 in the village of Sageston turning onto the B4318 for Tenby. Caravan park is 300 yards on the right, 60 foot entrance.
Acreage 7½ **Open** 1 March **to** 9 January
Access Good **Site** Level
Sites Available **Total** 120
Facilities
Nearby Facilities
Tenby
Carew Castle and Mill 1 mile, Dinosaur Park 2 miles and Oakwood Amusement Park 7 miles.

TENBY

Kiln Park Holiday Centre, Marsh Road, Tenby, Pembrokeshire, SA70 7RB.
Std: 01834 **Tel:** 844121
Nearest Town/Resort Tenby.
Directions Follow the A478 to Tenby, signposted from Tenby.
Acreage 150 **Open** March **to** October
Access Good **Site** Level
Sites Available **Total** 300
Facilities
Nearby Facilities
Tenby.
✓✓✓✓Graded Park. 5 minutes walk from sandy beach. Tenby has usual resort amusements. Childrens Club and a full family entertainment programme. Burger King and Pizza Hut on park.

TENBY

Lodge Farm Caravan & Camping Park, Lodge Farm, New Hedges, Tenby, Pembrokeshire.
Std: 01834 **Tel:** 842468
Nearest Town/Resort Tenby/ Saundersfoot
Directions Approaching Tenby on A478, turn left at New Hedges roundabout, first right, through village, Lodge farm entrance opposite minimarket.
Acreage 10 **Open** April **to** October
Access Good **Site** Level
Sites Available **Total** 65+
Facilities
Nearby Facilities
Tenby
Near beaches. Sky Television in club. Camping and Caravan Club Listed Site and AA 2 Pennants.

TENBY

Milton Bridge Caravan Park, Milton, Nr. Tenby, Pembrokeshire, SA70 8PH.
Std: 01646 **Tel:** 651204
Std: 01646 **Fax:** 651204
Nearest Town/Resort Tenby
Directions Half way between Kilgetty and Pembroke Dock on the A477.
Acreage 3 **Open** March **to** October
Access Good **Site** Lev/Slope
Sites Available **Total** 15
Facilities
Nearby Facilities
Lamphey
✓✓✓✓✓Graded Park. Small, friendly park situated on a tidal river. Ideal base for exploring the many attractions in the area.

TENBY

Rowston Holiday Park, New Hedges, Tenby, Pembrokeshire, SA70 8TL.
Std: 01834 **Tel:** 842178
Std: 01834 **Fax:** 842178
Nearest Town/Resort Tenby/ Saundersfoot
Directions 1½ miles north of Tenby, in village of New Hedges.
Acreage 8 **Open** March **to** October
Access Good **Site** Lev/Slope
Sites Available **Total** 110
Facilities
Nearby Facilities
Tenby
✓✓✓✓✓Graded Park. 10 minutes walk through woods to secluded Waterwynch Cove. No dogs Mid July/August. Cafe/Diner.

TENBY

Rumbleway Caravan & Tent Park, New Hedges, Tenby, Pembrokeshire, SA70 8TR.
Std: 01834 **Tel:** 845155
Std: 01834 **Fax:** 845155
Nearest Town/Resort Tenby/ Saundersfoot
Directions Take the A477 from Carmarthen to the A478 Tenby road. Site is 1 mile before Tenby on the right.
Acreage 6 **Open** April **to** September
Access Good **Site** Lev/Slope
Sites Available **Total** 110
Facilities
Nearby Facilities
Tenby
15 minute walk to the beach. Heated swimming pool on site.

TENBY

Trefalun Park, Devonshire Drive, St Florence, Tenby, Pembrokeshire, SA70 8RD.
Std: 01646 **Tel:** 651514
Std: 01646 **Fax:** 651746
Nearest Town/Resort Tenby
Directions From Kilgetty take the A477 to Sageston, turn left onto the B4318. At Manor House Wildlife Park turn left into Devonshire Drive, Trefalun is the second entrance on the left.
Acreage 10 **Open** April **to** October
Access Good **Site** Level
Sites Available **Total** 50
Facilities
Nearby Facilities
Tenby
✓✓✓✓✓Graded Park. Shop, club and swimming pool available at adjoining park for a moderate charge.

TENBY

Tudor Glen Caravan Park, Jameston, Nr. Tenby, Pembrokeshire, SA70 7SS.
Std: 01834 **Tel:** 871417
Std: 01834 **Fax:** 871832
Nearest Town/Resort Tenby
Directions From Tenby take the A4139 Coast Road west for 6 miles. Site is on the right before entering village of Jameston.
Acreage 6 **Open** March **to** October
Access Good **Site** Lev/Slope
Sites Available **Total** 46
Facilities
Nearby Facilities
Manorbier
✓✓✓✓Graded Park. Family run site, ideal touring base.

TENBY

Well Park Caravans, Tenby, Pembrokeshire, SA70 8TL.
Std: 01834 **Tel:** 842179
Nearest Town/Resort Tenby.
Directions On righthand side of main Tenby (A478) road 1 mile north of Tenby.
Acreage 10 **Open** April **to** October
Access Good **Site** Lev/Slope
Sites Available **Total** 100
Facilities
Nearby Facilities
Tenby.
✓✓✓✓✓Graded Park. A family run site, situated in pleasant surroundings. Excellent facilities. Very central and convenient for the beautiful beaches and places of interest along the Pembrokeshire coast. Wales in Bloom Award Winning Park, Daffodil Award and AA 4 Pennants.

TENBY

Whitewell Camping Park, Lydstep Beach, Penally, Tenby, Pembrokeshire, SA70 7RY.
Std: 01834 **Tel:** 842200
Nearest Town/Resort Tenby.
Acreage 13 **Open** April **to** September
Access Good **Site** Level
Sites Available **Total** 120
Facilities
Nearby Facilities
Tenby.
½ mile Lydstep Beach, green countryside on all sides.

TENBY

Windmills Camping Park, Narberth Road, Tenby, Pembrokeshire, SA70 8TJ.
Std: 01834 **Tel:** 842200
Nearest Town/Resort Tenby
Acreage 4 **Open** Easter **to** September
Site Lev/Slope
Sites Available **Total** 40
Facilities
Nearby Facilities
Tenby
Sea views, ¾ mile Tenby town centre.

TENBY

Wood Park Caravans, New Hedges, Tenby, Pembrokeshire, SA70 8TL.
Std: 01834 **Tel:** 843414
Nearest Town/Resort Tenby.
Directions 1 mile north of Tenby off A478. West side of New Hedges bypass
Acreage 2 **Open** Easter **to** September
Access Good **Site** Lev/Slope
Sites Available **Total** 60
Facilities
Nearby Facilities
Tenby.
✓✓✓✓Graded Park. Ideally situated between Tenby and Saundersfoot. Waterwynch beach 1 mile, scenic views. Ideal touring. Battery charging. No dogs end July and August, small dogs at other times. Licensed bar on site.

POWYS

BRECON

Anchorage Caravan Park, Bronllys, Brecon, Powys, LD3 0LD.
Std: 01874 **Tel:** 711246
Nearest Town/Resort Brecon.
Directions On the A438, 8 miles north east of Brecon on the west side of Bronllys Village.
Acreage 8 **Open** All Year
Access Good **Site** Lev/Slope
Sites Available **Total** 110
Facilities
Nearby Facilities
Abergavenny.
✓✓✓✓✓Graded Park. Overlooking the Brecon Beacons National Park. Ideally situated for touring and walking mid and South Wales. Baby bath. AA 3 Pennants.

BRECON

Brynich Caravan Park, Brecon, Powys, LD3 7SH.
Std: 01874 **Tel:** 623325
Std: 01874 **Fax:** 623325
Nearest Town/Resort Brecon.
Directions 1 mile east of Brecon on A470. 250 yards from A40/A470 roundabout.
Acreage 20 **Open** Easter **to** October
Access Very Easy **Site** Level
Sites Available **Total** 130
Facilities
Nearby Facilities
Abergavenny/Merthyr Tydfil.
✓✓✓✓✓Graded Park. Ideal centre for touring and discovering the many scenic views of central Wales. Calor Award for Most Improved Park in Wales 1998, AA 3 Pennent and RAC Appointed. Adventure playground, excellent facilities including two shower blocks with free hot water, two disabled shower rooms. Baby room with bath. NEW for 1997 - A 2 acre tented area allowing for larger overall pitch sizes.

BUILTH WELLS

Fforest Fields, Hundred House, Builth Wells, Powys, LD1 5RT.
Std: 01982 **Tel:** 570406
Std: 01982 **Fax:** 570444
Nearest Town/Resort Builth Wells
Directions 4 miles east of Builth Wells on A481 signposted Hundred House and New Radnor.
Acreage 7 **Open** Easter **to** October
Access Good **Site** Level
Sites Available **Total** 40
Facilities
Nearby Facilities
Builth Road
✓✓✓✓Graded Park. No clubhouse or statics on this beautiful, award winning, family run site. Very peaceful with stunning views. Pristine, free toilet and shower facilities. Woodland and moorland walks direct from the site. AA 3 Pennants and Attractive Environment Award 1997/98.

BUILTH WELLS

Irfon Caravan Park, Upper Chapel Road, Garth, Builth Wells, Powys, LD4 4BH.
Std: 01591 **Tel:** 620310
Nearest Town/Resort Builth Wells.
Directions 500 yards along the B4519 out of Garth (Garth is 6 miles west of Builth Wells along the A483).
Acreage 6½ **Open** Easter **to** October
Access Good **Site** Lev/Slope
Sites Available **Total** 36
Facilities
Nearby Facilities
Garth.
✓✓✓✓✓Graded Park. Quiet site alongside river. Scenic views, ideal touring in the beauty of mountains and forest.

CLYRO

Forest Park Caravan & Camping Site, Clyro, Hay-on-Wye, Powys, HR3 5SG.
Std: 01497 **Tel:** 820156
Std: 01497 **Fax:** 821469
Nearest Town/Resort Hay-on-Wye
Directions From Hereford take the A438 towards Brecon to the village of Clyro. Take the Painscastle Road out of Clyro, caravan park is approx. ¾ mile on Painscastle Road on the right hand side. 2 miles from Hay-on-Wye.
Acreage 10 **Open** All Year
Site Sloping
Sites Available **Total** 28
Facilities
Nearby Facilities
Hereford
Salmon and Trout fishing on the Wye. Two golf courses within 2 miles. Walking on the Black Mountains, Offa's Dyke Path and the Brecon Beacons. Pitches for Tourers and Motorhomes are level.

CRICKHOWELL

Riverside Caravan & Camping Park New Road, Crickhowell, Powys, NP8 1AY.
Std: 01873 **Tel:** 810397
Nearest Town/Resort Crickhowell
Directions Between A40 and A4077 at Crickhowell.
Acreage 3¼ **Open** March **to** October
Access Good **Site** Level
Sites Available **Total** 65
Facilities
Nearby Facilities
Abergavenny
✓✓✓✓Graded Park. ADULTS ONLY, No children under 18 years, over 18 years at owners discretion. Near river, mountain and canal walks, pony trekking and fishing. Town 5 mins walk, in National Park. New improved toilet, shower block with laundry (with drying facilities). A.A. 3 Pennants, R.A.C. Appointed. No hang gliders and paragliders.

CRICKHOWELL

The Bell Inn, Glangrwyney, Crickhowell, Powys, NP8 1EH.
Std: 01873 **Tel:** 810247
Std: 01873 **Fax:** 812155
Nearest Town/Resort Abergavenny
Directions Situated on the A40 between Abergavenny and Brecon, just before the army camp.
Acreage ¾ **Open** April **to** October
Access Good **Site** Level
Sites Available **Total** 10
Facilities
Nearby Facilities
Abergavenny
National parkland, alongside a stream and 100yds from a river. Trout fishing available.

HAY-ON-WYE

Hollybush Caravan and Tenting Site, Hollybush Inn, Hay-on-Wye, Powys, HR3 5PS.
Std: 01497 **Tel:** 847371
Nearest Town/Resort Hay-on-Wye.
Directions 2 miles west of Hay-on-Wye on B4350 Brecon Road.
Acreage 3 **Open** Easter **to** October
Access Good **Site** Level
Sites Available **Total** 22
Facilities
Nearby Facilities
Hereford.
Canoe launch.

LLANBISTER

Brynithon Caravan Site, Llananno, Llanbister, Nr. Llandrindod Wells, Powys, LD1 6TR.
Std: 01597 **Tel:** 840231
Nearest Town/Resort Llanbister Village.
Directions 10 miles north of Llandrindod Wells, 15 miles south of Newtown. Signposted. On A483.
Acreage 2 **Open** March **to** October
Access Good **Site** Level
Sites Available **Total** 30
Facilities
Nearby Facilities
Llandrindod Wells
Good area for rambling. Public telephone ½ mile.

LLANBRYNMAIR

Cringoed Caravan & Camping Park, Llanbrynmair, Powys, SY19 7DR.
Std: 01650 **Tel:** 521237
Nearest Town/Resort Newtown
Directions Take the A470 from Newtown to Llanbrynmair for 18 miles, turn onto the B4518 for 1 mile, site is on the right.
Acreage 5 **Open** Easter/1 April **to** Oct
Access Good **Site** Level
Sites Available **Total** 50
Facilities
Nearby Facilities
Machynlleth
✓✓✓✓Graded Park. Ideal base by the river for touring the many beaches, railways, castles, slate mines, nature reserves and the Alternative Technology Centre.

LLANDRINDOD WELLS

Bryncrach Caravan Site, Bryncrach, Hundred House, Llandrindod Wells, Powys, LD1 5RY.
Std: 01982 **Tel:** 570291
Nearest Town/Resort Builth Wells
Directions Hundred House is on the A481 between Builth Wells and the A44. Turn left signposted Franks Bridge immediately before the public house, after 250 yards turn left into farm road.
Acreage 1¾ **Open** All Year
Access Good **Site** Level
Sites Available **Total** 15
Facilities
Nearby Facilities
Llandrindod Wells
Quiet site with splendid views and walks. Fishing and riding can be arranged. River nearby.

LLANDRINDOD WELLS

Dalmore Caravan Park, Howey, Llandrindod Wells, Powys, LD1 5RG.
Std: 01597 **Tel:** 822483
Std: 01597 **Fax:** 822483
Nearest Town/Resort Llandrindod Wells.
Directions 2 miles south of Llandrindod on main A483, towards Builth Wells.
Acreage 2 **Open** March **to** October
Access Good **Site** Lev/Gentle Slope
Sites Available **Total** 20
Facilities
Nearby Facilities
Llandrindod.
✓✓✓✓Graded Park. Ideal base for hiking and touring Mid Wales, scenic views.

LLANDRINDOD WELLS

Disserth Caravan Park, Howey, Llandrindod Wells, Powys, LD1 6NL.
Std: 01597 **Tel:** 860277
Std: 01597 **Fax:** 860277
Nearest Town/Resort Llandrindod Wells.
Open March **to** October
Access Good **Site** Level
Sites Available **Total** 40
Facilities
Nearby Facilities
Llandrindod Wells.
Alongside river, Ideal touring, fishing. Two static caravans for hire.

LLANDRINDOD WELLS

The Park Motel, Crossgates, Llandrindod Wells, Powys, LD1 6RF.
Std: 01597 **Tel:** 851201
Nearest Town/Resort Llandrindod Wells.
Directions 3 miles north of Llandrindod Wells. Follow the A483 to Crossgates, turn left at the roundabout onto A44 (Rhayader). Park is ¼ mile on the left.
Acreage 1 **Open** March **to** October
Access Good **Site** Level
Sites Available **Total** 15
Facilities
Nearby Facilities
Penybont.
✓✓✓Graded Park. Set in 3 acres of beautiful Mid-Wales countryside yet conveniently situated on the A44. Ideal for touring.

LLANFAIR CAEREINION

Riverbend Caravan Park, Llangadfan, Near Welshpool, Powys, SY21 0PP.
Std: 01938 **Tel:** 820356
Std: 01938 **Fax:** 820356
Nearest Town/Resort Welshpool
Directions Take the A458 from Welshpool to Dolgellau, after 17 miles turn left at Cann Office Public House in the village of Llangadfan.
Acreage 3 **Open** April **to** September
Access Good **Site** Level
Sites Available **Total** 50
Facilities
Nearby Facilities
Welshpool
Alongside the quiet and restful River Banwy, idyllic situation.

LLANFYLLIN

Henstent Caravan Park, Llangynog, Nr. Oswestry, Powys, SY10 0EP.
Std: 01691 **Tel:** 860479
Nearest Town/Resort Bala
Directions Situated on the B4391. Follow signs for Bala from Oswestry. 18 miles from Oswestry, 12 miles from Bala.
Acreage 1 **Open** March **to** October
Access Good **Site** Sloping
Sites Available **Total** 35
Facilities
Nearby Facilities
Gobowen.
Views of Berwyn Mountains. Alongside River Tanat, fishing and walking. Heated toilet block.

LLANGAMMARCH WELLS

Riverside Caravan Park, Llangammarch Wells, Powys, LD4 4BY.
Std: 01591 **Tel:** 620465/620629
Nearest Town/Resort Builth Wells.
Directions From Builth take A483 towards Garth, signposted in Garth Llangannarch 2 miles.
Acreage 3 **Open** April **to** October
Access Good **Site** Level
Sites Available **Total** 25
Facilities
Nearby Facilities
Llangammarch Wells.
Alongside river, scenic views, ideal touring. Cafe/restaurant nearby.

LLANGORSE

Lakeside Caravan Park, Llangorse, Nr. Brecon, Powys.
Std: 01874 **Tel:** 658226
Std: 01874 **Fax:** 658430
Nearest Town/Resort Brecon.
Directions A40 Brecon/Abergavenny junction at B4560 at Bwlch to Llangorse Village. Site adjacent to common leading to lake.
Acreage 14 **Open** April **to** October
Access Good **Site** Level
Sites Available
Facilities
Nearby Facilities
Abergavenny.
✓✓✓✓Graded Park. Best coarse fishing in Wales. We hire boats for fishing, sailing, windsurfing and canoeing. A.A. and R.A.C. Appointed. Caravans available for hire.

LLANIDLOES

Dol-Llys Farm Caravan Site, Dol-Llys Farm, Llanidloes, Powys, SY18 6JA.
Std: 01686 **Tel:** 412694
Nearest Town/Resort Llanidloes.
Directions From Llanidloes take the B4569, past hospital, fork right onto the Oakley Park Road, Dol-Llys is the first farm on the right.
Acreage 3 **Open** March **to** October
Access Good **Site** Level
Sites Available **Total** 20
Facilities
Nearby Facilities
Caersws
Alongside the banks of the River Severn. Ideal for walkers, fishing and touring Mid Wales. Sports centre nearby.

LLANSANTFFRAID

Vyrnwy Caravan Park, Llansantffraid-Ym-Mechain, Powys.
Std: 01691 **Tel:** 828217
Std: 01691 **Fax:** 828669
Nearest Town/Resort Oswestry/ Welshpool
Directions Take the A483 then the B4393. 8 miles from Oswestry and 8 miles from Welshpool.
Open April **to** October
Access Good **Site** Level
Sites Available **Total** 40
Facilities
Nearby Facilities
Gobowen
Alongside a river.

LLANWDDYN

Fronheulog, Lake Vyrnwy, Via Oswestry, Powys.
Std: 01691 **Tel:** Llanwyddyn 870662
Nearest Town/Resort Lake Vyrnwy.
Directions 2 miles south of Lake Vyrnwy on B4393. 8 miles from Llanfyllin, Bala 18 miles.

Acreage 2 **Open** March **to** October
Access Good **Site** Level
Sites Available **Total** 22
Facilities
Nearby Facilities
ADULTS ONLY. Pre-booking necessary. RSPB reserve nearby. Ideal centre for touring. Cold water tap. Price Guide £2.00 per person per night.

MIDDLETOWN

Bank Farm Caravan Park, Middletown, Welshpool, Powys, SY21 8EJ.
Std: 01938 **Tel:** 570260/570526
Nearest Town/Resort Welshpool.
Directions On A458 5½ miles east of Welshpool and 13¼ miles west of Shrewsbury
Acreage 2 **Open** March **to** October
Access Good **Site** Lev/Slope
Sites Available **Total** 20
Facilities
Nearby Facilities
Welshpool.
✓✓✓✓Graded Park. Scenic views, touring area.

MONTGOMERY

Bacheldre Watermill, Churchstoke, Montgomery, Powys, SY15 6TE.
Std: 01588 **Tel:** 620489
Std: 01588 **Fax:** 620489
Nearest Town/Resort Bishops Castle
Directions Head north west on the B4385 for 5 miles. Turn left at the crossroads onto the A489, continue for ½ mile then turn left.
Acreage 2 **Open** Easter **to** October
Access Good **Site** Level
Sites Available **Total** 25
Facilities
Nearby Facilities
Welshpool
✓✓✓✓Graded Park. Ideal for touring and walking.

NEWBRIDGE-ON-WYE

Pont-ar-Ithon Caravan Site, Pont-ar-Ithon, Newbridge-on-Wye, Builth Wells, Powys, LD2 3SA.
Std: 01597 **Tel:** 860203
Nearest Town/Resort Llandrindod Wells
Directions 4 miles from Builth Wells, 5 miles from Llandrindod Wells and 8 miles from Rhayader and Elan Valley.
Open March **to** October
Access Good **Site** Level
Sites Available
Facilities
Nearby Facilities
On the River Ithon. 40 miles from Aberystwyth and Borth.

NEWTOWN

Llwyn Celyn Holiday Park, Adfa, Nr. Newtown, Powys, SY16 3DG.
Std: 01938 **Tel:** 810720
Nearest Town/Resort Newtown
Directions Bypass round Welshpool on the A483, take turn to Berriew on the B4390. Follow to Newmills, ¼ mile turn right for Adfa, through Adfa Village and first left. Park is on the left.
Acreage 14 **Open** Wk Before Easter **to** Oct
Access Good **Site** Level
Sites Available **Total** 16
Facilities
Nearby Facilities
Welshpool
Scenic views, good walking and bird watching. Take-away meals available.

NEWTOWN

Smithy Caravan Park, Abermule, Newtown, Powys, SY15 6ND.
Std: 01584 **Tel:** 711280
Std: 01584 **Fax:** 711460
Nearest Town/Resort Newtown
Directions Leave the A483 3 miles north Newtown and enter the village of Abermule. Turn down lane opposite village shop and post office.
Acreage 4 **Open** All Year
Access Good **Site** Level
Sites Available **Total** 30
Facilities
Nearby Facilities
Newtown
Outstanding quality park, maintained to the highest standards. 2 miles of fishing on the River Severn. Bowling and tennis courts nearby.

NEWTOWN

Tynycwm Camping & Caravan Site, Tynycwm, Aberhafesp, Newtown, Powys, SY16 3JF.
Std: 01686 **Tel:** 688651
Nearest Town/Resort Newtown.
Directions 7 miles north west of Newtown via A489 to Caersws, then B4569 north signposted Aberhafesp, cross B4568 ignore sign for Aberhafesp and continue to next crossroads. Turn left signposted Bwlch y Garreg. Farm and site 1 mile on right.
Acreage 3 **Open** May **to** October
Access Good **Site** Level
Sites Available **Total** 50
Facilities
Nearby Facilities
Caersws.
Scenic views, pony trekking close, farm site.

PRESTEIGNE

Rockbridge Park, Presteigne, Powys, LD8 2NF.
Std: 01547 **Tel:** 560300
Nearest Town/Resort Presteigne.
Directions 1 mile west of Presteigne on the B4356.
Acreage 3 **Open** April **to** September
Access Good **Site** Level
Sites Available **Total** 20
Facilities
Nearby Facilities
Knighton.
Alongside river, sceinc views, peaceful and relaxing.

RHAYADER

Gigrin Farm, South Road, Rhayader, Powys.
Std: 01597 **Tel:** 810243
Std: 01597 **Fax:** 810357
Nearest Town/Resort Rhayader.
Directions ¼ mile south of Rhayader, just off the A470. Turn at Farm Trail sign.
Acreage 2 **Open** All Year except Xmas
Access Good **Site** Level
Sites Available **Total** 15
Facilities
Nearby Facilities
Llandrindod Wells
Ideal touring area, beautiful views. 2 mile Nature Trail and Wildlife Interpretive Centre. Bed and breakfast available in the farm house. Fishing and RSPB reserve, near Elan Valley Dams. Red Kite Feeding October to May at 2 o'clock GMT. Mountain bike riding nearby.

TALGARTH

Riverside International Caravan Park, Bronllys, Talgarth, Nr Brecon, Powys, LD3 0HL.
Std: 01874 **Tel:** 711320
Std: 01874 **Fax:** 712064
Nearest Town/Resort Brecon.
Directions Leave Brecon on A438 8 miles to Bronllys, turn right in the village for Talgarth, site ¼ mile on right - opposite Bronllys Castle.
Acreage 9 **Open** Easter **to** October
Access Good **Site** Lev/Slope
Sites Available **Total** 85
Facilities
Nearby Facilities
Abergavenny
✓✓✓✓✓Graded Park. Edge of Brecon Beacon National Park. Free freezer service and ice packs.

WELSHPOOL

Maes-Yr-Afon Caravan Park, Berriew, Welshpool, Powys, SY21 8QB.
Std: 01686 **Tel:** 640587
Std: 01686 **Fax:** 640587
Nearest Town/Resort Welshpool.
Directions A483 Welshpool to Newtown road, then 5 miles before Newtown take the B4390 to Berriew. Park is 2 miles towards Manafon on the left.
Acreage 2 **Open** March **to** October
Access Good **Site** Level
Sites Available **Total** 20
Facilities
Nearby Facilities
Welshpool

YSTRADGYNLAIS

Dan-Yr-Ogof Caravan & Tenting Park, Dan-Yr-Ogof, Abercrave, Powys, SA9 1GJ.
Std: 01639 **Tel:** 730284
Std: 01639 **Fax:** 730293
Nearest Town/Resort Brecon
Directions Midway between Brecon and Swansea on the A4067, within the Brecon Beacons National Park.
Acreage 10 **Open** Easter **to** October
Access Good **Site** Sloping
Sites Available **Total** 60
Facilities
Nearby Facilities
Neath
Situated in a National Park, alongside a river with wooded surroundings. Cafe/restaurant ¼ mile and dry ski slope nearby.

SWANSEA

LLANGENNITH

Hillend Camping Park, Hillend, Llangennith, Gower, Swansea, SA3 1JD.
Std: 01792 **Tel:** 386204
Std: 01792 **Fax:** 386204
Nearest Town/Resort Swansea
Directions Exit M4 junction 47, follow the A483 (Swansea), A484 (Llanelli), B4296 (Gower), B4295 (Gower) to Llangennith, then signposts to Hillend.
Acreage 14 **Open** April **to** October
Access Good **Site** Level
Sites Available **Total** 250
Facilities
Nearby Facilities
Swansea
100yds from Rhossilli Bay in Britain's first area of outstanding natural beauty. Ideal for surfing, canoeing, walking, fishing, windsurfing, bathing and hang gliding.

LLANMADOC

Llanmadoc Camping Site, Llanmadoc, Gower Coast, Swansea, SA3 1DE.
Std: 01792 **Tel:** 386202
Nearest Town/Resort Swansea
Directions M4 come off at junction 47 A483, signposted to Gower left at traffic lights Gorseinon, right at Gonerton.
Acreage 11 **Open** April **to** October
Access Good **Site** Lev/Slope
Sites Available **Total** 250
Facilities
Nearby Facilities
Swansea
Adjoining sandy beach and a National Trust and nature conservancy. Area of outstanding natural beauty.

OXWICH

Oxwich Camping Park, Oxwich, Gower, Swansea, SA3 1LS.
Std: 01792 **Tel:** 390777
Nearest Town/Resort Swansea.
Directions A4118 from Swansea, 10 miles turn left. 1¼ miles turn right at crossroads, ¼ mile on right hand side.
Acreage 10 **Open** April **to** September
Site Lev/Slope
Sites Available **Total** 180
Facilities
Nearby Facilities
Swansea
✓✓✓✓Graded Park. Near sandy beach. Water sports and nature reserve.

PORT EYNON

Bank Farm, Norton, Gower, Swansea, SA3 1LL.
Std: 01792 **Tel:** 390228
Std: 01792 **Fax:** 391282
Nearest Town/Resort Swansea
Directions Take the A4118 from Swansea towards Port Eynon, turn left for Horton 1 mile before Port Eynon, turn right at the site entrance after 200 yards.
Acreage 80 **Open** March **to** 15 November
Access Good **Site** Sloping
Sites Available **Total** 230
Facilities
Nearby Facilities
Swansea
✓✓✓Graded Park. Overlooking the beach. Heated swimming pool.

PORT EYNON

Newpark Holiday Park, Port Eynon, Gower, Swansea, SA3 1NP.
Std: 01792 **Tel:** 390292
Std: 01792 **Fax:** 391245
Nearest Town/Resort Port Eynon/ Swansea
Directions From Swansea take the A4118. Turn left as the hill begins to descend into Port Eynon Village.
Acreage 14 **Open** April/Good Friday **to** Oct
Access Good **Site** Level
Sites Available **Total** 172
Facilities
Nearby Facilities
Swansea
Family site with panoramic views of Port Eynon Bay. Full facilities for tourers, trailer tents and tents. 5 minute walk to a Blue Flag beach and the village. ½ hour by car to Swansea.

RHOSSILI

Pitton Cross Caravan & Camping Park, Rhossili, Swansea, SA3 1PH.
Std: 01792 **Tel:** 390593
Std: 01792 **Fax:** 391010
Nearest Town/Resort Swansea
Acreage 6 **Open** April **to** October
Access Good **Site** Level
Sites Available **Total** 100
Facilities
Nearby Facilities
Swansea
✓✓✓ Graded Park. Quiet site.

SWANSEA

Riverside Caravan Park, Ynysforgan Farm, Morriston, Swansea.
Std: 01792 **Tel:** 775587
Nearest Town/Resort Swansea
Directions Direct access to site from roundabout under motorway junction 45 on M4.
Acreage 7 **Open** All Year
Access Good **Site** Level
Sites Available **Total** 120
Facilities
Nearby Facilities
Swansea
✓✓✓ Graded Park. Alongside river, ideal touring, flat level grassy site. Indoor swimming pool and jaccuzi. Television room. Dogs are welcome but no dangerous breeds.

SWANSEA

Three Cliffs Bay Caravan Site, North Hills Farm, Penmaen, Gower, Swansea, SA3 2HB.
Std: 01792 **Tel:** 371218
Nearest Town/Resort Swansea
Directions Take the A4118 from Swansea, site is signposted in the village of Penmaen.
Acreage 5 **Open** Easter **to** October
Access Good **Site** Lev/Slope
Sites Available **Total** 95
Facilities
Nearby Facilities
Swansea
Overlooking Three Cliffs Bay.

VALE OF GLAMORGAN

BARRY

Vale Touring Caravan Park, Port Road (West), Barry, Vale of Glamorgan, CF6 9AZ.
Std: 01446 **Tel:** 719311
Nearest Town/Resort Barry Island.
Directions The park is located 2 miles west of Barry on the A4226. When you reach the roundabout with sculpture arrows turn left, park is on your right.
Acreage 2 **Open** April **to** October
Access Good **Site** Level
Sites Available **Total** 40
Facilities
Nearby Facilities
Barry
✓✓ Graded Park. Ideal touring, beach 2 miles away.

COWBRIDGE

Llandow Touring Caravan Park, Llandow, Cowbridge, Vale of Glamorgan.
Std: 01446 **Tel:** 794527
Std: 01446 **Fax:** 792462
Nearest Town/Resort Cowbridge
Directions From the A48 turn onto the B4268 to Llantwit Major, follow brown signs to the caravan park.
Acreage 5 **Open** February **to** November
Access Good **Site** Level
Sites Available **Total** 100
Facilities
Nearby Facilities
Bridgend
✓✓✓✓ Graded Park. Sheltered, secluded park set in the heart of the Vale of Glamorgan. 4 minutes from the Heritage Coast and 20 minutes from Cardiff.

LLANTWIT MAJOR

Acorn Camping & Caravanning, Rosedew Farm, Hamlane South, Llantwit Major, Vale of Glamorgan, CF61 1RP.
Std: 01446 **Tel:** 794024
Std: 01446 **Fax:** 794024
Nearest Town/Resort Llantwit Major
Directions From M4 junction 33 follow signs Cardiff Airport then B4265 for Llantwit Major. Approach site from the town centre via Beach Road or via Ham Lane East through Ham Manor Park.
Acreage 4 **Open** February **to** 8 December
Access Good **Site** Level
Sites Available **Total** 90
Facilities
Nearby Facilities
Barry
✓✓✓✓ Graded Park. 1 mile from beach, 1 mile from town, coastal walks, ideal base for touring. Holiday hire caravans available, one suitable for wheelchair.

WREXHAM

WREXHAM

Camping & Caravanning Club Site, c/o The Racecourse, Overton Road, Bangor-y-Coed, Wrexham, LL13 0DA.
Std: 01978 **Tel:** 781009
Directions From the A525 follow racecourse and international camping signs through the village. Turn left immediately opposite the Buck Hotel signposted racecourse, site is approx. 1 mile on the right hand side.
Acreage 6 **Open** 22 March **to** 1 Nov
Site Lev/Slope
Sites Available **Total** 100
Facilities
Nearby Facilities
Located on the racecourse, just 5 miles from Wrexham.

IT WILL HELP US TO CONTINUE PROVIDING THIS INFORMATION IF YOU WOULD KINDLY MENTION CADE'S WHEN REPLYING TO OUR ADVERTISERS

SCOTLAND

ABERDEENSHIRE

ABERDEEN

Lower Deeside Holiday Park, South Deeside Road, Maryculter, Aberdeenshire, AB12 5FX.
Std: 01224 **Tel:** 733860
Std: 01224 **Fax:** 732490
Nearest Town/Resort Aberdeen
Directions On the B9077 5 miles south west of Aberdeen.
Acreage 14 **Open** All Year
Access Good **Site** Level
Sites Available **Total** 45
Facilities
Nearby Facilities
Aberdeen
✓✓✓✓Graded Park. Peaceful country site. Ideal for touring Royal Deeside and the scenic north east coast and exploring local historic castles. Only 10 minutes from the granite city of Aberdeen with its wide range of leisure and recreational facilities for all ages.

ABERDEEN

Nigg Touring Park, Altens Farm Road, Nigg, Aberdeen, Aberdeenshire, AB1 4HX.
Std: 01224 **Tel:** 896633/696679
Std: 01224 **Fax:** 696988
Nearest Town/Resort Aberdeen
Directions From all directions follow the Lorry Park signs, when reaching the Lorry Park follow caravan park signs.
Acreage 4 **Open** All Year
Access Good **Site** Lev/Slope
Sites Available **Total** 64
Facilities
Nearby Facilities
Aberdeen
Gently sloping site with panoramic views of Aberdeen City.

ABOYNE

Aboyne Loch Caravan Park, Aboyne, Aberdeenshire, AB34 5BR.
Std: 013398 **Tel:** 86244
Std: 01330 **Fax:** 811669
Nearest Town/Resort Aberdeen.
Directions ½ mile east of Aboyne Village on the A93 Aberdeen to Braemar road.
Acreage 8 **Open** April **to** October
Access Good **Site** Level
Sites Available **Total** 65
Facilities
Nearby Facilities
Aberdeen.
Situated on a wooded promontory of land, surrounded on three sides by a loch.

ABOYNE

Camping & Caravanning Club Site, Drummie Hill, Tarland, By Aboyne, Aberdeenshire, AB34 4UP.
Std: 01339 **Tel:** 881388
Directions From southwest on the B9119 approaching Tarland bear left before the bridge, continue for 600 yards and the site is on the left.
Acreage 4 **Open** 22 March **to** 1 Nov
Site Level
Sites Available **Total** 40
Facilities
Nearby Facilities
✓✓✓✓Graded Park. Close to the village of Tarland.

BANCHORY

Campfield Caravan Site, Banchory, Aberdeenshire, AB31 4DN.
Std: 013398 **Tel:** 82250
Nearest Town/Resort Banchory.
Directions On A980 road, 5 miles north of Banchory.
Acreage 2 **Open** April **to** September
Access Good **Site** Level
Sites Available **Total** 14
Facilities
Nearby Facilities
Aberdeen.
✓✓✓✓Graded Park. Scenic views ideal for touring and exploring Deeside.

BANCHORY

Feughside Caravan Park, Strachan, Banchory, Aberdeenshire, AB31 6NT.
Std: 01330 **Tel:** 850669
Nearest Town/Resort Banchory.
Directions Take B974 to Strachan, 3 miles. Continue straight on B976, 2 miles to Feughside Inn. Site is directly behind Inn, turn right directly after Inn.
Open April **to** Mid October
Access Good **Site** Level
Sites Available **Total** 20
Facilities
Nearby Facilities
Stonehaven.
✓✓✓✓✓Graded Park. Scenic views. Near river. Ideal touring area. Good walks. Family site in country. Fishing nearby Trout Loch, hotel 100 yards, pitch and putt nearby. Thistle Award Holiday Homes for hire.

BANCHORY

Silver Ladies Caravan Park, Strachan, By Banchory, Aberdeenshire, AB31 6NL.
Std: 01330 **Tel:** 822800
Std: 01330 **Fax:** 825701
Nearest Town/Resort Banchory
Directions 1 mile south of Banchory on left of B974 Fettercairn road.
Acreage 7 **Open** April **to** October
Access Good **Site** Level
Sites Available **Total** 17
Facilities
Nearby Facilities
Aberdeen
✓✓✓✓✓Graded Park. Near River Dee, scenic views. Ideal base for exploring Royal Deeside.

GOURDON

Gourdon Caravan Park, Old Railway Station, Gourdon, Near Montrose, Aberdeenshire, DD10 0LA.
Std: 01561 **Tel:** 361475
Nearest Town/Resort Montrose
Directions 12 miles north of Montrose on the A94.
Acreage 1 **Open** April **to** October
Access Good **Site** Level
Sites Available **Total** 18
Facilities
Nearby Facilities
Montrose
Ideal for a relaxing holiday. In the centre of a fishing village, 100 yards from the sea. Coastal walks. Ideal touring base for the surrounding area and Royal Deeside.

JOHNSHAVEN

Wairds Park, Beach Road, Johnshaven, Nr. Montrose, Aberdeenshire, DD10 0HD.
Std: 01561 **Tel:** 362395
Nearest Town/Resort Montrose
Directions 10 miles north of Montrose on the A92. Turn right at the signpost for the village.
Acreage 6 **Open** 1 April **to** 15 October
Access Good **Site** Level
Sites Available **Total** 20
Facilities
Nearby Facilities
Montrose
✓✓✓✓Graded Park. On the seafront ina village with a small harbour. All weather bowling green.

KINTORE

Hillhead Caravan Park, Kintore, Aberdeenshire, AB51 0YX.
Std: 01467 **Tel:** 632809
Std: 01467 **Fax:** 633173
Nearest Town/Resort Kintore
Directions Turn off the A96 in the centre of Kintore onto a road signposted Ratch Hill, in ½ mile turn left signposted Blairs/Hillhead Caravan Park. In ½ mile turn left into park. Or follow camping and caravan signs on the B996 3 miles.
Acreage 1½ **Open** Easter **to** October
Access Good **Site** Level
Sites Available **Total** 29
Facilities
Nearby Facilities
Inverurie
✓✓✓✓Graded Park. Quiet, sheltered park. Easy access to Castle and Malt Whisky Trails, Aberdeen and Royal Deeside.

LAURENCEKIRK

Brownmuir Caravan Park, Fordoun, Laurencekirk, Aberdeenshire, AB30 1SJ.
Std: 01561 **Tel:** 320786
Nearest Town/Resort Stonehaven
Directions Follow the A90 north to Aberdeen. 4 miles north of Laurencekirk turn left at Fordoun and follow signs for 1 mile, site is on the right.
Acreage 4 **Open** April **to** October
Access Good **Site** Level
Sites Available **Total** 10
Facilities
Nearby Facilities
Stonehaven
Scenic views and ideal for touring around Royal Deeside.

LAURENCEKIRK

Dovecot Caravan Park, Northwaterbridge, By Laurencekirk, Aberdeenshire, AB30 1QL.
Std: 01674 **Tel:** 840630
Std: 01674 **Fax:** 840630
Nearest Town/Resort Laurencekirk
Directions Turn off the A90 5 miles south of Laurencekirk at R.A.F. Edzell. Site is 500 yards on the left.
Acreage 6 **Open** April **to** Mid October
Access Good **Site** Level
Sites Available **Total** 25
Facilities
Nearby Facilities
Montrose
✓✓✓✓Graded Park. Alongside the River Esk in a warm hollow. Ideal touring base.

MACDUFF

Wester Bonnyton Farm Site, Gamrie, Banff, Aberdeenshire, AB45 3EP.
Std: 01261 **Tel:** 832470
Std: 01261 **Fax:** 832470
Nearest Town/Resort Macduff/Banff
Directions 2 miles east of Macduff on the B9031 and 1 mile off the A98 Banff to

Fraserburgh road.
Acreage 2 **Open** March **to** Sept
Access Good **Site** Level
Sites Available **Total** 8
Facilities
Nearby Facilities
Keith
✓✓✓Graded Park. Quiet, farm site overlooking the Moray Firth. Many local tourist attractions.

PORTSOY

Sandend Caravan Park, Sandend, Portsoy, Aberdeenshire, AB45 2UA.
Std: 01261 **Tel:** 842660
Nearest Town/Resort Portsoy
Directions 3 miles from Portsoy on the A98.
Acreage 4½ **Open** April **to** 4 October
Access Good **Site** Level
Sites Available **Total** 52
Facilities
Nearby Facilities
Keith
✓✓✓✓✓Graded Park. In a conservation village overlooking a sandy beach. Ideal for touring and The Whisky Trail.

ST. CYRUS

East Bowstrips Caravan Park, St. Cyrus, Nr Montrose, Aberdeenshire, DD10 0DE.
Std: 01674 **Tel:** 850328
Std: 01674 **Fax:** 850328
Nearest Town/Resort Montrose.
Directions Approx 6 miles north of Montrose. Follow A92, enter village of St. Cyrus, first left after Hotel, second right.
Acreage 4 **Open** April **to** October
Access Good **Site** Lev/Slope
Sites Available **Total** 30
Facilities
Nearby Facilities
Montrose.
✓✓✓✓✓Graded Park. Quiet, family park by the coast. Ideal touring base. Excellent facilities. Beautiful sandy beach and nature reserve approx 1 mile. Special facilities for disabled visitors including adapted caravan for hire. AA 4 Pennants.

TURRIFF

East Balthangie Caravan Park, East Balthangie, Cuminestown, Turriff, Aberdeenshire, AB53 5XY.
Std: 01888 **Tel:** 544921/544261
Std: 01888 **Fax:** 544261
Nearest Town/Resort Turriff
Directions Take the A92 from Aberdeen to Ellon, turn onto the B9107 to Cuminestown. After New Deer turn right to New Byth, caravan park is 3 miles on the right.
Acreage 5 **Open** March **to** October
Access Good **Site** Level
Sites Available **Total** 12
Facilities
Nearby Facilities
Aberdeen
Good base for touring.

ANGUS

ARBROATH

Elliot Caravan Park, Dundee Road, Arbroath, Angus.
Std: 01241 **Tel:** 873466
Nearest Town/Resort Arbroath
Directions On the A92, ½ mile from town.
Acreage 2 **Open** April **to** September
Access Good **Site** Level
Sites Available **Total** 8
Facilities
Nearby Facilities
Arbroath
Near the beach, across from a golf club. Ideal for touring and sea fishing.

CARNOUSTIE

Woodlands Caravan Park, Newton Road, Carnoustie, Angus, DD7 6HR.
Std: 01241 **Tel:** 854430
Nearest Town/Resort Carnoustie
Directions Off the A92 Dundee to Arbroath road signed Carnoustie with caravan symbol. After 1 mile turn right into Newton Road and follow signs.
Acreage 4½ **Open** March **to** Mid October
Access Good **Site** Level
Sites Available **Total** 120
Facilities
Nearby Facilities
Carnoustie
✓✓✓✓✓Graded Park. ½ mile from the beach and open golf course. Ideal for touring the glens of Angus and the wildlife trails on the local cliffs.

FORFAR

The Glens Caravan & Camping Park, Memus, By Forfar, Angus, DD8 3TY.
Std: 01307 **Tel:** 860258
Std: 01307 **Fax:** 860258
Nearest Town/Resort Kirriemuir.
Directions From the A90 Dundee to Aberdeen dual carriageway) take the B9128 signed Forfar. Turn first right signposted Memus and follow Memus and caravan site signs for 4 miles. From Kirriemuir take the Roods and Shiel Hill road for 5 miles.
Acreage 1 **Open** April **to** October
Access Good **Site** Level
Sites Available **Total** 30
Facilities
Nearby Facilities
Dundee.
Set at the foot of the Angus Glens. Ideal for touring, walking, cycling, bird watching, fishing, shooting and golfing. Towns and coast within easy reach.

MONIFIETH

Riverview Caravan Park, Marine Drive, Monifieth, By Dundee, Angus, DD5 4NN.
Std: 01382 **Tel:** 535471
Std: 01382 **Fax:** 535375
Nearest Town/Resort Dundee
Directions A92 Dundee to Arbroath road, after 3 miles turn right into Monifieth, site is well signposted.
Acreage 5½ **Open** April **to** October
Access Good **Site** Level
Sites Available **Total** 50
Facilities
Nearby Facilities
Dundee
✓✓✓✓✓Graded Park. Private access to a sandy beach. Magnificent views. Supermarket, village shops and two golf courses within a 5 minute walk.

MONIFIETH

Tayview Holiday Park, Marine Parade, Monifieth, Angus, DD5 4NH.
Std: 01382 **Tel:** 532837
Std: 01382 **Fax:** 534444
Nearest Town/Resort Monifieth
Directions In Monifieth pass below the railway bridge, pass the local authority site and turn right, site is in view.
Acreage 10 **Open** March **to** October
Access Good **Site** Level
Sites Available **Total** 80
Facilities
Nearby Facilities
Dundee/Monifieth
Outdoor sports facilities and the beach.

MONTROSE

Littlewood Holiday Park, Brechin Road, Montrose, Angus, DD10 9LE.
Std: 01674 **Tel:** 672973
Nearest Town/Resort Montrose
Directions Situated on the A935 Brechin to Montrose road, on the north west edge of Montrose.
Acreage 3½ **Open** April **to** October
Access Good **Site** Level
Sites Available **Total** 10
Facilities
Nearby Facilities
Montrose
✓✓✓✓✓Graded Park. On the edge of Montrose Basin Nature Reserve. Near to the National Trust's House of Dun.

ARGYLL & BUTE

ARDLUI

Ardlui Holiday Home Park, Ardlui, Loch Lomond, Argyll & Bute, G83 7EB.
Std: 01301 **Tel:** 704243
Std: 01301 **Fax:** 704268
Nearest Town/Resort Helensburgh
Directions 25 miles on the A82 to Helensburgh, on the Clyde Coast.
Acreage 1 **Open** All Year
Access Good **Site** Sloping
Sites Available **Total** 20
Facilities
Nearby Facilities
Ardlui
✓✓✓✓Graded Park. On the shores of Loch Lomond. Ideal for touring or walking the West Highland Way.

ARROCHAR

Ardgartan - Forestry Commission, Ardgartan, Arrochar, Argyll & Bute, G83 7AR.
Std: 01301 **Tel:** 702293
Nearest Town/Resort Arrochar
Directions 2 miles west of Arrochar on the A83 Glasgow to Inverary road.
Acreage 17 **Open** 25 March **to** 30 Oct
Access Good **Site** Level
Sites Available **Total** 200
Facilities
Nearby Facilities
✓✓✓✓Graded Park. On the shores of Loch Long, surrounded by the magnificent mountain scenery of Argyll Forest Park. Ideal for outdoor activities.

BLAIRMORE

Gairletter Caravan Park, Blairmore, By Dunoon, Argyll & Bute, PA23 8TP.
Std: 01369 **Tel:** 810208
Std: 01369 **Fax:** 810208
Nearest Town/Resort Dunoon
Acreage 5½ **Open** March **to** October
Access Good **Site** Level
Sites Available **Total** 40
Facilities
Nearby Facilities
Gourock
✓✓✓✓Graded Park. On a beach with two slipways for boating. No roads for children to cross. Ideal touring. AA 3 Pennants.

CAMPBELTOWN

Peninver Sands Holiday Park, Peninver, By Campbeltown, Argyll & Bute, PA28 6QP.
Std: 01586 **Tel:** 552262
Std: 01586 **Fax:** 552262
Nearest Town/Resort Campbeltown
Directions From Campbeltown take the B842 for 4½ miles. Park is on the right as you enter Peninver.
Acreage 2¾ **Open** April **to** October
Access Good **Site** Lev/Slope
Sites Available **Total** 25
Facilities
Nearby Facilities
Oban
✓✓✓✓Graded Park. Peaceful, family run park with outstanding views towards Arran and Ayrshire. Near the beach.

CARRADALE

Carradale Bay Caravan Park, Carradale, Kintyre, Argyll & Bute, PA28 6QG.
Std: 01583 **Tel:** 431665
Nearest Town/Resort Campbeltown.
Directions From Campbeltown B842, turn right onto the B879 (signposted Carradale). In ¼ mile at caravan park sign turn right onto a single track road. Site entrance within ¼ mile.
Acreage 12 **Open** Easter **to** September
Access Good **Site** Level
Sites Available **Total** 65
Facilities
Nearby Facilities
✓✓✓✓Graded Park. Situated on a safe, sloping, sandy beach with a river running alongside.

CONNEL

Camping & Caravanning Club Site, Barcaldine, By Connel, Argyll & Bute, PA37 1SG.
Std: 01631 **Tel:** 720348
Directions Heading North on the A828, 7 miles from the Connel bridge turn into site at the Camping Club sign on the right. Opposite the Marine Resource Centre proceed through the large iron gates.
Acreage 4 **Open** 22 March **to** 1 Nov
Site Level
Sites Available **Total** 90
Facilities
Nearby Facilities
Oban
✓✓✓✓Graded Park. Public house with restaurant on site. 1 mile from Sea Life Centre. Ideally located for the Highlands and Islands.

CRAIGNURE

Shieling Holidays, Craignure, Isle of Mull, Argyll & Bute, PA65 6AY.
Std: 01680 **Tel:** 812496
Std: 01680 **Fax:** 812496
Nearest Town/Resort Craignure.
Directions From Craignure Ferry turn left on A849 to Iona for 400 metres, then left again at church.
Acreage 7½ **Open** April **to** October
Access Good **Site** Level
Sites Available **Total** 42
Facilities
Nearby Facilities
Oban
✓✓✓✓✓Graded Park. Enchanting location by the sea. Boats and canoes. Hostel beds. Website: www.zynet.co.uk/mull/members/shieling.

DUNOON

Stratheck Caravan Park, Loch Eck, By Dunoon, Argyll & Bute, PA23 8SG.
Std: 01369 **Tel:** 840472
Std: 01369 **Fax:** 840472
Nearest Town/Resort Dunoon.
Directions A815 to Glasgow from Dunoon, about 6 miles from Dunoon. ½ mile past entrance to Benmore Gardens.
Acreage 13 **Open** March **to** October
Access Good **Site** Level
Sites Available **Total** 50
Facilities
Nearby Facilities
Gourock
✓✓✓✓Graded Park. Alongside river, amidst magnificent Highlands mountains and Lochs.

GLENBARR

Killegruer Caravan Site, Woodend, Glenbarr, Tarbert, Argyll & Bute.
Std: 01583 **Tel:** 421241
Nearest Town/Resort Campbeltown.
Directions 12 miles north of Campbeltown on the A83.
Acreage 1¼ **Open** April **to** September
Access Good **Site** Level
Sites Available **Total** 25
Facilities
Nearby Facilities
Oban.
Overlooks a sandy beach with views of the Inner Hebrides and the Mull of Kintyre. Site facilities have recently been upgraded. Close to ferry link to Northern Ireland and the Inner Hebrides.

GLENDARUEL

Glendaruel Caravan Park, Glendaruel, Argyll & Bute, PA22 3AB.
Std: 01369 **Tel:** 820267
Std: 01369 **Fax:** 820367
Nearest Town/Resort Tighnabruaich
Directions 13 miles south Strachur on A886 or by ferry to Dunoon and then on the B836. B836 not recommended for touring caravans - 1 in 5 gradient.
Acreage 6 **Open** April **to** October
Access Good **Site** Level
Sites Available **Total** 45
Facilities
Nearby Facilities
Gourock.
✓✓✓✓✓Graded Park. Peaceful secluded site within a 22 acre country park. Kyles of Bute 5 miles. Bicycles for hire. Ideal centre touring and walking. Dogs by arrangement only. Sea trout and Salmon fishing. Winner of the Calor Environmental Award 'Most Improved Park in Scotland'. Best Caravan & Camping Park in Argyll the Isles Loch Lomond, Stirling & Trossachs Tourist Board and Antartex Tourism Award.

INVERUGLAS

Loch Lomond Holiday Park, Inveruglas, Near Tarbet, Argyll & Bute, G83 7DW.
Std: 01301 **Tel:** 704224
Std: 01301 **Fax:** 704206
Nearest Town/Resort Tarbet.
Directions 3 miles north of Tarbet on the A82.
Acreage 1 **Open** March **to** October
Access Good **Site** Level
Sites Available **Total** 18
Facilities
Nearby Facilities
Tarbet.
✓✓✓✓✓Graded Park. Own beach in a superb location. Ideal for hill walking and touring.

LOCHGILPHEAD

Lochgilphead Caravan Park, Bank Park, Lochgilphead, Argyll & Bute, PA31 8NX.
Std: 01546 **Tel:** 602003
Std: 01546 **Fax:** 603699
Nearest Town/Resort Lochgilphead
Directions Within the town of Lochgilphead, close to junction of the A83 and the A816.
Acreage 7 **Open** April **to** October
Access Good **Site** Level
Sites Available **Total** 70
Facilities
Nearby Facilities
Oban
✓✓✓✓✓Graded Park. Adjacent to Loch Fyne, Crinan Canal and the town.

MACHRIHANISH

Camping & Caravanning Club Site, East Trodigal, Machrihanish, Campbeltown, Mull of Kintyre, Argyll & Bute, PA28 6PT.
Std: 01586 **Tel:** 810366
Nearest Town/Resort Campbeltown
Directions On the A83 from Glasgow to Campbeltown, take the B843 to Machrihanish. Site entrance is on the right 200 yards past chimney.
Acreage 8 **Open** 22 March **to** 27 Sept
Access Good **Site** Level
Sites Available **Total** 90
Facilities
Nearby Facilities
Tarbet
✓✓✓✓Graded Park. Set in a seaside village, ½ mile to a sandy beach. Close to the fishing port of Campbeltown. Watersports close to site. Washing machine on site.

OBAN

Oban Caravan & Camping Park, Gallanachmore Farm, Gallanach Road, Oban, Argyll & Bute, PA34 4QH.
Std: 01631 **Tel:** 562425
Std: 01631 **Fax:** 566624
Nearest Town/Resort Oban
Directions From Oban town centre follow signs for Gallanach (past the main ferry terminal).
Acreage 15 **Open** Easter **to** Mid October
Access Good **Site** Lev/Slope
Sites Available **Total** 180
Facilities
Nearby Facilities
Oban
✓✓✓✓✓Graded Park.

OBAN

Oban Divers Caravan Park, Glenshellach Road, Oban, Argyll & Bute, PA34 4QJ.
Std: 01631 **Tel:** 562755
Std: 01631 **Fax:** 562755
Nearest Town/Resort Oban
Directions From north go through Oban to the traffic island, take ferry and caravan signs into Albany Street then first or second left. take the first right, then first left signposted caravans/tents. Glenshellach Road is 1½ miles.
Acreage 4 **Open** Mid March **to** End Oct
Access Good **Site** Lev/Slope
Sites Available **Total** 45
Facilities
Nearby Facilities
Oban
✓✓✓✓✓Graded Park. Quiet, scenic park on different levels with a stream running through. Member of Countryside Discovery.

SOUTHEND

Machribeg Caravan Site, Southend, By Campbeltown, Argyll & Bute, PA28 6RW.
Std: 01586 **Tel:** 830249
Nearest Town/Resort Campbeltown.
Directions Take the B843 from Campbeltown for 10 miles. Site is situated 250yds through Southend Village on the left by the beach.
Acreage 4 **Open** Easter **to** September
Access Good **Site** Sloping
Sites Available **Total** 80
Facilities
Nearby Facilities
Near the beach with good views, very quiet location. 18 hole golf course.

TAYINLOAN

Point Sands, Tayinloan, Argyll & Bute, PA29 6XG.
Std: 01583 **Tel:** 441263
Nearest Town/Resort Tarbert
Directions On the A83 19 miles north of Campbeltown.
Acreage 13 **Open** April **to** October
Access Good **Site** Level
Sites Available **Total** 65
Facilities
Nearby Facilities
✓✓✓✓Graded Park. On a safe sandy beach. Ideal for touring and visiting the Isles of Gigha and Arran.

TAYNUILT

Crunachy Caravan & Camping Park, Bridge of Awe, Taynuilt, Argyll & Bute, PA35 1HT.
Std: 01866 **Tel:** 822612
Nearest Town/Resort Oban.
Directions Alongside main A85 Tyndrum to Oban 14 miles east of Oban outside the village of Taynuilt.
Acreage 9 **Open** March **to** November
Access Good **Site** Level
Sites Available **Total** 80
Facilities
Nearby Facilities
Taynuilt.
Alongside the River Awe at the foot of Ben Cruachan.

TAYVALLICH

Leachive Caravan Site, Leachive Farm, Tayvallich, By Lochgilphead, Argyll & Bute, PA31 8PL.
Std: 01546 **Tel:** 870206
Nearest Town/Resort Lochgilphead
Directions From Lochgilphead follow the A816 for 2 miles, turn onto the B841 for 4 miles then onto the B8025 for 5 miles.
Acreage 2 **Open** April **to** October
Access Good **Site** Level
Sites Available **Total** 15
Facilities
Nearby Facilities
Beside a sea loch, ideal for all water activities including sailing, diving and canoeing.

AYRSHIRE (EAST)

HOLLYBUSH

Skeldon Caravan Park, Hollybush, By Ayr, East Ayrshire, KA6 7EB.
Std: 01292 **Tel:** 560502
Nearest Town/Resort Ayr.
Directions From A77 (Ayr Bypass) turn onto A713 (direction of Castle Douglas) after 4 miles turn right after passing the Hollybush Inn and follow sign for caravan park (¼ mile). From castle Douglas on the A713, turn left at Hollybush sign, 4 miles from Ayr.
Acreage 3 **Open** April **to** September
Access Good **Site** Level
Sites Available **Total** 30
Facilities
Nearby Facilities
Ayr.
Sheltered southern aspect on Bank of River Doon.

PATNA

Carskeoch House Caravan Park, Patna, East Ayrshire, KA6 7NR.
Std: 01292 **Tel:** 531205
Nearest Town/Resort Ayr
Acreage 13 **Open** March **to** October
Access Good
Sites Available **Total** 30
Facilities
Nearby Facilities
Ayr
Hill walking and fishing.

AYRSHIRE (NORTH)

IRVINE

Cunningham Head Estate Caravan Park, Cunningham Head, Nr. Kilmarnock, North Ayrshire.
Std: 01294 **Tel:** 850238
Nearest Town/Resort Irvine.
Directions From Irvine take A736 Glasgow road at Stanecastle roundabout turn east onto B769 Stewarton road. Park is 2 miles on left.
Acreage 20 **Open** April **to** September
Access Good **Site** Level
Sites Available **Total** 90
Facilities
Nearby Facilities
On grounds of mansion house (now gone). Ideal for touring Burns Country and Clyde coast resorts. Near Magnum Leisure Centre.

IRVINE

Tynepark Leisure, Torranyard, Kilwinning, North Ayrshire, KA13 7RD.
Std: 01294 **Tel:** 850286
Std: 01294 **Fax:** 850486
Nearest Town/Resort Irvine
Directions 5 miles north east of Irvine on the A736 (Glasgow road), at Torranyard crossroads, behind tandoori restaurant.
Acreage 19 **Open** April **to** October
Access Good **Site** Level
Sites Available **Total** 350
Facilities
Nearby Facilities
Irvine
Ideal location for exploring the south west coast of Scotland. 49 golf courses. Robert Burns.

ISLE OF ARRAN

Kildonan Hotel Camping & Touring Site, Kildonan, Isle of Arran, North Ayrshire, KA27 8SE.
Std: 01770 **Tel:** 820320
Std: 01770 **Fax:** 820320
Nearest Town/Resort Brodick
Directions From Brodick take the A841 south for 12 miles. Located on the southern most point of Arran.
Acreage 2¾ **Open** March **to** October
Access Good **Site** Lev/Slope
Sites Available **Total** 20
Facilities
Nearby Facilities
Ardrossan
✓✓✓Graded Park. Situated in hotel grounds, alongside our own private beach for sea swimming. Overlooking Pladda and Ailsa Craig Islands. Colony of seals in front of the site, fantastic wildlife and uninterupted views. Disabled pitches available.

SKELMORLIE

Skelmorlie Mains Caravan & Camping Site, Skelmorlie Mains, Skelmorlie, North Ayrshire.
Std: 01475 **Tel:** 520794
Std: 01475 **Fax:** 520794
Nearest Town/Resort Largs.
Directions ½ mile from A78 south of Skelmorlie.
Acreage 4 **Open** April **to** October
Access Good **Site** Sloping
Sites Available **Total** 100
Facilities
Nearby Facilities
Wemyss Bay.
✓✓✓Graded Park. Scenic view of Cumbrae, Arran, Bute Islands and Firth of Clyde.

AYRSHIRE (SOUTH)

AYR

Middlemuir Park, Tarbolton, Nr. Ayr, South Ayrshire, KA5 5NR.
Std: 01292 **Tel:** 541647
Std: 01292 **Fax:** 541649
Nearest Town/Resort Ayr
Directions From Ayr take the B743 signposted Mauchline, after approx. 5 miles take the third turning for Tarbolton.
Acreage 2 **Open** March **to** October
Access Good **Site** Level
Sites Available **Total** 30
Facilities
Nearby Facilities
✓✓✓✓Graded Park.

AYR

Sundrum Castle Holiday Park, Coylton, By Ayr, South Ayrshire, KA6 5JH.
Std: 01292 **Tel:** 570057
Std: 01292 **Fax:** 570065
Nearest Town/Resort Ayr
Directions From Ayr on the A70 to the village of Coylton, park is on the left hand side just before Coylton.
Acreage 30 **Open** March **to** October
Access Good **Site** Level
Sites Available **Total** 52
Facilities
Nearby Facilities
Ayr
✓✓✓✓Graded Park. Beautiful Ayrshire coast, famous golf courses nearby. Race meetings. Coach outings to the Isle of Arran, Edinburgh and Northern Ireland. Abundance of local tourist attractions.

BALLANTRAE

Laggan House Leisure Park, Ballantrae, Nr. Girvan, South Ayrshire, KA26 0LL.
Std: 01465 **Tel:** 831229
Std: 01465 **Fax:** 831511
Nearest Town/Resort Girvan.
Directions Going south on the A77, after leaving Ballantrae, cross over bridge and take the first left, follow signs.
Acreage 6 **Open** Early March **to** October
Access Good **Site** Level
Sites Available **Total** 15
Facilities

Nearby Facilities
Girvan
✓✓✓✓Graded Park. Walking, touring, bird watching, fishing and swimming. Sauna and solarium.

BARRHILL

Queensland Holiday Park, Barrhill, Girvan, South Ayrshire, KA26 0PZ.
Std: 01465 **Tel:** 821364
Std: 01465 **Fax:** 821364
Nearest Town/Resort Girvan
Directions 11 miles south east of Girvan on the A714.
Acreage 1 **Open** March **to** October
Access Good **Site** Level
Sites Available **Total** 15
Facilities
Nearby Facilities
Barrhill
✓✓✓✓Graded Park. Ideal location for walking and cycling in Galloway Forest, or for touring South Scotland. Good local rivers.

GIRVAN

Bennane Shore Holiday Park, Lendalfoot, Girvan, South Ayrshire, KA26 0JG.
Std: 01465 **Tel:** 891233
Std: 01465 **Fax:** 891233
Nearest Town/Resort Girvan.
Directions 8 miles south of Girvan on the A77 Stranraer to Glasgow trunk road.
Acreage 7 **Open** March **to** October
Access Good **Site** Level
Sites Available **Total** 25
Facilities
Nearby Facilities
Girvan
✓✓✓✓Graded Park. Beach front, scenic views. Private slipway for the boating enthusiasts. Ideal touring.

GIRVAN

Carleton Caravan Park, Carleton Lodge, Lendalfoot, Girvan, South Ayrshire, KA26 0JF.
Std: 01465 **Tel:** 891215
Nearest Town/Resort Girvan.
Directions Off A77 Girvan/Stranraer road at Lendalfoot village. 800 yards on unclassified road.
Acreage 9 **Open** March **to** October
Access Good **Site** Terraced
Sites Available **Total** 10
Facilities
Nearby Facilities
Girvan.
Small quiet site, near sea, ideal touring area.

GIRVAN

Windsor Holiday Park, Barrhill, Nr. Girvan, South Ayrshire, KA26 0PZ.
Std: 01465 **Tel:** 821355
Std: 01465 **Fax:** 821355
Nearest Town/Resort Girvan.
Directions A714 Newton Stewart 17 miles, Girvan 11 miles.
Acreage 6 **Open** March **to** October
Access Good **Site** Level
Sites Available **Total** 30
Facilities
Nearby Facilities
Barrhill.
✓✓✓Graded Park. Ideal touring. Cycle hire available.

MAIDENS

Arlochan Hotel & Caravan Park, Maidens, Culzean, South Ayrshire, KA19 8LA.
Std: 01655 **Tel:** 760254
Nearest Town/Resort Girvan
Open March **to** September
Access Good **Site** Level
Sites Available **Total** 4
Facilities
Nearby Facilities
Girvan
Situated off the beach. Within walking distance of Culzean Castle and Turnberry Golf Course.

MAYBOLE

Camping & Caravanning Club Site, Glenside, Culzean Castle, Maybole, South Ayrshire, KA19 8JK.
Std: 01655 **Tel:** 760627
Directions From North on the A77 turn right in Maybole onto the B7023 signposted Culzean and Maidens. After 100 yards turn left, site is on the right in 4 miles. From South on the A77 turn left onto the A719 signposted Turnbury and Maidens, site is on the left in 4 miles.
Open 22 March **to** 1 Nov
Site Lev/Slope
Sites Available **Total** 90
Facilities
Nearby Facilities
✓✓✓✓Graded Park. In the grounds of Culzean Castle on the west coast of Scotland.

TROON

St. Meddans Caravan Site, Low St. Meddans, Troon, South Ayrshire, KA10 6NS.
Std: 01292 **Tel:** 312957
Nearest Town/Resort Troon
Directions On the A759 off number 2 Dundonald Road.
Acreage 1½ **Open** March **to** October
Access Good **Site** Level
Sites Available **Total** 27
Facilities
Nearby Facilities
Troon
Beaches, golf courses, town centre and swimming pool all within a 5 minute walk.

CLACKMANNANSHIRE

DOLLAR

Riverside Caravan Park, Dollarfield, Dollar, Clackmannan, FK14 7LX.
Std: 01259 **Tel:** 742896
Directions From Dollar take the B913 (signposted Dunfermline). Park is ½ mile south.
Acreage 5 **Open** April **to** September
Access Good **Site** Level
Sites Available **Total** 30
Facilities
Nearby Facilities
Stirling.
Near the attractive village of Dollar with wooded glen and Castle Campbell.

DUMFRIES & GALLOWAY

ANNAN

Galabank Caravan & Camping Site, North Street, Annan, Dumfries & Galloway, DG1 2SB.
Std: 01556 **Tel:** 502521 Office Only
Nearest Town/Resort Annan.
Open May **to** Early Sept
Access Good **Site** Level
Sites Available **Total** 30
Facilities
Nearby Facilities
Annan.
✓✓Graded Park. Alongside a river with river walks. Putting in the adjacent park. Swimming pool nearby. Ideal touring. Dogs are welcome if kept on leads.

ANNAN

Queensberry Bay Caravan Park, Powfoot, Annan, Dumfries & Galloway, DG12 5PU.
Std: 01461 **Tel:** 700205
Nearest Town/Resort Annan
Directions 3 miles from Annan on the B724, take an unclassified road to Powfoot for 2 miles.
Acreage 5 **Open** April **to** October
Access Good **Site** Level
Sites Available **Total** 75
Facilities
Nearby Facilities
Annan
Near the beach. Ideal touring centre.

AUCHENMALG

Cock Inn Caravan Park, Auchenmalg, Nr. Glenluce, Newton Stewart, Dumfries & Galloway, DG8 0JT.
Std: 01581 **Tel:** 500227
Nearest Town/Resort Stranraer.
Acreage 6½ **Open** March **to** October
Access Good **Site** Lev/Slope
Sites Available **Total** 70
Facilities
Nearby Facilities
Stranraer.
✓✓✓✓Graded Park. Near beach.

BEATTOCK

Craigielands Country Park, Beattock, Nr Moffat, Dumfries & Galloway, DG10 9RB.
Std: 01683 **Tel:** 300591/300650
Std: 01683 **Fax:** 300425
Nearest Town/Resort Moffat
Directions 13 miles north of Lockerbie left from the M6 signed Beattock/Moffat. Situated at the south end of Beattock Village.
Acreage 56 **Open** All Year
Access Good **Site** Lev/Slope
Sites Available **Total** 125
Facilities
Nearby Facilities
Lockerbie
Own loch for fishing and boating.

BORGUE

Brighouse Bay Holiday Park, Borgue, Kirkcudbright, Dumfries & Galloway, DG6 4TS.
Std: 01557 **Tel:** 870267
Std: 01557 **Fax:** 870319
Nearest Town/Resort Kirkcudbright.
Directions From Kirkcudbright take the A755 signposted Gatehouse of Fleet, west over river. On outskirts of town take B727 signposted Borgue. After 4 miles turn left at Brighouse Bay sign. Park is on the left, behind trees, in 2 miles.
Acreage 25 **Open** All Year
Access Good **Site** Lev/Slope
Sites Available **Total** 180
Facilities
Nearby Facilities
Dumfries.
✓✓✓✓✓Graded Park. Beautifully situated on a quiet peninsula with its own sandy beach and working farm, family park with exceptional on-site recreational facilities including an indoor pool complex, members lounge, spa facilities, fitness room, quad and mountain bikes, pony trekking centre, 18 hole golf course, fishing, boating and slipway.

CAIRNRYAN

Cairnryan Caravan Park, Cairnryan, Stranraer, Dumfries & Galloway, DG9 8QX.
Std: 01581 **Tel:** 200231
Std: 01581 **Fax:** 200207

Nearest Town/Resort Stranraer
Directions 5 miles north of Stranraer on the A77. Directly opposite the P&O Ferry terminal.
Acreage 7½ **Open** March **to** October
Access Good **Site** Lev/Slope
Sites Available **Total** 15
Facilities
Nearby Facilities
Stranraer
✓✓✓✓Graded Park. Overlooking the sea.

CASTLE DOUGLAS

Lochside Caravan & Camping Site, Lochside Park, Castle Douglas, Dumfries & Galloway.
Std: 01556 **Tel:** 502949
Nearest Town/Resort Castle Douglas.
Directions Well signposted in town centre of Castle Douglas.
Acreage 6 **Open** Easter **to** October
Access Good **Site** Level
Sites Available **Total** 161
Facilities
Nearby Facilities
Dumfries.
✓✓✓Graded Park. Beside Loch, ideal touring. Nearby squash courts, putting, swimming pool and bowling green. Dogs are welcome if kept on leads.

CREETOWN

Castle Cary Holiday Park, Creetown, Newton Stewart, Dumfries & Galloway, DG8 7DQ.
Std: 01671 **Tel:** 820264
Std: 01671 **Fax:** 820670
Nearest Town/Resort Creetown
Directions Approaching from the south on the A75 Euro-route, ¼ mile before Creetown Village, entrance to the park is on the right hand side.
Acreage 6 **Open** All Year
Access Good **Site** Level
Sites Available **Total** 80
Facilities
Nearby Facilities
Barrhill
✓✓✓✓✓Graded Park. Superb parkland setting close to beaches, river and mountains. Ideal touring and camping park. Fully stocked coarse fishing loch. Mountain bike hire and crazy golf. AA Scottish "Campsite of the Year" 1996.

CREETOWN

Creetown Caravan Park, Silver Street, Creetown, Dumfries & Galloway, DG8 7HU.
Std: 01671 **Tel:** 820377
Std: 01671 **Fax:** 820377
Nearest Town/Resort Newton Stewart
Directions 45 miles west of Dumfries. 6 miles east of Newton Stewart. Follow the A75 to Creetown, turn down between Ellangowan Hotel and Clock Tower.
Acreage 3½ **Open** March **to** October
Access Good **Site** Level
Sites Available **Total** 70
Facilities
Nearby Facilities
Barrhill
✓✓✓✓✓Graded Park. Alongside a river, within the village of Creetown.

CREETOWN

Ferry Croft Caravan Site, Creetown, Dumfries & Galloway, DG8 7JS.
Std: 01671 **Tel:** 820502
Nearest Town/Resort Newton Stewart
Directions 6 miles from Newton Stewart on the A75, turn off for Creetown. When reaching the clock tower turn up the hill following the signs for Ferry Croft Caravan Site.
Acreage ½ **Open** Easter **to** End Sept
Access Good **Site** Level
Sites Available **Total** 8
Facilities
Nearby Facilities
Stranraer
Small, quiet, attractive site at the edge of the village of Creetown. Close to the coast and hills, within easy reach of good beaches, golf, fishing and forest walks. Ideal touring.

CROCKETFORD

Park of Brandedleys, Crocketford, Dumfries & Galloway, DG2 8RG.
Std: 01556 **Tel:** 690250
Std: 01556 **Fax:** 690681
Nearest Town/Resort Dumfries.
Directions Turn left off A75 Dumfries/Castle Douglas road on edge of Crocketford village onto unclassified road. Site on right 150 yards.
Acreage 20 **Open** March **to** October
Access Good **Site** Lev/Slope
Sites Available **Total** 80
Facilities
Nearby Facilities
Dumfries.
✓✓✓✓✓Graded Park. Ideal touring centre, set in beautiful countryside overlooking loch and hills. Sauna. Caravans for sale. Caravans, chalet, log cabins and cottage for hire. Calor Award "Best Park in Scotland 1995"

DALBEATTIE

Islecroft Caravan & Camping Site, Mill Street, Dalbeattie, Dumfries & Galloway.
Std: 01556 **Tel:** 610012

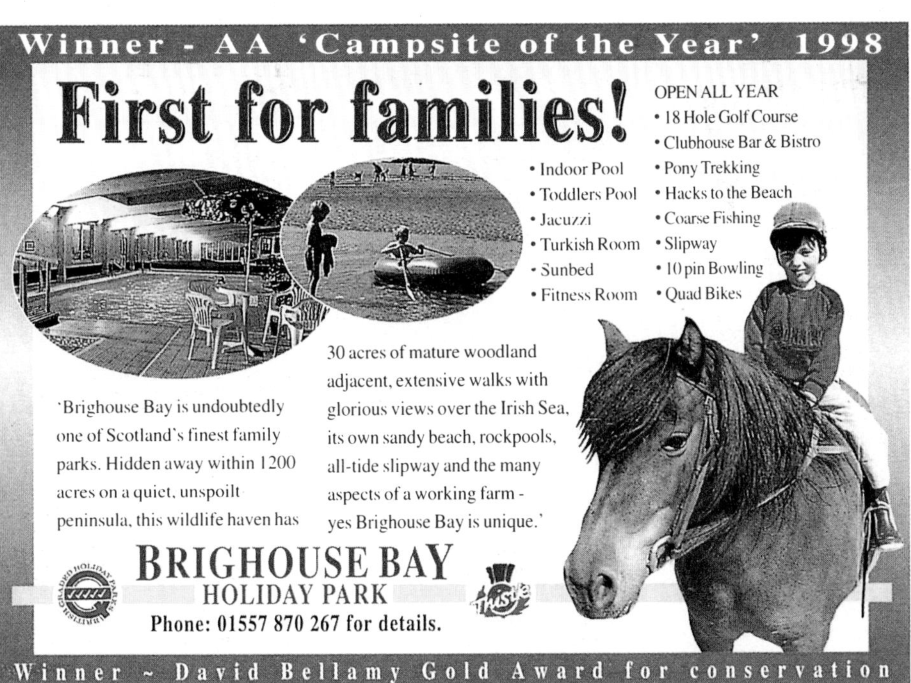

Nearest Town/Resort Dalbeattie
Directions Adjacent to Colliston Park, off Mill Street in the centre of Dalbeattie.
Acreage 3¼ **Open** Easter **to** September
Access Good **Site** Level
Sites Available **Total** 74
Facilities
Nearby Facilities
Dumfries.
✓✓✓Graded Park. Ideal position for touring inland and coastal areas of the region. Dogs are welcome if kept on leads.

DALBEATTIE

Kippford Caravan Park, Kippford, Dalbeattie, Dumfries & Galloway, DG5 4LF.
Std: 01556 **Tel:** 620636
Std: 01556 **Fax:** 620636
Directions From Dumfries take the A711 to Dalbeattie, then turn left onto the A710 signposted Solway Coast. The park entrance is on the main road in 3½ miles, 200yds after the branch road to Kippford.
Acreage 18
Access Good **Site** Sloping
Sites Available **Total** 184
Facilities
Nearby Facilities
Dumfries
✓✓✓✓✓Graded Park. Junior childrens play area and adventure playground. Swimming nearby.

DALBEATTIE

Sandyhills Bay Leisure Park, Sandyhills, Dalbeattie, Dumfries & Galloway, DG5 4NY.
Std: 01387 **Tel:** 780257
Nearest Town/Resort Dalbeattie.
Directions On A710 coast road from Dumfries to Dalbeattie, next Sandyhills Village and Colvend Golf Course.
Acreage 6 **Open** 1st April **to** 31st October
Access Good **Site** Level
Sites Available **Total** 60
Facilities
Nearby Facilities
Dumfries.
✓✓✓✓✓Graded Park. A unique park only yards from a fabulous sandy beach with golf, riding, fishing and eating out within ¼ mile. Magnificent coastal walks. Take-away food. Thistle Commended holiday caravans.

DUMFRIES

Barnsoul Farm, Irongray, Dumfries, Dumfries & Galloway, DG2 9SQ.
Std: 01387 **Tel:** 730249
Std: 01387 **Fax:** 730249
Nearest Town/Resort Dumfries
Directions Leave Dumfries on the A75, travel 6 miles in the direction of Stranraer. Turn right at the sign for "Shawhead" and "Barnsoul Farm 2½ Miles". Go into Shawhead Village turn right then left following signs for Barnsoul.
Acreage 200 **Open** April **to** October
Access Good **Site** Lev/Slope
Sites Available **Total** 20
Facilities
Nearby Facilities
Dumfries
✓✓✓Graded Park. Very scenic inland site, woods and fields. Hire caravans and chalets. AA 2 Pennants.

DUMFRIES

Beeswing Caravan Park, Kirkgunzeon, By Dumfries, Dumfries & Galloway, DG2 8JL.
Std: 01387 **Tel:** 760242
Std: 01387 **Fax:** 760242
Nearest Town/Resort Dumfries
Directions Take the A711 from Dumfries towards Dalbeattie, ¾ miles after the village of Beeswing turn right and follow the lane to the park entrance.
Acreage 6½ **Open** March **to** October
Access Good **Site** Lev/Slope
Sites Available **Total** 25
Facilities
Nearby Facilities
Dumfries
✓✓✓Graded Park. Quiet, country site with an abundance of wildlife. Excellent for touring.

DUMFRIES

Mouswald Place Caravan Site, Mouswald Place, Mouswald, Dumfries, Dumfries & Galloway, DG1 4JS.
Std: 01387 **Tel:** 830226
Std: 01387 **Fax:** 830226
Nearest Town/Resort Dumfries
Directions From Dumfries take the A75 for 2½ miles. Take the right fork to Mouswald and Caravan Park, ¾ mile on the right.
Acreage 5½ **Open** March **to** October
Site Lev/Slope
Sites Available **Total** 30
Facilities
Nearby Facilities
Dumfries
Small, quiet, woodland park.

ECCLEFECHAN

Cressfield Caravan Park, Ecclefechan, Nr Lockerbie, Dumfries & Galloway, DG11 3DR.
Std: 01576 **Tel:** 300702
Std: 01576 **Fax:** 300702
Nearest Town/Resort Lockerbie.
Directions Leave A74(M) at Ecclefechan -

junction 19 (5 miles south of Lockerbie, 8 miles north of Gretna). Follow the B7076 for ½ mile to south side of village.
Acreage 15 **Open** All Year
Access Good **Site** Level
Sites Available **Total** 115
Facilities
Nearby Facilities
Lockerbie.
✓✓✓✓Graded Park. Peaceful country park with excellent facilities, just north of the border. Ideal touring base or night halt.

ECCLEFECHAN

Hoddom Castle Caravan Park, Hoddom, Lockerbie, Dumfries & Galloway, DG11 1AS.
Std: 01576 **Tel:** 300251
Nearest Town/Resort Lockerbie.
Directions Exit A74/M74 at Ecclefechan (junction 19). At church in village turn west on the B725 (Dalton). 2½ miles to entrance at Hoddom Bridge.
Acreage 24 **Open** April **to** October
Access Good **Site** Lev/Slope
Sites Available **Total** 180
Facilities
Nearby Facilities
✓✓✓✓Graded Park. Quiet site in parkland of a castle. Nature trails and woodland walks on land adjoining park. 9 hole golf course on site.

GATEHOUSE OF FLEET

Mossyard Caravan Park, Mossyard, Gatehouse of Fleet, Castle Douglas, Dumfries & Galloway, DG7 2ET.
Std: 01557 **Tel:** 840226
Std: 01557 **Fax:** 840226
Nearest Town/Resort Gatehouse of Fleet.
Directions 4 miles west of Gatehouse of Fleet on the A75. Turn left at signpost to the caravan park.
Acreage 6¼ **Open** April **to** October
Access Good **Site** Lev/Slope
Sites Available **Total** 55
Facilities
Nearby Facilities
Dumfries.
✓✓✓✓Graded Park. Sandy beaches within 200yds.

GATEHOUSE OF FLEET

Sandgreen Caravan Park, Sandgreen, Gatehouse of Fleet, Dumfries & Galloway, DG7.
Std: 01557 **Tel:** 814351
Std: 01557 **Fax:** 814351
Nearest Town/Resort Gatehouse of Fleet
Directions From Dumfries take the A75 west, leave at Gatehouse turning left for Sandgreen (3 miles off the A75).
Acreage 44 **Open** March **to** October
Access Good **Site** Lev/Slope
Sites Available **Total** 25
Facilities
Nearby Facilities
Dumfries
✓✓✓Graded Park. Quiet, unspoilt, natural site next to a sandy beach. Ideal for swimming and watersports. Hillwalking nearby.

GLENLUCE

Glenluce Caravan Park, Glenluce Village, Dumfries & Galloway, DG8 0QR.
Std: 01581 **Tel:** 300412
Nearest Town/Resort Stranraer.
Directions 10 miles east of Stranraer on A75 Dumfries/Stranraer road. Entrance to park at telephone kiosk in centre of village opposite the Inglenook Restaurant.
Acreage 5 **Open** Mid March **to** Mid Oct
Access Good **Site** Lev/Slope
Sites Available **Total** 40
Facilities
Nearby Facilities
Stranraer.
✓✓✓✓Graded Park. Secluded sun trap park in the private grounds of a former estate mansion house. Family operated, close to village. Near to the beach and golf, with bowling, pony trekking, fishing and superb walks all within 1 mile.

GLENLUCE

Whitecairn Farm Caravan Park, Glenluce, Newton Stewart, Dumfries & Galloway, DG8 0NZ.
Std: 01581 **Tel:** 300267
Std: 01581 **Fax:** 300267
Nearest Town/Resort Stranraer.
Directions 1½ miles north of Glenluce village.
Acreage 4 **Open** March **to** Oct
Access Good **Site** Level
Sites Available **Total** 30
Facilities
Nearby Facilities
Stranraer.
✓✓✓✓Graded Park. Central location for touring Wigtownshire. Very peacful park, away from the main road. 2 miles from A75.

GRETNA

The Braids Caravan Park, Annan Road, Gretna, Dumfries & Galloway, DG16 5DQ.
Std: 01461 **Tel:** 337409
Std: 01461 **Fax:** 337409
Directions From the M6 run straight onto the A74. Take the A75 signposted Dumfries/Stranraer. In 1 mile take the second left for Gretna (B721), park is 600yds on the left.
Acreage 5 **Open** All Year
Access Good **Site** Lev/Slope
Sites Available **Total** 84
Facilities
Nearby Facilities
Gretna
✓✓✓✓Graded Park. Ideal touring centre, advice given. Fishing can be arranged. Good area for bird watching. On board tank waste disposal point. Small rallies welcome, rally building available.

ISLE OF WHITHORN

Burrowhead Holiday Village, Isle of Whithorn, Newton Stewart, Dumfries & Galloway, DG8 8JB.
Std: 01988 **Tel:** 500252
Std: 01988 **Fax:** 500855
Nearest Town/Resort Newton Stewart
Directions Take the A75 to Newton Stewart, turn south on the A714 through Wigtown onto the A746 and the B7004 to the Isle of Whithorn. Burrowhead is signposted on the right.
Acreage 100 **Open** April **to** October
Access Good **Site** Lev/Slope
Sites Available **Total** 200
Facilities
Nearby Facilities
✓✓✓Graded Park. Well run park with facilities for the whole family. Scenic views over sea to the Isle of Man. 100 acres of land. Phone for a free brochure.

ISLE OF WHITHORN

Castlewigg Caravan Park, Whithorn, Newton Stewart, Dumfries & Galloway, DG8 8DP.
Std: 01988 **Tel:** 500616
Std: 01988 **Fax:** 500616
Nearest Town/Resort Newton Stewart.
Directions From roundabout at Newton Stewart turn onto the A714 to Wigtown. Just before Wigtown take the A746 to Whithorn. 3 miles after Sorbie site on the right.
Acreage 4¼ **Open** March **to** October
Access Good **Site** Level
Sites Available **Total** 15
Facilities
Nearby Facilities
Stranraer
Scenic views, central location. Award winning gardens.

KIRKCOWAN

Three Lochs Holiday Park, Balminoch, Kirkcowan, Newton Stewart, Dumfries & Galloway, DG8 0EP.

Std: 01671 **Tel:** 830304
Std: 01671 **Fax:** 830335
Nearest Town/Resort Newton Stewart.
Acreage 15 **Open** Easter **to** October
Access Good **Site** Level
Sites Available **Total** 80
Facilities
Nearby Facilities
✓✓✓✓Graded Park. Three Lochs for coarse or trout fishing and sailing. Full size snooker.

KIRKCUDBRIGHT

Seaward Caravan Park, Dhoon Bay, Kirkcudbright, Dumfries & Galloway.
Std: 01557 **Tel:** 331079
Nearest Town/Resort Kirkcudbright.
Directions Take A755 signposted Gatehouse of Fleet, west from Kirkcudbright. On outskirts turn left onto the B727 signposted Borgue. Park is on the right in 2 miles.
Acreage 6¼ **Open** 1st March **to** 31st Oct
Access Good **Site** Level
Sites Available **Total** 50
Facilities
Nearby Facilities
Dumfries.
✓✓✓✓✓Graded Park. An exclusive park beautifully situated with exceptional views over Kirkcudbright Bay. Many on-site amenities plus all the activities at nearby Brighouse Bay. NEW indoor complex. 9 hole golf course. Sea adjacent for angling and sandy beach ¼ mile away. Thistle Commended caravans for hire. For Bookings please telephone 01557 870267.

KIRKCUDBRIGHT

Silvercraigs Caravan Site, Silvercraigs Road, Kirkcudbright, Dumfries & Galloway.
Std: 01557 **Tel:** 330123
Nearest Town/Resort Kirkcudbright.
Directions Turn left from St. Mary's Street to St. Mary's Place, follow Barrhill Road and Silvercraigs Road, site on left.
Acreage 5¼ **Open** Easter **to** October
Access Good **Site** Sloping
Sites Available **Total** 50
Facilities
Nearby Facilities
Dumfries.
✓✓✓Graded Park. Ideal touring, near sea. Laundry facilities available. Wildlife Park nearby. Pets welcome if kept on leads.

KIRKPATRICK FLEMING

"King Robert the Bruce's Cave" Caravan & Camping Site, Cove Lodge, Kirkpatrick Fleming, By Lockerbie, Dumfries & Galloway, DG11 3AT.
Std: 01461 **Tel:** 800285
Nearest Town/Resort Gretna
Directions Turn off A74 M74 at Kirkpatrick Fleming, then in Kirkpatrick follow all signs to Bruces Cave.
Acreage 80 **Open** All Year
Access Good **Site** Level
Sites Available **Total** 40
Facilities
Nearby Facilities
Annan
In grounds of 80 acre estate, peacefull and quiet and secluded, famous ancient monument of King Robert the Bruce's cave in grounds of site, free fishing on 3 mile stretch of river for Trout, Sea Trout, Salmon. New disabled toilet block and laundry room.

LANGHOLM

Whitshiels Caravan Park, Langholm, Dumfries & Galloway, DG13 0HG.
Std: 013873 **Tel:** 80494
Nearest Town/Resort Langholm
Directions 300 yards north of Langholm on the A7.
Acreage ½ **Open** All Year
Access Good **Site** Lev/Slope
Sites Available **Total** 8
Facilities
Nearby Facilities
Carlisle
✓✓✓Graded Park. Border regions, the Lake District, Tibeten Monastery and fishing.

LOCHMABEN

Kirkloch Caravan & Camping Site, Kirkloch Brae, Lochmaben, Dumfries & Galloway.
Std: 01556 **Tel:** 502521 Office Only
Nearest Town/Resort Lochmaben
Acreage 1½ **Open** Easter **to** October
Access Good **Site** Level
Sites Available **Total** 30
Facilities
Nearby Facilities
Dumfries
✓✓✓Graded Park. Beside a loch and adjacent to a golf course. Ideal touring. Dogs are welcome if kept on leads.

LOCHNAW

Drumlochart Caravan Park, Lochnaw, Leswalt, By Stranraer, Dumfries & Galloway, DG9 0RN.
Std: 01776 **Tel:** 870232
Std: 01776 **Fax:** 870276
Nearest Town/Resort Stranraer
Acreage 22 **Open** March **to** October
Access Good **Site** Level
Sites Available **Total** 30
Facilities
Nearby Facilities
Stranraer
✓✓✓✓✓Graded Park. Woodland setting with a 10 acre loch for rowing boats and fishing.

LOCKERBIE

Halleaths Caravan Park, Halleaths, Lochmaben, Lockerbie, Dumfries & Galloway, DG11 1NA.
Std: 01387 **Tel:** 810630
Std: 01387 **Fax:** 810630
Nearest Town/Resort Lochmaben/ Lockerbie.
Directions From Lockerbie on M74, take A709 to Lochmaben. ½ mile on the right after crossing the River Annan.
Acreage 8 **Open** March **to** November
Access Good **Site** Level
Sites Available **Total** 70
Facilities
Nearby Facilities
Lockerbie.
✓✓✓✓Graded Park. Bowling, tennis, yachting, boating, golf and both coarse and game fishing, all within 1 mile of park.

MOFFAT

Camping & Caravanning Club Site, Hammerlands Farm, Moffat, Dumfries & Galloway, DG10 9QL.
Std: 01683 **Tel:** 220436
Nearest Town/Resort Moffat
Directions Take the Moffat sign off the A74, in 1 mile turn right by the Bank of Scotland, right again in 200 yards, signposted on the right, follow road round to the site.
Acreage 14 **Open** 22 March **to** 1 Nov
Access Good **Site** Level
Sites Available **Total** 200
Facilities
Nearby Facilities
Lockerbie
✓✓✓✓Graded Park. Very flat site for camping. Perfect stopover or base for touring Scotland. Walks from the site. Good for fishing and golf.

MONREITH

Knock School Caravan Park, Monreith, Newton Stewart, Dumfries & Galloway.
Std: 01988 **Tel:** 700414/700409
Nearest Town/Resort Port William.
Directions 3 miles south on A747 at crossroads to golf course.
Acreage 1 **Open** Easter **to** October
Access Good **Site** Lev/Slope
Sites Available **Total** 15
Facilities
Nearby Facilities
Near sandy beaches and golf.

MONREITH

Monreith Sands Holiday Park, Newton Stewart, Dumfries & Galloway, DG8 9LJ.
Std: 01998 **Tel:** 700218
Nearest Town/Resort Port William.
Directions 2 miles south of Port William.
Acreage 2
Access Good **Site** Lev/Slope
Sites Available **Total** 20
Facilities
Nearby Facilities
Stranraer.
Beach 200 yards, quiet site. Golf 1 mile.

NEWTON STEWART

Caldons Campsite - Forestry Commission, Glentrool, Newton Stewart, Dumfries & Galloway, DG8 6SU.
Std: 01671 **Tel:** 840218
Nearest Town/Resort Newton Stewart
Directions Take the A714 from Newton Stewart to Bargrennan and follow signs.
Acreage 47 **Open** 24 March **to** 30 Sept
Access Good **Site** Level
Sites Available **Total** 160
Facilities
Nearby Facilities
✓✓✓Graded Park. Situated in beautiful Glen

Trool, in the heart of Galloway Forest Park. The Southern Upland Way passes the site.

NEWTON STEWART

Creebridge Caravan Park, Newton Stewart, Dumfries & Galloway, DG8 6AJ.
Std: 01671 **Tel:** 402324
Std: 01671 **Fax:** 402324
Nearest Town/Resort Newton Stewart.
Directions From east, 1 mile east of Newton Stewart turn right then left immediately, park is ½ mile on the left.
Acreage 4 **Open** March **to** October
Access Good **Site** Level
Sites Available **Total** 40
Facilities
Nearby Facilities
Barrhill.
✓✓✓✓Graded Park. On the edge of a market town. Hill walking, forest, fishing, bowls and golf.

NEWTON STEWART

Glen Trool Holiday Park, Glentrool, Nr. Newton Stewart, Dumfries & Galloway, DG8 6RN.
Std: 01671 **Tel:** 840280
Nearest Town/Resort Glentrool.
Directions Situated off the A714, 9 miles north of Newton Stewart, ½ mile south of Glentrool Village.
Acreage 3 **Open** March **to** October
Access Good **Site** Level
Sites Available **Total** 14
Facilities
Nearby Facilities
Barhill
✓✓✓✓✓Graded Park. On edge of forest, ideal touring.

NEWTON STEWART

Talnotry Campsite - Forestry Commission, Queens Way, Newton Stewart, Dumfries & Galloway, DG8 7BL.
Std: 01671 **Tel:** 402420
Nearest Town/Resort Newton Stewart
Directions Take the A712 (Queens Way) from Newton Stewart for 7 miles. We are on the right.
Acreage 22¼ **Open** April **to** September
Access Good **Site** Level
Sites Available **Total** 60
Facilities
Nearby Facilities
Barrhill
Scenic views.

PARTON

Loch Ken Holiday Park, Parton, Castle Douglas, Dumfries & Galloway, DG7 3NE.
Std: 01644 **Tel:** 470282
Std: 01644 **Fax:** 470297
Nearest Town/Resort Castle Douglas
Directions 7 miles north of Castle Douglas on the A713, easy access.
Acreage 7 **Open** March **to** October
Access Good **Site** Level
Sites Available **Total** 85
Facilities
Nearby Facilities
Dumfries
✓✓✓✓✓Graded Park. Terraced site on a lochside with sandy beaches and easy access to the water for coarse fishing, boating, sailing and swimming.

PORTPATRICK

Castle Bay Caravan Park, Portpatrick, Dumfries & Galloway, DG9 9AA.
Std: 01776 **Tel:** 810462
Std: 01776 **Fax:** 810462
Nearest Town/Resort Stranraer
Directions Entering Portpatrick, pass the war memorial and turn first left opposite the Old Mill Restaurant. Continue for ¾ mile, go under the old railway bridge, site entrance is 50 yards ahead.
Acreage 12 **Open** March **to** October
Access Good **Site** Lev/Slope
Sites Available **Total** 30
Facilities
Nearby Facilities
Stranraer
✓✓✓✓Graded Park. Sea views. Amusements, pool table and video games on site.

PORTPATRICK

Galloway Point Holiday Park, Portree Farm, Portpatrick, Stranraer, Dumfries & Galloway, DG9 9AA.
Std: 01776 **Tel:** 810561
Std: 01776 **Fax:** 810561
Nearest Town/Resort Portpatrick.
Directions A75 from Dumfries. A77 from Glasgow and Stranraer. ½ mile south of Portpatrick.
Acreage 17 **Open** Easter **to** Mid October
Access Good **Site** Lev/Slope
Sites Available **Total** 100
Facilities
Nearby Facilities
Stranraer.
✓✓✓✓Graded Park. Overlooking Irish Sea. Only ten minutes walk to fishing village of Portpatrick. Botanical gardens nearby. AA 3 Pennants and Environment Award, RAC Appointed, Thistle Award.

PORTPATRICK

Sunnymeade Caravan Park, Portpatrick, Nr. Stranraer, Dumfries & Galloway, DG9 8LN.
Std: 01776 **Tel:** 810293
Std: 01776 **Fax:** 810293
Nearest Town/Resort Portpatrick
Directions A77 to Portpatrick. First left on entering village, park is ¼ mile on the left.
Open Easter **to** October
Access Good **Site** Lev/Slope
Sites Available
Facilities
Nearby Facilities
Stranraer
✓✓✓✓Graded Park. Overlooking Irish Sea, near golf, beach, bowling, fishing etc. Private fishing pond on the park.

PORTWILLIAM

West Barr Caravan Park, West Barr, Portwilliam, Newton Stewart, Dumfries & Galloway, DG8 9QS.
Std: 01988 **Tel:** 700367
Nearest Town/Resort Portwilliam
Directions 1½ miles north of Portwilliam on the A747.
Open April **to** October
Access Good **Site** Level
Sites Available **Total** 6
Facilities
Nearby Facilities
Stranraer
Small site on the shores of Luce Bay. Ideal for touring Galloway.

ROCKCLIFFE

Castle Point Caravan Park, Barcloy Road, Rockcliffe by Dalbeattie, Dumfries & Galloway, DG5 4QL.
Std: 01556 **Tel:** 630248
Nearest Town/Resort Rockcliffe
Directions In Dalbeattie take A710. 5 miles turn right to Rockcliffe. Sign for park in 1 mile near entrance to village.
Acreage 3 **Open** March **to** October
Access Good **Site** Level
Sites Available **Total** 37
Facilities
Nearby Facilities
Dumfries
✓✓✓✓Graded Park. Overlooking sea and Rockcliffe Bay, (shore 200yds), very quiet, and well kept. Lovely view.

SANDHEAD

Sands of Luce Caravan Park, Sandhead, Stranraer, Dumfries & Galloway, DG9 9JR.
Std: 01776 **Tel:** 830456
Std: 01776 **Fax:** 830456

Nearest Town/Resort Stranraer.
Directions From Stranraer follow the A77 to the A716. Site entrance is 1 mile south of Stoneykirk Village at the junction of the A716 and the B7084.
Acreage 5 **Open** Mid March **to** October
Access Good **Site** Lev/Slope
Sites Available **Total** 90
Facilities
Nearby Facilities
Stranraer.
✓✓✓✓Graded Park. Site extends directly onto a wide sandy beach. Ideal for children and watersports.

SANQUHAR

Castleview Caravan Site, Townfoot, Sanquhar, Dumfries & Galloway, DG4 6AX.
Std: 01659 **Tel:** 50291
Nearest Town/Resort Sanquhar
Directions On the A76, within a built up area at the south end of the town (i.e. approaching from Dumfries).
Open March **to** October
Access Good **Site** Level
Sites Available **Total** 15
Facilities
Nearby Facilities
Sanquhar
On the southern upland route, fishing on the River Nith.

SOUTHERNESS

Lighthouse Leisure, Southerness, Near Dumfries, Dumfries & Galloway, DG2 8AZ.
Std: 01387 **Tel:** 880277
Std: 01387 **Fax:** 880298
Nearest Town/Resort Dumfries
Directions 15 miles from Dumfries on the A710, via New Abbey and Kirkbean. 1 mile after Kirkbean turn left to Southerness (signposted). Park office is on the right as you enter the village.
Acreage 1 **Open** March **to** October
Access Good **Site** Level
Sites Available **Total** 16
Facilities
Nearby Facilities
Dumfries
✓✓✓✓Graded Park. Near the beach.

STRANRAER

Aird Donald Caravan Park, Stranraer, Dumfries & Galloway, DG9 8RN.
Std: 01776 **Tel:** 702025
Nearest Town/Resort Stranraer.
Directions Off A75 entering Stranraer. Signposted.
Acreage 12 **Open** All Year
Access Good **Site** Level
Sites Available **Total** 100
Facilities
Nearby Facilities
Stranraer.
✓✓✓✓Graded Park. Only 1 mile east of Stranraer town. Ideal touring. Also tarmac hard standing for touring caravans in wet weather. Ideal site for ferry to Ireland. New toilet and shower block. Leisure centre nearby.

THORNHILL

Penpont Caravan & Camping Park, Penpont, Thornhill, Dumfries & Galloway, DG3 4BH.
Std: 01848 **Tel:** 330470
Nearest Town/Resort Thornhill
Directions 2 miles west of Thornhill on A702, on the left just before Penpont Village.
Acreage 1¾ **Open** April **to** October
Access Good **Site** Lev/Slope
Sites Available **Total** 40
Facilities
Nearby Facilities
Dumfries
✓✓✓Graded Park. Ideal touring centre in lovely countryside. Cycling, walking, fishing and bird watching.

DUNBARTONSHIRE (WEST)

BALLOCH

Tullichewan Holiday Park, Old Luss Road, Balloch, West Dunbartonshire, G83 8QP.
Std: 01389 **Tel:** 759475
Std: 01389 **Fax:** 755563
Nearest Town/Resort Balloch.
Directions Follow international direction signs from A82 onto the A811 to Balloch.
Acreage 13 **Open** All Year
Access Good **Site** Level
Sites Available **Total** 140
Facilities
Nearby Facilities
Balloch.
✓✓✓✓✓Graded Park. Premier family park. Ideal centre for touring Loch Lomond, Trossachs and the West Highlands. Close to Glasgow.

FIFE

CRAIL

Ashburn House Caravan Site, St Andrews Road, Crail, Fife, KY10 3UL.
Std: 01333 **Tel:** 450314
Nearest Town/Resort Crail
Directions A917 coast road to St Andrews.
Acreage 3 **Open** March **to** October
Access Good **Site** Level
Sites Available **Total** 65
Facilities
Nearby Facilities
Leuchars
Near beach. Ideal for touring and golf. Now - coastal walks.

KINGHORN

Pettycur Bay Holiday Park, Burntisland Road, Kinghorn, Fife.
Std: 01592 **Tel:** 890321
Nearest Town/Resort Kinghorn
Directions From Forth Bridge take the A921 cut off. Follow coast road to Burntisland. Park is ½ mile east.
Acreage 2 **Open** March **to** October
Access Good **Site** Level
Sites Available **Total** 55
Facilities
Nearby Facilities
Kinghorn.
Overlooking 2 miles of golden sands. Panoramic seascape in a prime tourist area.

LEVEN

Letham Feus Caravan Park, Cupar Road, Leven, Fife, KY8 5NT.
Std: 01333 **Tel:** 351900
Std: 01333 **Fax:** 351900
Nearest Town/Resort Leven
Directions On the A916 2 miles north east of Kennoway.
Acreage 3 **Open** April **to** September
Access Good **Site** Gently Sloping
Sites Available **Total** 21
Facilities
Nearby Facilities
Cupar
✓✓✓✓Graded Park. Small, peaceful site with wonderful sea views. 5 minutes from Letham, 3 minutes from East Neuk and golf courses galore. Ideal for St Andrews. Holiday Home hire and sales.

ST. ANDREWS

Cairnsmill Caravan Park, Largo Road, St. Andrews, Fife, KY16 8NN.
Nearest Town/Resort St Andrews
Directions Follow A915 approx 1 mile.
Open April **to** October
Access Good **Site** Level
Sites Available
Facilities
Nearby Facilities
Leuchars
✓✓✓✓Graded Park. Near beach, ideal touring.

ST. ANDREWS

Clayton Caravan Park, Clayton, St. Andrews, Fife, KY16 9YE.
Std: 01334 **Tel:** 870242
Std: 01334 **Fax:** 870057
Nearest Town/Resort St Andrews
Directions On the A91 between Cupar and St Andrews.
Acreage 40 **Open** March **to** October
Access Good **Site** Lev/Slope
Sites Available **Total** 50
Facilities
Nearby Facilities
Leuchars
✓✓✓✓Graded Park. In quiet countryside with our own stretch of river for fishing. Close to many golf courses and beaches. Ideal for touring Scotland.

ST. ANDREWS

Craigtoun Meadows Holiday Park, Mount Melville, St. Andrews, Fife, KY16 8PQ.
Std: 01334 **Tel:** 475959
Std: 01334 **Fax:** 476424
Nearest Town/Resort St. Andrews.
Directions A91 - St Andrews - turn right at Guardbridge - Strathkinness - at second crossroads after Strathkinness turn left.
Open 1st March **to** 31st October
Access Good **Site** Level
Sites Available **Total** 98
Facilities
Nearby Facilities
Leuchars.
✓✓✓✓✓Graded Park. Close to beaches and many golf courses.

ST. MONANS

St. Monans Caravan Park, St. Monans, Fife, KY10 2DN.
Std: 01333 **Tel:** 730778
Std: 01333 **Fax:** 730466
Nearest Town/Resort St. Andrews.
Directions Park is on the A917 at east end of St. Monans.
Acreage 1 **Open** 21 March **to** October
Access Good **Site** Level
Sites Available **Total** 18
Facilities
Nearby Facilities
Leuchars
✓✓✓Graded Park. Small, quiet park, near the sea and small villages with harbours.

HIGHLAND

ACHARACLE

Resipole Farm Caravan & Camping Park, Loch Sunart, Acharacle, Highland, PH36 4HX.
Std: 01967 **Tel:** 431235
Std: 01967 **Fax:** 431777
Nearest Town/Resort Fort William.
Directions Take A82 south from Fort William across Corran Ferry then A861 to Strontian and Salen. Site 7¼ miles west of Strontian on roadside.
Acreage 6 **Open** April **to** September
Access Good **Site** Level
Sites Available **Total** 60
Facilities
Nearby Facilities
Fort William.
✓✓✓✓✓Graded Park. Scenic views, loch side, central for touring the area. Roomy site.

ARISAIG

Camusdarach, Arisaig, Highland, PH39 4NT.
Std: 01687 **Tel:** 450221
Std: 01687 **Fax:** 450221
Nearest Town/Resort Mallaig.
Directions Take the A830 from Fort William to Mallaig. 4 miles after Arisaig entrance to Camusdarach is on the left.
Acreage 2¾ **Open** April **to** October
Access Good **Site** Undulating
Sites Available **Total** 42
Facilities
Nearby Facilities
Arisaig.
✓✓✓✓Graded Park. Panoramic views over Skye and Inner Hebrides. 500yds from superb beaches by footpath.

ARISAIG

Gorton Sands Caravan Site, Gorton Farm, Arisaig, Highland, PH39 4NS.
Std: 01687 **Tel:** 450283
Nearest Town/Resort Arisaig.
Directions A830 Fort William/Mallaig road, 2 miles west of Arisaig, turn left at sign 'Back of Keppoch', ¾ mile to road end across cattle grid.
Acreage 6 **Open** April **to** September
Access Good **Site** Level
Sites Available **Total** 45
Facilities
Nearby Facilities
Arisaig.
✓✓✓✓Graded Park. On sandy beach, views of Isles of Skye, Eigg and Rhum. Boat trips to Isles, hill walking, ideal for bathing or boating.

ARISAIG

Invercaimbe Caravan & Camp Site, Invercaimbe, Arisaig, Highland, PH39 4NT.
Std: 01687 **Tel:** 450375
Nearest Town/Resort Arisaig
Directions Take the A830 from Fortwilliam (38 miles), we are 1½ miles past the village of Arisaig.
Acreage 1 **Open** Easter **to** October
Access Good **Site** Level
Sites Available **Total** 26
Facilities
Nearby Facilities
Arisaig
Directly on the beach with very good views.

ARISAIG

Portnardoran Caravan Site, Arisaig, Highland, PH39 4NT.
Std: 01687 **Tel:** 450267
Std: 01687 **Fax:** 450267
Nearest Town/Resort Mallaig.
Directions 2 miles north of Arisaig village, on Fort William - Arisaig road A830.
Acreage 2 **Open** Easter **to** October
Access Good **Site** Level
Sites Available **Total** 40
Facilities
Nearby Facilities
Arisaig.
Beside silver sands, scenic views of inner Hebrides, safe for swimming.

ARISAIG

Silverbeach Caravan & Camping, Silverbeach, 5 Bunnacaimbe, Arisaig, Highland, PH39 4NT.
Std: 01687 **Tel:** 450630
Nearest Town/Resort Arisaig
Directions 2 miles north of Arisaig Village on the A830 Fort William to Mallaig road.
Acreage 2 **Open** May **to** September
Access Good **Site** Lev/Slope
Sites Available **Total** 10
Facilities
Nearby Facilities
Arisaig
On the shoreline of a beautiful, sandy beach with views of the Isles of Eigg, Rum and Skye. Ideal for young families.

ARISAIG

Skyeview, Arisaig, Highland, PH39 4NJ.
Std: 01687 **Tel:** 450209
Nearest Town/Resort Arisaig.
Directions 1 mile north of Arisaig just off the A830.
Acreage 1 **Open** April **to** October
Access Good **Site** Sloping
Sites Available **Total** 10
Facilities
Nearby Facilities
Arisaig.
Panoramic views of Skye and the Inner Hebrides. Ideal for hill walking, fishing, golfing and boat trips.

AVIEMORE

Aviemore Mountain Resort Caravan Park, Aviemore, Highland, PH22 1PF.
Std: 01479 **Tel:** 810751
Std: 01479 **Fax:** 810862
Nearest Town/Resort Aviemore.
Directions Entrance to the park is off the main A9 at the south end of Aviemore, adjacent to the Tourist Information Centre.
Acreage 6 **Open** December **to** October
Access Good
Sites Available **Total** 90
Facilities
Nearby Facilities
Aviemore.
✓✓✓✓Graded Park. Santa Claus land, ice rink and cinema nearby. Good for walking, fishing and ski-ing.

AVIEMORE

Glenmore - Forestry Commission, Glenmore, Near Aviemore, Highland, PH22 1QU.
Std: 01479 **Tel:** 861271
Nearest Town/Resort Aviemore
Directions From the A9 turn onto the B9152 south of Aviemore. At Aviemore turn right onto the B970, site is 5 miles.
Acreage 20 **Open** January **to** 3 November
Access Good **Site** Level
Sites Available **Total** 220
Facilities
Nearby Facilities
Aviemore
✓✓✓✓Graded Park. In the heart of The Cairngorms. Near to Loch Morlich with its sandy beaches. Ideal for walking, cycling, mountaineering and winter sports. Near ski slopes.

AVIEMORE

Rothiemurchus Camp & Caravan Park, Coylumbridge, Nr. Aviemore, Highland, PH22 1QU.
Std: 01479 **Tel:** 812800
Std: 01479 **Fax:** 812800
Nearest Town/Resort Aviemore.
Directions From Aviemore take the ski road towards Glenmore. Park on right in 1¼ miles.
Acreage 4 **Open** All Year
Access Good **Site** Level
Sites Available **Total** 39
Facilities
Nearby Facilities
Aviemore.
✓✓✓✓✓Graded Park. Alongside river, in pinewood setting. Close to Aviemore, ideal for ski-ing, boating, walking et cetera.

BALMACARA

Reraig Caravan Site, Balmacara, Kyle of Lochalsh, Highland, IV40 8DH.
Std: 01599 **Tel:** 566215
Nearest Town/Resort Kyle of Lochalsh.
Directions On the A87, 1¾ miles west of junction with A890.
Acreage 2 **Open** May **to** September
Access Good **Site** Level
Sites Available **Total** 45
Facilities
Nearby Facilities
Kyle of Lochalsh.
✓✓✓✓Graded Park. Hotel adjacent to site. Dishwashing sinks, hairdryers. Forest walks adjacent to site. No bookings by telephone. No large tents. No awnings during July and August.

BEAULY

Lovat Bridge Caravan Park, Lovat Bridge, Beauly, Highland, IV4 7AY.
Std: 01463 **Tel:** 782374
Nearest Town/Resort Beauly
Directions On the A862. South from Beauly 1 mile, north from Inverness 12 miles.
Acreage 12 **Open** March **to** October
Access Good **Site** Level
Sites Available **Total** 40
Facilities
Nearby Facilities
Muir of Ord
✓✓✓Graded Park. Sheltered site alongside a river. Ideal touring.

BETTYHILL

Craigdhu Caravan & Camping, Bettyhill, Nr. Thurso, Highland.
Std: 01641 **Tel:** 521273
Nearest Town/Resort Thurso.
Directions Main Thurso/Tongue road.
Acreage 4½ **Open** April **to** October
Access Good **Site** Lev/Slope
Sites Available **Total** 90
Facilities
Nearby Facilities
Kinbrace.
Near beautiful beaches, river, fishing. Scenic views. Ideal touring. Rare plants. New swimming pool, telephone, cafe/restaurant and licensed club nearby.

BOAT OF GARTEN

Boat of Garten Caravan & Camping Park, Boat of Garten, Highland, PH24 3BN.
Std: 01479 **Tel:** 831652
Std: 01479 **Fax:** 831652
Nearest Town/Resort Aviemore
Acreage 9 **Open** All Year
Access Good **Site** Lev/Slope
Sites Available **Total** 97
Facilities
Nearby Facilities
Aviemore
✓✓✓✓✓Graded Park. Ideal for fishing, golf and skiing.

BOAT OF GARTEN

Croft Na Carn Caravan Park, Loch Garten Road, Boat of Garten, Highland, PH24 3BY.
Std: 01343 **Tel:** 830880
Std: 01343 **Fax:** 830880
Nearest Town/Resort Aviemore
Directions Follow the AA and Osprey road signs.
Acreage 3 **Open** All Year
Access Good **Site** Lev/Slope
Sites Available **Total** 30
Facilities
Nearby Facilities
Aviemore
✓✓✓✓Graded Park. Adjacent to RSPB Nature Reserve. Ideal base for fishing, golf, walking, climbing, skiing and touring.

BROADFORD

Campbell's "Cullin View" Caravan & Camping Site, Breakish, Isle of Skye, Highland.
Std: 01471 **Tel:** Broadford 822248
Nearest Town/Resort Broadford.
Directions 6 miles from Skye Bridge ferry at side of garage.
Acreage 4 **Open** All Year
Access Good **Site** Lev/Slope
Sites Available
Facilities
Nearby Facilities
Kyle of Lochalsh.
Scenic views.

CANNICH

Cannich Caravan & Camping Park, Cannich, By Beauly, Highland, IV4 7LN.
Std: 01456 **Tel:** 415364
Std: 01456 **Fax:** 415263
Nearest Town/Resort Inverness.
Directions A82 from Inverness, at Drumnadrochit take the A831 to Cannich.
Acreage 7 **Open** March **to** December
Access Good **Site** Level
Sites Available **Total** 100
Facilities
Nearby Facilities
Inverness
Scenic views, own stretch of river for trout fishing.

DINGWALL

Camping & Caravanning Club Site, Jubilee Park Road, Dingwall, Highland, IV15 9QZ.
Std: 01349 **Tel:** 862236
Nearest Town/Resort Dingwall
Directions From northeast on the A862 go into Dingwall, turn left at sign for Town Centre, take the next left and go over railway bridge, then first left signposted.
Acreage 10 **Open** 22 March **to** 1 Nov
Access Good **Site** Level
Sites Available **Total** 85
Facilities
Nearby Facilities
Dingwall
✓✓✓✓✓Graded Park. Central for touring the Highlands. Train and ferry links to the Isle of Skye. Close to the city of Inverness.

DORNIE

Ardelve, Dornie, Kyle, Highland.
Nearest Town/Resort Kyle of Lochalsh.
Directions Just off A87, Invergarry/Kyle road.
Acreage 2 **Open** May **to** September
Access Good **Site** Sloping
Sites Available
Facilities
Nearby Facilities
Kyle of Lochalsh.
Ideal for touring Skye. Near Eilan Donan Castle. Static caravans for hire.

DORNOCH

Dornoch Caravan & Camping Park, The Links, Dornoch, Highland, IV25 3LX.
Std: 01862 **Tel:** 810423
Std: 01862 **Fax:** 810423
Nearest Town/Resort Dornoch
Directions From A9, 6 miles north of Tain, turn right into Dornoch. Turn right at the bottom of the square.
Acreage 25 **Open** April **to** 22nd October
Access Good **Site** Level
Sites Available **Total** 130
Facilities
Nearby Facilities
Tain
✓✓✓✓Graded Park. Beach, championship golf course, cathedral town. Scenic views, ideal touring.

DORNOCH

Grannie's Heilan' Hame, Embo, Dornoch, Highland, IV25 3QD.
Std: 01862 **Tel:** 810383
Std: 01862 **Fax:** 810368
Nearest Town/Resort Dornoch.
Directions Follow the A9 from Inverness northwards. Turn right onto the A949 to Dornoch, then left after Dornoch Cathedral. 2 miles north of Dornoch turn right for Embo.
Acreage 60 **Open** March **to** October
Access Good **Site** Level
Sites Available **Total** 226
Facilities
Nearby Facilities
Tain (9-10 miles).
✓✓✓✓✓Graded Park. Positioned overlooking sea of Dornoch Firth. Sauna, solarium, two tennis courts and "Bowleasy" mini ten pin bowling. Bird watchers paradise, excellent touring area.

DORNOCH

Seaview Farm Caravan Park, Hilton, Dornoch, Highland, IV25 3PW.
Std: 01862 **Tel:** 810294
Nearest Town/Resort Dornoch
Directions From Dornoch square take Embo road. Site 1½ miles on right, entrance opposite telephone box.
Acreage 3½ **Open** May **to** September
Access Good **Site** Level
Sites Available **Total** 25
Facilities
Nearby Facilities
Ardgay
✓✓✓Graded Park. Near beach, scenic views, good centre for touring, small quiet site.

DRUMNADROCHIT

Borlum Farm Caravan & Camping Park, Drumnadrochit, Highland, IV3 6XN.
Std: 01456 **Tel:** 450220
Std: 01456 **Fax:** 450358
Nearest Town/Resort Drumnadrochit
Directions Take A82 from Drumnadrochit towards Fort William site is on right.
Acreage 2 **Open** April **to** October
Access Good **Site** Lev/Slope
Sites Available **Total** 25
Facilities
Nearby Facilities
Inverness
✓✓✓Graded Park. Overlooking Loch Ness, Ideal touring centre.

DUNDONNELL

Badrallach Bothy & Camp Site, Croft 9, Badrallach, Dundonnell, Highland, IV23 2QP.
Std: 01854 **Tel:** 633281
Nearest Town/Resort Ullapool/Gairloch
Directions Off the A832, 1 mile east of the Dundonnell Hotel take a left turn onto a single track road to Badrallach, 7 miles to lochshore site.
Acreage 1 **Open** All Year
Access Poor **Site** Level
Sites Available **Total** 15
Facilities
Nearby Facilities

Garve/Inverness
✓✓✓Graded Park. Lochshore site on a working croft, overlooking Anteallach on the Scoraig Peninsular. Bothy, peat stove. Otters, porpoises, Golden Eagles and wild flowers galore. Total peace and quiet - Perfect!

DURNESS

Sango Sands Caravan & Camping Site, Durness, Sutherland, Highlands, IV27 4PP.
Std: 01971 **Tel:** 511262/511222
Std: 01971 **Fax:** 511205
Nearest Town/Resort Durness
Directions On the A838 in the centre of Durness Village.
Acreage 12 **Open** April **to** 15 October
Access Good **Site** Level
Sites Available **Total** 82
Facilities
Nearby Facilities
Lairg
Overlooking Sango Bay.

EDINBANE

Loch Greshornish Caravan & Camping Site, Borve, Arnisort, Edinbane, Isle of Skye, Highland, IV51 9PS.
Std: 01470 582 **Tel:** 230
Nearest Town/Resort Portree
Directions 12 miles from Portree on the A850 Portree/Dunvegan road.
Acreage 5 **Open** April **to** October
Access Good **Site** Level
Sites Available **Total** 130
Facilities
Nearby Facilities
✓✓✓✓Graded Park. Beside the sea, ideal centre for touring.

EVANTON

Black Rock Caravan & Camping Park, Evanton, Highland, IV16 9UN.
Std: 01349 **Tel:** 830917
Std: 01349 **Fax:** 830321
Nearest Town/Resort Dingwall.
Directions A9 north from Inverness for 12 miles. Turn left for Evanton B817, proceed for ¾ mile.
Acreage 4½ **Open** April **to** October
Access Good **Site** Level
Sites Available **Total** 67
Facilities
Nearby Facilities
Dingwall.
✓✓✓✓✓Graded Park. Centrally situated for touring the Highlands. Bordered on one side by River Glass. 16 bed hotel on site.

FORT AUGUSTUS

Fort Augustus Caravan & Camping Park, Market Hill, Fort Augustus, Highland.
Std: 01320 **Tel:** 366618
Std: 01320 **Fax:** 366360
Nearest Town/Resort Fort Augustus.
Directions ¼ mile south of Fort Augustus on the A82.
Acreage 3¼ **Open** May **to** September
Access Good **Site** Level
Sites Available **Total** 50
Facilities
Nearby Facilities
Spean Bridge
Ideal touring alongside golf course, near Loch Ness, scenic views and hill walking.

FORT WILLIAM

Glen Nevis Caravan & Camping Park, Glen Nevis, Fort William, Highland, PH33 6SX.
Std: 01397 **Tel:** 702191
Std: 01397 **Fax:** 703904
Nearest Town/Resort Fort William.
Directions On north side of Fort William (A82). East at Glen Nevis signpost. Site 2½ miles up Glen Nevis.
Acreage 19 **Open** Mid March **to** October
Access Good **Site** Lev/Slope
Sites Available **Total** 380
Facilities
Nearby Facilities
Fort William.
✓✓✓✓✓Graded Park. Close to Ben Nevis. Situated in Glen Nevis. Excellent centre for tours in all directions.

FORT WILLIAM

Linnhe Caravan & Chalet Park, Corpach, Fort William, Highland, PH33 7NL.
Std: 01397 **Tel:** 772376
Std: 01397 **Fax:** 772007
Nearest Town/Resort Fort William.
Directions On the A830, 1 mile west of Corpach village, 5 miles from Fort William.
Acreage 14 **Open** 15th Dec **to** 31st Oct
Access Good **Site** Level
Sites Available **Total** 75
Facilities
Nearby Facilities
Corpach.
✓✓✓✓✓Graded Park. The best in the west. Magnificent scenery from top quality park, private beach and boat slipway. Mains serviced pitches available. Toddlers play room. Holiday chalets and caravans for hire.

FORTROSE

Camping & Caravanning Club Site, Rosemarkie, Fortrose, Highlands, IV10 8UW.
Std: 01381 **Tel:** 621117
Directions From the A9 at Tore roundabout take the A832 Fortrose to Cromarty road. Go through Avoch, in Fortrose turn right at the Police Station into Ness Road signposted golf course and leisure centre. Take the first turn left (NB small turning signposted golf course and caravan site), follow the road for 400 yards to the site entrance.
Acreage 5 **Open** 22 March **to** 27 Sept
Site Level
Sites Available **Total** 60
Facilities
Nearby Facilities
Inverness
✓✓✓✓Graded Park. On the shores of the Black Isle, overlooking the Moray and Cromarty Firths. Next door to a golf course.

GAIRLOCH

Gairloch Holiday Park, Strath, Gairloch, Highland, IV21 2BX.
Std: 01445 **Tel:** 712373
Nearest Town/Resort Gairloch
Directions Turn off the A832 at Auchtercairn onto the B8021. In approx. ¼ mile turn right by Millcroft Hotel then immediately right into the site.
Acreage 6 **Open** Easter **to** Mid October
Access Good **Site** Level
Sites Available **Total** 75
Facilities
Nearby Facilities
Achnasheen
✓✓✓✓Graded Park. Near the beach. In the village centre for shops, hotels and restaurants. AA 3 Pennants.

GAIRLOCH

Sands Holiday Centre, Gairloch, Highland, IV21 2DL.
Std: 01445 **Tel:** 712152
Std: 01445 **Fax:** 712518
Nearest Town/Resort Gairloch.
Directions Turn west off the A832 onto the B8012. Site 3 miles on, beside sandy beach.
Acreage 55 **Open** April **to** September
Access Good **Site** Lev/Slope
Sites Available **Total** 250
Facilities
Nearby Facilities
Achnasheen.
✓✓✓✓Graded Park. Site is near beach, scenic views, river, loch fishing and launching slip. Tennis and climbing wall in Gairloch Leisure Centre.

GLENCOE

Invercoe Caravans, Glencoe, Ballachulish, Highland, PA39 4HP.
Std: 01855 **Tel:** 811210
Std: 01855 **Fax:** 811210
Nearest Town/Resort Fort William.
Directions On B863 (off A82) about ¼ mile from Glencoe crossroads.
Acreage 5 **Open** Easter **to** October
Access Good **Site** Level
Sites Available **Total** 60
Facilities
Nearby Facilities
Fort William.
✓✓✓✓Graded Park. Ideal centre for touring West Highlands. Beautiful scenery. No advanced bookings.

GLENCOE

Red Squirrel Campsite, Leacantuim Farm, Glencoe, Highland, PA39 4HX.
Std: 01855 **Tel:** 811256
Nearest Town/Resort Fort William
Directions Off the main A82 in Glencoe Village, follow signs.
Acreage 20 **Open** All Year
Site Lev/Slope
Sites Available
Facilities
Nearby Facilities
Fort William
✓✓Graded Park. Casual and very different site. River for swimming and centre of the mountains. 500 yards from a public telephone.

GRANTOWN-ON-SPEY

Grantown-on-Spey Caravan Park, Seafield Avenue, Grantown-on-Spey, Highland, PH26 3JQ.
Std: 01479 **Tel:** 872474
Nearest Town/Resort Grantown-on-Spey
Directions From Aviemore come into Grantown high street, through the traffic lights and turn left at the Bank of Scotland, site signposted.
Acreage 27½ **Open** Easter **to** September
Access Good **Site** Level
Sites Available **Total** 150
Facilities
Nearby Facilities
Aviemore
✓✓✓✓✓Graded Park. Quiet park, central for touring the Highlands and the Whisky Trail. Good fishing, walking and golf.

INVERGARRY

Faichem Park, Ardgarry Farm, Faichem, Invergarry, Highland, PH35 4HG.
Std: 01809 **Tel:** 501226
Nearest Town/Resort Invergarry.
Directions From the A82 at Invergarry take the A87, continue for 1 mile. Turn right at Faichem signpost, bear left up hill, first entrance on the right.
Acreage 2 **Open** April **to** October
Access Good **Site** Lev/Slope
Sites Available **Total** 30
Facilities
Nearby Facilities
Spean Bridge.
✓✓✓✓✓Graded Park. Panoramic views across Glengarry.

INVERGARRY

Faichemard Farm Camp Site, Faichemard Farm, Invergarry, Highland, PH35 4HG.
Std: 01809 501 **Tel:** 314
Nearest Town/Resort Fort William.
Directions Take A82 to Invergarry (25 miles) travel west on A87 for 1 mile, take side road on right at sign for Faichem, go past Ardgarry Farm and Faichem Park Camp Site to signpost A & D Grant.
Acreage 10 **Open** April **to** October
Access Good **Site** Lev/Slope
Sites Available **Total** 40
Facilities
Nearby Facilities
Spean Bridge.
✓✓✓✓Graded Park. Hill walking, bird watching, space and quiet. Pitch price £6, every pitch has its own picnic table.

INVERMORISTON

Loch Ness Caravan & Camping Park, Easter Port Clair, Invermorriston, Highland, IV3 6YE.
Std: 01320 **Tel:** 351207
Std: 01320 **Fax:** 351207
Nearest Town/Resort Inverness-shire
Directions Main A82 road between Inverness and Fort William. 35 miles either way.
Acreage 8 **Open** End March **to** 31 October
Access Good **Site** Level
Sites Available **Total** 85
Facilities
Nearby Facilities
Inverness
✓✓✓✓✓Graded Park. Loch side site with scenic views. Ideal touring.

INVERNESS

Auchnahillin Caravan & Camping Centre, Daviot East, Inverness, Highland, IV1 2XQ.
Std: 01463 **Tel:** 772286
Std: 01463 **Fax:** 772282
Nearest Town/Resort Inverness.
Directions Drive south on the A9 from Inverness for 5 miles, turn left onto the B9154. Park is 1 mile from this junction in Daviot East.
Acreage 12 **Open** Easter **to** October
Access Good **Site** Level
Sites Available **Total** 100
Facilities
Nearby Facilities
Inverness
✓✓✓✓Graded Park. Ideal touring area to discover grandeur of Highlands. Scenic views. E-mail - auch@zetnet.co.uk

INVERNESS

Scaniport Caravan & Camping Park, Scaniport, Inverness, Highland, IV1 2DL.
Std: 01463 **Tel:** 751351
Nearest Town/Resort Inverness
Directions Situated on the B862 Inverness to Foyers road, approx. 5 miles south of Inverness, opposite the public telephone box in Scaniport.
Acreage 2 **Open** Easter **to** September
Access Good **Site** Level
Sites Available **Total** 30
Facilities
Nearby Facilities
Inverness
✓✓✓Graded Park.

JOHN O'GROATS

John O'Groats Caravan & Camping Site, John O'Groats, Nr. Wick, Highland, KW1 4YS.
Std: 01955 **Tel:** 611329
Nearest Town/Resort John O' Groats
Directions End of A99 beside last house.
Acreage 4 **Open** April **to** October
Access Good **Site** Level
Sites Available **Total** 90
Facilities
Nearby Facilities
Wick.
✓✓✓✓Graded Park. On sea shore with clear view of Orkney Islands. Day trips to Orkney by passenger ferry, jetty nearby. Hotel and snack bar within 150 yards. Cliff scenery and sea birds 1½ miles.

JOHN O'GROATS

Stroma View Huna, Wick, Highland.
Std: 01955 **Tel:** John O'Groats 611313
Nearest Town/Resort John O'Groats.
Directions A9 to John O'Groats, 1½ miles west on A836 Thurso. Well signposted.
Acreage 1 **Open** April **to** October
Access Good **Site** Level
Sites Available **Total** 30
Facilities
Nearby Facilities
Wick.
Near beach, sand. Views of Stroma, Orkney Isles. Dairy produce on site. Seal colony at Gills Bay, 1½ miles west of site. Ferry from Jog to Orkney daily. Free showers. Fast offshore sea cruises and fishing trips, weather permitting, on 105 "Tiger Lilly". 2-6 Berth caravans. All mod cons.

KINLOCHBERVIE

Oldshoremore Caravan Site, 152 Oldshoremore, Kinlochbervie, Highland, IV27 4RS.
Std: 01971 **Tel:** 521281
Nearest Town/Resort Kinlochbervie
Directions Take the A838 to Rhiconich, join the B801 for 4 miles. Then take an unclassified road to Oldshoremore, 2 miles.
Acreage 1 **Open** April **to** September
Access Good **Site** Lev/Slope
Sites Available **Total** 15
Facilities
Nearby Facilities
Lairg
Spectacular scenery.10 minute walk to the beach. Ideal touring, fishing and hill climbing.

KYLE OF LOCHALSH

Balmacara - Forestry Commission, Balmacara, Near Kyle of Lochalsh, Highland, IV40 8DN.
Std: 01599 **Tel:** 566374
Nearest Town/Resort Kyle of Lochalsh
Directions From the east on the A87 take the second turning right after Reraig Village.
Acreage 7½ **Open** 24 March **to** 29 September
Access Good **Site** Level
Sites Available **Total** 120
Facilities
Nearby Facilities
Kyle of Lochalsh
Just a few minutes away from the Skye Bridge. An ideal touring base for Skye and the northwest Highlands.

LAIDE

Gruinard Bay Caravan Park, Laide, Highland, IV22 2ND.
Std: 01445 **Tel:** 731225
Std: 01445 **Fax:** 731225
Nearest Town/Resort Gairloch
Directions 15 miles north of Gairloch on the A832.
Acreage 3¼ **Open** April **to** October
Access Good **Site** Level
Sites Available **Total** 55
Facilities
Nearby Facilities
Achnasheen
✓✓✓✓Graded Park. Beachside park, beautiful views. Ideal touring and walking base.

LAIRG

Dunroamin Caravan & Camping Park, Main Street, Lairg, Highland, IV27 4AR.
Std: 01549 **Tel:** 402447
Std: 01549 **Fax:** 402447
Nearest Town/Resort Lairg
Directions 300yds east of Loch Shin on the A839 on Main Street Lairg.
Acreage 4 **Open** April **to** October
Access Good **Site** Level
Sites Available **Total** 50
Facilities
Nearby Facilities
Lairg
✓✓✓✓✓Graded Park. Ideal centre for touring, fishing and sight seeing. Close to Loch Shin and all amenities.

LAIRG

Woodend Caravan & Camping Park, Woodend, Achnairn, Lairg, Highland.
Std: 01549 **Tel:** 402248
Std: 01549 **Fax:** 402248
Nearest Town/Resort Lairg
Directions A836 from Lairg onto A838 and follow site signs.
Acreage 4 **Open** April **to** September
Access Good **Site** Lev/Slope
Sites Available **Total** 45
Facilities
Nearby Facilities
Lairg
Overlooking Loch Shin, fishing and scenic views. Campers Kitchen is a small building where campers can take their cooking stores to prepare food, with table, chairs and a dish washing area. Ideal touring centre for north west. AA 3 Pennants.

MELVICH

Halladale Inn Caravan Park, Melvich, Highland, KW14 7YJ.
Std: 01641 **Tel:** 531282
Std: 01641 **Fax:** 541282
Nearest Town/Resort Thurso
Directions 17 miles west of Thurso on the A836 north coast road.
Open April **to** October
Access Good **Site** Level
Sites Available **Total** 14
Facilities
Nearby Facilities
Thurso/Forsinard
✓✓✓✓Graded Park. Sandy beaches and sea fishing, wild brown trout and salmon fishing. Bird watching, surfing and diving.

MUIR OF ORD

Druimorrin Caravan & Camping Park, Orrin Bridge, Urray, Muir of Ord, Highland, IV6 7UL.
Std: 019997 **Tel:** 433252
Nearest Town/Resort Muir of Ord
Directions From Inverness take the A9 north to Tore roundabout, then the A832 west through Muir of Ord. The park is situated on the A832 2½ miles west of Muir of Ord.
Acreage 5½ **Open** Easter **to** End September
Access Good **Site** Level
Sites Available **Total** 60
Facilities
Nearby Facilities
Muir of Ord
✓✓✓✓Graded Park. Ideal touring and fishing centre for North and East Highlands.

NAIRN

Delnies Woods Caravan Park, Delnies Woods, Nairn, Highland, IV12 5NX.
Std: 01667 **Tel:** 455281
Std: 01667 **Fax:** 455437
Nearest Town/Resort Nairn
Directions On the A96 2 miles west of Nairn.
Acreage 5 **Open** Easter **to** End October
Access Good **Site** Level
Sites Available **Total** 100
Facilities
Nearby Facilities
Nairn
✓✓✓✓✓Graded Park. Set in mature pine woods. 15 miles from the Whisky Trail to the east and 15 miles from Loch Ness to the west.

NAIRN

Spindrift Caravan & Camping Park, Little Kildrummie, Nairn, Highland, IV12 5QU.
Std: 01667 **Tel:** 453992
Nearest Town/Resort Nairn
Directions From Nairn take the B9090 south for 1¼ miles. Turn right at sharp left hand bend signposted Little Kildrummie onto unclassified road and the entrance is 400yds on the left hand side.
Acreage 3 **Open** 1st April **to** 31st October
Access Good **Site** Level
Sites Available **Total** 40
Facilities
Nearby Facilities
Nairn
✓✓✓✓✓Graded Park. A quiet grassy site, sheltered by trees, overlooking the River Nairn. Fishing permits available from reception. AA 4 Pennants.

ONICH

Corran Caravans, Moss Cottage, Onich, By Fort William, Highland, PH33 6SE.
Std: 01855 **Tel:** 821208
Nearest Town/Resort Fort William
Directions Take the A82 for 8 miles, turn first right after Corran Ferry down a single track road, at T-Junction turn right.
Open March **to** October
Access Good **Site** Level
Sites Available **Total** 20
Facilities
Nearby Facilities
Fort William
✓✓✓✓Graded Park.

POOLEWE

Camping & Caravanning Club Site, Inverewe Gardens, Poolewe, Achnasheen, Highlands, IV22 2LF.
Std: 01445 **Tel:** 781249
Directions Site entrance is on the A832, north of the village of Poolewe.
Acreage 3½ **Open** 22 March **to** 1 Nov
Site Level
Sites Available **Total** 55
Facilities
Nearby Facilities
✓✓✓✓✓Graded Park. Close to Inverewe Gardens and Loch Ewe.

PORTREE

Torvaig Caravan & Camping Site, Torvaig, Staffin Road, Portree, Isle of Skye, Highland, IV51 9HU.
Std: 01478 **Tel:** 612209
Nearest Town/Resort Portree
Directions 1 mile north of Portree on main Staffin road A855.
Acreage 3 **Open** April **to** November
Access Good **Site** Sloping
Sites Available **Total** 120
Facilities
Nearby Facilities
Kyle of Lochash
✓✓✓✓Graded Park. Scenic views and ideal base for touring Skye.

REAY

Dunvegan Camp Site, Reay, Highland, KW14 7RQ.
Std: 01847 **Tel:** 811405
Nearest Town/Resort Thurso
Directions Adjacent to the A836 Thurso to Tongue road, in the village of Reay.
Acreage 2 **Open** April **to** October
Access Good **Site** Level
Sites Available **Total** 15
Facilities
Nearby Facilities
Thurso

ROY BRIDGE

Bunroy Holiday Park, Roy Bridge, Highland, PH31 4AG.
Std: 01397 **Tel:** 712332
Std: 01397 **Fax:** 712045
Nearest Town/Resort Fort William.
Acreage 3½ **Open** March **to** October
Access Good **Site** Level
Sites Available **Total** 20
Facilities
Nearby Facilities
Roy Bridge.
In broad leaf woodland with river boundary, an area of scenic beauty. Central for touring, walking, climbing and outdoor pursuits.

ROY BRIDGE

Inveroy Caravan Park, Roy Bridge, Highland, PH31 4AQ.
Std: 01397 **Tel:** 712275
Nearest Town/Resort Fort William
Directions 12 miles from Fort William on the A82 and the A86.
Open All Year
Access Good **Site** Level
Sites Available
Facilities
Nearby Facilities
Roy Bridge

SCOURIE

Scourie Caravan & Camping Park, Harbour Road, Scourie, Highland, IV27 4TG.
Std: 01971 **Tel:** 2060/2217
Nearest Town/Resort Scourie.
Directions On A894 Ullapool to Durness road, overlooking Scourie Bay.
Acreage 4 **Open** April **to** September
Access Good **Site** Level
Sites Available **Total** 60
Facilities
Nearby Facilities
Lairg.
Ideal base for touring Northwest Scotland. Bird watching, hill walking, loch and sea fishing. Restaurant closed on Sundays. No advance booking except by phone day prior to or morning of arrival. Electrics first come first served. Palm trees, Highland cattle and beautiful birds like Black and Redthroated Divers seen from your pitches.

SPEAN BRIDGE

Gairlochy Holiday Park, Old Station, Gairlochy Road, Spean Bridge, Highland, PH34 4EQ.
Std: 01397 **Tel:** 712711
Std: 01397 **Fax:** 712712
Nearest Town/Resort Fort William

Directions Turn off the A82 at the Commando War Memorial ½ mile north of Spean Bridge onto the B8004. Site is 1 mile on the left and signposted.
Acreage 2½ **Open** April **to** October
Access Good **Site** Level
Sites Available **Total** 20
Facilities
Nearby Facilities
Spean Bridge
✓✓✓✓Graded Park. Ideal for touring, walking and mountain biking. Free fishing. 15 minute walk to the Caledonian Canal.

SPEAN BRIDGE

Stronaba Caravan & Camping Site, Stronaba Farm, Spean Bridge, Highland, PH34 4DX.
Std: 01397 **Tel:** 712259
Nearest Town/Resort Spean Bridge
Directions On the main A82 Fort William to Inverness road. 2¼ miles north of Spean Bridge, on the left hand side just beyond A.A. phone box.
Acreage 4 **Open** Easter **to** October
Access Good **Site** Lev/Slope
Sites Available **Total** 25
Facilities
Nearby Facilities
Spean Bridge.
✓✓✓Graded Park. Scenic views, ideal touring. Gas, telephone and cafe/restaurant all within 2¼ miles.

STAFFIN

Staffin Caravan & Camping Site, Staffin, Isle of Skye, Highland, IV51 9JX.
Std: 01470 562 **Tel:** 213
Nearest Town/Resort Portree.
Directions South side of Staffin village.
Acreage 1½ **Open** April **to** September
Access Good **Site** Lev/Slope
Sites Available **Total** 80
Facilities
Nearby Facilities
Kyle.
✓✓✓✓Graded Park. Sandy beaches 1 mile. Site overlooking Staffin Bay. Free hot showers. Public telephone ½ mile, local cafe/restaurant.

TAIN

Meikle Ferry Caravan Park, Meikle Ferry, By Tain, Highland, IV19 1JX.
Std: 01862 **Tel:** Tain 892292
Nearest Town/Resort Tain.
Directions 2 miles north of Tain, just off the A9.
Acreage 3¼ **Open** All Year
Access Good **Site** Level
Sites Available **Total** 30
Facilities
Nearby Facilities
Tain.
✓✓✓✓✓Graded Park. Good views. Ideal touring centre. Inn/restaurant adjacent.

THURSO

Thurso Caravan Park, Scrabster Road, Thurso, Highland, KW14 7JY.
Std: 01847 **Tel:** 895503
Std: 01955 **Fax:** 604524
Nearest Town/Resort Thurso
Directions On the A836 within Thurso town.
Acreage 4½ **Open** May **to** September
Access Good **Site** Level
Sites Available **Total** 80
Facilities
Nearby Facilities
Thurso
✓✓✓✓Graded Park. Overlooking Thurso Bay. Ideal for touring Caithness and the North Coast.

TONGUE

Kincraig Caravan & Camping Site, Tongue, By Lairg, Highland, IV27 4XF.
Std: 01847 **Tel:** 611218
Nearest Town/Resort Thurso
Directions Turn off the A838 into Tongue Village.
Acreage 1½ **Open** May **to** October
Access Good **Site** Lev/Slope
Sites Available **Total** 15
Facilities
Nearby Facilities
Lairg
Hill walking and scenery.

ULLAPOOL

Ardmair Point Caravan Site, Ullapool, Highland, IV26 2TN.
Std: 01854 **Tel:** 612054
Std: 01854 **Fax:** 612757
Nearest Town/Resort Ullapool
Directions 3½ miles north of Ullapool on A835.
Acreage 3½ **Open** May **to** September
Access Good **Site** Level
Sites Available **Total** 45
Facilities
Nearby Facilities
Garve
✓✓✓✓Graded Park. Beautiful location with outstanding views from the site over sea to 'Summer Isles'. Boating centre, hire of boats.

ULLAPOOL

Broomfield Holiday Park, Shore Street, Ullapool, Highland, IV26 2SX.
Nearest Town/Resort Ullapool
Directions Turn right past Ullapool Harbour.
Acreage 11 **Open** Easter **to** September
Access Good **Site** Level
Sites Available **Total** 140
Facilities
Nearby Facilities
Garve
✓✓✓✓Graded Park. On the sea front. Beside a cafe/restaurant and adjacent to a golf course.

LANARKSHIRE (NORTH)

GLASGOW

Craigendmuir Caravan Park, Craigendmuir Park, Stepps, Nr. Glasgow, North Lanarkshire, G33 6AF.
Std: 0141 **Tel:** 779 4159
Std: 0141 **Fax:** 779 4057
Nearest Town/Resort Glasgow
Directions Take the A80 to Cumbernauld and exit at Stepps, Buchanaw Business Park, Cardowan Road, follow signs.
Acreage 2 **Open** All Year
Access Good **Site** Level
Sites Available **Total** 90
Facilities
Nearby Facilities
Stepps
✓✓✓✓Graded Park. Close proximity to Glasgow and near all major roads.

LANARKSHIRE (SOUTH)

LANARK

Clyde Valley Caravan Park, Kirkfieldbank, Nr. Lanark, South Lanarkshire.
Std: 01555 **Tel:** 663951
Std: 01698 **Fax:** 357684
Nearest Town/Resort Lanark
Directions Leave the M74 onto the A73 for Lanark, ½ mile north to Kirkfieldbank.
Acreage 5 **Open** April **to** October
Access Good **Site** Level
Sites Available **Total** 50
Facilities
Nearby Facilities
Lanark
Two fishing river run past the site.

LANARK

Newhouse Caravan & Camping Park, Ravenstruther, Lanark, South Lanarkshire, ML11 8NP.
Std: 01555 **Tel:** 870228
Nearest Town/Resort Lanark.
Directions On A70 Edinburgh road from Lanark, 3 miles east on left.
Acreage 8 **Open** Mid March **to** Mid October
Access Good **Site** Level
Sites Available **Total** 45
Facilities
Nearby Facilities
✓✓✓✓✓Graded Park. Ideal touring, near Clyde Valley, 40 minutes from Edinburgh and Glasgow. Near New Lanark Conservation Village.

LOTHIAN (EAST)

ABERLADY

Aberlady Caravan Park, Aberlady Station, Aberlady, East Lothian, EH32 0PZ.
Std: 01875 **Tel:** 870666
Std: 01875 **Fax:** 870666
Nearest Town/Resort Edinburgh
Directions Take the A1 then the A1637.
Acreage 4½ **Open** March **to** October
Access Good **Site** Level
Sites Available **Total** 15
Facilities
Nearby Facilities
Longniddry
✓✓✓Graded Park. Near the beach.

DUNBAR

Battleblent Touring Caravan Park, Edinburgh Road, West Barns, Dunbar, East Lothian, EH42 1TS.
Std: 01368 **Tel:** 862234
Std: 01368 **Fax:** 862234
Nearest Town/Resort Dunbar
Directions 1 mile from Dunbar town centre on the A1087 Edinburgh road, at West Barns.
Acreage 1 **Open** Easter **to** October
Access Good **Site** Level
Sites Available **Total** 10
Facilities
Nearby Facilities
Dunbar
Belhaven Bay and beach. 30 minutes from Edinburgh. Bar and restaurant. Ideal touring.

DUNBAR

Thurston Manor Holiday Home Park, Innerwick, Dunbar, East Lothian, EH42 1SA.
Std: 01368 **Tel:** 840643
Std: 01368 **Fax:** 840261
Nearest Town/Resort Dunbar
Directions 4 miles south of Dunbar on the A1 take the Innerwick sign. Park is ½ mile on the right. Tourist signs can be seen from the A1.
Acreage 250 **Open** 1 March **to** 31 October
Access Good **Site** Level
Sites Available **Total** 100
Facilities
Nearby Facilities
Dunbar
✓✓✓✓✓Graded Park. 5 Star facilities and our own woodland valley of great natural beauty. Ideal touring park.

HADDINGTON

The Monks' Muir, Haddington, East Lothian, EH41 3SB.
Std: 01620 **Tel:** 860340
Std: 01620 **Fax:** 861770
Nearest Town/Resort Haddington
Directions Direct access from the main A1 road, very well signposted, between East Linton and Haddington. Approx. 15 minutes from Edinburgh boundary.
Acreage 7½ **Open** All Year
Access Good **Site** Level
Sites Available **Total** 93
Facilities
Nearby Facilities
Drem/Dunbar
✓✓✓✓✓Graded Park. Award winning environmental park with fish, frogs, guinea-pigs, rabbits, owls and bats. Glorious landscaping and plantings. High quality shop/ Bistro and garden centre. Superb views. Mobile shop for veg and fish. David Bellamy Gold Conservation Award.

LONGNIDDRY

Seton Sands Holiday Centre, Longniddry, East Lothian, EH32 0QF.
Std: 01875 **Tel:** 813333
Std: 01875 **Fax:** 813531
Nearest Town/Resort Edinburgh.
Directions From Tranent roundabout turn onto the B6371 for Cockenzie, then turn right onto the B1348, the park is 1 mile on the right.
Open March **to** October
Access Good **Site** Level
Sites Available **Total** 60
Facilities
Nearby Facilities
Longniddry
✓✓✓✓Graded Park. Scenic and peaceful site right opposite the sea. Kids Club and family entertainment. Bike hire, Pitch & Putt and a multi-sports court. Near to Edinburgh. Dogs are allowed but not in peak season. Thistle Award.

MUSSELBURGH

Drum Mohr Caravan Park, Levenhall, Musselburgh, East Lothian, EH21 8JS.
Std: 0131 **Tel:** 665 6867
Std: 0131 **Fax:** 653 6859
Nearest Town/Resort Edinburgh
Directions From Edinburgh take the A1, Berwick Upon Tweed turn off at slip road to Walleyford signposted caravan park and Mining Museum. From south on A1 turn off at A199 signposted Musselburgh and then as above.
Acreage 10 **Open** March **to** October
Access Good **Site** Lev/Slope
Sites Available **Total** 120
Facilities
Nearby Facilities
Edinburgh
✓✓✓✓✓Graded Park. Golf adjacent to site, near Edinburgh.

NORTH BERWICK

Gilsland Caravan & Camping Park, Grange Road, North Berwick, East Lothian, EH39 5JA.
Std: 01620 **Tel:** 892205
Nearest Town/Resort North Berwick
Directions From the centre of North Berwick take road south to the high school and sports centre. Turn right along Grange Road for ½ mile.
Acreage 20 **Open** Mid March **to** Mid October
Access Good **Site** Level
Sites Available **Total** 180
Facilities
Nearby Facilities
North Berwick
✓✓✓✓Graded Park. 1 mile from the beach, town centre and harbour. ½ mile from a swimming pool and sports centre.

LOTHIAN (WEST)

BLACKBURN

Mosshall Farm Caravan Park, Mosshall Farm, Blackburn, West Lothian, EH47 7DB.
Std: 01501 **Tel:** 762318
Directions Leave the M8 at junction 4 and take the road for Whitburn. At T-Junction A705 take a left turn towards Blackburn, we are 300 yards on the right.
Acreage ¾ **Open** All Year
Access Good **Site** Level
Sites Available **Total** 15
Facilities
Nearby Facilities
Bathgate
✓✓✓Graded Park. Situated half way between Edinburgh and Glasgow.

EAST CALDER

Linwater Caravan Park, West Clifton, By East Calder, West Lothian, EH53 0HT.
Std: 0131 **Tel:** 333 3326
Std: 0131 **Fax:** 449 3699
Nearest Town/Resort Edinburgh
Directions At Newbridge junction of the M8/ M9/A8 take the B7030. Continue for 2 miles then turn right at signpost for East Calder, park is through West Clifton on the right.
Acreage 5 **Open** March **to** October
Access Good **Site** Level
Sites Available **Total** 60
Facilities
Nearby Facilities
Edinburgh
✓✓✓✓Graded Park. Ideal for visiting Edinburgh, Royal Highland Showground and touring.

LINLITHGOW

Beecraigs Country Park Caravan & Camping Site, The Park Centre, Nr. Linlithgow, West Lothian, EH49 6PL.
Std: 01506 **Tel:** 844516
Std: 01506 **Fax:** 846256
Nearest Town/Resort Linlithgow
Directions Follow the signs for Beecraigs Country Park taking you approximately 2 miles up Preston Road. At the top of the hill road turn left following signs for Beecraigs Loch and Restaurant. Take the first right, restaurant is reception area.
Acreage 6½ **Open** All Year
Access Good **Site** Level
Sites Available **Total** 54
Facilities
Nearby Facilities
Linlithgow
✓✓✓✓✓Graded Park. Within a 913 acre Country Park which offers a wide range of leisure and recreational interests - fishing, outdoor activities, play area, Red Deer Farm and woodland walks.

MIDLOTHIAN

DALKEITH

Fordel Caravan & Camping Park, Lauder Road, Dalkeith, Midlothian, EH22 2PH.
Std: 0131 **Tel:** 660 3921
Std: 0131 **Fax:** 663 8891
Nearest Town/Resort Dalkeith
Directions On the A68 8 miles south of Edinburgh and only 2 miles south of Dalkeith.
Acreage 3 **Open** April **to** October
Access Good **Site** Level
Sites Available **Total** 45
Facilities
Nearby Facilities
Edinburgh
✓✓✓✓Graded Park. Edinburgh and lots of local tourist attractions.

MORAYSHIRE

ABERLOUR

Aberlour Garden Caravan Park, Aberlour-on-Spey, Moray, AB38 9LD.
Std: 01340 **Tel:** 871586
Std: 01340 **Fax:** 871586
Directions Turn off the A95 midway between Aberlour and Craigellachie, site signposted 500 yards. Vehicles over 10' 6" high should use the A941 to Dufftown, site signposted.
Acreage 3½ **Open** April **to** October
Access Good **Site** Level
Sites Available **Total** 56
Facilities
Nearby Facilities
Elgin
✓✓✓✓✓ Graded Park. Close to Speyside Way and on the malt whisky and castle trail.

BUCKIE

Strathlene Caravan Park, Great Western Road, Portessie, Buckie, Moray, AB56 1SR.
Std: 01542 **Tel:** 834851
Std: 01224 **Fax:** 696988
Nearest Town/Resort Buckie
Acreage 9 **Open** March **to** October
Access Good **Site** Level
Sites Available **Total** 60
Facilities
Nearby Facilities
Keith
✓✓✓✓ Graded Park.

BURGHEAD

The Red Craig Hotel & Caravan & Camping Park, Masonhaugh, Burghead, Moray, IV30 2XX.
Std: 01343 **Tel:** 835663
Std: 01343 **Fax:** 835663
Nearest Town/Resort Elgin
Directions Turn off the A96 Elgin to Inverness road onto the A9013 Burghead road. Turn right just before the village onto the B9040, site is 300 yards on the left.
Acreage 4 **Open** April **to** October
Access Good **Site** Level
Sites Available **Total** 38
Facilities
Nearby Facilities
Elgin
✓✓✓✓ Graded Park. Panoramic views across the Moray Firth.

ELGIN

North Alves Caravan Park, Alves, By Elgin, Moray, IV36 3XD.
Std: 01343 **Tel:** 850223
Nearest Town/Resort Elgin/Forres.
Directions Turn off the A96 half way between Forres and Elgin.
Acreage 12 **Open** April **to** October
Access Good **Site** Level
Sites Available **Total** 75
Facilities
Nearby Facilities
Elgin
✓✓✓✓ Graded Park. Finest safe, sandy beach 1 mile. Various golf courses nearby. Many attractions within easy reach.

FINDHORN

Findhorn Sands Caravan Park, Findhorn, Moray, IV36 0YZ.
Std: 01309 **Tel:** 690324
Nearest Town/Resort Elgin
Directions Turn off the main A96 onto the B9011 to Kinloss at Forres roundabout. Turn left to Findhorn Village, site is on the beach.
Open April **to** October
Access Good **Site** Level
Sites Available **Total** 45
Facilities
Nearby Facilities
Forres
✓✓✓✓ Graded Park. Near a sandy beach and only 100 yards from the village of Findhorn.

FOCHABERS

Burnside Caravan Site, Fochabers, Moray.
Std: 01343 **Tel:** 820362/820511
Std: 01343 **Fax:** 821291
Nearest Town/Resort Elgin
Directions Situated in Fochabers on the A96 trunk road.
Open April **to** October
Access Good **Site** Level
Sites Available **Total** 120
Facilities
Nearby Facilities
Elgin
Ideal touring centre for north east Scotland.

FORRES

Old Mill Caravan Park, Brodie, Moray, IV30 0TD.
Std: 01309 **Tel:** 641244
Nearest Town/Resort Forres
Directions 3 miles east of Forres on the A96.
Acreage 6 **Open** April **to** September
Access Good **Site** Level
Sites Available **Total** 74
Facilities
Nearby Facilities
Forres
✓✓✓✓✓ Graded Park. Sheltered park with modern facilities. Adjacent to the grounds of Brodie Castle with its lake and woodland walks.

HOPEMAN

Station Caravan Park, Hopeman, Nr. Elgin, Moray.
Std: 01343 **Tel:** 830880
Std: 01343 **Fax:** 830880
Nearest Town/Resort Elgin
Acreage 13 **Open** March **to** November
Access Good **Site** Level
Sites Available **Total** 37
Facilities
Nearby Facilities
Elgin.
✓✓✓ Graded Park. On a beach on Moray Firth coast.

LOSSIEMOUTH

Silver Sands Leisure Park, Covesea West Beach, Lossiemouth, Moray, IV31 6SP.
Std: 01343 **Tel:** 813262
Nearest Town/Resort Lossiemouth
Directions Elgin/Lossiemouth A941, turn left 1 mile before Lossiemouth continue 1¼ miles, past R.A.F. camp, turn left, site beside lighthouse.
Acreage 14 **Open** April **to** October
Access Good **Site** Level
Sites Available **Total** 140
Facilities
Nearby Facilities
Elgin.
✓✓✓✓ Graded Park. Beautiful unspoilt golden beach next to park, no roads to cross. Ideal touring area for fishing villages, castles and distilleries.

SPEY BAY

Spey Bay Caravan & Camping Park, Spey Bay, Moray, IV32 7PJ.
Std: 01343 **Tel:** 820424
Directions From the A96 at Fochabers take the B9104 Spey Bay road to the sea.
Acreage 3 **Open** April **to** October
Access Good **Site** Level
Sites Available **Total** 25
Facilities
Nearby Facilities
Elgin
✓✓✓✓ Graded Park. On the sea shore, adjacent to a golf complex and nature area.

PERTH & KINROSS

ABERFELDY

Aberfeldy Caravan Park, Dunkeld Road, Aberfeldy, Perth & Kinross, PH15 2AQ.
Std: 01887 **Tel:** 820662
Std: 01738 **Fax:** 475210
Nearest Town/Resort Aberfeldy
Directions 9 miles east of the A9 take the Ballinluig turn off onto the A827, on the east outskirts of the town.
Open End March **to** End October
Access Good **Site** Level
Sites Available
Facilities
Nearby Facilities
Pitlochry
✓✓✓✓✓ Graded Park. In spectacular, open countryside on a quiet stretch of the River Tay. Off-season discounts. Motorcycles by arrangement. 5 Star discount card for games and retail outlets. Renowned for hospitality.

ABERFELDY

Glengoulandie Deer Park, Glengoulandie, Foss, By Pitlochry, Perth & Kinross, PH15 6NL.
Std: 01887 **Tel:** 830261
Nearest Town/Resort Aberfeldy.
Directions B846 road from Aberfeldy to Kinloch Rannoch for 8 miles, on left hand side.
Acreage 3 **Open** April **to** 1 Nov
Access Good **Site** Level
Sites Available **Total** 10

Facilities
Nearby Facilities
Pitlochry.
Adjoining a wildlife park.

ABERFELDY

Kenmore Caravan & Camping Park, Aberfeldy, Perth & Kinross, PH15 2HN.
Std: 01887 **Tel:** 830226
Std: 01887 **Fax:** 830211
Nearest Town/Resort Aberfeldy.
Directions 6 miles west on A827 from Aberfeldy to Killin.
Acreage 14 **Open** April **to** October
Access Good **Site** Level
Sites Available **Total** 160
Facilities
Nearby Facilities
Pitlochry.
✓✓✓✓✓Graded Park. By river near loch. Touring centre. All outdoor pursuits and water sports. AA 5 Pennants. Excellent par 70 golf course on site.

AUCHTERARDER

Auchterarder Caravan Park, Nether Coul, Auchterarder, Perth & Kinross, PH3 1ET.
Std: 01764 **Tel:** 663119
Nearest Town/Resort Auchterarder/Perth
Directions Situated between the A9 and the A824 east of Auchterarder Village, 1½ miles from the main road. Reached by turning onto the B8062 (Dunning) from the A824.
Acreage 5 **Open** All Year
Access Good **Site** Level
Sites Available **Total** 23
Facilities
Nearby Facilities
Gleneagles
✓✓✓✓✓Graded Park. Bordered by Pairney Water with private fishing. Ideal central location in the heart of Perthshire.

BLAIR ATHOLL

Blair Castle Caravan Park, Blair Atholl, Pitlochry, Perth & Kinross, PH18 5SR.
Std: 01796 **Tel:** 481263
Std: 01796 **Fax:** 481587
Nearest Town/Resort Pitlochry.
Directions Follow A9 north past Pitlochry, after 6 miles turn off following signs to Blair Atholl. After 1¼ miles turn right into caravan park.
Acreage 35 **Open** April **to** Late Oct
Access Good **Site** Level
Sites Available **Total** 283
Facilities
Nearby Facilities
Blair Atholl.
✓✓✓✓✓Graded Park. Blair Castle. Queens view and the road to the Isles.

BLAIRGOWRIE

Ballintuim Caravan Park & Hotel, Ballintuim, By Blairgowrie, Perth & Kinross, PH10 7NH.
Std: 01250 **Tel:** 886276
Nearest Town/Resort Blairgowrie
Directions From Blairgowrie take the A93 towards Braemar, turn left onto the A924 towards Pitlochry for 3 miles.
Acreage 18 **Open** All Year
Access Good **Site** Lev/Slope
Sites Available **Total** 20
Facilities
Nearby Facilities
Perth
✓✓✓✓Graded Park. Set on a hillside, near a river, in a Perthshire valley. Picnic by the pond on site.

BLAIRGOWRIE

Beech Hedge Caravan Park, Cargill, Perth & Kinross.
Std: 0125 0883 **Tel:** Meikleour 249
Nearest Town/Resort Blairgowrie.
Directions 8 miles north of Perth on A93 Breamar road.
Acreage 2 **Open** March **to** October
Access Good **Site** Level
Sites Available **Total** 20
Facilities
Nearby Facilities
Perth.
Scenic views, ideal touring centre.

BLAIRGOWRIE

Blairgowrie Holiday Park, Rattray, Blairgowrie, Perth & Kinross, PH10 7AL.
Std: 01250 **Tel:** 872941
Std: 01250 **Fax:** 874535
Nearest Town/Resort Blairgowrie.
Directions 1 mile north of Blairgowrie town centre off the A93. Turn right past Keathbank Mill and the petrol station. Park is on the left in 250yds following international signs.
Acreage 15 **Open** All Year
Access Good **Site** Level
Sites Available **Total** 30
Facilities
Nearby Facilities
Perth.
✓✓✓✓✓Graded Park. Beautiful landscaped, family park. Ideal centre for touring Perthshire, Angus, Glens and Royal Deeside. Local swimming pool.

BLAIRGOWRIE

Nether Craig Caravan Park, By Alyth, Blairgowrie, Perth & Kinross, PH11 8HN.
Std: 01575 **Tel:** 560204
Std: 01575 **Fax:** 560315
Nearest Town/Resort Alyth
Directions At roundabout south of Alyth, join the B954 signposted Glenisla. Follow caravan signs for 4½ miles (DO NOT go into Alyth).
Acreage 4 **Open** 15 March **to** 31 October
Access Good **Site** Level
Sites Available **Total** 40
Facilities
Nearby Facilities
Dundee
✓✓✓✓✓Graded Park. Peaceful, rural, touring park with unspoilt views. Ideal country pursuits and touring.

BRIDGE OF CALLY

Corriefodly Holiday Park, Bridge of Cally, Perth & Kinross, PH10 7JG.
Std: 01250 **Tel:** 886236
Nearest Town/Resort Blairgowrie.
Directions From Blairgowrie take A93 north for 6 miles. Turn onto A924 Pitlochry road, site approx 200yds from junction of A93 and A924.
Acreage 17½ **Open** Dec **to** Oct
Access Good **Site** Level
Sites Available **Total** 165
Facilities
Nearby Facilities
Perth.
Riverside setting with scenic views. Level hardstanding pitches and grass. Private bowling on site. Ideal touring base.

COMRIE

Riverside Caravan Park, Old Station Road, Comrie, Perth & Kinross, PH6 2EA.
Std: 01764 **Tel:** 670555
Std: 01764 **Fax:** 670207
Nearest Town/Resort Crieff
Directions On the A85 7 miles north of Crieff and 30 miles from Perth or Stirling.
Open April **to** October
Access Good **Site** Level
Sites Available **Total** 14
Facilities
Nearby Facilities
Perth
Good centre for touring. 6 caravans for hire. Sorry no dogs.

COMRIE

Twenty Shilling Wood Caravan Park, St, Fillans Road, Comrie, Perth & Kinross, PH6 2JY.
Std: 01764 **Tel:** 670411
Std: 01764 **Fax:** 670411
Nearest Town/Resort Crieff.
Directions ¼ mile west of Comrie on A85.
Acreage 10¼ **Open** Late March **to** 20 Oct
Access Good **Site** Level
Sites Available **Total** 16
Facilities
Nearby Facilities
Perth.
✓✓✓✓✓Graded Park. Family run, spotless, peaceful sheltered park in woodlands visted by deer and many woodland birds. Individual pitches. All season. David Bellamy Silver Conservation Award.

COMRIE

West Lodge Caravan Park, Comrie, Perth & Kinross, PH6 2LS.
Std: 01764 **Tel:** 670354
Nearest Town/Resort Comrie.
Directions On A85, 5 miles from Crieff. 1 mile from Comrie.
Acreage 3 **Open** 1 April **to** 31 October
Access Good **Site** Level
Sites Available **Total** 20
Facilities
Nearby Facilities
Perth.
✓✓✓✓Graded Park. Sheltered friendly site, ideal for touring, set in beautiful country area. Caravans for hire nightly or weekly.

CRIEFF

Crieff Holiday Village, Turret Bank, Crieff, Perth & Kinross, PH7 4JN.
Std: 01764 **Tel:** 653513
Std: 01764 **Fax:** 655028
Nearest Town/Resort Crieff.
Directions Follow A85 Crieff/Comrie road, turn left ¼ mile from Crieff at first crossroads. Site 300 yards on left, well signposted.
Acreage 2 **Open** All Year
Access Good **Site** Level
Sites Available **Total** 45
Facilities
Nearby Facilities
Gleneagles.
✓✓✓✓Graded Park. Beautifully situated, bounded by River Turret. Adjacent to public parks. Ideal touring centre.

CRIEFF

East Buchanty, Glenalmond, Perth, Perth & Kinross.
Std: 01738 **Tel:** 880293

Nearest Town/Resort Crieff
Directions 7 miles north east of Crieff, A85 Gilmerton, then B8063 at Buchanty
Acreage 12 **Open** All Year
Site Level
Sites Available
Facilities
Nearby Facilities
Perth
Scenic views, ideal touring. No Dogs. No amenities except running water. £3.00 per night.

DUNKELD

Erigmore House Holiday Park, Birnam, Dunkeld, Perth & Kinross, PH8 9XX.
Std: 01350 **Tel:** 727236
Std: 01350 **Fax:** 728636
Nearest Town/Resort Dunkeld
Directions 12 miles north of Perth, leave the A9 and turn east at the sign for Birnam. Turn right after garage and follow driveway up to the house.
Acreage 18 **Open** March **to** October
Access Good **Site** Sloping
Sites Available **Total** 26
Facilities
Nearby Facilities
Dunkeld
✓✓✓✓Graded Park. Situated within Macbeth's Birnam Wood and borders the mighty River Tay where Beatrix Potter wrote Peter Rabbit. Superb Highland scenery, lochs, mountains and glens. The view beyond is "Eastwoods".

DUNKELD

Inver Mill Farm Caravan Site, Invermill, Inver, Dunkeld, Perth & Kinross, PA8 0JR.
Std: 01350 **Tel:** 727477
Nearest Town/Resort Dunkeld.
Directions 1 mile from Dunkeld. Following the A822 to Crieff for 30yds and turn immediate right to village signed Inver. 15 miles north of Perth just off the A9.
Acreage 5 **Open** April **to** October
Access Good **Site** Level
Sites Available **Total** 65
Facilities
Nearby Facilities
Dunkeld.
✓✓✓✓Graded Park. Situated by river, walks and tranquility. Golf and fishing. Ideal touring.

GLENDEVON

Glendevon Holiday Park, Glendevon, By Dollar, Perth & Kinross, FK14 7JY.
Std: 01259 **Tel:** 781208
Std: 01259 **Fax:** 781570
Nearest Town/Resort Dollar
Directions On the A823 halfway between Dunfermline and Crieff.
Acreage 16 **Open** April **to** October
Access Good **Site** Level
Sites Available **Total** 160
Facilities
Nearby Facilities
Gleneagles
Free fishing on the River Devon. Activity Centre for shooting, fishing, off-road quad hire and gold panning. Ideal touring centre.

KINLOCH RANNOCH

Kilvrecht Camp Site, By Kinloch Rannoch, Pitlochry, Perth & Kinross.
Std: 01350 **Tel:** 727284
Std: 01350 **Fax:** 728635
Nearest Town/Resort Kinloch Rannoch
Directions Go through Kinloch Rannoch and take the south Loch Rannoch road. Heading west for 3½ miles, site well signposted.
Acreage 25 **Open** Easter **to** End October
Access Good **Site** Level
Sites Available **Total** 90
Facilities
Nearby Facilities
Pitlochry
Secluded, quiet and peaceful.

PERTH

Cleeve Caravan Park, Glasgow Road, Perth, Perth & Kinross, PH2 0PH.
Std: 01738 **Tel:** 639521
Std: 01738 **Fax:** 475210
Nearest Town/Resort Perth
Acreage 5 **Open** Late March **to** End Oct
Access Good **Site** Level
Sites Available **Total** 100
Facilities
Nearby Facilities
Perth
✓✓✓✓✓Graded Park. Quiet, woodland park. Within easy access of historic Perth (5 minutes). 50+ off season discounts! 5 Star discount cards available for 2 nights or over.

PITLOCHRY

Milton of Fonab Caravan Site, Bridge Road, Pitlochry, Perth & Kinross, PH16 5NA.
Std: 01796 **Tel:** 472882
Std: 01796 **Fax:** 474363
Nearest Town/Resort Pitlochry
Directions ½ mile south of Pitlochry, opposite Bell's Distillery.
Acreage 15 **Open** End March **to** Beginning Oct
Access Good **Site** Level
Sites Available **Total** 154
Facilities
Nearby Facilities
Pitlochry
✓✓✓✓Graded Park. On the banks of the River Tummel. 5 minute walk to Pitlochry Festival Theatre and a 10 minute walk to Dam and Fish Ladder.

ST. FILLANS

Loch Earn Caravan Park, South Shore Road, St. Fillans, Perth & Kinross, PH6 2NL.
Std: 01786 **Tel:** 685270
Std: 01786 **Fax:** 685270
Nearest Town/Resort Crieff.
Directions Turn off the A85 when entering St. Fillans from the east, signposted South Loch Earn Road. Park is 1 mile along this road.
Acreage 2 **Open** End March **to** October
Access Good **Site** Level
Sites Available **Total** 24
Facilities
Nearby Facilities
✓✓✓✓Graded Park. Lochside park with ½ mile of beach. Water sports and fishing.

TUMMEL BRIDGE

Tummel Valley Holiday Park, Tummel Bridge, Pitlochry, Perth & Kinross, PH16 5SA.
Std: 01882 **Tel:** 634221
Std: 01882 **Fax:** 634302
Nearest Town/Resort Pitlochry
Directions Take the A9 and by-pass Pitlochry, then the B8019 to Tummel Bridge. Park is 11 miles down this road on the left.
Acreage 55 **Open** March **to** November
Access Good **Site** Sloping
Sites Available **Total** 50
Facilities
Nearby Facilities
Pitlochry
✓✓✓✓✓Graded Park. An area of outstanding natural beauty, positioned alongside the River Tummel. Fabulous views. Ideal country for walking, riding and fishing.

SCOTTISH BORDERS

COCKBURNSPATH

Chesterfield Caravan Park, The Neuk, Cockburnspath, Borders, TD13 5YH.
Std: 01368 **Tel:** 830459
Std: 01368 **Fax:** 830540
Nearest Town/Resort Eyemouth
Directions From the A1 bypass, follow signs to Abbey St. Bathans. Caravan park is situated ½ mile on the left from this junction.
Open April **to** Mid October
Access Good **Site** Level
Sites Available
Facilities
Nearby Facilities
Dunbar
✓✓✓✓✓Graded Park. Quiet, tidy, clean, country site with scenic views. Within easy reach of the A1, Scottish Borders, Edinburgh, Berwick-on-Tweed. Nearest beach 3 miles.

COLDINGHAM

Scoutscroft Holiday Centre, St Abbs Road, Coldingham, Eyemouth, Borders, TD14 5NB.
Std: 01890 **Tel:** 771338
Std: 01890 **Fax:** 771746
Nearest Town/Resort Berwick-on-Tweed
Directions 12 miles north of Berwick-on-Tweed turn off the A1 onto the A1107. In Coldingham take the B6438 to St Abbs and look for signs.
Acreage 20 **Open** March **to** October
Access Good **Site** Sloping
Sites Available **Total** 170
Facilities
Nearby Facilities
Berwick-on-Tweed
✓✓✓✓✓Graded Park. Coldingham Bay and a Scuba Diving Watersports Centre.

ETTRICK

Honey Cottage Caravan Park, Hope House, Ettrick Valley, Borders, TD7 5HU.
Std: 01750 **Tel:** 62246
Nearest Town/Resort Selkirk
Directions On the B709 Langholm road. 30 minutes from Selkirk on the B7009 and Hawick (B711).
Open All Year
Access Good **Site** Level
Sites Available **Total** 30
Facilities
Nearby Facilities
✓✓✓Graded Park. Ettrick water right outside pitches. Beautiful Ettrick Hills for walkers and climbers. Quiet roads for cyclists. Ideal for touring the Scottish Borders. Restaurant 1 mile.

HAWICK

Bonchester Bridge Caravan Park, Bonchester Bridge, Hawick, Scottish Borders, TD9 8JN.
Std: 01450 **Tel:** 860676
Nearest Town/Resort Hawick/Jedburgh.
Directions Take the A6088 from Hawick.
Acreage 3 **Open** April **to** October
Access Good **Site** Level
Sites Available **Total** 25

Facilities
Nearby Facilities
Berwick-upon-Tweed
Peaceful site in central Borders, good for fishing, golf, walking and falconry.

HAWICK

Riverside Caravan Park, Hornshole, Hawick, Borders, TD9 8SY
Std: 01450 **Tel:** 373785
Nearest Town/Resort Hawick.
Directions A689 Hawick/Jedburgh, site 2 miles on left. A68 turn left at the Scottish Border and follow signs for Hawick for 10 minutes. From the A7 follow signs for Hawick, go through the town centre, 2 miles on the left.
Acreage 8 **Open** March **to** 31 October
Access Good **Site** Level
Sites Available **Total** 44
Facilities
Nearby Facilities
Berwick-on-Tweed.
✓✓✓✓Graded Park. On the banks of the River Teviot.

JEDBURGH

Jedwater Caravan Park, Jedburgh, Borders, TD8 6PJ.
Std: 01835 **Tel:** 840219
Std: 01835 **Fax:** 840219
Nearest Town/Resort Jedburgh
Directions 4 miles south of Jedburgh on the A68.
Acreage 10 **Open** Easter **to** October
Access Good **Site** Level
Sites Available **Total** 120
Facilities
Nearby Facilities
Berwick
✓✓✓✓✓Graded Park. Sheltered park alongside a river. Ideal spot for visiting historical Border towns.

LAUDER

Thirlestane Castle Caravan & Camping Park, Lauder, Borders, TD2 6RU.
Std: 01578 **Tel:** 722254
Std: 01578 **Fax:** 718749
Nearest Town/Resort Lauder
Directions ½ mile south of Lauder on the A68, A697 signed off at Lauder.
Acreage 4½ **Open** Easter **to** 1 October
Access Good **Site** Level
Sites Available **Total** 50
Facilities
Nearby Facilities
Berwick-on-Tweed/Edinburgh
✓✓✓✓Graded Park. Ideal touring, 45 minutes from Edinburgh.

PEEBLES

Crossburn Caravan Park, Edinburgh Road, Peebles, Borders, EH45 8ED.
Std: 01721 **Tel:** 720501
Std: 01721 **Fax:** 720501
Nearest Town/Resort Peebles
Directions ½ mile north of Peebles on the A703.
Acreage 6 **Open** 1 April/Easter **to** Oct
Access Good **Site** Level
Sites Available **Total** 35
Facilities
Nearby Facilities
Edinburgh
✓✓✓✓✓Graded Park. Alongside a river. Mountain bikes for hire. Hill walking. Ideal touring centre.

PEEBLES

Rosetta Caravan & Camping Park, Rosetta Road, Peebles, Borders, EH45 8PG.
Std: 01721 **Tel:** 720770
Std: 01721 **Fax:** 720623
Nearest Town/Resort Peebles
Directions 1 mile from Peebles, well signposted from all main roads.
Acreage 27 **Open** April **to** October
Access Good **Site** Level
Sites Available **Total** 130
Facilities
Nearby Facilities
Edinburgh
✓✓✓✓✓Graded Park. Scenic views, touring, fishing on the River Tweed, golf course adjacent.

SELKIRK

Victoria Park, Buccleuch Road, Selkirk, Borders, TD7 5DN.
Std: 01750 **Tel:** 20897
Std: 01750 **Fax:** 20897
Nearest Town/Resort Selkirk
Directions Convenient to both the A7 and the A68 north and south routes.
Open April **to** October
Access Good **Site** Level
Sites Available **Total** 60
Facilities
Nearby Facilities
Edinburgh
✓✓✓✓Graded Park. Next to the River Ettrick. Pleasant location on the edge of the Historic Royal Burgh of Selkirk. Ideal touring base for scenic Ettrick and Yarrow or Walter Scott Country.

SHETLAND ISLANDS

LERWICK

Clickimin Camping & Caravan Site, Clickimin Centre, Lochside, Lerwick, Shetland Islands, ZE1 0PJ.
Std: 01595 **Tel:** 741000
Std: 01595 **Fax:** 741001
Nearest Town/Resort Lerwick
Open End April **to** End Sept
Access Good **Site** Level
Sites Available **Total** 60
Facilities
Nearby Facilities
✓✓✓✓✓Graded Park. On the grounds of a large leisure complex. Ideally situated to tour the whole island. Ideal for nature lovers. Licensed bar on site.

STIRLINGSHIRE

ABERFOYLE

Cobleland - Forestry Commission, Aberfoyle, Stirling, FK8 3UX.
Std: 01877 **Tel:** 382392
Nearest Town/Resort Aberfoyle
Directions Just off the A81 on an unclassified road, about 1½ miles south of Aberfoyle.
Open 24 March **to** 30 October
Access Good **Site** Level
Sites Available
Facilities
Nearby Facilities
Stirling
✓✓✓Graded Park. On the banks of the River Forth. Ideal for touring in the Trossachs.

ABERFOYLE

Trossachs Holiday Park, Aberfoyle, Stirling, FK8 3SA.
Std: 01877 **Tel:** 382614
Std: 01877 **Fax:** 382732
Nearest Town/Resort Aberfoyle
Directions On the east side of the A81, 3 miles south of Aberfoyle.
Acreage 40 **Open** March **to** October
Access Good **Site** Sloping
Sites Available **Total** 124
Facilities
Nearby Facilities
Stirling
✓✓✓✓✓Graded Park. The perfect location for touring the Trossachs. David Bellamy Gold Award Environmental Park. Cycle hire available.

BLAIRLOGIE

Witches Craig Caravan & Camping Park, Blairlogie, Nr. Stirling, Stirlingshire, FK9 5PX.
Std: 01786 **Tel:** 474947
Nearest Town/Resort Stirling.
Directions A91 Stirling to St. Andrews road.
Acreage 4 **Open** April **to** October
Access Good **Site** Level
Sites Available **Total** 60
Facilities
Nearby Facilities
Stirling.
✓✓✓✓✓Graded Park. Scenic views. Hill walking.

CALLANDER

Gart Caravan Park, Stirling Road, Callander, Stirling, FK17 8LE.
Std: 01877 **Tel:** 330002
Nearest Town/Resort Callander
Directions Situated on the main A84 road, 1 mile south of Callander Town Centre, on the left hand side.
Open 1 April **to** 15 October
Access Good **Site** Level
Sites Available **Total** 131
Facilities
Nearby Facilities
Stirling
✓✓✓✓✓Graded Park. Ideal centre for walking, climbing, water sports, golf, fishing, pony trekking and off-road cycling. Or simply relax and enjoy the stunning scenery.

CALLANDER

Keltie Bridge Caravan Park, Callander, Stirlingshire, FK17 8LQ.
Std: 01877 **Tel:** 330811
Nearest Town/Resort Callander
Directions Signposted from the A84 between Doune and Callander.
Acreage 12 **Open** April **to** October
Access Good **Site** Level
Sites Available **Total** 40
Facilities
Nearby Facilities
Dunblane
✓✓✓✓Graded Park. Riverside setting with views of Trossachs Hills. New facilities for 1996.

CALLANDER

Mains Farm Camping Site, Main Farm, Thornhill, Stirling.
Std: 01786 **Tel:** Thornhill 850605
Std: 01786 **Fax:** 850605
Nearest Town/Resort Callander.

Directions In Thornhill village next to public park. 5½ miles south of Callander on B822.
Acreage 5 **Open** March **to** End October
Access Good **Site** Level
Sites Available **Total** 50
Facilities
Nearby Facilities
Stirling.
Scenic views, ideal touring centre. Trossachs area.

DRYMEN

Camping & Caravanning Club Site, Milarrochy Bay, Nr. Drymen, Stirlingshire, G63 0AL.
Std: 01360 **Tel:** 870236
Directions From the A811 Balloch to Stirling road, take the Drymen turnoff. In Drymen turn onto the B837 (junction is by the War Memorial) towards Balmaha. After approx. 5 miles the road turns sharp right up a steep hill from Balmaha, the site is 1½ miles.
Acreage 14 **Open** 22 March **to** 1 Nov
Site Lev/Slope
Sites Available **Total** 150
Facilities
Nearby Facilities
Balloch
√√√√Graded Park. On the east bank of Loch Lomond, fishing on site. In the heart of Rob Roy country.

DRYMEN

Cashel - Forestry Commission, Near Rowardennan, Stirlingshire, G63 0AW.
Std: 01360 **Tel:** 870234
Nearest Town/Resort Drymen
Directions On the B837 Drymen to Rowardennan road, 3 miles north of Balmaha.
Acreage 11 **Open** 22 March **to** 30 October
Access Good **Site** Level
Sites Available **Total** 250
Facilities
Nearby Facilities
√√√Graded Park. On the shores of Loch Lomond, ideal for boating, cycling and walking. The West Highland Way passes the entrance and Ben Lomond towers above.

FINTRY

Balgair Castle Caravan Park, Fintry, Stirlingshire, G63 0LP.
Std: 01360 **Tel:** 860283
Std: 01360 **Fax:** 860300
Nearest Town/Resort Stirling
Open March **to** October
Access Good **Site** Level
Sites Available **Total** 63
Facilities
Nearby Facilities
Stirling
√√√√√Graded Park. Riverbank site.

KILLIN

Cruachan Caravan & Camping Park, Cruachan, Killin, Stirling, FK21 8TY.
Std: 01567 **Tel:** 820302
Nearest Town/Resort Killin.
Directions 3 miles east of Killin on the A827.
Acreage 6 **Open** Mid March **to** October
Access Good **Site** Lev/Slope
Sites Available **Total** 50
Facilities
Nearby Facilities
Crianlarich.
√√√Graded Park. Forest walks, family farm and adjacent to a park. Coffee shop. Horse riding next door. Ideal touring and hillwalking area. Self catering also available.

KILLIN

High Creagan Caravan Park, Killin, Stirling, FK21 8TX.
Std: 01567 **Tel:** 820449
Nearest Town/Resort Killin.
Directions A827, 2¼ miles from Killin.
Acreage 4 **Open** March **to** October
Access Good **Site** Level
Sites Available **Total** 30
Facilities
Nearby Facilities
Stirling.

LOCHEARNHEAD

Balquhidder Braes Caravan Park, Balquhidder Station, Lochearnhead, Stirling, FK19 8NX.
Std: 01567 **Tel:** 830293
Nearest Town/Resort Lochearnhead
Directions From Callander follow the A84 north for approx. 12 miles. Going south we are approx. 2 miles from Lochearnhead on the A84.
Acreage 4 **Open** March **to** October
Access Good **Site** Level
Sites Available **Total** 50
Facilities
Nearby Facilities
Stirling
√√√√Graded Park. Ideal touring. Cafe/restaurant just across the road.

STIRLING

Auchenbowie Caravan Site, By Stirling, Stirling, FK7 8HE.
Std: 01324 **Tel:** 823999
Std: 01324 **Fax:** 822950
Nearest Town/Resort Stirling.
Directions ¼ mile south of junction 9 M80/M9 on A872 towards Denny turn right for ¼ mile.
Acreage 3¼ **Open** April **to** October
Access Good **Site** Lev/Slope
Sites Available **Total** 60
Facilities
Nearby Facilities
Stirling.
√√√Graded Park. Rural area ideal for touring.

TYNDRUM

Pine Trees Leisure Park, Tyndrum, Stirling, FK20 8RY.
Std: 01838 **Tel:** 400243
Std: 01838 **Fax:** 400314
Nearest Town/Resort Oban/Fort William/Stirling
Directions At the junction of the A82 and the A85 on the main Glasgow to Oban road, Glasgow to Fort William and Stirling to Oban/Fort William road. 37 miles from Oban, 47 miles from Fort William, 50 miles from Stirling and 55 miles from Glasgow.
Acreage 8 **Open** All Year
Access Good **Site** Level
Sites Available **Total** 90
Facilities
Nearby Facilities
Tyndrum
Ideal touring centre for Glencoe, Oban, Stirling, the Trossachs and Loch Lomond. Good for climbing, hill walking, fishing, etc..

WESTERN ISLES

HARRIS

Laig House Caravan Site, 10 Drinnis Hadder, Harris, Western Isles, HS3.
Std: 01859 **Tel:** 511207
Nearest Town/Resort Tarbert
Directions 4½ miles south of Tarbert on the east coast.
Acreage 2½ **Open** April **to** October
Access Good **Site** Level
Sites Available **Total** 20
Facilities
Nearby Facilities
Kyle of Lochalsh
Ideal touring, free fishing on coast. Hill walking and excellent beaches.

HARRIS

Minch View Caravan Site, 10 Drinishader, Isle of Harris, Western Isles, HS3 3DX.
Std: 01859 **Tel:** 511207
Nearest Town/Resort Tarbert
Directions South east of Tarbert along the A859 (5 miles). Turn off the A859 at Drinishader road end. From car ferry turn left at all junctions.
Acreage 3 **Open** April **to** October
Access Good **Site** Level
Sites Available **Total** 26
Facilities
Nearby Facilities
Kyle of Lochalsh
Alongside the sea and a fresh water loch with scenic views. Ideal touring.

STORNOWAY

Laxdale Holiday Park, 6 Laxdale Lane, Laxdale, Isle of Lewis, Western Isles, HS2 0DR.
Std: 01851 **Tel:** 706966/703234
Std: 01851 **Fax:** 706966
Nearest Town/Resort Stornoway
Directions From Stornoway take the A857 north for 1 mile, directly before the Laxdale River turn left and the park is 150 metres on the left.
Acreage 2 **Open** March **to** October
Access Good **Site** Lev/Slope
Sites Available **Total** 43
Facilities
Nearby Facilities
√√√√√Graded Park. Peaceful, tree lined site, ideal for touring the islands of Lewis and Harris. Modern facilities. Purpose-built bunkhouse with cooking facilities on site.
E-mail:gordon@laxdaleholidaypark.force9.co.uk

ALWAYS REMEMBER TO BOOK IN PEAK SEASON

CADE'S **FIFTY PENCE**

CAMPING, TOURING & MOTOR CARAVAN SITE GUIDE 1999

PRESENT THIS VOUCHER TO THE SITE OPERATOR WHEN PAYING TO RECEIVE FIFTY PENCE DISCOUNT PER VOUCHER, PER NIGHT. SEE CONDITIONS OVERLEAF. VALID UNTIL 31-12-99.

CADE'S **FIFTY PENCE**

CAMPING, TOURING & MOTOR CARAVAN SITE GUIDE 1999

PRESENT THIS VOUCHER TO THE SITE OPERATOR WHEN PAYING TO RECEIVE FIFTY PENCE DISCOUNT PER VOUCHER, PER NIGHT. SEE CONDITIONS OVERLEAF. VALID UNTIL 31-12-99.

CADE'S **FIFTY PENCE**

CAMPING, TOURING & MOTOR CARAVAN SITE GUIDE 1999

PRESENT THIS VOUCHER TO THE SITE OPERATOR WHEN PAYING TO RECEIVE FIFTY PENCE DISCOUNT PER VOUCHER, PER NIGHT. SEE CONDITIONS OVERLEAF. VALID UNTIL 31-12-99.

CADE'S **FIFTY PENCE**

CAMPING, TOURING & MOTOR CARAVAN SITE GUIDE 1999

PRESENT THIS VOUCHER TO THE SITE OPERATOR WHEN PAYING TO RECEIVE FIFTY PENCE DISCOUNT PER VOUCHER, PER NIGHT. SEE CONDITIONS OVERLEAF. VALID UNTIL 31-12-99.

CADE'S **FIFTY PENCE**

CAMPING, TOURING & MOTOR CARAVAN SITE GUIDE 1999

PRESENT THIS VOUCHER TO THE SITE OPERATOR WHEN PAYING TO RECEIVE FIFTY PENCE DISCOUNT PER VOUCHER, PER NIGHT. SEE CONDITIONS OVERLEAF. VALID UNTIL 31-12-99.

CADE'S **FIFTY PENCE**

CAMPING, TOURING & MOTOR CARAVAN SITE GUIDE 1999

PRESENT THIS VOUCHER TO THE SITE OPERATOR WHEN PAYING TO RECEIVE FIFTY PENCE DISCOUNT PER VOUCHER, PER NIGHT. SEE CONDITIONS OVERLEAF. VALID UNTIL 31-12-99.

CADE'S **FIFTY PENCE**

CAMPING, TOURING & MOTOR CARAVAN SITE GUIDE 1999

PRESENT THIS VOUCHER TO THE SITE OPERATOR WHEN PAYING TO RECEIVE FIFTY PENCE DISCOUNT PER VOUCHER, PER NIGHT. SEE CONDITIONS OVERLEAF. VALID UNTIL 31-12-99.

CADE'S **FIFTY PENCE**

CAMPING, TOURING & MOTOR CARAVAN SITE GUIDE 1999

PRESENT THIS VOUCHER TO THE SITE OPERATOR WHEN PAYING TO RECEIVE FIFTY PENCE DISCOUNT PER VOUCHER, PER NIGHT. SEE CONDITIONS OVERLEAF. VALID UNTIL 31-12-99.

CADE'S **FIFTY PENCE**

CAMPING, TOURING & MOTOR CARAVAN SITE GUIDE 1999

PRESENT THIS VOUCHER TO THE SITE OPERATOR WHEN PAYING TO RECEIVE FIFTY PENCE DISCOUNT PER VOUCHER, PER NIGHT. SEE CONDITIONS OVERLEAF. VALID UNTIL 31-12-99.

CADE'S **FIFTY PENCE**

CAMPING, TOURING & MOTOR CARAVAN SITE GUIDE 1999

PRESENT THIS VOUCHER TO THE SITE OPERATOR WHEN PAYING TO RECEIVE FIFTY PENCE DISCOUNT PER VOUCHER, PER NIGHT. SEE CONDITIONS OVERLEAF. VALID UNTIL 31-12-99.

CONDITIONS OF USE

Vouchers will only be redeemed by those sites featuring a symbol in the *facilities* line of their County entry. Presentation of this voucher to the Site Operator at the time of paying your balance will entitle you to a fifty pence discount per voucher, per night. (Only one voucher per night). Vouchers may be used in multiples i.e. five vouchers presented for a five night stay will entitle you to a discount of £2.50.

A **CADE'S CAMPING, TOURING & MOTOR CARAVAN SITE GUIDE 1999 EDITION** must be presented at the time of payment. Vouchers are valid for accommodation only. Vouchers may not be exchanged for cash. Valid until 31-12-99.

CONDITIONS OF USE

Vouchers will only be redeemed by those sites featuring a symbol in the *facilities* line of their County entry. Presentation of this voucher to the Site Operator at the time of paying your balance will entitle you to a fifty pence discount per voucher, per night. (Only one voucher per night). Vouchers may be used in multiples i.e. five vouchers presented for a five night stay will entitle you to a discount of £2.50.

A **CADE'S CAMPING, TOURING & MOTOR CARAVAN SITE GUIDE 1999 EDITION** must be presented at the time of payment. Vouchers are valid for accommodation only. Vouchers may not be exchanged for cash. Valid until 31-12-99.

CONDITIONS OF USE

Vouchers will only be redeemed by those sites featuring a symbol in the *facilities* line of their County entry. Presentation of this voucher to the Site Operator at the time of paying your balance will entitle you to a fifty pence discount per voucher, per night. (Only one voucher per night). Vouchers may be used in multiples i.e. five vouchers presented for a five night stay will entitle you to a discount of £2.50.

A **CADE'S CAMPING, TOURING & MOTOR CARAVAN SITE GUIDE 1999 EDITION** must be presented at the time of payment. Vouchers are valid for accommodation only. Vouchers may not be exchanged for cash. Valid until 31-12-99.

CONDITIONS OF USE

Vouchers will only be redeemed by those sites featuring a symbol in the *facilities* line of their County entry. Presentation of this voucher to the Site Operator at the time of paying your balance will entitle you to a fifty pence discount per voucher, per night. (Only one voucher per night). Vouchers may be used in multiples i.e. five vouchers presented for a five night stay will entitle you to a discount of £2.50.

A **CADE'S CAMPING, TOURING & MOTOR CARAVAN SITE GUIDE 1999 EDITION** must be presented at the time of payment. Vouchers are valid for accommodation only. Vouchers may not be exchanged for cash. Valid until 31-12-99.

CONDITIONS OF USE

Vouchers will only be redeemed by those sites featuring a symbol in the *facilities* line of their County entry. Presentation of this voucher to the Site Operator at the time of paying your balance will entitle you to a fifty pence discount per voucher, per night. (Only one voucher per night). Vouchers may be used in multiples i.e. five vouchers presented for a five night stay will entitle you to a discount of £2.50.

A **CADE'S CAMPING, TOURING & MOTOR CARAVAN SITE GUIDE 1999 EDITION** must be presented at the time of payment. Vouchers are valid for accommodation only. Vouchers may not be exchanged for cash. Valid until 31-12-99.

CONDITIONS OF USE

Vouchers will only be redeemed by those sites featuring a symbol in the *facilities* line of their County entry. Presentation of this voucher to the Site Operator at the time of paying your balance will entitle you to a fifty pence discount per voucher, per night. (Only one voucher per night). Vouchers may be used in multiples i.e. five vouchers presented for a five night stay will entitle you to a discount of £2.50.

A **CADE'S CAMPING, TOURING & MOTOR CARAVAN SITE GUIDE 1999 EDITION** must be presented at the time of payment. Vouchers are valid for accommodation only. Vouchers may not be exchanged for cash. Valid until 31-12-99.

CONDITIONS OF USE

Vouchers will only be redeemed by those sites featuring a symbol in the *facilities* line of their County entry. Presentation of this voucher to the Site Operator at the time of paying your balance will entitle you to a fifty pence discount per voucher, per night. (Only one voucher per night). Vouchers may be used in multiples i.e. five vouchers presented for a five night stay will entitle you to a discount of £2.50.

A **CADE'S CAMPING, TOURING & MOTOR CARAVAN SITE GUIDE 1999 EDITION** must be presented at the time of payment. Vouchers are valid for accommodation only. Vouchers may not be exchanged for cash. Valid until 31-12-99.

CONDITIONS OF USE

Vouchers will only be redeemed by those sites featuring a symbol in the *facilities* line of their County entry. Presentation of this voucher to the Site Operator at the time of paying your balance will entitle you to a fifty pence discount per voucher, per night. (Only one voucher per night). Vouchers may be used in multiples i.e. five vouchers presented for a five night stay will entitle you to a discount of £2.50.

A **CADE'S CAMPING, TOURING & MOTOR CARAVAN SITE GUIDE 1999 EDITION** must be presented at the time of payment. Vouchers are valid for accommodation only. Vouchers may not be exchanged for cash. Valid until 31-12-99.

CONDITIONS OF USE

Vouchers will only be redeemed by those sites featuring a symbol in the *facilities* line of their County entry. Presentation of this voucher to the Site Operator at the time of paying your balance will entitle you to a fifty pence discount per voucher, per night. (Only one voucher per night). Vouchers may be used in multiples i.e. five vouchers presented for a five night stay will entitle you to a discount of £2.50.

A **CADE'S CAMPING, TOURING & MOTOR CARAVAN SITE GUIDE 1999 EDITION** must be presented at the time of payment. Vouchers are valid for accommodation only. Vouchers may not be exchanged for cash. Valid until 31-12-99.

CONDITIONS OF USE

Vouchers will only be redeemed by those sites featuring a symbol in the *facilities* line of their County entry. Presentation of this voucher to the Site Operator at the time of paying your balance will entitle you to a fifty pence discount per voucher, per night. (Only one voucher per night). Vouchers may be used in multiples i.e. five vouchers presented for a five night stay will entitle you to a discount of £2.50.

A **CADE'S CAMPING, TOURING & MOTOR CARAVAN SITE GUIDE 1999 EDITION** must be presented at the time of payment. Vouchers are valid for accommodation only. Vouchers may not be exchanged for cash. Valid until 31-12-99.

CADE'S FIFTY PENCE

CAMPING, TOURING & MOTOR CARAVAN SITE GUIDE 1999

PRESENT THIS VOUCHER TO THE SITE OPERATOR WHEN PAYING TO RECEIVE FIFTY PENCE DISCOUNT PER VOUCHER, PER NIGHT. SEE CONDITIONS OVERLEAF. VALID UNTIL 31-12-99.

CADE'S FIFTY PENCE

CAMPING, TOURING & MOTOR CARAVAN SITE GUIDE 1999

PRESENT THIS VOUCHER TO THE SITE OPERATOR WHEN PAYING TO RECEIVE FIFTY PENCE DISCOUNT PER VOUCHER, PER NIGHT. SEE CONDITIONS OVERLEAF. VALID UNTIL 31-12-99.

CADE'S FIFTY PENCE

CAMPING, TOURING & MOTOR CARAVAN SITE GUIDE 1999

PRESENT THIS VOUCHER TO THE SITE OPERATOR WHEN PAYING TO RECEIVE FIFTY PENCE DISCOUNT PER VOUCHER, PER NIGHT. SEE CONDITIONS OVERLEAF. VALID UNTIL 31-12-99.

CADE'S FIFTY PENCE

CAMPING, TOURING & MOTOR CARAVAN SITE GUIDE 1999

PRESENT THIS VOUCHER TO THE SITE OPERATOR WHEN PAYING TO RECEIVE FIFTY PENCE DISCOUNT PER VOUCHER, PER NIGHT. SEE CONDITIONS OVERLEAF. VALID UNTIL 31-12-99.

CADE'S FIFTY PENCE

CAMPING, TOURING & MOTOR CARAVAN SITE GUIDE 1999

PRESENT THIS VOUCHER TO THE SITE OPERATOR WHEN PAYING TO RECEIVE FIFTY PENCE DISCOUNT PER VOUCHER, PER NIGHT. SEE CONDITIONS OVERLEAF. VALID UNTIL 31-12-99.

CADE'S FIFTY PENCE

CAMPING, TOURING & MOTOR CARAVAN SITE GUIDE 1999

PRESENT THIS VOUCHER TO THE SITE OPERATOR WHEN PAYING TO RECEIVE FIFTY PENCE DISCOUNT PER VOUCHER, PER NIGHT. SEE CONDITIONS OVERLEAF. VALID UNTIL 31-12-99.

CADE'S FIFTY PENCE

CAMPING, TOURING & MOTOR CARAVAN SITE GUIDE 1999

PRESENT THIS VOUCHER TO THE SITE OPERATOR WHEN PAYING TO RECEIVE FIFTY PENCE DISCOUNT PER VOUCHER, PER NIGHT. SEE CONDITIONS OVERLEAF. VALID UNTIL 31-12-99.

CADE'S FIFTY PENCE

CAMPING, TOURING & MOTOR CARAVAN SITE GUIDE 1999

PRESENT THIS VOUCHER TO THE SITE OPERATOR WHEN PAYING TO RECEIVE FIFTY PENCE DISCOUNT PER VOUCHER, PER NIGHT. SEE CONDITIONS OVERLEAF. VALID UNTIL 31-12-99.

CADE'S FIFTY PENCE

CAMPING, TOURING & MOTOR CARAVAN SITE GUIDE 1999

PRESENT THIS VOUCHER TO THE SITE OPERATOR WHEN PAYING TO RECEIVE FIFTY PENCE DISCOUNT PER VOUCHER, PER NIGHT. SEE CONDITIONS OVERLEAF. VALID UNTIL 31-12-99.

CADE'S FIFTY PENCE

CAMPING, TOURING & MOTOR CARAVAN SITE GUIDE 1999

PRESENT THIS VOUCHER TO THE SITE OPERATOR WHEN PAYING TO RECEIVE FIFTY PENCE DISCOUNT PER VOUCHER, PER NIGHT. SEE CONDITIONS OVERLEAF. VALID UNTIL 31-12-99.

MONEY OFF VOUCHERS

CONDITIONS OF USE

Vouchers will only be redeemed by those sites featuring a ▣ symbol in the *facilities* line of their County entry. Presentation of this voucher to the Site Operator at the time of paying your balance will entitle you to a fifty pence discount per voucher, per night. (Only one voucher per night). Vouchers may be used in multiples i.e. five vouchers presented for a five night stay will entitle you to a discount of £2.50.

A **CADE'S CAMPING, TOURING & MOTOR CARAVAN SITE GUIDE 1999 EDITION** must be presented at the time of payment. Vouchers are valid for accommodation only. Vouchers may not be exchanged for cash. Valid until 31-12-99.

CONDITIONS OF USE

Vouchers will only be redeemed by those sites featuring a ▣ symbol in the *facilities* line of their County entry. Presentation of this voucher to the Site Operator at the time of paying your balance will entitle you to a fifty pence discount per voucher, per night. (Only one voucher per night). Vouchers may be used in multiples i.e. five vouchers presented for a five night stay will entitle you to a discount of £2.50.

A **CADE'S CAMPING, TOURING & MOTOR CARAVAN SITE GUIDE 1999 EDITION** must be presented at the time of payment. Vouchers are valid for accommodation only. Vouchers may not be exchanged for cash. Valid until 31-12-99.

CONDITIONS OF USE

Vouchers will only be redeemed by those sites featuring a ▣ symbol in the *facilities* line of their County entry. Presentation of this voucher to the Site Operator at the time of paying your balance will entitle you to a fifty pence discount per voucher, per night. (Only one voucher per night). Vouchers may be used in multiples i.e. five vouchers presented for a five night stay will entitle you to a discount of £2.50.

A **CADE'S CAMPING, TOURING & MOTOR CARAVAN SITE GUIDE 1999 EDITION** must be presented at the time of payment. Vouchers are valid for accommodation only. Vouchers may not be exchanged for cash. Valid until 31-12-99.

CONDITIONS OF USE

Vouchers will only be redeemed by those sites featuring a ▣ symbol in the *facilities* line of their County entry. Presentation of this voucher to the Site Operator at the time of paying your balance will entitle you to a fifty pence discount per voucher, per night. (Only one voucher per night). Vouchers may be used in multiples i.e. five vouchers presented for a five night stay will entitle you to a discount of £2.50.

A **CADE'S CAMPING, TOURING & MOTOR CARAVAN SITE GUIDE 1999 EDITION** must be presented at the time of payment. Vouchers are valid for accommodation only. Vouchers may not be exchanged for cash. Valid until 31-12-99.

CONDITIONS OF USE

Vouchers will only be redeemed by those sites featuring a ▣ symbol in the *facilities* line of their County entry. Presentation of this voucher to the Site Operator at the time of paying your balance will entitle you to a fifty pence discount per voucher, per night. (Only one voucher per night). Vouchers may be used in multiples i.e. five vouchers presented for a five night stay will entitle you to a discount of £2.50.

A **CADE'S CAMPING, TOURING & MOTOR CARAVAN SITE GUIDE 1999 EDITION** must be presented at the time of payment. Vouchers are valid for accommodation only. Vouchers may not be exchanged for cash. Valid until 31-12-99.

CONDITIONS OF USE

Vouchers will only be redeemed by those sites featuring a ▣ symbol in the *facilities* line of their County entry. Presentation of this voucher to the Site Operator at the time of paying your balance will entitle you to a fifty pence discount per voucher, per night. (Only one voucher per night). Vouchers may be used in multiples i.e. five vouchers presented for a five night stay will entitle you to a discount of £2.50.

A **CADE'S CAMPING, TOURING & MOTOR CARAVAN SITE GUIDE 1999 EDITION** must be presented at the time of payment. Vouchers are valid for accommodation only. Vouchers may not be exchanged for cash. Valid until 31-12-99.

CONDITIONS OF USE

Vouchers will only be redeemed by those sites featuring a ▣ symbol in the *facilities* line of their County entry. Presentation of this voucher to the Site Operator at the time of paying your balance will entitle you to a fifty pence discount per voucher, per night. (Only one voucher per night). Vouchers may be used in multiples i.e. five vouchers presented for a five night stay will entitle you to a discount of £2.50.

A **CADE'S CAMPING, TOURING & MOTOR CARAVAN SITE GUIDE 1999 EDITION** must be presented at the time of payment. Vouchers are valid for accommodation only. Vouchers may not be exchanged for cash. Valid until 31-12-99.

CONDITIONS OF USE

Vouchers will only be redeemed by those sites featuring a ▣ symbol in the *facilities* line of their County entry. Presentation of this voucher to the Site Operator at the time of paying your balance will entitle you to a fifty pence discount per voucher, per night. (Only one voucher per night). Vouchers may be used in multiples i.e. five vouchers presented for a five night stay will entitle you to a discount of £2.50.

A **CADE'S CAMPING, TOURING & MOTOR CARAVAN SITE GUIDE 1999 EDITION** must be presented at the time of payment. Vouchers are valid for accommodation only. Vouchers may not be exchanged for cash. Valid until 31-12-99.

CONDITIONS OF USE

Vouchers will only be redeemed by those sites featuring a ▣ symbol in the *facilities* line of their County entry. Presentation of this voucher to the Site Operator at the time of paying your balance will entitle you to a fifty pence discount per voucher, per night. (Only one voucher per night). Vouchers may be used in multiples i.e. five vouchers presented for a five night stay will entitle you to a discount of £2.50.

A **CADE'S CAMPING, TOURING & MOTOR CARAVAN SITE GUIDE 1999 EDITION** must be presented at the time of payment. Vouchers are valid for accommodation only. Vouchers may not be exchanged for cash. Valid until 31-12-99.

CONDITIONS OF USE

Vouchers will only be redeemed by those sites featuring a ▣ symbol in the *facilities* line of their County entry. Presentation of this voucher to the Site Operator at the time of paying your balance will entitle you to a fifty pence discount per voucher, per night. (Only one voucher per night). Vouchers may be used in multiples i.e. five vouchers presented for a five night stay will entitle you to a discount of £2.50.

A **CADE'S CAMPING, TOURING & MOTOR CARAVAN SITE GUIDE 1999 EDITION** must be presented at the time of payment. Vouchers are valid for accommodation only. Vouchers may not be exchanged for cash. Valid until 31-12-99.

MAP SECTION

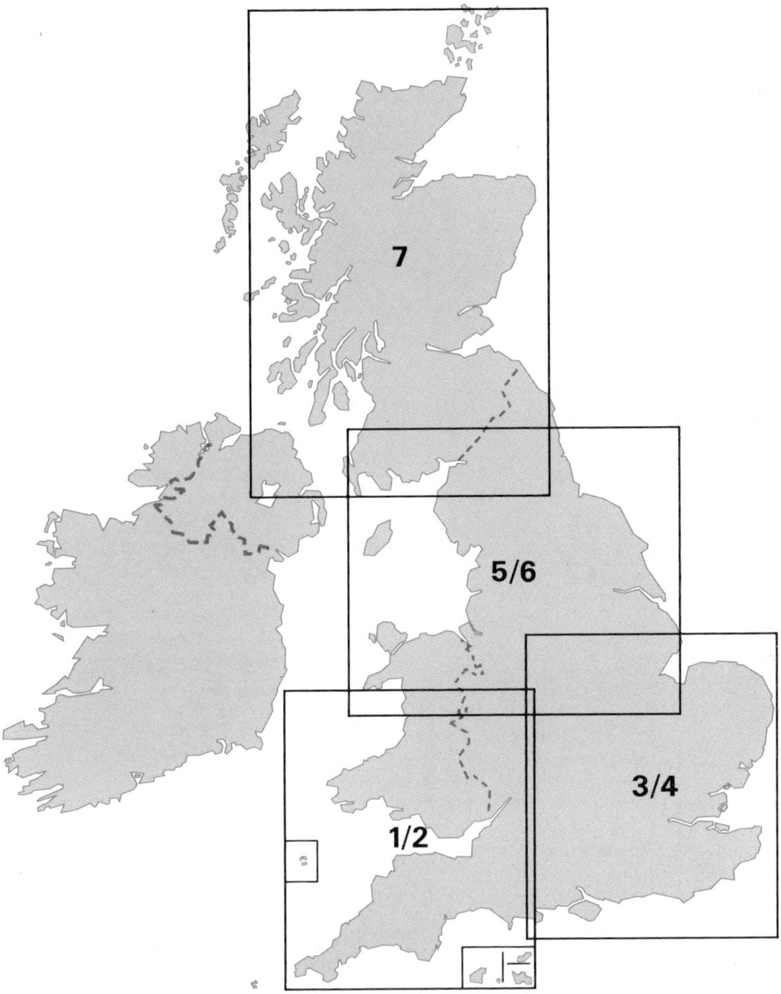

7

5/6

3/4

1/2

Maps designed and produced by GEOprojects (UK) Ltd., Reading, Berkshire. RG1 4QS.

1

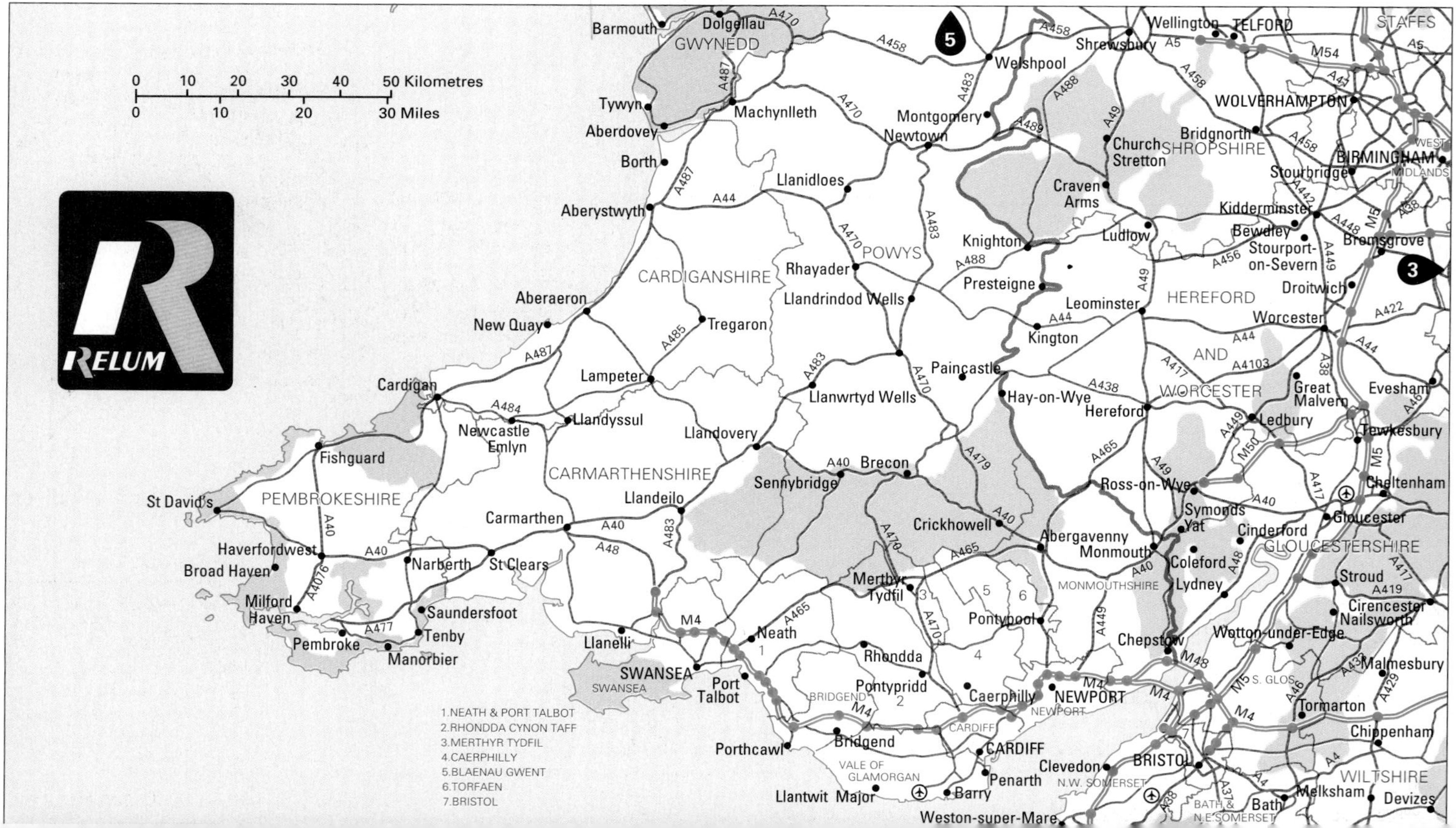
0 10 20 30 40 50 Kilometres
0 10 20 30 Miles
RELUM
GWYNEDD
CARDIGANSHIRE
POWYS
CARMARTHENSHIRE
PEMBROKESHIRE
SHROPSHIRE
HEREFORD
AND
WORCESTER
GLOUCESTERSHIRE
MONMOUTHSHIRE
WILTSHIRE
STAFFS
WEST MIDLANDS
VALE OF GLAMORGAN
SWANSEA
BRIDGEND
CARDIFF
NEWPORT
N.W. SOMERSET
BATH & N.E.SOMERSET
S. GLOS
Barmouth
Dolgellau
Tywyn
Aberdovey
Machynlleth
Borth
Aberystwyth
Aberaeron
New Quay
Cardigan
Fishguard
St David's
Haverfordwest
Broad Haven
Milford Haven
Pembroke
Manorbier
Tenby
Saundersfoot
Narberth
St Clears
Carmarthen
Newcastle Emlyn
Llandyssul
Lampeter
Tregaron
Llandovery
Llandeilo
Llanelli
SWANSEA
Port Talbot
Neath
Porthcawl
Bridgend
Llantwit Major
Barry
Penarth
CARDIFF
Weston-super-Mare
Clevedon
BRISTOL
Bath
Melksham
Devizes
Chippenham
Tormarton
Malmesbury
Cirencester
Nailsworth
Wotton-under-Edge
Stroud
Gloucester
Cheltenham
Tewkesbury
Evesham
Great Malvern
Ledbury
Worcester
Droitwich
Bromsgrove
Stourport-on-Severn
Bewdley
Kidderminster
Stourbridge
BIRMINGHAM
WOLVERHAMPTON
Bridgnorth
TELFORD
Wellington
Shrewsbury
Welshpool
Montgomery
Newtown
Llanidloes
Rhayader
Llandrindod Wells
Llanwrtyd Wells
Brecon
Sennybridge
Paincastle
Hay-on-Wye
Kington
Presteigne
Knighton
Craven Arms
Church Stretton
Ludlow
Leominster
Hereford
Ross-on-Wye
Symonds Yat
Cinderford
Coleford
Lydney
Monmouth
Abergavenny
Crickhowell
Merthyr Tydfil
Pontypool
Chepstow
NEWPORT
Caerphilly
Pontypridd
Rhondda
1.NEATH & PORT TALBOT
2.RHONDDA CYNON TAFF
3.MERTHYR TYDFIL
4.CAERPHILLY
5.BLAENAU GWENT
6.TORFAEN
7.BRISTOL

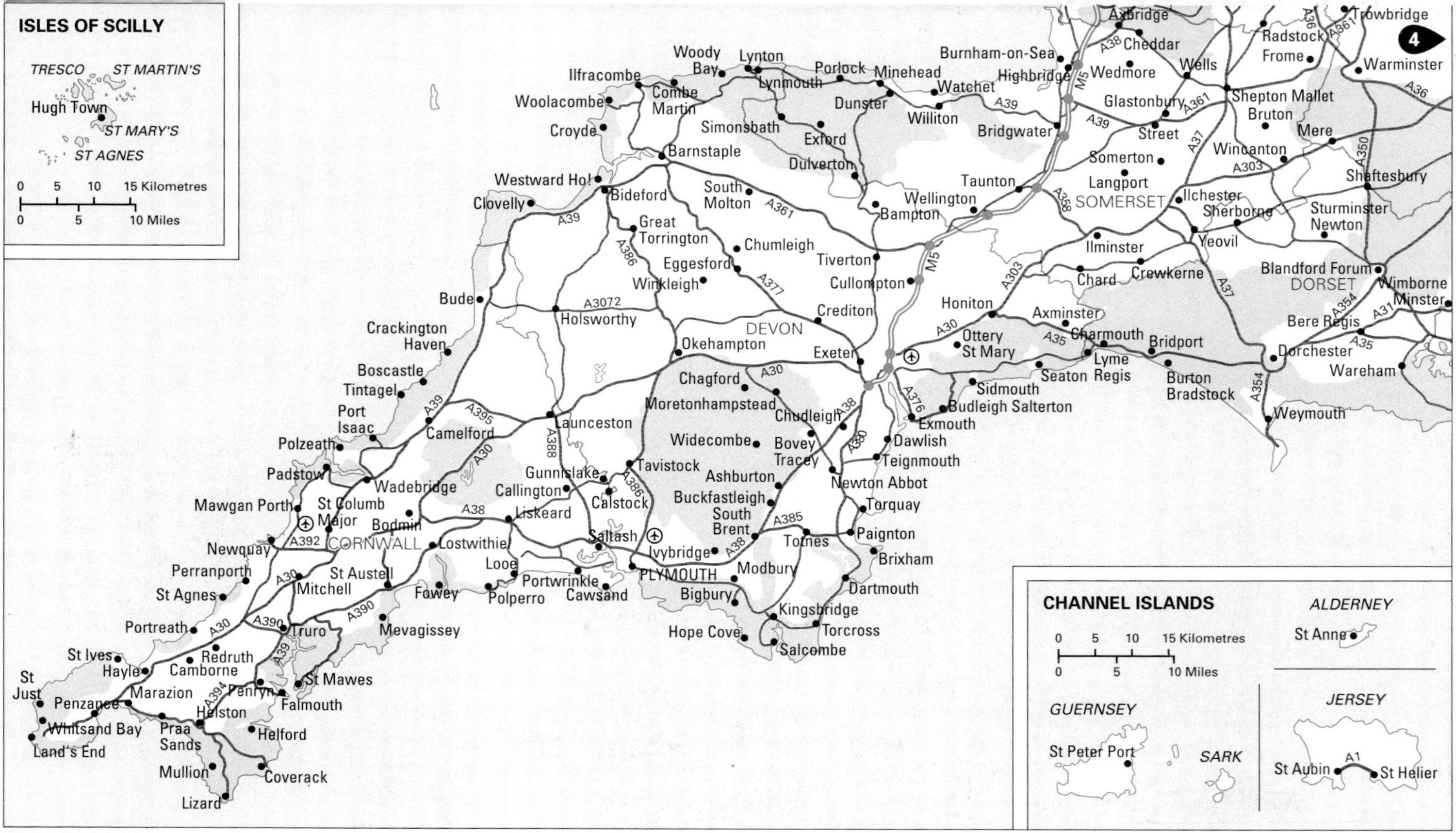

ISLES OF SCILLY

TRESCO
ST MARTIN'S
Hugh Town
ST MARY'S
ST AGNES
0 5 10 15 Kilometres
0 5 10 Miles

Ilfracombe
Woody Bay
Lynton
Lynmouth
Porlock
Minehead
Watchet
Burnham-on-Sea
Highbridge
Axbridge
Cheddar
Wedmore
Wells
Radstock
Trowbridge
Frome
Warminster
Woolacombe
Combe Martin
Dunster
Williton
Bridgwater
Glastonbury
Street
Shepton Mallet
Bruton
Mere
Croyde
Simonsbath
Exford
Barnstaple
Dulverton
Somerton
Langport
Wincanton
Shaftesbury
Westward Ho!
Bideford
South Molton
Taunton
Wellington
Bampton
SOMERSET
Ilchester
Sherborne
Sturminster Newton
Clovelly
Great Torrington
Chumleigh
Tiverton
Ilminster
Yeovil
Eggesford
Winkleigh
Cullompton
Chard
Crewkerne
Blandford Forum
DORSET
Wimborne Minster
Bude
Holsworthy
Crediton
Honiton
Axminster
Bere Regis
Crackington Haven
Okehampton
DEVON
Exeter
Ottery St Mary
Charmouth
Bridport
Lyme Regis
Dorchester
Wareham
Boscastle
Tintagel
Chagford
Seaton
Burton Bradstock
Sidmouth
Port Isaac
Moretonhampstead
Budleigh Salterton
Weymouth
Camelford
Launceston
Chudleigh
Exmouth
Polzeath
Widecombe
Bovey Tracey
Dawlish
Teignmouth
Padstow
Wadebridge
Gunnislake
Tavistock
Ashburton
Newton Abbot
Mawgan Porth
St Columb Major
Callington
Calstock
Buckfastleigh
Torquay
Bodmin
Liskeard
South Brent
Paignton
CORNWALL
Lostwithiel
Saltash
Totnes
Newquay
Ivybridge
Brixham
Perranporth
St Austell
Looe
Portwrinkle
PLYMOUTH
Modbury
Mitchell
Fowey
Polperro
Cawsand
Dartmouth
St Agnes
Bigbury
Kingsbridge
Portreath
Truro
Mevagissey
Hope Cove
Torcross
Salcombe
St Ives
Redruth
Hayle
Camborne
St Mawes
St Just
Marazion
Penryn
Penzance
Falmouth
Helston
Whitsand Bay
Praa Sands
Helford
Land's End
Mullion
Coverack
Lizard

A36 A361 A38 M5 A39 A37 A350 A303 A358 A361 A386 A377 A3072 A30 A35 A354 A31 A37 A376 A38 A380 A385 A395 A388 A386 A38 A392 A30 A390 A39 A394 A354

4

CHANNEL ISLANDS

0 5 10 15 Kilometres
0 5 10 Miles

ALDERNEY
St Anne
GUERNSEY
St Peter Port
SARK
JERSEY
St Aubin
A1
St Helier

2

3

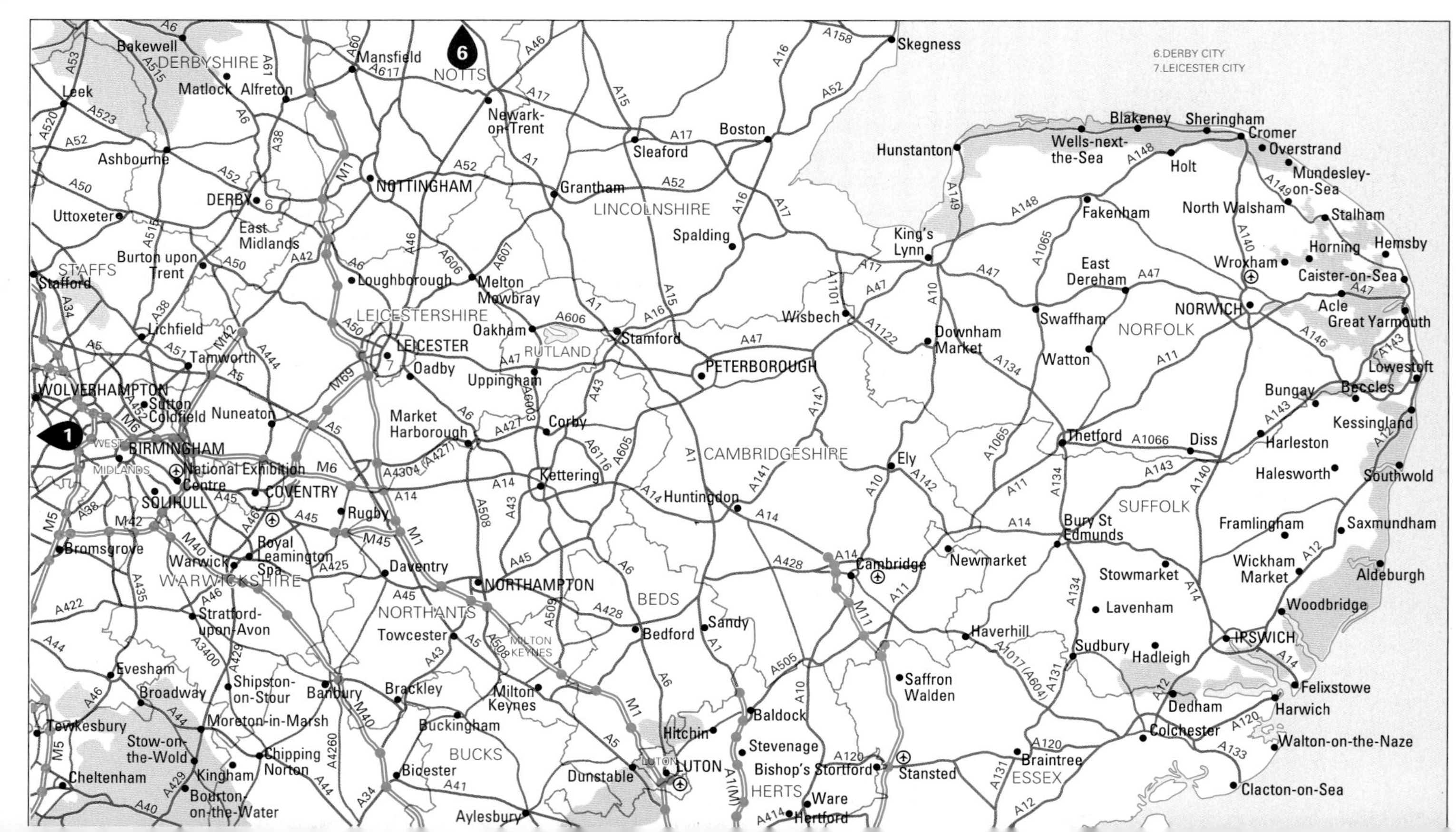

6.DERBY CITY
7.LEICESTER CITY
DERBYSHIRE
NOTTS
LINCOLNSHIRE
NORFOLK
SUFFOLK
LEICESTERSHIRE
RUTLAND
CAMBRIDGESHIRE
STAFFS
WEST MIDLANDS
WARWICKSHIRE
NORTHANTS
BEDS
BUCKS
HERTS
ESSEX
MILTON KEYNES
Bakewell
Mansfield
Skegness
Leek
Matlock
Alfreton
Newark-on-Trent
Boston
Sleaford
Hunstanton
Wells-next-the-Sea
Blakeney
Sheringham
Cromer
Overstrand
Holt
Mundesley-on-Sea
Ashbourne
NOTTINGHAM
Grantham
DERBY
Uttoxeter
East Midlands
Spalding
King's Lynn
Fakenham
North Walsham
Stalham
Horning
Hemsby
Wroxham
Caister-on-Sea
East Dereham
NORWICH
Acle
Great Yarmouth
Burton upon Trent
Stafford
Loughborough
Melton Mowbray
Oakham
Stamford
Wisbech
Downham Market
Swaffham
Watton
Lowestoft
Lichfield
Tamworth
LEICESTER
Oadby
Uppingham
PETERBOROUGH
Bungay
Beccles
Kessingland
WOLVERHAMPTON
Sutton Coldfield
Nuneaton
Market Harborough
Corby
Thetford
Diss
Harleston
BIRMINGHAM
National Exhibition Centre
COVENTRY
SOLIHULL
Kettering
Ely
Halesworth
Southwold
Rugby
Huntingdon
Bury St Edmunds
Framlingham
Saxmundham
Bromsgrove
Royal Leamington Spa
Warwick
Daventry
NORTHAMPTON
Cambridge
Newmarket
Stowmarket
Wickham Market
Aldeburgh
Stratford-upon-Avon
Towcester
Bedford
Sandy
Lavenham
Woodbridge
Haverhill
Sudbury
Hadleigh
IPSWICH
Evesham
Shipston-on-Stour
Banbury
Brackley
Milton Keynes
Saffron Walden
Felixstowe
Broadway
Moreton-in-Marsh
Buckingham
Baldock
Dedham
Harwich
Tewkesbury
Stow-on-the-Wold
Hitchin
Stevenage
Colchester
Walton-on-the-Naze
Chipping Norton
Braintree
Cheltenham
Kingham
Bicester
Dunstable
LUTON
Bishop's Stortford
Stansted
Clacton-on-Sea
Bourton-on-the-Water
Aylesbury
Ware
Hertford

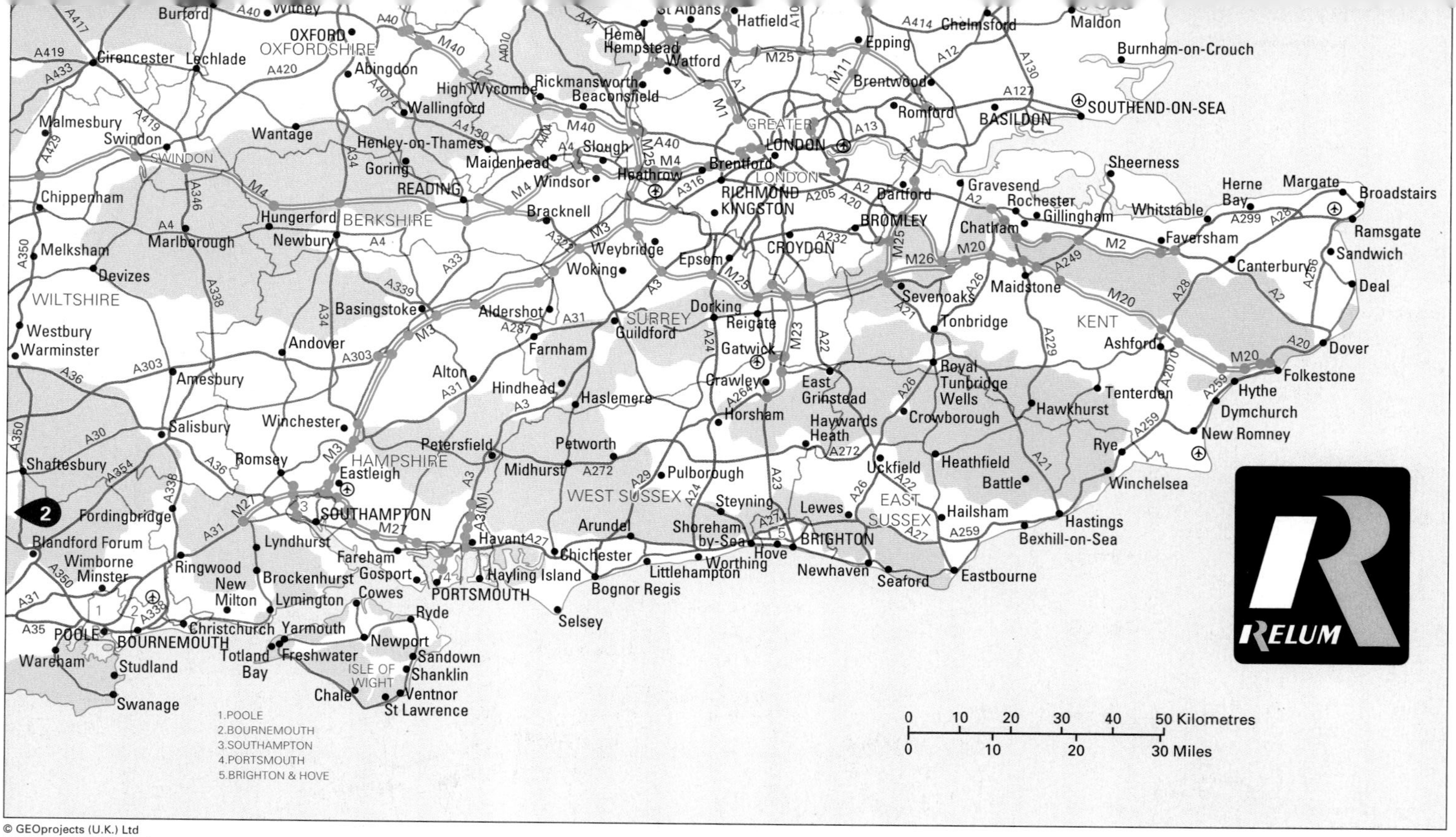

RELUM

Burford
Witney
OXFORD
OXFORDSHIRE
Cirencester
Lechlade
Abingdon
Wallingford
High Wycombe
Rickmansworth
Beaconsfield
Hemel Hempstead
St Albans
Hatfield
Watford
Epping
Chelmsford
Maldon
Burnham-on-Crouch
Brentwood
Romford
BASILDON
SOUTHEND-ON-SEA
GREATER LONDON
LONDON
Malmesbury
Swindon
SWINDON
Wantage
Henley-on-Thames
Goring
Maidenhead
Slough
Windsor
Heathrow
Brentford
RICHMOND
KINGSTON
Dartford
BROMLEY
CROYDON
Gravesend
Rochester
Gillingham
Chatham
Sheerness
Whitstable
Herne Bay
Margate
Broadstairs
Ramsgate
Sandwich
Deal
Faversham
Canterbury
Chippenham
READING
Hungerford
BERKSHIRE
Newbury
Bracknell
Weybridge
Woking
Epsom
Melksham
Marlborough
Devizes
WILTSHIRE
Westbury
Warminster
Basingstoke
Aldershot
Farnham
Guildford
SURREY
Dorking
Reigate
Gatwick
Sevenoaks
Tonbridge
Maidstone
KENT
Ashford
Dover
Folkestone
Hythe
Dymchurch
New Romney
Andover
Amesbury
Salisbury
Alton
Hindhead
Haslemere
Crawley
Horsham
East Grinstead
Royal Tunbridge Wells
Crowborough
Hawkhurst
Tenterden
Rye
Winchelsea
Winchester
Romsey
Petersfield
Petworth
Midhurst
Pulborough
Haywards Heath
Uckfield
Heathfield
Battle
Shaftesbury
Eastleigh
HAMPSHIRE
WEST SUSSEX
EAST SUSSEX
Steyning
Lewes
Hailsham
Hastings
Bexhill-on-Sea
Fordingbridge
SOUTHAMPTON
Havant
Arundel
Shoreham-by-Sea
BRIGHTON
Hove
Blandford Forum
Wimborne Minster
Lyndhurst
Fareham
Chichester
Worthing
Littlehampton
Newhaven
Seaford
Eastbourne
Ringwood
New Milton
Brockenhurst
Gosport
PORTSMOUTH
Hayling Island
Bognor Regis
Selsey
Lymington
Cowes
Ryde
POOLE
BOURNEMOUTH
Christchurch
Yarmouth
Newport
Wareham
Studland
Totland Bay
Freshwater
ISLE OF WIGHT
Sandown
Shanklin
Chale
Ventnor
St Lawrence
Swanage

1.POOLE
2.BOURNEMOUTH
3.SOUTHAMPTON
4.PORTSMOUTH
5.BRIGHTON & HOVE

0 10 20 30 40 50 Kilometres
0 10 20 30 Miles

5

A713
A76
Lockerbie
7
Langholm
Bellingham
New Galloway
DUMFRIES AND GALLOWAY
Dumfries
A75
A74(M)
A7
Longtown
Gretna
Annan
Greenhead
A69
Newton Stewart
Castle Douglas
A75
Dalbeattie
Brampton
A74
A686
A75
Gatehouse of Fleet
Carlisle
A689
A69
A689
Silloth
Wigtown
Kirkcudbright
Wigton
Alston
A596
A595
M6
Port William
A686
Maryport
Cockermouth
Bassenthwaite
Penrith
A66
A66
Workington
Thornthwaite
Keswick
Appleby-in-Westmorland
Brampton
CUMBRIA
A66
Whitehaven
Ullswater
Shap
Ennerdale Bridge
A591
A685
Little Langdale
Ambleside
Kirkby Stephen
Gosforth
A595
Troutbeck
A6
Seascale
Hawkshead
Coniston
Windermere
Sedbergh
Hawes
A10
Ramsey
Ravenglass
Kendal
Newby Bridge
Broughton-in-Furness
A590
ISLE OF MAN
Peel
A2
A1
Millom
A590
Grange-over-Sands
A65
Kirkby Lonsdale
Ulverston
Ingleton
A27
Douglas
M6
A25
Carnforth
Port Erin
A683
Settle
Castletown
Barrow-in-Furness
Morecambe
Port St Mary
Lancaster
LANCASHIRE
Fleetwood
A6
Clitheroe
A59
M65
A585
M55
BLACKPOOL
A583
Lytham St Anne's
PRESTON
BLACKBURN
A565
Southport
A570
A59
M6
Chorley
A666
M61
M66
A6
BOLTON
Ormskirk
Formby
Wigan
M58
MANCHESTER
M62
MERSEYSIDE
WARRINGTON
Amlwch
Hoylake
BIRKENHEAD
LIVERPOOL
Widnes
Llanerchymedd
Prestatyn
M53
M56
M56
Holyhead
ANGLESEY
Llandudno
Colwyn Bay
Rhyl
M6
Llangefni
Beaumaris
Conwy
A55
A556
Northwich
Knutsford
A55
Abergele
FLINTSHIRE
Ellesmere Port
A5
Menai Bridge
Bangor
A54
CHESHIRE
A34
A54
Denbigh
Mold
A470
A55
Chester
Llanrwst
ABERCONWY & COLWYN
A494
Caernarfon
A5
Ruthin
A483
A534
A49
A51
Crewe
Llanberis
Nantwich
A500
Betws-y-Coed
DENBIGHSHIRE
A487
Wrexham
WREXHAM
A41
Newcastle-under-Lyme
A525
A5
Corwen
Llangollen
Ffestiniog
Whitchurch
A51
Nefyn
Porthmadog
Ellesmere
A495
A53
Criccieth
Penrhyndeudraeth
A494
Bala
Market Drayton
Pwllheli
Oswestry
Wem
Llanbedrog
A470
A483
A5
A49
A41
Harlech
A442
A518
Aberdaron
Abersoch
GWYNEDD
Llanfyllin
SHROPSHIRE
Dolgellau
Wellington
POWYS
Shrewsbury
TELFORD
Barmouth
A487
A470
Welshpool
A458
A5
A458
M54
A470
A483
Tywyn
Machynlleth
Montgomery
1
A489
A49
Newtown
Bridgnorth

0 10 20 30 40 50 Kilometres
0 10 20 30 Miles

RELUM

1.HARTLEPOOL
2.DARLINGTON
3.STOCKTON-ON-TEES
4.MIDDLESBROUGH
5.REDCAR & CLEVELAND

6.KINGSTON UPON HULL
7.STOKE-ON-TRENT
8.DERBY CITY
9.LEICESTER CITY

Morpeth
Ashington
Whitley Bay
Tynemouth
SOUTH SHIELDS
NEWCASTLE UPON TYNE
Corbridge
TYNE AND WEAR
SUNDERLAND
Washington
Consett
Durham
Tow Law
Peterlee
Hartlepool
Bishop Auckland
Middleton-in-Teesdale
Redcar
Saltburn-by-the-Sea
MIDDLESBROUGH
STOCKTON-ON-TEES
Barnard Castle
Darlington
Guisborough
Whitby
Stokesley
Richmond
Northallerton
Leyburn
Middleham
Thirsk
Helmsley
Pickering
Scarborough
Cayton bay
Filey
NORTH YORKSHIRE
Castle Howard
Flamborough
Ripon
Malton
Sledmere
Bridlington
Huby
Grassington
Knaresborough
Stamford Bridge
Great Driffield
Skipton
Harrogate
YORK
Wetherby
Hornsea
Ilkley
EAST RIDING OF YORKSHIRE
Keighley
Bingley
Horsforth
Beverley
LEEDS
Selby
W. YORKS
BRADFORD
Halifax
KINGSTON UPON HULL
Withernsea
Goole
Wakefield
HUDDERSFIELD
Kirkburton
Holmfirth
NORTH LINCOLNSHIRE
Scunthorpe
Grimsby
Cleethorpes
N.E. LINCS.
Barnsley
Doncaster
OLDHAM
SOUTH YORKS
Glossop
Rotherham
Gainsborough
Market Rasen
Louth
Mablethorpe
STOCKPORT
SHEFFIELD
Castleton
Worksop
Whaley Bridge
Alford
Macclesfield
Chesterfield
Lincoln
Horncastle
Skegness
Buxton
Bakewell
Clay Cross
LINCOLNSHIRE
Woodhall Spa
DERBYSHIRE
Mansfield
Congleton
Matlock
NOTTS
Alfreton
Leek
Newark-on-Trent
Boston
Sleaford
STOKE-ON-TRENT
Ashbourne
NOTTINGHAM
Grantham
Uttoxeter
DERBY
East Midlands
Spalding
STAFFS
Stafford
Burton upon Trent
Loughborough
Melton Mowbray
LEICESTERSHIRE
Wisbech
Lichfield
Oakham
Stamford
RUTLAND
Tamworth
LEICESTER
PETERBOROUGH
March
WALSALL
Atherstone
Uppingham
Whittlesey
WOLVERHAMPTON
Hinckley
CAMBRIDGESHIRE
Littleport
Nuneaton
Corby
Ramsey
Bedworth
Market Harborough
Oundle
Chatteris

7

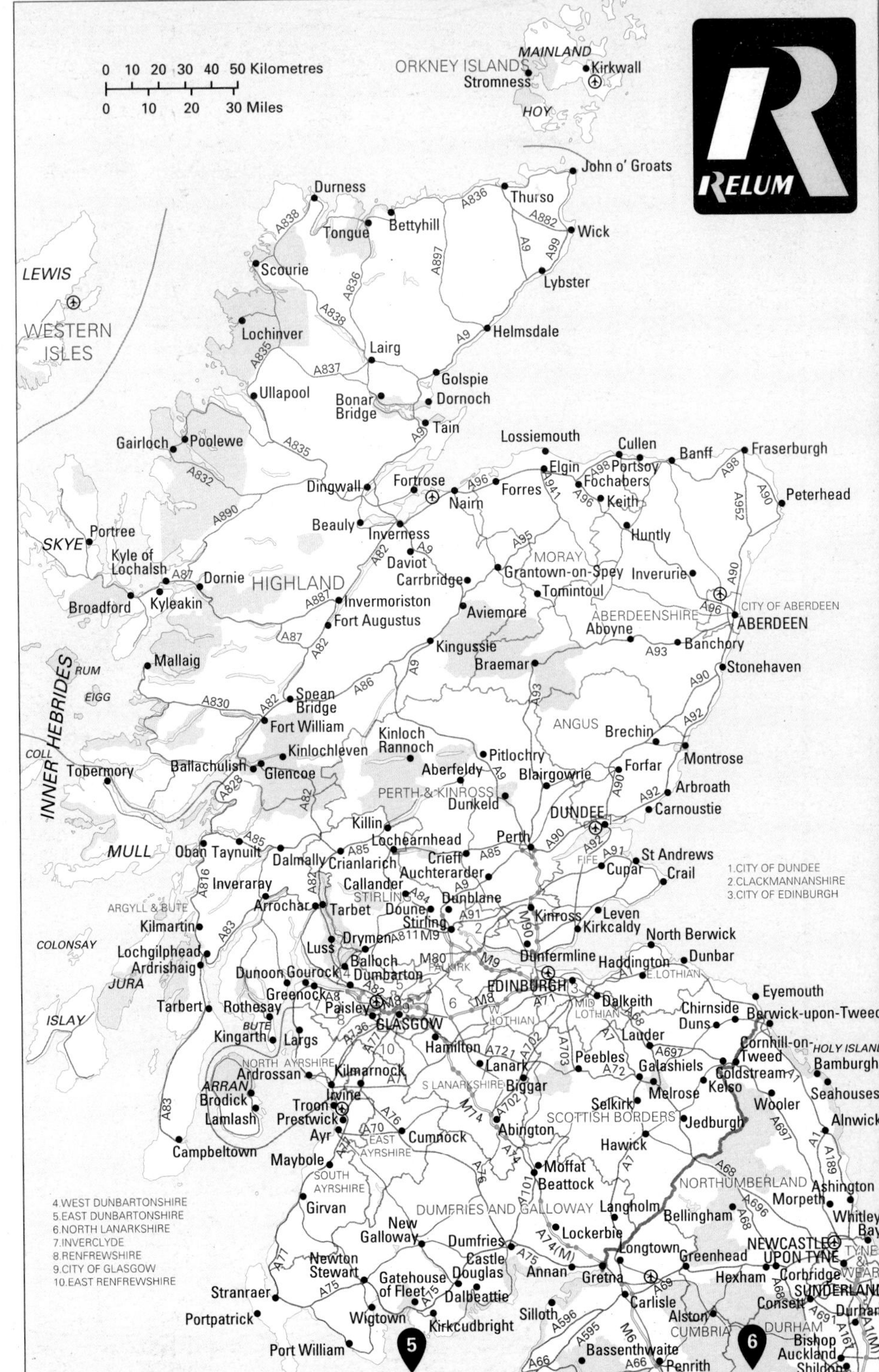

0 10 20 30 40 50 Kilometres
0 10 20 30 Miles
RELUM
ORKNEY ISLANDS
MAINLAND
Kirkwall
Stromness
HOY
John o' Groats
Thurso
Wick
Lybster
Helmsdale
Durness
Tongue
Bettyhill
Scourie
Lochinver
Lairg
Golspie
Dornoch
Ullapool
Bonar Bridge
Tain
LEWIS
WESTERN ISLES
Gairloch
Poolewe
Dingwall
Fortrose
Nairn
Forres
Lossiemouth
Elgin
Cullen
Portsoy
Banff
Fraserburgh
Fochabers
Keith
Huntly
Peterhead
Beauly
Inverness
Daviot
Carrbridge
Grantown-on-Spey
MORAY
Tomintoul
Inverurie
SKYE
Portree
Kyle of Lochalsh
Dornie
Kyleakin
Broadford
HIGHLAND
Invermoriston
Fort Augustus
Aviemore
ABERDEENSHIRE
CITY OF ABERDEEN
ABERDEEN
Aboyne
Banchory
Kingussie
Braemar
Stonehaven
Mallaig
RUM
EIGG
INNER HEBRIDES
Spean Bridge
Fort William
ANGUS
Brechin
Montrose
Kinlochleven
Kinloch Rannoch
Pitlochry
Forfar
COLL
Tobermory
Ballachulish
Glencoe
Aberfeldy
Blairgowrie
Arbroath
PERTH & KINROSS
Dunkeld
Carnoustie
DUNDEE
Killin
Lochearnhead
Perth
MULL
Oban
Taynuilt
Dalmally
Crianlarich
Crieff
Auchterarder
FIFE
Cupar
St Andrews
Crail
1.CITY OF DUNDEE
2.CLACKMANNANSHIRE
3.CITY OF EDINBURGH
Inveraray
Callander
STIRLING
Doune
Dunblane
ARGYLL & BUTE
Arrochar
Tarbet
Stirling
Kinross
Leven
Kirkcaldy
Kilmartin
COLONSAY
Lochgilphead
Ardrishaig
Luss
Drymen
Balloch
FALKIRK
Dunfermline
North Berwick
Dunbar
Haddington
E.LOTHIAN
JURA
Dunoon
Gourock
Dumbarton
Greenock
EDINBURGH
Dalkeith
MID LOTHIAN
W. LOTHIAN
Eyemouth
Tarbert
Rothesay
BUTE
Paisley
GLASGOW
Chirnside
Duns
Berwick-upon-Tweed
ISLAY
Kingarth
Largs
Hamilton
Lanark
Lauder
Cornhill-on-Tweed
HOLY ISLAND
NORTH AYRSHIRE
Peebles
Galashiels
Coldstream
Bamburgh
ARRAN
Ardrossan
Kilmarnock
S LANARKSHIRE
Biggar
Melrose
Kelso
Seahouses
Brodick
Irvine
Troon
Selkirk
Wooler
Lamlash
Prestwick
SCOTTISH BORDERS
Jedburgh
Alnwick
Ayr
Cumnock
Abington
Hawick
Campbeltown
EAST AYRSHIRE
Maybole
Moffat
Beattock
NORTHUMBERLAND
Ashington
SOUTH AYRSHIRE
Morpeth
Girvan
DUMFRIES AND GALLOWAY
Langholm
Bellingham
Whitley Bay
4.WEST DUNBARTONSHIRE
5.EAST DUNBARTONSHIRE
6.NORTH LANARKSHIRE
7.INVERCLYDE
8.RENFREWSHIRE
9.CITY OF GLASGOW
10.EAST RENFREWSHIRE
New Galloway
Lockerbie
Dumfries
Newton Stewart
Castle Douglas
Longtown
Greenhead
NEWCASTLE UPON TYNE
TYNE & WEAR
Gatehouse of Fleet
Annan
Gretna
Hexham
Corbridge
SUNDERLAND
Stranraer
Dalbeattie
Carlisle
Consett
Durham
Portpatrick
Wigtown
Kirkcudbright
Silloth
Alston
CUMBRIA
DURHAM
Port William
Bassenthwaite
Penrith
Bishop Auckland
Shildon
5
6